# POPULAR VOICES IN LATIN AMERICAN

# CATHOLICISM

# STUDIES IN CHURCH AND STATE

JOHN F. WILSON, EDITOR

---

*The Restructuring of American Religion:*
*Society and Faith since World War II*
by Robert Wuthnow

*Shintō and the State, 1868–1988*
by Helen Hardacre

*Redeeming Politics*
by Peter Iver Kaufman

*Undermined Establishment: Church-State*
*Relations in America, 1880–1920*
by Robert T. Handy

*Popular Voices in Latin American Catholicism*
by Daniel H. Levine

# POPULAR VOICES IN LATIN AMERICAN CATHOLICISM

*Daniel H. Levine*

PRINCETON UNIVERSITY PRESS

PRINCETON, NEW JERSEY

*LIBRARY OF CONGRESS CATALOGING-IN-PUBLICATION DATA*

LEVINE, DANIEL H.

POPULAR VOICES IN LATIN AMERICAN CATHOLICISM / DANIEL H. LEVINE.

P. CM. — (STUDIES IN CHURCH AND STATE)

INCLUDES BIBLIOGRAPHICAL REFERENCES AND INDEX.

ISBN 0-691-08754-7 (ALK. PAPER)—ISBN 0-691-02459-6 (PBK.: ALK. PAPER)

1. CATHOLIC CHURCH—COLOMBIA—HISTORY—20TH CENTURY. 2. CATHOLIC

CHURCH—VENEZUELA—HISTORY—20TH CENTURY. 3. COLOMBIA—CHURCH

HISTORY. 4. VENEZUELA—CHURCH HISTORY. I. TITLE. II. SERIES.

BX1470.2.L48   1992   282'.861'09049—DC20   91-39180   CIP


THIS BOOK HAS BEEN COMPOSED IN LINOTRON TIMES ROMAN

PRINCETON UNIVERSITY PRESS BOOKS ARE PRINTED

ON ACID-FREE PAPER AND MEET THE GUIDELINES FOR

PERMANENCE AND DURABILITY OF THE COMMITTEE ON

PRODUCTION GUIDELINES FOR BOOK LONGEVITY

OF THE COUNCIL ON LIBRARY RESOURCES

PRINTED IN THE UNITED STATES OF AMERICA

1   3   5   7   9   10   8   6   4   2

1   3   5   7   9   10   8   6   4   2

(PBK.)

*For S.L. and for the Memory of D.L.*

I would not give five cents for a God who could not help me here on the earth, for such a God is not a God at hand. He is only an imagination. It is a false delusion—trying to make you think you had just as well go ahead and suffer and be enslaved and be lynched and everything else here, and after a while you are going to Heaven someplace. If God cannot prepare Heaven here for you, you are not going anywhere.

—Father Divine

# CONTENTS

LIST OF FIGURES    xiii

LIST OF TABLES    xv

FOREWORD    xvii

PREFACE AND ACKNOWLEDGMENTS    xix

NOTE ON THE INTERVIEWS    xxiii

**PART I:** ISSUES AND CONTEXTS

ONE

Popular Voices    3

*Defining and Finding Popular Groups*    6
*Initial Perspectives on Theory and Practice*    13
*Studies in Latin America*    20
*Studying Popular Groups, Hearing Popular Voices*    23
*The Structure of This Book*    29

TWO

Liberation Theology, Base Communities, and the Pattern of Change in
Latin America    31

*Context and Conjuncture: The Pattern of Change in Latin America*    32
*Central Ideas in Liberation Theology*    39
*Liberation Theology and Base Communities: Ideas and Action*    44
*Conclusion*    51

THREE

Colombia and Venezuela: Nations, Churches, and Programs    54

*State, Politics, and Associational Life*    55
*Socioeconomic and Demographic Contrasts*    59
*The Churches: Contrasts in Structure, Ideology, and
Organizational Strategy*    65
*Popular Work: Alternative Views*    82
*Conclusion*    91

FOUR

Colombia and Venezuela: Dioceses, Villages, and Barrios    94

*Facatativá*    94
*Barquisimeto*    107
*Cali*    116
*Comparative Perspectives*    124

**PART II:** ACTORS AND EXPERIENCES

**FIVE**

Being Religious, Reading the Bible, Becoming Church    133

*Being Religious and Reading the Bible*    134
*Biblical Texts and Readings*    139
*Becoming Church: Varieties of Popular Experience*    146
*Transforming Popular Religion*    167
*Conclusion*    177

**SIX**

Popular Needs and Popular Ideals    181

*Being Poor*    182
*Fellowship, Sociability, and Self-Image*    193
*Images of Church and Clergy*    199
*Empowering the Poor*    207

**SEVEN**

Priests, Sisters, and Pastoral Agents    213

*Background and Personal History*    215
*Working*    230
*Opting for the Poor, Popular Religion, and the Nature of Groups*    242
*Two Matched Profiles*    252
*Conclusion*    270

**EIGHT**

Selected Life Histories    272

*Huberto Vanegas: A Lay Pastoral Agent*    273
*Two Colombian Women: Olga Ceballos and Susanna Madrid*    280
*Two Peasant Men: Fortunato Duque and Patricio Alvarez*    294
*Conclusion*    310

**PART III:** THEORETICAL AND COMPARATIVE REFLECTIONS

**NINE**

Linking Everyday Life with Big Structures    317

*Consciousness, Ideology, and Culture*    322
*Mediators, Mediations, and the Question of Democracy*    335
*A Note on Class*    344
*Conclusion*    350

**TEN**

The Future of Popular Voices    353

*Reprise*    354

*Explaining Change*  362
*Are Popular Voices Unique?*  365
*Facing the Future*  368
*Knowing about the Future*  371
*Envoi*  374

BIBLIOGRAPHY  375

INDEX  397

# FIGURES

| 3.1 | Colombia, Percentage Change since 1940 | 68 |
| 3.2 | Venezuela, Percentage Change since 1940 | 69 |
| 4.1 | Facatativá, Percentage Change since 1962 | 96 |
| 4.2 | Barquisimeto, Percentage Change since 1960 | 107 |
| 4.3 | Cali, Percentage Change since 1960 | 117 |
| 4.4 | Fieldwork, Research Levels | 124 |

# TABLES

| | | |
|---|---|---|
| 2.1 | Change and Conflict in Latin American Catholicism, by Periods | 34 |
| 2.2 | A Typology of Base Communities | 48 |
| 3.1 | Social and Economic Indicators for Venezuela and Colombia, Selected Years | 61 |
| 3.2 | Venezuela and Colombia, Selected Indexes | 64 |
| 3.3 | Selected Indexes on the Church in Venezuela and Colombia, 1950–1980 | 67 |
| 4.1 | Facatativá, Cali, and Barquisimeto, Selected Years | 95 |
| 5.1 | Field Research Sites, Selected Traits | 165 |
| 5.2 | Key Questions on Base Communities | 166 |
| 7.1 | Priests and Sisters, Selected Traits | 217 |
| 7.2 | Priests and Sisters, A Typology of Positions on Key Issues | 250 |
| 8.1 | Responses to Statements of Opinion | 312 |

# FOREWORD

*P*OPULAR *Voices in Latin American Catholicism* is the fifth volume in the series "Studies in Church and State," which is published by the Princeton University Press. This series is sponsored by the Project on Church and State at Princeton University, an undertaking originally funded by the Lilly Endowment. The Project has been guided by two objectives. One has been to sponsor scholarly publications on the interaction of religion and its political environment, primarily but not exclusively in the context of the history of the United States. The other has been to draw on disciplines in addition to those routinely concerned with church-state issues to investigate this interaction.

The studies published in this series are designed to fulfill these goals. The initial volume, by Robert Wuthnow, explored how religion and its place in American society have changed since World War II. Helen Hardacre's volume analyzed the tradition of Shintō and its relation to the Japanese state. The next volume, by Peter I. Kaufman, examined some of the ways religious and political authority interacted in the medieval and early modern West after Constantine made Christianity his empire's official religion. The most recently published study, by Robert T. Handy, concerns the undermining of Protestant Christianity's influence in American society and politics in the closing decades of the nineteenth century and initial ones of the twentieth. Additional volumes will examine aspects of church-state issues in India and in modern Europe, and in several other decisive periods of U.S. history, including the Revolutionary and the Jacksonian eras. A community study of a multiethnic, medium-size industrial city in the Northeast will also appear in the series. Finally, a summary volume exploring these issues as they have developed in our history as a nation will complete the Studies in Church and State series.

The Project on Church and State has also sponsored a two-volume bibliographical guide to literature on church-state issues in American history, edited by John F. Wilson, and a casebook on church-state law compiled by John T. Noonan, Jr.[1]

The members of the Project's steering committee recognize that it cannot commission studies on many additional topics that deserve scholarly treatment, but we hope that the publications already available, as well as those yet to come, will demonstrate that new work will broaden discussion of these perennial questions. In turn, we hope such recognition will stimulate further scholarship.

---

[1] John F. Wilson, ed., *Church and State in America: A Bibliographical Guide*, vol. 1, *The Colonial and Early National Periods*; vol. 2, *The Civil War to the Present Day* (Westport, Conn., 1986, 1987); John T. Noonan, Jr., *The Believers and the Powers That Are* (New York, 1987).

Daniel Levine's study follows his earlier scholarship on the role of the Catholic church in contemporary Latin American societies. It is constructed around extensive fieldwork that yields a rather new and arresting perspective on the subject. In exploring the appeal of Christianity at the level of the folk, he uncovers some of the sources of religion's power among the people. By juxtaposing studies of different regions, he suggests not only the richness of religious life but the range of its influence. Above all, he sets base communities in their social contexts and helps to locate the significance of the "liberation" that is claimed and experienced. An additional strength of the study is its use of scholarly insights from a wide array of disciplines, developed in various cultural locations. We believe that *Popular Voices in Latin American Catholicism* will simultaneously enrich the study of religion's interaction with regimes in South and Central America and help to relate that issue to scholarship more broadly conceived.

The Project on Church and State began under the guidance and with the support of Robert Wood Lynn of the Lilly Endowment. We thank Vice-President Lynn and his successor, Craig Dykstra, for their continued interest and confidence in our work. Throughout its formative years, the Project benefited from the dedication and experience of its coordinator, Yoma Ullman, as well as from her skill and demanding standards. Princeton University Press has provided support and encouragement, as well as exemplary working relationships. We wish especially to thank its director, Walter H. Lippincott, and the current religion editor, Ann Wald. In the early years of working with the Press, Gail Ullman's interest and close involvement as history editor was invaluable.

John F. Wilson
Robert T. Handy
Stanley N. Katz
Albert J. Raboteau

# PREFACE AND ACKNOWLEDGMENTS

THIS IS a book about ordinary people in Latin America, their religion and their culture. It is a book about how those people come to see themselves in new ways, and in the process create and justify new fields of thought and action, sparking and reinforcing transformations that reach beyond personal life to change family, community, and the big structures of church and politics. The experiences of these ordinary and, for the most part, poor and unschooled men and women open windows on how social and cultural transformations begin and what makes them endure. Their creative efforts throw strong, clear, and fresh light on the vital role religion continues to play in human affairs. They further affirm the capacity average people have for innovations that fuse values, experience, and community in meaningful and enduring collective action.

Scattered across all of Latin America, men and women in grass-roots Christian communities are reaching for a voice and a place of their own. They do not do all this alone. Popular culture is not well understood if it is approached as a pure or spontaneous product of "the people," created in isolation from other groups, institutions, or from long-standing identities and traditions. Reality is more complex. Changes in popular culture emerge as part of continuing ties between ordinary people and everyday life, on the one hand, and "big structures"—institutions of power and meaning that shape alternatives and understandings for society as a whole—on the other. This linkage is critical for popular groups and institutional elites alike. Popular groups and the individuals comprised by them prize the "ties that bind" for the sense of identity and continuity they carry. They use these ties to legitimize their hopes and their ideals and to secure much-needed resources. Elites also require and value linkages, if only to validate their claims to leadership: there are no leaders without followers, at least not for very long.

When a new kind of popular culture is formed, these complex ties are not abandoned but instead gain new meaning. Crucial to the construction of these new meanings are the creative efforts of ordinary people, of elites, and of those men, women, and organized groups who create and occupy mediating roles, roles like teacher or community organizer that bind everyday life and big structures in new and meaningful ways.

I am grateful to the ordinary men and women of Venezuela and Colombia who have generously shared their lives and experiences with me. I feel truly fortunate—blessed is not too strong a word—to have gotten to know them. I have made a faithful effort in this book to let their voices speak with minimal distortion. In this I have been moved by a commitment to record these voices, a commitment that has gained a sense of urgency with the passage of time.

Under the papacy of John Paul II, increasing pressure has been brought to bear on popular groups and on those who promote and work with them. The long-term impact of these pressures is still not clear, but whatever the future holds, there are grounds for concern: groups are vulnerable; programs can be terminated. It is therefore vital to record popular voices and to listen to what they have to say. My effort in this book is thus in part testimonial, but at the same time reaches beyond mere recording to explain how and why these voices emerge and find words and a place to speak and be heard.

My decision to focus on transformations in the religion, culture, and organized life of popular groups means that a number of doubtless important questions are addressed only tangentially here. Thus, with the exception of liberation theology, I do not take up theological issues. Analysis of the development and character of international or national church institutions is also restricted, except where such matters impinge directly on the communities included in my fieldwork. I have discussed many of these issues elsewhere, and an extensive and increasingly strong literature analyzes these critical dimensions of cultural and political change in rich and comparative detail. For present purposes, we take these questions up primarily as they appear to affect, shape, and be reshaped in the consciousness and experience of ordinary believers and of those who work with them.

The research and writing of this book led me to travel widely in and between Venezuela and Colombia over a period of more than two years. I observed countless group meetings and training sessions and returned periodically to peasant villages and urban neighborhoods in the two countries for re-interviews, including life histories taken from clergy, sisters, and selected group members. Throughout, I have sought the general in the particular, and I have found the source of new and freer popular voices in the solidarities ordinary people construct and value as they craft a more democratic kind of everyday life.

In this book, we shall listen to many voices and trace the history of communities and of the men and women who make up and work with them. In doing the research on which this book is based, and throughout the lengthy process of organizing materials and writing the results, I have incurred many debts that it is my pleasure to acknowledge here. I want to thank some of the people who made the research possible by helping to open doors and by generously serving as sounding boards for my initial efforts to make sense of what I was seeing and hearing. In Colombia, my gratitude goes in particular to Alberto Mayor, Carminia Navia, Hector Torres Rojas, Msgr. Jaime Prieto, Huberto Vanegas, and Francisco Zuluaga. In Venezuela, I must make special mention of Alberto Dorremochea, Alberto Gruson, Alberto Micheo, and Arturo Sosa. I have also been helped by many others who have preferred to remain unnamed here.

Initial field studies were undertaken with support from a Faculty Fellowship and Research Grant provided by the Horace H. Rackham School of Graduate

Studies of the University of Michigan. The National Endowment for the Humanities provided a generous Basic Research Grant (#RO 20172-82), which made it possible for research to go forward over an extended period. I am indebted to these institutions for their support. I was already working through my findings and beginning to write when I was approached by John Wilson, who invited me to incorporate my work into the general framework of the Project on Church and State. Association with the Project on Church and State has brought me many benefits, not least among them the intellectual stimulation and encouragement of John Wilson and other colleagues. Through the Project, I also received important financial support from the Lilly Foundation, which enabled me to devote substantial time to writing—time that would otherwise have been available only in bits and pieces. I have also had the good fortune to be a Residential Fellow of the Kellogg Institute at the University of Notre Dame. The Institute provided time, space, and a uniquely stimulating and collegial atmosphere for writing. I am grateful to colleagues and to the staff at Kellogg for all their cheerful help and helpful criticism.

Some of the material in this book has appeared earlier. Specifically, I want to acknowledge previous publication of the following: portions of chapter 2 in "Assessing the Impacts of Liberation Theology in Latin America," *Review of Politics* 50, no. 2 (Spring 1988); material from chapters 1–6 in "Popular Groups, Popular Culture, and Popular Religion," *Comparative Studies in Society and History* 32, no. 4 (October 1990); material from chapters 2–6 in "Religion and Popular Protest in Latin America: Contrasting Experiences" (jointly with Scott Mainwaring), in Susan Eckstein, ed., *Power and Popular Protest: Latin American Social Movements* (Berkeley: University of California Press, 1989); portions of chapters 1 and 9 in "Religion and Politics in Comparative and Historical Perspective," *Comparative Politics* 19, no. 1 (October 1986), and "Holiness, Faith, Power, Politics," *Journal for the Scientific Study of Religion* 26, no. 4 (December 1987); portions of chapters 1–3 in "Continuities in Colombia," *Journal of Latin American Studies* 17, no. 2 (November 1985); portions of chapters 1–4 in "Colombia: The Institutional Church and the Popular," in my edited volume, *Religion and Political Conflict in Latin America* (Chapel Hill: University of North Carolina Press, 1986); and parts of chapter 1 in "Religion, the Poor, and Politics in Latin America Today" and "Conflict and Renewal," both in *Religion and Political Conflict in Latin America*. In addition, all translations from works in Spanish are my own, unless otherwise indicated.

As I write these lines, I am closing in on almost two decades of research and publication in the general area of politics, culture, and religion in Latin America. Through much of this period, I have also taught a series of seminars at the University of Michigan devoted to critical analysis and review of current issues and studies in this field, including but not limited to my own work. I am grateful to all the graduate and undergraduate students who have allowed me to share my ideas with them and who have given me a chance to benefit from the freshness and originality of their own views.

I have also learned much from those colleagues and friends who together constitute "the usual suspects" at work in this corner of the social science vineyard. In particular, I wish to thank the following people, listed here in alphabetical order: Phillip Berryman, Thomas Bruneau, Edward Cleary, Margaret Crahan, Michael Dodson, Susan Eckstein, Raymond Grew, Thomas Kselman, Michael Lowy, Otto Maduro, Scott Mainwaring, Catalina Romero, Brian Smith, John Wilson, and Robert Wuthnow. I want to make special mention of Penny Lernoux, whose untimely death robbed us all of a good friend and an insightful, impassioned writer. Penny Lernoux was generous of her time and knowledge with me, as she was with so many others. She is sorely missed.

In addition to the names already cited, the following colleagues gave me the benefit of careful, critical readings of earlier articles in this general area and of specific chapters in this book: Joel Aberbach, Susan Eckstein, Gary Hawes, Don Herzog, Michael Lowy, Cecilia Mariz, Ric Northrup, Guy Petit-demanges, Robert Putnam, Thomas Quigley, Steven Rosenstone, Arlene Saxonhouse, Rebecca Scott, and Alexander Wilde. The entire manuscript was read with care and useful critical comments were provided by Phillip Berryman, Michael Dodson, Thomas Kselman, Scott Mainwaring, John Wilson, and one anonymous reviewer. I have also benefited greatly from editorial comments by Yoma Ullman for the Project on Church and State and by Gail Ullman for Princeton University Press. I am particularly grateful to Scott Mainwaring, who has been a valued collaborator, colleague, and friend.

I must thank Teresa Calle, who conducted important parts of the field interviewing in Colombia. She is a creative and insightful observer and a truly gifted interviewer. Bryan Froehle put his intellectual acumen and organizational skills to the task of making it possible to work through mountains of raw interview transcript. He has also been a sharp but generous critic. Brian Crisp and Sue Crisp helped with the figures and the tables. John Transue carefully proofread the whole text.

Now more than ever, I am grateful to my wife, Phyllis Levine, who is not only a careful and sympathetic critic of what I write and do, but also a true friend, tried and tested. Among the many things for which I have to thank her, in particular I want to acknowledge here the key role she played in organizing field studies at sites in both Venezuela and Colombia and in conducting interviews. My debt to her is incalculable on all dimensions; its true extent remains a secret between us.

When this book was first completed, it was dedicated to my parents, Sylvia and David Levine. Since that time, my father has died. I now rededicate the book to my mother and to the memory of my father.

Ann Arbor, 1991

# NOTE ON THE INTERVIEWS

INTERVIEWS for this book were conducted at the national, diocesan, local, and community levels. Elite and informational types of interviewing were combined with the use of two standard questionnaires: one for members and leaders of groups, another for priests and sisters. Life histories were taken from group members, pastoral agents, priests, and sisters, and much time was spent in observing group meetings at all the sites. The questionnaires were administered only after extensive preliminary work of this kind, and often led to re-interviews.

In all, about 250 interviews were conducted over a three-year period. This number includes many informational interviews and re-interviews. The questionnaires were given to a total of 69 lay persons (53 Colombians and 16 Venezuelans; 38 men and 31 women) and 13 clerics (6 Colombians and 7 Venezuelans; 5 priests and 8 sisters). After transcription, interviews were organized and bound into volumes according to location. Interview transcripts run to more than twenty-three hundred pages. All quotations from interviews used in this book are identified by a code that denotes the site and specifies a page in the corresponding volume. Thus, C 71 identifies an interview from Caparrapí, and a passage found on page 71 of that volume.

The following codes are used:

G = General interviews for Venezuela and Colombia.

For rural Colombia: F = Facatativá, C = Caparrapí, Q = Quebradanegra and La Magdalena, S = San Isidro, A = Agua Fría, T = Tabio, R = Río Frío.

For urban Colombia: CR = Cali in general and Barrio El Rodeo, CA = Barrio Meléndez.

For rural Venezuela: V = Villanueva and surrounding hamlets.

For urban Venezuela, B = barrios in Barquisimeto.

# PART I

## ISSUES AND CONTEXTS

O Lord, thou art my God;
I will exalt thee, I will praise thy name;
for Thou hast done wonderful things,
plans formed of old, faithful and sure.

For Thou hast been a stronghold to the poor,
   a stronghold to the needy in his distress,
   a shelter from the storm and a shade from the heat;
For the blast of the ruthless is like a storm against a wall,
   like heat in a dry place.

Thou dost subdue the noise of the aliens;
as heat by the shade of a cloud,
so the song of the ruthless is stilled.

          —Isaiah 25:1, 4–5


    The Spirit of the Lord is upon me,
    because he has anointed me to preach
      good news to the poor.
    He has sent me to proclaim release of
      the captives
    and recovering of sight to the blind,
    to set at liberty those who are oppressed,
    to proclaim the acceptable year of the Lord.

          —Luke 4:18–19

# ONE

## POPULAR VOICES

DANIEL VIRGUEZ, a Colombian peasant, has sought out adult education, ventured far beyond the confines of his village, and become a respected and effective leader in his church and society. Pastora Chirinos, a woman from the slums of urban Venezuela, became literate and active, forming groups of friends and neighbors who meet to talk about their faith, read the Bible, and work together on community needs for housing and health, education, water, and bus service. Huberto Vanegas grew up illiterate and alone. To survive, he shined shoes in the street, sold beer in a whorehouse, and worked as a migrant laborer. He is now a rural extension agent for the church, founding cooperatives and self-help projects throughout an extensive rural zone. Once isolated, dispirited, and unorganized, Daniel, Pastora, and Huberto have become active, articulate, and confident citizens. They are not revolutionaries, not even very radical. But there is no question that these three people have changed themselves through their involvement in a changing church that has begun to redefine the meaning of religious faith while making a new and legitimate place for the poor in its guiding ideas and core structures.

These individuals have learned to have confidence in their own critical judgment and in their capacity to reason and decide for themselves. They have taught themselves to create and use organizations, and in the process have nurtured a disposition to organization and collective action in general. All this has furthered an ever-fresh re-creation of community: the idea itself, and also the bonds of solidarity and identity on which it rests.

These three dimensions of change—reason, sociability, and community—lie at the heart of the popular experiences reviewed in this book and explain their more general significance. The convergence of reason, sociability, and community constitutes a bridge linking recent Latin American experience to moments of change in other times and places, when cultural and social innovation have come together to reshape the moral and social landscape. Cases in point include the Puritan revolution (and the Reformation generally), the Iranian revolution, a number of cultural affirmations in the face of colonialism, and the whole experience of black religion and culture in America leading to and manifest in the civil rights movement.

The lives of Daniel Virguez, Pastora Chirinos, and Huberto Vanegas are not isolated instances. They share in a broad movement of transformation through which ordinary men and women all over Latin America have found voices of their own: voices they use to praise God, talk with one another, and discuss issues that make a difference to themselves and to their families, churches, communities, and nations. Reflect for a moment on how difficult it must be for people to find an authentic voice when they have long been given to understand that their opinions have no value or—to be more precise—*that they have no opinions*. Voices are found only through a long process compounded of discovery, conscious self-invention, and struggle. In this book, I explain how these popular voices emerge among the Latin American poor and how they find the words to speak, the confidence to make these words known, and the friends and allies required for successful and enduring action.

The meaning of popular voices in religion has lately been the subject of sharp debate and bitter conflict in Latin America, as elsewhere in the modern world.[1] Struggle has centered on what popular groups of religious inspiration will believe, say, and do; on selection and orientation of leaders; and on control of the groups' relations to institutions of power and meaning in the larger society. The whole process is political in a few related senses. The institutional churches create programs, train people, and project messages that affect government and "politics" as conventionally understood at all levels. This kind of politics is familiar to us all.

But there is more. Leaders and ordinary faithful in the churches learn about politics and the political not only from these explicit messages but also from the implicit models of power and legitimate authority they encounter in the ordinary practice of church and community.[2] When new popular groups find a voice and press for greater autonomy and more democratic forms of governance, they challenge established models of power and authority throughout the social order. They do so partly by example, since their very existence and activities reinforce the legitimacy of such initiatives. Their challenge also comes indirectly, as group life elicits and empowers new types of leaders whose experience, though limited at first to a local ambit, may still provide a basis of skills and self-confidence for activism on a larger canvas. Because religion is a central culture-forming institution, the stakes in all this go well beyond the short-term outcomes of any particular conflict to include the shaping of core concepts about activism and passivity, hierarchy and equality, equity, justice, and legitimacy.

I want to underscore the novelty that independent popular voices constitute in religion as a whole and, specifically, in Latin America. It is not that religions have no place for the poor. To the contrary, throughout history religious institutions have attended to and spoken for poor people. Charity has been

---

[1] I review some of the relevant literature in "Religion and Politics in Comparative and Historical Perspective" and in "Holiness, Faith, Power, Politics."

[2] Cf. Juan Luis Segundo, *The Hidden Motives of Pastoral Actions: Latin American Reflections*; and John Gaventa, *Power and Powerlessness: Quiescence and Rebellion in an Appalachian Valley*.

provided, the sick cared for, and the cause of the helpless represented before public authorities and the powerful. Poverty has repeatedly been held up as a symbol of the simple and virtuous life. Images and concerns like these have a long and legitimate pedigree in many religions. They also have a central place in Christian traditions, and specifically in Latin American Catholicism. But the broad currents of change in the Catholic church that crystallized with the Second Vatican Council changed the tenor of these commitments in subtle but significant ways. The Council stressed that the church had to understand and promote change and had to change itself. Church leaders and members were urged to listen and learn from ordinary experience and to make a greater place for participation by ordinary people in church, society, and politics. In practical terms, these commitments (among others) gave renewed legitimacy to the old prophetic task: to cut religion's ties with principalities and powers and to serve above all, as *voice for the voiceless*.

The church as *voice for the voiceless* has become a familiar metaphor in contemporary Latin America. The phrase carries with it images of fearless advocacy for the marginal and for those without power or position. Across the region, church leaders and activists have taken up the cause of human rights, promoted and empowered grass-roots groups, and helped stake out legitimate new fields for religiously inspired criticism and collective action: housing, land, jobs, unions, to name only a few. Not surprisingly, all this has generated enormous conflict, for example, concerning the church's proper relation to politics and the state, to Marxism and revolution, to popular movements, and to violence or social conflict generally. Civil and military authorities long accustomed to unquestioning support from church elites and religious institutions have been particularly embittered by what they see as a betrayal of the church they were brought up to revere and defend, and of its authentic values and proper alliances. As a result, church-state conflicts in Latin America have arguably been sharper over the past few decades than at any time in the previous century.

Being a "voice for the voiceless" can therefore be difficult and often dangerous. The effort has indeed exposed numerous bishops, clergy, sisters, and countless ordinary people to harassment, abuse, and death.[3] But however arduous the task may be, the role of voice for the voiceless maintains longstanding distinctions between the church and those it leads. Without voices, the mass of ordinary faithful remain silent *objects*. The church acts in their name, providing leadership and authoritative guidance. What happens when these silent masses begin to speak and act for themselves? It is one thing to

[3] See, among others: Anna Carrigan, *Salvador Witness: The Life and Calling of Jean Donovan*; Judith Noone, *The Same Fate as the Poor*; Penny Lernoux, *Cry of the People*, and her last book, *People of God*; Phillip Berryman, *Religious Roots of Rebellion: Christians in the Central American Revolutions*; Emilio Mignone, *Witness to the Truth*; and Donna Witson Brett and Edward T. Brett, *Murdered in Central America: The Stories of Eleven U.S. Missionaries*.

speak for, or, to use another phrase that will echo throughout this book, to "opt" for the poor; it is quite another to accept and even promote or empower efforts by the poor to opt and speak for themselves: creating groups, finding leaders, and taking initiatives apart from and possibly in conflict with hierarchical tutelage.

Being a voice for the voiceless is less difficult and demanding for institutions like the churches than is listening to what the hitherto voiceless have to say and giving them space and tools with which to act. The emergence of popular groups and of popular voices able to speak and act for themselves has changed the landscape of religion, politics, and culture in contemporary Latin America. As average men and women move from silence to voice, from the status of objects to subjects, their words and deeds touch sensitive issues of power and meaning in every institution. This complex process of self-creation, conflict, and change is the subject of this book.

## Defining and Finding Popular Groups

A few words of definition are appropriate here to clarify the meaning of the term "popular." Contemporary Latin American usage derives the "popular" quality of religion, art, music, and the like not from their popularity (something favored by many) but rather from their fit to a sense of what constitutes the *populus*—the central defining traits of the population. From this perspective, the term "popular" (*lo popular* in Spanish) summons images of inequality and subordination and directs attention to the poor conceived as "popular" groups or classes. Reference to *lo popular* also commonly evokes a sense of collective identity and a claim to group autonomy and self-governance, in particular with regard to choosing leaders, setting group agendas, and explicating the religious significance of all this.

In all these ways, attention to *lo popular* points analysis and action to the ideas, beliefs, practices, and conditions of poor people however defined and, by extension, to the kinds of ties that bind them to structures of power, privilege, and meaning. Whatever else the word may stand for in Latin American Catholicism, "popular" therefore necessarily denotes activities by large numbers of poor people within church structures. This general definition masks a substantial shift in the meaning and value given to things "popular" in the recent theory and practice of Latin American Catholicism.

Not long ago, reference to *lo popular* called up images of ignorance, magic, and superstition. Popular religion was taken to mean saints, feast days, shrines, pilgrimages, or processions. Popular groups were depicted as occasional agglomerations of the poor and humble, at best logical extensions of major institutions (confraternities that "keep the saints," parish groups) or simply arms of the church like Catholic Action. From this vantage point, popular culture and action remained subordinate to and ultimately derived from institutions and elites. But the same reference now commonly evokes class identity (the popular as "the people"—specifically peasants, proletarians, etc.), comes wrapped in claims to autonomy and collective self-governance by such people, and is identified in ordinary discourse with values like authenticity, sharing, solidarity, and sacrifice. Reflecting the new status of popular groups (no longer just sheep to be led in a "flock"), verbs like *accompany* have entered the Catholic lexicon, replacing earlier stress on direction, instruction, and purification.

Why this focus on the poor? To begin with, the poor are obviously the majority of the population, and naturally the churches want to reach and orient them in changing and often difficult circumstances. Poverty and the poor have always held a privileged place in Christian thought. This means that efforts to rethink the sources and meaning of poverty and to work with poor people in new ways engage contexts of religious significance in ways that easily turn into central points of conflict.

These general predispositions have been reinforced and extended in Latin America by the development of theologies (e.g., liberation theology) and related institutional programs dedicated to empowering popular groups and giving them a legitimate place in religion, society, and politics. In situations of economic and political crisis, like those of the past few decades in Latin America, any attempt to reach, orient, and organize the poor is likely to be viewed with fear and suspicion by civil and military authorities. In particular, the ability to shape and direct the organizations of the poor and to train and orient those who link the institutional churches to the poor in daily practice (priests, sisters, catechists, and lay leaders—"pastoral agents" of all kinds) becomes politically explosive and has lately emerged as a central arena of ideological and bureaucratic conflict.

The attention churches, social movements, politicians, and state elites have devoted to popular groups and the intensity of the conflicts centered on them cannot be explained by the numbers they attract. Most accounts agree that membership figures (unreliable in any case) are small and that rates of participation vary enormously from case to case.[4] Supposed "politicization of religion" or accelerated social mobilization through religious groups also fails to account for the energies concentrated on them. At issue here is no simple

---

[4] Full citations on this point are provided in the next chapter. The following remain among the most thorough and reliable sources: Thomas Bruneau, *The Church in Brazil: The Politics of Religion*; Marcelo de Azevedo, *Basic Ecclesial Communities in Brazil: The Challenge of a New Way of Being Church*; and W. E. Hewitt, "The Influence of Social Class on Activity Preferences of Comunidades Eclesiales de Base (CEBs) in the Archdiocese of São Paulo," and his exhaustive *Base Christian Communities and Social Change in Brazil*. See also the cases collected in Daniel H. Levine, ed., *Religion and Political Conflict in Latin America*; and in Scott Mainwaring and Alexander Wilde, eds., *The Progressive Church in Latin America*.

opposition of religion to political power; for this, Latin American history provides ample precedent. In any event, no political parties fly the banners of liberation theology; no mass movement claims direct inspiration from its tenets. Nowhere in Latin America have theologians, churches, or related popular movements brought down a government or altered basic structures of economic, social, or political power. The Iranian revolution, in short, has no parallel in the Western Hemisphere.

The key to understanding the sources and patterns of conflict lies elsewhere. First, there is less unquestioned unity around core religious institutions led by bishops. Second, the ideological direction of criticism has shifted to embrace considerable religious dissatisfaction with capitalism. This has been fused in practice with challenges to authoritarian rule and abuses of power. Finally, the social location of the process has shifted as popular groups assume a more salient and independent role. Popular religious groups advance claims to autonomy along with commitments in theory and practice to more egalitarian concepts of authority. This means that apart from explicit programs or activities that may lead to confrontations with the powerful, popular groups also challenge prevailing understandings of politics, of religion, and of the church, which have long been founded on expectations of hierarchy and inequality.[5]

The implications of new understandings of the popular are major, for the churches turn on the meanings given to poverty, class, authority, and church in Catholic discourse. Who are the poor, why are they poor, and why does poverty grow? As noted earlier, concern with poverty and the poor is nothing new; the churches have always dealt with the poor in some way. But new understandings of poverty can change the stance institutions take and thus lay the basis for new sorts of relations with the poor in everyday life. The change has been deceptively simple. Once attributed largely to *individual* failings, poverty now increasingly appears in church discourse as the product of *structural* inequalities. Poverty is thus no longer an inevitable and universal condition. Now it is treated as the product of certain historically specific structures of power created by human beings and, hence, changeable. Because their condition is contingent on power, the poor need not be "always" with us. Arrangements of power are human creations, subject to challenge and change.

Note that this is a sociological definition of poverty, which cuts across Catholicism's traditional stress on "the poor in spirit" and highlights instead the need for solidarity with the materially poor. Several important implications flow from the shift to sociological categories. As poverty is defined in structural terms, stress is placed on class and on the opposition of classes as a social fact that the church must recognize. This places the church in the midst of conflict and raises troubling questions for its traditional message of reconcili-

---

[5] Cf. Leonardo Boff, *Church: Charism and Power. Liberation Theology and the Institutional Church.*

ation.[6] Emphasis on class gains added significance because of changes since the Second Vatican Council that have enhanced the religious value accorded to the experience and understanding of ordinary people. In the discourse of Latin American Catholicism, older assumptions about the ignorance of the masses have yielded with remarkably little opposition to a view stressing sharing and solidarity with the poor on the grounds that poverty gives them a more authentic and religiously valid perspective. There are powerful strains of religious populism in all this, manifest in an urge to go to, share with, and be like "the people," which will appear repeatedly throughout this book. Such identification is increasingly taken as a sign of religious authenticity. The resulting actions and the religious justifications advanced by priests, sisters, and lay activists suggest that the poor are no longer to be taken simply as the uninstructed waiting to be led by their betters.

Changes in sociological analysis are intertwined with theological and doctrinal debates over the nature of the church, and the proper organization and exercise of authority within it. The way Catholic leaders understand the church shapes how they see themselves, the institutions they lead, and their proper relation to social and political issues. These visions of the church (ecclesiologies) provide an important mediation through which religious ideas are crystallized in structures of organizational life, patterns of authority, and legitimate goals, commitments, and actions.

We can usefully begin by distinguishing two meanings of "church." Contemporary debates often oppose a model stressing hierarchy, juridically defined roles, and the guiding force of authoritative doctrine (Church as Institution) to one seeing the church primarily as a historical community of believers and highlighting values of solidarity, shared experience, and multiple sources of power and authority (Church as Community, as People of God).[7] These models define very different projects for the church, particularly through the contrasting senses of unity and belonging on which they rest. The first builds unity around ecclesiastical structures, with average members in a distinct and subordinate relation to clergy. The second builds unity on solidarities of community and shared experience. Institutional unity thus is taken to rest on social unity; community and class-based groups are stressed; and clerical dominance is undercut.

These contrasting ecclesiologies fit closely to different notions of what the

---

[6] See, for example, Brian H. Smith, *The Church and Politics in Chile: Challenges to Modern Catholicism*; Scott Mainwaring, *The Catholic Church and Politics in Brazil, 1916–1985*; Berryman, *Religious Roots*, part 3; and Michael Dodson and Laura O'Shaughnessy, *Nicaragua's Other Revolution: Religious Faith and Political Struggle*.

[7] I discuss alternatives in greater detail and provide fuller references in the following: "Authority in Church and Society: Latin American Models"; *Religion and Politics in Latin America: The Catholic Church in Venezuela and Colombia*; and "Colombia: The Institutional Church and the Popular." A useful account remains Avery Dulles, *Models of the Church*.

popular is all about. Two related concepts undergird variations in theory and practice: "popular," as, for example, in popular religion; and "base," as used in base communities, the small groups whose members and characteristic experiences will occupy us throughout this book. The "popular" character of popular religion has taken on distinct meanings in recent debates: a pattern of inherited belief and practice centered on magic and superstition, which is to be purified through reinforced ties to the church; a spiritual tradition of the poor and humble *in general*, who are encouraged to express their faith in renewed structures of community and participation; and finally, the beliefs and practices of popular classes, rooted in their class situation and expressing its contradictions and dilemmas. Although all three usages rest on a sense of class (with "popular" roughly equivalent to "poor"), this social identity is put to very different uses in each. The first two take poverty in the abstract, removed from the structures of any specific society. From this vantage point, it is the poor and humble in general who are at issue, not peasants, urban workers, slum dwellers, Indians, or the like. Only in the last usage does class provide independent grounds for reflection and action.[8]

The concept of "base" has a comparable set of meanings, which find expression in the organization and structure of groups and of their ties with the church. Briefly, *base* is used to denote both a subunit in the hierarchical structures of the institutional church and a "basic" social group, like a class. The first points to the "base" of institutional pyramids; the second locates "base" in terms of social structure and relations of power. Each of these usages advances a distinct view of the proper relation between popular religion (and *lo popular* in general) and the institutional church. Abstracting the "popular" from social class and tying base to the hierarchical structures of the church binds expressions of popular religion tightly to institutional membership and clerical control. With purification or enhanced participation of the poor and humble in general at issue, any link to religiously legitimate goals depends on the mediation of clergy and the sanction of authoritative doctrine (the Social

---

[8] Catholicism has traditionally insisted on maintaining an appeal to all classes, nations, and social conditions. The issue of class and class division was joined at the 1979 conference of Latin American bishops at Puebla. There, prelates were divided between those who saw secularization as the church's central challenge, and who attributed social conflict above all to the "strains of modernization," and others who insisted on a structural analysis of inequality, conflict, and injustice. The words of Salvadoran Archbishop Oscar A. Romero, murdered little more than a year after Puebla, state the latter position clearly and point to its implications for the church. "The church's option for the poor explains the political dimension of the faith in its fundamentals and in its basic outline. Because the church has opted for the truly poor, not for the fictitiously poor, because it has opted for those who really are oppressed and repressed, the church lives in a political world, and it fulfills itself as church also through politics. It cannot be otherwise if the church, like Jesus, is to turn itself toward the poor." From his address at the University of Louvain on February 2, 1980, cited in Archbishop Oscar Romero, *Voice of the Voiceless: The Four Pastoral Letters and Other Statements*, pp. 182–83. On Puebla, see Phillip Berryman, "What Happened at Puebla"; and my "Religion, the Poor, and Politics in Latin America Today."

Thought of the Church). Membership is socially heterogeneous, and ties to hierarchy remain central to the legitimate constitution of any group. In contrast, grounding base and popular in class and community makes membership socially homogeneous. The legitimate constitution of a group is less dependent on ties to the hierarchy than on solidarity and reflection on shared experience. These are taken to provide a guide to action apart from authoritative doctrine. In this second usage, sociology and ecclesiology combine to make it possible for religiously legitimate group orientations to emerge from reflection on ordinary experience and shared needs, not only from elite direction.

Alternative concepts of "popular" and "base" combine to undergird very different working definitions of authority. At issue here are not only the pattern of institutional-popular relations and the way it is legitimated but also the scope and likely content of change in religious belief and practice. At any given moment, a wide range of religious beliefs and practices are available to ordinary people: prayer, processions and pilgrimages, devotions to particular saints, attitudes to death and spirits, amulets and holy water, study of the Bible, and so forth. Participation as an equal in community and religious life (for example, through shared Bible study) brings confidence in one's own judgment and reasoning ability. Reliance on elite intercession and trust in magical manipulations yields to stress on personal responsibility and community solidarity. At issue here is not the religious character of groups; that is not in question. What is happening at the grass-roots level must instead be understood as the creation, or, better, as the reassembly, of a new vocabulary of meaning and moral concern. The effort is organized and made sense of in different ways according to the distinctions between base and popular, community and institution just outlined. In particular, I will show that the center of gravity of religious sensibility shifts substantially as groups become more rooted in community and less dependent on hierarchical control and institutional mediation.

In *Democracy in America*, de Tocqueville pointed out the importance of religion to the culture and practice of American democracy in terms that are relevant here. In his view, the separation of religion from state power enhanced the vitality of associational life that he found to be characteristic of American life. "Religion," he wrote,

> which never intervenes directly in the government of American society, should therefore be considered as the first of their political institutions, for although it did not give them the taste for liberty, it singularly facilitates their use thereof. . . . The religious atmosphere of the country was the first thing that struck me on arrival in the United States. The longer I stayed in the country, the more conscious I became of the important political consequences resulting from this novel situation.[9]

[9] *Democracy in America*, 1:292, 295.

De Tocqueville argued that American religion fit into a broad pattern of "mores" (manners, styles of social interaction, family patterns, prevailing norms about hierarchy, equality, and authority, and reinforcing links between civil and political associations) that gave American democracy its special character and strength. He gave particular emphasis to associations, which in his view undergirded American democracy by making habits of expression and association legitimate and possible in all walks of life. Citizens could practice equality and liberty every day, and as a result,

> in democratic countries the science of association is the mother of science; the progress of all the rest depends on the progress it has made. . . . When citizens can only meet in public for certain purposes, they regard such meetings as a strange proceeding of rare occurrence, and they rarely think at all about it. When they are allowed to meet freely for all purposes, they ultimately look on public association as the universal, or in a manner, the sole means which men can employ to accomplish the different purposes they may have in view. Every new want constantly revives the notion. The art of association then becomes, as I have said before, the mother of action, studied and applied by all.[10]

Applying de Tocqueville's insights to contemporary Latin America suggests a focus on several related issues. The first involves the character and influence of new religious organizations. Are they more democratic in practice as well as in theory? Do they have discernable impact beyond the boundaries of religion, narrowly defined? The second concerns the origins and character of the new groups. How and why do groups get started in the first place? Do differences in origin make for variations in the nature of the group? What turns isolated instances of change into enduring solidarities and produces the capabilities and commitments required for sustained, independent, collective action? What is the characteristic link between groups and larger institutions (e.g., church and state), and what difference do such links make to the culture and practice of groups on a day-to-day basis? These considerations direct our attention to changes in religion itself that may arise as part of these developments. Is involvement in different kinds of groups associated with distinct patterns of spirituality, belief, and practice? What are the implications of all these changes for the long-term development of politics and culture?

Study of base communities (or CEBs, from the Spanish *comunidades eclesiales de base*) provides a particularly useful window on how (if at all) these changes find expression in church and community. Base communities have drawn considerable attention lately from students of religious and social change in Latin America. Their origins and character are central to the analysis of this book and are considered in detail below, especially in chapters 2, 5, and 6. Here it suffices to note that base communities are small, religiously

---

[10] Ibid., pp. 138, 140.

focused groups of friends and neighbors. Typically established through the initiative of agents of the institutional church (priests, sisters, lay activists), base communities throughout Latin America have been intended to provide a place for religious activities (prayer, Bible study, and so forth) combined with activities directed at community improvement. Many have expected these communities to further cultural and political change by eliciting and legitimizing active, informed participation in familiar, accessible, and manageable settings. But as a practical matter, base communities range in emphasis from highly pietistic and devotional to socially activist, in structure from authoritarian to democratic, and in status from autonomous to utterly reliant on elites and institutions for guidance. These brief considerations suggest that the proper way to undertake analysis of base communities is not to see them as a necessary core of change but rather to explore the conditions under which change can begin and take hold in such contexts. The link between base communities and broader cultural change then becomes an empirical question.

The preceding comments suggest how much the issues raised by popular religious groups transcend the achievement of short-term goals. Apart from the acheivement of proximate objectives like building a school, laying a water line, or founding a cooperative, experience in groups also furthers the construction of languages, universes of discourse, and expectations. To explore these matters, this book grounds analysis of cultural change in evolving links between ideas, group structure and practice, class, and institutions. I give particular attention to the convergence of religious experience and associational life in the development of a new vocabulary and structural basis for independent moral judgment and group solidarity. The process is complex, and the next section outlines the theoretical and empirical foundations of the approach taken in this book.

## Initial Perspectives on Theory and Practice

Empirical change and theoretical reassessment go hand in hand in the matter of religion, culture, and politics.[11] Recent experience offers many examples of intense mobilization and bitter conflict in religion, as between religious and political organizations and institutions across a wide range of regions and cultures. In Latin America, as in Europe, Asia, Africa, the Middle East, and the United States, struggle has been joined at all levels to control the formation and agenda of groups, to set their characteristic commitments and styles of

---

[11] The theoretical issues raised in this section are discussed where appropriate throughout the text, but extended comparative and theoretical analysis is reserved to the last two chapters.

action, and to shape common understandings of authority in institutional life and everyday practice.[12]

The vitality and continued salience of religion has confounded the expectations of much conventional social science, which for long made secularization inevitable and desirable. Change in religion was either ignored or derived from supposedly more primary factors in the economic or political order. But a closer look affirms that religion's social and political impact follows an autonomous logic, which cannot be derived in any simple deductive fashion from factors like class or political affiliation.

Long before crises such as the Iranian revolution, or the political upheaval in Poland and in Central America made religion and politics a focus for public and official concern, scholars working in different disciplines and religious/political traditions had begun to develop a common set of themes. The following points, among others, help make this a coherent literature: a stance that sees change in religion as normal and continuous; from this, a common attempt to grasp its impact on politics not as aberrant or irrational but as a logical outgrowth of central religious themes and structures; a shared concern to reassess "popular religion," placing it in the context of ongoing links to dominant institutions of power and meaning; and finally, a commitment to reread history "from below," and thus to see the links between everyday life and the high politics of "state and church" (however defined in a particular society) in a radically new light. At a general theoretical level, these themes reveal a shared focus on the sources of change in ideas and on their links to class, context, and institutional transformations. They also point to reassessment of religion's role in social and political change.

Why this renewed concern with religion and politics, and why in these particular ways? Much of the answer lies in a reaction to long-prevailing assumptions in the social sciences that made religion secondary to supposedly more immediate, "real," or rational social, economic, or political forces. Three assumptions are especially critical here: The first makes religion *epiphenomenal*; the second takes religious motives or groups as less-evolved *alternatives* to politics, at best "prepolitical" way stations; the third awaits an inevitable secularization—here, religion appears mostly as a survivor from the past, doomed to privatization and disappearance. Much early work on "moderniza-

[12] Relevant sources on issues in the study of popular religion include the following: Natalie Davis, "Some Tasks and Themes in the Study of Popular Religion"; James Obelkevich, ed., *Religion and the People, 800–1700*; Carlo Ginzburg, *The Cheese and the Worms: The Cosmos of a Sixteenth Century Miller*; Thomas Kselman, "Ambivalence and Assumption in the Study of Popular Religion," and his edited *Belief in History; Innovative Approaches to Religious History in Europe and North America*. A recent collection of anthropological studies is Ellen Badone, ed., *Religious Orthodoxy and Popular Faith in European Society*. On the changing dimensions of popular religion in the United States, see Peter Williams, *Popular Religion in America*; and Nathan Hatch, *The Democratization of American Christianity*.

tion'' took these premises for granted.[13] Recent scholarship has turned the theoretical and methodological tables. Writers like Ajami, Arjomand, Berryman, Bruneau, Comaroff, Davis, Fields, Gilsenan, Ileto, Mainwaring, Mardin, Smith, Wuthnow, and others have challenged conventional expectations of secularization, showing that religion is dynamic not static, primary not epiphenomenal.[14] In so doing, they moved research about religion decisively beyond the study of documents, elite-directed programs, or classic church-state issues. Instead, there has been notable stress on discovering the sources of change in popular religion and popular culture and on understanding its evolving links to dominant institutions of power and meaning.

Like churches and religion generally, popular practices and usages also evolve to address new issues and circumstances. Just as elites reach out to shape popular groups, popular groups come to institutions like the churches with their own vision of what is right, wrong, and necessary. Change at either level requires careful, systematic attention; neither level of change can be deduced from the other. Although analysis must go beyond the formal limits of institutions, the continued impact of institutions cannot be ignored. Institutions are more than just machines for grinding out documents or allocating roles and statuses in a formalized way. They are vital, changing structures that help form the contexts in which experience is lived and judged. They provide identity, continuity, and nets of solidarity that are much valued by members, despite possible rejection by group members of specific institutional leaders or positions. Identification with and loyalty to institutions binds individual or group action to broad moral horizons and shared traditions.

This is not to make popular groups mere clay in the hands of elites but simply to note that links between them are of mutual interest: ties that neither side is quick to abandon. Analysis that forgets the binding quality of religious institutions and looks only to gross concepts like ''elite manipulation'' or ''popular struggle'' misses much of the reason why people join religious groups in the first place. It fails to see how *religious* motives and values undergird other aspects of group life and keep them going in the face of possible adversity. Whatever else the groups examined in these pages may claim to be, whatever other ends they serve, their original and continuing identity is reli-

[13] Ronald Inglehart discusses studies of political culture in relevant terms in his ''The Renaissance of Political Culture.'' See also his *Culture Shift in Advanced Industrial Society*.

[14] Fouad Ajami, *The Vanished Imam: Musa Al Sadr and the Shia of Lebanon*; Said A. Arjomand, ''Iran's Islamic Revolution in Comparative Perspective,'' ''Religion, Political Order, and Societal Change: With Special Reference to Shi'ite Islam,'' and *The Turban for the Crown*; Berryman, *Religious Roots*; Bruneau, *The Church in Brazil*, and also ''Church and Politics in Brazil: The Genesis of Change''; Karen Fields, *Revival and Rebellion in Colonial Central Africa*; Jean Comaroff, *Body of Power, Spirit of Resistance*; Michael Gilsenan, *Recognizing Islam*; Reyaldo Ileto, *Pasyón and Revolution*; David Lan, *Guns and Rain: Guerrillas and Spirit Mediums in Zimbabwe*; Mainwaring, *The Catholic Church*; Smith, *The Church and Politics*; Robert Wuthnow, *The Restructuring of American Religion*.

gious. The continuing power of religious belief and commitment provides a basis for enduring solidarities and the construction of meaningful vocabularies of moral concern. For this reason, if for no other, we must pay close attention to the content of popular belief and spirituality. Their transformation, not their abandonment for other ideals, is what lies at the root of whatever cultural, social, or political changes such groups may spur or legitimize in the larger society.[15]

Why religion? Why should religion be a perennial source of political meaning and action? What conditions make for change in religion and combine to give religious ideas a ready audience at any given historical moment? Scholars have often been content to follow Max Weber, noting the "elective affinities" between religious and political ideas, institutional forms, and practices. This perspective is enormously fruitful, but I would suggest that exclusive concern with elective affinities hinders understanding by accepting conjuncture as an explanation in itself.[16]

By stressing conjuncture and fit so much, an unreconstructed Weberian analysis gives too much weight (albeit unwittingly) to equilibrium and homeostatic balance and not enough to dimensions of power, conflict, and change within religion itself and between religion and politics. Demonstrating the "fit" of particular ethical norms or organizational forms to the life pattern of different groups is important, but it is excessively passive and gives too little place to the sources and pathways of change. It also fails to acknowledge religion's tremendous *consolidating* power. I refer to the peculiar ability of religious metaphors, places, and rituals to sum up and intensify experience. They do this by joining everyday events to a sense of supernatural intervention and by reinforcing religious ideas with material resources and a net of repeated human interactions.[17] This is what religious organizations and rituals *do*, and this is why they work so powerfully to unify behavior across social levels and in different arenas and walks of life.

---

[15] Berryman's description of how groups and group consciousness evolved in Aguilares, El Salvador, is relevant. In his words, the goal of those working with local residents "was certainly not to turn them from religiosity to activism, but to deepen the traditional religious vision and to transform it from an attitude of passivity (accepting things the way they are as the 'will of God') to one of active struggle for change" (*Religious Roots*, p. 108).

[16] I return to the concept of elective affinity in chapter 9, below.

[17] Karen Fields insists on this point to great effect throughout *Revival and Rebellion*. Analyses of millenarian movements that underscore the way they combine supernatural power with highly rationalized organization include the following: Susan Asch, *L'Eglise du Prophète Kimbangu de ses origines a son role actuel au Zaire*; Wyatt MacGaffey, *Modern Kongo Prophets: Religion in a Plural Society*, and also his *Religion and Society in Central Africa: The Bakongo of Lower Zaire*; Ralph Della Cava, *Miracle at Joaseiro*, and also his "Brazilian Messianism and National Institutions: A Reappraisal of Canudos and Joaseiro"; Lan, *Guns and Rain*; and Ileto, *Pasyón*. Terence Ranger provides an illuminating general review of religion's changing place in studies of Africa in "Religious Movements and Politics in Sub-Saharan Africa."

Further reflection suggests that conventional concepts have confined our sense of the issues within unduly narrow limits. Scholarly and public attention has focused too much on explicitly political ideas or vehicles (parties, elections, or direct manipulation of religious events). Research in this vein latches on to the apparent political *result* of religious action, with little sense of how or why religion may have stimulated or sustained action in the first place. But religious ideas, structures, and practices have a logic of their own. Individual and group action may be governed as much by that logic as by adherence to related social or political agendas. Analysis that remains within the contours of conventionally defined political events is likely to misread the process. By focusing on immediate concerns, and then projecting current configurations into the past, it reifies a particular form of religious-political convergence, without regard for understanding how the issues came to take on their present character and structure.

To be sure, explicitly political vehicles are important. Politicians and public officials often use religion for their own purposes, and religious leaders attempt in all kinds of ways to shape political outcomes and shape the public agenda. But if analysis starts here, a great deal is missed. Much of the theoretical and practical import of religion and politics lies less in conventional outcomes of this kind as in the way changes within religion are associated at once with new kinds of social organization and with the legitimation of new ideas about activism, power, and governance in ordinary life. This is what lays down a cultural foundation for authority (or for resistance to its claims).[18] It is here that the human solidarities are built which make any action endure. In this light, explicitly political events appear as the end of a long chain of events, not as its beginning.

All this suggests a need to reformulate common questions about the ideological direction of "politicized religion." I have already indicated some of the problems this concept raises. Instead of asking if religion is "revolutionary," "moderate," or "conservative" (or even "politicized"), it might be more profitable to look at structural issues, especially those affecting the link of popular and institutional levels to one another. Research would then consider how religious change provides a medium for the crystallization, organized expression, and potential enhancement of popular culture and action. Ideological direction of course varies with the specifics of tradition, context, and circumstances.[19] But the contrast between social and cultural "levels" remains.

[18] The relation between the black churches and the civil rights movement is a case in point. See for example Aldon Morris, *The Origins of the Civil Rights Movement*; and Taylor Branch, *Parting the Waters: America in the King Years, 1954–1963*.

[19] As Peter Worsely puts it, "Religion, it ought to be said, is neither intrinsically conservative nor revolutionary. It can be infused with any kind of social content, notably political: there are both religions of the oppressed . . . and the kinds of religions that have been summed up in the

The point is simultaneously theoretical and methodological. To understand how religion and politics interact and change together, analysis must accept the logic of religious belief and practice. This requires a conscious effort to hear it as expressed, to see it as practiced, and to construct or reconstruct the context in which these religious ideas resonate. Only then can we grasp how and why religion helps people make sense of the world, and organize themselves and others to deal with it. All this adds up to the need for scholarship to begin with what religious groups and people *actually do* and not with an account of why they do not do things of interest to social scientists, such as engaging in explicitly political activities. Jean Comaroff puts the matter well: "If we confine our scrutiny to the zero-sum heroics of revolution successfully achieved, we discount the vast proportion of human social action which is played out, perforce, on a more humble scale. We also evade, by teleological reasoning, the real questions that remain as to what *are* the transformative motors of history."[20]

The perspective outlined here requires a systematic effort to go beyond intellectualized and elite-focused categories. Consider the question of doctrine and ideology. How do average people perceive and act upon the formal ideas of religion and politics? No simple deduction from doctrine to motivation and practice is possible. The links are not direct but mediated in all instances by elements like context, class, gender, and institutional affiliations. The case of liberation theology, discussed in detail in chapter 2, illustrates the point well. Most of the scholarly and polemical literature devoted to this subject continues to address liberation theology *as a system of ideas*.[21] But the theologians stress the wisdom of the people. They take theology less as a tightly drawn set of ideas than as a group of reflections made about, and from within, a world of injustice and oppression. Their whole position thus enhances the value of popular insight. I do not mean to suggest that the ideas themselves lack importance; as we shall see, they have legitimized new goals and new kinds of organization with great and enduring impact. But the process does not operate in a neat, deductive fashion. Rather, throughout Latin America popular groups have taken these ideas and reworked them in the context of urgent everyday needs and conflicts. Along the way, religious symbols, ideas, and celebrations acquire new meaning, spurring and underscoring a changed appreciation of the proper bases of society and politics while at the same time empowering new commitments for change.

---

label given to the Church of England as 'the Conservative Party at prayer.' The relationship of religious beliefs, let alone movements and organizations, to the established power system thus varies, and is not a matter for metaphysical pronouncement disguised as sociological generalization. It requires empirical investigation to see what the case is" (*The Trumpet Shall Sound*, p. xxix).

[20] *Body of Power*, p. 261.

[21] I discuss liberation theology in detail in chapter 2, below.

Thinking about ideology in this way clarifies the issues of linkage, leadership, and legitimacy. Whatever linkage exists, however it may be organized and mediated, traffic along its pathways is never one way only. Institutions reach out to popular groups; popular groups select and rework. All this is unobjectionable, but attention to linkage conceals much ambiguity as to just *what* (or who) is "linked." In this book, I use the concept of linkage in several senses. In structural and class terms, linkage "joins" popular groups with elites and with the institutions they control and operate. Linkages also knit the concerns of everyday life and local grass-roots contexts with formally organized expressions of culture and power. The values of individuals are thereby connected in regular ways with organized group ideologies and broad cultural norms.

Legitimations and leadership are related. Much of the struggle around religion and politics in Latin America, as elsewhere, centers in some way on legitimation. Legitimation is contested at many levels, in struggles to claim the moral authority of religion and divine will (however defined) for different sorts of group practice and commitment and for alternative structures of power. Legitimation thus involves setting religion *as a unit* ("church," *ulema*, etc.) for or against some structure of power and authority. At the same time, disputes about legitimacy also arise *within* religions as alternative concepts of authority struggle to gain voice, audience, and routine expression. These provide a basis for common action and also a set of "spaces" (literally, groups, buildings, practices, rituals) in which such new ideas can be worked out, shared, and reinforced.

The central issue in terms of leadership is less *which* leader is endorsed or promoted than what makes any leader legitimate in the first place. One tradition looks for traits of inherited power, authority of office, or some special "gift" of divine inspiration. But these Weberian categories (traditional, legal-rational, charismatic) are not especially helpful. They fail to address how religious change at once legitimates new kinds of leaders (for example, prophetic rather than clerical) while eliciting potential leadership cadres from hitherto passive or suppressed groups. New, religiously inspired theories and structures can enhance the value of participation while providing experience in participation and self-governance. Once underway, the process rapidly becomes self-sustaining.[22]

[22] Latin America is only one example among many. Similar changes were notable among the Puritans, whose leaders were a new class in seventeenth-century England. Similar new leadership groups appeared in colonial Vietnam and Central Africa early in this century, have long been visible in the Philippines, and can now be seen in Southern Africa and in the upsurge of Shi'ite activism. Recent studies of American Evangelicals suggests that much the same thing is going on in the United States today. See my "Religion and Politics in Comparative and Historical Perspective" for a review of the evidence.

## Studies in Latin America

Over the last few decades, research and writing on Latin America have made significant, innovative contributions to the study of religion, culture, and politics. Not long ago, the shelves were sparse. Those seeking enlightenment found little more than formalistic accounts of church-state ties. Work of this kind rarely strayed beyond the confines of elite pronouncements, legal documents, and codified arrangements, or occasional impressionistic pieces.[23] North Americans and a handful of European scholars, as well as a creative and articulate group of Latin Americans who write as analysts and as interested participants, have brought forth a wealth of excellent studies on a wide range of specific topics in the last few decades.

The changing organization and political orientation of national churches has been examined in cases ranging from Brazil, Chile, or Central America to Argentina, Peru, Venezuela, and Colombia.[24] There has also been growing concern with the international dimensions of religious change.[25] Scholarship and polemic about ideological change and theological innovation, including liberation theology, has been extensive.[26]

[23] J. Lloyd Mecham's classic *Church and State in Latin America*, first published in 1934, long set the tone for research in the field. Attention was focused on legal relationships, documents and treaties were the basic data, and nations were presumed to provide the relevant units of analysis. Both church and state appeared in static terms, with little reference to broader political, social, or cultural dynamics, or to the relation between institution and other levels of analysis. I discuss the recent history of research in my "Religion" in Paula Covington, ed., *Latin American and Caribbean Studies: A Critical Guide to Research*.

[24] See the studies collected in Mainwaring and Wilde, *The Progressive Church*; Levine, *Religion and Political Conflict*; and for particular cases, the following: on Brazil: Azevedo, *Basic Ecclesial communities*; Bruneau, *Church in Brazil*; Mainwaring, *Catholic Church and Politics*; Della Cava, *Miracle*; and also his "Catholicism and Society in Twentieth Century Brazil"; Madeleine Adriance, *Opting for the Poor*; and Diana De G. Brown, *Umbanda*; on Chile: Smith, *Church and Politics in Chile*; on Central America: Berryman, *Religious Roots*; Dodson and O'Shaughnessy, *Nicaragua's Other Revolution*; Andres Opazo Bernales, *Popular Religious Movements and Social Change in Central America*; Jenny Pearce, *The Promised Land: Peasant Rebellion in Chalatenango, El Salvador*; Phillip A. Williams, *The Catholic Church and Politics in Nicaragua and Costa Rica*; Roger Lancaster, *Thanks to God and the Revolution: Popular Religion and Class Consciousness in Nicaragua*; and Jorge Cáceres, "Political Radicalization and Popular Pastoral Practices in El Salvador, 1969–1985"; on Argentina: Mignone, *Witness to the Truth*; on Peru: Luis Pasara, "Peru: The Leftist Angels," and also his *Radicalización y conflicto en la iglesia peruana*; and Catalina Romero, "The Peruvian Church: Change and Continuity"; on Venezuela and Colombia: Levine, *Religion and Politics in Latin America*.

[25] Among others see Eric Hansen, *The Catholic Church in World Politics*; and Lernoux, *People of God*.

[26] The literature is vast, but among major works one must cite the following: Gustavio Gutiérrez, *A Theology of Liberation*; *The Power of the Poor in History*, and *We Drink from Our Own Wells*; Leonardo Boff, *Jesus Christ Liberator*; *Ecclesiogenesis*; *Church: Charism and Power*; and *When Theology Listens to the Poor*; Juan Luis Segundo, *Theology for Artisans of a New Human-*

In recent years, a number of systematic efforts have been undertaken to examine the nature of progressive and conservative elements in the churches and to trace patterns of conflict between them. We thus have the benefit of substantial work on religion and revolution,[27] religion and authoritarianism,[28] and most recently of a handful of studies linking religious change to prospects for democratization.[29] A small group of scholars has also begun serious and systematic study of the social movements associated with religious change. Particular attention has been given to the composition and goals of membership, to movements' links with the churches, and to these movements' possible long-term impact on culture and politics. Evolving aspects of belief and practice have received less attention, although recent studies have begun to shed light on the extent to which broad-scale religious, political, and economic transformations translate into new kinds of everyday usage. The literature has been further enriched by biographies and life histories that give human depth and color to these general trends.[30]

This expanding body of scholarship did not emerge in a void. It draws strength and inspiration not only from the theoretical reassessments discussed earlier but also from the tremendous changes Latin America's society, economy, politics, and religion have undergone since the early 1960s. I provide detail on these transformations in the next few chapters. Here it suffices to underscore the points that make Latin America of particular interest. In brief, whether we begin with politics, with economics, or with the organization of social life, it is clear that, with rare exceptions, the last thirty years have brought rapid change and hard times to ordinary people throughout the region. Accelerated agrarian concentration, rapid economic growth, and intense migration to the cities in the postwar period proved repeatedly to be preludes for stagnation, heightened social conflict, and unprecedented levels of state repression and violence, including several civil wars and two successful revolutions (Cuba in 1959, Nicaragua in 1979).

---

ity; *The Liberation of Theology*; and *Theology and the Church*; Jon Sobrino, *Christology at the Crossroads*, and *Spirituality of Liberation*; Enrique Dussel, *History and Theology of Liberation: A Latin American Perspective*; *Ethics and the Theology of Liberation*; and *Ethics and Community*. Important commentaries include Ricardo Antoncich, *Christians in the Face of Injustice*; Phillip Berryman, *Liberation Theology*; Arthur McGovern, *Liberation Theology and Its Critics*; Michael Novak, *Will It Liberate? Questions about Liberation Theology*; and Paul Sigmund, *Liberation Theology at the Crossroads*.

[27] Dodson and O' Shaughnessy, *Nicaragua's Other Revolution*; Phillip Williams, *The Catholic Church*; John Kirk, *Between God and the Party: Religion in Revolutionary Cuba*; and Berryman, *Religious Roots*.

[28] Mignone, *Witness*; Mainwaring, *Catholic Church and Politics*; and Joseph Comblin, *The Church and the National Security State*.

[29] Daniel H. Levine and Scott Mainwaring, "Religion and Popular Protest: Contrasting Experiences"; and Edward Cleary, ed., *Born of the Poor: The Latin American Church since Medellín*.

[30] Carrigan, *Salvador Witness*; Pearce, *The Promised Land*; James G. Carney, *To Be a Christian Is to Be a Revolutionary*; James Brockman, *The Word Remains: A Life of Oscar Romero*.

Crises of this kind are commonly expected to stimulate a turn to religion, as individuals and communities bring their new and urgent needs to the encounter with God and with the churches. The last few decades have indeed witnessed a remarkable spurt of religious innovation throughout Latin America, resulting in a heightened role for the churches as institutions and enhanced participation by ordinary believers. In a crude way, one might even say that innovation and conflict in religion have been most intense where socioeconomic and political crisis has been the sharpest; Central America, Chile, Brazil, and Peru come to mind immediately. But Latin American experience presents several twists that together cast doubt on this "crisis-solace" model of religious growth.

To begin with, the model is too static. It assumes that both churches and their clienteles remain unchanged except for the external pressure of crisis. But these are active subjects, and the historical record shows considerable self-moved change at all levels. For their part, the churches have undergone deep ideological and organizational transformations. As noted, these have been manifest most notably in new attitudes toward poverty and the poor and in the creation of activist groups of clergy and sisters dedicated to working with the poor. These men and women seek to promote not only religious values (including solace where appropriate) but also material improvement and activism in general. Those who come to religious institutions have changed as well. New work routines, growing literacy and access to media, and migration on a large scale have combined to change the ordinary rhythms of life, making popular sectors available to hear new kinds of messages and to work effectively with innovative organizational forms.

The crisis-solace model also suffers from an unfortunately patronizing tone. The expectation that a turn to religion is sparked above all by the search for solace and escape rests on the same assumptions that have long dismissed religious belief and action as epiphenomenal, presumably doomed to privatization and ultimate disappearance. As my comments thus far indicate, this view is deeply flawed. To confine religion to a desire for escape is to misread the meaning of crisis and the role religion can play in crafting and supporting a response to crisis. In addition to presenting occasions for solace and escape, crisis is an opportunity for change and creative action that is eagerly seized on by ordinary people. In this book, I will show that given minimal support, legitimacy, and access to resources, ordinary people readily take crisis as a springboard for personal and collective change, creating self, family, and community according to a new image.[31]

The convergence of economic, social, political, and cultural changes in recent Latin American experience has helped shift the central axis of response in the region's Catholicism away from solace, the counsel of resignation, es-

---

[31] For a comparative example, see Samuel L. Popkin, *The Rational Peasant: The Political Economy of Rural Society in Vietnam*, chap. 5.

cape, or even just the provision of urgently needed help.[32] There has also been little promotion of traditional celebrations like pilgrimages, and there have been no major new visions or shrines. Such phenomena of course remain,[33] but on the larger scene they have been overshadowed by ideological critiques (including criticism by the churches of economic and political injustice) and by the emergence of new organizations and new forms of collective action among the poor.

Despite all this change, and the associated outpouring of research and commentary, important theoretical, empirical, and methodological gaps remain. For practical and financial reasons, most research has remained within a single country or set of communities. There are few genuinely comparative studies. At the same time, an unfortunate convergence of rigid disciplinary boundaries and reliance on elite-dominated categories of analysis has tended to separate in research what is joined in practice. Most studies thus focus either on elites or masses, documents or attitudes, institutions or movements. There has been little systematic attention paid to how institutional churches reach out to contact and shape popular religion and popular organization. Even less effort has gone into understanding the impact of this process on the churches themselves, not to mention into examining how change looks from the ground up: from the point of view of average men and women.

But of course neither institutions nor popular groups can be understood in isolation. There are no leaders without followers, at least not for very long. By the same token, popular groups, beliefs, and practices do not spring full-blown "from the people." They cannot be understood as autonomous, somehow "natural" products but must instead be seen as historical creations that emerge out of long-standing relations between subordinate groups and dominant institutions, among them the churches. The continuing importance of these links suggests that complete understanding requires analysis to take account of the way religious, cultural, and political change spills over formal ideological and institutional limits, shaping and drawing strength from the everyday experience of meaning and power.

## Studying Popular Groups, Hearing Popular Voices

This book is based primarily on original field research I carried out between 1981 and 1983 in peasant villages and popular urban neighborhoods in Vene-

---

[32] The development and spectacular recent growth of evangelical Protestantism in Latin America is another story. Among others see the following: David Stoll, *Is Latin America Turning Protestant?*; Lernoux, *People of God*; Jean Pierre Bastien, "Protestantismos latinoamericanos entre la resistencía y la sumisión, 1961–1983"; Deborah L. Huntington, "The Salvation Brokers: Conservative Envangelicals in Central America"; Susan Rose and Steve Brouwer, "Guatemalan Upper Classes Join the Evangelicals"; and Cecilia L. Mariz, "Popular Culture, Base Communities, and Pentecostal Churches in Brazil."

[33] See Candace Slater, *Trail of Miracles*.

zuela and Colombia. This is not a book about Venezuela and Colombia or even about the sources of variation in group and personal life uncovered at different levels in each country or church. Like base communities, the nations, churches, and communities studied here constitute the setting, not the subject, of this inquiry. My subject is religious change and cultural transformation: how these transformations begin, who carries them forward, and what makes them endure. I do not mean to suggest that context is not important. To the contrary, variations in the structure and traditions of national life, in patterns of opportunity and organization, and in the character of central institutions like the churches set important parameters for cultural and political change.

I chose to work in Venezuela and Colombia for both practical and theoretical reasons. In practical terms, my earlier research in these countries made it possible to build on established contacts and to examine change over time. In theoretical terms, these countries provide important contrasts not only to one another but also, taken together, to Latin America as a whole. Strong and continuing differences in economy, social structure, politics, religion, and the character of dominant institutions give popular issues a very different tone and character in the two cases. Because at the time of research each remained relatively open and democratic, analysis of popular experience in these countries offers a window on change that differs substantially from the examination of countries in extremes of crisis (e.g., in Central America) that have dominated much work on the subject. The peculiar conditions of revolution and civil war made popular religious groups in Central America more directly and explicitly political than has been the case elsewhere. Attention to less extreme settings may therefore shed light on more representative patterns of change.[34]

The structure and argument of this book, and of the research on which it is based, reflect a particular understanding of how best to approach the study of popular groups and to grasp the implications popular voices hold for cultural and political change. The whole effort grew out of my ongoing work on religion and politics. When I first addressed the issues through studies in Venezuela and Colombia, one of my goals was to understand the evolving organizational culture of the churches—to see the world as church leaders saw it, and then to explain how this worldview came to be. This suggests a perspective that examines change from the inside out. Fieldwork for that study was completed in the early 1970s. These were the years during which popular groups and all the debate and struggle associated with them (and with liberation theology) in Latin America began to occupy center stage. I finished writing the book while living in Central America, where popular groups played a central role in extremes of conflict.

Reflecting on these developments, I began searching for ways to grasp the

---

[34] This expectation is reinforced by the important role Colombia plays in continental church institutions, and by its position as standard bearer for Vatican policies throughout the region.

dynamics of religious change and its ties to culture and politics that would move analysis beyond exclusive focus on elite categories and on the institutional church alone. In particular, I wanted to understand transformations in popular culture without sacrificing attention to continuities of need, interest, identity, and affect that bind popular groups to religion and religious institutions over the long haul. My solution was to follow the example of popular groups themselves, and incorporate ordinary people into my working definition of ''church.'' Hence the stress I have placed in this book on relationships and linkages, and on the detailed attention given not only to elite views of the popular and official programs to capture and control them but also to popular images of dominant institutions and their agents: church, state, clergy and priests, politicians and bureaucrats, soldiers and police.

I conducted extensive preliminary research at the national level in both Venezuela and Colombia to locate central issues and actors, and to identify official and competing programs intended to work with popular groups. On this basis, dioceses and communities in the two countries were selected for closer examination, with a view to wide variation in context, structure, and orientation: rural and urban, devotional and socially activist, autonomous or controlled, progressive or conservative. The next step was to identify groups, study their development, and explore central patterns of organizational and cultural change. These complexities dictated an eclectic but structured bag of methodological tricks. Thus, I did not rely on narrative history or documents alone, although these helped set the stage. Instead, I worked to reconstruct organizational and personal histories through analysis of archival material, travel, observation of meetings, and depth interviewing.

Rather than attempt a general survey, I combined elite and informational interviewing (at national and diocesan levels) with two standard questionnaires: one for members and leaders of lay groups, another for priests and sisters. I also collected life histories of selected group members, sisters, and pastoral agents. The structure of research thus builds in variation of many kinds both between and within nations, institutions, groups, and categories of individuals such as peasants and city dwellers, men and women, laity and clergy. This comparative and multilevel structure allows for a more thorough exploration of the origins and pathways of change than would be possible with a focus on any single case or dimension of the process.[35]

[35] One solution to obstacles of distance, decentralization, and language has been the classic anthropological strategy of intense community studies and immersion in local life. Extended residence in a particular village or neighborhood can facilitate efforts to recognize general issues in the particularities of local actors, events, and circumstances. But although this approach has been enormously fruitful, several problems made it inappropriate for this research. Such methods commonly risk exaggerating the independence of local life by ignoring formative and continuing links with economic, cultural, and political structures. Further, the typical concentration those methods encourage on microlevel analysis makes them ill-suited to comparative work. My theoretical con-

Although it sounds simple and straightforward enough, in fact listening to popular voices and hearing what they say commonly runs up against a number of intellectual and practical obstacles. I have already indicated the theoretical ground from which these difficulties arise, including excessive reliance on elite categories of analysis and a disposition (inherited from nineteenth-century liberal and Marxist prejudices) to assume that religion is static and epiphenomenal. In addition, several practical problems discourage researchers and distort understanding of changes at the popular level.

Distance complicates the process of making contact with popular groups. Considerable travel and a great deal of persistence are required to reach groups, identify and locate members, and watch them grow and operate in situ. Getting there can be difficult, and repeated efforts may be needed before a sufficient base of trust is established to make reliable interviewing possible. Peasant communities are isolated and scattered, communications are irregular at best, roads are poor, and bus or jeep transport can be very unreliable. Urban communities are no less isolated, despite their greater proximity in physical terms. Transport to the slums and barrios of Latin America's cities is arduous and infrequent. One is commonly told that "no one goes there" and warned about the dangers of unaccompanied travel. Distance is as much social and cultural as physical. Peasants and city dwellers alike have good reason to distrust outsiders who come asking questions. Their experience of public officials has been far from happy. Success in overcoming obstacles like these requires patience and a careful effort to build legitimacy and extend contacts from one level to another.[36]

Classic models of Catholic organization underscore values of hierarchy, clerical supervision, and tight control of issues, leaders, and programs: Catholic Action is a case in point.[37] The contrast to popular groups like base communities is noteworthy. Base communities lack permanent staff and for the most part carry on without regular, structured ties to the national level. Decentralization is the norm. Members and leaders are expected to remain in their communities and to continue working at their jobs and caring for family and local needs. As a practical matter, this means that visits to communities and groups are often frustrated. Key people are likely to be elsewhere: visiting relatives, busy with harvest, working at another job, or simply not available. Again, extensive preparation and repeated visits are the only solutions.

---

cerns dictated a different approach, combining insofar as possible the virtues of community studies with the strengths of institutional and comparative analysis.

[36] I worked my way down the organizational chain, armed in one case with letters of introduction from the bishop and vicar-general of a diocese, and in other instances with personal introductions from activists and pastoral agents. The letters helped me overcome potentially nasty encounters with the military in rural areas of Colombia. See chapter 4 for details.

[37] Gianfranco Poggi, *Catholic Action in Italy*; and Levine, *Religion and Politics in Latin America*, chap. 8.

Language poses complex issues in which practical obstacles combine with theoretical difficulties. To begin with, ordinary people rarely use the discourse of social science to discuss issues that matter to them. General concepts such as class, politics, or even "religion" find little place in everyday conversation or group discussions. But group members cannot therefore be dismissed as indifferent on such matters. To the contrary, they think about their poverty, discuss it at length among themselves, and try to understand its sources. They are also politically informed. They listen to radios, talk with travelers, and worry about the impact of national politics on people like themselves. They pray together and debate how best to achieve an authentic and satisfying religious life.

All this effort is couched in specific, not general or abstract, terms. Group members may not read books or newpapers very often, and they certainly do not read liberation theology, but as we shall see, they read the Bible and use it as a basis for reflection on the meaning of events. In the groups I studied, the following issues occupy center stage when people talk with one another: faith and the need to serve others while serving God; the moral and social bases of community; a search for individual and collective ways to overcome the vulnerability that comes with being marginal and powerless; specifics like water supply, education, bridge building, or the establishment of cooperative arrangments for buying, selling, and saving; and friendship, trust, and the value of sociability. These and other issues are explored in detail in subsequent chapters. Here I wish to stress two points. First, in each case, the issue is specific in character (rooted in local life and problems) but at the same time has a capacity to range across personal, family, community, and institutional life. Sociability and trust are good examples, as is the persistent stress on linking faith to working together to serve others. Each provides a necessary foundation for action, drawing people together in hitherto unknown ways, getting them to share experiences and to think about pooling efforts and resources. The second point concerns how best to grasp the general implications of such localized and specific discussions. The approach I follow depends on putting words in context, searching for their origins, and then elucidating in fine-grained detail the practice in which they are embedded.[38]

The methodological issues outlined in this section involve more than matters of technique. They are theory laden and have important theoretical consequences. This formulation is one of the cliches of today's social sciences; specification is therefore in order. The research and writing of this book takes off from a phenomenological perspective and works insofar as possible with the categories people use in ordinary discourse. As a practical matter, this means taking statements of belief and action at face value. Although I checked

---

[38] On this point, see James Scott, *Weapons of the Weak: Everyday Forms of Peasant Resistance*, especially chap. 2, "Normal Exploitation, Normal Resistance."

assertions of fact and descriptions of programs with one another and against the documentary record, I resisted the temptation to explain away elements of religious belief or experience like visions or occasional encounters with spirits.[39]

Working with the categories in people's heads rather than with externally derived concerns can be tricky. Some element of distance and externality always remains and must be accounted for. Care is also needed to avoid taking categories of belief as frozen, once and forever the same. People think about these things, chew them over, and change in overt as well as in unstated ways. It is therefore vital to know the history of categories and to understand how styles of thought evolve. I did this by asking directly about change and also by tracing the institutional rootedness of ideas and the organizational forms through which these ideas are diffused. Analysis of official and competing efforts to create materials for popular groups and to train pastoral agents and group leaders was also important in this regard.

Belief and action must be placed in meaningful social contexts. This is because beliefs rarely appear in the abstract: they are learned and held by particular people in circumstances that make sense to them. I provided for meaningful contexts by stressing connections between communities, groups, and individuals and by building these into the structure of research. This is the logic of working from the national level to grass-roots communities through dense institutional networks that match links maintained through churches (dioceses, religious orders, parishes, etc.) with parallel ties established by state agencies, employment, the military, marketing patterns, cooperatives, and so forth.

In sum, popular voices find expression in contexts shaped by institutions and their agents, and by the needs and understandings (derived from class, economic circumstance, gender, politics, and communty tradition) that popular individuals and groups bring to their encounter with instituions.[40] A series of ongoing links between popular groups and the big structures of politics,

---

[39] Cf. Scott, *Weapons*, p. 46: "The approach taken here certainly relies heavily on what is known as phenomenology or ethnomethodology. But it is not confined to that approach, for it is only slightly more true that people speak for themselves than that behavior speaks for itself. Pure phenomenology has its own pitfalls. A good deal of behavior, including speech, is automatic and unreflective, based on understandings that are seldom if ever raised to the level of consciousness. A careful observer must provide an interpretation of such behavior that is more than just a repetition of the commonsense knowledge of participants." Scott builds on Max Weber's call for a social science that combines external verification with internal "insight." See Weber's classic essay, "The Concept of Following a Rule."

[40] I share the views outlined by Susan Eckstein in the methodological appendix to *The Poverty of Revolution*: "Perfecting my sources of information within an individualistic paradigm in itself would never have led me to my present understanding of the sources and consequences of urban poverty" (p. 229). On the virtues of working at the intersect of biography, structure, and history, see also C. Wright Mills, *The Sociological Imagination*.

economy, and culture provide critical organizational and symbolic ladders on which issues and resources move across social levels. Relations between the church and other key institutions such as the state give a specific tone and character to this encounter. They project models of proper behavior, leadership, and organization that can encourage hierarchy or equality, activism or passivity. By argument and example, they also advance contrasting notions of what religious faith requires in terms of equity, justice, and solidarity with others. The changing issues of religion and politics provide the context, but it is the individuals, movements, and groups that breathe life into the process. Ordinary people have a central role to play, and their ideas are as vital to analysis and understanding as are the more easily documented positions of elites and formal institutions. It is difficult to combine so many kinds and levels of reality, but the task is essential if we are to grasp the process of change in all its richness and to achieve durable, reliable understanding.

## The Structure of This Book

This book will begin with general issues, move to close analysis of particulars, and return in conclusion to general and comparative reflections. I chose this structure in part because it best reflects the nature of the research process. It also provides an apt framework through which popular voices can speak with minimal comment or interpretation. After establishing the historical line and central dimensions of change in Latin America as a whole, I gradually sharpen the focus and increase the magnification, moving first from region to country, diocese and community, and then to groups, mediators, and life histories. This pattern gives the reader the required context, followed by a chance to get accustomed gradually to the words, images, and speech rhythms that ordinary people use to explain themselves and their view of the world.

Moving through the book, the reader will find ordinary lives coming to the surface in all their richness and complexity. The men and women of Venezuela and Colombia who appear in these pages are both specific persons and something larger than themselves. As individuals, they carry a full weight of family and community and come to their encounter with big structures with a host of specific needs and expectations. Although they are particular (if they were not particular, they would not be fully human), what they do and say is neither accidental nor the result of conjuncture alone. Like the weather, human lives make patterns and move with forces beyond themselves. Individual peasants have much in common with others; women carry a particular burden of restriction and oppression; migrants to cities are recognizable the world over, despite variations in their language, outlook, and in the physical circumstances of city life. Combining particular with general dimensions of change helps to build human agency into the process in systematic ways. Change is never automatic, nor can it be understood with reference to "social forces" unmediated by consciousness and experience. By combining structural and cultural issues and joining collective with individual levels of change, the approach taken in this book sets transformations in religion (ideas, structures, and practices) in the context of changes that make these transformations resonate and ring true to ordinary people.

Why do popular groups turn to religion in the first place, and what do they find there? The men and women we will listen to in these pages all seek greater self-understanding and a better life, and they do so beginning with religion. For too long, popular religion has been dismissed as the simple faith of the unlettered—more emotional than reflective, more a matter of coming to terms with day-to-day survival than of intellectual apprehension of the changes at work in the surrounding world. Popular religion has been too easily identified as static and fatalistic, a prime source for escapism and mass apathy.[41] This book should help lay those long-established and false images to rest.

[41] Cf. Kselman, "Ambivalence and Assumption," and also his *Belief in History*.

# TWO

## LIBERATION THEOLOGY, BASE COMMUNITIES, AND

## THE PATTERN OF CHANGE IN LATIN AMERICA

IN A SMALL rural community in Colombia, I once interviewed a priest who managed in very few words to sum up much of the reason for the intense interest and conflict that surround Latin American Catholicism today. As we talked about the role that the church could and should assume in social and political life, he said firmly that ''I believe that Jesus Christ did not come to found a new religion, but rather to bring an integral liberation which reaches into all aspects of life'' (C 40). Both the man himself and his words are of interest here.

For years this priest has lived and worked in poor rural communities. His manner is simple and direct; in dress and life-style he identifies closely with the peasants he serves. His day-to-day activities center on promoting a new consciousness, sense of self-worth, and capacity for action among poor people. These efforts are worked out in practice through the creation of grass-roots organizations in which new forms of religious participation emerge and are closely linked to community-directed efforts at social, economic, and political change. His words point to a role for religion that transcends the institutional and ideological boundaries of formal church structures. They suggest that religion has a primary role to play in human liberation, and that in the search for liberation, transmitting the Gospel message of salvation cannot be separated from the creation of a better life, here and now.

All this is new in Latin America. For centuries, religion stood as a bulwark for conservatism in this part of the world, and the Catholic church remained firmly allied with elites opposed to change in the established order of things generally. Church leaders particularly set themselves against popular activism and protest of any kind. When protest came under Catholic banners, matters remained mostly under firm elite control and direction. But over the last few decades, significant elements in the Catholic church have moved to the active promotion of change, empowering and legitimating popular protest all across the region. Once seen as a cultural reservoir for apathy and fatalistic resignation, religion, and above all the Catholicism of popular classes, now commonly appears synonymous with solidarity and resistance to injustice and repression in cases otherwise as different as Brazil, Chile, or El Salvador.

The dynamic force of this process rests on the way transformations in religion have cut across changes in society and politics. Influence has run in both directions: change in religion has reshaped the agenda of social and political life in significant ways, while at the same time it has drawn new strength, allies, and models of action and organization from surrounding society. In this context, particular attention has gone lately to liberation theology and to base communities, which together have provided an anchor for debate and struggle throughout the period. This chapter examines the origins and key concepts of liberation theology, explores its relation to base communities, and assesses the impact of these innovations on the theory and practice of religion, politics, and social movements and on the relations among them in Latin America today.[1]

## Context and Conjuncture: The Pattern of Change in Latin America

Before I get into particulars, an important theoretical reservation is in order. By stressing context and conjuncture here, I do not mean to suggest that liberation theology's possible impacts are simply by-products of other forces. This commonly held view roots religious change in a process of *radicalization* that drives theologians and average people to more activist positions in response to extremes of exploitation and repression. Radicalization is a suggestive but inadequate tool for the explanation of change. Many have indeed been radicalized in Latin America lately, but the concept is too passive. It stresses reactions to repression, when in fact we are dealing with active, creative subjects whose vision of faith and commitments was open to radicalization from the outset. Liberation theology's core ideas, in particular their notable stress on themes of activism, participation, justice, and equality, have autonomous roots in religious change. The religious legitimacy of these ideas makes believers especially sensitive to undercurrents of power and privilege in any situation.

Liberation theology crystallized at a difficult moment in modern Latin American history, a period full of change, controversy, and unresolved conflict. The first major book with this title was published in 1971, capping a long period of writing and reflection.[2] In terms of intrachurch debates, liberation theology appears not long after the landmark meeting of the region's Catholic

---

[1] Apart from the commentary in and on Latin America cited in chapter 1, liberation theology has also drawn emulation and stirred sharp debate elsewhere. In the Philippines, for example, there has been much discussion of liberation theology and its links to grass-roots movements. See *Liberation Theology and the Vatican Document*, vol. 1, *The Vatican Document and Some Commentaries*; and vol. 2, *A Philippine Perspective*. The transformation of American black religion from quiescence and resignation to activism is relevant to these debates. See Albert J. Raboteau, *Slave Religion*, chaps. 5 and 6; and Morris, *Origins*.

[2] Gutiérrez, *Teología de la liberación*.

bishops at Medellín (1968), which set new dimensions for the church's role in all aspects of regional life. The struggles that first surfaced at Medellín were part of a general effort to reorient Latin American Catholicism in the light of the Second Vatican Council, which had concluded in Rome only three years earlier. The pattern of debate, conflict, and organizational change that followed the Medellín meetings emerged at the next general conference of Catholic bishops in 1979, at Puebla, and has continued openly ever since.

This remarkable and for the most part unanticipated combination of innovation, organizational growth, and intense ideological as well as political struggle surrounding Latin American Catholicism has inspired a vast literature, and I do not wish to go over that familiar ground here. A brief summary will suffice to set the scene.[3] For present purposes, recent Latin American history can be broken down into four broad periods: from the end of World War II to 1958; 1958 to 1968; 1968 to about 1979; and 1979 to the present. Major patterns are summarized in table 2.1

Despite scattered reforms and sporadic innovations, it is fair to say that until the late 1950s, the Latin American churches had a well-deserved reputation for stodgy conservatism. Long-standing alliances with political and economic powers were rarely challenged, and for the most part, the churches remained frozen in a defensive stance, suspicious of change, and strongly insistent on their guiding role in national culture. Their image of popular groups stressed the traditional view that the poor would be "always with us" and would require constant instruction and guidance to overcome a heritage of ignorant superstition.

By the end of this period, evidence began to surface of interest in reform in the churches, manifest in tolerance of a range of innovations. The common impression that Vatican II was the sole source and spark for change in the Latin American churches requires modification. The historical record shows that reform was underway on a broad front in Latin America before Vatican II. Examples include efforts to strengthen lay movements (among workers, peasants, or students), bureaucratic and educational change, and a series of "Pastoral Weeks" intended to review the overall pattern of church action and involvement.[4] These and related efforts suggest the presence of a broad disposition to change in Latin American Catholicism that was legitimized and enhanced, but not created de novo, by the encyclicals of Pope John XXIII and the Council.

Much of the Council's impact in the churches of Latin America can be

---

[3] See the sources cited in chapter 1.

[4] Examples abound: for Central America, see Berryman, *Religious Roots* and works already cited by Cáceres, Carney, Dodson and O'Shaughnessy, Opazo, and Phillip Williams; for the important but less studied case of Peru, see works cited by Pasara and Romero; Mainwaring, Bruneau, and Adriance (works cited) provide details for Brazil, albeit from different points of view.

**TABLE 2.1**

Change and Conflict in Latin American Catholicism, by Periods

| | Pope | Key Political Events | Key Church Events | Church Ideology (Key Issue) | Ideal Church Organization | Image of the Popular | Model Latin American Case |
|---|---|---|---|---|---|---|---|
| Post-War–1958 | Pius XII | Cold War | — | Christendom (defense) | Catholic Action Christian Democrats | Massive phenomena Ignorance (popular "piety") | Chile Brazil (Leme) |
| 1958–1968 | John XXIII Paul VI | Cuban revolution Democratic alternatives | Vatican II Medellín | Neo-Christendom Modernization Flirtations with Marxism (reform) | Decline of Catholic Action Rise of Christian Democracy | Massive phenomena Ignorance (popular "piety") | Chile Colombia |
| 1968–1979 | Paul VI | Rise of authoritarianism Civil war in Central America | Medellín Puebla Shift in CELAM | Emergence of Liberation Theology Splits (politics) | Decentralized Groups Base communities | Popular as the *class* of poor | Brazil Colombia |
| 1979–? | John Paul I John Paul II | Central American crisis Redemocratization | Puebla Papal Visits | Splits (popular) | Base Communities | Popular as the *class* of poor | El Salvador Brazil Colombia |

*Trends:* 1. Rise and decline of Christian Democracy as a model
2. Succession of key issues for church: Marxism, politics, violence, human rights, "popular," unity
3. Succession of preferred organizational vehicles: Catholic Action, Christian Democracy, popular/base communities

traced to three sources. First, as a general matter, conciliar stress on the need for the church to read and adapt to the "signs of the times" encouraged a more open stance to change, while at the same time undergirding a search for more effective sociological tools with which to understand change and participate actively in it. If the signs of the times were to be read, who better to read them than the men (and, grudgingly, the women) actively engaged in the work of the world? Second, as we have seen, conciliar innovations like the translation of liturgies into local languages opened dramatic new horizons of religious participation for ordinary believers. Participation became not only possible but also encouraged. Moreover, not any participation would do; since the Council, stress has been placed on participation that is active and informed. Conventional focus on administration of the sacraments and participation in pilgrimages, festivals, and the like has increasingly been dismissed as a mere "numbers game" that misses the point of religious authenticity. Third, the Council encouraged new kinds of interaction and organization within and among the Latin American churches. Many of the region's bishops met for the first time at Council sessions, and their exchanges reinforced a sense of common identity and shared problems. The Council also gave new legitimacy and impetus to national episcopal conferences as well as to regional structure. Most important among these are CELAM (the Latin American Conference of Bishops), which organized the meetings at Medellín and Puebla, and CLAR (the Latin American Conference of Religious Congregations), which has sponsored important reforms among religious orders. CELAM and CLAR each sponsor conferences, support publications, and serve as important arenas in which the church's continental agenda is debated and set.

The notion of the "signs of the times" warrants separate comment. This biblical concept (Matt. 16:3) was revived and given new force by Pope John XXIII, who made it a centerpiece of his convocation to the Council. Emphasis on reading the signs of the times undergirds a position that is open to change, with notable implications for the long-term ties of religion and politics. As with the emergence of models of the Church as People of God, reading the signs of the times undercuts traditional distinctions of "church" from "world." Reading the signs of the times thus affirms the value of ordinary experience, opening the door to egalitarian perspectives on knowledge and action. Alongside the hierarchical, trickle-down models long identified as typically Catholic, democratic views begin to find expression and room to grow. Average people have something to offer apart from faith and passive obedience; elites lose their monopoly on truth and inspiration. The church itself is enjoined to change; as part of the world, it shares in changing circumstances, and must learn from them.[5]

[5] In *Humanae Salutis*, his formal convocation to the Council, Pope John stated that "we should make our own Jesus' advice that we should know how to discern the 'signs of the times.' " Cited

In social and political terms, the 1960s were on the whole an open and optimistic period for the churches. The 1968 conference of Latin American bishops at Medellín marked a high point in this process and shaped the outlines of a critical and prophetic stance for the churches, along with efforts to implement many liturgical, structural, and pastoral innovations. But soon after Medellín, significant polarization appeared between those committed to a more thorough and radical promotion of change and others content to modernize within the church as they looked toward gradual reform in society and politics. After the overthrow of Allende in Chile, Marxism came into official disfavor in the churches, and there was a changing of the guard in major ecclesiastical institutions. This was manifest above all in the new and aggressively conservative leadership of CELAM, especially in the person of Msgr. Alfonso López Trujillo of Colombia, who became first the secretary-general and then the president of the organization. These changes led to a growing split that found CELAM and most of the area's episcopal hierarchies on one side and major religious congregations on the other. Through CLAR, the religious orders expressed a decidedly more progressive stance, with particular stress on the need for clergy and sisters to identify and side with the people.[6]

The tensions of this period came to a head at the 1979 Puebla meeting, which introduced a vigorous new pope to the scene, a pope who has since made Latin America a special priority. Puebla itself took place at the height of struggle in Central America, a struggle that claimed many church people as victims. Indeed, the meeting was convened only scant months before the triumph of the Nicaraguan revolution. At Puebla, a bitter and unusually public struggle between progressives and conservatives ended in something of a standoff.[7] No one was condemned, and each side continued its activities. The bishops affirmed their "preferential option for the poor," radicals persisted in their goals, and numbers of prelates went home determined to rein in potentially divisive elements in the base communities and to reinforce hierarchical

---

in Peter Hebblethwaite, *John XXIII: Pope of the Council*, pp. 397–98. Hebblethwaite suggests that optimism (characteristic of John XXIII) is also central to this perspective. Discerning the signs of the times connotes searching, often in difficult circumstances, for evidence of the Spirit at work in the world. This does not require blessing all existing structures or events, but it does suggest faith in the positive aspects of change, and in the capacity of human beings to change themselves and their societies.

[6] I return to this theme in detail in chapter 7, below.

[7] The rise to revolution in Central America coincided with great change and dislocation in the Catholic church as a whole. The year of 1978 saw three popes in the Vatican. After fifteen years in office, Paul VI died in late August, and his successor, John Paul I, died scarcely a month later, on September 28. Pope John Paul II was elected on October 16, and soon after traveled to Latin America, coming to inaugurate the Puebla conference in January 1979. See Peter Hebblethwaite, *The Year of Three Popes*. Berryman sums up the standoff at Puebla by citing one participant's view that Puebla was "empate en cancha ajena": that is, the visiting team (liberationists) managed a tie. See his "What Happened at Puebla" for a full account.

authority in their own churches. Since 1979, conflict on these issues has continued unabated. Conservative voices in the region's Catholic churches have been amplified by the appointment of large numbers of relatively young and highly conservative bishops, by determined campaigns to rein in what are seen as dangerously independent and excessively politicized groups, by concerted efforts to purge seminaries and schools of the influence of liberation theology, and by related attempts to promote alternative and presumably more malleable popular organizations linked to the church.[8]

These founding events occurred amid intense social and economic transformation. With rare exceptions, governmental efforts to spur economic growth through industrialization failed, and the 1970s witnessed a long slide to debt and economic depression. The whole period since the late 1950s has been marked by accelerated urbanization, expanded literacy, and a series of agrarian changes, which impoverished and further proletarianized peasants on a massive scale throughout the region. Political transformations were equally dramatic. The end of the 1960s brought a turn to military-dominated bureaucratic authoritarianism in major South American countries (Brazil, Chile, Argentina) followed in the next decade by the crisis of reactionary rule in Central America. Successful revolution in Nicaragua and the Salvadoran slide to civil war both came at decade's end.[9]

In such a context, the ideas of liberation theology resonated strongly, and the organizational innovations they inspired and legitimated found a ready and available audience that in many ways simply *did not exist earlier*. In part, this clientele was the product of the social and economic changes of the postwar period. Agrarian proletarianization, urbanization, and the growth of literacy

---

[8] See Lernoux, *People of God*, for a thorough examination. On the Chilean case, where a rollback is especially visible, see Circulo de Análisis Social, "Análisis de Coyuntura Politico Eclesial."

[9] David Collier's *The New Authoritarianism in Latin America* remains a useful overview of political developments. On Central America, see Berryman, *Religious Roots*; Enrique Baloyra, "Reactionary Despotism in Central America"; Walter La Feber, *Inevitable Revolutions*; and James Dunkerly, *Power in the Isthmus*.

On agrarian transformations, see above all Merilee S. Grindle, *State and Countryside: Development Policy and Agrarian Politics in Latin America*. An important general review of recent economic changes is John Sheahan's *Patterns of Development in Latin America*. Lars Schoultz comments insightfully on the structure and political implications of Latin American poverty in *National Security and United States Policy toward Latin America*, especially part 1. On the origins and impact of the debt, see, among others, Pedro-Pablo Kuczynski, *Latin American Debt*; Barbara Stallings and Robert Kaufman, eds., *Debt and Democracy in Latin America*; and William L. Canak, ed., *Lost Promises: Debt, Austerity, and Development in Latin America*.

Alejandro Portes reviews the implications of economic and political change for class formation, social structure, and organizational life in "Latin American Class Structures: Their Composition and Change during the Last Decades," and "Latin American Urbanization in the Years of the Crisis." See also Susan Eckstein, "Power and Popular Protest in Latin America," in her edited volume, *Power and Popular Protest: Latin American Social Movements*.

and mass communications cut many populations loose from the social bonds that had structured and made sense of daily life to that point. But the intense and expanded repression of the period also closed alternatives like political parties or trade unions, driving popular groups to the churches almost by default. The churches thus sought a new role and at the same time had one thrust upon them. Inspired by the ideas soon to be crystallized in liberation theology, elements in the churches began reaching out, developing strategies to promote popular interests and enhancing an independent role for popular groups. Groups themselves were attracted and gradually convinced by the new stress in Catholic discourse about equality, by the prophetic critique of injustice, and by the innovative forms of practice to which these gave rise. Spurred by urgent needs for material aid, protection, and moral support, they turned increasingly to the churches.

In retrospect, it is clear that the abundant state terror and violence that unfortunately characterize much of Latin America over the last twenty-five years provided a growth medium for popular religious movements. If violence was intended to cow activists and eliminate the drive to organization through the churches, it mostly failed. Organization was stimulated in several related ways. First, violence and repression made biblical and prophetic messages ring true. Jenny Pearce quotes one Salvadoran peasant who links the Bible with everyday life in ways that will echo throughout these pages.

> What made me first realize the path of our farmworkers' union was when I compared the conditions we were living in with those that I saw in the Scriptures: the situation of the Israelites for example . . . where Moses had to struggle to take them out of Egypt to the Promised Land. . . . Then I compared it with the situation of slavery in which we were living. For example, when we asked for changes in the work rates on the plantations, instead of reducing them for us, the following day they increased it, just like the Pharaoh did with the Hebrew People making bricks, right? . . . Our struggle is the same: Moses and his people had to cross the desert as we are crossing one right now; and for me, I find that we are crossing a desert full of a thousand hardships, of hunger, misery and of exploitation.[10]

Repression drove activists and potential clients to the churches. Often there was no place else to go. Working within the umbrella of the institutional church's decentralized structures, activists and pastoral agents were in many cases harder to trace and control than were the national groups that already had been eliminated by the police and army.[11] Clients came to the churches with urgent needs and found material as well as ideological help, along with solidarity and assistance in organization, which together made resistance easier. The self-reinforcing aspect of community is critical to and precedes any

---

[10] *The Promised Land*, p. 118.
[11] Adriance stresses this point in *Opting for the Poor*.

direct political action. As we shall see, explicitly political messages, identities, and commitments typically come later. The root religious motive is what makes for commitment and endurance in the face of adversity.

To round out this general review, I wish to mention briefly the role played by Christian Democratic parties. At one point in the early 1960s, these parties seemed to hold great hope for the future of Latin American politics and for the direction of Catholic political energies in democratic channels. Although such hopes have generally faded, it is worth reflecting on the relation between these parties and the popular movements that concern us here. The relationship is clearly inverse. The political successes of Christian Democracy in the 1960s (Chile, Venezuela, and, to a much smaller degree, El Salvador) had a mostly retarding effect on popular religious movements. Religiously inspired social and political activism was channeled into party and electoral molds, under the firm control of civilian political elites. Where Christian Democracy was weak or absent (Peru, most of Central America, Colombia, and Brazil), religious activism moved more directly to the kinds of popular movements at issue here—that is, those that were linked to the church but emphasized autonomy, were biblically inspired, and that stressed social action.

## Central Ideas of Liberation Theology

Liberation theology is part of a general Latin American response to the changes in Catholicism since the Second Vatican Council. Theologians and activists identified with this school share a concern with historical change, insist on the necessity and primacy of action to promote justice, and give place of preference to everyday experience as a source of religiously valid values. From these foundations, liberation theology has spurred and legitimized organizational innovation while undergirding a notable clerical populism throughout the region, which has sent sympathetic priests, sisters, and pastoral agents "to the people." Their notion of religious service embraces values of solidarity and shared experience and identifies strongly with people whose lives are deformed by oppressive structures. Phillip Berryman's definition points up the complexities at issue in liberation theology: (1) an interpretation of Christian faith out of the suffering and hope of the poor; (2) a critique of society and of the ideologies sustaining it; and (3) a critique of the activity of the church and of Christians from the angle of the poor.[12]

Liberation theology comes together as a theory and a set of guidelines for action around issues of poverty and the poor. The theologians explain poverty in structural terms, using Marxist categories of class, conflict, and exploitation as the basis for a critical social analysis. They also insist on the need to see

[12] *Liberation Theology*, pp. 6, 205.

issues through the eyes of the poor, to share their conditions, and to live with them in ways that undercut long-established social and cultural distances between the church and average believers. Poverty is distinguished from misery. The former may have virtues of simplicity and lack of commitment to earthly things, but the latter has no virtues. Misery stunts human potential, making a fully Christian life impossible. Four closely related themes lie at the heart of liberation theology: first, a concern with history and historical change; second, the return to biblical sources; third, a stress on the poor, and a related emphasis on doing theology in a way that enhances the value of everyday experience and the insight of average people; and finally, close and complex relations with Marxism.

Concern with history hinges on attempts to grasp the meaning and direction of historical change. Change itself is depicted as inevitable, normal, and good; all societies and institutions change continuously. The proper task of religion and of theology is thus not to defend some static structures or ideas that are treated as eternal and unchanging, a "sacred deposit of faith" in traditional terms, but rather to participate creatively *from within the process*. This requires theologians to see the church itself in historical terms, as a community of believers living and changing over time and space. The experience of this community then becomes a basis for defining "the church," and for locating its proper place in the world. The very distinction of "church" from "world," so central to conventional Catholic discourse, yields here to a desire to "read the signs of the times," valuing and learning from the world in which the church is intimately and inextricably entangled.

The return to biblical sources draws strength from the reforms of Vatican II, which put ritual and liturgy into local languages. This technical innovation has altered the quality of religious participation and spurred great popular interest and concern with Bible study. Making shared Bible study central to religious practice has enormous impact in societies whose majority is often poor and illiterate, where most poor people have long been given to understand that their opinions are of no value (or, more precisely, *that they have no opinions*). If all can read and comment on the Bible, the value of popular insights is enhanced and traditional distinctions of rank in religious life are undercut. Equal access to the Bible can be a great leveler, as the experience of the Puritan revolution in seventeenth-century England reminds us.[13]

Given their concern with historical experience, it is not surprising that liberation theologians should look to the Hebrew Prophets and emphasize Old Testament images of God as an active presence in the world. For prophets like Isaiah, Amos, or Jeremiah, as also throughout the whole Exodus story, au-

[13] On this point see David Zaret, *The Heavenly Contract: Ideology and Organization in Pre-Revolutionary Puritanism*; and two books by Christopher Hill: *The World Turned Upside Down: Radical Ideas in the English Revolution*, and *The Century of Revolution*.

thentic faith is most fully expressed in actions to promote justice.[14] Liberation theology enhances *prophetic roles*, those which by teaching and example criticize injustice and work toward a better society. The figure and impact of Jesus Christ have been reinterpreted; themes of passive suffering and sacrifice have been downplayed in favor of themes that highlight Jesus' concern for justice, equity, and sharing.[15]

Liberation theology's overwhelming stress on the poor flows easily from the two previous points. Of course, concern for the poor is not new. Poverty and the poor have long held privileged status in the Christian scheme of things. The churches have always attended to the poor, for example, through charity, protection of the abandoned, or the promotion of programs *for the poor* like agrarian or political reform. What changes in liberation theology is less the fact of poverty or the notion of involvement with the poor than the way poverty is explained and the role that is created and promoted for the poor in church, society, and politics.

The social centrality and core religious value of poverty together undergird a view that accords poor people a privileged insight into reality.[16] This hermeneutical position drives liberation theologians to enhance the value of ordinary experience as a guide to reflection and action. The poor have something of special value for theology and for religion generally. Moreover, this contribution is best expressed in efforts initiated and carried out by the poor themselves, not by others acting in their name. In this way, the poor appear in the texts of liberation theology less as objects of the church's actions or programs than as active subjects. Acting *for the poor* therefore yields to sharing with, learning from, and accompanying them in organizations that poor people themselves have a major hand in running. Liberation theologians repeatedly affirm that the basic questions of theology center on poor people and on the meaning of their experience. Unlike much modern European theology, the basic interlocutor of liberation theology is therefore less the unbeliever than the poor, the basic problem less atheism than idolatry and suffering.[17]

---

[14] Michael Walzer provides a good overview in *Exodus and Revolution*. See also H. Mark Roelofs, "Liberation Theology: The Recovery of Biblical Radicalism." The exodus paradigm of oppression followed by wanderings in the desert and ending in the promised land runs through much liberation theology. In this vein, Gustavo Gutiérrez compares being poor in Latin America to being in a foreign land in these words: "Exiled, therefore, by unjust social structures from a land that in the final analysis belongs to God alone . . . but aware that they have been despoiled of it, the poor are actively entering into Latin American history, and are taking part in an exodus that will restore them what is rightfully theirs" (*We Drink from Our Own Wells*, p. 11).

[15] Claus Bussmann reviews the issues well in *Who Do You Say? Jesus Christ in Latin American Theology*.

[16] Cf. Monika Hellwig, "Good News to the Poor: Do They Understand it Better?"

[17] Leonardo and Clodovis Boff put the matter sharply, noting that "to pretend to 'discuss liberation theology' *without seeing the poor* is to miss the whole point, for one fails to see the central

The preceding considerations point up the centrality of questions of method. In liberation theology, the very enterprise of doing theology moves from a deductive and axiomatic logic to become an interpretive discipline, shaped and limited by the context in which it evolves and by the interests and experiences of the Christian community itself. As a practical matter, these interests and experiences are the way they are because of historical realities of exploitation, injustice, and oppression. By framing the matter in these terms, liberation theology commits itself to listening to the poor and learning about the world as they see and experience it. Commitment and involvement with struggles for liberation are central, and therefore stances of dispassionate neutrality are dismissed as unrealistic and hypocritical. The development of such ideas laid a foundation for the more general church commitment outlined in 1979 at Puebla, to a "preferential option for the poor."[18]

The relation of all this to Marxism is highly controversial and has provided much of the ground for ecclesiastical and political attacks on liberation theologians and those associated with them. Critics paint it as tainted by Marxist ideas and subordinate in practice to Marxist political agendas of class conflict, violence, and revolution. The truth of the matter is complex and must be sorted out with great care.[19] Much of liberation theology's basic sociological apparatus is clearly borrowed from Marxism. Concepts and categories like class, conflict, and exploitation are prominent and mix with general notions about dependence to forge a unified analysis of Latin American reality. The theologians see using Marxist sociology as simply realistic. In their view, conceptual borrowing does not require political alliance, and can be undertaken in any case without calling into question the religious roots of belief and commitment.[20]

Liberation theology also has more subtle links to Marxism. Its pervasive stress on action (especially self-moved mass participation) echoes a number

---

problem of the theology being discussed. For the kernel and core of liberation theology is not theology, but liberation" (*Liberation Theology: From Confrontation to Dialogue*, p. 11).

[18] The phrase has come to symbolize the conclusions reached at this important meeting of Latin America's Catholic bishops. For the complete text of the Puebla documents, along with selected commentaries, see John Eagleson and Phillip Scharper, eds., *Puebla and Beyond*.

[19] The best and most balanced of recent studies is Arthur McGovern's *Liberation Theology and Its Critics*. See also Michael Lowy's insightful review of the issues in *Marxisme et théologie de la liberation*. For critical views, see Sigmund, *Liberation Theology at the Crossroads*; Novak, *Will It Liberate?*; and the two Vatican instructions on liberation theology written by Joseph Cardinal Ratzinger, prefect of the Congregation for the Doctrine of the Faith. The first, "Instruction on Certain Aspects of the 'Theology of Liberation,' " is harsher in tone than the second, "Instruction on Christian Freedom and Liberation." I review a selection of recent works in "How Not to Understand Liberation Theology, Nicaragua, or Both" and "Considering Liberation Theology as Utopia." On the general controversy, see also Joseph Cardinal Ratzinger, *The Ratzinger Report*; Segundo, *Theology and the Church*; Antoncich, *Christians*; and Rosino Gibellini, *The Liberation Theology Debate*.

[20] Cf. Michael Dodson, "Liberation Theology and Christian Radicalism in Contemporary Latin America."

of Marx's original insights. Marx had much more to say about religion than the famous and often misrepresented comment about its being an "opiate of the people." The *Theses on Feuerbach*, for example, underscore the need for action and the urgency of learning from action in ways that inform and sharpen further action toward the common goal. Liberation theology's great stress on doing, on praxis, and on action to promote justice recall Marx's statement that "the philosophers have only *interpreted* the world in various ways; the point, however, is to change it" (no. 11). It also echoes his description of social life as "essentially practical" (no. 8), as well as his much-ignored warning against simplistic materialism: "The materialist doctrine that men are products of circumstance and upbringing, and that, therefore, changed men are changed products of other circumstances and upbringing, forgets that it is men who change circumstances, and that it is essential to educate the educator himself" (no. 3).[21]

Specific Marxist-Christian alliances are the least significant aspect of the relation. Individual theologians have certainly commented favorably on such common action, but after a short-lived flurry centered on Chile in the early 1970s, no broad movement has been visible. Indeed, the failure in Chile spurred a considerable backlash against such alliances. Where Marxist-Christian alliances do appear, as for example in Central America lately, at issue is more a set of practical, grass-roots cooperations, a unity "from below," than the result of some general program (presumably inspired by liberation theology) to draw the two sides together in a common effort.[22]

This account of liberation theology underscores its characteristic fusion of religious understanding, social analysis, and activism. It is vital to keep these elements in balance and not to assume that religious belief, practice, or spirituality are secondary, mere adjuncts to the basic tasks of social or political transformation. In the words of Gustavo Gutiérrez, "It is a serious mistake to reduce what is happening among us today to a social or political problem." To the contrary, a new spirituality is emerging: "The spirituality being born in Latin America is the spirituality of the church of the poor . . . the spirituality of an ecclesial community that is trying to make effective its solidarity with the poorest of the world. It is a collective, ecclesial spirituality that, without losing anything of its universal perspective, is stamped with the religious outlook of an exploited and believing people. . . . It is a new spirituality because the love of the Lord who urges us to reject inertia and inspires us to creativity is itself always new."[23]

Liberation theology's core ideas gained added force in Latin America from

---

[21] Citations from the *Theses on Feuerbach* are from the text in Robert Tucker, ed., *The Marx-Engels Reader*.

[22] Berryman, *Religious Roots*; and works cited by Williams, Dodson and O'Shaughnessy, and Cáceres.

[23] *We Drink from Our Own Wells*, pp. 2, 29. Transformations in popular spirituality are detailed in chapter 5, below.

the particular conjuncture in which they emerged. An understanding of the social transformations and political dynamics of this period makes sense of liberation theology's impact in three related ways: (1) the visibility of specific ideas and their role in shaping the agenda of public discourse and debate; (2) the emergence of new popular clienteles for church action of any kind; and (3) the specific appeal to this clientele of structures emphasizing grass-roots autonomy, such as the base communities that developed across the region around the same time.

## Liberation Theology and Base Communities: Ideas and Action

The clearest ideological impact of liberation theology has come through its capacity to shape discourse, creating and promoting issues as legitimate topics of debate in society, politics, and in the churches. Three issues warrant separate attention: human rights, popular participation, and authority. The Latin American churches have been central to the promotion and defense of human rights in Latin America since the late 1960s. They have articulated a broad critique of injustice and abuses of power, have protected groups and individuals, and have aided victims of oppression in many ways.[24] It is worth asking why. Why did human rights move to the center of church agendas at this particular time? After all, repression is nothing new.

The ideas of liberation theology played a key role in this process. They underscored the legitimacy of a critical and "prophetic" role for the churches. Further, by stressing the centrality of popular insight and experience, they turned discourse away from traditional stress on inter-elite contacts and negotiations toward solidarity and shared experience with repression's victims. This general stance was reinforced by the move of many pastoral agents to "live with the people," sharing their lives in often difficult and dangerous conditions.[25] As these agents came under attack, church leaders responded in their defense, and thereby became entangled in broader political issues and confrontations. Finally, liberation theology's characteristic sociology, rooting poverty and injustice in structural economic conditions, spurred concern not only with abuses of civil liberties but also with the kinds of social and economic systems that make such abuses likely in the first place. The whole package of agency and influence converging around human rights is a good example of what is involved in "educating the educator."

Issues of popular participation and authority are closely linked for liberation theology. Theological arguments for the autonomous value of popular insight have structural and organizational consequences, in particular for the way au-

[24] Brian H. Smith, "Churches and Human Rights: Recent Trends on the Subcontinent."
[25] See chapter 7, below, for a full discussion.

thority is justified and exercised in religion and in politics. These emerge most clearly in the relation between liberation theology and base communities.

Liberation theology and base communities are linked historically, and it is fair to say that they are related as theory is to practice. This neat phrase has several specific meanings. It points up the time sequence: the major growth of base communities dates from the mid-1970s, drawing strength from the conjuncture noted above between church initiatives and social/political transformations. The phrase further suggests that the spread of base communities is spurred by the way liberation theology's ideas motivate church leaders and pastoral agents to sponsor and promote such initiatives. Finally, it implies that the ordinary experience of base communities reinforces ideas of egalitarianism and collective action, and that this experience undergirds continuing commitments to action in the promotion of justice as an outgrowth of a transformed religious faith.

Elsewhere I have described this position as a "Radical Ideal" of base communities.[26] In this view, base communities generate new values, orientations, and forms of action that reach out from religion to revolutionize social and political life as a whole. The Radical Ideal is suggestive but needs substantial modification to serve as a guide to accurate and complete understanding. As a practical matter, it is approximated only in a handful of cases that are mostly drawn from extreme situations like Central America or Brazil in the late 1970s. Most experiences are mixed, variation is more notable, and the immediate political thrust of base communities is less obvious, as is the possible impact of liberation theology in the process.

A common working definition takes off from the three elements of the name "ecclesial base community": striving for *community* (small, homogeneous); stress on the *ecclesial* (links to the church); and a sense in which the group constitutes a *base* (either the faithful at the base of the church's hierarchy or the poor at the base of a class and power pyramid). Whatever else they may be, at a minimum, most base communities are small groups of ten to thirty people, are ordinarily homogeneous in social composition, and are usually made up of poor people. Whatever else they may do, at a minimum they gather regularly (once every week or two) to read and comment on the Bible, to discuss common concerns, and occasionally to act together toward some concrete end.

Within these general contours, there is much dispute over what constitutes a base community. Widely varying kinds of organizations are often lumped together and presented under this heading. What passes for a base community in El Salvador or Brazil often bears little relation to groups of the same name encountered in Colombia or Argentina. Conversely, a group that meets all of the normal definitions may not call itself a base community. There is also

[26] "Religion, the Poor, and Politics."

intense competition within countries between alternative models, as progressives and conservatives each try to advance their goals through groups with this name.

Base communities are rarely spontaneous creations, springing unbidden and full blown "from the people." They are born linked to the churches, specifically to initiatives by bishops, religious orders, priests, nuns, or lay agents commissioned by the church. These ties are maintained through a regular routine of courses, visits by clergy, and especially sisters, and through the distribution of mimeographed circulars, instructional material, and cassettes. Base communities may be popular in social composition, but they are not autonomous or isolated from the institutional church. Rather, they are constantly influenced by it and often subject to its monitoring and control.[27]

A close look at the process of grass-roots organization reveals a clear and common pattern. The first step comes as pastoral agents began reworking ties between churches and popular classes. In large numbers they went to live in popular comunities and work alongside residents on a day-to-day basis. There are clear populist echoes here. Groups were formed after some such contact, and only with a few years of experience did a more elaborate and articulated vision begin to appear of what, as base communities, they were supposed to be like. Base communities thus begin with pastoral agents reaching out to popular sectors. But since they involve a relation *between* the church and popular groups, it is essential to explore the bases of popular receptivity.

This receptivity is not unlimited. There are countless cases where clerics have tried but failed to create base communities. Failure has been more likely when pastoral agents attempted to encourage the formation of highly politicized groups from the outset. Success has been more common in cases where religion and community were principal initial goals. Popular receptivity has been greater where traditional religious values and practices (e.g., respect for images, processions, veneration of saints) were upheld, even as other aspects of popular religiosity changed. Members also respect and venerate religious authorities, and remain loyal to them even if they reject specific policies these leaders may advance. For this reason, direct attacks on bishops or on the pope by radical activists have often backfired.

These considerations suggest that attention to base communities' political character should not obscure their original and enduring religious nature. If we ask what base communities actually do every day, we find that in practice they are much more conventionally religious than is commonly realized. Members pray a lot, both individually and as a group. They also value and practice a number of traditional prayers and rites (rosaries, nocturnal vigils,

[27] The literature on base communities is large and growing fast. Recent works with useful bibliographies include Azevedo, *Basic Ecclesial Communities*; Bruneau, *The Church in Brazil*; W. E. Hewitt, *Base Christian Communities*, "Strategies," and "The Influence"; and Levine and Mainwaring, "Religion and Popular Protest."

adorations, and celebrations like processions and pilgrimages), many of which are spurned lately by Catholic radicals. The clash of popular desires for liturgy with activist stress on "useful" collective action is a permanent feature of much base community life.[28]

The preceding comments lay the bases for a typology of base communities, which is presented in summary form in table 2.2, below. Groups are distinguished on dimensions such as their origins, their prevailing ecclesiology, the source of each group's agenda, the group's prevalent scope of action, and so forth. The implications of this typology will be drawn out more fully in subsequent chapters, as a range of grass-roots experiences with base communities is examined. For the moment, it suffices to note the broad outlines of two prominent alternatives to the Radical Ideal, denominated here as a "Conservative Ideal" and an ideal of "Sociocultural Transformation." The first of these provides a mirror image to radical understandings of what base communities ought to be like. In the Conservative Ideal, autonomy is replaced by hierarchical control, stress on independence by emphasis on deference to authority, broad-gauged activism by efforts confined for the most part to the ambit of family and community. Tight top-down control of groups and of their agendas is ensured here by careful provision for training the leaders and monitoring the everyday life of groups. In contrast, those promoting what I have termed an ideal of sociocultural transformation have much in common with radicals but differ on several key points. Politics, especially partisan affiliations and open confrontations with the hierarchy, is played down. Religious activities are valued and enhanced, and there is a generally open and accepting attitude to expressions of popular piety. This stands in sharp contrast not only to conservatives, who typically dismiss popular religion as the heterodox product of ignorance and superstition, but also to radicals, who, as mentioned, often see popular desires for traditional celebrations as alienated expressions of class exploitation, diversions on the road to an all-out commitment to liberation.

The three types present very different images of the ideal group, member, and leader. For radicals, the ideal group is focused on social action and consciousness raising. The ideal member is a politically informed person whose faith inspired activism in community and nation. For conservatives, the ideal group is dependent on the church and serves above all as an occasion for prayer, reflection, and Bible study. The ideal member appears here as a pious client of the clergy, and when possible, local leaders are incorporated into some kind of miniclerical status such as deacon or lay minister. Those working toward sociocultural transformation give greater scope to local leaders. Such groups typically are started not by activists (radical or conservative clergy) but

[28] Azevedo makes this point forcefully in *Basic Ecclesial Communities*, pp. 80–98, and 119–57. See also Nicholas Wolterstorff, *Until Justice and Peace Embrace*, especially chap. 7.

rather by local men and women who, inspired by motivational sessions that often lead to a vivid sense of conversion, return home determined to "do something" in and for the community.

From ground level, what average people in Latin America see is not some monolith comprised of liberation theology/base communities, as the Radical Ideal would lead us to expect, but rather competing projects that advance very different visions of what base communities ought to mean and how they ought to act in practice. The alternative before them is not so much "base communities or nothing" as a choice among competing packages. The competition is played out on several levels, as those promoting different visions of base communities (and of religion and politics more broadly) struggle to control scarce resources and to gain access to grass-roots groups. Occasionally, open competition rages in the same community. This has been the case in struggles over the popular church in Nicaragua and is also common where evangelical Protestant chuches have begun to make inroads.[29] But the more common case finds

TABLE 2.2
A Typology of Base Communities

|  | Radical Ideal | Sociocultural Transformation | Conservative Ideal |
|---|---|---|---|
| Origins | Early 1970s | Early to mid-1970s | Late 1970s |
| Exemplars | El Salvador 1970s Chile 1970s | Peru Brazil | Colombia |
| Prevailing Ecclesiology | People of God (Liberationist) | People of God (Liberationist) | Institution Christendom |
| Prevailing Image of "Popular Religion" | Religion of the oppressed | Religion/Culture of the poor | Religion of the ignorant |
| Key Values | Authenticity Solidarity | Authenticity Solidarity | Loyalty Unity |
| Local Automony | Yes | Yes | No |
| Agenda Source | Bible and "reality testing" | Bible and "reality testing" | Bible and official guides |
| Scope of Action | Local/National | Mostly local | All local |
| Politics | Confrontational | Local/Within group | "None"(?) |
| Links to Church | Strong/Backing to popular | Coordination | Strong, vertical control |

[29] See the sources cited in chapter 1.

alternative visions of base communities, each ensconced in a specific territory, where they are protected and supported by some element of the institutional church, be it a diocese, a religious order (like Jesuits or Maryknolls), or a group of foreign clergy.

No matter what the social or political agenda may be, from child care to sewing circles, from cooperatives to strikes or land invasions, in all instances there is great stress on prayer, Bible study, and liturgy. In any event, most of the social and political agenda at issue is quite conventional. Typical activities include sewing, visiting the sick, or "social action," which usually means collecting money, clothing, or food for those in extreme need. There are also commonly attempts to found cooperatives, which generally remain limited to very small-scale savings and loan operations or, at most, to collective marketing or common purchase arrangements.

All this is innocuous, and its salience in base community life raises thorny questions about impact. If normal practice continues along these tracks, where is the change? I would argue that even within these parameters, experience in the base communities represents a notable break with hitherto normal religous practice. Consider daily practice once again. Members meet regularly to read and discuss the Bible, to pray, and to celebrate liturgies as a group. *None of this was true on any significant scale before the mid-1960s.* Until recently, most popular religious life was sporadic, centered around celebrations of mass on major holidays or on occasional visits to church coinciding with key sacraments like birth, marriages, or funerals. Scarcity of clergy meant that many people's only contact with the official church, especially in rural areas, came on such isolated occasions.

The promotion of base communities, Bible study, and the change to local languages (Spanish and Portuguese) for ritual and liturgy has been particularly important. Group meetings make religious life more regular and familiar. Direct access to the Bible lessens dependence on traditional authority figures for guidance and interpretation. Moreover, shared reading and discussion elicit ideas, interests, and leadership skills that otherwise would surely have remained latent. The whole process promotes new criteria of legitimate action and introduces ideas about leadership different from those the community is likely to have encountered before. Berryman underscores the depth and impact of these changes, noting that "today the Bible is read in small villages or barrio level groups by people sitting on benches, often in the dim light of a kerosene lamp. Previously accustomed to seeing the church as the priest, or the large building down in the town, or an organization with its own authorities like those of the government, they now begin to see themselves as the church."[30]

A critical element in setting long-term impact is the quality of experience

[30] *Liberation Theology*, p. 56.

group life provides and promotes. In chapters 5 and 6 I will show how egalitarian and participatory practice builds confidence and promotes new capabilities for self-expression and leadership. The solidarities thus created may then spill over to undergird collective action in other areas (unions, cooperatives, local associations), countering traditions of fatalism and mutual suspicion. Genuine group autonomy furthers such spillover by providing legitimate room for experimentation and self-initiated contacts with other local groups. As group life democratizes, the process has a chance to become self-sustaining; if ordinary practice remains authoritarian (despite what may sound like "progressive" programs), change is self-limiting and has little chance to take root in everyday life.

The role played by clerical populism in diffusing the ideas of liberation theology and linking them in practice to base communities has varied with circumstances. El Salvador, Brazil, and Chile provide radically different constraints and opportunities from those encountered in Costa Rica, Mexico, Colombia, and Venezuela. But in all cases, clerical populism and the accompanying adulation of the popular by progressive groups has come wrapped around an intense fight for power. An old-fashioned, bitter political struggle rages throughout the region to control popular groups and, especially, to control programs that prepare and train pastoral agents and that produce materials for group use. At issue is who will staff the institutes, run the photocopy and mimeograph machines, record and distribute the cassettes, organize and pay for travel, and visit the groups and coordinate their activities. In short, who will set the agenda of the base communities? Will they stress spiritual matters to the exclusion of social and political issues, will they emphasize the reverse, or will some combination of the two emerge?[31]

The initial impetus behind the formation and growth of base communities was clearly religious, not political. Throughout Latin America, base communities were established as part of a broad church strategy to reach and hold popular clienteles more effectively. They developed in ways that responded to the needs of popular sectors for participatory experiences that could provide meaning, structure, and support as they faced a difficult and changing world. All this was appealing and would have had some impact in any event. But in those countries where the communities later became prominent (e.g., El Salvador, Nicaragua, Chile, and Brazil), political closure decisively magnified their impact. Instead of frightening activists into apathy, official threats and violence reinforced the dedication of numerous bishops and pastoral agents, who intensified efforts to create and defend base communities.

At issue here is a complex process of exchange and mutual influence between new church commitments to the poor (with all the theological and or-

---

[31] As we shall see (chapters 4 through 7, below) this includes control over precisely which biblical passages are read and discussed and influence over the way they are interpreted.

ganizational underpinnings reviewed in this chapter), social changes, and repression. When the churches began to promote ideas about justice, rooting
them in participatory, reinforcing group structures, they found a ready audience. The moral sanction of the churches, reinforced by solidarity and mutual
support in the groups, helped sustain membership and uphold its commitments
as possible and correct, even in the face of great danger.[32] Initially limited
religious agendas thus broadened as the needs of members were echoed and
reinforced by guiding ideas derived from liberation theology. Together these
changes undergirded a range of new commitments and activities. Ironically, it
is precisely those regimes who complain most bitterly about the "political"
impact of liberation theology and base communities, and about excessive "politicization" of the churches generally, which have been prime creators of
what they deplore and condemn so strongly. Their own intense repression created a clientele and made the logic of resistance and activism all the more
meaningful. In Latin America, authoritarianism was a prime growth medium
for popular religous movements.

## Conclusion

This chapter has considered liberation theology and base communities in the
context of the broad changes that have reshaped religion, social life, and politics in Latin America over the past three decades. In conclusion, I wish to
underscore once more that the impact of liberation theology is not well understood in deductive terms, nor does its influence run in any single direction—
be it from theologians to group agendas or from "the people" to the pens of
the theologians themselves. Ideas are received in light of concrete circumstances and needs, and are elaborated and reworked constantly in daily practice. All the groups in question take off from a religious agenda, often limited
at first to traditional notions of catechism and moral renovation. Through a
dialectic of reflection and action, this agenda is gradually refashioned to embrace a broader range of issues, edging easily over into social and political
arenas.

The precise direction of these interests and energies is set by circumstances.
Central American or Chilean realities make extreme political dilemmas immediately pressing; the open conditions of Venezuela or Costa Rica allow for
a focus on economic and social transformations to be both possible and appealing. But regardless of the specifics of the case, for the groups, social and

[32] Repression alone does not suffice to set these dialectics in motion. Changes in the discourse,
organization, and action of the churches have autonomous sources and play an independent role.
Cases like Uruguay and especially Argentina affirm that in the absence of such prior transformations, repression at best makes for passive acceptance, at worst for active collaboration from the
churches.

political issues are not separate from religious questions, nor are they prior. They are part of the same process. This suggests that no matter what empirical focus discussions of impact may take, the matter is not well addressed in one-dimensional terms, as if this were some simple index that rises or falls, marking levels on a hypothetical impact thermometer. Change is not so much a matter of *more or less impact* than of figuring out what goals will be pursued and how they will be implemented.

Liberation theology's most enduring impacts are likely to come through the development of new structures, mediating agents, and new styles of leaders drawn from hitherto oppressed and quiescent social strata. Pastoral agents play a key role in carrying ideas and getting the new groups going. Many agents experience vast transformations in their own lives and vocations through this involvement with popular groups. They carry that sense of conversion forward in energetic group promotion.[33] Others, above all in more recent years, come to the role (say of priest, nun, or lay missioner) because of the appeal of such activities. In either case, the centrality of pastoral agents underscores the importance of general developments in the church for the long-term future of liberation theology and base communities.

In practical terms, problems arise from the difficulty many clerical personnel have in shedding paternalistic habits of domination and direction. It is common to encounter the anomaly of "progressive" priests and pastoral agents who promote a liberationist agenda in authoritarian ways. But rhetoric is not enough. Promoting these ideas without providing for their expression in new kinds of self-controlled organizations and actions dooms the group to stagnation and disappearance. If and when the "good" father or sister leaves, what will sustain action and conviction if no autonomous capacity for setting directions and managing events has been developed? While a sympathetic bishop or religious order can sustain and shield groups with human, material, and symbolic resources, by the same token, hostile church structures can scuttle the strongest groups or keep them from appearing in the first place.

These reflections suggest that liberationist ideas are likely to have their deepest and most enduring impact where the process is most genuinely democratic and least directive. Such a process does not require breaking ties to the institutional churches or confronting hierarchically structured church authorities. Most groups and their members want to remain in the church. They venerate authority and strongly value conventional religious practice. Nonetheless, they stir the fears of many church elites because of the challenge they pose to established notions of authority. Such fears have been manifested lately in repeated Vatican attacks on liberation theology and on the supposed

---

[33] See chapter 7, below, for details. Two examples of North American pastoral agents killed in Latin America are James Guadelupe Carney and Jean Donovan. See Carrigan's *Salvador Witness*; and James Carney's revealing autobiography, *To Be a Christian*. I review the broader implications of Donovan's life and death in my "'Whose Heart Could Be So Staunch?'"

dangers of a "popular church." But in point of fact, breaks are rarely initiated from the bottom up: there is no large-scale desertion from the churches and no formal schism in Latin America.

Structures are of fundamental importance. They reinforce general commitments with bonds of human solidarity and work primary group affiliation and personal conviction together with collective action. They also provide concrete material and organizational links to other levels to form a collection of ladders reaching up and out from the group to other arenas and levels of institutional life. This capacity to mediate between everyday life and big structures is critical to whatever possible impact liberation theology may have, now or in the future.

Assessing the long-term viability of structures and programs requires attention to the social and political processes that *create a place* for pastoral agents and their initiatives. As we have seen, the conjuncture of such social and political changes with incipient transformations in the churches was decisive. To be sure, liberation theology, base communities, and related initiatives each had independent merit, but their development and subsequent impact have everywhere been strongly conditioned by the kind of hearing and the sort of audience the conditions of their birth created around them. The next two chapters bring us closer to these day-to-day realities through a detailed look at national- and local-level transformations in the politics, economies, social life, and religious institutions of Venezuela and Colombia.

# THREE

## COLOMBIA AND VENEZUELA: NATIONS,

## CHURCHES, AND PROGRAMS

THE CENTRAL theoretical and empirical goal of this book is to understand and explain changes in the culture, associational life, and religious expression of popular groups, and to explore what politics means to their daily lives. Most of the description and analysis presented in these pages centers therefore on communities, organizations, and individuals. As we have seen, however, complete understanding requires us to look beyond the popular level. Transformations in popular groups cannot be addressed in a void but must instead be studied in terms of their characteristic relation with institutions, manifest, for example, in the place these big structures accord to popular groups and popular expression of any kind in the discourse and practice of politics, social life, and culture, including religion.

In the following consideration of Venezuela and Colombia, there is no attempt at comprehensive description or analysis of the institutional development or social movements each has witnessed in recent years. I have discussed these matters in detail elsewhere; there is also a substantial literature.[1] I build here on those foundations; I do not repeat them. Instead, I focus on four dimensions of change that have combined to make Colombia and Venezuela into

[1] In addition to the sources cited in chapters 1 and 2, above, I draw freely on the following: Jonathan Hartlyn, *The Politics of Coalition Rule in Colombia*; John Peeler, *Latin American Democracies: Colombia, Costa Rica, and Venezuela*; Albert Berry, Ronald Hellman, and Mauricio Solaun, eds., *The Politics of Compromise: Coalition Government in Colombia*; Paul Oquist, *Violence, Conflict, and Politics in Colombia*; Bruce Bagley, *The State and the Peasantry in Contemporary Colombia*; Miguel Urrutia, *Winners and Losers in Colombia's Economic Growth of the 1970s*; Marco Palacios, *Coffee in Colombia, 1850–1970: An Economic, Social, and Political History*; Leon Zamosc, *The Agrarian Question and the Peasant Movement in Colombia*; Gonzalo Sánchez and Donny Meertens, *Bandoleros, gamonales, y campesinos: El caso de la violencia en Colombia*; Charles Bergquist, *Labor in Latin America: Comparative Essays on Chile, Argentina, Venezuela, and Colombia*; Lise Margolies, ed., *The Venezuelan Peasant in Country and City*; William Roseberry, *Coffee and Capitalism in the Venezuelan Andes*; John Sheahan, *Patterns of Development in Latin America*; Alejandro Portes and John Walton, *Urban Latin America: The Political Condition from Above and from Below*; and James Lang, *Inside Development in Latin America*. My own relevant publications include *Conflict and Political Change in Venezuela*; *Religion and Politics in Latin America*; "Venezuela: The Sources, Nature and Future Prospects of Democracy"; "Colombia: The Institutional Church and the Popular"; "Continuities in Colombia"; "Democracy and the Church in Venezuela"; (with Scott Mainwaring) "Religion and Popular Protest"; and "Popular Groups, Popular Culture, and Popular Religion."

very different kinds of places: state, politics, and associational life; socioeconomic and demographic change; church ideology, institutional structures, and organizational strategies; and variation in the character of alternatives to official church programs. Together, these dimensions will shed light on how ideology and structure, elites and masses, and national, regional, and grass-roots phenomena combine in distinct and enduring patterns.

## State, Politics, and Associational Life

Differences in state organization and national politics between Venezuela and Colombia have deep historical roots and have been accentuated by the changes of the twentieth century. The power and role of the state differs, the character of elites and pattern of political organization vary sharply, and prevailing concepts of authority, above all with respect to elite-mass relations, stand opposed in the two cases. Each state is centralized, and both have relied heavily on elite pacts and accommodations to mute social conflict and guarantee political stability. But similarity on these points should not obscure important contrasts in the way politics is conceived and carried out.

The Colombian system, known as the National Front, was much more far-reaching and clearly was intended to demobilize. This agreement, written into the national constitution in 1958, provided for stability by ensuring that the two dominant parties alternate in power. The pact was engineered by leaders of the Liberal and Conservative parties as a means of ending more than a decade of savage civil strife, known in Colombia simply as The Violence. By the mid-1950s, signs had begun to appear of a shift in the fighting from interparty strife to insurrection fueled by class conflict. By reestablishing and stabilizing civilian rule and party domination, the National Front brought peace and an effective end to such developments.[2]

[2] On The Violence and ensuing National Front arrangements, see Oquist, *Violence*; and Hartlyn, *The Politics*. On the triggering incidents in April 1948, see above all Arturo Alape, *El Bogotazo: Memorias del olvido*; and Herbert Braun, *The Assassination of Gaitán: Public Life and Urban Violence in Colombia*. The character of The Violence has been graphically depicted in Colombian literature. See, for example, Eduardo Caballero Calderón's *El Cristo de espaldas*, and *Siervo sin tierra*; or Daniel Caicedo's account of violence in the Valle del Cauca, *Viento seco*. The distant and overbearing character of most leaders, combined with the parties' acknowledged role in sparking and sustaining The Violence, has given both parties and "politics" an enduring bad name in Colombia. As we shall see, both the fear of violence and its reality remain a constant in modern Colombian life. The level of conflict began rising sharply again in the late 1970s, as long-established guerrilla movements became more active, new ones were founded, and an escalating pattern of repression, insurrection, and, lately, drug-linked murder got underway. See Amnesty International, *Colombia Briefing*; Americas Watch, *The Central Americanization of Colombia? Human Rights and the Peace Process*; Washington Office on Latin America, *Colombia Besieged: Political Violence and State Responsibility*; and Gonzalo Sánchez, *Colombia: Violencia y democracia, informe presentado al ministerio de gobierno*.

This stress on control and demobilization is understandable in light of the character and public image of the country's main political parties. Only in Colombia do the Liberal and Conservative parties that dominated nineteenth-century politics throughout Latin America survive as key political actors. Both parties have a decidedly nineteenth century character: loosely structured, electorally focused, and highly elitist. Their elitism is manifest both in the social origins of party leaders (often linked to competing networks of elite families) and in the well-documented tendency of party structures to rely on existing social hierarchies and local bosses (*gamonales*) to get things done.[3] The Colombian political elite has long resisted mass mobilization of any kind. The dominant elite concept of politics revolved around agreements among gentlemen. Authority was thought to rest among such gentlemen, whose common upbringing and culture prepared them to rule in civilized ways. They were known in the parlance of the time as *convivialistas*, those who "got along." The system was severely challenged in the 1940s when Jorge Eliécer Gaitán captured control of the Liberal party with a campaign of mass mobilization stressing that "the people are superior to their leaders." Gaitán's assassination in downtown Bogotá on April 9, 1948, sparked massive riots and widespread insurrection. This fighting provided the spark for The Violence, which was brought to a (temporary) close with the formation of the National Front. As Braun points out, intense fear among the elite led them to identify "the people" with violence, mobilization with danger, and politics in big public spaces (rather than in the salons of gentlemen) with lack of civilization.

> The fear that the *pueblo* [the people] would vent its primitive passions was never far from many minds. According to this idea, "everyone" participated in the riot. Only those who were not part of "everyone," only those who were not *pueblo* did not participate. . . . The *convivialistas*, respectable citizens, the upper classes, and parts of the middle classes as well as workers associated with the most advanced factories remained on the side of the law.[4]

Pervasive elite fear of popular movements served as the ideological underpinnings for a pattern of organization best described as preemptive fragmentation. Like political groups, most secondary associations operate on clientelistic lines, whose power is invoked to reinforce vertical ties to leaders while breaking up and isolating class-based initiatives. Signs of independence have sparked swift and for the most part effective countermeasures. Party and state elites regularly sponsor dependent organizations, for example, among peasants or trade unions. Autonomous popular groups, above all those taking class

---

[3] On parties and party systems, see Hartlyn, *The Politics*; and also Francisco Leal Buitrago, *Estado y política en Colombia*. Braun's *The Assassination* provides an insightful review of the history and culture of parties.

[4] *The Assassination*, p. 202.

or community as a basis for organization, are rejected, delegitimized, and destroyed wherever possible.[5]

Pacts, parties, and violence are also salient in modern Venezuela but have substantially different sources and implications. When military rule was overthrown in early 1958, leaders of the major political parties made a series of pacts that stabilized the transition to democratic politics and civilian rule. They pledged to support elections, oppose military conspiracies, and commit themselves to a common minimum program for the next government, no matter who won. Formal coalition rule lasted through the first two post-1958 governments, followed by working agreements to hinder fragmentation and excesses of conflict that might give antidemocratic elements an excuse to intervene. In contrast to Colombia, none of this was written into the constitution nor was alternation of power guaranteed; elections were free and open.

The character of Venezuelan political parties gave these accords a special tone. Colombia's tangled networks of elite families, patron-client linkages, and upper-class disdain and fear of the people find little echo here. Indeed, little in the way of nineteenth-century institutions, elites, or issues carries over into the life of modern Venezuela. When the parties that still dominate Venezuelan politics were founded in the 1940s, they represented something genuinely new in the life of the nation: socially heterogeneous, year-round organizations that combined mass mobilization with a drive for electoral politics and state power. They drew strength from the social changes set in motion by the petroleum industry, building alliances between small-town, middle-class youth and the dispossessed masses of the country's periphery.[6]

Venezuela has experienced considerable violence, though never as extensive or socially destructive as in Colombia—at least not in this century. Until 1958, Venezuela was one of Latin America's prime exemplars of military coups and rapacious, brutalizing dictatorship, with a long and sorry history of secret police, torture, forced labor, and concentration camps. The country was

[5] See for example, the accounts in Levine, *Religion and Politics in Latin America*; Bagley, *The State*; Zamosc, *The Agrarian Question*; and Hartlyn, *The Politics*. Malcolm Deas's account of labor organizing during the 1920s suggests that the problem has deep historical roots. After noting that the working class was small and atomized, he continues: "This problem was compounded by one of consciousness. The best accounts of early agitation in Colombia show recurring frustrations that are particularly Colombian. Efforts to form an autonomous working class movement had to contend with the power of absorption of conventional politics, particularly Liberal politics. . . . A second source of frustration derived from the nature of Colombian society, and worked in favor of Conservative governments as well as the Liberal opposition. The nature of social distances in Colombia did not foster working class consciousness" ("Colombia, Ecuador and Venezuela, c. 1880–1930," p. 660).

[6] Among others, see Levine, *Conflict*, and "Venezuela," and the sources cited there; Ramón J. Velásquez, *La caída del liberalismo amarillo*; Arturo Sosa and Eloi Lengrand, *Del garibaldismo estudiantil a la izquierda criolla, 1928–1935*; and Steve Ellner, *Generational Identification and Political Fragmentation in Venezuelan Politics in the Late 1960s*.

also a major theater for guerrilla insurrection during the first half of the 1960s, and fear of guerrilla victory clearly spurred elites to make pacts and stick to them. The insurgency did not last very long in Venezuela, and guerillas never achieved much of a popular base. Despite grumblings and discontent with the specific acts of particular individuals and governments, Venezuelans of all classes have mostly positive images of parties, politics, and democracy.[7] Electoral participation has been high, abstention generally low.

$\rightarrow$ Venezuelan political parties grew up simultaneously with trade unions and peasant movements, and party organizers have long made strenuous efforts to penetrate and control all kinds of associations. In the discourse of public life, praise and encouragement of the general idea of organization is accompanied by constant efforts to co-opt groups and leaders into the party-run system. This complex system began to change in the 1980s. Social and economic changes detailed in the next section have often outstripped the organizational capabilities of the parties, leaving a growing number of groups beyond the reach of party-related networks. Key political parties have also put a growing proportion of their resources into mass media, leaving older structures for neighborhood organization and ward-heeler activity to decline. Together, these trends have left an open field, and a vigorous net of "new" social movements has started to appear in selected cities and rural areas.

The preceding observations suggest that institutional patterns, elite formation, and public discourse about politics combine to very different ends in the two cases. Colombian elites expect a hierarchical order of things, press for control, and, where possible, preempt independent organization. Class issues have little place in the discourse of public life. Autonomous popular groups are commonly depicted as illegitimate threats to the established order.[8] In Venezuela, the absence of carryover from the past has fostered more open and less hierarchical norms. Associational life flourishes, and the operative norms of most associations are deliberately modeled on those of national politics: equality, competitive elections, participation, and rights of opposition. These pat-

[7] In the nineteenth century, civil wars did spark major rearrangements of Venezuela's population, as residents of the plains area fled to the safety of mountain communities. I review the evidence on migration, on the character of military rule (including the concentration camps of the 1950s), and on support for the guerrilla movement in *Conflict* and "Venezuela." See also Richard Gott, *Guerrillas in Latin America*; and Timothy Wickham-Crowley, "Winners, Losers, and Also-Rans: Toward a Comparative Sociology of Latin American Guerrilla Movements," pp. 170–71.

[8] Bergquist argues that conservative settlement of land conflicts in the 1930s helped consolidate a pattern of social relations and public discourse in Colombia in which class issues and autonomous popular groups were weakened and pushed to the margins with few allies. See his *Labor*. On the self-image of social classes in Venezuela, see (among others) William Roseberry, "Images of the Peasant in the Consciousness of the Venezuelan Proletariat"; N. S. Relensberg, H. Karner, and V. Köhler, *Los pobres de Venezuela*; and Jeanette Abouhammad, *Los hombres de Venezuela: Sus Necesidades, sus Aspiraciones*.

terns make sense when set against the modern evolution of social and economic structures and the demographic patterns of each country.

## Socioeconomic and Demographic Contrasts

The patterns established over the past half-century have helped create popular sectors with characteristically different experiences and needs in the two cases. Venezuela has changed more quickly and thoroughly than has its neighbor. A population that in the 1920s was overwhelmingly rural, illiterate, and disease-ridden, had, by the late 1950s, moved to the cities, started school, and began to live longer and in most cases healthier lives. Regional distinctions faded as a genuine national market developed in politics, culture, and economic life.[9] Combined with the political openness democracy has brought since 1958, these changes undergird a sense of movement and openness throughout the social order. Lisa Peattie comments on the Venezuela she encountered in the 1960s.

> The roads, radios, and schools financed by oil meant not only a sharp rise in literacy—illiteracy dropped from 71 percent in 1936 to an estimated 26 to 28 percent in 1960—but also a general spread of sophistication of several kinds. There was sophistication in self-presentation; I have seen girls in isolated rural settlements to the south of Ciudad Guayana wearing tight slacks and upswept hairdos in completely urban style. There began to develop that sense of social process which makes it possible for a semi-educated worker to say "I have had a historic life" or for another woman, totally illiterate and at the economic margins, to tell me that "education is the future of the people." . . . A country like Venezuela lives in hope and optimism, but also in jeopardy. Its situation is that of a moving disequilibrium. It can no more stop or go backward than can a boy going down hill on a bicycle with his feet on the handlebars.[10]

The fate of Venezuelan agriculture is a useful index of the nature and impact of change. The oil boom touched off a massive rural depression. Landholdings were dramatically consolidated, farms abandoned, and peasants pushed off the land in great numbers. From the 1920s on, Venezuelan agriculture declined steadily, both as an employer of labor and as a share of gross domestic product (GDP), leaving the nation with one of the smallest agricultural sectors in all of Latin America. Peasants were not only pushed off the land, they were also pulled to cities. They traveled on the new roads paid for by oil revenues and

---

[9] I review the evidence in "Venezuela."

[10] *The View from the Barrio*, pp. 23, 143. Peattie is less sanguine now, as her recent *Planning: Ciudad Guayana Reconsidered* indicates. A life history that captures the flavor of Venezuela's social and cultural transformations is Carmen Elena Busquets, *La ruta de Don Miguel*.

found jobs in public works and also in what soon became an urban service-oriented economy.

Economic change has been slower in Colombia, and quite different in character. Despite providing a steadily dropping share of jobs and GDP, agriculture has remained vital and important. It has also changed in significant ways. The fact that agricultural employment has fallen more quickly than has agriculture's share of GDP points to high levels of capitalization, the expansion of profitable agribusinesses, and the gradual decline of Colombia's peasantry. These developments were spurred by the relative peace of the National Front. They accelerated in the late 1960s, as declining elite fears of rural unrest combined with overall expansion elsewhere in the economy to move public policy away from agrarian reform to active promotion of capitalist enterprise in the rural sector. The 1960s brought substantial land concentration, expulsions of peasant farmers, and a sharp drop in rural real wages, which until that point had risen steadily since the 1920s. Many rural families became temporary or permanent agricultural wage workers.[11] The economic patterns and differences outlined to this point are summarized in table 3.1.

The poverty and insecurity of Colombian rural life have increased sharply in recent years, despite a general pattern of economic progress. Macroeconomic indicators that show steady growth, expanding employment, and rising levels of welfare (including access to health, education, and the like) over much of the postwar period obscure evidence of a growing sense of crisis in the day-to-day lives of most Colombians, especially but not only in the countryside.[12] Growth in the Colombian economy has reinforced inequality and buttressed a system that sharply constrains chances for mobility. Sandilands comments that despite "many obvious and spreading signs of modernization in all sectors and of bloodless statistics indicating that the gross national product has perhaps tripled over this period, it would be hard to demonstrate, even on grounds of formal economic welfare criteria, that the benefits of those who have gained from the process of change have outweighed the increased misery of the growing number of losers."[13]

Although Colombia has long had more inhabitants and more big cities, urbanization has been substantially slower than in Venezuela.[14] In part this is because potential migrants to Colombia's cities have had rural alternatives not

[11] On this point, see Bagley, *The State*, p. 24. On wages and levels of living, see above all Albert Berry, "Rural Poverty in Twentieth Century Colombia." Grindle, *State and Countryside*, provides a general review of trends in Colombian agriculture.

[12] Sheahan argues on the basis of statistics of this kind, but see Urrutia, *Winners and Losers*; Lang, *Inside*; and the discussion in chapters 5 and 8, below.

[13] Cited in Bagley, *The State*, p. 25.

[14] See my *Religion and Politics in Latin America* for a review of the evidence; and also Levine, "Venezuela"; Hartlyn, *The Politics*; Portes and Walton, *Urban*; Lang, *Inside*; and Sheahan, *Patterns*.

**TABLE 3.1**

Social and Economic Indicators for Venezuela and Colombia, Selected Years

| | Total Population | % School Enrollment, Ages 6–11 | % Labor Force in | | | Agriculture as Share Total GDP | Inflation Rate |
| | | | Agriculture | Industry | Services | | |
|---|---|---|---|---|---|---|---|
| **Venezuela** | | | | | | | |
| 1950 | 5,034,838 | — | 42.9 | 21.4 | 35.8 | — | — |
| 1960 | 7,523,999 | 69 | 33.4 | 22.5 | 44.2 | 7.9 | 1.0 (1960–70) |
| 1970 | 10,721,822 | 78* | 26.0 | 24.8 | 49.3 | 7.5 | 8.4 (1970–80) |
| 1980 | 15,024,000 | 83 | 16.1 | 28.4 | 55.6 | 6.5 | 11.0 (1980–84) |
| **Colombia** | | | | | | | |
| 1950 | 11,548,172 | — | 57.2 | 17.9 | 24.9 | — | — |
| 1960 | 17,484,508 | 48 | 50.2 | 19.5 | 30.4 | 32.7 | 11.2 (1960–70) |
| 1970 | 21,070,115 | 64* | 39.3 | 23.3 | 37.4 | 28.6 | 21.1 (1970–80) |
| 1980 | 24,933,000 | 70 | 34.3 | 23.5 | 42.3 | 25.8 | 21.9 (1980–84) |

*Sources:* Adapted from data in the following: Inter-American Development Bank, *Economic and Social Progress in Latin America, 1986, Special Section: Agricultural Development*; Inter-American Development Bank, *Economic and Social Progress in Latin America, 1987, Special Section: Labor Force in Employment*; Sheahan, *Patterns of Development in Latin America*; Grindle, *State and Countryside*.

*1975

available to their Venezuelan counterparts. Agricultural diversification has created substantial numbers of new jobs, for example, as wage laborers in the expanding sugar, rice, and flower industries.[15] This intranational rural migration continues earlier trends that include a tradition of spontaneous colonization. Until the political stabilization of the late 1960s, a widespread popular "solution" to The Violence in Colombia was for peasant families to vote with their feet, fleeing to frontier areas, especially in the eastern plains and in the southeast. Moreover, from the mid-1950s until the recent economic crisis, there was a steady stream of legal and illegal Colombian migration to Venezuela.

City life in the two countries also differs, although the contrasts are less sharp than they are for agriculture. For example, there are fewer resources to go around in Colombia's main cities. The relative weakness of Colombia's central state has combined with the greater strength of its local and regional elites (e.g., in cities like Medellín or Cali) to make for a slower and more tension-filled process of urban incorporation. With relatively little public money available to fund construction in Colombia, informal sector employment has been the overwhelming norm for popular urban groups. The economic and social patterns outlined here have major consequences for the development and character of popular groups.

In the countryside, the greater density of rural life in Colombia, and its rapid transformation in situ, created a clientele that was both increasingly available and in need. This sparked sharp competition to organize both the growing agroproletarian sector and peasant small-holders. In the Colombian pattern, state agencies sponsored the organization of rural workers in the late 1960s then turned against these new groups as more radical demands began to emerge.[16] The church has been most active in the peasant sector, which is concentrated in the country's most traditionally Catholic regions (the core coffee producing departments of Antioquia, Caldas, Huila, Cundinamarca, Risaralda, and Tolima).[17]

Venezuela's experience of rural organization is ambiguous. Although the national peasant organization has long been dominated by the political parties, the peasantry's sharp drop in numbers, reinforced by agriculture's overall decline, has made rural efforts less important to the parties. The unintended effect of these changes has been to open rural organization to competing groups, most notably those promoting independent community organizations, including cooperatives and religiously linked groups. Their efforts have been eased by the fact that most of Venezuela's remaining peasantry is located in Andean

[15] See the data in Sheahan, *Patterns*.
[16] Zamosc, *The Agrarian Question*; or Bagley, *The State*.
[17] On church-run peasant groups, see Levine, *Religion and Politics in Latin America*, chap. 7.

states (Lara, Trujillo, Mérida, Táchira), which are traditionally the most devoutly Catholic in the nation.

In the cities, associational life is shaped by the pace and character of urban growth and industrialization. The fact that industrial employment has grown more slowly than have commerce or services reinforces the social heterogeneity of urban popular neighborhoods. But despite this apparent melting-pot atmosphere, the absence of shared economic experiences inhibits the melting and undercuts organization rooted in economic interests.

> This pattern follows from the fluid and temporal character of their employment, which militates against organized struggles for better wages or more security. This limitation does not mean, however, that the informal proletariat does not participate in popular mobilizations. In general, the interests around which informal workers coalesce have to do less with control over the means of production than with minimal access to the means of collective reproduction, such as transportation, water and other basic services, and shelter.[18]

Portes goes on to suggest that because mobilizations center more on residence than occupation, such movements commonly advance neighborhood and community demands more than class issues.[19]

> For this reason, mobilizations around collective reproduction issues are more broadly based in a class sense than those involving exclusively wages and working conditions of the formal proletariat. [Moreover,] not only do these mobilizations represent a distinct form of popular struggle that parallels the more traditional forms involving the formal proletariat, but their relative incidence has increased in recent years.[20]

Experience in Venezuela and Colombia affirms this pattern, with predictable shadings for each case.[21] In Venezuela, apart from those in industrial cities like Valencia or Ciudad Guayana, urban movements have been decidedly heterogeneous and territorially focused. Because national organizational networks in Venezuela depend so heavily on party-union-associational linkages, new movements lacking a foothold in the trade-union sector often slip through the cracks of the existing system. There is both opportunity and weakness here. Opportunity arises from the parties' demonstrated inability to build enduring structures in the cities. Weakness lies in the resulting absence of

---

[18] Portes, "Latin American Class Structures," p. 31.

[19] On this point, see Manuel Castells, *The City and the Grassroots*; Larissa Lomnitz, *Networks and Marginality*; and for a general review, Susan Eckstein, *Power and Popular Protest*.

[20] Portes, "Latin American Class Structures," p. 32.

[21] For Colombian cities see Portes and Walton, *Urban*; and also Jaime Giraldo, *Paros y movimientos Cívicos en Colombia*. For Venezuela, see Talton Ray, *The Politics of the Barrios of Venezuela*; Peattie, *The View* and *Planning*; and Daniel H. Levine, "Urbanization, Migrants, and Politics in Venezuela."

linkage between such "new groups" and the system of power managed by party organizations. Urban popular groups in Colombia are weak for similar reasons, but their debility is amplified by resource scarcity and by the indifference and active hostility of state agencies and political parties. The result has been a proliferation of short-lived groups, punctuated by periodic mobilizations and sporadic enthusiasm for opposition movements. Colombian groups end up trapped between verbal radicalization and organizational vulnerability. The pattern outlined thus far has continued even though the edge of contrast has blurred in certain respects. For example, by the mid-1980s, Colombia had begun to close the gap with Venezuela in areas like access to schooling, levels of literacy, and life expectancy.[22] But as the statistical gap between them has narrowed, our two countries appear to have moved in opposite directions. Table 3.2 provides a summary of patterns in the 1980s.

In Colombia, political decay and resurgent violence are prominent. Although violence has not returned to the civil war levels of earlier decades, the combination of kidnappings, assassinations, and riots with growing insur-

**TABLE 3.2**
Venezuela and Colombia Selected Indexes

|  | *Venezuela* | *Colombia* |
|---|---|---|
| Surface Area (kms²) | 898,805 | 1,138,338 |
| Population (1986) | 17,914,000 | 29,058,000 |
| % Urban (1986) | 81.3% | 66.6% |
| Life Expectancy at Birth | 69.0 (1985) | 62.1 (1981) |
| Infant Mortality per 1,000 | 26.1 (1985) | 60.9 (1981) |
| Annual Population Growth Rate (1970–85) | 2.9 | 1.6 |
| % Literate | 85.95 (1984) | 81 (1981) |
| Annual Growth Rate GDP Cumulative Variation (1981–85) | −9.6 | 11.2 |
| 1985 Growth Rate | −1.2 | 2.6 |
| Inflation Rate (%) (1960–70) | 1.0 | 11.2 |
| (1970–80) | 8.4 | 21.1 |
| (1980–84) | 11.4 | 24 |

*Source*: See sources for table 3.1.

[22] See the data in John Sloan, "The Policy Capabilities of Democratic Regimes in Latin America."

gency, right-wing death squads, and the power of the drug cartels has led many Colombian observers to speak freely about the "Central Americanization" of their country. Initially hopeful signs connected with official amnesties and government-insurgent peace talks collapsed utterly by the mid-1980s.[23] Along with continued political stability, the same decade has brought economic stagnation and a sense of closing opportunities to Venezuela. The collapse of world oil prices and accumulating debt burdens sparked a sharp devaluation of the currency in the years after 1983. The whole decade has witnessed negative economic growth and accelerating inflation, leading Venezuelans to lose their hitherto widespread confidence in the future and point increasingly to the "Latin Americanization" of their country. These developments were brought into sharp focus in early 1989 by urban riots that came in reaction to official austerity programs. This was the first significant urban violence and the first time troops and police had gone into the streets since the early days of guerrilla war.[24] It is worth pointing to the ironies that contrasting social and political developments in these two countries present to the observer. Abel shows that during the 1930s and 1940s Colombian elites feared that impending changes in Venezuela might spill over into their country, upsetting its stable social and political order.[25] By the late 1980s, these roles were reversed, and Venezuelan elites now fear that disorder, unrest, and decay may spill over from Colombia into their own country.

## The Churches: Contrasts in Structure, Ideology, and Organizational Strategy

In Colombia, institutional decay and political crisis underscore the church's stance as an institution that can control resources, mount programs, and command loyalties in an increasingly difficult and restrictive situation. This fits well with traditions giving the church a prominent role in setting the agenda

[23] Americas Watch, *The Central Americanization*; and also R. Santamaría Salamanca and G. Silva Luján, "Colombia in the 1980s: A Political Regime in Transition." An old Colombian adage sums things up well: "In Colombia, which is the land of curious things, civilians make war and the miltiary brings peace" (En Colombia, que es el país de las cosas singulares, dan guerra los civiles, dan paz los militares).

[24] Cf. Miriam Kornblith, "Deuda y democracia en Venezuela: Los sucesos del 27 y 28 de febrero de 1989"; Sergio Antillo Armas, Frank Bracho, and Sara Aniyar, *El venezolano ante la crisis*; and Frank De Armas and Manuel Rodríguez Mena, *La crisis: Responsabilidades y salidas*.

[25] This was the period when a new generation of activists and mass publics began to challenge long-standing patterns of rule. At the time, Colombian elites still relied on informal mechanisms of domination: ideological control via the churches, nets of kinship, and patronage run through the political parties. The army was still very small, and there was no national police. The Violence changed all this, and the old pattern has never been successfully reconstructed. See Christopher Abel, *Política, iglesia, y partidos en Colombia*.

of national life. Recent changes also reinforce a cast of mind among church leaders that associates stability with idyllic images of rural life; urbanization, mobilization, and "politics" with disorder and chaos.[26] Change is painted as dangerous and abnormal, conflict as the momentary (and lamentable) by-product of transition from one stable state to another. In Venezuela, emerging "crisis" presents different issues to the institutional church. Poor, weak, and not much accustomed to taking a leading role, the Venezuelan church after 1958 reached a happy and for the most part comfortable accommodation with the democratic system.

Elsewhere I have documented the historical roots of the difference between these two churches.[27] Briefly, the colonial period left a stronger heritage of ecclesiastical structures and religious presence in Colombia than in Venezuela. This pattern was reinforced by the outcome of nineteenth-century civil wars. These were won in Colombia by Conservatives, who strongly affirmed the church's leading role. In Venezuela, Liberals took control and stripped the Venezuelan church of what little property and resources it controlled, leaving it thoroughly subordinate to state power.

The two churches differ sharply in terms of the resources they control: administrative structures like dioceses and parishes; numbers of clerical personnel (priests and sisters); and educational, charitable, and related institutions. The data in table 3.3 indicate that the Colombian church has a strong and enduring advantage on all counts. Having greater numbers of dioceses and parishes provides greater coverage and administrative flexibility and lets the church's leaders adapt and distribute resources more effectively. Colombians have been very active in this regard. More dioceses have been created over Colombian territory during this century than in all the years from the Conquest to 1900. The total number of parishes has almost tripled over the past five decades, with slower growth in personnel, especially male clergy. Despite these efforts, as figure 3.1 indicates, the Colombian church (like most of its Latin American counterparts) has gradually fallen behind the rate of population growth. There is a deeper structural problem as well: Not only do resources fail to keep pace with population, they are also in the wrong places. Because clerical personnel remain concentrated in existing institutions (particularly schools), areas of rapid growth like the urban popular sector are left largely unattended.

The Venezuelan church has also grown substantially during this century. Since 1940, dioceses have tripled, and total clergy has doubled. The number of sisters has increased by over a third since 1960, the first year for which reliable data are available. Because the initial totals were also small, absolute numbers remain limited, and Venezuela's bishops have relied heavily on for-

---

[26] See Levine, "Continuities in Colombia."
[27] *Religion and Politics*, chap. 2.

**TABLE 3.3**

Selected Indexes on the Church in Venezuela and Colombia, 1950–1980

| | Dioceses | Parishes | | Priests | | Sisters | |
|---|---|---|---|---|---|---|---|
| | | Number | Persons per | Number | Persons per | Number | Persons per |
| Venezuela | | | | | | | |
| pre-1900 | 6 | — | — | — | — | — | — |
| 1950 | 13 | 465 | 10,828 | 786 | 6,406 | — | — |
| 1960 | 20 | 582 | 12,928 | 1,218 | 6,177 | 2,919 | 2,578 |
| 1970 | 26 | 1,232 | 8,703 | 1,976 | 5,426 | 4,032 | 2,659 |
| 1980 | 28 | 1,459 | 10,297 | 1,995 | 7,531 | 4,345 | 3,458 |
| Colombia | | | | | | | |
| pre-1900 | 7 | — | — | — | — | — | — |
| 1950 | 33 | 1,127 | 10,247 | 3,003 | 3,846 | 8,865 | 1,303 |
| 1960 | 48 | 1,433 | 12,201 | 4,094 | 4,271 | 15,329 | 1,141 |
| 1970 | 56 | 1,850 | 11,389 | 4,864 | 4,332 | 17,699 | 1,190 |
| 1980 | 59 | 2,212 | 11,272 | 5,330 | 4,678 | 17,654 | 1,412 |

*Sources:* Adapted from data in the following: Levine, *Religion and Politics in Latin America,* p. 73; Levine, "Continuities in Colombia," p. 307; *Statistical Abstract for Latin America,* vol. 23; *Catholic Almanac,* selected years; *Statistical Yearbook of the Church,* selected years.

**FIGURE 3.1.**
Colombia, Percentage Change since 1940

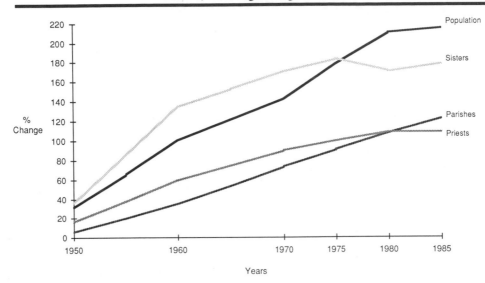

eign clergy. Much of the increase in male clergy after 1960 can be attributed to new church-state agreements that significantly eased the process of bringing foreign personnel into the country. Even so, as figure 3.2 shows, growth has leveled off in recent years. This reflects worldwide shortages of clergy as well as decisions by church leaders, especially in the religious orders, to nationalize their ranks, relying in the future on native-born clergy even if this means sharply reduced numbers.[28]

The national bureaucratic structures of the two churches also differ sharply, with advantage once again to the Colombians. The Colombian Bishops' Conference is advised by a large, permanent secretariat with a professional staff organized into fifteen departments. Each department is supervised by an episcopal commission and headed by trusted clergy drawn from dioceses all over the country. They conduct studies, produce reports, organize training programs, conferences, and seminars, draft episcopal documents, and the like. The secretariat is a high-powered and generally effective organization, giving the bishops a national outlook and providing them with information and tools with which to see and comment on national issues. Nothing comparable exists in Venezuela. A permanent secretariat was organized some time ago, but ef-

[28] By 1970, 60 percent of all clerical personnel were foreign-born, including an overwhelming majority of priests, especially those in religious orders. The figure is widely agreed on: see Juan Carlos Navarro, *Contestación en la iglesia venezolana, 1966–1972*; or Luis Ugalde, "La nueva presencia de la iglesia en los procesos históricos de la sociedad."

**FIGURE 3.2.**

Venezuela, Percentage Change since 1940 (Sisters, Percentage Change since 1960)

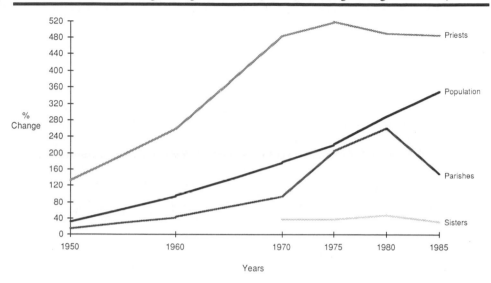

forts to provide regular staff, resources, and a measure of authority collapsed in the 1970s, leaving the organization with part-time personnel and little to do.

Differences in resources and organization tell only part of the story. To understand what church leaders do with the resources they command, we must go beyond numbers to address the self-image, central norms, and perceived role by which these churches order their respective lives. I begin with the Colombian church, which has been described as the "leading edge of the old wave."[29] The phrase suggests a vigorous mix of conservative ideals with aggressive innovation. Elites in this church are anything but static. Not content with rearguard actions against change, they work at home and abroad to create initiatives to penetrate popular sectors while remaining faithful to traditional concepts of the Church as Institution. Colombian prelates dominate CELAM (itself headquartered in Bogotá) and are regarded throughout Latin America as leading spokesmen for current Vatican policy in the region.

Although ecclesiological debates in Colombia follow the general lines traced in Latin America and in the church at large over the past three decades, there are striking continuities with the past. Three are especially noteworthy: a concept of authority that makes hierarchy central to church life; a concern for unity seen as the joining of a heterogeneous base around hierarchy, clergy, and the structures they control; and a related vision of the link between church

[29] Levine and Mainwaring, "Religion and Popular Protest."

and society in which the church (properly constituted) provides values and guidelines to the world.

All institutions embody some notion of authority, but authority is not the same everywhere. Not all authority is authoritarian. Colombia's bishops have long claimed authority of broad scope, and have rooted their claim in the hierarchical nature of authority, as evidenced in the church's juridical structure. Authority as hierarchy is the core of an institution whose unity is built and legitimized around the leadership of the church's "official" agents: bishops and clergy. Vertical ties are stressed and laity subordinate in the church as in society at large. With this base, the church *as an institution* then goes to society, providing authoritative orientation and guidance. The whole perspective reveals an underlying commitment to concepts of *Christendom*, according to which the good society is founded upon, guided by, and suffused with Christian principles. These principles are to be defined exclusively by official church leaders working from a stock of authoritative doctrine. What is not acceptable in this scheme of things is the construction of autonomous, grassroots initiatives of any kind.

The only public evidence of reconsideration of this position came in a 1969 document entitled *La iglesia ante el cambio* (The church facing change).[30] Spurred perhaps by the recently concluded Medellín conference, the bishops pointed to a "state of crisis" whose resolution required full-scale rethinking about the nature of the church, the world, and the relation between them. They drew explicit links between social change, intrachurch relations, and recognition of the changing nature of authority in the church. Thus, "in the search for these new relations, the greatest difficulties arise on issues of authority, the teaching office of the church, the sacramental ministry, and social change: four areas closely linked in the life of the church, and of the church in the world."[31]

This tentative interest in innovation soon faded, and signs of doubt and caution have dominated subsequent discourse. As it became clear that new models of authority, innovations in the ministry, and greater openness to social change had the practical effect of giving average believers, as well as lower clergy and religious, the right to create autonomous programs with minimal control, the hierarchy drew back sharply. Bishops attacked the new ecclesiologies, condemned notions of a "popular church" that began to surface in the 1970s, and reaffirmed the central role of the hierarchy as a constitutive element of church life.[32]

---

[30] Conferencia Episcopal de Colombia, *La iglesia ante el cambio*. Although Colombia's bishops are clearly aware of debates about authority in the church as a whole, they see its reformulation in theory and practice as at best a secondary priority, at worst a threat to the church and society in which they live. For details, see my *Religion and Politics*, part 2.

[31] Conferencia Episopal, *La iglesia*, par. 335, pp. 128–29

[32] See particularly Conferencia Episcopal de Colombia, *Identidad cristiana en la acción por la*

One document chosen from many may help clarify matters for the Colombian case. As part of the preparations for 1979 meeting of Latin America's bishops at Puebla, each of the region's episcopal conferences submitted a detailed report to CELAM summarizing its own situation and position.[33] The Colombian contribution is one of the longest (almost three hundred pages) and pays special attention to matters of popular religion and popular religiosity. The bishops work on the concept of the church and reaffirm traditional positions, taking special pains to refute the concept of a "popular church" as a "church of poor." They utterly reject translation of traditional Catholic concepts into sociological categories: the Gospel poor into the proletariat, sin into social injustice, and evangelization into social and political reflection and action. Such conceptual innovation is seen to gut Catholicism of its transcendental core, undermining the apostolic authority of the bishops in the process. The church's mysteries are reaffirmed instead, and the necessary role of clergy and bishops in their interpretation is underscored.

Unity is stressed above all: the unity of laity, clergy, and bishops; the unity of all social classes in the church; and the unity of meaning and action in this world and the next. Religious organizations and any manifestion of religiosity are acceptable only if situated in contexts where the authority of hierarchy and its officially designated agents have a central role. Links to bishops and clergy are presented as the only core around which a coherent and legitimate religious life can be built. The loosening and constant questioning of these links is taken as a source of social and political troubles; their reaffirmation is seen as the only sure foundation for resolution of national problems. Definitions of church unity rooted in sociological criteria like class or community are specifically ruled out. Indeed, the very existence of the church is threatened by attempts

> to question the age-old structures of the church, and to begin only from the people, from their values, struggles, and contradictions; to rethink faith only from the perspective of the commitment to liberation of the poor and oppressed; to revive prophetic charisms in the very heart of existing ecclesiastical institutions, in order then to condemn anything not in line with these premises.[34]

Popular religion is depicted above all in terms of ignorance and "superstition." In the documents of the Colombian church, the poor appear mostly as humble but faithful masses. They constitute the "base" of the church in the

---

*justicia*. A counterdocument was issued one year later by radical groups: *Identidad cristiana en la acción por la justicia: Una versión alternativa*. The controversy is reviewed with care in Wilde, "Creating Neo-Christendom in Colombia." In taking these positions, Colombia's bishops reflect and provide leadership for broader trends in the Latin American church, which have themselves been reinforced by recent Vatican policies.

[33] "Aporte de la Conferencia Episcopal de Colombia," pp. 77–354, in CELAM, *Aportes de las conferencias episcopales: Libro auxiliar 3*.

[34] Ibid., pp. 161–62.

sense that they fill the lowest rungs of its hierarchically ordered structures. Like authority, knowledge and religious authenticity are seen to flow from the top down. The whole package reinforces the role of clerical mediation and makes unity around the formal structures of the institution a critical legitimating element. Articulating the link between unity and authority has been the special public concern of Msgr. Alfonso López Trujillo, past president of CELAM and now cardinal archbishop of Medellín. In one communication, he argues that the church faces dangerous currents of "laicism," which if unchecked could eventually overrun and eliminate the hierarchy. He squarely rejects "horizontal" models of the church, which stress shared experience and the diffusion of power and legitimate authority. These are foreign to Catholic thinking.

> Working above all from a sociological perspective, the kind of structure of the church is thrown into question. Horizontal relations are to replace vertical ones. The fabric of [base] communities must not be vertical (bishop-priest-layman on the same level). Why the recourse to such spatial images? If the goal is to avoid the extremes of "clericalism" or "authoritarianism" which would make the communities domains at the pleasure of hierarchy, with no real space for lay action, then the intent is not censurable. But if such "horizontal" structuring produces a confusion of the missions [that] different statuses and vocations hold in the church, then the matter is one of grave concern.[35]

In sum, with the brief exception of *La iglesia ante el cambio*, Colombia's bishops have consistently upheld the centrality of hierarchy to church structures, practices, and the legitimacy of religious expression in general. At the same time, they have staked out an increasingly critical social role. The traditional Colombian mix of triumphalism with anticommunism and moral lamentation has yielded to studied denunciations of poverty, inequality, and injustice. But in this case, criticism is approached not in the "prophetic sense" we have encountered elsewhere but rather from the position of an institution whose guidance is offered as part of a general re-Christianization of the social order.

In documents and public statements, the bishops are highly critical of injustice, inequality, and political disorganization. They denounce violence and speak of a situation that has "touched bottom" and desperately needs change. They call for transformations in the way Colombia's central institutions operate and for greater justice in all aspects of national life. But the bishops' view of society and politics limits the scope of their commentary and constrains the role they define for the church and the groups it sponsors. Their analysis rests on concepts of modernization and development. Inequality, injustice, and vi-

---

[35] *Opciones e interpretaciones a la luz de Puebla*, pp. 32–33. See also his *De Medellín a Puebla*.

olence are attributed primarily to the strains associated with transition from a "traditional" rural society to a supposedly "modern" urban one. Although this position marks an advance over the individualistic moralism of the past and reflects the church's turn to sociological analysis, there is no hint that structurally rooted ties of domination or inequality may play a strategic part. Class conflict is to be avoided at all costs, and whatever else it may do, the church should not be understood to sanction or promote it.[36]

Problems like inequality, corruption, violence or alchoholism are listed but rarely linked to one another in systematic ways. The result is anomalous. Harshly critical social and political judgments, couched in the language of sociology, are followed by attributions of cause that are at best mildly reformist and, more commonly, moralistic. Moral crises are cited extensively. Thus, "it is in the disregard of God's commandments and of spiritual values that we can find the source of the overwhelming flood of evils which now threatens Colombia."[37] When the bishops turn to consider politics, they shy away from direct involvement and stress the need to insulate church-sponsored groups from the perils of activism. They resort to long-standing distinctions between politics as the pursuit of the common good and politics as partisan organization and action, embracing the first but leaving the second to others. The church's role is clear:

> Her task is to specify the basic values of the community as a whole. . . . She also defines the proper means and ethics of social relations. In this broad sense politics concerns the Church and its pastors [who are] ministers of unity. . . . The Church contributes by promoting the values which must inspire politics. . . . She does so through her testimony, through her teachings, and through her many faceted pastoral action.[38]

The ambiguities of this position are apparent.[39] The distinction itself assumes that the church (as an institution) can remain "above politics," despite the fact that it is enmeshed in politics of all kinds, every day. Even a studied neutrality has political implications, if only by leaving established patterns unchallenged. In any event, blanket restrictions on political involvement by church-related groups are simply not workable. Pastoral activities undertaken in the real world of Colombian society soon run up against structures of power

[36] Reference to touching bottom is made in the Pastoral Message issued by the Third-Sixth Plenary Assembly of the Bishops' Conference in 1981. For a representative selection of views, see Conferencia Episcopal de Colombia, *Aproximación a la realidad colombiana*. Wilde reviews recent statements in "Creating Neo-Christendom." See also Edward Cleary, ed., *Paths From Puebla*.

[37] *Aproximación*, p. 125.

[38] Ibid., p. 132.

[39] For details see Poggi, *Catholic Action*; Michael Dodson, "The Christian Left in Latin American Politics"; Jean-Guy Vallancourt, *Papal Power*; and my *Religion and Politics in Latin America*, chap. 7.

that limit and shape any action, no matter how "apolitical" their stated intent. In any event, as groups develop and acquire resources, experience, and leadership, they often clash with bishops and priests. Group leaders seek a vital organization, and hence try to respond to the needs of the membership. But these trends conflict with the hierarchy's demands for subordination and reliability and its pressure for constant external control and supervision. With rare exceptions, Colombian bishops are also suspicious of borrowing from and cooperating with non-Catholic and secular elements, and make determined efforts to restrict such activities. This ensures that any criticism will remain under clerical control.

In sum, ecclesiastical leadership in Colombia seeks to modernize church structures and reach out to society without a basic reshaping of either. Democratization or reform are rejected: the church remains highly clerical and authoritarian, society remains grounded in unquestioned relations of class and power. There is little echo here of arguments advanced in Central America or in Brazil, according to which the church should "accompany" popular groups. That would require a thorough reworking of prevailing models of the church, changing the balance between institution and community and thus recognizing that other sectors and levels of the social order have something of value to offer for reflection and action.

The long-standing weakness of the Venezuelan church makes its self-image and goals predictably more modest. As leaders of a weak institution in a pluralist society, Venezuela's bishops aim for steady growth and safe strategies. They seek accommodation and fear rocking the boat. Because until recently this has not been an intellectual church, it is wise to give less weight to official documents and programs (which are mostly conventional and unreflective) and more to practice, where as noted there has been considerable scope for initiative and openness to alternatives.

The restoration of democracy after 1958 had enormous impact on the church in Venezuela. New civilian regimes brought concrete benefits, including improved legal status, increased official subsidies, eased rules for the import of clergy, and a cardinalcy.[40] Accommodation to political democracy and social pluralism made for new understandings of society and of the church itself, and for a growing desire to work with popular groups, which themselves gained legitimacy in church eyes throughout the period. Few of these developments came without conflict, but the Colombian model of unremitting official hostility finds little parallel here.

---

[40] The church collaborated in overthrowing the dictatorship and made sustained efforts to legitimize the new democracy. The prominent role of Christian Democratic politicans in the post-1958 coalitions helped ease the fears of church elites. For details, see my "Democracy and the Church."

Reading through the pastoral letters and public statements of the period,[41] one is left with complex and often contradictory impressions. The ecclesiology at work here is highly conventional. Venezuelan prelates depict the church above all as an institution, distinguished from surrounding society as a perfect and unchanging set of structures. This view underpins a series of messages focused on technical aspects of religious practice and conventional moral themes. The abstract and general character of such positions was nurtured by a general mood of optimism and accommodation that marked the church's relations to politics and to the social order generally after 1958. The Venezuelan church felt no threat from the state and, with the definitive elimination of leftist insurgency by the mid-1960s, no threat from popular movements or politics either.[42]

All this explains the limited resonance Medellín had in Venezuela. The social issues so prominent at Medellín seemed irrelevant. Denunciations of "institutionalized violence" and delineation of a prophetic stance for the churches appeared to have little place in the Venezuelan scheme of things. Around the time of Puebla, an articulate liberationist line had begun to manifest itself in Venezuelan Catholicism. Colombian prelates might have reacted harshly, but a review of the Venezuelan bishops' contribution to Puebla turns up little fear and no sense of threat or impending crisis. The report is short (less than twenty pages) and focuses on technical issues in catechism and liturgy, complaints about the shortage of clergy, popular religious ignorance, moral decay, and so forth. The overall tone is highly positive, with praise scattered all around—to the drafters of the document, to the heritage of Medellín, to the theology of liberation, to base communities, and, of course, to the church's own efforts.

This general portrait of complacent accommodation in Venezuela requires modification on several counts. After 1958, there was growing interest by church groups in work with popular sectors. With the church's social and political position secure for the first time in modern memory, Catholic leaders reached beyond elite-focused alliances and strategies to initiatives directed at the poor. There were programs of free schools and artisanal training typically begun by isolated groups of clergy or sisters and then taken up and blessed by the hierarchy. By the late 1960s, a few religious congregations began to articulate a liberationist position. Their members went to "live with the people," got involved in neighborhood and community organizations, and, in the process, soon came face-to-face with persisting poverty and inequality. These new experiences cast doubt on the overall picture of peace, prosperity, and progress endorsed by the institutional church.

[41] As collected in Conferencia Episcopal Venezolana, *Cartas, instrucciones y mensajes, 1883–1977*, vol. 1–A.

[42] As Arturo Sosa aptly notes, democracy thus gave the church a chance for "convalescence." See "Iglesia y democracia en Venezuela."

First came efforts to "help marginal groups" in order to facilitate their incorporation into "development." However, the move to living in poor areas, sharing their problems and feeling them in the flesh worked a gradual shift in perspectives that produced a new understanding of social relations. To borrow the title of one reflection on the process, "We saw with new eyes." Barrios and the inhuman conditions their residents endure were no accident, nor was the issue one of more time for development to take hold. To the contrary, they were the result of the established order, and the deepest commitments of religious life required active efforts for social transformation.[43]

In the flurry of controversy and open conflict that ensued, church leaders made a point of reaffirming support for the government and accommodation to the existing order. As I show in the next section, they collaborated in the expulsion of activist foreign clergy and made efforts (in the Colombian style) to ensure greater ideological control by purging seminaries and theological faculties and terminating a few threatening organizational experiments. But these efforts were limited by bureaucratic weaknesses; resulting campaigns had shorter lives and less success than those in Colombia. Bureaucratic weakness also hindered the church's capacity to control alternatives.

It is difficult to think of a single major effort at group promotion that has stemmed from the bishops. There is no coordinated national policy for work with popular groups of any kind, including base communities. As we shall see, most initiatives are started by independent groups of activist lay people and clergy (especially sisters) or by religious congregations. Another example of limited success concerns the attempted purge of seminaries and theological faculties mentioned above. This was followed not long after by the creation of an alternative system of clerical higher studies cosponsored by the religious congregations. Official efforts to limit this new institution have had only modest impact.[44]

The bishops' underlying view of popular groups emerges most clearly when they turn their attention to popular religion. Like their Colombian colleagues, Venezuelan prelates restrict discussions of popular religion to matters of piety and religious practice. There is little reference to what popular experience or insight might have to say to organized religion or to faith generally. Poor people are depicted as inherently spiritual and religious, requiring only adequate instruction to rid themselves of superstition and distorted practices. Popular religion appears in static terms, as something people have or do not have, understand or fail to grasp. But such a view conflates religiosity with culture in general. In effect, it removes the poor themselves from any role in defining

---

[43] Ibid., p. 17.

[44] My account is based on interviews with founders and students of ITER, Instituto de Teología para Religiosos, a joint effort by male and female religious orders to provide advanced studies. See chapter 7 for more details.

or changing their values and orientations, or the way these are expressed. After a generally sympathetic review of the bishops' public statements on this issue, one Venezuelan author (himself now a bishop) comments that

> facing the challenge of finding new ways to deal with popular religiosity, it is important to remember how much our approach has been marked by concepts of a "clerical church", images that probably continue to influence us, if only at a subconscious level. In this view, lay people have little access to the essentials of Catholicism. They find themselves in a wholly clerical world and their field of action is limited to devotions, for reasons that have nothing to do with the character of their religiosity itself.[45]

Most of the public commentaries by Venezuela's Catholic bishops since 1958 prize the fact that the church is accepted by all groups, enemy of none. They also remain strongly supportive of the country's democratic political institutions, but temper this stance with acknowledgment of problems that include corruption, decay of the judicial system, unemployment and inequality, and to be sure, the "moral deterioration of the last thirty years." In contrast to the church's official stance in Colombia, the tone here is tentative. In a document issued to mark the thirtieth anniversary of the current democracy, the bishops specifically reject the notion that they have authoritative solutions or guidance to offer. Theirs is a voice of ethical reflection, no more.[46] Responding to the widespread urban rioting of early 1989, the Episcopal Conference continued in the same vein. They deplored violence, called for moral renovation, reaffirmed support for democracy, and urged more equitable sharing of the burdens economic crisis has brought. The work of clergy, sisters, and lay people active among the poor was acknowledged and supported "more than ever," but like the poor, these individuals were urged to remain in close communion with the ecclesiastical institution to ensure that true justice, charity, and reconciliation were served.[47] Throughout, problems are listed, with little effort made to put them into a pattern, to weigh causes and implications, or to assess the likelihood that structural causes, not accidental circumstances, may be at work. Popular groups are painted in passive terms: they are acted upon, not actors. Injustice is done to them; they are victims who deserve better. What they are not is independent actors or potential sources of a different pattern of social arrangements.

Because the Venezuelan system was open and seemed to offer opportunity, accommodation appeared less problematic to the church leaders than it might have been in other cases. The bishops' stated goal has been to spread the mes-

[45] Baltazar Porras, *Los obispos y los problemas de Venezuela*, pp. 281–82.
[46] Conferencia Episcopal Venezolana, "Declaración," par. 3.1.
[47] Conferencia Episcopal Venezolana, "La voz de la iglesia."

sage and build a base for the church while, if possible, offending no one. One long-time observer sums things up as follows:

> What has been established here is that the church denies its political role, or accepts it only in a secondary position. So that when the church does take a position, its political role is focused on two points: first, on not appearing in the vanguard of anything—never to take on a direct role with respect to the state, either in support or opposition; second, on a deeper level, in the sense of personal socialization, just in case something should happen, the idea is that if the church preaches peace, people will feel bad when faced with options of conflict or struggle. Therefore they focus on peace, on personal virtues, on morality. (G 166)

The organizational strategies followed by each national church warrant separate attention. Bishops in both countries like to think of lay organizations as available resources, as bridges extending hierarchical authority into society. They speak freely of "our groups" in ways that assume an identity of interest that is not always present. In particular, church leaders in Colombia have long experimented in a search for effective means of penetrating popular and working-class sectors under changing circumstances. The history of official Catholic organizations in Colombia falls easily into the following periods. Decentralized social action and charity was the norm until about 1930, when it was superseded by the cultivation of Catholic Action movements, with particular stress on organizing workers and peasants. When these movements began to decay in the 1960s, matters were taken under the direct control of the national bishops' conference, and distinctions were drawn between pastoral and political action. Beginning in the mid-1970s, stress has been placed on the creation of small groups whose ties with the hierarchy are ensured by tight control over training pastoral agents and lay ministers and over the whole process of promoting base communities.[48]

The transition from Catholic Action to the centrally controlled promotion of small groups is a good example of the hierarchy's long-term orientation to reliability, loyalty, and control. Inspired by European Catholic Action, the Colombian bishops, beginning in the 1930s, sponsored the formation of a series of labor and peasant groups, entrusting their day-to-day management to the Jesuit-run National Coordination for Social Action. This Jesuit presence was meant to ensure orthodoxy, loyalty, and subordination, with priests training lay leaders and serving as "moral advisers" at all levels. By the late 1960s, ideological and generational changes in the Jesuit order made the bishops lose confidence in Jesuit programs. At the same time, established groups such as trade unions struck out for greater autonomy, resisting episcopal pres-

---

[48] This periodization is similar to the one used in training materials for lay leaders issued by the Bishops' Conference. See, for example, Conferencia Episcopal de Colombia, "Lección no. 9: La pastoral social en Colombia."

sure for control and reliability. In reaction, the hierarchy centralized control, removing management of groups and training programs from the Jesuits and giving it to a new department of the bishops' conference. Suspect training institutes were purged, "unreliable" clerical advisers replaced, and stress was placed on developing leaders who would be loyal to the institutional church. Considerable effort went to the design of grass-roots programs, including instruction on formation of a proper agenda, details of how chairs and tables should be placed in group meetings, and elaborate manuals for training potential leaders. Ideological reliability and institutional loyalty are the basic desiderata in all these materials. One example from a correspondence course suffices to make the point.

> Any ideological position which Christians assume must be taken in accord with the general doctrine of the church and with the teachings of the bishop in particular. It makes no sense to uphold as Christian an ideological position already condemned by the church. Unfortunately, this sort of thing makes for ambiguities. Christians must be radical in their loyalty to the church.[49]

Along with ensuring the maintenance of internal hierarchy and control, this insistence on loyalty serves to deny dangerous (i.e., radical activist) political involvements a prominent place in church-related groups. Once again, Msgr. López Trujillo puts the issue sharply. He notes that in speaking of *the people*,

> defending their rights is not the same as giving free rein to class struggle. Bear in mind that it is a law of language that some expressions are so ideologically contaminated that it is a difficult business to rescue their original content and tone. To organize for class struggle, even if we judge it compatible with our faith, has consequences of its own. . . . A confused people sees a sterile division in the heart of the Church, robbing [it of] its true mission and mediating capacity.
>
> Language gains not the instrumental force of communication and dialogue, but of harangue alone: catechism sows slogans and nurtures reflexes of violence; homilies become fiery political speeches which may gain applause on the stage, but which elsewhere produce only the short circuit of bitterness.[50]

The bishops' stance and the vehemence of their public positions rest on fear, above all, fear of class division and of politics. These are feared for their potential impact on the church's place in society and for the potential challenge they embody to relations of power and authority within the church. The hierarchy's studied response to the challenge posed by popular groups and by what they see as a "popular church" in their midst is well illustrated by three official programs: training pastoral agents; developing base communities; and promoting deacons and lay ministries generally.

[49] Ibid., Lección no. 10: "Compromiso político del cristiano." The lesson goes on to list coherence between faith and political options as a necessary complementary criterion.

[50] *Opciones e interpretaciones*, p. 21.

The institutional church in Colombia jealously guards the identification, training, and legitimation of pastoral agents. A program called One Hundred Pastoral Agents is of particular interest in this regard. With financing from the West German church, this program was started by the bishops' conference in an effort to identify and train rural leaders. The goal was to work closely with dioceses and parishes in order to strengthen existing nets of community groups while creating leaders for the future. The project was offered to twenty dioceses, was accepted by twelve, and, over a three-year period, sponsored courses that were ultimately completed by sixty local "leaders." I asked the national director of this program what was meant by "pastoral agent." His response suggests the thrust of the whole effort. "Just like it says there [in the documents]," he told me, "our line has been to form 'Christian leaders.' We haven't taken it much beyond that, simply a Christian leader, one who works as an apostle in the community" (G 159). Note how narrow and tightly linked to the institutional church this definition is. It assumes an agenda defined from above and anticipates a sphere of action limited to explicitly religious functions: those activities proper to an "apostle".

Instructional materials for this and other such courses ground all reflection and any consideration of action in authoritative and lengthy expositions of official Catholic social doctrine. The dominant role of clergy is stressed throughout, and much effort goes to clarifying the meaning of "laity" and the proper place of lay people in the church. As a rule, the laity are praised for their important role but are confined to the bottom of the ladder. Strict distinctions are maintained between lay and clerical roles and activities, with the former subordinate to the latter. Training programs are clearly pitched to the production of reliable intermediaries, men and women who will faithfully represent the institution's central interests in work with popular classes. This means binding such classes to bishops and clergy in ties of symbolic legitimation and controlled membership. Stern warnings are made about the danger posed by false prophets, those who "pay little heed to announcing the true Gospel message. The temptations of political acclaim seduce them [and] laden with revolutionary promises they divide the community. They do not give the word of God, but speak only the language of men."[51]

Church documents and guidelines for the formation of base communities make it clear that the bishops take "base" to mean simply "lowest level" or "beginning"—" base" as in "basic." As a result, base communities in Colombia are seen primarily as small-scale incarnations of the church, cellular units linked tightly to existing structures.[52] Reliability is further enhanced

---

[51] Conferencia Episcopal de Colombia, *Agentes de comunión y participación: Diáconos permanentes y ministros laicos*, p. 15.

[52] This interpretation is apparent, for example, in Conferencia Episcopal de Colombia, "Las comunidades eclesiales de base y la parroquia"; and in Ivan Marín, "Experiencia de ministerios en Colombia," pp. 104–6. One official pamphlet lists eight constitutive traits, giving most de-

when lay people are turned into official or semiofficial agents of the institutional church: clergy or, more precisely, miniclergy. In the report to Puebla cited earlier, the Colombian stance is made very clear.

> The best conditions for nurturing a vocation of service to the church are found in the heart of the Christian community. The Holy Spirit never stops enriching the church with varied gifts and charisms to be placed in service to the community. It is the hierarchy which is charged with discerning their proper content and exercise. Today, these different conditions converge principally in the [base communities] as the beginning of an era of lay ministries in the church. The same holds for permanent deacons. CEBs are a fertile ground, as much to find and nurture vocations of deacons as to exercise their ministry as promoter, animator, and unifying link between the communities and their pastors (parish priests and bishops). Many CEBs already have lay ministers officially named by the hierarchy. They also have fine conditions for permanent deacons. Many have sent young people to seminaries and religious orders.[53]

The status of permanent deacons and lay ministers warrants a word of its own. These older, often ancient offices and functions have been revived throughout Latin America, partly in response to the scarcity of clergy and also as an expression of the desire to stimulate lay activity. In theory, new lay ministers remain rooted in their communities and social groups and therefore sensitive to local needs and desires. As we shall see, such individuals often have important impact in the community: leading Bible study groups, encouraging openness and broader participation, and stimulating social and political awareness by linking religious reflection directly to the experiences of daily life. But the Colombian hierarchy's goals are manifestly more narrow. Their overwhelming concern with security and reliability generates a push toward clericalism: continued control by clergy and the production of new (if lesser) clergy.

In contrast to all this, the organizational record of the Venezuelan church is sparse. Until the late 1960s, four kinds of groups occupied the bishops' attention: traditional parish societies; a weak collection of Catholic Action organizations; carefully nurtured and socially powerful Catholic schools and related parents' groups (directed, for the most part, at a middle-class clientele); and the indirect legitimating effects of the Christian Democratic party, COPEI. Throughout, as one long-term adviser to the bishops puts it: "The lay person who is well viewed here is the one who says 'amen.' They don't want active people, people with ideas and a spirit of cooperation, capable of deciding for themselves" (G 228). Working from a marginal and resource-poor position,

---

tailed attention to the requirement that such communities be "hierarchically structured with a ministerial quality" (Conferencia Episcopal de Colombia, *Vivamos la iglesia comunidad eclesial*, p. 30).

[53] Conferencia Episcopal de Colombia, "Aporte," p. 179.

the hierarchy's goal had to be to extend and project, not to preserve and defend positions of strength.

Venezuela's bishops have also attempted to promote base communities. They created the National Pastoral Institute (in 1966), which, on starting operations in 1971, dedicated itself to the development of courses and instructional materials and to the organization of sporadic regional and national meetings. But the Institute exists mostly on paper. Its newsletter appears irregularly and has only limited circulation. There is no effort at national coordination, and I could find no instance of a community whose origin owed anything to the Institute. All the groups in place have all been founded by structures outside the control of the hierarchy.

## Popular Work: Alternative Views

The character and limitations of official church programs for popular work stand out sharply when challenges and alternatives are considered. In both Colombia and Venezuela, the 1960s constitute the prehistory of radical popular work. In these years, individual priests or small groups of clergy accompanied by lay activists began intensive efforts at reflection and action punctuated by highly publicized clashes with bishops and with public authorities. With rare exceptions, such initiatives were led by clergy and stressed the composition and public diffusion of critical documents. Little effort was invested in the day-to-day work of building mass organizations. In short, these were movements with neither structures nor followers. Not surprisingly, they left little that was tangible behind. Their heritage amounts to this: They promoted the idea that criticism from within the church (indeed, of the church) was legitimate, prefiguring much of the discourse later crystallized in liberation theology.

The prehistory of alternative popular work in Colombia is dominated by the meteoric career of Camilo Torres and the later rise, defeat, and dispersal of two movements of radical clergy: the Golconda Group and SAL (Sacerdotes para America Latina, or Priests for Latin America).[54] All three demanded that the church take radical and prophetic stands in the promotion of social justice and political change. These cases are as interesting for what they were *not* and did *not* do as for their role as precursors. Repeated claims to speak and act for the people cannot hide the fact that the people themselves played little role: there was no mass organization and no breach of clerical dominance. Despite

[54] They have much in common with initiatives that sprang up elsewhere in Latin America around the same time, including Argentina's Movement of Third World Priests and Peru's ONIS (National Office for Social Information). All of these predate the Medellín conference, the crystallization of liberation theology, the emergence of base communities, and the appearance of what has come to be called the "popular church."

occasional participation by lay activists, the activities of all three clearly revolved around clergy.

Each of these experiences has been extensively documented. Only a brief account is possible here.[55] Camilo Torres's appeal drew heavily on his initial curiosity value as a radical priest in a country of conservative clerical traditions. Golconda was a loose amalgam of clergy with a few sympathetic bishops, and limited itself for the most part to writing documents. SAL's very name suggests its clerical character. Although SAL's leadership tried for alliances with unions and vocally supported a number of strikes, the group remained limited in base and elitist in character. Together, the experiences of Camilo Torres, Golconda, and SAL meant that the Colombian church was embroiled in a series of sharp public conflicts from the mid-1960s to the late 1970s. The net result was further to radicalize and marginalize already radical groups while reinforcing the power of conservatives in the hierarchy. The latter moved swiftly and effectively to eliminate what they saw as a radical threat. Many left the priesthood; they either were expelled or left in voluntary search of different paths to serve popular causes. Urban Colombia is now littered with small foundations, bookstores, and the like run by clerics who left the priesthood around this time.

Recent expressions of radical activism have taken a more cautious and explicitly long-range strategy. There is less stress on documents and statements of position, more concern with building networks of grass-roots organizations. Open confrontaton with bishops or state authorities is avoided. Documenting this new generation of efforts can be difficult: groups and activists are suspicious of outsiders. They fear repression by civil and ecclesiastical authorities and prefer, therefore, to work with minimal publicity. One organizer reminded me that "this is not Brazil, where one has the bishops' support. Here in Colombia the hierarchy is opposed, and as we are few, it is easy to destroy us. So this is our plan: sow the seeds, let them grow, and later, when these seeds become trees, with strength of their own, *then* to be ready for the ecclesiastical and official onslaught. Should it come now, when the people are not mature, all this will collapse" (G 92).

Two institutions have been central to the construction of popular alternatives in Colombian Catholicism: CINEP (Centro de Investigación y Educación Popular), a Jesuit research and social action center, and *Solidaridad*, a radical journal founded in 1978. Together, they have mounted a challenge on all fronts to the hierarchy's vision of the popular. Combining forces, they work to document popular movements, to empower them (with resources, organi-

[55] On Camilo Torres, see William J. Broderick, *Camilo Torres*; and Oscar Maldonado, Guiteme Oliveri, and Germán Zabala, *Cristianismo y revolucion*; and for a general dissussion, Daniel H. Levine and Alexander Wilde, "The Catholic Church, 'Politics,' and Violence: The Colombian Case." On SAL and Golconda, see the documents collected in *SAL: Un compromiso sacerdotal en la lucha de clases. Documentos, 1972–1978.*

zational help, training materials, etc.), and to coordinate scattered efforts on a regional and national scale. Beginning in 1982, biennial meetings have drawn members from affiliated base communities across the country. There have also been related gatherings of pastoral agents, whose role appears here in much broader and more activist terms than that allowed for by the country's bishops.[56]

The following issues get special stress and are frequently discussed in the pages of *Solidaridad*: class unity as the basis of popular religious organization; the utility of Marxist analysis; the need for new structures of authority that will empower popular groups in both church and society; and the primary role of political action in religious organization and commitment. *Solidaridad*'s June 1981 issue, for example, is devoted to the meaning of a "popular church." Articles (all unsigned, for fear of repression) take special pains to challenge the hierarchy's stress on lay ministries, which is described as an evasion of the real problems the "base" confronts. The central issue is not the reform of church structures but the reworking of their social and political position in the context of needed revolutionary change. For *Solidaridad*, the bishops' obsession with control and loyalty is driven by fear of losing ties to power and privilege. They stress control so much that innovation is completely choked off and alternatives are driven out of the church.

> This gives a special tone to the relations of Christians to popular struggle in Colombia. Or, to state it differently, to the birth of our own popular church. Our groups of Christians feel like spiritual orphans. Communion with the hierarchy is very hard, and this explains why in so many instances there has been such stress on breaking. A hierarchy which doggedly turns its back on the people, in the long run creates a people which turns its back on the hierarchy. This situation has forced many priests to work clandestinely, weakening the impact of their work with the masses. In our country, fidelity to the church is particularly conflictful.[57]

Survival is an immediate problem for those linked to the CINEP-*Solidaridad* line. There is a loose network of popular groups, and constant effort is made to retain links with central church institutions. But leaders and activists alike face a constant threat of being forced out of the church and thus losing the moral authority and the symbolic legitimation membership provides. This leads them, wherever possible, to step back from direct conflict with the bishops. One CINEP organizer states:

---

[56] CINEP arose out of a complex ideological and generational split among Colombia's Jesuits. In addition to its social action programs, CINEP sponsors, often with external funding, extensive research and publication. CINEP works with a broad national focus. Efforts to mount similar initiatives regionally, for example, in the Universidad Obrera (in Cali) and the Universidad Campesina and Instituto Mayor Campesino (in Buga) failed. For an instance of the impact of these programs, see the life history of Huberto Vanegas in chapter 8, below.

[57] "Desde la perspectiva de la iglesia de los pobres," p. 35.

We have evaluated these experiences and discovered that the hierarchy does have power. Of course, we knew this, but we had not felt it in practice, not in the flesh. But then we found that they do have the power to destroy all this. So it is foolish to attack them so openly. At the same time, we drew another conclusion: The hierarchy has meaning to the people. Attacking the hierarchy means losing contact with the people. Attacking the hierarchy only sows suspicions toward us among the people. Another conclusion is that we gave all this an overly political cast. Christian commitment, yes, but very political. All in good faith, of course, but the result was documents which were too political. We were Christian groups, but we looked like political groups, with a commitment which was above all political. (G 87)

These comments suggest that radicals in the Colombian Church are searching for a new operative style that can balance political goals with the appeal of religious symbols and activities. Articles in *Solidaridad* have thus begun to emphasize the value of popular culture (including popular religion) and to argue that efforts to respect and to work within the typical expressions of this culture are the best foundation for organization and action over the long haul. The following statement in the journal's tenth anniversary edition sums up *Solidaridad*'s view of the significance of the "church of the poor" in national life:

Through day-to-day effort and from the pages of *Solidaridad*, the Church of the Poor has contributed to the development of popular culture in all its various aspects (ideological, political, artistic . . .) and to the renovation of methodologies for popular work and organization. . . . A broad sector of the [national] Alternative Popular Movement acknowledges the need for a christian presence in the process of liberation of our people, and not only accepts but demands it.[58]

The net result of all this is a collection of groups that operate quietly, scattered in the interstices of church structures and protected by a sympathetic bishop here, a religious order there. In the process, groups form and dissolve as occasion arises, and the very notion of centralized, nationally structured organizations begins to fade. As one key figure in CINEP told me, "Beyond the fact that groups form and dissolve, far more important is the dissolution of the very notion of Christendom. This is gone, and hence the groups built on that vision also fade away" (G 74).

This is optimistic, for as we have seen, Christendom is far from gone in Colombia. Its resurgent strength gives real foundation to the fears of radical organizers and the popular groups they inspire. Difficult and "unreliable" clergy really are suspended or transferred on short notice, seminaries really are purged, training institutes really are shut down. To bring CINEP to heel, the bishops launched a major lobbying campaign in the international church.

[58] *Solidaridad* (November 1988): 10.

They managed to have the organization's leadership changed, to hinder publication efforts, and to attack its funding sources. The campaign was kicked off in 1981 with an unprecedented public denunciation.

> With pastoral distress, and impelled by the requirements of truth and ecclesial unity, we must declare that our call to those priests who are a notable part of institutions of investigation or study centers, and who share the theses of "Christians for Socialism" has proven fruitless. They persist in ideological goals which break the communion of the Lord's church. Hence, in the spirit of the Apostolic Call for Reconciliation, we declare that CINEP, its publication "Controversy," the journal *Solidaridad*, as well as the popular ecclesial communities, are infused with ideologies and goals in grave conflict with the doctrine and discipline of the church.[59]

The bishops seem to fear that the new radical strategy may work. Even though only a scattered handful of base communities are affiliated with the CINEP-*Solidaridad* line, and despite the fact that as a practical matter no national plan or coordination exists, the bishops found a significant threat. In a document on base communities issued in Febrary 1986, they denounced all such groups as ideological, not ecclesial in character, and noted that they now appear in Colombia

> with links and coordinating centers of a supposedly ecclesial character [this refers to the Jesuits] but which lack approval by the bishops and the Episcopal Conference. We have information that there have been national meetings, all without informing the bishops or getting their assent. . . . Any base communities which are not expressly approved by the bishops in their dioceses and by the Episcopal Conference nationally have no validity either in their operations or in their coordination. We will gather data about base communities that lack such approval and we will do all we can to ensure that the church avoids such evils. . . . We commit ourselves to denounce and deauthorize all those which depart from church doctrine.[60]

Developments in Venezuela have followed a similar trajectory, albeit with reduced conflict and a softer edge to debate. Here, too, the prehistory of alternative strategies for popular work is found in the middle to late 1960s. Movements had only limited impact and were dominated by clergy with small groups of students and political activists.[61] Inspired by Vatican II, small groups of priests began meeting on a regular basis around 1966. They articulated a critical vision of church and society, and hoped to find bases for a new presence by the church in national life. They argued in particular that clergy

[59] Conferencia Episcopal de Colombia, *Mensaje pastoral* (1981), p. 31.
[60] Cited in *Solidaridad*'s tenth anniversary edition, p. 8.
[61] This account draws heavily on Navarro, *Contestación*; Sosa, "Iglesia y democracia"; and Ugalde, "La nueva presencia."

and sisters had to go to the poor, share their lives and struggles, and help them organize. The stage was set for later conflicts. Groups of clergy (with a few nuns) who were independent of mainline structures like dioceses or the priests' councils then being formed popped up around the country. For about five years, members met periodically and kept in touch in other ways, coming to public view in occasional documents and sporadic protests undertaken by students with whom they worked. Three incidents (chosen from among many) show how matters came to a head, sparking a crackdown.

In 1969, students organized a series of occupations of prominent churches (including the Barquisimeto Cathedral and the Basilica of San Francisco in Caracas). They protested luxury and ostentation in the church, called themselves "the People of God on the march," and demanded active commitment to the poor. Police were called in, and the students were arrested and charged, despite heated protests. Not long after, there was a much-publicized arrest and expulsion of Father Francis Wuytack, a Belgian priest. Wuytack was charged with "political activities" stemming from his involvement with community organizations in the Caracas barrio of La Vega, where he lived.[62] Church authorities supported these actions, and the anomaly of bishops cooperating with a Christian Democratic government to expel a priest for serving the people was widely noted. Once again, there were extensive protests, including unprecedented public demonstrations by priests and sisters. The last incident came in connection with a national Catholic Congress on the Integral Development of Man, held in the city of Barquisimeto in 1971. The hierarchy placed great store in this gathering, which it saw as a showcase for Catholic ideas and programs about development. These hopes were spoiled by students who mounted protests, disrupted the meetings, and pushed debates in a new direction. They insisted that Venezuela's problems made little sense in terms of "development" and rejected solutions of a specifically Catholic stripe as irrelevant. Structural inequalities required active commitment to struggle for change: capitalism was the problem; Catholics were only one element in a collective effort to promote justice. The hierarchy's showcase was spoiled, its allies in the business community and in COPEI were outraged, and a broad crackdown ensued.[63]

Two initiatives from this period survived to play a key role in later efforts. These were the Centro Gumilla (a Jesuit center for research and social action) and CESAP (Centro al Servicio de la Acción Popular), which offers courses and related services to popular organizations. The founding of Centro Gumilla

[62] For details on the Wuytack case, see my *Religion and Politics in Latin America*, chap. 6.

[63] The bishops' efforts to establish control came not long after leaders in COPEI expelled a group of young radicals from the party's youth movement. These student leaders (concentrated at the Central University in Caracas) formed a short-lived Christian Left movement, and then dispersed to other activities, including militance in new leftist parties. There was no counterpart in Venezuela to the radical Christian movements that allied with the Allende government in Chile.

in 1969 reflected the coming to power of a new generation in Venezuela's Jesuit community. These men have made the Centro Gumilla into a major national voice promoting alternative visions of church and society and working for the empowerment of popular groups. They took over publication of *SIC*, a Jesuit monthly that has appeared regularly since 1938, and changed it from a sleepy journal of limited circulation focused almost entirely on church questions into one of Venezuela's best and most cited sources of news and commentary. The Center also sponsors a broad range of publications including pamphlet series on educational reform, national history, agriculture, industrial development, liberation theology, and contemporary reworkings of Bible stories or psalms. These are distributed widely and provide a basis for numerous local-level study groups.

There are two distinct "centers" to the Centro Gumilla. The first is situated in Caracas, where most research and publication efforts, including *SIC*, are housed. The second is located in the western city of Barquisimeto. From this base, Jesuits have assumed a leading role in developing cooperatives and community groups throughout the surrounding region.

Although both Centro Gumilla and CINEP are Jesuit organizations, differences abound. Venezuelans have avoided becoming marginalized in church or in politics. They have played the game of church politics with great skill, as evidenced by their continued leadership of the nation's Jesuit community, their influence in schools and in the Catholic University, and their role as regional actors. One former provincial (who was also head of the Centro Gumilla) has served as president of CLAR. Centro Gumilla's publications are also much less polemical and overtly political. The commitment to work with and empower popular culture is more central to their efforts and occupies a greater share of Centro Gumilla's attention and resources. Examination of a range of publications, projects, and case histories reveals an underlying respect for popular culture and concern to work with its expressions as part of the general process of organizational growth and community empowerment.[64] Popular religion, for example, is depicted in ways that underscore links with the experiences and values of real social groups. The concept is neither limited to heterodox practices nor painted as a stumbling block to popular action. To the contrary, as a representative contribution to *SIC* argues, "The religion of the people is not a passive hiding place or refuge, but rather an arm of resistance and even of active defense." Popular religion is so important to the culture and orientations of ordinary people that those with power and privilege strive constantly to promote "a kind of religion far removed from history, spiritualized in the negative sense of the word, mystical and superstitious."[65]

[64] See, for example, Pedro Trigo, "La cultura en los barrios." The Centro Gumilla also issues a series of pamphlets that put Bible stories into contemporary language, using lots of popular slang and a question-and-answer format.
[65] Alberto Micheo, "La religión del pobre," p. 418.

Many of the Centro Gumilla's grass-roots projects involve close collaboration with CESAP. Ordinary members attend courses that CESAP sponsors on topics ranging from accounting or how to start cooperatives to national politics and church issues. CESAP was founded in 1974 by a Belgian priest who had previously been director of Jovenes de Acción (Youth for Action), a student group terminated as part of the bishops' crackdown.[66] To avoid the fate of that organization, CESAP has maintained legal and financial independence from the beginning. Despite these clearly religious origins, CESAP has always aimed beyond explicitly Catholic groups to popular organizations generally. As a rule, CESAP directs its energies less to starting groups than to responding to local requests for help and providing coordination. With support from international foundations, supplemented by revenues from the sale of services and publications, the organization established three regional centers (one near Caracas, one in Barquisimeto, and one in eastern Venezuela). Each center runs courses, lending libraries, and outreach programs such as nutritional, health, or literacy campaigns.

Independence from the institutional church is critical to CESAP's guiding concept of popular empowerment. When programs remain bound to the institution and its view of the world, leaders and activists have a hard time grasping how reality looks and feels from the bottom up. One observer told me that "organization is certainly needed, but not organization in the name of the church" (G 167). In the words of a CESAP leader, the goal is to have "groups and organizations become more independent and autonomous every day, so that they really belong to the members. Our role as a center at the service of popular action is to offer services they can't generate on their own, which they need in order to work better" (G 178). Although formal ties with the church might make life easier in some respects, the strings attached would gut CESAP's original intent.

> The institutional church seeks its own power and finds us difficult to comprehend. . . . They will accept us if we ask to form part of the hierarchical church. But once inside, we would have to subordinate [literally, *vender*, or "to sell"] the people's own initiatives. We might end up as quite an active movement, but with little beyond the organization itself. That's not our goal, that's not what we want to do. (G 186)

Since 1974, CESAP has organized hundreds of courses and published extensive instructional material, including numerous pamphlets intended as guides for group discussion. Throughout, the stated goal of popular organization is described as replacing capitalism with a just, participatory, and classless society. A more immediate purpose is to promote class consciousness and egalitarian social relations in family and community. Groups are urged to join

---

[66] I discuss this group in *Religion and Politics in Latin America*, chap. 7.

with others in order to learn from similar experiences while they gain strength through coordinated effort. Education is critical, not only for the young, but throughout life.[67]

Two pamphlets on Puebla give the flavor of this orientation.[68] They present first peasants, then workers discussing Puebla and trying to relate it to their own situation. Justice is a central theme, along with the meaning of Christ's death and resurrection. Christ lived among the poor not because poverty is good but to underscore that the poor are also human beings with a right to freedom and a better life. Throughout, poverty is attributed to the impact of sinful economic and political structures. Attempts by some members to say that people are poor because of laziness or indifference are rejected by the group. Christ sided with the poor, and in the same way, Mary is not so much an idealized virgin mother as a poor woman who refused to accept things passively. Christ was killed by the rich and powerful of the time, but his resurrection shows that victory over death is possible.

Both pamphlets argue that religion requires involvement in politics for the simple reason that religion involves people whose lives and needs embrace religious and political issues at one and the same time. Authentic Christian work requires raising consciousness, condemning oppression and violence. It is ill-served by groups that ostentatiously claim to be for Christians only. This issue is played out in a long debate that concludes when one woman gets a friend to join by showing that the group is not for Catholics only. Christianity, she argues, means accepting all persons as persons and working together without distinctions.

The preceding comparison of alternative programs for popular work in Colombia and Venezuela reveals parallels as well as contrasts. The parallels draw on elements common to Latin America as a whole: a prominent role for Jesuits; the emergence of activist Catholic groups independent of the hierarchy; increasing concern with popular culture; and a slow expansion of the role of women. Contrasts arise from strong contextual variations, including the relative power each institutional church wields and the social foundations and political climate for popular work as a whole. Within the churches, prevailing concepts of popular culture are a particularly good index of the general view taken of popular groups. In contrast to developments in Venezuela, Colombian organizers all across the ideological spectrum downgrade the validity of popular culture. They paint it either as crystallized ignorance and superstition (the hierarchy's view) or as the product of alienation caused by political oppression and by the economic injustices of capitalist development (the radical

---

[67] See, for example, CESAP, *Formación y organización popular: Conceptos educativos y elementos metodológicos del trabajo de CESAP* (1981); or *Un centro al servicio de la Acción Popular*.

[68] CESAP, *Nosotros y Puebla I: El designo de Dios en la realidad de America Latina*, and *Nosotros y Puebla II: Los obispos y la realidad*.

position). Popular culture appears as part of the problem, not part of the solution. It must be changed before the "real work" (of church practices or
political mobilization) can get underway. One is tempted to say that this is no
more than the latest of long-standing Colombian traditions that have elites and
institutions telling popular groups what to do and how to do it.

## Conclusion

At the beginning of this chapter, I asked if democracy makes a difference. As
stated, the question is too broad, and answers are necessarily ambiguous. It is
too broad because democracy means different things in the politics and in the
day-to-day life of each nation. It leads to ambiguities because there is another
question hidden deep within. This deeper question concerns the relation between democratization of culture and ordinary life and democratic politics at
the level of institutions. Consider the evidence again.

In Colombia, "democracy" has meant civilian rule, party competition, and
limited mobilization. Prevailing norms have not furthered the extension of
democratic ideals to social relations or associational life generally. To the contrary, hierarchy has been the order of the day in Colombia, with little legitimate place provided either for popular mobilization or for the construction of
democratic patterns of governance within organizations. The institutional
church has long since abandoned the overt pro-Conservative partisanship of
earlier years. In the wake of The Violence, Colombia's hierarchy became a
solid supporter of the National Front and, through it, of government and public
authority in general. Ironically, as national political conflicts ceased to provide
a central axis of conflict for the church, politics moved within, leading the
hierarchy to focus its fears and energies on the threat posed by autonomous
popular movements, especially those claiming to act out of religious motives
or affiliations.

Conflict over the popular has been extensive and bitter. The Colombian
hierarchy attacks the "popular church" so often and with a vehemence so
disproportionate to reality that one suspects that they see in it a basic challenge
to the church and to their authority. In this case, it is hard to keep the two
separate, for as we have seen, Colombia's bishops put hierarchy at the very
core of church life. The institutional church in Colombia sees a threat in the
popular because its leaders see the stress on class, solidarity, and shared authority as a challenge to the structure of power within the ecclesiastical institution and, hence, to the very survival of the church as they know it.

In Venezuela, "democracy" has also meant competitive politics. But in this
case, the combination of rapid socioeconomic change and extensive mobilization with political norms that value equality and participation over hierarchy
and subordination have given both activism and independent organizations a

legitimate place in national culture. Democratic governance within organizations also poses little threat. These general patterns have had visible impact in the church. It is not that religious leaders encourage democratizing grass-roots elements. With rare exceptions, they do not. But their self-image and the role they set for themselves encourage toleration and accommodation rather than aggressive strategies of control. The prevailing culture of politics and associational life in this case means that groups have more than an even chance of survival once they get underway. The hierarchy is unlikely to embark on sustained or effective repression, allies can be found, and the clientele is available, confident, and open to ideas about the legitimacy of action on their part.

The concepts and self-images that dominate the praxis of the Catholic church in both Venezuela and Colombia spring as much from inner sources (doctrine, theology tradition, organizational routines) as from the bishops' specific attitude to popular groups and to those opting to work with them. In Colombia, pervasive elite fear of the popular fits well with the clientelistic mentalities and structures that dominate national politics and culture. More is at issue here than a simple dichotomy of control or openness might indicate. The inner continuities of the Colombian church suggest that even if the threat of the moment should pass, any group the church promotes is likely to have a characteristic structure and style of action. New organizations may indeed penetrate popular classes, but links of authority and institutional membership cut across lines of class to reaffirm hierarchy at every turn. As a result, no matter how critical or progressive officially sponsored groups may appear to be, they are likely to remain authoritarian in spirit, popular in name alone. The situation in Venezuela differs because in this case, self-image, structure, and context combine to encourage openness, not tightfisted control. General orientations are tempered here by the impact of social formations and available opportunities on prevailing notions of what is proper and acceptable.

Contrasts between the two cases appear most clearly when attention is directed to alternative rather than official programs. Official programs share a common rationale and are distinguished mostly by available resources and by traditions that set a more limited role for the church in the Venezuelan case. But alternatives reveal differences with deeper roots. In the last analysis, they rest on heightened awareness among Venezuelans of the values popular groups embody and of the self-initiating and self-directing role popular groups can undertake.

The way we think about things organizes how we act, what we seek, and how we see and interpret events. The predominant ideas of any culture come linked to structures. They are the underpinnings of what we take as routine, the stuff of common sense. Religion stands out among major social institutions by virtue of its remarkable capacity to reach across social and cultural levels. Ideas are powerfully structured, nowhere more so than in highly bureaucratized traditions like Catholicism, with its complex and overlapping nets of dioceses, parishes, religious orders, and related institutions. Although recent innovations have enhanced the role of national church bureaucracies, for most purposes, the fundamental administrative unit of the churches remains the diocese.

Like national churches, individual dioceses reflect the history and predominant social, economic, and cultural patterns of the area. This does not make them mere captives of local society. Dioceses can lead as well as follow, stimulate change or snuff it out. Outcomes depend on how religious ideas are interpreted, worked into regular routines of action, and carried from theory to practice by specific agents who link up with available clienteles. The next chapter takes a close look at experience in three dioceses: in Colombia, rural Facatativá and urban Cali; in Venezuela, Barquisimeto, where both urban and rural settings were studied.

# FOUR

## COLOMBIA AND VENEZUELA: DIOCESES, VILLAGES, AND BARRIOS

T HE DEVELOPMENT of popular groups in the dioceses of Facatativá and Cali in Colombia and of Barquisimeto in Venezuela offers a sample of the styles and approaches to popular work, and of the programs now at issue in these nations as well as in the region as a whole. As a group, these experiences fall somewhere between the highly politicized and conflict-ridden extremes of Nicaragua or El Salvador or the popular church of Brazil, and the stolid conservative passivity or even active reactionary stance of cases like Argentina. That outcomes should fall in this middle range should come as no surprise, given the relatively open and democratic character of national society in Venezuela and Colombia. Still, the results are neither automatic nor inevitable. As we shall see, they grow out of carefully considered and elaborately put together programs.

That groups in Facatativá, Cali, and Barquisimeto fall in a middle range does not make them all the same. There are sharp contrasts whose magnitude is only suggested by the data statistics collected in table 4.1. A more complete explanation of these differences finds their origins in long-term commitments to contrasting visions of change that are put to work in very different kinds of social, economic, and cultural contexts.

### Facatativá

The diocese of Facatativá was founded in 1962 and, to date, has had only two bishops, each with a national reputation for steady, progressive leadership. The diocese lies in a varied agricultural region to the west and south of the capital city of Bogotá. Its territory runs through a number of miniclimates, from the cold mountain plain near Bogotá to the tropical valleys of the Magdalena River. The specific focus of agricultural activities depends on local ecology but normally includes coffee, corn, sugar, and beans, with a mix of cash cropping (e.g., vegetables or hops), some low-level processing, and limited subsistence production. A few highly profitable, capital-intensive commercial enterprises (especially cattle, cereals, the cultivation of flowers for export) coexist here with a host of small holdings where peasant cultivators raise crops for sale in local markets. The area's rough and varied topography

**TABLE 4.1**
Facatativá, Cali, and Barquisimeto, Selected Years

|  | Area (kms²) | Population | Parishes | Priests | Sisters | Educational Institutions |
|---|---|---|---|---|---|---|
| Facatativá |  |  |  |  |  |  |
| 1962 | 8,000 | 233,000 | 32 | 20 | — | — |
| 1970 | 8,000 | 350,000 | 34 | 65 | 191 | 17 |
| 1975 | 6,788 | 374,000 | 32 | 65 | 196 | 28 |
| 1980 | 6,788 | 483,000 | 32 | 61 | 230 | 12 |
| 1985 | 6,788 | 550,000 | 28 | 55 | 220 | 14 |
| Cali |  |  |  |  |  |  |
| 1960 | 6,555 | 906,891 | 55 | 189 | 682 | 44 |
| 1970 | 2,712 | 980,000 | 57 | 190 | 1,000 | 59 |
| 1975 | 2,712 | 1,250,000 | 68 | 231 | 1,172 | 53* |
| 1980 | 2,712 | 1,296,000 | 74 | 181 | 859 | 90 |
| 1985 | 2,712 | 1,633,669 | 81 | 185 | 976 | 113 |
| Barquisimeto |  |  |  |  |  |  |
| 1960 | 26,906 | 502,820 | 52 | 82 | 80 | 21 |
| 1970 | 19,800 | 550,000 | 67 | 136 | 200 | 25 |
| 1975 | 19,800 | 733,635 | 72 | 144 | 227 | 37 |
| 1980 | 19,800 | 836,700 | 79 | 148 | 255 | 40 |
| 1985 | 19,800 | 1,115,000 | 88 | 186 | 232 | 64 |

Source: Annuario Pontificio, selected years.
*1976

isolates towns and villages from one another, especially in the rainy season, when roads turn to mud and travel is difficult and time-consuming. Telephone and telegraph services, like regular power, schools, or water, are rare and, for the most part, limited to the largest towns.

Throughout its brief history, the diocese has had modest ecclesiastical resources and has had difficulty keeping pace with population growth: population has more than doubled, while the number of parishes, priests, sisters, and church institutions has remained static (see fig. 4.1). The numbers mask considerable innovation, especially in efforts to use existing personnel better and to avoid overlap and duplication of efforts. Religious congregations (male and female) have been incorporated fully into diocesan planning, and attempts have been made to reduce the concentration of personnel in the schools and hospitals located at the diocesan center. More priests and sisters have been dedicated to live and work full-time in the diocese's many scattered rural settlements. Groups of sisters have also been placed in autonomous pastoral roles (Vicarías de Religiosas) in particularly remote areas. The diocese has also chosen pilot regions and parishes, and has concentrated human and material resources in these areas. There has been considerable stress on mobilizing lay people, including catechists, agricultural promoters, and a range of groups affiliated with the church.

Facatativá was the site of much early experimentation. One high-ranking prelate states that "from the beginning, the diocese has been a pillar of base communities in Colombia, and was chosen for pilot programs in this area" (F 3). By the late 1960s, diocesan documents emphasized the need to promote base communities. The first formal plan for base communities dates from 1972, and the documentation for the diocese's general pastoral plan for that year speaks of three goals: formation of base communities; "mentalization" of clergy to bring them up to date with trends in the church; and the integral promotion (spiritual, economic, and cultural) of the peasant population. The bishop insists that change is the central goal.

> For us, the most important goal is to encourage transformations. We've got to renovate continuously. Otherwise, what good is any of this? Any one of these movements, any project, any community—they've all got to contribute to change. . . . If all we do is further stagnation, none of this has any reason for being. (F 43)

In his view, despite its relative weakness and poverty, the church can contribute positively to change, above all by innovating in ways that set out paths others can follow. Agenda setting of this kind is difficult; more than words are needed.

**FIGURE 4.1.**

Facatativá, Percentage Change since 1962 (Sisters, Percentage Change since 1965)

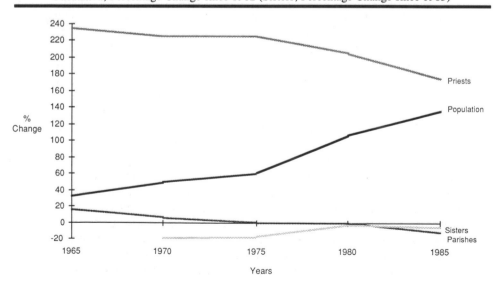

You've got to do things, create visible works. But you know, an individual, a parish or diocese, and even the church working in the country as a whole, cannot accomplish very much. It's just a drop in the bucket, small projects—that's all we can do. A real effort requires resources only the state can command. So the church's role is to fight for changes in the state, but the problem is how. (F 44)

The diocese took an important step forward in 1970 with the arrival of a Spanish priest, Román Cortés. Cortés was brought to Facatativá in order to spur and coordinate the promotion of base communities throughout the diocese, in close concert with the National Advisory Team on Base Communities and Lay Ministries of the Colombian Bishops Conference, of which he was a member. For eight years, he worked as the bishop's special envoy, setting up base-level groups and creating a support structure for them throughout the diocese. He traveled constantly and worked in collaboration with, but independently of, the ordinary structure of parishes and movements. A close aide remarked that

> we went through an intense preparatory period, above all with the first groups we identified and trained in the villages to establish courses and base communities in their areas. We worked at this for about six or seven years, practically the entire time that Román served as roving delegate. We organized parish and diocesan meetings, regular monthly gatherings for the animators of local groups. In these meetings, we would try to advance a common theme, for example concerning identity, or the role of the laity in today's world. (F 129)

In 1978, Cortés was named parish priest of Caparrapí and pastoral vicar of the entire surrounding area, consisting of three extensive parishes (Caparrapí, Yacopí, and La Palma) and hundreds of isolated hamlets scattered over one of the poorest, most conflict ridden, and abandoned zones in the region. Guerrilla movements have a forty-year history in this area,[1] and residents remain trapped between insurgents and the heavy hand of a large, often abusive military presence. After the move to Caparrapí, Cortés focused his energies in this region, which served the diocese as a model and pilot program.

Until his sudden death from cancer in 1981, Cortés worked feverishly to establish a network of base communities and local activists. It was not easy. He had to overcome suspicion from the military and from local residents fearful of any outsiders as well as from local clergy accustomed to waiting for the faithful to come to them. Cortés insisted on an active, outgoing stance, and managed to draw together the human and material resources necessary to make his strategy work. A pamphlet commemorating the diocese's twentieth anniversary underscored the need to "renovate" the clergy as a first step in crafting an effective option for the poor. There were many obstacles.

---

[1] See Gonzalo Sánchez, *Los días de la revolución: Gaitanismo y el nueve de abril en provincia.*

It has not been easy, given the scarcity of clergy to staff the parishes, the heterogeneity of our local priests, and certain diverging tendencies and theories which we are only now able to clarify, as part of a deliberate search for better models of priestly life. . . . There have also been failures of coordination and planning, and problems in finding adequate support for the clergy now in place.[2]

Cortés had a tremendous impact on religion and community life throughout the territory of Facatativá. He got countless groups started, motivated many hitherto apathetic residents, and in general shook up the staid and conventional ecclesiastical structures of the area. One of his original lieutenants argued that the problem

is that priests were used to a very independent life in the parishes. Sometimes it seems that the diocese is irrelevant to them. They act like independent republics within its structures. To be sure, they respect the bishop a lot, and all that, when it comes down to action, each one does his own thing. (F 11)

Román Cortés's normal mode of operation warrants closer examination. To organize communities, he began with *cursillos de cristiandad*, or "little courses in Christianity." On arrival in a particular town or hamlet, he would invite residents to attend what he called a "course on Christian fundamentals." Participants would then join a two- or three-day enterprise of prayer, reflection, and personal confrontation with one another and with the priest who led each *cursillo*. The result was a series of profound conversion experiences. In later chapters, I present detailed accounts of what goes on in *cursillos* and of the effect they have on individuals and communities. The following comment by one peasant man suffices here to give a flavor of the experience. I asked how he first got involved in the base community, and why.

There was no base community here. All we had was a community, just an ordinary hamlet with a little community organization [Acción Comunal, a government-mandated structure]. There was a *junta* (a directive committee) but it didn't work like it should have. Well, in any case, we did the *cursillo*, spurred on by Román. You know, people were even afraid of him. When Román came here, at first people hid. I was like that, I was afraid of him. I don't know what the problem was, maybe too much respect, or just plain fear. I don't know.

After the *cursillo*, we were completely changed. It's like being two persons. You go out old and come back new, renovated in spiritual and material terms. And [then] you're able to see the wrong in what you did only the day before. And that's a big change: a change in material things, in spiritual life, in the community, in the way we live, each one of us in the community. The whole idea was to live in community and to lead our lives more focused on the church. (A 34)

[2] *Diocesis de Facatativá, 1962–1982: 20 años de lucha y esperanza.*

The *cursillo* movement is a perfect vehicle for creating groups consonant with the Colombian church's predilection for hierarchical structures and authority patterns. The *cursillo* movement was founded in Spain during the 1950s. In theory and practice, it stresses intense personal conversion combined with service to the institutional church. Deference to established hierarchy is a constant thread in pamphlets, sermons, and discussion.[3] In Facatativá, this created an approach to community organization that underscored the need for tight linkages between popular groups and the church, linkages monitored on a regular basis by official agents of the church itself. As in the Colombian church generally, communities in Facatativá were seen as a source of recruits for semiclerical roles like lay ministers or permanent deacons; the ideal member was depicted as a kind of subordinate minicleric.

A few years after Román Cortés died, the diocese issued a book with his last "messages" to clergy, pastoral agents, and laity.[4] The volume also contains remembrances of him and his work contributed by friends and collaborators. Extraordinary insight is provided into the kind of base communities desired in Facatativá. They are to be firmly grounded in "religious fundamentals" and in ties to the church. Cortés believed that conversion and spiritual renovation was a prerequisite; hence the *cursillos*. Groups should operate so as to make sacraments, love of and loyalty to the church, and attention to family and community central, in that order. Cortés foresaw a normal path for groups, from individual religious conversion through reorganization of family life and reinforcement of mutual trust and solidarity in the community. Concerns about ecology and community followed, leading to the organization of cooperatives and small self-help projects like road repair, bridge construction, or water piping. He stressed that *cursillos* were only a means: "We do *cursillos* so that people will form groups and communities: we don't create communities so that people will go to *cursillos*. The community is the splendor of the garden whose gateway is the *cursillo*."

What precisely does "community" mean in these discussions? In the diocese of Facatativá, what exactly does it mean to form a community, to live in a community? Cortés stressed simultaneous commitment to Christ and to the community. He acknowledged how hard this can be, and urged base communities to seek help and guidance from the church. Viable communities required links to the church, the root of all other enduring relationships.

> Learning to live in a communitarian way in such an individualistic world is not a matter of a moment. Do not despair! Try and try again. Seek the help of the Diocese. Seek the help of your parish priests to live in community. Try communitarian living. Learn to pray together, to love together, to share together the Word, the Mass, food, money, life, being a person. Learn to share as brothers and

---

[3] I discuss *cursillos* in more detail in *Religion and Politics in Latin America*, pp. 233–37.
[4] Román Cortes Tossal, "Testimonio y mensajes del P. Román Cortes Tossal."

sisters, and to form yourselves and help yourselves and commit yourselves together. Those who are already living a communitarian life will give you the message: commitment, commitment, commitment. No one can be a good *cursillista* who is not living in community, no one is truly living in community without commitment.

Founding *cursillos* is a little like holding revival meetings: follow-up is critical. To ensure that *cursillos* would evolve in the proper way, Cortés designed an elaborate structure of training programs and regular contact with local groups. Parishes, communities, schools, and members were visited regularly, either by Cortés or his small staff, which until the late 1970s consisted of one or two full-time aides working out of diocesan offices. Regular "leadership schools" were also established in six centrally located parishes. These "schools" have operated continuously since the mid-1970s. Participants travel long distances to attend—often at considerable expense in bus fares, lost work time, and so forth. Meetings usually last a full day and follow a standard agenda that begins with prayer, Bible study, and singing and then moves on to development and evaluation of diocesan goals and local needs and projects. Themes and suggested issues are provided on mimeographed sheets sent out by the diocese. Diocesan publications provide extensive detail on how best to get groups started and organize meetings effectively. For example, leaders are reminded to have groups form a circle, not sit in rows; to include songs, create posters, and so forth. Instructions are also given on which kinds of themes to raise and in what order.[5]

The monthly leadership schools serve to keep up community spirits and to prepare a corps of local "animators" who will spur and monitor grass roots. Potential animators are first identified in the *cursillos* through which contact was made with a given community. After a period of orientation, animators are relied on to facilitate regular contact between diocese and community. They make sure meetings are held and take care that agendas fit with diocesan guidelines. They also provide a reservoir for identifying and training the lay ministers and permanent deacons of the future.

This elaborate structure provides an effective means for monitoring and controlling groups. The typical group agenda is cleared with the diocese or its formal agents and, for the most part, is kept within narrow boundaries. Local innovation is discouraged; independent contact with nonreligious groups in the area (e.g., peasant associations or educational groups) is frowned upon. Once outside the immediate circle of friends and neighbors, most ties are vertical, managed through sisters and clergy and reinforced by regular visits, training sessions, and the promotion of lay ministries as an ideal outcome. This means

[5] Diocesis de Facatativá, "Experiencia de comunidades eclesiales de base y ministerios laicales en la diocesis de Facatativá, Colombia," pp. 2–3.

that although the program of *cursillos*, base communities, and schools covers much of the diocese, the scale and scope of any particular effort is limited.

Working with *cursillos* clearly simplified the whole effort. Their rigid structure and devotional agenda let Cortés and his aides tap local traditions of religiosity and respect for clergy. Initial barriers of shyness or distrust of outsiders were thus more easily overcome; residents got involved and active with minimal delay. But once involved in groups and in their networks, members encountered a number of restraints. Agendas were confined to local issues, and authority structures reinforced deference to hierarchy and continued reliance on clergy. The likelihoood of effective, independent leadership emerging in the communities was thus very limited.[6]

The egalitarianism and group autonomy associated elsewhere with the Radical Ideal of base communities are unlikely to find much welcome in Facatativá. The kind of leader or lay agent created as a result of these efforts is considerably less independent and self-starting than, for example, the Delegates of the Word that emerged in Central America at around the same time.[7] But efforts like those in Facatativá cannot therefore be dismissed as inauthentic. It is false and misleading to assume that some abstract model of the good base community exists: a Platonic ideal to which reality must accommodate. Facatativá offers a real alternative, not just a false image.

Cortés's success and the sheer power of his personality encouraged others to try their hand in the receptive environment of Facatativá. By the mid-1970s, similar but independent initiatives had sprung up in large numbers. There were schools for training peasant girls, who were to return to their communities as promoters. There were also general programs for economic development, literacy, and leadership. A case in point was Hogar-Escuela (Home-School), a complex effort designed to promote adult literacy among peasants through work with audio cassettes and to tie literacy training to a range of small-scale community development projects. After its founding in 1975 (by a group of Dominican sisters), Hogar-Escuela soon had agents and branches at work in a large number of towns and villages. The organization's statement of goals fits the Colombian church perfectly. Change and hierarchy, material progress and spiritual growth are stressed together.

> So it is clear, then, that the entire Christian community, united around its legitimate pastors and guided by them, constitutes the responsible subject of its own liberation and human promotion. The church's doctrine brings its own vision of

---

[6] Ibid. This document underscores the need for close ties with parish and diocese, especially in the formation of group agendas and the selection and orientation of leaders. An earlier special issue (no. 91, [September 1978]) of *Comunidad diocesana* (the diocese's magazine) sets these concerns specifically in the context of the needs of Facatativá's peasantry and of plans to organize and work with them.

[7] See Pearce, *The Promised Land*; Dodson and O'Shaughessy, *Nicaragua's Other Revolution*; and Berryman, *Religious Roots*.

man and humanity [which] is always the promotion of an integral liberation of the human person in his earthly and transcendent dimensions, contributing in this way to building the definitive Kingdom, without confusing earthly progress with the growth of Christ's realm.[8]

After a while, these activities grew well beyond the diocese's management capacity. There was duplication, wasted effort, and a nagging sense that this scattered collection of programs barely scratched the surface of peasant needs and interests. Around 1977, systematic efforts at coordination began. The diocese's bureaucracy was thoroughly reorganized, bringing scattered efforts together under a single structure—the vicarate of Pastoral Action. This was placed under the energetic leadership of Msgr. Jaime Prieto, a priest whose extensive background in social issues combined study with work experience and lengthy administrative service in social action groups. Prieto's authority was reinforced by his designation as vicar-general (second in command) of the diocese. Among his most important goals were providing a solid, long-range financial basis to diocesan efforts, engaging a permanent staff, and ensuring that religious promotion and socioeconomic projects were linked at all stages of the process. With full backing from the bishop, he undertook negotiations with the Colombian offices of Catholic Relief Services of the United States (CRS). One CRS official comments:

> This all began around 1978, mid-1977 to be exact. Jaime Prieto came to the office to tell us that he was now Director of Social Pastoral, and wanted to set up a program for the diocese. So we began meeting, we had lots of meetings. But it was very difficult, because at that time lots of groups were working on their own. There were no shared criteria, and in any case, there was not enough personnel. Jaime was by himself, and he was the only one who knew what this kind of work was all about. . . . As a result, we had trouble getting an overall vision of things, and it was awfully difficult to organize a program that included everything. (F 148)

The resulting program, called Procampesinos, involved a three-year agreement in which CRS pleged to provide funding and project supervision while the diocese committed itself to a long-range plan for work with peasant communities. Procampesinos looked to implement a practical option for the poor by sponsoring numerous small-scale programs of immediate material benefit. Unlike many such internationally funded programs in Latin America, little effort was devoted here to physical structures: buildings or vehicles. Instead, CRS underwrote a revolving fund earmarked to provide start-up money for local projects and to cover part of the costs of a series of courses to be undertaken on religious, economic, social, and cultural issues throughout the diocese. This arrangement was intended to avoid beginning projects until ade-

---

[8] *Hogar Escuela*, n.p.

quate groundwork, above all in the form of visits, contacts, and courses in the local area, had been laid. All projects were to be economically self-sustaining and were organized to maximize participation.

These concerns pointed to the need for extensive, long-term contact between the diocese and local communities and led to the second pillar of the program, the organization of a full-time diocesan staff, known in Facatativá as the "Mobile Team." This consisted of a catechist, two rural promoters (a specialist in agricultural projects and one in cooperatives), an accountant and project evaluator, and a related group of educators and individuals designated to offer courses on a broad range of topics (theology, catechism, health care, sewing, etc.) Popular demand moved courses in a practical direction. According to one CRS official,

> At first, the courses were all very abstract, about Christ, the church, things like that. But soon the peasants themselves began to ask for more concrete things, for example, courses about cooperatives. In this way you could see the bases of organization emerge among the people, in the formation of base-level organizations around specific projects like water piping. (F 150)

The Mobile Team evaluated requests for help that came in from local communities, requests often forwarded and endorsed by the parish priest. They also developed specific projects like cooperatives, water lines, or local stores and then took the plans to the field, convincing and mobilizing residents in the effort. Members of the team often spent months in isolated areas, exploring local situations and developing a basis of trust with peasants in the region as a foundation for the later work on specific projects. They worked closely with pastoral agents and group members who were already active throughout the diocese as a result of Román Cortés's efforts.

As part of the agreement with CRS, a sociological study of the diocese was undertaken to provide more precise data on local needs and desires.[9] The study was carried out over a three-year period, with active participation by local groups. Findings underscored the acute and growing poverty of most of the population, the absence of strong peasant organizations and, hence, of access to available services like credit or medical attention, pervasive violence and insecurity, and a series of specific deficiencies in health, education, property rights and working conditions, housing, transportation, light and water, and religious attention.[10] Data from the study were used to set priorities and to design and target programs more effectively. Throughout, stress was given to maximizing peasant participation within a framework that bound local con-

[9] Dioceses of Facatativá, *Premonografía*.

[10] See ibid.; the special number of *Comunidad diocesana* cited in note 6, above; and a mimeographed circular entitled "Aspectos de la realidad local y diocesana observadas por los promotores y comunidades eclesiales de base (para confrontar posteriormente con las realidades sentidas por las mismas comunidades)." This is attached to "Experiencia," cited in note 5, above.

cerns to the overall objectives of the diocese. In one 1978 document, the bishop highlighted the need for peasants to organize.

> Only you can overcome this situation of marginality through your own organization, and organization that you can then turn into pressure groups, into economic power, and into the means for sharing rightfully in deciding the destinies of the nation.[11]

The diocese chose a few parishes as pilots, including the region around Caparrapí (where Román Cortés was already at work) and the parish of Quebradanegra, where two nuns were located permanently in the nearby village of La Magdalena and charged with spurring and regularly monitoring local groups. The Mobile Team's efforts were multiplied by the continuing structure of leadership schools as well as by reorganization of diocesan resources to provide for greater coordination of local efforts. Regular communication between groups and the diocese was maintained through the Mobile Team and the sisters, and also by means of a series of courses to which local promoters and animators were regularly invited. A final piece to the puzzle was provided in 1983 with construction and operation of a pastoral center in the diocese (housed in the seminary) named after Román Cortés and intended as a central location for the many meetings, courses, and group gatherings.

The three-year term of the Procampesinos agreement was drawing to a close at the time of my field research, and there was general consensus in the diocese and in CRS itself that much had been accomplished. Hundreds of courses had been given to thousands of peasants, scores of local groups and small-scale enterprises had been launched, savings and loan organizations had been established and affiliated with Cupocrédito (a national organization of credit unions), and a regular monitoring, control and visiting system was firmly in place. I asked one CRS official if the program had been successful.

> Absolutely. We got to know and work in this area which had been completely marginal to any efforts at social promotion. Peasants participated in nothing, and that was that. An area that contained zones of violence like Caparrapí and Yacopí, where no one from the outside had ever entered. That also housed a growing industrial zone near Bogotá. A new image of the church has also been created, or rather, the image of the church has been restored, an image of caring and involvement that had been lost. (F 154)

The efforts of Román Cortés, the diocese, and CRS all evince a clear vision of the proper group, the ideal member, and the desired pattern of change. To put these efforts into practice required adapting general strategies to the specifics of different communities. I conducted field studies in three: Caparrapí,

[11] Msgr. Hernando Velásquez Lutero, ''Alocución del Monseñor Hernando Velásquez Lutero en el encuentro campesino.''

Quebradanegra, and Tabio. In each case, I interviewed the priest and members of local groups, explored the history of organization, and visited outlying hamlets. Caparrapí, Quebradanegra, and Tabio provide contrasting settings for popular organizations and yield distinctly mixed results. Because the names of these communities will recur repeatedly in the next few chapters, a brief note on each is appropriate here.[12]

The municipality of Caparrapí itself is reached from Facatativá after a ten-hour bus ride (two buses daily), and roads are often impassable in the rainy season. The town sits around a barren main square with a broken fountain, where a weekly market is held. The square itself is dominated on one side by parish offices and a large church (built some time ago by American priests). Offices of the Federation of Coffee Growers, the Agrarian Bank, cooperatives, and the bus agency occupy another. The remainder is filled out by municipal offices, a police station, agricultural implement and feed stores, and a small hotel (the Residencias Hilton).

From the town center, visitors face lengthy and difficult trips by jeep and then horse or mule to get to the 90 percent of local population that lives in the hundreds of hamlets scattered in surrounding hillsides and valleys. The parish held about twenty thousand people in 1980, most of whom worked as isolated small farmers operating with limited resources and low technology to grow subsistence crops along with small amounts of coffee, sugar, and corn for sale. Poverty is the norm. The land is fertile enough, but rough terrain and poor communications combine here with pervasive guerrilla violence and military occupation to impede progress and constrain organization. The vast majority of hamlets lack electric light, running water, and regular access to formal education beyond the first few years of primary school. I gave special attention to three hamlets with important group development: San Carlos, San Pedro, and Barro Blanco. The latter two lie in the heart of guerrilla territory; residents report constant harassment by both army and insurgents.

After the death of Román Cortés, the diocese continued to focus human and material resources in Caparrapí. Four young priests combined efforts to try to fill his shoes. They were aided by several groups of sisters, six women in all, some of whom live in the parish center and travel out for specific projects while others work full-time in the Vicarías de Religiosas mentioned earlier. Pastoral efforts in the post-Cortés era hinge on the *cursillos*, base communities, and efforts to promote cooperatives, local water systems, and small but economically viable projects like beekeeping or raising rabbits or chickens. The latter have been funded by CRS-Procampesinos, which also made Caparrapí a pilot zone.

The second parish, Quebradanegra, is centered on the small, dusty village

---

[12] These data are drawn from statistics in the diocese's *Premonografía* checked against other sources and verified in visits and interviews.

of Quebradanegra. The town itself could easily have been lifted from the pages of a story by Gabriel García Márquez.[13] The main square is framed by a small store, a barracks with police and soldiers lounging around, a school, a church and rectory, and again, a small hotel. Quebradanegra is easily accessible by bus from Facatativá (about five hours) and lies close to the important regional market town of Villeta. As in Caparrapí, more than 90 percent of the parish's population (approximately five thousand in 1980) is scattered across a large number of isolated hamlets. Agriculture dominates the local economy, and the crops are similar to those raised in Caparrapí. Quebradanegra plays a key role in the diocese's plans for base communities. As noted, two nuns are permanently based in nearby La Magdalena and are charged with promoting and monitoring base communities in the entire surrounding area. We shall see one of them in action in the next chapter.

From the many hamlets this parish contains, I selected two for a closer look. The first is Agua Fría, a small and easily accessible settlement of about seventy-five families. The second is San Isidro, a remote hilltop village reachable only after a full day's travel from Facatativá by bus, on horse or mule, and on foot. Both communities have active base groups and regularly send representatives to parish leadership schools and diocesan courses. Agua Fría has also developed a cooperative and small local store. Agua Fría's base community is one of the oldest in the diocese and has achieved unusual levels of independence and internal democracy.

The final parish studied, Tabio, is a prosperous farming and commercial center of about eight thousand people close to the capital city of Bogotá (just forty minutes by bus). Because it is close to Bogotá, Tabio has access to urban services like water, light, schools, and even telephones. Agriculture is quite profitable here. Soils are rich and well watered, transport is good, and proximity to the capital city lets farmers grow high-yield items for the urban market. Potatoes, carrots, and onions are common, as are grains and hops for Bogotá's breweries. Well-to-do families from the capital also maintain weekend homes in the area. The parish is thus wealthier and more socially diverse than either Caparrapí or Quebradanegra. In contrast to Caparrapí and Quebradanegra, fully four-fifths of parish residents live in Tabio itself, with the remainder scattered in a dozen hamlets in surrounding valleys. Apart from studying the urban core of Tabio, I paid particular attention to the rich agricultural hamlet of Río Frío, where a long-term effort at promoting a community store and related projects failed utterly in the face of local indifference and entrenched factionalism. Although the store (EMCO, for Empresa Comunitaria, or "communitarian enterprise") still existed at the time of my visits, it was little used. The community was riven by envy, gossip, and petty intrigue. In the chapters that follow, I use data from Tabio mostly for compar-

---

[13] See, for example, the stories in his *La mala hora*.

ative purposes—there is no extensive network of base communities like those found in the other two parishes.

## Barquisimeto

The archdiocese of Barquisimeto lies in Venezuela's western mountains. Its territory corresponds to the state of Lara and comprises the commercial and industrial city of Barquisimeto along with a rich and varied agricultural hinterland. The archdiocese's total population has more than doubled over the past quarter century, and the archdiocese has gradually expanded its resources in an attempt to keep pace (see fig. 4.2). These efforts have been supplemented by the activities of a substantial concentration of Jesuits who have long been involved in education, social promotion, and cooperative organizing in the area.

The Barquisimeto region shares a few important traits with Facatativá. This is also an area of considerable religiosity: piety and deference to clergy are common, especially in the countryside. Rural Barquisimeto also has a long history of violence and insurrection. The areas that now constitute the core of popular religious groups and peasant cooperatives in the region were a major center of Venezuela's guerrilla war in the 1960s. As in Facatativá, agriculture here includes a small number of highly profitable enterprises (dedicated to sugar, rice, or cattle) along with a host of marginal small holdings. These are

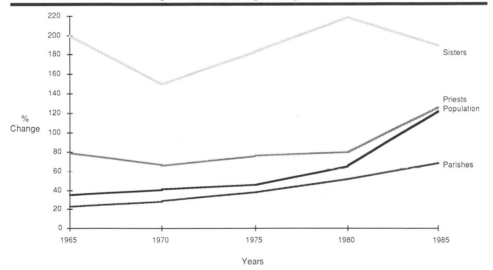

**FIGURE 4.2.**
Barquisimeto, Percentage Change since 1960

devoted almost exclusively to coffee. Since the nineteenth century, peasants here have had commercial dealings with middlemen who advance credit and buy raw beans for sale to processors who roast and market coffee nationally.[14]

Popular religious organization in this region is divided between groups linked to peasant cooperatives in the mountain villages and a combination of community organizations, base communities, and cooperatives in the barrios of the city of Barquisimeto itself. I begin with a sketch of the origins and growth of rural organization, which is more complex and structurally developed than its urban counterpart.

In 1969, Father Vincent Arthur, an Australian priest known locally as Padre Vicente, began founding units of the Legion of Mary in a series of isolated rural hamlets. He started work with a team of Australians in charge of a vast rural parish centered on the town of Guárico. When his compatriots were called home in the mid-1970s, Vicente opted to stay and finish his life in Venezuela. For Vicente, a firm religious base was the necessary prerequisite to any other action. Only with a foundation of clear and proper relations with God and a commitment to decent and morally upright lives in family and community could enduring social activities of any kind be undertaken. Vertical ties (with God) were primary; with those in order, horizontal ties (among men and women) would follow easily. Working through the medium of the Legion of Mary, Padre Vicente thus strove at first for spiritual and moral goals: promoting religious practice and reflection, fighting drunkenness, and combating free union and spousal abandonment.

Padre Vicente maintained a chapel and small residence in the market town of Villanueva. From this base, he set out regularly in a jeep to ford rivers and climb through clouds of dust or seas of mud (depending on the season) to reach widely scattered hamlets (called *caseríos* in Venezuela) on a regular schedule. But he could not be everywhere at once, and with rare exceptions, he had no clerics to help him. For all practical purposes, communities had to meet and carry on independently. At each Legion session (biweekly for the most part), biblical passages would be read, mass celebrated (if Vicente was present), local needs and achievements discussed, and a plan for future action set.

As was the case with the *cursillos* used by Román Cortés in Facatativá, Vicente's recourse to the Legion of Mary was a happy choice. The Legion of Mary had been founded early in this century in Ireland. From the beginning, the Legion has combined intense spirituality with an ethic of participation and service to church and community. A strong mystique of membership is built around complex and detailed rules, a nomenclature modeled on the Roman legions (local groups are *curiae*, regional structures are *presidiae*, and so

---

[14] Coffee production here is a vestige of what was one of Venezuela's major economic activities before the petroleum boom of the 1920s definitively undercut the nation's agriculture. See Roseberry, *Coffee*; and Leonardo Mora, "Café amargo."

forth), and operating guidelines that stress internal equality (members commonly address one another as "brother" or "sister") and let members run the group on their own. Together, these elements allow the Legion to appeal to traditional religiosity while encouraging isolated groups to carry on without clerical supervision.

Motivation and perseverance were high. This is understandable in view of the urgent needs and previous abandonment of the region as a whole. These were doubtless reinforced by the compelling character of Padre Vicente himself. Vicente is a gentle and utterly unpretentious old man, thin, frail, and silver-haired, highly spiritual and completely devoted to others. He is widely regarded in the area as a saint and has clearly earned great trust among a population with good reason to be suspicious of outsiders. By the late 1970s, an extensive net of local organizations and a cadre of dedicated and capable leaders were in place throughout the region. At this point, Vicente felt it essential to include work for direct social and economic improvement. In his words,

> Well, as I've said already, we began some thirteen years ago [1970] with the spiritual, that is with the Legion of Mary. Some seven or eight years ago, a *caserío* very removed from Villanueva said they had problems with getting their coffee to market at a reasonable price. I spoke to the fathers in [Centro] Gumilla, the Jesuit fathers, and they immediately became interested, organized a community jeep so that now they'd be able to get the coffee to market at a reasonable price, and at the same time they organized credit societies and coffee cooperatives where they buy and sell in a cooperative way. And they have done a great deal during the past seven years to improve the material lot of the campesino. (V 171)

The conjunction of the Legion of Mary with the cooperatives has been critical for the development of popular organization. Each has nurtured and encouraged the other. Legion members are the core of cooperative leadership, and as we shall see, the habits of self-expression and group governance learned in Legion meetings serve members well in running the cooperative. The values of mutual trust, faith, and solidarity inculcated through the Legion also provide a solid underpinning for cooperative activities like the extension of credit. As one Jesuit commentary points out, "In this specific context, the most effective arguments for motivating community cohesion involve religion or participation in some shared religious experience. These work even in situations where sociologically oriented arguments run up against unbreachable barriers, like those presented by family feuds."[15] In turn, the cooperative has supported the Legion, for example, by improving the material circumstances of its members and opening new fields for action to them, including access to education, better health care, dietary reform, and organizational participation of all kinds.

---

[15] Centro Gumilla, "Rescatando campesinos caficultores," p. 30.

The Jesuits first responded to Vicente's invitation by conducting a detailed socioeconomic study of the region. The results underscored the centrality of the coffee crop and pointed up the problems and abuses that the area's many scattered small-scale producers encountered on a day-to-day basis. One early report describes the area this way:

> These *caseríos* are not concentrations of dwellings, but rather small administrative centers, generally comprising a store, school, and chapel. They are more locales for periodic meetings than residential centers. For the most part, they are situated alongside the main road that runs across the mountain saddle. Peasant farmsteads are scattered side by side over the slopes.[16]

Organizational levels were unusually high:

> It is rare to encounter an area so well attended to in the religious sense. Apart from his personal presence, two pastoral tools support Vicente's efforts: (1) the selection and training of peasants to exercise religious responsibilities, such as celebrations of the word, distribution of Communion, helping the sick, catechisms; and (2) the Legion of Mary as an apostolic instrument. Working with the mystique and the apostolic commitment this kind of group generates, Vicente managed to form a group of peasants able to take charge of religious attention throughout the countryside.[17]

The economic dilemma faced by local cultivators arose from the limited size and low technical level of their farms. Lacking capital, individual farmers were subject to a vicious circle of dependence on middlemen. Limited financing also forced peasants in the area to pay excessive costs for transport and agricultural inputs; they could not share in the more profitable parts of the coffee business, such as the roasting or marketing of already processed beans. The Jesuit study found that those agencies intended to provide small farmers with credit and services were not much help: they were more a part of the problem than of the solution.

> The poor peasant, who lacks enough capital to buy shares, thus ends up as the victim of an endless series of insults and robberies. Their coffee is bought as low quality grades and then resold as high quality, with the agencies pocketing the difference. The scales are fixed to make sure peasants get less. They are required to turn in their coffee in new sacks, sacks which are neither paid for nor returned. . . . The worst abuse is that payments for coffee are held up for months as agency officials work with money that belongs to the peasants. Meanwhile, peasants spend much of their advance money in three, four, five or more trips to

[16] Centro Gumilla, "Proyecto campesino," p. 2.
[17] Centro Gumilla, "Rescatando campesinos caficultores," p. 27.

the town where, after hours on the road, they are told: "the money's not here yet, come back next week."[18]

The Jesuits' economic analysis underscored the centrality of debt and the social cost of interests rates that commonly stood at more than 10 percent monthly:

> This is a structural indebtedness, which has become a way of life. We tried to specify ideas and methods we could use to confront all this. From the outset, we tried to inculcate three basic ideas: (1) acting on their own, individuals had no hope of escape; (2) the only way to make progress was through some kind of group or community action; (3) acting together in this way is a concrete way of living as brothers, which is the ideal of the Legion of Mary and of all Christians.
>
> In this way, we tried to ensure that social and community work would not be marginal to religious life, and conversely, that the religious sense of brotherhood in the Legion would find ever-growing channels of practical expression. This seems to us to be a way to integrate Faith and Justice.[19]

Early on, the Jesuits made a point of getting to any and all meetings, regardless of weather or road conditions. This was essential to building a foundation of trust and mutual respect. They worked carefully from the ground up, beginning in 1977 with the establishment of small savings and loan cooperatives in four widely scattered hamlets. After a small amount was reserved for capital, pooled savings were plowed back into specific material improvements: a truck purchased and used in common; seed, fertilizer, and equipment; water piping; repairs to community buildings; payment for medical emergencies; and so forth. These small victories reinforced a sense of immediate effectiveness, legitimated the group, and kept it going.

After three years, the number of local units had increased substantially, regional organizations were created, and buying and selling on a regional scale was undertaken. At this point (September 1980), seventeen local groups representing over a thousand farmers formed a regional coffee cooperative, CRAMCO (Centro Regional de Abastecimiento y Mercadeo Centro Occidental). Official permission was sought and received for CRAMCO to act as a credit-granting agency. The formation of CRAMCO put peasants in a position to buy and sell coffee, to store and hold it off the market for better prices, and to act as intermediaries for the allocation of official credits to producers. They had replaced the middlemen. By 1982, a complex structure was in place: fourty-four local unions, which met monthly and undertook extensive educational work of all kinds; five subregional nucleuses located in the area's major marketing towns (Guárico, Chabasquen, Biscucuy, Calderas, and Batatal);

---

[18] Ibid., p. 26. Coffee is negotiated in standard sacks calculated to hold a *quintal* (forty-five kilograms) of beans.

[19] Ibid., p. 28.

and a regional cooperative with a major impact on the peasant households. Capabilities for large-scale collective action were also reinforced. Accumulated funds made possible the collective purchase of costly machinery for the processing of raw coffee, the construction of community stores in certain *caseríos*, and lower transport charges across the board. A start was also made on building local and regional warehouses and sheds for storing crops and inputs.

As the cooperative grew, other functions were added. A group of Medical Mission Sisters (all North Americans) began extensive educational and preventive efforts. They took their mobile clinic from its base in the city of Barquisimeto to the countryside to organize health-care committees and train local health promoters. Around the same time, a Spanish priest associated with Padre Vicente, Father Manuel Moreno (known locally as Padre Manolo) started a complex effort at dietary reform and natural medicine. Local diets are traditionally high in starches and fats, with few proteins and almost no use of locally available fruits, vegetables, or dairy products. Moreno promoted demonstration vegetable gardens and urged peasants to broaden their diet with natural foods instead of expensive canned items. He also encouraged natural and holistic medicine as alternatives to the expensive pharmacists and doctors of nearby towns. One Jesuit likens the process to baking and serving a cake.

> That's why I always say that Vicente made the base of the cake, Vicente is the one who made the place we went to. We baked the cake. And Manolo has come to put on the last decorations before we take the cake out and serve it, right? That's how I describe it to the peasants, half seriously and half as a joke. I tell them that if Vicente had not come, we wouldn't have had a plate to put our cake. And if Manolo hadn't found the groups we organized, he would not have been able to do what he did either. And why? Because the groups were already in place, so when someone says there is a meeting, there's something important to be done about this or that issue, people are always ready to get together. (V 215)

Successful creation of so much organization over so little time is a remarkable achievement, especially given the initially low levels of resources available in the area. Experience in the Legion of Mary gave members confidence in their ability to act independently and sufficient trust in one another to make openings for action in other areas of life a real possibility. Participation in those religious settings prepared these individuals to take an active role in the cooperatives. Urgent needs were married here with real opportunities for change, as members worked off a base of mutual trust and concrete benefits.

Membership in the cooperative requires discipline and perseverance. Groups meet biweekly as a rule, with regular attendance required. More than four unexcused absences in a single year leads to dismissal, which carries with it exclusion from credit and mutual aid. Allocating credit is of central importance to the group and to all its members. Care must be taken to ensure creditworthiness, because if loans are not repaid, the whole organization can easily founder. CRAMCO's local units employ a system of solidary credit that effectively reinforces group cohesion and participation. Each local unit holds special sessions twice yearly to consider credit applications. The whole unit is responsible for credits and must cover individual defaults. Great care is therefore taken to evaluate requests: local groups even send commissions to individual farms if it seems necessary.

The ordinary rules and procedures of the cooperative also enhance individual self-confidence and leadership abilities. Meetings are run openly, participation is encouraged, and members elect leaders freely from among themselves. The norm of competitive elections, which is central to political life at all levels in Venezuela, has reached even this remote corner of the nation. Observation of many local meetings confirms that although Jesuit advisers enjoy great respect, in no sense do they manage or run the groups, either openly or under the table. In designing and carrying out their activities, Jesuits were also careful to provide for their own long-term fade-out, turning functions over to ordinary members as soon as possible. They have taught local groups how to keep books, helped them meet regulations for legal recognition, and set them going. At the time of my research, the Jesuit role had shrunk to quarterly visits intended to check the books. One Jesuit argued that their role could and should diminish as peasant confidence and ability to act grew. It was difficult at first:

> The first problem concerned their life in common, learning to express themselves and to speak in public. At first, no one would talk in public. That was five years ago. But now they even argue publicly. These are such basic things, for instance I would say one thing and Micheo [another Jesuit] would hold the contrary: "No Dorre, I think we should do this another way." And so, in front of the peasants we would argue it out, giving pros and cons. They would stare at us and say, the two priests arguing, how can such a thing be?
>
> At first, we didn't realize what was going on. But later some of them asked us why were we fighting. I said, "No, it's not that we are fighting. We're just contrasting our two opinions. He is giving his opinion because he believes it's better to start from there. And I was telling him that it would be better to start from here. And you've got to learn this."
>
> But they saw it as a lack of respect between the two of us. Even that, even something as basic as dialogue or the contrast of opinions. And doing it conversationally, but in public, in front of them. But as you can see, by now they have learned to talk and to argue the opposite side of any question. (V 215–16)

The evolution of popular religious groups in the city of Barquisimeto offers an interesting complement to these rural experiences. As mentioned earlier, Barquisimeto has long been one of Venezuela's centers for the development of base communities, spurred by the Centro Gumilla, in sporadic cooperation with CESAP and the National Pastoral Institute. The Jesuit effort has been concentrated in the expanding popular barrios that now contain about 60 percent of the city's population.[20] Since the early 1970s, Jesuits have worked out the parish of Cristo Rey, which holds approximately 100,000 people spread across four distinct middle- and lower-class barrios: Barrio Nuevo, Titicare, Brisas del Aeropuerto, and La Carucieña. Of these, Brisas del Aeropuerto and La Carucieña have been particular targets for organizational development. Brisas del Aeropuerto is an older, now mostly lower-middle-class neighborhood located, as its name suggests, near the city's airport. La Carucieña is a large settlement formed not long ago through the invasion of an unfinished public housing project.

Here as in the countryside, Jesuit organizers work with a broad range of collaborators. These include lay activists as well as priests and especially sisters from national and foreign religious orders. There is also a substantial group of novices (from the Jesuit and other congregations) whose work in the communities forms an integral part of their education and training. Two groups of women warrant separate mention. First is the Medical Mission Sisters we have already encountered in the highland villages. They are also based in the parish of Cristo Rey and operate their mobile clinic throughout the barrios. They focus on preventive health care, prenatal attention, and emergency help. They have also been instrumental in forming health committees that work to improve sanitation, reform diets, and ensure better access to health-related services in the barrios.[21] A second group consists of four to six sisters from the congregation of San José de Tarbes who left their order's elite school for girls to live and work with popular groups. They rent a house in La Carucieña, and from this base engage in a broad range of pastoral efforts combining explicitly religious themes with community organization. The presence of this large collection of sisters who have exchanged their traditional work in schools or hospitals for a way of life radically identified with the poor is one of the most fascinating aspects of developments in Barquisimeto (see chapter 7, below, for details).

Popular organization has been more halting and sporadic in the city than in the peasant areas described earlier. Barquisimeto's rapid growth, much of it through invasion and squatter settlements on the periphery, has given it a highly diverse population. The pattern of urban settlement and employment reinforces the effects of heterogeneity. Unemployment is high (up to 60 percent in poor barrios) and available opportunities are concentrated in sporadic service jobs. Barrios are more accumulations of dwellings than centers of economic, social and cultural activities; most people with jobs work elsewhere. There is much organizational diversity as well, as unions, political groups,

---

[20] Relensberg, Karner and Köhler, *Los pobres*, pp. 95–96, 98.

[21] See Juanita Ortega, "La salud es un derecho: Una experiencia popular"; or Nacho Reyes Oviedo, "Los comités de salud."

sporting leagues, and Protestant churches compete for the same clientele. There are no traces here of the church's rural monopoly.

Popular organization of a religious cast has worked through the following vehicles: (1) a net of base communities, above all in Brisas del Aeropuerto and the older barrios of the parish; (2) a series of small cooperatives and health committees founded in conjunction with the Centro Gumilla and the Medical Mission Sisters; (3) scattered efforts at catechism and religious education; and (4) occasional community-wide mobilizations pitched to issues like housing or services such as health, water, police posts, or transportation. As a rule, collective action hinges more on community organization and socioeconomic issues than on religion per se. Stress has been placed on reaching out to hitherto abandoned groups and on forming communities with them. Explicitly religious activities such as catechism, mass attendance, or the construction of church buildings are expected to follow the construction of community, not to precede it. Two sisters comment:

> To me, that is the most important thing the church can do, because without such efforts, we lose sight of the human person involved and we accomplish nothing. That's the reason so many have been lost, that's why we have so many problems now. So many of the problems barrio people have . . . stem from lack of attention by the church. We share a lot of the blame for this; there has been a great abandonment on our part. We just sat there waiting for people to come to us, and we kept ourselves aloof, very high. We didn't realize that they are the majority and we have left them abandoned. (B 138)

> Integral promotion, the church has got to see what can be done in that sense. It's not just a matter of salvation, and anyway salvation isn't going to the beyond, to your own little bit of heaven. Salvation begins here on earth. It's not just for the beyond. To save means, hmm, to save means helping someone find solutions to their situation right now. It's not just for the beyond. (B 165)

Priests, sisters, and neighborhood leaders meet regularly (at least biweekly) to discuss issues of common concern and to plan joint efforts like innoculations, barrio clean-up campaigns, and celebrations like Christmas or Holy Week. There is little formal citywide coordination through the archdiocese. Connections with the Jesuits and the sisters offer a potential medium for planning and collective action, but this function is invoked only in moments of crisis. More common is a series of groups and alliances that come and go with the issues of the moment. This suggests that pastoral efforts here have been directed less at creating groups than at promoting a kind of consciousness and ferment likely to generate involvement and activism on the whole. One local woman put the typical urban Barquisimeto mix in terms that will find broad echo in later chapters.

I work together with Sister Sarah and Sister Juanita on an equal footing, we are equal. They always push things along, but when they are gone, I am in charge. We also have a training group, and an education committee directed by Sister Gladys. We are all equally responsible for making sure that the groups do the right thing and that everyone's opinion is respected. Last December, we tried to organize a cleanup for the area, and decorations, but things didn't work out as we had hoped. A little, but not everything. More recently, we put out a bulletin, informing people about who is selling contaminated foods and adulterated medicines. Then it's each person's responsibility. (B 97)

The same woman goes on to comment that

on the level of religion, things have been more religious, there's more relation with the church, going to mass and working for the community. That's how to be a real Christian. You can do it without going to mass. Feeling your neighbor's pain is also a way of being Christian. That's how real salvation begins. Our separated brothers [Protestants] say that you've got to work for souls on their own, but the real glory comes in working for equality. Christ died to give us glory here among ourselves. Salvation. If I work for the good of my community, I save my soul. (B 100)

# Cali

Cali offers interesting parallels and contrasts to urban Barquisimeto. Cali has also grown rapidly, more than doubling in population over the last quarter century. The city's early economic focus on agricultural processing and transport (tied to the rich Cauca Valley) has also been augmented lately by industrial growth and by a massive migration to the city from all over the south and west of Colombia. Cali combines a powerful local business elite and militant unions with a powerful tradition of protest, including strong local support for insurrectionary groups.[22]

Beginning in the early 1960s, the archdiocese of Cali tried to respond to change by reorganizing its programs and mobilizing fresh resources, especially from the business elite. Multifunctional parish centers were developed in close cooperation with private enterprise, which provided permanent funding through an independent foundation (Fundación Carvajal) holding 40 percent of the stock in one of Colombia's major industrial enterprises. The Fundación Carvajal has also dedicated substantial resources to underwriting small businesses throughout the poor barrios of the city. During my first visits to Cali in 1972 and 1973, I studied the parish centers in detail. On returning in 1982, I found that although the centers have matured and consolidated, no

[22] William Medhurst, *The Church and Labour in Colombia*, pp. 179–80.

new initiatives have been taken. The archdiocese has drifted and, as figure 4.3 indicates, has steadily lost ground in the face of population growth.

The archdiocese is weakly structured. There is no central office devoted to lay organization, no systematic training or promotion of lay ministries, and little coherent vision of grass-roots promotion. There is also minimal coordination between zones in the city or across levels of action, joining city to barrio, parish, or neighborhood. Cali thus lacks either the consolidated official vision of Facatativá, or the integrated alternative presented by Venezuela's Jesuits. The predominant regional culture is also low in markers of traditional religiosity. This convergence of an expanding and notably heterogeneous population with weak organization and low religiosity makes any effort to build grass-roots religious groups all the harder.

The geography of urban Cali also has a decided impact on popular organization.[23] The city's traditional core lies in a handful of neighborhoods close to the Cali River, which winds along the base of low mountains that block expansion to the north. These natural features have confined urban growth almost exclusively to a growing band of invasion barrios strung like a fan from south to west around the city center. The newest barrios are farthest out; those of ten- or twenty-year vintage are now generally considered to be within urban Cali but themselves derive from haciendas and other properties invaded and settled not long ago.

**FIGURE 4.3.**
Cali, Percentage Change since 1960

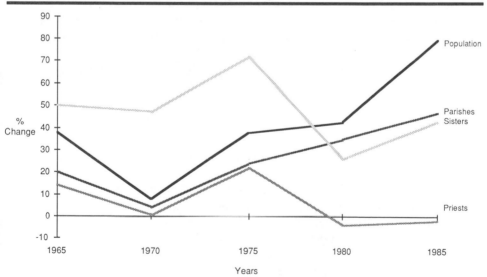

[23] For all practical purposes, the diocese coincides with the metropolitan area of the city. A few rural parishes remain, but they hold little population and lack importance.

The organizational vacuum in Cali's religious life has been filled by independent initiatives scattered over the city's popular barrios. Many of these efforts rely on the resources and energies of foreign religious congregations, which provide individuals or small groups who work on their own, either within the confines of a single barrio or moving from one to another, as continued urban growth throws up new and ever more urgent opportunities for popular work. In preliminary fieldwork, I visited a half-dozen parishes and neighborhoods throughout the city. After discussions at regional and diocesan levels and a series of barrio visits, I chose two for detailed study: Barrio El Rodeo and Barrio Meléndez.

Barrio El Rodeo lies in Cali's south-central periphery. This large settlement (about twenty-five thousand residents in the early 1980s) was founded in 1963 after a series of violent invasion attempts marked by repeated expulsions, reinvasions, and much armed conflict. The invasions were organized and led by men and women who worked in the outdoor markets (*galerías*) of the central city as vendors, shoemakers, day laborers, and the like. From these beginnings, the barrio has maintained an image of militant radicalism throughout Cali.

For much of the barrio's history, organization has been closely associated with the efforts of a group of Basque priests who arrived and founded a parish in the area not long after the barrio itself had been formed. They had come from Spain precisely in order to live and work "with the people." From the beginning, they focused on covering basic socioeconomic needs while simultaneously developing a critical consciousness in the population. One barrio activist comments that "they really work well here, they do what they can. They find out what's going on, and they pitch in, working with a pickax or with a shovel, to help build a shack or whatever. I'm telling you this as a neighbor, because you know I'm not one of those praying types, I don't go to mass except if someone dies or gets married. But we're good friends. I get along well with all the priests here" (CR 107).

The specific choice of Barrio El Rodeo as a site for their work was more or less accidental. One of the priests explains:

> It was really quite simple. One day I went to Cali, just like we always do. I went to the archdiocese and I told then that we were four young priests from a religious order who wanted to work in one of these barrios. That we would be entirely at the service of the archdiocese, not of our order, so that if it turned out that they did not like us, we would leave and make no problems for anyone. I think the Curia got worried and even a little frightened, because at the same time they had other groups of religious who were asking for the "high life" of Cali. So right then and there the Chancellor took me in his car to see a few barrios. And entering Rodeo over there, his car got stuck in the mud. And I said, this is the place, and so it was.

And you know it was really something then. It had been raining heavily, and the whole barrio was covered in a yellowish mud, with sewage running freely everywhere. It was really the poorest of the poor. An invasion barrio, and not just any invasion barrio, but one with strong features. There had been seventeen separate invasions: only the seventeenth was finally successful. (CR 85, 86)

Like many such urban communities in recent Latin American experience, over the years Barrio El Rodeo has gradually changed from a precarious collection of squatters facing a constant threat of expulsion into a relatively stable zone of lower- and lower-middle-class settlement. Streets within the barrio remain unpaved; garbage collection and provision for sewage are still problematic. But most residents now hold legal title to lots and houses and have access to city services, including public transport, primary and secondary schools, and regular light and water. Together these changes have blunted much of the barrio's initial radicalism. The reputation remains, but the sharp edge of urgent needs has been softened, and the militant recourse to mobilization and confrontation has become less attractive for many residents.

The same holds for the priests. Three remain from the group that founded the parish in 1970. The fourth has moved to Bogotá and has been replaced by another member of his order. They live in a modest rented house across the street from the parish center they helped build. Grouped around the parish center are some of the institutions promoted over the years: a center of popular culture, a small lending library (now in disuse), a school and a health post, including a nutrition center, and a group of low-cost housing units. On the theory that organization itself was the critical element, for over a decade they willingly lent facilities and support to *any* local group. Their pastoral efforts therefore downplayed explicitly religious messages in favor of building communities. Like the sisters in Barquisimeto, they believed that religious values could not be taken in isolation but rather had to emerge as part of an integral project of liberation undertaken in and by the community.

But by the early 1980s, disillusionment had set in. Little commitment to religious values had resulted. The priests felt used by others, above all for political purposes. On reflection, they concluded that the problem came from an ingenuous determination to "follow the people," pursuing general goals of liberation without care for their ideological or structural connection with religion. Two of the priests comment:

So we took steps to shut that down, and to reflect on the meaning of it all, why things were undertaken, for whom and for what ends. We had never done a general reflection of this kind before. We just saw the need and did the work, period. I think that if we had to go through all that again, we would be more careful to look at things from the situation of the people, to interpret things from their point of view, not just our own. There would be a much lengthier preparatory process, and a long-term structuring of the effort. (CR 87)

From the beginning, we set our religious, Christian identity aside, and failed to search for the dynamics of our faith. After all, we thought, in purely human terms, working for the people was the critical thing. Working for humanity was sufficient, and therefore it was not necessary to be explicit about our faith. That point of view guided our work for many years. Not insisting on the maturation of people's faith, but rather on their maturation as human beings.

*So what happened?*

Well, for example, our insistence that any group was good, that groups need not be Christian, as a practical matter led to the flourishing of political organizations, groups that eventually created all sorts of problems for the parish itself. Some of them were revolutionaries, who used us purely for their own ends. They infiltrated the parish and took over everything, all the groups. The community of faith was nothing but a facade for them. So eventually we had to break with all that, expel those individuals. This happened around the end of 1980. (CR 50, 51)

After ten years of militant effort, the priests reaffirmed traditional identities and linkages around the parish center. Even the original goal was rejected, because, as one of the group stated, "It's clear to me now that the goal is not liberation, but rather communion" (CR 89). Previous emphasis on militant action and organization were now reduced in favor of building community around church structures. The experience of Barrio El Rodeo occupies one end of the spectrum of popular religious organization visible in Cali. Efforts here were concentrated in a coordinated set of neighborhood groups that were highly militant in language and action and were supported and actively promoted by clergy. For the most part, activities were confined to local initiatives and mobilizations and were isolated from efforts in other barrios or in the church as a whole.

Barrio Meléndez is an instructive contrast. This barrio lies on the western edge of Cali, along the road out of the city. Settlements have long existed in this site but, until recently, were rural in tone. As one woman remarked, "Around here, at least when I first came, no one ever said that they lived in Cali. Instead, people would say that they lived in the country. It was hard to get here; there was only one bus from the center" (CA 173). The Meléndez area is also known in Cali for a series of dance halls that draw a big weekend clientele, which comes out from the city center for the music and also to swim and picnic along the river that gives the barrio its name.

The barrio itself spreads in several sectors over varied terrain running from the main road (Fifth Street) through a central core (Meléndez proper) and up a series of hills to the poorer and more remote neighborhoods of El Jordán and Polvorines. Urban services are concentrated in the lower-lying regions. There is limited bus service into the barrio itself, even more limited as one tries to go up to El Jordán and Polvorines, on the hill. Most residents are lower- or lower-middle-class, holding jobs ranging from laborer and messenger to cook, policeman, or cabdriver. The majority came to the city from other parts of the Cauca Valley during the early 1950s. The move to Meléndez came only after prior residence in other parts of the city. Meléndez was and remains a step up from the slums of the central city.

Several developments have combined in recent years to break the barrio's long-standing isolation from city life. There is an important military barracks not far from the barrio's center, putting the repressive power of government just next door. As land has become scarcer and more expensive in the city center, extensive commercial and institutional growth also got underway on the outskirts of the city. For example, in the late 1960s a new campus for the local university (Universidad del Valle) was also built nearby. More recently, a chain of shopping centers constructed locales just across the road from the barrio. This complex, known as Unicentro, has provided a pole for further development, and services the middle- and upper-class housing units that around this time began to locate on the cheaper land of Cali's western fringes. A number of elite secondary schools attracted by the low cost of land, also located here. Stimulated by all these changes, transportation improved and extensive urban services such as light, water, and telephone began to be installed. As land values rise, property taxes and the cost of services have begun to move beyond the means of most residents. Many fear that the barrio they know will disappear in the next twenty years, and they will be forced to move.

For a long time, Meléndez had little in the way of organized social life. Things began to change with the arrival of four Spanish priests who took over the newly founded parish in 1977. On arrival, they began a careful effort aimed at promoting group formation and spurring popular involvement in barrio affairs and in the church. The four cultivated an easygoing, informal style and made themselves familiar and trusted figures in the barrio. They soon recruited a core of people (mostly women) to serve as founders and multipliers of groups. One local woman comments:

> Well, you know, we were just ordinary people, going to mass once in a while. And that mass was the kind we had been used to, you prayed a little and that was that, right? We each lived our own lives and thought only about ourselves. But then when the priests came here, the ones who went back to Spain a little while ago, they got us organized. They were very good priests, really committed to the poor. (CA 270)

The priests were soon followed to the barrio by a group of young Colombian women, sisters of the Javierian Institute. These women came to the barrio committed to identify with the poor and immerse themselves in popular milieus. They had a clear and explicit rationale for their work with popular culture, their vision of which has profoundly shaped the subsequent development of base communities and related groups in the barrio. The sisters see culture in general and popular culture in particular as deeply marked by sharp, structural inequalities of knowledge, wealth, and power. In their view, urban popular culture in Colombia is an important and apt medium for organization and change. As things stand, this culture is manipulated by mass media and by major institutions like business, the political parties, schools, and the church in ways that reinforce alienation, passive resignation, and apathy. For sustained efforts at popular organization to have any hope of success, residents must first break this ideological stranglehold and create independent visions of self, community, society, and politics. This is best done through work that combines specifics of local interest (e.g., struggle for jobs, water, roads, or schools) with a continuous effort at study and critical reflection. In a programmatic article, one of the sisters argues that

> like factories in Europe in the past, among us the barrio is now becoming a critical meeting place and arena of combat. It is also clear that in the specific case of our Colombian cities, marked as they are by a large lumpen proletariat, by extensive unemployment, underemployment, occasional street vending, that there is no gathering place as secure as the barrio. It is here that the lives and the possibilities of our people begin and end. Popular barrios are the space that belongs to the popular masses. . . .
>
> Possibilities arise for [creating] theater groups, arts and reading workshops, discussion groups and programs of popular education that after a while, through a continuous effort, can become expressions of *popular power*, capable of autonomous decision, programming, and organization. Through these groups or workshops, the people can begin to reclaim the right to make their own decisions about taste, or the use of spare time. . . . The point is to seize control of blocks of time and areas of life from the bourgeois power. . . . Popular Libraries and Centers of Popular Education can provide the means for systematizing efforts at this level.[24]

The Javierian sisters are less devoted to action per se than were the priests in Barrio El Rodeo and are more concerned with providing a cultural foundation that can inform *any* action and give it meaning. Articulating an alternative religious vision is central to this effort. To this end, the sisters work closely with the base communities first organized by the Spanish priests. They have organized an attractive and much used Center for Popular Culture, which includes a lending library, almost unique in this area. The Center provides a series of courses on topics ranging from Colombian history to cooperatives, liberation theology to Bible study, sewing to hairdressing. A special effort is made to hold courses at night as a means of actively involving men more. All these initiatives provide a familiar, easily accessible, and nonthreatening environment for the transformation of local culture and practice. The sisters have

[24] Carminia Navia V., "Las semanas culturales y el problema de la organización popular," pp. 40, 41, 42.

also made a sustained effort to reform traditional religious practices, for example, discouraging pilgrimages and changing the tone and emphasis of Holy Week celebrations.

Through the Javierian nuns, local groups are connected with others in the city and across the country in loose networks affililated with CINEP and *Solidaridad*. Representatives from Meléndez even managed to attend a 1983 national meeting of base communities near Bogotá, a major and costly undertaking for poor people. In a report prepared for that meeting, one group recounts its history in these words:

> Some of us joined in order to deepen our faith; to understand religion better and practice it more fully. Others joined for the opportunity to study the Bible and understand it; to know how to apply the Bible to everyday life. To understand God better. To be able to communicate the Gospel message. Also to achieve greater comprehension with our neighbors and with other people generally; to put egoism behind us. Others joined because we oppose the way today's social structures operate, and because we believe that when poor people are united in groups, that makes it possible to fight for improvements and to achieve a more genuinely fraternal life. Finally, a number of us joined seeking a way to improve ourselves, to study and express ourselves better.[25]

Their evaluation of results is modest but points to concrete changes in personal and community life. They cite improved family life and better relations with friends and neighbors. In addition,

> the groups have helped us change how we think, we have undergone a spiritual transformation. Now we understand social injustice better, we identify more fully with our neighbors. We have learned to recognize our human rights and demand them, and we know that the rights of others also must be respected. Through the community, we have come to understand the Bible, and to believe in a concrete God who is close at hand, a God who is relevant to our lives, our feelings and desires, and to our struggles.

Shortly before the time of my fieldwork, the four Spanish priests, along with colleagues in Cali's industrial suburb of Yumbo, suddenly had their contracts terminated and were compelled to return to Spain. They were replaced by a priest notably hostile to this kind of grass-roots organization. The barrio's base communities and related groups continued but found themselves more dependent than ever on the sisters for guidance and moral support. Strong backing from their congregation has enabled the four sisters to continue working in the barrio. They own or rent their own facilities and are technically independent of the archdiocese. They have thus remained active, continuing

---

[25] "Presentación de la experiencia de las comunidades cristianas populares del Barrio Meléndez (Cali)."

in a consistent focus on cultural transformations as the key to long-term change. Activism of the Rodeo sort is deliberately avoided, in large measure as a practical effort to avoid the problems confrontational tactics cause for popular groups. Of course, this stance is consistent with the overall CINEP-Solidaridad line, noted earlier, of avoiding open conflict where possible.

## Comparative Perspectives

Relations between the dioceses, parishes, villages, and barrios considered in this chapter are indicated in figure 4.4. There are parallels and differences between these cases, not only in terms of the broad strategies and programs at issue in each but also in the way such efforts appear to popular groups and acquire substance and legitimacy in their lives. Explicit ties to the institutional church are present in every instance. As I have argued here, popular groups hardly ever spring full blown "from the people." They are not spontaneously created, "pure" popular alternatives to elite-designed structures. To the contrary, in every case they arise out of enduring links with institutions, links that play a critical role in shaping how groups see themselves and understand what they are about in the first place.

Pastoral agents play an important mediating role, carrying messages and bearing symbols of authority, guidelines for action, and specific human and

**FIGURE 4.4.**
Fieldwork, Research Levels

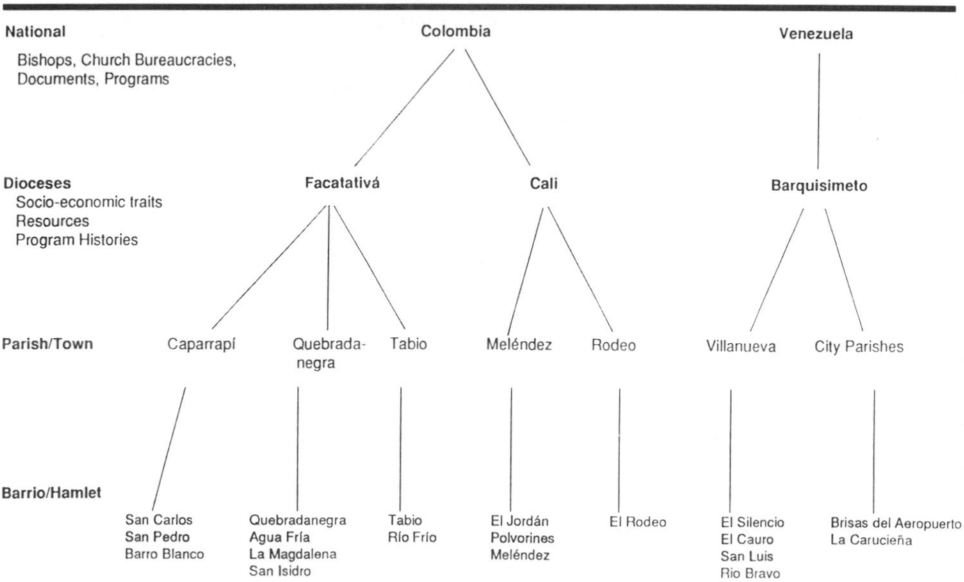

| National | Colombia | | Venezuela |
|---|---|---|---|
| Bishops, Church Bureaucracies, Documents, Programs | | | |

| Dioceses | Facatativá | Cali | Barquisimeto |
|---|---|---|---|
| Socio-economic traits Resources Program Histories | | | |

| Parish/Town | Caparrapí | Quebrada-negra | Tabio | Meléndez | Rodeo | Villanueva | City Parishes |
|---|---|---|---|---|---|---|---|

| Barrio/Hamlet | San Carlos San Pedro Barro Blanco | Quebradanegra Agua Fría La Magdalena San Isidro | Tabio Río Frío | El Jordán Polvorines Meléndez | El Rodeo | El Silencio El Cauro San Luis Río Bravo | Brisas del Aeropuerto La Carucieña |
|---|---|---|---|---|---|---|---|

material resources from one level to another. How this role is conceived and carried out depends in large measure on the place a particular group occupies in the church and on the ideology and programmatic vision that drives its efforts. The Jesuits of rural Venezuela operate apart from mainline ecclesiastical structures. They represent a conscious alternative to the centralizing, neo-Colombian model increasingly visible in their own national church. Structural independence and a commitment to respect popular culture and empower popular organizations makes them comfortable with groups that move into new fields and reach for greater autonomy. All this stands in contrast to Facatativá, where even with the best of intentions, provision for continued clerical supervision and ongoing ties to diocese and parish structures has unintended consequences, limiting the scope of group interests and constraining the emergence of independent leadership and capacities for growth.

Class appears to be less important in setting the character, agenda, and typical activities of groups than is commonly supposed. Among groups of similar class and perceived needs, sharp differences emerge according to the character and orientation of pastoral agents.[26] The impact of class and community context is everywhere mediated by enduring ties to institutions. In any event, variation among the groups is not well addressed by arguing that some are "more religious" and others "more social"; that one is tied to clerical plans and the other springs directly "from the people." Albeit in different ways, all are religious, all stem from deliberate efforts by pastoral agents, all combine religious with social interests.

Important contrasts are also apparent in the scale and scope of specific programs and in their links to ecclesiastical structures. Scale and linkage are important: they provide an infrastructure that allows groups to expand into new areas. They make it easier for additional pastoral agents to enter the scene once things get started. The highly coordinated and relatively well-financed experiences in Facatativá or Jesuit-aided efforts in Barquisimeto are thus distinct from the isolated collection of barrio level initiatives we have considered in Cali. In the first two cases, popular religious groups arise out of a deliberate and carefully thought out strategy. Organizers here bring substantial external resources (human, material, and financial) to the task. They produce and distribute masses of material in a continuous effort to shape the agenda and concerns of local groups. They also visit groups on a regular basis, to monitor and spur ongoing efforts. The deliberate quality of these experiences makes linkage easier to trace and also puts prevailing ideological formations (the proper group, the model member) up front in an unusually clear fashion.

The proper group in Facatativá is bounded by church-directed structures; the model member combines piety and social (not political) activism with deference to clerical authority. Legitimate guidelines and authority both trickle

[26] Cf. Hewitt, *Base Christian Communities.*

down from the top. In Barquisimeto, the proper group is much less tied to formal church structures. Groups have moved sharply beyond initial church-defined boundaries, and the model member appears as an independent, self-moved actor. The contrast between Facatativá and Barquisimeto is especially striking if we recall that grass-roots groups in both cases share a common origin in highly traditional Catholic structures—*cursillos* and the Legion of Mary. This suggests that linkage to institutions does not by itself determine group orientation. The key difference is made by the model of *church* and of the *popular* at work in the two cases.

Barrio groups in Cali present an interesting contrast. To begin with, there is no centrally planned or coordinated effort of any kind. Indeed, the archdiocese intervenes hardly at all in most popular barrios. At the same time, the pattern of urban growth in Cali has created substantial opportunities for independent action, while attracting numbers of pastoral agents anxious to work closely with popular groups. The results are ambiguous. Grass-roots initiatives in the popular barrios of Cali appear to be much more radical in rhetoric and action than in either Facatativá or Barquisimeto. But they are also more cut off from supportive infrastructures. Links to church structures (parishes, priests, and sisters) are visible, but they are are smaller in scale and more limited in scope and reach, remaining for the most part confined to the barrio itself. The structural isolation of groups and pastoral agents makes initiatives highly vulnerable to setbacks or hostilities from other levels.

Unusual concentrations of pastoral agents played a major role in the development of popular groups in all our cases. In Facatativá, this results from a deliberate strategy by the diocese. Elsewhere, mutual attraction makes for abundant personnel: one group gets things going, this comes to the attention of others, and so forth. The initial presence of Jesuits draws Medical Mission Sisters and other women religious to the barrios of Barquisimeto; Padre Vicente's work provides the base for Jesuits and later for the health-oriented work of Manolo Moreno. In all cases, deliberate efforts at teamwork have superseded traditional patterns that have a single parish priest responsible for a far-flung territory.

The central mediating and legitimating role played by pastoral agents should not obscure the importance of popular expectations in making the whole effort work. At issue is not only or even primarily a matter of institutional imposition. Potential members also value ties to the church because religious experience and affiliation is central to them. They prize the moral values church membership offers and appreciate the solidarity and mutual support group participation makes possible. This suggests that the growth of popular religious groups and the operation of base communities in particular cannot be grasped solely in terms of the material benefits, neighborhood projects, or political programs the group's formal agenda may espouse. Members also find enduring religious values through affiliation with the group and, in the process, create new understandings of what being religious is all about. From their vantage point, sharp distinctions between social, religious, and political dimensions of group life have lost much of their compelling force and meaning. Each dimension is involved in the other, and the issue for believers is to find appropriate syntheses, not to draw artificially sharp demarcations.

To this point I have stressed elements that appear most sharply when taken from the perspective of the institutional churches, looking "out and down": out to society and down to potential popular clients. Such a perspective is useful as a beginning but is too limited by itself to yield a satisfactory portrait of the formation and character of popular groups. If we turn the tables and ask how all these structures, programs, groups, and the like may appear from the bottom up, other concerns, other context-forming experiences, and other issues come to center stage. Many of these are explored in detail in the following chapters. Three warrant underscoring here: the centrality of religious values and structures; the experience of poverty; and the salience of violence.

The importance of religious issues should come as no surprise. After all, these are churches and religious groups. But observers have become so accustomed to search for social, economic, or political results that they may in the process obscure the close and continuing link between religious identities and practices and organizational vitality as a whole. Each nurtures the other; they grow and change together. Indeed, in the cases considered here, it is clear that the trust and solidarity built into religious participation is what provides the bedrock for any activity. Reflecting on the role of religious elements in popular organization, one Venezuelan Jesuit argues that views which paint religion as little more than a flight from the world, a source of passive resignation, must be abandoned.

> We have seen that religious values centered on a concrete and nearby God, on brotherhood, and on personal virtues like hospitality, honesty, and reliability are the most effective qualities for achieving and maintaining group cohesion. It is evident that introducing religious values as a means of energizing popular organizations for justice constitutes a new kind of pastoral action. At issue here is not the creation of new values, distinct from those already in place, but rather extending and reorienting the values that are already there. To do this, it is essential first to understand these values from within, and in this way to grasp their true meaning in the concrete circumstances of each group's life.[27]

For popular groups to take hold and endure, religious motivation must be married to some attempt to meet specific concrete social, cultural, and material needs. As we shall see, poor people think about their needs a great deal, discuss the situation with one another, and look to institutions and their leaders for help. With rare exceptions, they seek neither confrontation nor major

[27] Alberto Micheo, "La religión del pobre," p. 419.

structural change. More modestly, they hope for a better life for family and community. This suggests the wisdom of organizations that build on small victories and reach only gradually for new fields of action. The Venezuelan Jesuit just cited notes (in another contribution) that starting with broad political goals can be self-defeating:

> For those working at the level of practical action, this is like asking a peasant who is building a slingshot for killing birds if he has thought about constructing an atomic bomb. . . . It's much too remote. The people grow and learn according to the logic of facts and events, not concepts.[28]

Violence bears further reflection. Earlier, I noted how repression has energized and occasionally radicalized communities and pastoral agents throughout Latin America. Violence is also relevant for the popular groups reviewed in this chapter. The rural zones of Facatativá and Barquisimeto where church efforts are concentrated and peasant groups have been successful are also areas with well-known histories of violence and guerrilla war. Rural insurgency died out in Venezuela by the late 1960s, but major sections of Facatativá's territory remain under permanent military garrison, with some guerrilla groups now entering their fifth decade of struggle.

The centrality of violence in recent memory and current experience has a double-edged impact on peasant organization. It makes peasants suspicious of outsiders. Many hide or run away on the first appearance of pastoral agents or priests in the area, for fear that they are guerrilla fighters in disguise. Lengthy effort has been required to gain and hold popular trust. Once this barrier has been overcome, however, the precarious quality of ordinary life, coupled with the sense of abandonment and marginality that many residents feel, has predisposed them to welcome affiliation with the churches, which they perceived as a legitimate, politically neutral tie. Ties to the church give peasants a valued sense that they are not alone.

Violence in the cities has a different but no less noteworthy impact. The land invasions that created most popular barrios put residents up against considerable repressive force. They suffered greatly before gaining rights of occupation and, ultimately, title to their dwellings. Memories of the invasion remain fresh and are regularly called on as spurs to solidarity and common action. Residents of Barrio El Rodeo commemorate the invasion every year with a week of skits, plays, parades, and discussion groups. The men and women of the barrios do more than remember past violence. In addition, they see current urban institutions (e.g., city planning offices, police, schools, bus companies, water-supply agencies) as wreaking violence on them, either by abusive treatment, excessive costs, or simple negligence and humiliation.

---

[28] Micheo, "Una experiencia campesina," p. 7. This article was part of a symposium on "popular power" presented in the January 1981 issue of *SIC*.

They commonly state a willingness for direct confrontation, despite their own recognized weakness.[29]

In this and the preceding chapter, I have centered attention on the institutional and structural contexts of popular organization. Transforming popular culture in lasting ways is more likely if activities in various walks of life are institutionalized and deliberately made to reinforce one another. This means providing a material substructure to group activity that connects local leaders and members with larger structures at the same time it makes a series of specific channels of action and organizational ladders available to them.

More than words are needed for culture to change. Of course words and language are important. They can legitimize new goals and provide symbols of meaning and belonging that sustain communities and groups through hard times. But for words to have enduring effect, they must come embedded within routine patterns of organization and action. They must crystallize as the common sense of everyday life. Ties with institutions play a critical role in this process, shaping the way formal agendas are turned into enduring values, understandings, and social ties.

To this point, analysis has remained at the level of structures and organizations. In the four chapters that follow, level and focus shift, as we consider the origins, pathways, and meaning of change through the eyes and with the words of those involved.

---

[29] Violence in Cali has escalated sharply in recent years, as part of the general upsurge of conflict among the Left, the Right, the drug dealers, and the state that contributed so much to the decay of Colombian politics in the 1980s.

# PART II

## ACTORS AND EXPERIENCES

Take away from me the noise of your songs;
To the melody of your harps I will not listen.
But let justice roll down like the waters,
And righteousness like an everflowing stream.

—Amos 5:23–24

If anyone says, ''I love God,'' and hates his
    brother, he is a liar;
for he who does not love his brother whom he
    has seen, cannot love God whom he has not seen.
And this commandment we have from him, that he
    who loves God should love his brother also.

—1 John 4:20–21

# FIVE

## BEING RELIGIOUS, READING THE BIBLE,

## BECOMING CHURCH

I F RELIGION is to have a role in the transformation of popular culture, religion itself has to change. Religious ideas and structures must evolve in new directions, and the way religion is experienced and understood within popular culture must also be transformed. Religious elites or pastoral agents cannot simply mandate a new agenda or direct popular groups to take on new values, roles, or commitments. To be enduring, change has to be incorporated into the common sense of everyday life, reinforced by daily routine, and worked into the expectations that ordinary people bring to bear on decisions about legitimate priorities, commitments, and kinds of action. This chapter explores these issues through a close look at changing popular views of what being religious is all about and at the kinds of everyday practice that reflect and reinforce these general notions in concrete experience. Together, these ideas, practices, and commitments constitute a package that undergirds new concepts of self-worth, equality, participation, and activism while providing a foundation for sustained organizational life.

It is worth reflecting for a moment on what being religious means. Clearly, this cannot be reduced to the holding of particular ideas, as if ideas themselves simply come and go "in the air," with no relation to context or circumstance. How ideas are taken up is as important as their content. This is because changing ways of being religious are closely associated with a series of specific transformations in the material and organizational setting in which ideas are acquired and held. In particular, the shift from sporadic church attendance, very occasional sacraments, and reliance on charms, promises, and pilgrimages to the intense ambience of groups like base communities as the central axis of religious experience changes the meaning of being religious and alters its implications for perception and action in society generally. Personal change and collective transformation are thus fused in popular experience, bound together by new religious norms and structures.

This should come as no surprise, for religion is much more than a matter of individual experience. Indeed, the ability to join personal and collective experience through shared symbols, rituals, and valued institutional links is a universal feature of religious life. Religion has always been closely linked to community and public life, in Latin America as elsewhere. All this sounds obvious but nonetheless runs counter to much of the received wisdom of contemporary sociology, which for long has stressed the gradual and inevitable privatization of religion as part of an overall secularization of society and culture. Bryan Wilson's recent statement is representative:

> In this private sphere, religion often continues, and even acquires new forms of expression, many of them much less related to other aspects of culture than were the relations of the past. . . . The very rationalization of society's operation and its dessicating effect on everyday life may provide their own inducement for individuals privately to take up the vestiges of ancient myths and arcane lore and ceremonies, in the search for authentic fantasy, power, possibilities of manipulation, and alternative sources of private gratification. In this sense, religion remains an alternative culture, observed as unthreatening to the modern social system in much the same way that entertainment is seen as unthreatening. It offers another world to explore as an escape from the rigors of technological order and the ennui that is the incidental by-product of an increasingly programmed world.[1]

The popular voices we are about to hear have a different vision, one that stems not from ennui or escape but rather from an effort to engage the world on better terms—better for individuals and better for the communities in which they live. The characteristic fusion of faith, organization, and action found in these experiences cannot be dismissed as primitive, traditional, or as the mere by-product of a supposedly incomplete "transition" to modernity. To the contrary, the evolving vision of being religious that moves these men and women is the result of careful debate and reflection, conscious innovation, and sustained common effort.

## Being Religious and Reading the Bible

Reading the Bible was greatly prized in every group I studied. Direct access to the Bible was also widely viewed as an indispensable basis for profound changes in the meaning and practice of religion. These changes are anchored by three dimensions of transformation that together provide coherence to the emerging sense of self of the groups and their members: first, a belief that earlier religious practice had been stunted and inadequate; second, a sense of conversion as a life-changing experience; and finally, an emphasis on how Bible study turns attention and energies away from personal devotions and individual salvation toward solidarity with others and activism in and for the community.

When group members talk about their own childhood experience of religion, they underscore the prominence of rote learning and the extent to which religion was confined to a limited range of beliefs and practices. For the most

---

[1] "Secularization: The Inherited Model," p. 20.

part, religious instruction came from parents or relatives; contact with the institutional church was at best sporadic. As one man from Meléndez put it,

Our parents taught us a lot, but really it was only what they themselves knew, for example about hearing mass or carrying on customs like saying the holy rosary, but they never told me about reading the Bible. Nobody knew about it there. Yes, my family was very Catholic, very religious. We tried to go to mass as often as possible, [but] that meant long walks on the road—or better, on the path, because you know all we had there were paths, not real roads. Anyway, it was five kilometers from my hamlet down to the church, which was in the town center—that's where the parish was. So whoever was able to make the trip went to the church; the others had to pray at home. (CA 143)

Memories like this are echoed in most of the groups, whose members would agree with this man from Agua Fría, who told me that "in the old days, the religion our parents gave to us was different, they filled you with a lot of nonsense. . . . I remember that I had to memorize my prayers [and] they warned me to be careful when I took Communion, not to chew the host because that would be a sin" (AF 68). The general feeling that earlier training in religion was stunted and inadequate magnifies the profound sense of conversion that comes with involvement in new kinds of groups. For average men and women, joining the *cursillo*, the Legion of Mary, or the local base community means committing themselves to personal and community transformation. Sticking with the group is a sign of success. One of the original founders of Agua Fría's base community states that he was afraid at first, in awe of clergy and shy of outsiders generally.

So anyway we took the *cursillo*. Román got us involved; we were kind of afraid of him. You know, when Román first came here, people ran away and hid from him. I was one of them; I was afraid of him. I don't know what the problem was, maybe too much respect or just fear, I'm not sure. That's the way it is sometimes with a person you don't know, someone from the outside [que no sea de su patio].

*What do you remember about the* cursillo?

We started thinking, we were very different. You're like two people, you go out old and return all new—new spiritually and new materially. And we began to realize the bad things we had been doing. So all this is a change in our way of living, each of us as part of the community. The whole idea was to live as a community, to live more focused on the church. (AF 34)

The intense process of conversion and the sense of becoming a new person is amplified by access to the Bible on a regular basis.[2] Ordinary religious belief

[2] Cf. Susan Harding, "Convicted by the Holy Spirit"; Raboteau, *Slave Religion*; and the life histories in chapter 8, below.

and practice appear in a new light. Group members repeatedly characterize reading the Bible as "the best part" of religious experience. The high value placed on reading and talking about the Bible also reflects a conviction that understanding acquired in this way is deeper, longer lasting, and more authentic than that produced by the rote learning of childhood. New abilities to read and act independently are especially prized. At a minimum, access to the Bible makes it possible for members to share a religiously valid experience without the presence of clergy, who are notoriously scarce anyway in rural communities and popular urban barrios. Many of those I interviewed in fact became literate precisely because they wanted to read the Bible. Even in communities where illiteracy remains the rule, there is usually *someone* who knows how to read, and others enjoy listening and value the opportunity to discuss what it all means together with friends and neighbors.

The Bible is read individually (often on waking up or retiring), in family gatherings, or in regular group meetings. As one woman told me, "I read it every day, whenever I have my glasses. I find great things there, beautiful things" (CA 216–17). The following three comments from Cali highlight the special worth members place on the Bible:

> Yes of course, for us the most important thing is the fact of knowing, knowing the word of God, reading the Bible. For me that's been the most important of all. To be able to know God's word, to read the Bible, and to find the best way to put it into practice. Because everything the Bible says and everything it teaches is God's word, yes it is. That's why I like it so much. (CA 134)

> Yes, yes, let's say that no priest is available for a mass. Well then, we can come anyway, no? Participate, join in the church. Reading Scripture and talking about it is what's important anyway. So that's what we do, because after all, religion is really for us. As they say, God is in the people. . . . Before, we couldn't do that, because we were forbidden to read the Bible. But not now, now things are different, we have more alternatives. (CA 120–21)

> What I like best about the Bible is that every passage you read fits exactly with the way our lives are right now. If you read a piece of the Gospel and then you consider the problems we have, there's enough there to talk about for a whole night. (CA 176)

Reading and studying the Bible in a group of friends and neighbors gives members practical experience in working together as equals and reinforces confidence in their ability to reason, evaluate, and act independently. As one Venezuelan peasant told me, "Now we're accustomed to the idea that everyone should participate in mass, and comment on the readings. A person learns more that way" (V 70). A woman from La Carucieña echoes these views and underscores that "before we had no idea; you just went to mass, no more. But we didn't think about our own part. Now we share the responsibility" (B 99).

The development of confidence in one's ability to judge and act independently of guidance from elites (civil or ecclesiastical) adds a new dimension
to popular life.[3] Traditional combinations of private anger and resentment with
public silence and deference yield here to confident self-expression and a conviction that organization is both right and possible.[4] Two particular aspects of
the Bible's role in community life undergird this process. Bible study underscores links between religion and daily life and thus requires and leads to action in ways that traditional prayer and attendance at sacraments do not. The
second highlights the impact of specific settings and of the particular way Bible study is undertaken on the process of eliciting and reinforcing capabilities
for action.

One reason Bible study is seen to require radically different ways of being
religious is that learning about religion through reflection on the Bible is very
much one's own creation. As such, it leaves a deeper mark on consciousness
and experience than is the case with traditional practices.[5] In the words of this
rural leader, regular get-togethers for Bible study meant that "between us all
we can be a greater light. We can help others, and in that way see everything
more clearly" (S 69). When I asked one woman from Meléndez to describe
an ordinary meeting, she replied in the following terms:

> Well, it's like this, we develop it this way. We all work to understand better, even
> me. Because you know, there are so many things a person doesn't know. Right?
> The Bible. We read the Gospels and we study every little bit. And here we have
> people who have never known anything. They read it there [in church], the priest
> reads the Gospel and that's that. Because he says a world of things people pay no
> attention to. But here we try to explain things ourselves. We don't have them
> explained to us, but ourselves we draw it out, we discover what we think. (CA
> 40)

In her view, more was learned this way, because

> there's more closeness, more dialogue. Not just the priest in the pulpit telling you
> not to sin, not to do this or that, to repent. Because you know, a person hears that
> stuff and then goes home and forgets it all. (CA 46)

Exclusive attention to personal spirituality or prayer without explicit efforts
to help others or some involvement in the community is commonly seen as a
lesser kind of religion: less authentic and less enduring. Indeed, one woman
from Meléndez argues that because the religion of her girlhood was so over-

---

[3] Popular stress on these issues in Latin America recalls early Puritan accounts of the Bible,
which, as Zaret shows in *The Heavenly Contract*, encouraged independence and confidence in
one's own unaided reasoning abilities.

[4] Cf. Scott, *Weapons*, and *Domination and Arts of Resistance: Hidden Transcripts*.

[5] James Adams, "CEBs as Groups: The Implications of Social Influence Theory."

whelmingly concerned with ritual, sacrament, and rote learning, it bordered on idolatry. In her view, without the groups,

> we would just be the same as before. And really, we even committed idolatries, kneeling before Christ and thinking he was the true God, that praying to him all our problems would be over. Now we know better, we see God in our brother, God is reflected in our brothers, in the poor. Now we understand, you see, that you've got to stand with the poor, with those who suffer, because, well, doing good to your brother is doing good to God, and if you hurt your brother you hurt God too. That's what we understand. (CA 275–76)

One peasant man, a founder of the Legion of Mary in the Villanueva region, noted that the church itself needed to "take more initiative with society's problems, not be so totally spiritual or apart . . . not keep itself for rituals and nothing more"(V 32).

The process of learning together, and the general relation of study to action in base communities and similar groups, takes specific form as a result of the way reading and commenting on the Bible is incorporated into the regular fabric of group life. By providing a medium that explicitly encourages participation, base communities also help make that participation legitimate. All this runs counter to traditional images of knowledge in a Catholic context, which follow a trickle-down model, whereby lay persons are subordinate to sisters, sisters to priests, priests to bishops, and so on. A young man from Agua Fría put the matter well, noting that "before, no one ever talked about our role as laity. You didn't dare. Things are different now that we have institutions that legitimize us" (A 75–76).

The Bible's great importance in group life should not lead us to confuse ordinary members with fundamentalists. To these men and women, the Bible offers not an inerrant text to be followed to the letter but rather accessible values, ideals, and role models. The words they find in biblical passages speak to them across time and space, bringing words of encouragement and a sense that others have taken the same path and faced up to the same problems.[6] The way the Bible is discussed is indicative. Texts are rarely studied in a formal, analytical way. Instead, participants jump right in to discuss how what is spoken of in the Bible is happening here and now, to people like themselves. The lessons found in the Bible thus appear not as formulas to be applied in some mechanical fashion but as a set of values and ideals and as a glimpse of role models available to average men and women, now as in biblical times. The promised coming of the Kingdom of God is thus taken not as an injunction to prepare for personal salvation (to "get right with God," in the style of North American televangelism) but rather as a part of working with others to build a

---

[6] See Jean Pierre Wyssenbach, "La Biblia entre nosotros" and "Comunidad de barrio"; and also Pedro Trigo, "Vida é historia en America Latina."

better life, now. Echoing Luke 17:20–21 ("the Kingdom of God is not coming
with signs to be observed. . . . The Kingdom of God is in the midst of you"),
group members see building community and bettering family, spiritual, and
social life as integral parts of that Kingdom.

## Biblical Texts and Readings

The specific texts that group members take up in their regular meetings give a
characteristic tone and thrust to the whole process. Passages that might once
have been at the center of attention (such as Romans 13, on obeying constituted authority) are now commonly set aside in favor of texts that urge authenticity in faith and action, underscore God's preference for the poor, and demand action to promote justice. As I observed group meetings and talked with
pastoral agents and base community members, I encountered a clear pattern
in biblical citations. Three issues or messages together occupy the center of
popular biblical discourse. The first is a stress on authenticity, particularly as
seen in the link of faith to action. The second concerns solidarity, sharing, and
sacrifice in the community. The third points to the social nature of true Christian love.[7]

Popular concerns with authenticity and common action as the best expression of faith are confirmed in the Hebrew Prophets and in a rereading of the
life and death of Jesus. Isaiah, Jeremiah, Hosea, Amos, and Micah thunder
against injustice in terms that are familiar to ordinary people. They point to
oppression and call for freeing prisoners. They denounce the rich, especially
those who rob poor people of a chance to live decently and who, in the words
of the prophet Isaiah (5:8), "join house to house, who add field to field until
there is no more room, and you are made to dwell alone in the midst of the
land."[8] The experience of Exodus, in which oppressed people pass through
long periods of trial and struggle (the desert) as they move from bondage to
freedom (the promised land) also has vivid and immediate meaning for popular groups.

Being a prophet and acting in a prophetic manner has several specific meanings. As distinguished from clergy, prophets participate in religious life from
outside formally established structures. They are critics who denounce abuses
and demand authenticity in God's name. Prophets are thus more rooted in
ordinary life than are clergy, and bring its concerns (above all, concerns for
fairness and justice) to center stage. In this way, prophets might be said to
bridge the gap between everyday existence and religious faith, as they move

---

[7] In his *Liberation Theology*, Berryman points to these central concerns in popular readings of
the Bible: the goodness of creation, the Exodus story and the Hebrew Prophets, and a rereading
of the life and death of Jesus.

[8] Isaiah 25.

from the former to the latter. Weber notes that prophets are leaders who by teaching and example demonstrate the proper way to live and act.[9] The essence of prophetic leadership is not giving orders but accompanying others on the path to justice. This model of what a leader should be is alive in popular communities today, and as we shall see, profoundly shapes their emerging view of religion, faith, and church.

The Prophets speak in God's name, and affirm God's special concern to shelter, protect, and uplift the poor. Where Jesus cites the Prophets directly, as in his reading from Isaiah at the synagogue in Nazareth, much comment ensues. The words are well known:

> The Spirit of the Lord is upon me, because he has annointed me to preach good news to the poor. He has sent me to proclaim release to the captives, and recovering of sight to the blind, to set at liberty those who are oppressed, and to proclaim the acceptable year of the Lord. (Luke 4:18–19)

Although the Prophets regularly denounce the injustices human beings do to one another, they reserve particular scorn and anger for religious hypocrites. The rejection of empty "feasts and solemn assemblies" (Amos 5:21–24) is widely echoed, as is the corresponding injunction to link faith with active promotions of justice. Stress on authenticity as expressed in direct links of faith to the promotion of justice draws added strength from an emerging popular Christology that downplays conventional elements of mild meekness and resignation. Instead, stress is placed on how Jesus' life and death point to a practical love for others worked out in solidarity and common action. "We are like Jesus," one Venezuelan peasant commented in a meeting of the cooperative at Villanueva.

> Jesus was the first, he joined with people to see how they could get out from under. You can't separate the two things. Jesus came and celebrated, he got involved with people's problems. It's the same with us; a day's work always ends with a celebration. The two things. So you see, Jesus is here with us, doing the same work. (V 77)

He and his companions see themselves as "like Jesus" because they also place their trust in God while at the same time working together to help one another and to improve the community. In a further discussion sparked by a passage (Luke 13) where Jesus compares the Kingdom successively to a fig tree (that must be planted and nurtured for years before it bears fruit), to a grain of mustard seed (that later becomes a mighty tree), and finally to the yeast needed for bread to rise, one member argues that this recalls how CRAMCO (the coffee cooperative) got started in his town.

[9] *Economy and Society*, 1:439–67.

When we organized in El Cauro, at first there was no priest to help us. People told us no, priests don't get into all that, it is not of the church. But we know that priests are involved with all the problems people have, to see how they can get out from under. They are not only for praying. (V 76)

Of the many CRAMCO meetings I have attended, two in particular illustrate how reading and commenting on the Bible legitimizes common effort and reinforces solidarity among group members. One session was held in the crossroads hamlet of Río Bravo, where members had recently completed an impressive store and warehouse that served a large surrounding area. The meeting opened with a passage from John 15:12–13, which reads,

This is my commandment, that you love one another as I have loved you. Greater love has no man than this, that a man lay down his life for his friends.

In the ensuing discussion, one member stated that this meant "Jesus seeks us now through the family gardens, through the health committees. It is just like when God made the first man, he made a garden then." He went on to stress that passages of this kind show that their group is spiritual and material at one and the same time. He described the group's operative code as "praying and lending a hand" ("rezando y la mano dando") (V 242). Another meeting the next day in San Luis began with discussion of a passage in Matthew 23:24– 26, where Jesus denounces hypocrites and Pharisees who clean the outside of cups and plates but are not themselves clean within. The text was read haltingly and with obvious difficulty by the local group's president, Bernabé, whose turn it was. After finishing, Bernabé offered his own commentary to the effect that Jesus was telling all of them to "be clean" by working together, not just by meeting for the sake of having a social gathering. Discussion took off from there and ranged widely over local and regional concerns.

Scenes like these were repeated in almost every community gathering I visited in the Villanueva region. All follow a common agenda, beginning with the reading of a brief biblical passage followed by a discussion of its significance here and now. The group then takes up the minutes of the last meeting, reviews the quarterly report of the cooperative, and works through the ordinary business each local unit has before it. This includes issues like problems in the sorting and weighing of members' coffee, setting criteria for the allocation and repayment of credits, or deciding on specific cases of creditworthiness. All meetings are run entirely by elected officers in an atmosphere of free and open discussion.

Apart from its role in spurring group solidarity, Bible reading also clearly serves as a hook drawing residents into the general process of participation and common action. Beginning meetings with a reading from the Bible and then making reference to it throughout the session gives activism and participation a sense of rightness they might not otherwise enjoy. A Jesuit organizer comments:

> At first, we had some problems. There were a few groups who thought that all this went beyond the proper bounds of religion. Some even said it was bad, that it meant using the Legion for things for which it was not intended. I told them no, and used Gospel passages, like the multiplication of loaves and fishes. I said, "Do you know why five thousand were able to eat? Because one person put his food in common. If that person had kept his bread and fish in his own pocket, Christ would not have made the miracle. Yes, and Christ is willing to work miracles here too. But someone has to contribute his loaf, his fish, someone has to lend his hoe, lend his jeep, put something in common, so that Christ can perform the miracle." And so we got started. (V 194)

A similar use of the Bible appears in the base communities of Cali's Barrio Meléndez. Members gather every week in the evening, rotating among each other's houses. They start each session by reading a passage from the Bible and then explicitly set time aside for a discussion of local and national issues. One man put it this way:

> People come here with such and such a problem and we start from there. This is where one can really feel the work of the group, because you know in the life of poor people there is so much pressure, so many economic problems. . . . On the one hand, patience is needed to stay in the fight. On the other, well you have to learn to stand up and ask for help. Not to remain closed off but to communicate, tell your problems to your neighbors, to the group. This is the base of our activities, that all [of us] develop a critical awareness. Because in isolation nothing gets done, nothing can be accomplished. Not for oneself, not for others. (CA 106)

The perceived link between biblical texts and practice is mediated by an understanding of faith according to which belief in God is best expressed in love for others. Concern about the meaning of authentic love is a common thread in group discussions. The biblical passage I had repeated most often to me was 1 John 4:20–21:

> If any one says, "I love God" and hates his brother, he is a liar; for he who does not love his brother whom he has seen cannot love God whom he has not seen. And this commandment we have from him, that he who loves God should love his brother also.

Commentary on this text undergirds an evolving view of society, of class relations, and of what it means to "be church." Society and class relations are depicted in terms that downplay conflict and rancor. From this perspective, at issue between rich and poor, powerful and weak is less oppression or exploitation than insufficient communication and an absence of basic human kindness. Mutual understanding and greater sharing are thus stressed more than structural change or revolution.

Prevailing images of "the church" also undergo considerable change. In earlier chapters, I noted the central role that definitions of "the church" play in legitimizing and empowering popular religious groups. The next section of this chapter examines in great detail the various meanings given to the idea of "being church" in popular discourse. Here it suffices to note the growing importance ordinary men and women give to themselves as constitutive of "the church." In this light, "the church" no longer appears as the priest or the building down the street but rather as the members who work and live together—the people of God building community. Reflection on the passage from 1 John provides many with the foundation for a broad concept of what the church is and what it means to "be church." One Venezuelan peasant put it to me in the following terms:

> I believe we are nothing, not church, nothing, if we cannot feel for our brother. How can we [then] feel for other things? Look, the church tells us that if you love the God you cannot see, and you do not love the brother you do see, then you are a faker. So I believe that if we cannot feel for our brother, who is right here beside us, and we cannot give him a helping hand, then we can't do anything. We lose everything. To me, this is how to cooperate as a church. Because you are church and I am church. Doing your work you are making the church. This is the church we make as we work. You go about working not only for yourself but for the community. What is the use of this information? To learn about what is happening in the world. To get it moving. You are sent because someone sends you, there is one who moves you. If not, you can't see where you are. He is here with us both, guiding us and who knows here? So this is God's house, and this is the church. For me, this is what it is. (V 123)

Bible study thus promotes participation and legitimates collective action. Text and process converge to reinforce members' capacity to speak and act as equals and their sense of shared responsibility. The patterns of group life and consciousness depicted here approach the Radical Ideal of base communities (chapter 2). But before we assume the generalizability of a model that moves from Bible to group organization and activism, it is worth considering alternatives. At a minimum, the convergence of text and process outlined thus far suggests that a different selection of texts and a less democratic kind of group process might well generate other sorts of outcomes. More conventional ecclesiologies (stressing hierarchy over equality and obedience over activism) along with more authoritarian mediations provided by the institutional church itself (personnel and guidelines for group formation) may help to stop change far short of legitimizing class-based activism. The efforts set in motion throughout Facatativá by Román Cortés illustrate the point well.

In November 1982 I attended a lengthy session in the parish center of Caparrapí that was attended by promoters and animators from a broad range of
villages and hamlets. As we have seen, regularly scheduled meetings of this
kind are central to the organization of communities in Facatativá. This particular gathering was called to involve communities in organizing a full day's
celebration in honor of the memory of Román Cortés, whose recent death and
continuing impact on individuals and communities throughout the area gave
special importance to the business at hand.

The session began with discussion of two passages from Paul's letter to the
Ephesians. The first (4:7–16) distinguishes among the gifts of ministry granted
to various elements in the church. The second (5:6–20) urges believers to behave "as children of light," avoiding contact with evil and stressing spiritual
over material things in their daily activities. Together these passages present a
hierarchically structured image of "church." To begin with, stress on the varying nature and capacity of ministries in the church underscores the distinct
and particularly authoritative quality of the leadership exercised by clerical
personnel. Their calling and officially sanctioned status makes them different
kinds of people and grounds their leadership in sources of legitimation not
available to ordinary people. At the same time, by painting for group members
a self-image as "children of light," reflection on this text in effect encouraged
them to see themselves less as part of the whole community than as a special
group of the saved within it. In the discussion that followed, priests and sisters
took the lead, arguing that these passages showed the need for loyalty to the
institutional church and for work in harmony with the parish.

Two young priests (of the four then resident in the parish) chaired the meeting, which in short order turned into something like a game of charades. When
attention turned from the biblical text to the business of the day, the priests set
the agenda and thoroughly controlled the discussion. They began by laying
out a series of detailed plans and then calling on the group for comments.
Leaving little time for reaction from the membership—which by now had been
converted pretty much into an audience—they moved quickly from one facet
of the project to another until the whole day's events had been accounted for.
After one lengthy presentation on how to organize a parade that would include
representation from all the hamlets and communities, one of the priests asked,
"Well, what initiatives do you have? What else?" Before anyone could respond, the other (seated next to him) interrupted to say that "we have also
thought of doing an audio-visual presentation [a tape] on the parish. We
wanted this to come from you, but here it is anyway" (C 27).

The group remained silent: most rural Colombians are reluctant to challenge
a priest's right to speak, and in any case, those present at this gathering were
far too polite to think of interrupting. Later, the priests presented all this to me
as an example of "the people deciding," a model of base community life. But
of course the model visible in this experience is anything but participatory,

egalitarian, or democratic. No trace of the Radical Ideal can be found here. To the contrary, this slice of group life reveals a vision of faith and popular action molded tightly to the Conservative Ideal.

Deference to hierarchy is built into the process from the beginning. The very texts chosen for discussion emphasize purification of popular practices rather than a spur to common action. Clerics here do more than just monopolize discussion, in effect making learning a subordinate act. They also place any group action in a context where ecclesiastical control is the desired norm. For example, the priests in Caparrapí openly and repeatedly complained that cooperatives and similar groups are not sufficiently integrated into parish life. Their position drew this frustrated reaction from the diocese's main extension agent, who is a full-time lay employee.

> This is absurd. All our leaders are the same leaders promoted by education [Hogar-Escuela] or pastoral [the diocese] who are now in the cooperative. They are members, activists, leaders. They are presidents of local civic action committees, presidents of the cooperative. They do catechism in the villages, preparing couples for marriages, parents for baptisms. They are active in every social and civic program. How can they say that this is not linked to the parish? I just can't see it. They say this is not integrated, but I believe that no matter how tied a leader may be to the parish, this does not mean he must depend on the parish for everything. . . . What we need is coordination, not control. (F 184)

The preceding discussion suggests that the convergence of Bible study with self-moved activism that plays so central a part in group experiences in Venezuela or Cali is not much in evidence in the parish of Caparrapí. The absence is significant, although local groups were widely perceived to be in decline, few in leadership roles (clerics or lay people) linked their decay to the constriction of popular involvement. Instead of opening groups to greater and more equal participation, the common response in Caparrapí was to insist on closer links with parish structures, more continuous supervision, and a drive for tighter control of group agendas and day-to-day activities. The extension agent quoted above went on to lay the decline of the parish firmly at the feet of the clergy.

> Things have been difficult lately, precisely because they have not made a real political commitment. [Who?] The priests, the new ones. And as long as there is no real commitment, things will not go well. People want more. They now look for hard facts, works you can touch and see. People don't believe any more in the Eucharist all by itself. I think Jesus came not only to save souls but also to fill bodies. (F 185)

His comments indicate that the decay of local groups can be traced to the absence of structured provision for active involvement and participation from the communities. Without strong commitment by ordinary members, even constant clerical supervision will likely generate only flagging enthusiasm. Like the Colombian church as a whole, the diocese of Facatativá has succumbed to the temptation to call any small group a base community. One of Román Cortés's original collaborators in Caparrapí told me that "that is exactly what goes on here. The diocese likes to say that we have this number of communities and that number of projects, but *there is nothing like that*. And this makes it all the harder to achieve anything real. . . . Sometimes I think our local church has limited itself to false comforts [paño y agua tibia], giving aspirin to treat cancers. And in the end we are left with very little" (C 8).

## Becoming Church: Varieties of Popular Experience

In the discourse of Latin American Catholicism, intellectual circles, publications, official statements, and everyday speech are filled with references to the notion of *being church*. The matter is often posed as if a popular church springing directly from the people ("a church born of the people," to use one common formulation) were somehow distinguished from and set against an institutional church run by elites and put to work exclusively in fulfillment of their plans. This view keys the vision of many radical Catholic activists, for whom the opposition of popular to institutional churches is just another facet of the general confrontation between rich and poor, powerful and powerless.[10]

The meaning of *being church* also sparks lively discussion among popular groups, where one often hears that "we are all church" ("todos somos iglesia"). But when being or becoming "church" is seen through the lens that popular discourse and experience provides, the issues are much less cut-and-dried. To begin with, popular groups distinguish clearly between *the church* as an institution and *being church* as a community of faithful, the most obvious sense in which "we are all church." As I will show in the next chapter, most group members easily combine expectations of help from *the church* (the institution) with affirmations that "we are all church," insisting that the church as an institution live up to its own stated norms. Contrary to what both critics and proponents of a "popular church" occasionally pretend,[11] the distinctions drawn between these two meanings carry little sense of group or class struggle within the church. At issue is less some variant of class warfare in the churches than a set of personal and collective claims to be heard and to be

[10] For a sampling of these views, see the following: Lancaster, *Thanks to God*; Manzar Faroohar, *The Catholic Church and Social Change in Nicaragua*; Virginia Bouvier, *Alliance or Compliance: Implications of the Chilean Experience for the Catholic Church in Latin America*; Hugo Assmann, *Theology for a Nomad Church*; and Pablo Richard, *Death of Christendoms, Birth of the Church*. McGovern reviews the issues well in *Liberation Theology*.

[11] Cf. Lancaster, *Thanks to God*; or Pasara, "Peru."

valued equally with others. The stress on practical love noted earlier also suggests the importance of elements of reconciliation and a common emphasis on joining rather than on opposing.

Stating that "we are all church" has other noteworthy implications. It serves members as a shorthand expression for common notions of good behavior, providing guidelines for what a Christian person should do. When all are "church," all are expected to act in trustworthy and honorable ways. Examples of good behavior include the avoidance of negatives like drunkenness, slander, violence, or debt along with a general positive injunction to join faith to action that we have already seen. Values of sharing, solidarity, trust, honesty, and reliability have a prominent place in these discussions.[12] A useful way to get at the range of meanings hidden in the phrase "we are all church" is through detailed examination of the particularities of belonging and the arrangements for membership in the institutional church that are built into group experience. Among these are the way communities are founded, leaders selected, trained, and validated, and programs approved and set in motion. Do the popular religious groups visible "on the ground" in Venezuela and Colombia in fact represent new ways of "being church"? Let us take a closer look.

The elements common to base communities and similar groups are familiar by now. The vast majority are formed after some contact with the institutional church, for example, a visit by priests or sisters, a special campaign or mission to the area, or invitations to some church-sponsored course. Contact is then maintained through regular visits by pastoral agents, courses, circulation of materials (mimeographed sheets or cassettes), as well as through invitations to regular regional meetings. Groups rarely exceed twenty or twenty-five people and gather every week or ten days; as we have seen, sessions are typically organized around reading and commentary on the Bible, followed by a discussion of pressing local or national issues and some common action. In this way, groups provide members with easy access to legitimate religious participation while they facilitate regular social interaction of a kind that is rare, especially in the countryside.

Enumerating traits in this way is valuable but of limited use by itself if we are to grasp the way that group life works to create and promote a new sense of being religious, with specific impacts on personal, social, and community life. More complete understanding requires that we do more than list group traits; we must consider exactly how these traits are related to one another.[13]

---

[12] The repeated assertion that "we are all church" also advances personal and collective claims to take the measure of the institutional church, evaluating programs and judging the adequacy of priests, sisters, and pastoral agents. This is reinforced by a decline in long-standing social and cultural distances between clergy and ordinary people, manifest, for example, in speech, dress, and life-style. See chapter 6, below, for details.

[13] De Tocqueville's comments on the study of associational life in nineteenth-century America

In putting together the packages of organization, belief, and action that give each pattern of grass-roots life its distinctive character and social projection, the most critical elements are linkage to the institutional church and the extent to which members seek and receive an independent role in the management of group life. Together these elements underly the process of making independent sense of the Bible and of its meaning for personal and community life. Consider the contrasting experiences of Facatativá, Cali, and Villanueva.

The official model of base communities at work throughout Facatativá assumes close contact and continuous ties between popular groups and the churches. Documents, meetings, and training materials all underscore the need for close supervision and control of group agendas. Much effort goes to identifying and drawing out new leaders and linking them explicitly to church-defined roles. On this basis, spiritual and material issues are then addressed together, with emphasis placed on the gradual development of local self-help projects such as water lines, livestock raising, cooperatives, and community stores. All this is apparent from the vantage point of the diocese and its supporters in Catholic Relief Services. But if we consider base communities from the vantage point of the groups themselves, a good deal of variation emerges. San Isidro, Quebradanegra, Caparrapí, and Agua Fría illustrate the possibilities.

Although in all these cases groups got underway only after some contact with the official church, in San Isidro, Quebradanegra, and Caparrapí, the process hinged almost entirely on intense and continuous effort by clergy and sisters. Their continued presence is regarded as essential to sustaining group life in these communties. The reader will recall that the diocese of Facatativá gave explicit responsibility for developing and monitoring group life to two sisters based near Quebradanegra. When I asked one of them, Sister Sara Osorio, to describe her work, she said that it was difficult but nonetheless satisfying.

> It's difficult. One isn't accustomed to sleeping in so many different beds, eating so many kinds of food, or to those long treks through the country. It's difficult. And you know, that's exactly what my superiors told me: "You're healthy," they said. "You're neither too young nor too old for the job." . . . At first it was hard for me, it seemed like I had come here to do nothing, to do nothing at all, because the work is slow. (Q 5)

---

are relevant here. De Tocqueville regarded the art of association as "the mother of all action," and argued that "in democratic countries, the science of association is the mother of science; the progress of all the rest depends on the progress it has made" (2:133). Throughout *Democracy in America*, he underscored the need to see civil and political associations not as separate but rather as mutually reinforcing. "Is it enough to observe these things separately, or should we not discover the hidden tie which connects them?" (2:143).

Sister Sara operates like a circuit rider, organizing her time each month around a regular routine of visits to all the communities and *veredas* (rural Colombian territorial units) in her area. Each visit is planned and activities arranged with help from diocesan seminarians, students from area secondary schools, and other sisters. When they first arrive in a community, the group begins by knocking on doors and urging all local residents to attend. Those who accept the invitation are then involved in a program that can last up to a week. Bible study and prayer sessions are combined with workshops on local issues such as education, sewing, first aid, or the possibilities for forming stores or cooperatives.

Sister Sara is relied upon throughout the area for guidance on forming group agendas and for help in figuring out the requirements of the diocese's plans and programs. Once groups are established, Sara maintains contact, visiting each community at least once a month to "take its pulse" and keep spirits up. In her view, "communities flourish if you attend to them. [But] peasants are inconstant. You've got to keep your eye on the community at all times" (Q 5). Moreover,

any community that doesn't get visited decays right away. You've got to be constantly, constantly visiting and talking with them, to see where they're heading. Only very few are able to go it alone. (Q 7)

In theory, leaders emerge out of the consensus of the group. But Sister Sara's description of the process suggests something much less spontaneous.

When we do the motivational units, we keep an eye out for able people, sort of checking the group over. And when the motivational course is done, they themselves propose candidates. Usually these are the very same persons we have already identified as particularly capable and committed. Normally, they choose the leaders, but sometimes you've got to give them a nudge, right? (Q 8)

When people in Sister Sara's orbit talk about the origins of their base community and discuss why they joined in the first place, they highlight her guidance and directive role. In remote San Isidro, the base community was established after a lengthy mission carried out by Sara with assistance from Quebradanegra's parish priest as well as from seminarians, students, and what one local resident described as a "flock of nuns." Two representative accounts of the foundation follow: the first speaker is a young woman; the second an older man.

I really don't know. Some missionaries [nuns] came to the school about four years ago. Before that, we didn't know anything about it. They stayed a night, and later a sister came, Sister Sara came and told us a base community was going to be set up, people were needed, and who would volunteer. So she showed us how to organize the meetings and [now] we do it. (S 16)

How? Because they told us to [porque mandaron]. When Sister Sara and Father Mario came and told us, at first I said no. They never asked me to a meeting, because I would not go. I don't harm anyone, I don't steal, I am not bad. But I went anyway and I liked it. (S 61)

Groups established in this way require constant care and attention; dependence is built into the process from the very beginning. Agendas come from the outside (the diocese through Sister Sara), and with rare exceptions, groups stick closely to them. There is little independence in selecting issues for discussion or initiatives for action. For the most part, such groups are locally bounded, with all external contacts mediated through the church; there is little areawide organization. In any event, independent links to nonchurch groups are actively discouraged, and autonomy is viewed with concern.

Social issues are less salient here than is the pursuit of personal piety and individual spirituality. Communities of this kind typically define themselves in terms of a most conventional religiosity that distinguishes spiritual from material concerns, with heavy stress on the former. As one young woman in San Isidro put it, the groups give people a chance to "seek a little learning, to talk with God, be with God, and to discuss religion with others, with songs and prayer" (S 25). In the town of Quebradanegra (where the area's parish and parish priest are housed), questions about the character of groups and the proper way to organize them met with responses like this, from one long-time member:

It's lovely, because don't you see, it lets you be with God. That's the first thing, right? It's kind of like a withdrawal, a spiritual retreat, and it helps you avoid lots and lots of problems, lots of troubles, because you're committed to the community, and you feel it all the time. And so, when they need us, we organize retreats and we all attend.

*How many are in the group?*

Only around twenty or twenty-five. You know, it's hard work getting people to commit themselves to God's work. God's things are hard for them, but in contrast they find the things of this world easy enough. Just ask them to a dance and you'll see how fast the house fills up! Noise and trouble all night long. But when it comes to God's business, two little hours for a meeting, they complain about how much time it takes. (Q 31–32)

Concern with conventional religiosity and things of the church is reinforced by utter dependence on clergy and pastoral agents for finding leaders and putting together group agendas. Sister Sara's predominant role is a good case in point. She picks potential leaders from the people encountered in initial group meetings and in the local leadership schools. She then affirms these individuals in their roles and, through regular visits, ensures continued tight links (in theory and practice) to the institutional church. This pattern of close supervision and control of course does little to change prevailing cultural expectations about equality and authority. To the contrary, it reinforces the expectations most members start off with, in particular, their sense that hierarchy is normal and that clerical direction is the foundation of any legitimate standard operating procedure. One *animadora* from a hamlet in Caparrapí explains:

> It works like this. The parish puts out a program, for example, about preparations for Holy Week. We then call a community meeting and go through the program every week until we are ready. There was a time when more people came to our meetings, but now it's only a handful. Why? How can I explain it to you? At first, Sister Cecilia did the inviting, and we all followed her lead in our weekly meetings. But after a while, people stopped coming, and their excuse was that the Sister wasn't there. There's a lot of foolishness there; sometimes I don't know what to think. But I love my people, they're not all bad, you know. (C 75)

From the moment of their creation, therefore, groups like those in San Isidro, Quebradanegra, or Caparrapí depend on external guidance and stimulation. Susan Eckstein's comments on "the irony of organization" are relevant here.[14] Eckstein points out that organization can be as much a problem as a solution. When poor people are organized into groups that fit in a subordinate way within a dense net of hierarchical ties, they become weaker and more dependent on the institution and show little capacity for self-initiated action. Groups with authoritarian origins ("because they told us to") are likely to drop quickest of all. The closer links are to the institutional church, the swifter the decline once external support or supervision is reduced. This is particularly evident in Caparrapí, where the diocese concentrated its human and material resources and devoted the full-time efforts of Román Cortés, its most charismatic organizer, to the task of group formation. With his death, things came apart quickly.

Where linkages are weaker from the outset, groups appear that prove to be more capable of independent initiative and better able to bring personal and community experiences to the center of attention. Members get accustomed to setting their own agendas, for specific meetings and also for the group as a whole over the long haul. Leadership selection also becomes more open, with leaders chosen by and from within the group. Agua Fría's small base community was founded not by direct intervention of clergy or sisters but as a result of the efforts of two local residents who returned inspired from one of Román Cortés's early *cursillos*. The difference may seem minor, but it is substantial because it placed responsibility for the group on local shoulders from

---

[14] *The Poverty of Revolution*, chap. 4.

the very beginning. The two founders returned from their *cursillo* energized, as "new men" who had a sense that everything had changed. One of these men, Patricio Alvarez, later expanded his commitment to the church by becoming a lay minister (chap. 8, below). His companion describes the experience in these terms:

Well, I tell you all that happened a long time ago. We got our motivation from Román; he came through here twelve or thirteen years ago, stirring things up until he managed to get us to attend a special *cursillo* in El Ocaso. Patricio and I were the only ones who went, we were the very first. You know, before the *cursillo*, I was kind of bad, but with the orientations I got there, I improved a lot.

*Have things changed?*

Yes, I think so, because clergy aren't the only ones with rights. We can also participate at any time. For me it's wonderful to have a lay minister right here in the *vereda*. That's just the kind of thing we have been missing. So from now on the community is bound to do better. (A 66)

Agua Fría maintains steady contact with the diocese. Sister Sara is a visible presence here as well, explaining programs, inviting members to general gatherings, and the like. But in contrast to San Isidro, Quebradanegra, or Caparrapí, meetings in Agua Fría are run by locally elected leaders. The sessions are open, and members use them to exchange ideas and experiences as well as to make arrangements to work together and help one another. In this way, they begin to overcome the isolation that is traditional in much of rural life.

The group meets once a week, Saturdays in the afternoon. There's a specific leader: Patricio, Engracia, or myself. Patricio is the main one. Basically we do a celebration of the Word [read the Bible], and depending on what the Word says to us, we put it into practice. The truth is that men can't live alone; we live together in communities. And often when people are in trouble economically, well, we find a way to help each other out. (A 74–75)

As this young man suggests, base community members in Agua Fría move easily back and forth between Bible study and shared reflection and common action. Community efforts include the following, which have evolved sequentially over the years: a rotating system of voluntary labor, whereby members pool efforts to help others in greater need; the organization of a community store; and most recently, the formation of a cooperative. Unlike Quebradanegra or San Isidro, where the ideal group is depicted in pietistic terms ("to bring the cross to the people"[S 61]), the ideal base community for residents of Agua Fría is spiritual and material at one and the same time. The following three comments are representative.

Communities should be like the one we have. We don't devote ourselves to praying but we pray, we work, we give to the poor, we share what we have. About
seven years ago between us all we managed to build a house for one family here.
The poor woman was a widow. Her husband had died following the law of the
hoe, working his land. And the community built her house for her. (A 67)

We can't do it only with the spiritual. We need to complete both sides, spiritual
and material. Talking about religion does us no good at all if there is still misery
all around. Like we've seen with cases of mutual help, if we can't organize ourselves for specific tasks, then it has no use for us. Around here, the community
does a little of everything; any other approach is a waste of time. (A 77)

Here the whole group works. We don't just pray, but if prayer seems right, then
that's what we do. Whatever works. (A 59)

Agua Fría's base community started out with the usual focus on prayer and
Bible study, but the founders soon discovered that others in the *vereda* were
not taking them seriously. "We started to get word that some people were
making fun of us. We were told that in one place they mocked us because we
met to pray and to read the Bible, and that in another they laughed at us, and
said that we seemed like Protestants or Pentecostals because we did nothing
concrete, no work in the community" (A 20). By talking things over together,
they came to see their initial agenda as too limited. They began to share problems with one another, and in the process, soon discovered a common difficulty in the high cost of food and supplies, and the outlines of a common
solution in the establishment of a small, cooperatively owned community
store.

Someone said, "Why don't we do something, we're so beat up by the high price
of what we've got to buy. Why give all that profit just to one person so that he can
get rich, make himself into a capitalist, one of those people who shout at us, push
us around, and make us suffer? Let's join forces and set up a small shop that we
all own together. That way the profits will stay here with us. The store won't
belong to any one person; it will be everybody's property." (A 20)

The cooperative began on a very small scale in 1975 with pooled resources
to buy and sell at better prices in local markets. Later, a permanent structure
was built to house the community store, shelving and counters were put in,
and a small stock of merchandise was accumulated. A man who has managed
the store for years recalls that at first they were not sure how to proceed.

What should we do to get things rolling? First I throw in some money, and then
another throws in more, and then another and another. How to manage it then?
Our experience with community action had already taught us how to set things
up in the right way, with leaders, employees, and people to manage day-to-day

business. So we formed a regular board of directors, with a president, secretary, treasurer and all the rest. And what should we do then?

Well the idea was to buy things, to lay in a stock so that people wouldn't have to go to Villeta or anywhere else for their shopping. And that's what we did. People put in what they could: 20 pesos, 50 pesos. Putting things together in this way, and working really hard at it, we managed after a few months to collect about 750 pesos. We were ready to begin. Then we named a commission to do the marketing and decided where to go. That's how it all started. We used those 750 pesos to buy potatoes, rice, and goods like that, and then we sold them here for a little over a thousand. And from that point on we've continued to grow. (A 37)

Of all the communities in this general region, only Agua Fría seemed able and willing to alter the agendas and guidelines received from above. From the outset, members have been willing to try new things. They have also gained confidence in their ability to deal as equals with rich and powerful people who in other times would have been objects of bashful deference. They can also hold their own within the diocese, giving respect and deference to the bishop and his agents but at the same time tracing out their own course with considerable autonomy. One lay leader described the group's ties to the diocese this way:

Yes, programs come from the diocese, but lately they are difficult and boring, too long and complicated. So people get bored. And they have become more aware. They say, ''Let's talk concretely about the problems we have in the group, the families in our hamlet, and see what solutions we can find.'' So we search in the Gospels where Jesus tells his disciples do to this and that, and there we find ideas. Just as yesterday the Lord told this to his disciples, today he is speaking to us in the same way: do good for others, and there we end the meeting. . . . so we get together to discover what is going on, to see if we can solve things. We don't worry that there is hunger in Africa; we are hungry here. Or that in Africa, Vietnam, Israel, Egypt, or Korea there is war. Here we are also at war. What happens is that in some places the fight is one way and in others it is different. The whole thing doesn't bother me too much. (A 28)

I do not mean to paint Agua Fría as a miniature Athens in the Colombian countryside. But a close look at what sets this experience apart from the normal run of things in Facatativá is instructive. Agua Fría's experience is more independent across the board: the base community was founded by ordinary residents, leaders are locally elected, and, in general, the group goes about its business with relative autonomy. The fate of the community store reinforces the point. The success of Agua Fría's small effort, in contrast to the utter failure of a similar and much better funded enterprise in Río Frío, is clearly related to the fact that in Agua Fría, the initiative arose in the community itself rather than being imposed from the outside by well-meaning pastoral agents. Members are more involved in and committed to the fruit of their own labors.

One conclusion might be that Agua Fría represents an embryonic "popular church" opposed to the ecclesiastical institution. Nothing could be further from the truth. Members feel strong ties to the diocese, greatly prize the advice and resources the diocesan team has to offer, and are proud that one of their number has become a lay minister. Even in this case, the structural arrangements that prevail throughout the diocese of Facatativá have considerable impact on the scope of local efforts. Combined with the long-standing distrust of politicians and outsiders common to rural Colombia, the church's constant effort to manage ties to the larger society effectively contains most initiatives within narrow and localized boundaries. Still, it is fair to say that the way groups start and operate in Agua Fría clearly reinforces members' confidence and sense of dignity and self-worth. The group also gives them a place where these new capabilities can be practiced. To round out our discussion of how patterns of consciousness and group life work out "on the ground," let us compare experiences in Facatativá with those of Cali's Barrio Meléndez and rural Venezuela.

It helps to note a few basic differences between city and country. In contrast to rural areas, in the city, home and workplace are physically separate. Residents also have a much wider range of trades and occupations and for the most part have come from different places, having migrated to the city earlier in life. The long and tangled history of migration and movement one commonly encounters in the barrios reinforces feelings of heterogeneity, further complicating efforts to build a sense of community in the group. In addition, the city presents many alternatives to base communities, which face stiff competition for members' time and commitments from religious competitors like evangelical Protestant churches, spiritist centers, or charismatic groups, as well as from a range of trade unions, neighborhood associations, and political parties. Base communities in the barrios of Cali also share a number of features with their rural cousins. All began as a result of some contact with sympathetic clergy or sisters. Group practice also typically revolves around reading and studying the Bible combined with discussing local problems and efforts at common action. Finally, as in Facatativá (albeit for different reasons), initiatives begun in the base communities of Cali rarely reach beyond local confines.

Recall how in Barrio Meléndez base communities arose as a result of contacts between residents and a group of Spanish priests who came to the area to found a parish. The Javierian sisters arrived soon after, contributing an independent effort that has centered on the organization of cultural facilities and programs (a small lending library, a range of courses) along with events like a regular Week of Popular Culture, which combines music, theatrical presentations, films (if possible), and a range of group discussions. Group members in Meléndez readily acknowledge the central role that the Spanish priests played. Like the men and women of Facatativá, they believe that without co-operation from clergy, it is very difficult to get groups started or to sustain popular interest in their activities. One of the rare male participants put the matter plainly, noting that "the basic element for attracting people is the priest. He's got to be open, he's got to stand with the people, to know what's going on" (CA 117). A woman in the same group put the problem in more general terms. She wanted to get groups well established:

> Of course, that's what our work is all about, and we work hard at it. But around here people still lack true awareness of what it means. They believe that if every-thing isn't organized around the priest, then nothing can be done. No, they tell you, you just can't do that. . . . When problems come up, then they make every-thing into a question of revolution, and tell you about communism. That's the justification they use for calling anyone who claims his rights a rebel, someone bad. (CA 237–38)

The four Spaniards left so positive an impression in Meléndez that group members now see each as the very image or model of a "good priest": simple, straightforward, easy to deal with. One man recalls how they rejected formal titles:

> They would laugh about it, because they didn't even like us to call them "father," because our Father is in heaven. They said, just call us by our names, call us Isidro, call us Pedro, and after a while we got used to it. For example, I would say something like, "Hey Pedro, how's it going?" It's not how things used to be, your reverence and all that, the way we said it back home in my *vereda:* my reverend father; no, no. They told us to call them just by their names, nothing more. (CA 154–55)

The four are widely missed. As one woman told me,

> They taught us how to do so many things that even me, a person who criticizes everything, both good and bad (especially the bad!), even I've got to say that I have nothing critical to say about them, nothing at all. . . . They were very young priests, nice looking, with a religion that was really deep. We've all missed them a lot, because they got involved in everything, they were active throughout the barrio. They used to pass by my door every day, and I would ask where they were coming from. They would be all sweaty, and tell me that they were coming from the hills. That there was a sick woman there, a woman in need, suffering from hunger. (CA 41, 47)

Four and sometimes five different base communities operate in Meléndez. Each draws fifteen or twenty people together on a weekly basis; meetings are held in members' houses, with the specific location changing from week to week as members volunteer to host the gathering. Bible study is quite an active process here; members not only involve themselves in study but feel obligated to take the Bible as a guide to service to others.

> It's not just a question of reading it and that's that. You've got to put it into practice. Here it's like it was with Jesus himself, just like Christ devoted himself wholly to serving others, that's how it's got to be with us. You can't just read the Bible and that's an end of it; there's got to be service to others. (CA 131)

With the departure of the Spanish priests in 1981, the sisters took on a more central role. Through their contacts with the CINEP-*Solidaridad* network, they have brought residents a range of courses, speakers, and perspectives that otherwise would find little echo in a place like Meléndez or, indeed, in most Colombian parishes. One woman told me enthusiastically that through the sisters, she and her neighbors had access to all kinds of interesting ideas.

> In the group they explain lots of things to us. It's really nice, for example, they explain about national history, how the country was founded. They explain what the proletariat is, what that means, all kinds of things a person didn't know. In the group they tell us about interesting things. A professor from the university told us about the lumpen: we didn't know what that was, at least I had never heard of it. What is the proletariat, the upper classes, all of that. The sister or sometimes a professor explains things about the country and about society. It's all so interesting. (CA 37)

The sisters and their allies have little to offer beyond concepts and words. They control few financial resources and can provide no assistance with the sort of problems local groups face in the ordinary course of affairs: help with keeping books, paying for printing or transportation, or assistance in meeting legal requirements for group registration. Facing a now hostile priest, members have been thrown back on their own resources. It is a difficult and vulnerable position to be in, but members do the best they can. They are willing and able to conduct meetings on their own, even though doing so reminds them of the loss of valued ties to the institutional church. Losing the Spaniards was a blow; losing the sisters would be a disaster. Two members comment:

> The work those women have done is really something. Each one is involved in something else, in all kinds of activities, but still you've got to admit that there was more sense of community with the priests we had. In contrast, the one we've got now sees all this as if it were something bad being done to the barrio. He calls it subversion, and says that they're stirring up the people. That's what he's said in his sermons. I've only gone to a few. He tells you it's just a question of asking God for help; everything is supposed to fall from heaven. (CA 245)

> I like it when one of the Javierians comes because I feel kind of protected then, even when they don't say anything, like last night. We do the talking, but I always

let them explain things to me, they can explain what we don't manage to understand. . . . What will become of us [ay de nosotros] if they leave too? (CA 38)

A radicalized discourse is common in meetings of the Meléndez base communities and in conversations with members. The rhetoric in ordinary use here
gives a highly critical tone to group encounters and clearly contributes to the
barrio's "red" image. This makes for political problems, since members feel
unjustly accused of subversion and particularly victimized by their proximity
to battalion headquarters. Radical rhetoric added to the organizational weaknesses noted in chapter 4 means that when social activism does emerge, it
tends to come in short, sporadic outbursts. There are few enduring structures,
and no allies from outside the barrio available to help on a regular basis. A
protest over the cutoff of water supplies illustrates the matter well.

Water service to the barrio had been cut off without notice, presumably as
a result of work in the area. When the flow of water was not quickly restored,
a protest march was organized more or less on the spur of the moment. Residents from the higher portions of the barrio were most affected by the cutoff.
Carrying pots, pans, and hastily made placards, they moved to occupy the
main road (Fifth Street), inviting others to join them on the way. As one
woman described events, she and her family were eating lunch

> when we heard a lot of noise outside. I went out to see what was going on when
> a few people in the group invited me to come along. . . . "Walk with us, Doña
> Edilma, we're going down to protest the water cutoff. There's no water at all in
> the hills, and these children are sick." So right away I told my daughters to watch
> the house, took two pots of my own, and got moving down the hills. As we went
> along, more and more people kept joining us. And I tell you that we took Fifth
> Street. We shut it down and let no one pass."(CA 238)

Soon after blocking traffic completely on Fifth Street, they were attacked
by soldiers from the battalion, who had been called in by angry motorists—
the woman just quoted described them as spoiled rich kids ("hijos de papá y
mamá")—whose way in and out of the city was blocked by the protesters (CA
239). When the soldiers arrived, the group members were frightened and some
fled, but most resisted as well as they could until the day was saved by the
arrival of a local press photographer and by city police, who intervened to stop
the fighting. The next morning, local newspapers carried front-page coverage,
including photographs of the day's events. Water was restored immediately,
but no enduring organization ensued. Most of the residents I interviewed
agreed that the unity visible when Fifth Street was "taken" owed more to the
fact that water was something everybody in the barrio needed than to any long-
lasting disposition to organization and action.[15]

[15] For general comments on this point see Eckstein, *The Poverty*, and her "Power and Popular
Protest"; and Frances F. Piven and Richard Cloward, *Poor People's Movements*.

Members of the base communities in Meléndez find themselves in a contradictory situation. They believe strongly that their path is correct and value their newly acquired independence and critical judgment. But the new priest's hostility reinforces their sense of isolation, vulnerability, and powerlessness. They depend more than ever on the (mostly verbal) support they get from the Javierian sisters. Their analysis of the world is couched in a radical rhetoric, but, with the exception of outbursts like the water protest, most activities are innocuous: sewing circles, courses, and occasional charity. The only enduring organizational spin-off from the base communities that I could find in Meléndez was a group called Social Action, founded by seven women and dedicated to the distribution of clothing, medicine, and other needed items among the very poor.

To be sure, if placed in a different context, even activities like this can have an impact on consciousness and action. One woman told me how much she had been affected by her experience in distributing surplus food to the barrio's poorest families. Although she herself is poor, the depths of poverty elsewhere in the barrio still came as a shock. As a result, she has rethought her basic views on charity, and has come to resent bitterly the condescending attitudes still common among the rich and powerful. They think poor people are just an eyesore to be hidden or shunted aside. Moreover,

> they come here and provide help like it was a big deal, throwing things at people, and humiliating them. That's not right. . . . That shouldn't be, because you don't do favors for people in order to humiliate them. That's wrong. (CA 243a)

Exclusive focus on social and economic "output" misses the core of an experience like the one in Meléndez. When group members themselves discuss the base community's impact on their lives, they spend very little time on specific activities. Instead, they point to general changes that undergird a sense of independence and a new kind of religious consciousness. These make it possible for the men and women of the barrio to refashion their view of the world and of their own place in it. The following comments by an older woman in the barrio are widely echoed:

> Yes, what happens is that when people come to the meetings, each one brings what they know about community problems. Sometimes it's all the same big problem, like what we told you about the other night, what we call the march of the pots. Didn't we tell you about that? [*Yes, the water problem.*] Well, you know that's how it is, it's here in the marginal barrios that you get the worst abuses. . . . I don't know if you think it's the same everywhere in Latin America, but the way I see things, religion has been reformed, and I say reformed because they used to teach us that praying would solve everything, that praying was all you needed to satisfy God. But now the Bible makes us see things differently, because even

though it is true that praying is communicating with God, you've also got to be committed to act along with your brothers and sisters.

*And reading the Bible is something . . . ?*

Of course, because [with the Bible] you discover things that make sense of the reality in which you live. (CA 275)

Ordinary religious life for these men and women in Meléndez has clearly been transformed. The center of their religious sensibility has shifted away from sacraments or personal salvation. Getting together to pray is not enough. Like the Puritans of seventeenth-century England, members seek *edification* and a channel for active service.[16] Members believe that they are building a fuller and more authentic way of being religious. Without the Bible and the ideals of service to others that it brings, they would be little better than charismatics, all talk and no action. One woman put the matter in these evocative terms:

I tell everyone that we must be real Christians walking toward our faith, walking to truth, not the kind of Christians who sit all day long with rosaries in their hands, who wait every day for manna to fall from heaven. Because the manna is all used up, that's what I say. (CA 198)

Given the pervasive stress in Meléndez on being active, serving others, and the like, it is not surprising that traditional expressions of religiosity have been examined, found wanting, and reworked. A case in point is the Easter celebrations organized while I was visiting the barrio. Special efforts were undertaken to downplay traditionally elaborate reenactments of Christ's passion and death that involved lavish costumes, parades, and *tableaux vivants*. Instead, resurrection and new life were emphasized. The intense spirituality associated with Easter was refocused toward service to others—through donations for relief work as opposed to contributions for costumes.

The experience of Barrio Meléndez provides a window on efforts at cultural transformation associated with crippling organizational weakness. There is a beginning edge of independence and self-management, but the absence of regular ties with larger structures drastically restricts the potential scope and durability of any action. These limitations recall the situation in Facatativá, with the difference that groups in Facatativá stay well within conventional agendas and local confines precisely because their links to the church rule out other alternatives. Close proximity to the institutional church in Facatativá provides resources and a valued sense of legitimacy at the cost of independence. In both cases, we find groups that have evolved and had some impact on individuals and communities but that (albeit for different reasons) seem unlikely to result in the kind of structures that are required if incipient consciousness and com-

---

[16] For details, see Zaret, *The Heavenly Contract*.

mitment are to expand and endure. For a case where new ideas, organizational structures, and lasting ties to other levels converge, we must turn to the *caseríos* of rural Venezuela.

Recall the close association here between the Legion of Mary and the cooperative. As we have seen, the Legion combines intense piety and spirituality with rigid, multilayered structures and a commitment to community service. Legion meetings everywhere are organized on a common pattern, with stress placed on punctuality, personal and group reliability, and the maintenance of routines. Together these traits provide a firm basis for any organization. In Villanueva, they have been the glue holding the cooperative together. Most of the members I interviewed saw an easy connection between the Legion and the cooperative. The general point of view seemed to be that several different kinds of organization were now available, each with its specific purpose. If a goal could not be accomplished through one, then another path was open. Both have religious legitimation. "There are two groups here that have ties with the priests, and if we can't get things done on the social side, we try with the other" (V 46). Members have heard of base communities, but are not troubled by definitional niceties. One of the cooperative's founders responded to my question about base communities this way:

> There are no base communities here. There is the Legion of Mary, whose base has been spiritual, changing to other matters. Spiritual things give us a base for getting to the socioeconomic. When the Jesuits first came to this area, the Legion of Mary was already active, praying and drawing people together [rezando y acercando], and the cooperative started from there. (V 31–32)

There is considerable (though not total) overlap in membership between the Legion and the cooperative. The two groups meet weekly or biweekly, depending on circumstances like weather, travel conditions, or members' health. Ordinary members take part in every facet of group life: they contribute freely to discussions; evaluate requests for credits in open sessions; and elect leaders from their ranks. The following comments on leadership selection by two cooperative members underscore the contrast with rural Colombia. Emphasis is placed on local autonomy, and positive models of group life are drawn from the national scene. How are leaders picked?

> By the members themselves, that's how. Each person thinks about it, and in the groups we get to see who is capable, who would have the necessary abilities to run the assembly. Then we elect them, we remove them if they act badly, just like we removed the treasurer here awhile ago. That's right, the treasurer, who had been chosen three times in a row wasn't returned this time, we picked another. (V 87)

> The group chooses from among its own members, we do it in a meeting with secret ballots, *just like in any election*. We choose the best ones. (V 30)

Members commonly describe meetings by stressing that no single individual or closed group runs things. They distinguish between leadership in general (essential to any group) and a particular kind of overbearing bossism that is explicitly rejected. Thus, "everybody participates; no one runs things. Anyone can get up and speak his mind, anyone at all. Of course we have directors [of the group], but they're not bosses over anyone" (V 63). Common religious bonds do more than legitimize group origins; they also lay the base for ongoing mutual trust. On this foundation, the injunction to participate is taken very seriously. All have equal gifts, and all are obliged to join in. One long-term member comments that

> with the church, you can count on things being correct; the church insists on a healthy doctrine. That means no vices are allowed in the cooperative. Anyone can enter, from the greatest to the smallest. We've all got to be equal and we've all got to do our duty. The cooperative needs people who are responsible, people you can count on. We can't afford to have elements there who don't take things seriously. No. To the contrary, we've all got to be united, to cooperate and work together. Then we've really got something. (V 121)

The preceding observations suggest a number of parallels with Facatativá. In both cases, groups have their origins in very traditional religious organizations. Both areas have also been deeply marked by the inspiration and efforts of a dedicated and charismatic priest: Román Cortés in Facatativá and Padre Vicente Arthur in Villanueva. But from these common origins, the two cases soon parted company, above all with respect to the way group life evolved, to the quality of participation, and to the kinds of links binding each group to formal church structures. Group agendas in Villanueva expanded from their initial religious base to encompass cooperatives, farm gardens, and health committees. Once the initial step (forming the cooperative) was taken, members assumed new responsibilities easily and with remarkable speed, pushing themselves and their group into hitherto uncharted territory. One leader's account of the process recalls the experience of Agua Fría, but in notably less clericalized terms.

> Visiting the *caseríos*, we began to see things. We realized that the government wanted to help in some way, and so we began by calling a meeting in which a local group could be set up. You know, one of the major difficulties we coffee cultivators have is with the groups known as PACCA [the semiofficial marketing and credit organization]. They are supposed to be ours, but they pay no attention to us. That's been a real problem. So we called meetings to see if we could organize our own group, a group run by ourselves and for ourselves. . . . At first it was hard, because when we raised the idea of a group, people said we were dreaming, that it was a daydream to think that we coffee growers could have our own organization. Just a dream. (V 86)

The original nucleus of cooperative members was drawn from the Legion and, not surprisingly, remains very devout, dedicated to the cultivation of an intense personal and group spirituality. But they distinguish the respect and veneration in which they hold clergy (Padre Vicente, the Jesuits, the Medical Mission Sisters) from dependence on clergy for direction in all aspects of life. Both Legion and cooperative meetings are run by local leaders, without clergy present. Indeed, by the time of my visits, the shrinkage of Jesuit involvement in cooperative affairs had reached the point that initiatives were being discussed to remove the Jesuit adviser from his long-standing position as parliamentarian. The grounds are suggestive: no one wanted to offend him by disputing his rulings, but it was felt that the group could operate more freely without having a priest on the platform.

Why were these Venezuelan peasants able to assume new roles with so much greater ease and independence than their Colombian counterparts? Part of the reason clearly lies in the practical ecclesiology at work in Villanueva. Formal concepts that take the church as Pilgrim People of God are part of ordinary routine here. Translated into common speech and everyday practice, they make for a vision of the church where ideals of equality, mutual responsibility, and service are highlighted. If the church is indeed a Pilgrim People of God making its way through history, then this particular part of the church must also focus on joining in historical change, changing itself in the process. As we have seen, this stress on experience underscores the religious value of what ordinary people have to offer. All members of the church have capacities and gifts; all are expected to act and to share. At the same time, the routines and habits inculcated by the Legion (punctuality in meeting, keeping records, working together, etc.) created a group of "new men," spiritually regenerated and socially capable of independent initiative. Before the Legion, all this was unknown. Moreover:

> Well yes, I think that most of the people you now see working in the cooperative, before, most of them were people with no . . . most of them were full of vices— lazy, drinking, no commitment whatsoever. They led bad lives. But now you see them active in the cooperative and the Legion. There has been a real change in them as people. And it is precisely the area of getting together for religion [en lo católico] that has made the difference. Before, the only meetings we ever had in El Cauro were for celebrations, fiestas, Christmas, Easter, the annual mass. . . . Those were the only meetings. But now in the community, in every community, not a month passes without meetings, meetings where people participate. Now people are used to getting together, and they make new opportunities to join with one another. (V 93)

The similarities and differences between the three grass-roots experiences outlined here are drawn together in tables 5.1 and 5.2. If these summary characterizations are set against the overall typology of base communities outlined in chapter 2, a few points emerge that warrant separate mention. First, it is not difficult to fit the experience of group life we found in Facatativá, Cali, and Villanueva under the general headings that this typology offers. None reflects the Radical Ideal, although Cali comes close, especially if we take the matter from the point of view of pastoral agents. Most of Facatativá approaches the Conservative Ideal, with Villanueva, Cali, and some aspects of Agua Fría falling under the heading of commitments to Sociocultural Transformation.

Putting experiences into the boxes a typology provides is properly the beginning, not the end, of analysis. The proper task of research is explanation, not classification, and therefore, the activity of sorting out, which is appropriate to typologies, must always be subordinate to theoretical issues. The theoretical dimensions that inform the typology of base communities laid out in these pages bring elements of ideology and practice together in a context shaped by organizational and institutional mediations. Religious ideas (especially ecclesiologies) lay a foundation, legitimizing patterns of belief and action that can range, as we have seen, from the trickle-down images common in Facatativá to the participatory and egalitarian models Villanueva represents. Contrasting visions of the nature of membership (here, the meaning of *lo popular*) are also important. They locate any particular group's status in the larger social order, and in this way set out characteristic views of what constitutes the good member, the ideal leader, and the correct agenda for group life. Linkages make a difference by setting the parameters of local autonomy and empowering a kind of group process that joins Bible study to other social and cultural issues in characteristic ways.

The character of the groups and the way peasant consciousness has evolved within them together constitute necessary but not sufficient conditions for understanding how cultural and organizational change starts and takes hold. Complete analysis requires us to set these elements in the context of the sort of linkages that bind groups to larger structures. Popular religious groups in the Villanueva area arose not from the parish or other mainline church structures but from the Legion of Mary as promoted by a foreign priest. Continuing links with other levels of action are arranged through the Jesuits and, also, through the mechanisms the coffee cooperative has established. Unlike the situation in Facatativá, members here are willing and able to experiment, and experimentation is encouraged. Decisions are made at local and regional levels, not filtered down along hierarchically controlled channels. The ideal member is not the minicleric but the active citizen, respectful of the church and devoted to it but also committed to independent action.

Without democracy, there is no substantial change, either in religion or in social and cultural life more generally. Democracy requires autonomy and finds its fullest expression as active citizens create themselves through the groups. This is not necessarily a matter of finding or shaping heroes but rather of ordinary men and women coming to think and act on their own. To be sure,

**TABLE 5.1**
Field Research Sites, Selected Traits

| | Colombia | | Venezuela Barquisimeto | |
|---|---|---|---|---|
| | Facatativá | Cali | Rural | Urban |
| Main Program Line | Official bishops' pilot (CRS ties) | Independent | Jesuit | Jesuit |
| Social Context | Peasant Homogeneous | Urban Invasion barrios Heterogeneous | Peasant Homogeneous | Urban Invasion barrios Homogeneous |
| Traditional Religiosity | High | Low | High | Low |
| Key Religious Group | Cursillos | Base community | Legion of Mary | Various |
| Key Social Group | Cooperative Community stores | "Social action" Sporadic organizations | Cooperative, health committees | Cooperative, health committees |
| Hierarchical Control | Yes | No | No | No |
| Concentration of Religious Personnel | Yes | No | Yes | Yes |
| Pastoral Agent Goal | Evangelization and material Aid | Cultural change | Evangelization and material Aid | Material aid, then evangelization |
| Groups Explicitly Christian | Yes | Mixed | No | No |
| "Spillover" | Confined to locality | Limited | Yes | Limited |

**TABLE 5.2**
Key Questions on Base Communities

| | Facatativá | | Cali | Rural Venezuela |
|---|---|---|---|---|
| | Agua Fría | Caparrapí Quebradanegra San Isidro | Meléndez | Villanueva |
| How Founded | Cursillo graduates | Priests/sisters | Priests/local residents | Legion of Mary members |
| When Founded | 1970–72 | 1970–72 | 1977 | 1970–72 (cooperative later) |
| Meetings/Size | Weekly/15–20 | Weekly/12–20 | Weekly/10–15 | Biweekly/15–20 |
| Agenda Source | Diocese (adapted) | Diocese, pastoral agents | Bible study Discussion Alternative guides | Legion guides Cooperative |
| Leader Selection | Elected | Selected | Elected | Elected |
| Presence of Diocese | None | Through sisters | None | None |
| Relation to Priests and Sisters | Occasional | Strong | Localized contacts with Jesuits | Through cooperative |
| "Spillover" | Localized | No | Localized | Strong |
| Ideal Group | Spiritual/Social | Devotional/Activist | Spiritual/Activist | Spiritual/Activist |
| Ideal Member | Miniclergy | "Beato" | Activist | Activist |

the choice rarely appears in all-or-nothing terms. These are continuums, with many possible variants on the base community theme, many ways of building community in and through religion. But without independence and democracy, the long-term social and cultural transformations many expect from base communities are unlikely.

The preceding discussion of Bible study suggests that independence and democracy cannot be limited to issues that are explicitly social, economic, or political. To the extent that creating a "popular subject" involves building a new sense of self, marked by confidence in one's own judgment, it stands to reason that religion itself will not be exempt from change. The next section considers such changes, with special reference to links between group life, spirituality, and what is commonly called "popular religion."


## Transforming Popular Religion


Complete understanding of popular religious groups must take their religious beliefs and practices seriously. As I have stressed throughout, it is their characteristic transformation—not their abandonment for other norms and practices—that underlies any broader cultural, social, or political transformations such groups may spur or legitimize. It is important to be very clear about how this process works. More is at issue than just making sense of the world and adapting religious messages and understandings accordingly. Rather, through a subtle process that combines innovation in belief and everyday practice, popular religious groups of the kind examined here come to see themselves as potential and legitimate actors in any area, with a claim to freedom of action and to a share as valid as anyone's in its benefits. The world as perceived changes, and so does their own place in it.

Whatever else these groups may claim to be, whatever other ends they serve, their original and continuing bedrock identity is religious. For this reason, close attention to the content of popular piety and spirituality is required.[17] Gutiérrez argues that a new spirituality is now emerging among the Latin American poor. As poor people reflect on their experience and come to grips with its meaning in new and creative ways, they have made values of solidarity central, and in this way have provided "a concrete expression of Christian love today."

[17] Focusing on such dimensions does not assume that poor people are necessarily more religious or more spiritual than other social classes. This is a complete distortion, as is the common view that takes piety and spirituality as static—components of a "primitive" social consciousness destined to be replaced at some point by a more sociological, and presumably rationalized, understanding.

It may seem somewhat reckless to speak of a spirituality taking shape around the Latin American poor, but that is precisely what is happening as I see it. Perhaps some are surprised because they think of the struggle for liberation as taking place in the social and political sphere, and thus in an area that has nothing to do with the spiritual. Clearly everything depends on what one understands by spiritual. . . . The spirituality now being born in Latin America is the spirituality of the church of the poor . . . trying to make effective its solidarity with the poorest of the world. It is a collective, ecclesial spirituality.

Gutiérrez goes on to acknowledge that it may be too early for precise details on the new spirituality being crafted by popular groups in Latin America. "At present," he states,

we are in the position of those trying to decide whom a newborn child resembles. Some will say the father, others the mother; some will even find that the child has this grandfather's nose or that aunt's eyes, whereas still others will be of the opinion that the child does not remind them of any family features known to them. Better to photograph the child and decide later on whom it resembles.[18]

What does popular spirituality look like in the communities of Facatativá, Cali, and Venezuela? To understand these mattters more thoroughly, I explored beliefs and practices in the following areas, all conventionally lumped together under the rubric of "popular religiosity": first, prayer, pilgrimages and the use of holy water; second, prevailing understandings of Jesus, Mary, and the saints; and finally, expectations about life after death.[19]

Despite otherwise significant variations of every kind, in all the groups I studied all members pray regularly. They pray alone and in family gatherings, they pray in churches and in group meetings, and they pray on a wide range of other occasions. Prayer can be an exceptionally powerful experience, in which individual and collective speech, action, and memory are worked together with tremendous force and plasticity. In the words of Marcel Mauss, prayer is

infinitely flexible, and has assumed the most varied expressions, alternatively pleading and demanding, humble and menacing, dry and full of images, immutable and variable, mechanical and mental. It takes on the most diverse roles: here a brutal demand, an order, there a contract, an act of faith, a confession, a plea, a word of praise, a "hosanna!"[20]

---

[18] The three preceding citations are from *We Drink From Our Own Wells*, pp. 96, 29, and 92 respectively.

[19] These items were part of a series of questions that explored personal religious history and orientations, including recollections of religious learning, of First Communion and marriage (where appropriate), and details about family religious practice and possession of religious objects like rosaries, amulets, or pictures.

[20] "La oración", p. 95.

Much prayer remains conventional, devoted to giving thanks, making specific requests, or to carrying out conventional formulas such as the saying of rosaries. This pattern is particularly evident in groups with tighter links to the parishes and a less active and participatory view of Bible study. The following comments from two Quebradanegra men are representative:

Yes, one sends prayers to God and to the Holy Virgin who are, they are the chiefs [literally: *las cabezas*, or "heads"] that direct us.

*And what do you pray for?*

Well, prayer is to thank God for a day's work, for getting through the night, for making the rain stop, or for whatever favor or miracle God has performed. We thank God and we also make requests for the young people, for our families, and for ourselves as well. (Q 123)

[I pray] so that God will increase our faith, and also to ask for help with all the needs of our family and of the whole world. There are many needs, and so we have to ask God for help. Some people say that you shouldn't ask God for material things, but I always ask my God to let me have my own house some day. Father Jorge told me that no, you shouldn't be asking, because God already knows everyone's needs. It makes sense that God knows all our needs, but I ask anyway. It's like knocking on the door to make sure he remembers, that he does not forget. (Q 96)

Prayer helps many search for the strength they need to endure a difficult life. For this San Isidro man, "more than anything else, health is what we ask for. Always hopefully, with patience, and also to suffer patiently what must be suffered. With patience and intelligence" (S 68).[21] Requests for divine help also commonly extend beyond personal and family life. There are prayers for security, especially around Caparrapí. One man states that "every night I put my trust in God. A man never knows when he'll lose his life: with all this turmoil, you just can't be sure. But if they [guerrillas] come here, you've got to defend yourself. Anyone who comes to attack us will find us ready to fight. I ask God to give the valor I need" (C 63). His neighbor told me that he prays

every night to God and to the Virgin. I thank God for all the help he gives me, I offer him my concerns, my feelings, and I ask him to help me and my community so that wierd people [gentes raras] won't come. I don't want guerrillas here. (C 60)

The style and focus of prayer starts changing as groups become more participatory and place greater stress on shared reflection and common effort in the community. Prayer is then less an isolated individual (or at most a family-

[21] As Clifford Geertz comments, religion does not teach us to avoid suffering, but rather how to suffer ("Religion as a Cultural System," p. 104).

centered) act. Stress on the community context of prayer makes praying less a matter of asking for favors or even of thanksgiving (although these remain) than a means of identifying with others and, in this way, with God. The following statements illustrate the shift well: the first speaker is a man from Agua Fría, the second is a woman from Barrio El Rodeo in Cali.

> Yes, I pray continuously to find myself with the Lord. When I get up, when I go to bed, and lately, for a year or so now, I have become aware that when I am with other people, at work, playing, resting, I am praying then too, because I am communicating with my brothers. (A 13)

> [I pray] to identify myself, to identify myself a little with him. Not just to repeat a prayer, but rather to identify with the model he is, with being Christian. Identifying with one another, we can help ourselves. (CR 222)

A neighbor in the barrio adds to this view a sharp rejection of conventional external signs of faith such as tracing a cross on the forehead to mark Ash Wednesday. In this woman's view, authenticity is much more demanding, and real conversion requires solidarity with others.

> What a farce, to go there and put on a nice face for others when nothing changes inside. To my mind, the issue isn't my conversion to God but rather my conversion to others. I am converted to the extent that I give myself to others. It's not just a matter of converting myself alone. That's too easy, too comforting. When I convert myself before God, it's him and me, just the two of us. We know what's going on, but then what happens to the commitment to others? That's harder, a lot more demanding; that kind of commitment is much more far-reaching.

> To me, that's what conversion is all about. It's fine to convert yourself in repentance for having harmed your brother; offending your brother is like offending God, and all that. But the basic thing, what we need to see clearly, is that if we take no heed of others, if there is no love in what we do with others, then that will be the final judgment on us. (CR 326)

These comments exemplify the flavor of religious reform that is often associated with base communities. Members see themselves as having come, through participation in the groups, to a better and more authentic kind of religion. In their view, unnecessary or simply false accretions have been stripped away, leaving the true core of Christian belief and practice. This sense of purification emerges with particular clarity if we ask to whom people pray. The most notable area of change concerns the image and role of the saints.

A library of studies has addressed the importance of saints in the popular beliefs and practices of many religions.[22] In Christian tradition generally, and

---

[22] On the changing role and image of saints in European Christianity, see Victor Turner and

specifically in Latin America, saints have long been depicted as holy and powerful beings who can be influenced or persuaded to intercede in one's favor before God. This conventional portrait of the saints persists only in the most traditional communities. Residents there commonly stress the saints' powers and discuss their own ability to manipulate them through prayer, pilgrimages to specific shrines, or the performance of a devotion known to be pleasing to a given saint. These comments from a woman in San Isidro are representative: "God gave them the power to help us. We ask and they make God work miracles" (S 32).

But as a general matter, viewing the saints as lawyers or agents has fallen into disfavor and appears to be of dubious orthodoxy to most group members. Excessive attention to the saints is also felt to turn one's eyes away from God. One rural activist told me that "I used to make petitions to the saints, but then I saw that it was just a way of using 'pull' with God, that it was better to pray directly to Jesus" (C 71a). A woman from Meléndez concurred, noting that in any case, "lawyers are very expensive. If you talk with God, you don't need to pay" (CA 217). As prevailing views of the saints begin to change, traditional practices like pilgrimages or the making of specific promises (to bind saints to their word) have also lost popularity. Concern for orthodoxy and greater access to regular religious practice at home remove much of the clientele such devotions enjoyed. Why go to a distant shrine, incurring the costs of travel, lodging, fighting crowds, and running notable risks of robbery or accident when the same thing is now available close at hand? In Barrio Meléndez, for example, pilgrimages have clearly lost favor. Cali lies close to the well-known shrine of Our Lord of Miracles in Buga, which draws pilgrims from all over the south and west of the country. The following comment is representative of the Meléndez position:

Well, the truth is that I also used to like going there, but no more. For me that's over, it doesn't exist anymore. . . . Praying matters to me, being able to communicate with God, but I just can't see the sense of pilgrimages anymore because I know that God is everywhere, and that if I have faith, he will hear me no matter where I am. So I don't see the point, I just don't get it anymore. I used to like it, but now it seems absurd, medals and all that stuff. (CA 298)

Transformation of the common view of saints has been accompanied by intense devotion to Christ. The prevailing image of Jesus in popular discourse changes from passive sufferer/king on high to brother and guide. At the same time, frequent and regular Communion moves to the center of religious prac-

Edith Turner, *Image and Pilgrimage in Christian Culture*; Thomas Kselman, *Miracles and Prophecies in Nineteenth Century France*; and William Christian, *Local Religon in Sixteenth Century Spain*.

tice, further displacing local conventions like processions or the celebration of particular saints or feast days.[23]

These comments are not meant to suggest that saints have been abandoned or wholly removed from popular discourse. They remain but have been reconceived, appearing now as role models. In a more traditional variant of this position, some people cultivate devotion to specific saints because of parallels to their own lives. A case in point is this woman, who struggles to raise a family on her own after a bitter separation from her husband. "After God and the Holy Virgin" she told me she prays "to Saint Francis of Assisi and Mary Magdalene, because they were as fallen as I was" (C 83). To others, saints are just good people whose example teaches us how to live correctly. In this vein, one man from Agua Fría told me that "they cannot be powerful, because they are just apostles, like we can be" (A 89). His views are echoed first by a Venezuelan peasant, then by a woman from Cali.

So yes, there are saints, saints who were converted through their good works. And that is our goal, every person has a goal, and I tell you again, you come for your work to our communities, to our brothers. . . . You work according to your own image, from your community. You are sure that you are following a goal, searching for God. You go with God always, that is how life is, and so God is with you and that is what the saints were doing too. Many people became saints because of their good works, many. (V 129)

I respect them a lot, but there is no one I am particularly devoted to. To me they are people who managed to do something positive in their lives: I can do the same. Everything is according to its period. If they did to me what they did to Saint Teresa, I couldn't endure it. But really, they were people like me, they lived in a particular time and place, and perhaps with problems, and they were able to succeed. Well, can't I do it too? (CR 329)

From this vantage point, sainthood is not confined to a purely devotional ideal but is found in ordinary life. Anyone can become a saint, and in popular usage, the concept is often stretched well beyond the church's formal canon. In Cali, for example, one regularly finds homes and public transport plastered with decals of the Virgin Mary next to saints and portraits of Che Guevara, Camilo Torres, or perhaps John Kennedy. A resident of Barrio El Rodeo expressed her view of Mary and the saints as role models in the following terms:

I don't share the view of Mary as pure, puritanical, no. To me, she was a woman who was the mother of Christ, and who suffered like any mother, like any of our mothers who suffer so much every day—not that sanctified image. And I think the saints were just people who accomplished something important. Che could be

---

[23] Christian, *Local Religion*, pp. 175–208.

a saint, Camilo could be a saint, because they gave their lives for others, for the community, for the people's liberation. (CR 226)

Many accounts of popular religiosity pay special attention to beliefs about the dead, including spirits, ghosts, and apparitions. The matter is complex. When asked to define and discuss "popular religion," priests and pastoral agents commonly cite belief in spirits and a general cult of the dead as its most widespread and persistent manifestation. Cemeteries are crowded on All Saints Day, and clergy are regularly called upon for special prayers and devotions to the dead (see chap. 7). Direct questions about these phenomena typically meet with embarrassed and evasive responses from ordinary people. They know very well that conventional beliefs about spirits and apparitions are frowned upon in the orthodox circles to which they now belong. But belief persists anyway, and a common observation holds that "some people" (the elderly are usually cited) may still hold to that, "but not me." The following responses from Villanueva and Agua Fría come closer to the truth:

As for ghosts, let me say this—it's a superstition. I know they exist, but we're not supposed to believe that; it's just upsetting. Spirits are a different matter. Every person has a spirit, and we need to take care of that spirit, commission masses and things like that. It's okay to believe in those spirits. (V 126–27)

A little. As the saying goes, you're not supposed to believe in witches, but they fly anyway! (A 53)

Despite embarrassment, many individuals stubbornly maintain that they have had personal encounters with the supernatural. For example, a woman in Quebradanegra told me in all seriousness that "you can hear them, walking around, they don't let a person sleep. I believe in witches; they have played bad tricks on me. No spells, nothing like that, but they have stolen my underwear and replaced it with other people's. I asked around, and was told that it had to be a witch. Who knows what they were trying to do to me?" (Q 51). The dead are a constant and vivid presence in everyday life, as this experience (recounted by a schoolteacher from San Pedro) shows:

Yes, I for one have been scared by them. For example, once when a woman was dying, I was tremendously frightened. I was asleep, and I could feel someone climbing on me, someone icy cold who said to me, "Lola, I'm drowning, I'm drowning." So I lit some matches, and then I could see a small black shadow. The very next day that woman died, and they told me that she had been calling my name. Also, the day Padre Román died, the whole house was full of light. I think it was the flame from the altar candles—that was the light that filled the house. (C 48)

Unlike some of the beliefs and practices just discussed, holy water has a visible and legitimate place in ordinary church routines. Of course, water plays a major role in many cultures and religions. It is a common sign of life and is closely associated with healing. Shrines are typically located on the site of springs or wells, and the presence and use of water often accompanies reports of miracles and apparitions.[24] Water has a particularly central place in Catholic sacraments (such as baptism) and in ordinary church routines. The salient place that water holds in Christian imagery and practice draws on Jesus' well-known invitation, when

> on the last day of the feast, the great day, Jesus stood up and proclaimed, "If anyone thirst, let him come to me and drink. He who believes in me, as the scripture has said, 'Out of his heart shall flow rivers of living water.' " (John 7:37–38)

Popular recourse to holy water draws strength from all these elements and reaches well beyond the bounds of orthodoxy. Of all the practices commonly ascribed to "popular religion," extensive use of holy water is the most resistant to change, declining only in the most rigorously orthodox and Bible-centered groups, where, as we have seen, reading and common action tends to be stressed over ritual. For the Catholic church, holy water is technically a "sacramental," one of a group of items that, in the words of an old church manual, are "blessed or set aside by the Church for the purpose of exciting good thoughts or creating pious dispositions. . . . They do not possess any power in themselves. To hold that they do would be superstitious and idolatrous. They derive their efficacy from the fact that the Church blesses them and sets them aside as instruments capable of creating good thoughts and virtuous dispositions."[25] Despite these formal qualifications, ordinary people put holy water to a range of ritualistic, symbolic, and magical uses that together point to belief in the efficacy of the water itself to effect changes in behavior, to alter the odds in one's favor, and to manipulate the natural world in desired directions.

They regularly bring bottles and jugs of water to be blessed and then keep them at home for cases like the following: taking medicines with it to make them work better; keeping spouses faithful by sprinkling it on beds in the form of a cross; warding off spills, falls, spirits, witches, and bad luck in general by applying it regularly to corners, doorposts and gates of houses. One resident of Caparrapí reported asking the priest "to give me a little holy water to get rid of witches, because you know, even though I don't believe in them, it's a fact that they exist [que las hay las hay]. It also helps to undo spells" (C 71a). Another noted that although in her view holy water was effective in warding off evil, nonetheless, "I don't like to sprinkle it around in the house, because I am afraid to step on it" (C 55).

[24] Christian, *Local Religion*; Turner and Turner, *Image and Pilgrimage*; Obelkevich, *Religion and the People*; and Kselman, *Miracles*.

[25] See James E. McGavick, *Catholic Belief and Practice*, pp. 88–89. This manual was published in 1907.

The difficulties posed by popular reliance on holy water are evident in an encounter I witnessed while staying in the parish house of Caparrapí. After a meeting of the parish pastoral council, a small group of peasants arrived carrying several large jars of water. Their crops were being devastated by locusts, and they wanted to have the water blessed for later use in fighting off the danger. The general idea seemed to have been to sprinkle holy water on the crop as a charm. This request caused the young priests considerable anguish. They felt caught between their understanding that God does not violate natural law and their desire to avoid sending these men away empty-handed. Faced with a truly urgent request for support phrased in traditional religious terms, they opted for a predictable compromise: the water was blessed (making the petitioners happy), but the blessing was accompanied by a lecture about the true meaning of holy water.

The priests in Caparrapí felt weak when faced with this request. They were young and inexperienced, and suspected that their hold on popular loyalties was tenuous to begin with. In subsequent conversation, they contrasted their attitude with what they supposed Román Cortés would have said, which would have been to cut out the nonsense. The same response was found in the Jesuit parish of Cristo Rey in Barquisimeto. Residents there also put holy water to dubiously orthodox uses, and even though the priest was willing to accommodate a little, he drew the line.

> Around here, holy water is the remedy for everything, to bathe the eyes of a child born sick, to ward off spirits, and all the rest. Sometimes it's little more than witchcraft, but still you can't change that all of a sudden. Even so, sometimes they come after mass with big jars and jugs—at that point you've got to tell them no, that this is outrageous, it's wrong. (B 63)

There are suggestive parallels between the issue of holy water and evolving views about prayer and the saints. Refocusing prayer away from request and manipulation and toward community and mutual help pushes the center of religious sensibility away from individual gratification to life in common. In the same way, seeing the saints as role models rather than as lawyers or powerful intermediaries throws the burden of action back on individual and community, further enhancing the value and significance of one's own reason and one's own actions. In the process, magical practices and manipulations of the natural order are set aside. Just as all are equal before God, all are equal in nature. Further, nature itself is organized along rationally understandable lines. Interfering with these in a capricious or ad hoc way is fruitless, and the attempt itself is close to sacrilege. Locusts are unlikely to be kept away by holy water.

Concepts of death and the hereafter constitute our last indicator of "popular religion." Contrasts in the way religions prepare for and make sense of death provide a basis for strong differences in how they are lived. For example, unremitting emphasis on death's inevitability and imminence can lead to a stern and gloomy attitude focused on "getting right with God." On the other hand, religions can also stress ethical rules, and thus give more weight to living well over suffering and death. It is often said that Latin American Catholics have historically tended to worship either a baby Jesus or a crucified adult, thereby giving little stress either to life or to resurrection.[26] I found considerable and often startling variation.

Questions about what group members expect after death elicit responses ranging from conventional fears of condemnation and hopes for bodily resurrection in glory to concern for living as well as possible now and also for leaving something behind in the community. The contours of a conventional response are well illustrated by this woman from San Pedro, who said that "sometimes I fear that death is just nothing, just a complete disappearance of yourself. I get those doubts once in a while, but I'm more drawn and more fulfilled by the thought of finding myself face to face with Jesus" (C 48). Others cleave to religion and good behavior at least in part from fear of eternal condemnation. Retribution and ultimate judgment for one's acts are common themes when death is being talked about. This man from Agua Fría put it simply: "I guess salvation, what else is there to expect, other than going to hell. That would be bad" (A 89). A San Isidro woman concurred, stating that she wanted, above all, to be "granted a good death, not to be condemned, to present myself [clean] before the Lord, because you know we've got to pay for our sins" (S 32).

As these comments suggest, many come to the groups because they see participation as part of a general religious experience that insures salvation, or at least makes it possible. Less conventional responses underscore the value of continuing life (for example, in family and community) over death. A case in point comes in these comments by a man from Agua Fría. His words recall Salvadoran Archbishop Oscar Romero's well-known assertion that even if he was murdered, he would live on in the Salvadorean people.[27] To my query about death, this active and very orthodox man responded with hopes that his efforts would survive him.

> I ask God to have pity on me, on my spirit, and that what I have managed to sow with my witness, that after I die it may live on and continue and be fertile. (A 14)

[26] For example, John Mackay, *The Other Spanish Christ: A Study in the Spiritual History of Spain and South America*; and Claudio Veliz, *The Centralist Tradition of Latin America*, chap. 9.

[27] In an interivew with the Mexican newspaper *Excelsior* published two weeks before his murder, Romero stated that "I have frequently been threatened with death. I must say that, as a Christian, I do not believe in death but in the resurrection. If they kill me, I will rise again in the people of El Salvador. . . . A bishop will die, but the Church of God—the people—will never die." Cited in Sobrino, "A Theologian's View," pp. 50, 51. For other perspectives on Romero's life, see Berryman, *Religious Roots*; Brockman, *The Word Remains*; and Carrigan, *Salvador Witness*.

Most of those I interviewed distinguish clearly between salvation and condemnation. Heaven awaits the saved, hell is for the condemned. But not everyone concurs, and a substantial group of dissenters blurts out that although they are not sure what to expect, in no way do they believe in hell. No hell could be worse than the world they live in now. I heard this response most frequently in Cali, but it also appears scattered in all the groups. To be sure, such views can make death a release, as in the following comment from Barrio Meléndez: "I hope to rest in peace after all the tragedy this world causes. The heaven I see, that heaven is resting in peace from all these tragedies. . . . Hell is really in this world" (CA 222). As a rule, more radical conclusions prevail, as in the following comments by a neighbor and fellow group member who reserves particular scorn for the idea that devotion to the dead could make up for life's wrongs.

> I tell you sincerely that I don't think there can be any more hell than this world. That's right! What happens is that what you don't do right in this world, after death it amounts to nothing. I believe two things: that there is no more hell than this world, because in this world you live through everything; and that this business of arranging for masses and I don't know what—doing charity in the name of the dead. Hah! [a noise of scorn] If they didn't do it in life, much the less in death. So I ask you, what is the good of all that. I think that what you have to do, you have to do it in life. And you do it because it's right. You don't leave others to pay your debts. No! (CA 262–63)

This powerful rejection of conventional ideas about heaven, hell, and recompense needs to be put in context. The overall effect is similar to the changes in prayer and in the views of the saints noted earlier. Taking life as hell in the terms noted here removes fear from the center of spirituality, and thus frees members to concentrate on this life, to be confident that salvation is God's free gift. This position differs from traditional views that paint "this world" as a vale of tears to be endured (with resignation) until the moment of personal salvation. The commentary is much more bitter, and more decidedly sociological. These individuals are saying that day-to-day life in their communities is a living hell. Threats of hell therefore hold few terrors. They prefer to live as well as they can, not to avoid evil ends or condemnation but rather to express faith and solidarity with others.

## Conclusion

I began this chapter by stating that for religion to have a role in changing popular culture, religion itself had to change, not only in its relation to other institutions but also internally, through transformations in belief, practice, spirituality, and in the everyday life of individuals, organizations, and com-

munities. At this point, it is possible to begin identifying the common underpinnings of these changes, and to specify how they fit with one another. What
knits elements of Bible study, popular ecclesiology, links to the institutional
church, and evolving patterns of belief and practice together into coherent
packages?

Developing a sense of personal and community responsibility for action in
a rationally ordered world is of critical importance. Success in this effort turns
on the way individuals and groups see themselves in the process and on the
links they build to key institutions. Experience with participatory and egalitarian group life plays a key role here. By working together to understand religion and the world, and by acting together in ways that bridge the two, group
members assert themselves as capable, articulate, and confident men and
women. Whether the topic is Bible study, group process, or prayer, we come
back to if and how people see themselves as autonomous and capable actors,
and how they acquire confidence in the value of their own critical reason.
Weber's comments on the significance of congregational and ethical religion
are particularly relevant here.[28]

A congregational religion is what the name implies—a religion organized
in small, self-managed groups of believers where all presumably have equal
rights and capabilities. As Weber saw it, the viability of congregational forms
as they arose during the Protestant Reformation was strengthened by an
emerging religious discourse built around rationalized, ethical views of the
world. Congregational structures gave new weight and dignity to the views
and experiences of average members, who were enjoined to fuse religion with
daily life through continuous, self-moved ethical practice. In this context, the
term "ethical" does not imply that such beliefs are better or their holders more
virtuous than others. By reference to "ethical religion," Weber pointed to a
pattern of belief and practice whereby ordinary men and women were charged
with (or, more precisely, made themselves responsible for) following a common set of general ethical principles. If all believers have equal access to truth,
then all are responsible on their own for carrying out the divine guidelines
visible in the Bible, which all are expected to read. External interventions have
little place in this scheme of things. Magical practices and manipulations of
the natural order are also set aside. God enjoins the independent use of reason
and provides a natural world that is organized on rationally understandable
lines.

The resulting sense of independence and responsibility is at once individual
and collective. Each person is expected to order her or his behavior correctly,
according to God's will. The community provides a medium for discovering
that will in a common pursuit of edification. The groups provide spaces (literally and figuratively) where new religious sensibilities can be worked out.

---

[28] *Economy and Society*, 1:468–601.

Although clergy remain appreciated and often venerated teachers and leaders, their mystical and semisacred status as clerics is undercut. Through the community, members also create and nurture solidarity with one another, and bear witness to it in common actions. The rationalization of ethics is reinforced by the shift in religious sensibilities noted here, away from the conventions of "popular religion" (saints, pilgrimages, etc.) and toward a concentration on Bible study and the Eucharist. The long-term significance of the experiences reviewed in this chapter lies in how the setting, process, and content of religious change spur ordinary people to make explicit connections between personal life and collective condition, connections that let them see themselves as independent actors working in and on the world.

Whether or not change will get underway and exactly what paths it will follow are questions that cannot be answered with reference only to individuals, groups, or communities. The quality, direction, and durability of change at this level depend very much on how links to larger institutions are organized, legitimated, and used. Institutions that project a hierarchical and controlling image of the good group (and, by extension, the good member) strive to control group discourse, to keep their agents astride processes of leadership formation and selection, and in this way, to limit severely any possible religiocultural change, when they do not leave it strangled at birth. The experience of Facatativá suggests that groups of this kind are unlikely to be long-term sources of new leaders or of mobilizational energies that can spill over to other walks of life. Change is at best personal and confined to a local ambit. But with even a slight degree of institutional encouragement and openness, groups tend to flower, as they have in Agua Fría, filling the gap with voices hitherto silent and talents hitherto unrecognized. Given active backing for personal and group empowerment, the scale of action broadens, and the interconnections between religious change and social involvement are drawn more explicitly. Rural Venezuela and, in an organizationally weaker although rhetorically sharper fashion, urban Cali are cases in point.

Although explicitly political groups and actions (states, parties, strikes, even violence and revolutions) play only a minor role in the voices recorded here, politics involves more than is recognized in ordinary uses of the word. Politics is also played out in the construction of discourses and in ways of living together that provide a foundation for judging right and wrong and of standards for weighing legitimate and effective leadership. The transformation of popular images of self and community, and the attendant reworking of views on basic issues like activism, passivity, hierarchy, or equality, is an essential first step. Changing the theory and practice of ordinary life strengthens the impact institutions can have and makes changes in any aspect of life more meaningful and more likely to last.

In theoretical terms, the preceding observations require us to give greater weight to the conditions under which sociability begins and can be nurtured and, more broadly, to organizational mediations than to individual or group characteristics taken in isolation. It is the linkage that counts; controlling the linkage is critical to setting the course and general boundaries of future change. Religious change thus requires more than ideas alone. In any case, ideas never come in the abstract; they appear to particular people in specific historical and social circumstances. Ideas need audiences and mediators, groups of men and women who find the messages meaningful, work to diffuse them through time and space, and find the associated forms of practice logical in their own changing circumstances. Ideas and group structures evolve together; neither takes the lead. In his work on *Ideology and Utopia*, Mannheim put the matter of how change can begin and endure in particularly useful terms. In his view, individuals alone cannot turn utopian dreams into reality.

> Only when the utopian conception of the individual seizes upon currents already present in society and gives expression to them, when in this form it flows back into the outlook of the whole group and is translated into action by it, only then can the existing order be challenged by the striving for another order of existence.[29]

Mannheim's comment indicates that if we are to understand the possibilities for creating a popular subject in a thorough and systematic manner, detailed study of how the "outlook of the whole group" evolves and makes sense in context is indispensable. To this end, the next chapter looks in detail at changing personal and group experiences of poverty, gender, violence, and insecurity, considers popular self-images and prevailing explanations of poverty, and explores popular attitudes to the church and other major institutions.

[29] *Ideology and Utopia*, 207.

# SIX

## POPULAR NEEDS AND POPULAR IDEALS

THE PRECEDING chapter explored the origins and dynamics of change in religion, and pointed to possibilities and limitations for cultural and social change beginning in religion. Here I take up the other side of the coin, looking closely at the kinds of people making the changes and fitting them into their daily lives. As we listen to these men and women describe and comment on their experiences, needs, and evolving ideals, two themes will emerge and move to center stage. The first concerns the impact of poverty on personal and collective life. The second directs attention to popular notions of legitimacy, expressed most vividly here in discussions of what ideal members, leaders, and groups are like. These changing views about legitimacy serve as the basis for evolving popular critiques of church and clergy.

The men and women who join and participate in the groups discussed in this book are uniformly poor. Their youth and adult lives have been marked by scarcity and need. To be sure, they are not the very the poorest of the poor.[1] In the countryside, members are typically drawn from smallholding peasants and their families, with a smattering of local schoolteachers and tradespersons. City recruits come from the stable lower- and lower-middle classes: those with relatively secure jobs in commerce, public service, or industry. There are few migrant laborers, fewer residents of very new invasion barrios, and no one from the classic urban lumpen.

The poverty common to all these groups defines the way everyday life is organized and experienced and conditions how they see themselves as individuals and communities. In many ways, being poor mutes differences that otherwise set nations and communities apart: poor people have similar and urgent needs everywhere. But despite poverty's common features, the particularities of experience must be kept in focus. Poverty means different things and is associated with different obstacles and opportunities in Venezuela than in Colombia, in cities than in the countryside, among men and women. Seeing poverty through popular eyes lets us breathe life into the macroeconomic indexes so often tossed about in discussions of growth, debt, or programs for "development." Debates about the causes and nature of poverty are not confined to intellectuals or to the pages of learned journals. Poor people think a lot about

[1] Cf. Michael Lipton, *The Poor and the Poorest: Some Interim Findings*; Sheldon Annis and Peter Hakim, eds., *Direct to the Poor: Grass Roots Development in Latin America*; and Robert Wasserstrom, *Grass Roots Development in Latin America and the Caribbean: Oral Histories of Social Change*.

being poor and discuss it often among themselves in formal meetings and in occasional gatherings of family, friends, and neighbors. Listen to what being poor means.

## Being Poor

Poverty everywhere means scarcity, but what precisely is in short supply? The specific needs popular groups cite as most central fall into three overall categories. There are immediate material needs, including money and credit, better health, and access to benefits and services like water, education, and transport. Indirect, nonmaterial needs like fellowship, solidarity, and mutual support are also prominent, along with a general desire for sociability in the community. A final group of needs is best characterized as a need for legitimacy. I separate this from indirect needs as a whole because it is more general and because it expresses an evolving popular view of people who see themselves as entitled to better lives and in search of moral as well as material backing in the pursuit of that goal.

When poor people describe how poverty has shaped their lives, what emerges is not so much anger or class-related bitterness over having been shortchanged by poverty as sadness over the way poverty has truncated their lives, leaving them somehow less than they might otherwise be. Lack of education and persistent poor health are felt to be particularly crippling. Until recently, little formal schooling was available to the poor, especially in the countryside. One rarely encounters older rural people with more than two or three years of primary school. Poor diet, inadequate prenatal care, and an almost complete absence of nursing or medical attention have combined with unremitting hard physical labor to create a pattern of health problems ranging from anemia to arthritis, rotten teeth to hepatitis.[2] Infant mortality is high. One peasant from Agua Fría summed up the obstacles in his life in these terms:

> Not having been able to study. I would be better, more intelligent. Illness too, I have always been sick. I've always had problems. (A 12)

The needs and shortcomings manifest in personal and family life make sense when set in the context provided by economic opportunity and the nature of the communities where people grow up and make their lives. Apart from the differences outlined in chapters 3 and 4, above, communities also vary wideiy notably in terms of their openness to the outside world. Openness involves the extent to which residents live and work in the same way as their parents or grandparents. Openness is also defined in practice by the extent of

---

[2] For details see Berry, ''Rural Poverty''; and Vernon Childers, *Human Resources Development: Venezuela*.

residents' contact and interchange with individuals and groups from the outside and by the range of alternatives available to them on a regular basis. In these terms, the villages and *veredas* of Facatativá are relatively closed and isolated, and the *caseríos* of rural Venezuela have closer links with one another, while at the same time they enjoy greater access to the outside. The barrios of Cali and Barquisimeto are heterogeneous, not only in terms of the origins of residents but also in the alternatives they see before them. Let us take a closer look.

Most peasants in Facatativá live and work where they were born and brought up and do what their parents did. Like their mothers, women assume domestic responsibilities at a very young age, cooking, cleaning and caring for family members and often for livestock as well. They normally remain in parental households until marriage, after which they live with their husbands. Like their fathers, men begin agricultural work early, taking temporary breaks for military service or occasional stints as day laborers in harvest season. The scarcity of land often requires young men to pursue other trades, such as carpentry or general construction, barbering, or police work. But these are commonly seen as no more than temporary expedients, pauses to be endured before taking up the normal routine of peasant life. This man from San Isidro is typical. His primary work has been "in agriculture. I've also been a barber, a tailor and I've worked in construction. My parents always worked in agriculture" (S 67). Rural women report a much more limited range of employment. Apart from rare experiences in the cities as domestic servants (or, rarer still, as factory workers) most remain in the community all their lives, with only occasional trips outside.

A number of these women report going to considerable lengths in their pursuit of independence: eloping, marrying young, and in one case I encountered, joining a religious order to get away from oppressive and confining family circumstances. But these efforts rarely solve the problem: religious orders have their own noteworthy limitations, and marriage brings not freedom but simply a transfer of subordination to husband from parents. Women's lives thus remain confined by limited opportunity and subordination to men. This is reinforced by restricted access to education. Although the situation has improved in recent years, many women, above all those from an earlier generation, feel the lack of education with particular bitterness. The following comments (from San Isidro, Cali, and Río Frío, respectively) give a flavor of the situation.

> All my work is domestic. Since I got married, my jobs have been to cook, wash and iron, take care of the animals, cut sugar cane, help with the milling [of cane] and with the planting. Before marrying, I cooked for my brothers, and for my mother and father. Only after getting married have I managed to travel, once to Chiquinquirá [a well-known shrine]. Before then, I couldn't go anywhere because

my father hardly ever left the *vereda*, and everything had to be done with him. (S 29)

I only got through the fifth grade, because the idea then was that men could study, but women would later marry and have children, so why bother they said. We had to respect that, and so I was left with wishes for more study. So I started working, with nothing to do but think about them, about the house, and about my brothers. (CA 160–61)

The biggest problem here is that people don't value education. My sister Gladys and I wanted to continue our studies but they don't see the point. With children here it's the stick [beatings], nothing more. . . . Here people only care about working and making money, nothing else. Men say why go to school at all, if women are meant to marry and have babies, and men to handle a plow? (RF 62, 112)

Three important variations must be noted to this pattern whereby the sons and daughters of the poor follow the paths taken by their fathers and mothers. The first arises from the impact of The Violence on family life in rural Colombia. The second draws strength from the way outside groups or courses (often church-sponsored) provide new skills and perspectives, and thus facilitate a break with the patterns of the past. The third rests on the attraction of city life.

As we have seen, the decades following World War II brought massive violence to rural Colombia. By forcing many to flee their homes in search of security, The Violence broke traditional patterns of life and drove a generation of young peasants to make their way in the cities. Violence is more than a memory. The image and reality of violence continues to shape many poor people's view of the state, which they experience as powerful, overbearing, and given to physical abuse. Peasants feel the effects of state power not only as overt violence of the kinds cited here but also as a result of inequalities and patterns of economic control that leaves them with little room to maneuver between officially fixed prices, marketing regulations, and high prices for what they need to buy. In the cities, the violence that begins with the barrio invasions continues through disputes and confrontations over land titles, city services, taxes, unions, and the like.

Although official schooling remains scarce, costly, and often of low quality in Colombia, peasants have lately enjoyed growing access to alternative educational programs. These are provided by semiofficial entities like the Federation of Coffee Growers, by the National Apprenticeship Service (SENA), and by church-sponsored programs for adult education. Together these programs have facilitated adult literacy, trained cooperative organizers, diffused new agricultural techniques, and made a series of artisanal and mechanical skills available.[3] Apart from the specific subject matter each course imparts,

---

[3] I discuss one such program, Acción Cultural Popular, in *Religion and Politics in Latin Amer-*

these programs have broad social impact by drawing peasants out of their individual communities and thus reducing the isolation and distrust of outsiders common to much rural life. Two men from Caparrapí describe their experiences:

> I've done several: one on livestock at SENA, another on coffee processing machinery, that one by the Federation of Coffee Growers. Also a course on raising pigs, also from the Federation. (C 61)

> I never went to school [but] in Sutatenza, Boyacá, I did a four-month course for peasant leaders, there in the ACPO [Accíon Cultural Popular] institute. Then I worked for ACPO as a peasant organizer in six *veredas* in this region: in La Montaña, San Carlos, Taticito, San Pedro, Mesetas, and Loma de Aldana. I've also done five *cursillos de cristiandad*, four in Caparrapí and one in Facatativá itself. They were devoted above all to Christianity and base communities. (C 57)

Rural Venezuela is generally similar, although no continuing violence has impelled large numbers of people into or out of any particular region, at least in the modern period.[4] Overall educational levels are slightly higher, especially among younger people, although like Colombia, more remote Venezuelan settlements suffer from poor services of all kinds, education included. Most of the country people I interviewed in Venezuela also live and work where their parents did. One man describes his hometown and upbringing:

> Things are always in a critical state there. Everybody works hard but nobody has anything. People suffer a lot in those communities. . . . I never went to school. My mother taught me a little, and the rest I picked up along the way. There was an adult catechism course from El Hatillo [a seminary outside Caracas]. A local teacher organized a group, with classes, and I took the chance to join. We started an adult literacy program. That was the goal, and I also managed to catch a little education that way. (V 104, 109)

City life in both countries presents a sharp break from the rural norm of continuity. Almost none of the barrio residents interviewed for this study had family antecedents in the city. The sole exception I encountered in Cali was a young woman born in Barrio El Rodeo whose parents had been among the barrio's original invaders. Individual and family moves *to* the city were commonly followed by a series of moves *within* the city, until a stable location was found in Barrio Meléndez or Barrio El Rodeo. The personal and family history of migration and movement is similarly complex in urban Barquisimeto.

---

*ica*, chap. 7. See also David Clawson, ''Religious Allegiance and Economic Development in Rural Latin America.''

[4] Nineteenth-century civil wars spurred extensive internal migration. See my ''Venezuela'' for details and further references.

I pointed out earlier that establishing a barrio, making claims to land and housing, and actually moving in frequently entail extended, sometimes violent conflicts with public authorities. The two accounts that follow show the obvious pride of those who seized and held the barrio despite official attacks. The speakers go on to suggest how much the original invasion experience conditions subsequent community life. Invasions bring together a heterogeneous cast of characters, divided by background and occupation and united only by their common search for a cheap and secure place to live. In La Carucieña,

> what happened in this barrio was picturesque. This was invaded, it was an invasion barrio, we took this by force, like machos. We invaded these houses. [*Why?*] Because of needs, people here were desperate. I remember that I was living in Barrio Nuevo, and we heard that an invasion was going on in La Carucieña, we all jumped in, with our families and everything. I live over there in a house I have with my mother. And everything you see, for example especially around where the sisters live, all that was invaded, taken over. There was a lot of fighting; the Guard tried to throw us out. That would be in '79 or '78, around then. Yeah, people came here from all over, and that's why the barrio is so complicated, so difficult. Because there are all kinds of people here: good people who work hard, who study, but also bad people, people with vices and all sorts of problems. It's really a complex place, very complicated. (B 42)

> *Wasn't this a government project originally?*
>
> Yes, and we had signed up too. But when the lists came out, there were houses allocated to friends and relatives. The people from INAVI [National Housing Institute] were giving houses to their buddies and ignoring the poor, those who really needed help. That's the worst sin of all. And when people saw that even though they were on the list they would probably get nothing, in desperation they invaded. The houses were invaded, taken over by force. There was no sanitation, and people had to sleep on the floor—we spent a long time sleeping on the floor. You know, that's another thing that makes this barrio so interesting. The barrio has stayed more or less organized. There are lots of groups here, groups you can really count on. Experience has taught them that sometimes you've got to fight for things, fight for your rights. (B 43)

Recall that in Barrio El Rodeo it was only after numerous invasions and repeated pitched battles that residents were finally allowed to occupy the land and build their houses without challenge. It happened some time ago, but as this woman points out, people talk about it all the time.

> Nonetheless we heard about it, people told the story. About how they fought against the army, how they would sneak in to put up their shacks and at midnight the army would arrive and knock everything down, beat up everyone and throw them all in jail. So what people did was to organize things: while some slept,

others would stand guard. When the army started to arrive, they would wake everyone up. People grabbed whatever they could, threw it in a sack, and ran. . . . I've heard that the ones who actually did the invasion were the poorest, the lowest in all Cali. So you can guess what it must have been like, because this place drew everyone who had no place to live: the thieves, the drug addicts, all the pickpockets. There were also people who, even though they weren't like that, still had no place to live because they had maybe four or five children, and you know how it is, when you've got kids, no one wants you anywhere. The result of all that is that here we've got a little bit of everything. (CR 146–47)

These accounts suggest how complex the social landscape feels to barrio dwellers, especially at first. Residents come from very diverse areas, social conditions, and racial backgrounds. They often have more formal schooling than their rural cousins and have access to a much wider range of occupations. The jobs reported by urban group members include shoemaker, policeman, bus or taxi driver, operator of an independent petty commercial enterprise (e.g., street vending or running a food stall) domestic, carpenter, jeweler, engineer's assistant, bill collector, security guard, messenger, factory worker, and student. As in the country, the range is smaller for women: most are full-time housewives, although a number combine caring for husbands and family with work in small businesses like vending, food service, or such typically female roles as sewing or taking in laundry. There were also a few full-time students and one former nun now working as a teacher.

The diversity of urban life puts church-sponsored groups in quite a different light in the barrios than in the countryside. Potential members get home late from work. The very diversity of their employment means that problems do not necessarily mesh very well among neighbors. This makes it hard to transfer messages and norms effectively from work to neighborhood and church. Religious groups must also compete with others. In each of the barrios I visited in Cali and Barquisimeto, I found a wide range of alternatives competing for popular attention: not only access to mass media and to entertainment like the dance halls of Barrio Meléndez, but also faith healers, spiritists, storefront Protestant churches, political groups, and incipient unions, along with a host of general and specific neighborhood associations. There may also be competition among specifically Catholic groups, for example, between charismatics and base communities.

All this is difficult to imagine in the countryside, where something like a funnel effect operates, driving potential members to church groups in a logical and seemingly inexorable way. There are few alternatives to begin with, and those that do come on the scene typically lack the aura of trust which surrounds religiously inspired organizations, making them seem like a good bet to local residents. One woman from near Caparrapí put it succinctly. "If the church can't do something," she told me, "it probably can't be done at all" (C 79).

A man from a particularly remote *vereda* in the same parish described his own progression through available organizations in the following representative terms:

> Well, first I worked mostly with the Federation of Coffee Growers, but that lost strength, and I saw that the base community would be better, because of its religious ties, that's what our parents taught us. Padre Román founded the group; before that we didn't know anything about it. (C 62)

These comments point to a process whereby the church assumes a primary role as mediator for rural organization. Conventions of religiosity and deference to clergy combine with an absence of alternatives to reinforce the funnel effect noted here. There are clear and sometimes unintended consequences. For example, rural base communities often end up quite heterogeneous. Many residents will join *any* church-related group because they anticipate it will stress spirituality, enhance devotions, and thus help them pursue the "right" things. Such individuals may then find themselves side by side with others attracted by an organization's specific social or economic agenda or by the chance it offers for effective participation in community affairs.

Heterogeneity means something different in the barrios, where groups like base communities are under pressure to respond to the range of experiences and needs of their clientele. There is no funnel effect; members cannot simply be expected to arrive because it is the church that invites them. To find and hold members, urban groups (like all others) have to offer ideological and physical space (legitimacy and an actual place to meet) along with specific, concrete means of assistance. Of course, the matter is not limited to cities, but it does appear in sharper outline there, as this comment from a young activist in Barrio El Rodeo indicates:

> To me it's clear that being Christian isn't just a matter of believing in a God up in the skies, or going to church once a week. It's also not just being good, respecting others, and having that kind of bourgeois morality that goes on and on about respecting the family. None of that. To me, being really Christian means being really committed, ready to fight in any way necessary for the welfare of all. . . . Being Christian is also urging people to fight for what's theirs. Later you can be calm and think about saving your soul. To me, that's secondary, it comes after. (CR 215)

In sum, heterogeneity means that groups commonly draw a clientele with mixed motives. Alongside those attracted by economic or social programs, or by the general sense of protection and legitimacy that membership sometimes provides, are many whose agenda is primarily set in terms of piety or morals conventionally understood. When members point to the evils groups encounter and specify the needs to which they respond, it is therefore not surprising to find stress on moral decay (presumably combated through religion and "good behavior") in a prominent place. Concerns of this kind were particularly evident in places like Tabio, Río Frío, San Isidro, or Caparrapí, where commentary on local problems often stresses uncontrolled sexuality, immoral behavior, and a growing youthful indiscipline.

Members perceive an overall moral decline, and many pronounce themselves unhappy with changes in the church. Like this woman from Tabio, some believe that the old ways were better. "Sure," she told me, "there's more participation now, but there's also less piety. There was more piety before, and more respect too. Families need piety. You know, when I was young they used to treat us hard in school. We had to kneel and beg forgiveness for the slightest infraction. It was tough then, but I think it was better for us" (R 128). A man from Río Frío echoed these sentiments:

> Here we live under a small sky. But even so, morals are being lost, parents are not giving religion to their children. In the past, schoolkids here would line up every month to go to mass, but not anymore. That gentleman [the priest], you know the priest is part of the government; whenever we talk about government, the church is always there. I think he acted badly in this, because those kids wanted to go to mass every month. (RF 104)

According to this young female schoolteacher from rural Caparrapí, most problems in her community were caused by

> sex, an overwhelming sexuality everywhere, and libertine ways of living which leave women with no dignity at all. You know, in this world women have got to be more careful than men. But today's young people lack all purity and innocence. You see twelve-year-old girls walking around with their [birth control] pills. Drunkenness and drugs are also serious problems. Here we gets lots of drunkenness, but thank God we still don't see much of marijuana or drugs. (C 46)

Participation in group activities offers men and women with these views a chance to make a stand for moral improvement, or at least to stem the tide of decay. From their vantage point, inadequate religious education, general indiscipline, and deficient piety together constitute the root cause of the general immorality underlying all community and national problems. Thus, "In spiritual terms, we're very fallen here. Hardly anyone attends mass anymore, and spiritual life is ignored. All this comes from the lack of Christian instruction, of moral values in the home. If children don't get good examples at home, they become nothing. They're caught up in the very same vices that are doing us in" (C 70).

Concerns about moral decay and decline are also voiced in rural Venezuela, but matters are posed and resolved quite differently in this case. To the original members of the Legion of Mary, the group's explicitly religious character provided guarantees of honorability, making trust possible among people otherwise unknown to one another. This initial foundation for solidarity then served as a basis for developing capabilities for joint action in spheres other than the religious. As one peasant leader put it, from the beginning, Padre Vicente "got us to pray and get closer to God. He also helped us organize" (V 30). The men and women first recruited by Vicente now hold leadership positions in a number of groups throughout the region, and their presence serves members as a guarantee of reliability and moral uprightness.

Because participants see one another as free of vices, they can work together without fear of being swindled or left in the lurch. The individual just cited went on to state that as far as he was concerned, "a person who lives according to Christ's teaching makes no problems for society. So indirectly, he's collaborating in the life of society, showing the others the path to follow. He can do a lot that way" (V 32). A companion put the matter in the now familiar terms of what it means to "be church":

> Whenever we've talked about that, about separating social things, things that aren't the church's business, we've said that if we as church in fact have got a few things clear, for example, like you've got to act on social questions, well then as church, we also have to take actions. We've got to serve as a light for what we do, and that's promotion of the community. You know, if you consider everything we have, body and soul together, and then you say that the church should dedicate itself only to preaching salvation of the soul, then the question is this. When you come to social issues, should we then leave them in the hands of people who have no faith at all, no notion of how to act? (V 96)

When I asked respondents to discuss any major obstacles or disappointments they had experienced, they gave answers that ranged widely from lack of money or a steady job to the inability to find a marriage partner or to build a house of one's own. As suggested earlier, problems of health and inadequate education are uppermost in ordinary people's catalog of difficulties. Popular concern over health and vulnerability to illness is underscored by the frequency of youthful death. A high proportion of the rural people I interviewed had lost at least one child to illness. Children and adults also suffer from lingering illnesses such as intestinal worms, hepatitis, arthritis, or dental problems. Failing health is a personal and economic disaster for poor people. In more isolated rural communities, the only way to get help for a seriously ill resident is to fashion a litter, carry the patient to the nearest road, and hope that some transport (a bus or truck) appears without too much delay. The common outcome can easily be imagined. The following comment by a man from Agua Fría sums up many of the obstacles rural people experience:

> When you're born poor, it's nothing but obstacles. Poverty makes it that way. For example, I had an obstacle which was the death of my nine-year-old boy. He died about seven years ago. I managed to get him to Villeta [site of the regional hospital] and he died. He really liked to study. (A 63)

The limited availability of schooling makes education all the more valued. Poor people eagerly take advantage of opportunities for study that present themselves. Rural life raises a number of barriers to regular study: electric service is rare, lanterns or flashlights can be expensive to use, and candles are hard on the eyes. It isn't easy, particularly for adults, who are tired after a long day's work and find study difficult. Most people just turn in early. One young woman explains that in San Isidro the community established a small lending library.

> Right now it's in the treasurer's house; we have reading and study sessions there. There used to be a lending fee (six pesos per book) but that didn't work out; no one borrowed books. You see, country people are used to working so hard that when they do get home, they just go to sleep, nothing else. (S 17)

Although education is theoretically more available in the city, as a practical matter, many obstacles must still be overcome. Especially in Colombia, schools are few, fees are high, and there are never enough spaces to go around. One woman in Barrio Meléndez told me that she and her husband had managed to scrape together enough money to put their five children through secondary school only after considerable difficulties. In any event, access alone does not solve the problems education presents. Once children are in school, parents and children encounter scarce resources, unresponsive administrators, and teachers who often brutalize students. Beatings are common, and are resented bitterly.

Economic needs combine specifics like wages and access to housing or land with a general sense of powerlessness and vulnerability. Barrio dwellers mostly depend on selling their labor, and without organization or a vigorous union movement, they find themselves in a weak position. The high cost of living is the most frequently cited difficulty: things cost more every day, and incomes never rise fast enough to keep pace. One representative peasant view (from Agua Fría) points to "the cost of living, that's the worst thing, that's what keeps us down. Because everything we sell is cheap, and there are no takers. But what we need to buy, all that has a fixed price, and it's high" (A 59). Even though prices for their cash crops (like coffee) are set by the state, the market for required inputs (and needed consumer goods) is unregulated. A neighbor also cited the high cost of living in a Colombian variant of "the rich get richer and the poor get poorer":

> Of course it affects us because we're poor. Everything is controlled at the national level and we get screwed. Our products are worth nothing, what we buy is sky-high. You've got to accept the price buyers impose; no bargaining is possible for what we need to buy. (A 67)

Vulnerability and a sense of powerlessness also run through popular discussions of violence and insecurity. Insecurity is manifest especially in fear of the police and army and in a general resentment of the way rich and powerful people treat the poor. Long experience of violence and intimidation explains why peasants in both Caparrapí and Villanueva fled at their first encounter with Román Cortés and Vincent Arthur, for fear that each might be a *guerrillero* in disguise. Violence remains endemic around Caparrapí, and it is common to find men and women with nervous tics, bad dreams, and a pervasive fear of strangers. A brief account of life in the hamlet of San Pedro illustrates what violence can mean in day-to-day life.

San Pedro can be reached (in good weather) only after a difficult two-hour trip on one of the jeeps or trucks that leave the center of Caparrapí once a day. About seventy farming families live here. There is a small and poorly staffed school, but no regular water, light, or health services. San Pedro is officially classified as a police inspection station. Approximately 40 police, 150 soldiers, and a handful of officers are permanently garrisoned there. Residents are thus outnumbered by security forces, and feel the pressure. Soldiers keep tabs on individuals and groups. They regularly harass those at meetings and confiscate "subversive" materials. The garrison also blocks roads with little or no notice, in effect barring all travel into, out of, or through the area. As one man points out, this makes everything harder.

> Our main problem is that we are isolated from God's word. Right now we're sinking because we can't meet at all. When the armed forces see a meeting, they think it's all communism. We need some guidance. Sure, the priests and the sisters have helped. At least they opened the door for us, even a little bit. Before, we had nothing at all. (C 52)

As his comments suggest, even efforts by the diocese have been truncated by military review and control. Priests, sisters, and pastoral agents all report harassment and repeated confiscation of papers, books, and audio material. As a rule, outsiders are automatically suspect here; when they come asking questions, they are targets for expulsion. My assistant was warned by the lieutenant to leave San Pedro itself on short notice. I was personally interrogated at length by one military patrol, and released only with great reluctance, despite letters of presentation I carried from the diocese.

In a place like San Pedro, it is at best very difficult to establish a presence and work with groups. Without the limited protection official church sponsorship can give, it is impossible. One independent priest dedicated to "immersion" in the world of the poor tried living for a while in San Pedro. He rented a small house, worked as a laborer, and set about getting to know local families in an informal way. After a year or so, he began organizing small communities of young men, who lived and worked together, sharing religious reflection and social action. He was quickly denounced to civil, military, and church authorities. Román Cortés, who was then parish priest in Caparrapí, refused to defend him, and he was forced to leave the area, eventually relocating in Quebradanegra, where I interviewed him. In his words,

> Rumors started going around, about how the community was a front for the guerrillas, how we were really their agents. Our meetings were watched, and difficulties began. At that time there were (and there still are) lots of police—more than forty—in the town. I ask you, what are forty police going to do in a place like San Pedro? As you can well imagine, there were all kinds of abuses: insults, sexual assaults, public drunkenness. Sometimes they would just run around shooting in the air like crazies. I felt that I had to confront the situation, and it was after my meeting with the lieutenant that the problems really escalated. I began getting death threats, and so did the people working with me. I concluded that it was wrong for me to put them in danger, and so I advised them to go back to their homes. (C 36)

Cases of this kind are extreme but not uncommon. Activist groups throughout Colombia (like those elsewhere in Latin America) are very likely to draw the fire (often literally) of army and police. A long-time resident of San Pedro summed up how the world looks when seen from that small and suffering town by telling me, simply, that "from what I've seen, the rule is to kick the guy who's down" (C 71).

## Fellowship, Sociability, and Self-Image

Apart from the spiritual nourishment and direct social or economic benefits group participation brings, members greatly prize the simple fact of being able to get together regularly and meet new people. Groups fill a need for fellowship and sociability that is hard to satisfy, especially in the countryside, where impediments to travel are magnified by a long-standing suspicion of outsiders. Membership in groups makes it possible and legitimate to reach beyond the confines of family and locality. According to this young man from Agua Fría, "you know, man can't live alone. We're meant to live in community; alone it's hard" (A 75). He went on to tell me that in his life,

> maybe the biggest satisfaction of all has been the chance to share experiences and acquire new ones with my neighbors. That comes through the base community. (A 82)

One of the major impacts group formation can have is to establish traditions of sociability and to make the idea of forming groups (for any purpose) both legitimate and familiar.[5] Bear in mind that most of the communities reviewed in this study have only limited historical depth. I have already discussed the

---

[5] I return to this theme in more detail in chapters 9 and 10, below.

origins of barrios like Meléndez, El Rodeo, or La Carucieña. Despite their long history as urban foundations, Cali and Barquisimeto have both grown so spectacularly in the postwar period as to be for all practical purposes new. Immigration and land invasions have spurred a vast expansion of the urban popular sector in each city, as it has throughout Latin America. Many of the rural settlements we have examined are also relatively new, taking off only with the development of a market for coffee in the mid- to late-nineteenth century.[6]

This means that it is rare to find much in the way of established patterns of sociability on which current efforts can build. Traditional gatherings of the kind reported by Eugen Weber or Maurice Agulhon in their work on patterns of change in nineteenth-century rural France are absent here. There is no counterpart here to the rural *veillées* discussed by Weber, or to the *chambrées* that, according to Maurice Agulhon, laid a foundation for acceptance of democratic norms coming from the society at large.

> On the eve of 1848 *the spirit of democracy*, whether immanent or latent, was probably more important than the impact of democratic *ideas* from the *direct* influence of the ''enlightened'' minds of the village. But no less fundamental, even if less clearly detected, was the receptiveness that the *chambrées* showed—once again for structural reasons—to bourgeois influences both in the form of ideas and of modes of behaviour.[7]

Making friends, sharing experiences, and simply getting together on a regular basis clearly further a general growth in sociability, whose effects are widely believed to extend from person and community to family relations. Wives and husbands independently told me that participation in the group had helped improve family relations. There was greater respect and trust among spouses, less blatant machismo. A woman from Barrio Meléndez told me that ''it was hard at first, because my husband was against it. He thought it meant that I would ignore my household obligations. Or sometimes he would come home from work with a headache and complain that it was 'all because you're going there'! But now it's better, everyone understands, and even the kids help out'' (CA 255). A young woman from San Isidro put it simply, arguing that

> yes, there's more comprehension, and it's because of the meetings. There is greater love, greater integration, and more participation. I personally have become much more active, and I have more relations with others. I'm closer to people. We owe all this to the meetings. (S 17)

---

[6] On the social history of coffee, see Charles Bergquist, *Coffee and Conflict in Colombia*; Palacios, *Coffee in Colombia*; and Roseberry, *Coffee and Capitalism*.
[7] *The Republic in the Village*, p. 150.

I asked members to identify major national problems, and to describe their impact on the everyday life of people like themselves. Some found the effort too much to handle, like this man from Río Frío who told me that "there are lots of national problems, international too. But you can't pay too much attention to all that; you'll lose all hope. It's hard enough dealing with what we have around us" (RF 128). But many pointed to the way national institutions in culture and politics set up controlling expectations about leadership and good or proper behavior. Communities like their own drew inspiration from such sources, often with disastrous consequences. The example of corrupt or self-interested leaders reinforces selfishness and egoism that undermine efforts at collective action. The link between national models and local difficulties was stated explicitly by this Agua Fría man:

> Insecurity and the immorality of high government officials. Of course it affects us, because we are forming a community, and we have to pay attention to the examples we get. If the government is immoral, what can you expect from those down below? (A 52)

How can the powerless find and use effective tools for personal and community improvement? Under what circumstances can churches or the groups they sponsor help ordinary people craft a new self-image that breaks established cycles of isolation and despair? I have argued throughout that the potential which base communities and similar groups carry for change is best expressed where democratic norms, egalitarian participation, and group autonomy are put into practice. Ideals of equality are not enough. Words must be accompanied by visible and effective efforts to empower ordinary people in everything they do. But supposing that the point is granted, a prior question remains to be answered: *What makes ordinary people regard churches as reliable allies in the first place?*

Belief in God and in the church's legitimacy as a medium for salvation are important but insufficient by themselves as a basis for expecting help in this life. The initial grant of legitimacy given to the church (and, by extension, to groups it sponsors) is conditioned on popular belief that the church itself has broken traditional ties to the wealthy and powerful and to other dominant institutions like the state or armed forces. Only when such links are visibly replaced by trust in ordinary people, and when that trust is backed up by specific measures to legitimize and empower them, can the process of change traced out here get underway and have a chance to flower.

To understand better how perceived needs and experiences are tied to views about the general position of the church as an institution, I asked group members to comment on the idea of a "preferential option for the poor" and to discuss the role priests and sisters ought to assume in dealing with social problems. As we have seen, the phrase is well known. Reference to the "preferential option for the poor'' is commonly made in church documents, pamphlets, and group discussions. What do group members think of all this?

To my surprise, queries on Puebla drew a complete blank in several rural Colombian communities. Many knew nothing at all about it, like this woman from San Isidro who replied ''I've never heard anyone speak of Puebla. I don't know what it can be.'' Lacking details, but not wanting to be impolite, she fell back on convention for an answer, and told me that of course, ''it's important for the church to give preference to the poor, so that they can be taught about God's grace, get baptized and married'' (S 25–26). Others had attempted to read the Puebla documents, but found them tough going. The following comments by this relatively well educated man from Tabio reinforce the point made earlier, that people in church-related groups rarely read theological texts or church documents. What they read (if anything) is the Bible.

> The diocese of Facatativá tried to get us all involved with reading Puebla. So what happened? We began enthusiastically, ready to study and learn, but soon we let it drop. I'll tell you something: Puebla is written in a language that ordinary people just can't follow. At our meetings the priest was the only one who understood anything. It's funny. Christ's words are understandable, but it seems like that his successors have raised things to a level where no one can make any sense of what they say.
>
> I don't know, it's awfully hard to read. Here in the *comunidad* we tried to read Puebla; we even tried using a dictionary! Five meetings, but then no more. Because they were not speaking to us in Spanish. They used a very abstract, high-flown language. And that's supposed to be for peasants? Impossible! (RF 69)

Definitions of the ''option for the poor'' often hinge on figuring out exactly who the poor are and identifying the central aspect of their condition. Distinctions are often drawn between the spiritually and materially poor.[8] In more controlled and conventionally pietistic communities, a substantial number of respondents identified the poor spoken of at Puebla as the poor in spirit. Differences between rich and poor are acknowledged, but issues of social class are not thought to address the heart of the matter. All have urgent spiritual needs, and the proper role of the church is therefore to provide a message of salvation and moral instruction, along with material aid if possible. Two young group members comment: first a man from Quebradanegra, then a woman from Tabio.

> Well, really I would say that when you really talk about the poor, the truth is that lots of times a person can be rich but still poor in spirit. Or he can be poor materially and rich in spiritual terms. You've got to think about both kinds of poverty, and see the poverty each one can have. If someone is poor in goods, you try helping him out with what he needs. The same holds on the spiritual side, you've

[8] See chapter 9, below, for details.

got to search for spiritual riches. So I think Puebla is right to prefer the poor. (Q 120–21)

I agree completely, they should be the first! Someone who is materially rich is poor in spirit. You've got to give poor people spiritual wealth so that they can understand their situation. (RF 93)

These statements reveal more than a simple desire for greater emphasis on prayer and religious practice. They also reflect a belief that the root cause of poverty is less economic than cultural. In this light, material scarcity is not as problematic as the way available resources are used. Having more is not enough, because without some change in values (spiritual life), more will just mean more of the same. The solution lies in drinking less, treating spouses and families better, learning to read and write, and caring about the community—not just in having more. A young San Isidro woman put it this way:

Around here, lots of people are rich in land and cattle, but they never think about how they look, about fixing up their houses. There are others who have nothing, but who still try to live better. A person feels better that way. What's the point of having land and cattle and not living well? (S 3)

Underlying this position is an image of the world where poverty appears as simply a fact of life, a parameter that is unlikely to change or be changed. Social relations thus become natural facts, and the inevitability of poverty is reinforced by self-images that stress powerlessness, victimization, and disunity as normal attributes of poor people.[9] In communities like Quebradanegra or Río Frío, if one probes in conversation for why groups do not make more of a difference in local conditions or asks why it is so hard to convert religious membership into lasting socioeconomic cooperation, factors like egoism, gossip, and envy come up repeatedly.

To be sure, gossip and envy are the stuff of legend in small-town life. But more is at issue here. Among Colombian groups (both rural and urban), members believe that as overall levels of living rise, interest in collective efforts at material or spiritual improvement decline. Economic progress makes people selfish and self-satisfied, and thus bleeds commitment and energies away from community life.[10]

Envy and gossip also undermine efforts to get ahead in the first place. One older woman from Quebradanegra argued that in her town not even charity would work, because donors and recipients were both riven by jealousy. Her words are shot through with envy, jealousy, and discontent.

---

[9] Cf. Scott, *Weapons*; and also Jennifer Hochschild, *What's Fair? American Beliefs about Distributive Justice*.

[10] Cf. Daniel Goldrich, "Political Organization and the Politicization of the Poblador."

You know I'm not going to sanctify myself, I won't tell you that I am particularly charitable, or, how can I put it? That I have no faults, that I'm perfect just as I am. No! But I don't understand why people can't deal with each other, can't look out for one another. . . . It's like one time when we were to go and visit so and so. Well, then, yes sir, with pleasure, and we'll hold the meeting there too. But right away, someone complains that the meeting was supposed to be at her house, and another the same, and so it goes. It's the same with the collection in church. I put my five pesos in gladly, but then it turns out that others give only fifty cents or a peso. I never fail in these things, I never fail, but I do get disheartened when I'm the one who has to do everything.

You can see how poor this community is; nobody has very much, right? We're all suffering from poverty. But still some give and others don't. How can that be right? No sir, that means letting everything depend on just a few people. What I say is that in any case I always do my duty, just as I do my duty when I throw in five pesos and others give only fifty cents. (Q 25–26)

In these references to egoism and disunity as elements keeping the poor down, my examples have come entirely from Colombia. That is where I encountered them. I frankly am not sure why Colombians see these traits among themselves more than their Venezuelan neighbors do. But I suspect that such self-images have something to do with the overall weakness of class organizations and the absence of class-based discourse in national life. These structural conditions and prevailing cultural norms also make Colombian groups of all kinds (rural and urban alike) exceptionally sensitive to the orientations pastoral agents bring to the community and vulnerable to abandonment.

Even a casual glance at the terminology commonly used to describe self and community underscores the point. Vocabularies of class appear with regularity only in the cities, where, as we shall see, reference to workers, proletarians, and bourgeoisie is common. Rural Colombians typically describe themselves as "poor peasants" (*el pobre campesino*). The modifier is always used, with the word *poor* denoting not so much scarcity as vulnerability and a likelihood of victimization. The contrast to Venezuela is striking. Peasants in the communities around Villanueva describe themselves as "workers" (*trabajadores*) or, more commonly, as "coffee growers" (*caficultores*), thus underscoring their own productive role and highlighting an image of themselves as active elements in a larger net of relations. Independence and self-reliance are the common watchwords here. Group members are ready and willing to work together but expect few favors and want no charity. This spirit flavors attitudes to Puebla, as in the case of this young man from the remote *caserío* of El Palmarito:

I don't think the church needs to do anything special for the poor. Why should it? We all have the right to work and to achieve, to resolve our own everyday problems. The notion that just because I'm poor, I'll spend all my time in church, with the priest, or that he'll give me handouts that he won't give to others, that's not right. You end up like a parasite. (V 153)

If we compare the images presented in this chapter with the national and local patterns presented earlier, a few important configurations stand out clearly. Colombians are poorer and generally less well organized than are their Venezuelan counterparts. The same kinds of needs are present across the board, but in Colombia they typically appear in sharper terms and come more edged with violence. The organizational models Colombians draw from dominant national institutions are more authoritarian and hierarchical, just as the alternatives presented to them are commonly more radical than in Venezuela. Further, in all cases, women's experience of poverty differs from men's in ways that make group life particularly attractive to women. Because religion is generally regarded as legitimate for women, they find it easier to legitimize and sustain involvement in religious groups than in other kinds of organizations.[11] Groups also offer women opportunities that are otherwise not available, including education and the chance to reach beyond the confines of home, neighborhood, or community.

The heterogeneity common to all groups has different implications in rural and urban areas. The funnel effect noted earlier means that rural groups cast an especially broad net, attracting a membership whose interests range between poles of spiritual self-improvement to social activism. Heterogeneity in the barrios arises from the origins of the communities themselves (migration and invasion) and the dispersed nature of work and residence in the city. This means that even though rural populations are more homogeneous in terms of ordinary demographic traits, groups in the countryside are in fact likely to be more heterogeneous than those in the cities.

The images of self and world that characterize each of the communities studied here are not static. They vary in response to prevailing experiences in work and community and also according to the character of each group's image of the church and the specific pastoral agents it has encountered. The next section asks how popular groups see these men and women, and what they expect from them and from the church generally.

## Images of Church and Clergy

The concept of "being church" carries with it an implicit claim to take the measure of the existing church, and to evaluate the attitudes and practices of clergy, sisters, and pastoral agents associated with it. The shift is typically

[11] See Carol Drogus, "Reconstructing the Feminine: Women in São Paulo's Base CEBs"; Teresa Caldeira, *A política dos outros: O cotidiano dos moradores da periferia e o que pensam do poder e dos poderosos*; and Jane Jacquette, ed., *The Women's Movement in Latin America*.

seen not as a challenge to the special sacramental role of clergy, but rather as a reaffirmation of primitive Christian values and an extension of rough principles of equality throughout life.

The matter is complex, because popular views of the church combine stress on participation, equality, and responsibility (as in "we are all church") with a clear appreciation of the church as a separate set of powerful institutions. The material and symbolic resources at its command may or may not be put to the service of popular groups. Even where the institutional church does not have such resources in its own name, it may nonetheless control access to valued help from national and international sources. Not surprisingly, attention to this aspect of the church is especially pronounced in Colombia, where ecclesiastical structures have long had a visible and often dominant role. References to the institutional church were less frequent in Venezuela, where the church's overall presence in society and culture is weak. Comment here tended to center on "the church" as practiced and lived locally.

When popular groups in Colombia point to the failure of key institutions to provide adequate schools, health care, and employment, they do not exempt the church from these critiques. For centuries, ecclesiastical institutions were an integral part of the established system of power and did little to help ordinary people. The pastor was not a good shepherd; his flock was too often left to fend for itself. As this man from Caparrapí suggests, the impact of older stances and alliances is still felt today.

> Yes, things were different when I was young. Now there is more freedom; before we weren't even allowed to read the Bible. That's why we often say that today we are still behind, because even the church denied us a chance to learn. (C 53)

The perceived power of the church leads many to look for protection and for concrete expressions of support from its leaders and agents. Traditional images of the church as an alternate government (one of the "two swords" of medieval political theory) remain vivid for many ordinary people. Thus, a man from Agua Fría told me that he expected the church to make a contribution "through its own autonomy and also by advising others, because it is one of the chief figures in the state. There are two governments, civil and ecclesiastical." He then praised the church for its defense of the powerless.

> What I've heard is more or less that the ecclesiastical government has attacked the civil government for not treating people right, and has served as intermediary [for them]. (A 52, 53)

Popular commentary falls into a recognizable pattern after a while. The institutional church is seen to be powerful, historically allied with dominant classes and with the state, and slowly (too slowly) changing in ways that favor the poor. With rare exceptions, the church and its agents are viewed as trustworthy, certainly more so than government or political parties. Agents of the church are also widely regarded as honest, and therefore much less likely to swindle or cheat the poor. Here is the view of one woman from the area around Caparrapí. She had been complaining to me about the lack of services, especially from public schoolteachers who are paid but never show up.

> To me, the church is stronger than any government or any army. Wherever the church sets itself to resolving problems, progress is made. Like in Caparrapí, where the church has worked so hard, and you can see real advances. . . . You know, when the church picks people and prepares them to do a job, they are really careful about it, and they make sure the job gets done. But not the state or the government. Take the case of teachers. If the government would only give a little more care to how it trains teachers, none of this would happen. In contrast, you can depend on the church. The priests always find a way to come, even with mud or bad weather. . . . What's more, if the church sends out someone and they screw up, do a bad job, then at least with the church you can talk to their superiors, and tell them, that so-and-so screwed up. But with these people, there's no one, no one at all. (C 78, 79)

The actual degree of ecclesiastical commitment to the poor is a subject of much debate. Setting aside for a moment those who identify the poor primarily as the poor in spirit, remaining group members generally see the "preferential option for the poor" as an ideal only imperfectly realized in practice. Critical views are especially common in the cities, where ordinary people can see at first hand how differently church leaders deal with rich and poor. When the institutional church in Cali is viewed from the vantage point of barrios like Meléndez or El Rodeo, residents stress how much ecclesiastical structures and their leaders remain allied in practice with the rich and powerful. These two women from Barrio Meléndez set a tough standard:

> I say that if the church really wants to make a contribution, it's got to stop favoring the bourgeoisie and spending so much time working with them. Because in practical terms, they're the ones who are favored, not us. You know, if a priest says even one word in support of the poor, if he's a foreigner, he gets deported right away, while at the same time the church continues to stand alongside the powerful. At all levels they line up with the strong. . . . So as far as I can see, the church's real preference is for the rich, not the poor, and that's the truth. All those lunches and dinners and I don't know what that the bosses give. And then they have a benediction and it's the bishop with all his staff. So the real preference is for the rich, and poor people are pushed aside. That's what I see. (CA 255, 257)

> It seems to me that the church has remained apart from the suffering of the poor. The church has remained isolated, and we have yet to see any real commitment by the church with those who suffer. Whenever there are protests, say about some social problem, it seems to me that the church ought to take a leading role, play

an important part, but it has never happened. I don't know, but to me it seems that the church has always been closed to the people. (CA 277)

When I asked this very devout woman what the church should do, she replied simply that it ought to "place itself at the side of the poor, stay in touch with the people, and serve them whatever the need may be. Stay with the people not only in good times, but in bad times too" (CA 278). One of the men active in her group argued that the church in Cali really played its proper role only in the barrios. That's where they helped people get together and work collectively to defend themselves. In his view, this is what earns the church a real popular base. In contrast,

> you can go to mass at the Cathedral, or at San Francisco [a wealthy church], and there you'll never hear a sermon that has anything to do with your own economic life, with the people. No. Because rich people go to mass there, and they don't like to hear about things like that, about real economic problems. The truth is that the popular barrios are where you find the most problems, and there the church is the main thing people have to work with. (CA 115, 116)

One activist's experience at a citywide meeting of youth groups points up the "red" reputation places like Barrio El Rodeo enjoy. Her comments also underscore the ideological gap that accompanies the physical difference between urban center and periphery. The meeting in question was held in early 1979, at a time when revolutionary fighting was at its peak in Nicaragua. Early in the discussions, this young woman asked that a previously scheduled mass be postponed an hour or two in order to give members time to carry a message of solidarity with Nicaragua to the cardinal, who was then visiting Cali prior to a trip to Central America. As she spoke,

> the bishop turned red as a beet, and looked around to see who had spoken. Then a priest came over right away and said to me, "you're from Rodeo, right? What's your name?" And then he told me to be careful, that you couldn't say things like that here. So the whole conference remained in the clouds, you know? Talking about participation in the parishes by getting people to sell Bibles, or to pray the rosary once a week at home. All that is fine, it is all positive, but you can't stop there, the issues are much broader. . . . So I told myself, no. I wouldn't participate in another meeting of that kind. That's just a sale of Bibles, a praying of rosaries. It's fine to do all that, I don't deny it. But it's also important to participate more actively with the people. (CR 305, 306)

I found a parallel sense of ecclesiastical marginality reinforcing social isolation in rural zones deeply affected by violence. Residents there question the legitimacy of church efforts to retain long-standing alliances (e.g., with the military) and thus to avoid rocking the boat. Things were even worse in the past, when as one man from Tabio told me, it was very frustrating, especially during The Violence, when homilies were little more than attacks on a political party and the members of that party [Liberals] were all alienated. The religion we had then was mostly one based on fear and dread anyway. (R 84)

Even though the Colombian church no longer takes explicit sides in partisan politics, its stance with respect to continuing violence often falls short of popular ideals. The situation in San Pedro, discussed earlier in this chapter, is a case in point. Residents there feel trapped between guerrillas and an abusive local garrison, and see the church as reluctant to make the difficult and dangerous effort of reaching out. One man resorted to the traditional image of the church as a good shepherd in his critique:

Here we've got the same problem they have in El Salvador or in Guatemala: violence. And also the absence of a good shepherd who will search for his lost sheep. Now they're beginning to see the need for priests to start bringing together their flock in the countryside, in the *veredas*. You know, the Protestants have made a lot of progress because they're willing to go everywhere. (C 70)

Discussions of "the church" are rarely done in the abstract. Popular groups encounter a very specific church, and judge its performance in light of their own historical experience. Evaluations typically filter through perceptions of the clergy and sisters who, for all practical purposes, constitute "the church" that ordinary people encounter on a day-to-day basis. As a rule, popular groups feel closer to clergy and sisters now than in the past. They prize the reduction in previous social and cultural differences, and point approvingly to specific changes such as simplified life-styles, abandonment of distinctive clerical clothing, and elimination of special titles of address.[12] The current ease of contact with clergy is contrasted sharply with how things used to be, when nuns were distant and a little mysterious and a priest was "like a king, you had to request an audience with him. We looked at them with awe and fear" (RF 108). A woman from Cali comments in detail on the changes she has seen:

A priest was sort of sacred; you couldn't even say hello to him. And you see, that's why there was so little trust [*confianza*] between us and them. They were always so far off—just your reverence, your reverence. But not anymore. Now we know that they're really just people like us, the same, equal. We treat each other as equals; the priest is as much an equal as we are. So now when we deal with them, we no longer feel diminished. Instead, there's mutual confidence. (CA 246)

New feelings of equality and the greater ease of contact they bring do not undercut popular appreciation of the fact that clergy and sisters have access to

---

[12] See chapter 7, below, for evidence that clergy and sisters reciprocate these sentiments.

resources unavailable to ordinary people. For all their efforts to "opt for the poor," priests and sisters are still seen (correctly) by the poor themselves as emissaries from a world of power that is foreign to their experience. They hope that changed relations between themselves and clergy will legitimize community efforts and bring moral and material support as well. One peasant from Caparrapí noted simply that "from them we can hope for to get civilization" (C 66). Another from Agua Fría went further:

> Motivation first of all, and then for them also to give something of themselves, to contribute their own grain of sand, and not just sit back giving orders. . . . They have collaborated, so I guess we can't really complain, but lots of times they don't know how to motivate people, they don't give that enough importance. (A 67)

A companion agreed, but complained that in Agua Fría evidence of real commitment was still all too rare. Words were not enough:

> Take the priests, for example, They could help us more in the *vereda*, but they just give advice. Actually helping a poor person—the first case has yet to be seen. I tell you, the truth is that the diocese and the priests have money, and they could say, well, I have this much, and so I can help some poor person build a house, or buy groceries. Not just give advice! (A 59)

Although priests and sisters are not expected to solve local problems by themselves, they are expected to offer more than words. Just as the evolving sense of being religious detailed in the previous chapter requires ordinary believers to go beyond mass attendance and sacraments to solidarity with others, in the same way, group members call clergy and sisters to live in accord with their own stated principles of poverty, solidarity, and commitment. In this vein, one woman from Meléndez described the ideal parish priest as follows:

> For me, the ideal parish priest would be a priest who is more open to dialogue, simple and easy to talk with and to trust. A real person, an ordinary man, not aloof and uninterested [but rather] more conscious of his duty, of the real duty a priest has. Because you know, being a priest isn't just staying on your knees to pray. No! It is to see and know your neighbor, to be closer to those in need. That's what a real priest is like. (CA 256)

The relative scarcity of priests means that most of the formal contact ordinary people have with the institutional church (apart from sacraments, holidays, and the like) comes through their interaction with nuns. As a practical matter, sisters *are* the church for many groups, and for the most part, they appear less remote and forbidding than priests. Of course, there are many authoritarian nuns, and even with the best intentions, sisters have imposed programs on communities in a heavy-handed manner. But because they lack the sacramental authority of male clergy, sisters are viewed as less demanding and much less threatening.

A further point arises from the fact that women are the majority in most groups, especially in the cities. Contact with men outside the family (even celibate priests) raises sensitive questions about relations between the sexes. It is easier and less complicated for female members to deal with another woman. When I inquired of one group in La Carucieña about contact with the church, I was told firmly that "we don't know anything about the priest, we have nothing to do with him." In contrast, the nuns could always be counted on. Thus, "if it weren't for the sisters, we would really be stuck here" (B 152). A neighbor added these simple words: "Oh yes, the sisters. They're really friendly, they know how to behave. That's the way to be, they treat people well, they're decent" (B 75). I show in the next chapter that the nuns active in these Barquisimeto neighborhoods are particularly committed to a simple life-style, with direct and relatively undemanding involvement in the ordinary lives of residents. More conventional church figures, even women, are not welcome. As this woman from La Carucieña told me, "We don't want anything to do with those nuns who pass through just praying. They stink!" (B 99).

Meeting popular criteria for an ideal priest or nun means actively working with the poor, accompanying them in their efforts. It also requires that priests and nuns *become poor themselves*. From this vantage point, living alongside the poor and looking more or less like them are necessary but not sufficient. Complete solidarity requires that clerics become poor themselves. Only then can they appreciate what poverty means in the lives of ordinary people. This woman from Barrio El Rodeo put it sharply:

> They've got to take account of the poor. That's really it; nobody takes the poor into account. To do it, you've got to see things from the point of view of the poor, to opt for the poor. That's what it's all about, right? To stand with the poor, that means joining with them, seeing problems as they see them, working through them to analyze the situation we all are living in. It's not the same if a person doesn't experience for himself the way poor people really live, if he can't feel it in his own flesh. Without that, they'll never understand the poor and they'll never understand social problems. (CR 318)

This woman went on to specify that becoming being poor entailed more than simply not having things. In her view, an attitude of poverty also requires abandoning pretensions of authority, and thus breaking ingrained habits of ordering other people about.

> What priests and sisters have to do is become poor, and put themselves in poor people's shoes. For me, Jesus Christ is the best example. He became poor himself. He didn't just tell others—look, you've all got to opt for the poor, but not me. No. He made himself poor, he was born poor. And I think that's how priests and sisters ought to be. You know, I'm not just talking about material poverty. No.

There's also a spiritual poverty, knowing how to act with some humility, like an ordinary person, the way poor people do. It's knowing how to share with the poor, because you know the poor are really the only ones who know how to share. Not the rich, that's for sure. (CR 318)

As these observations suggest, "good" priests and sisters appear to popular groups as those able to shed authoritarian habits, share easily, and work alongside ordinary people. Two final comments will serve to round out this discussion. The first comes from Villanueva, where ideal and reality appear in close approximation. The second reflects frustration in Barrio Meléndez, where, as we have seen, the new priest is viewed with considerable hostility. Both speakers want more than spiritual instruction or sacramental attention. What should priests and sisters do?

They've got to take more initiative dealing with social problems, and not be completely spiritual, not be set off from the world. To participate, work together with families. That way they would value Christian work more, and not keep themselves just for religious services. (V 32)

As for priests and sisters, there has been what we could call real commitment. At least there was when the Spanish priests were here. But not anymore. Right after they left, a priest came here, somebody named Gustavo Adolfo, and for him everything was all walking with Christ. Walking with Christ, but for him it was always on your knees. He did nothing but pray from the beginning of mass to the end. That's the way it was with him. Later they sent us another priest, who took over the parish. [But] he has never accompanied us Christians, never stood with us at all. And that's what's got to be done, to fight with this family or struggle for that cause. But not him; he prefers the easy life. I've seen him around, and whenever I meet him he says that he's working, but he just stays in the parish office. He never moves himself from there. (C 208)

Let us be clear about what precisely is at issue in these calls for active solidarity. Popular groups are under no illusion that priests or sisters are identical to themselves. If the going gets rough, priests and sisters have options beyond the reach of ordinary people. They may be pulled out by superiors, be expelled, or simply decide to leave. In any case, there is too much visible difference in background, education, and access to resources for any realistic person to count priests or sisters as "us," not "them." Clerics are higher on the social ladder:

I'm not saying that they should solve all our problems for us. But even if they don't have resources themselves, they still have opportunities to talk with others, to put things to people who have good jobs. Then those people can talk with the higher-ups and tell them about the barrio. Tell them how things are there, about the people and the needs we have. You know, it's all a matter of dialogue, that's the way to do things. (CA 46–47)

Ordinary people are realistic, and know very well that even when clergy have the best intentions, opting for the poor is not the same as being poor. After all, only the nonpoor can make poverty a conscious option. "Us poor peasants work because we've got to, not because we love work" (C 70). Group members are also aware that opting for the poor in active ways can involve difficult and wrenching changes for priests and sisters brought up with traditional clerical expectations and trained in conventional roles. They know that it may be unrealistic to expect too much, and this knowledge tempers demands for solidarity with what often appears as bemused sympathy. The following comment, by a woman from Barrio Meléndez, suggests sympathy, and even a little pity.

One thing I would like is for priests and nuns to do things that get them into the poor barrios, that make them feel the problems there in their own flesh. I say that seeing all these things, they would be more aware of what's really going on. Sometimes I think that they're not responsible for the mentality they have, because you know, from the moment they begin their studies they're shut up in convents, right? And there it's just brainwashing, brainwashing, so that when they finally get out, it's like getting out of jail. They come out different from everything that goes on around them. *They know absolutely nothing.* One of the priests who later went to Bogotá told me that before he came here, his mentality was very different. For example, he thought everything was like what they told him in the seminary. He was from high society, so he had to get out and suffer, really suffer before he could understand. (CA 176–77)

## Empowering the Poor

The discussion to this point raises a series of questions about the character of organizational mediations and their impact on a community's self-image, capabilities, and dispositions for action. Must an organization be "specifically Christian" to constitute a valid option in the eyes of church people and ordinary believers? What are the implications of restricting group membership and orientation in this way? Why are church groups chosen in the first place?

I have already pointed to some of the underpinnings of a choice of specifically religious vehicles. There may be no other alternative, or at least no alternative considered worthy of trust. This is often the case in rural areas, where the funnel effect noted earlier draws groups to the church as a first and often only conceivable choice. Matters are considerably more complex in the cities. Not only is there greater choice, but at the same time, suspicion of government and continuous strife over services, land titles, and the like lead many to view all political parties and municipal or local government structures with a jaundiced eye. The barrios of Cali, for example, were central in the movement of civil strikes (*paros cívicos*) that swept Colombia in the mid-1970s. Like many such efforts in Colombia and elsewhere in Latin America, this rash of work stoppages, withheld payments, and the like was rarely converted into durable organizations. The movements just petered out. Still, their popularity speaks to the depth of urban distrust of established institutions and points to persisting organizational weaknesses.[13] One energetic organizer from Barrio El Rodeo explained that because the state did so little for ordinary people, they leaned to fend for themselves.

> We have come to believe that given the administrative inefficiency of the state, it's necessary to create our own forms of action, more as a response, or a defense of the people, than as a way of helping the state out. We don't believe that the state needs help. The state is supposed to have a bureaucracy that can deal with all this. The problem is that its structures don't even try to do much. (CR 121)

In the specific case of Cali, the initiatives that have come and gone in this way include youth groups, cultural organizations (e.g., popular theater, alternative media), independent trade unions, and neighborhood committees. All have tried to craft independent solutions to problems without becoming engaged with or dependent upon formal public structures such as planning agencies, corporations providing services like water or light, or the officially designated neighborhood boards. As a rule, politics enjoys low prestige in the barrios, and politicians themselves are regarded with distrust and derision. When I asked who should solve barrio problems, this Meléndez woman replied that ''I don't know who should solve them, because I have no use for all that political stuff. They tell me that I am a citizen, they've told me that, but I have never given my vote to anyone, I've never voted for anyone'' (CA 166). According to another woman from La Carucieña, problems never change: ''There's always inequality between rich and poor. Governments just use the poor. Now election time is coming, and you'll see, it's exploitation, that's all it is'' (B 99).

The plurality and short life of many urban alternatives complicates the matter of organizational choice for barrio dwellers. Although they fear co-optation and manipulation, they nonetheless still need some link to resources outside the barrio if they are to survive. One Barquisimeto activist told me that when he first heard about the cooperative being set up in La Carucieña,

> I remember that I wasn't much interested at first. Most of my activity had been with political parties, things like that. I've always searched for ways to organize

[13] On the movement of *paros cívicos*, see Pedro Santana, *Desarrollo regional y paros cívicos en Colombia*; and Jaime Giraldo, *Paros*. For general views, see Castells, *The City*; Portes and Walton, *Urban Latin America*; and Piven and Cloward, *Poor People's Movements*.

the people, to help the community with organization right here. That's my real concern, and so when I did get involved, I think it was really as part of that search, looking for some kind of tool that I could use working with people around here. (B 35)

Until his encounter with the cooperative, this man had little contact with the church or with religious organizations of any kind. "In terms of religion, I've never identified much with Catholic things," he told me. But in his view, this wasn't very important.

That's right. I've always said that when it comes to working, the important thing is to work. Anyway, to be a Christian, you don't have to be part of a religious group. You can also be committed in this kind of work. Around here we've talked about this a lot. That's how the cooperative got started, and [through it] everyone has participated in lots of things. (B 39)

The position staked out in these comments fits well with the overall stance taken by pastoral agents working in this area. In their view, a valid distinction exists between Christian groups and groups of Christians. The former are built on close, subordinate ties to church institutions. Their logic of their general orientation to work and to the community makes *re-Christianization* (of members, families, communities, and society at large) the principal and most urgent task at hand. But groups of Christians can work together for common purposes without the group itself necessarily assuming a Christian character or religious goals, or setting tests of piety as a standard of membership. From this standpoint, the religious meaning and value of any activities groups may undertake will be present regardless of formal affiliations.

This perspective reflects considerable trust in popular groups and a willingness by pastoral agents to take the group's definition of the situation (not formal institutional norms) as a starting point for reflection and action. One of the sisters working with health committees in La Carucieña remarked that "as for us, now we don't care whether people have a religious motivation or not. We didn't used to do this, but we learned the hard way" (B 190). The priest in charge of the parish in which this barrio falls supports this position. He sees his own primary task as that of reinforcing existing groups, not replacing them with organizations that would be more explicitly "Christian."

Before, the church organized its own groups, Catholic Action, for example, But our policy now is to organize people, the same people whose Christian faith later will help spur their own groups. That's what happened in Brisas [Barrio Brisas del Aeropuerto], where the Christian communities were the origin of the neighborhood committee. It was the very same Christian people. The same thing happened with the cooperative, which is an organization dedicated to serving the community.

Maybe that's why I see such strong differences among priests. Some priests devote all their efforts to organizing groups like the Legion of Mary or the *cursillos de cristiandad*, but they leave it at that. Our position is that of course there should be a Legion of Mary, why not? But that Legion of Mary has to serve the community, it has to be different. Like the health committees or the cooperative— they were initiatives of ours. What else is there? Even those groups that were formed for the "taking of the water." They didn't call themselves Christian groups, but they were all Christian people, formed in one group or another. For these reasons, the whole thing has been an issue in our meetings, and we've talked about it a lot. What is the Christian community? I've asked myself if a group of people that calls itself Christian is therefore a Christian community? Or would it be people who call themselves Christian and then join groups? You don't need a meeting, and certainly not a meeting that specifically calls itself Christian, to feel Christian in the first place. (B 62)

This point of view reflects the relatively declericalized atmosphere of Venezuelan society and draws further strength from the overall stance of that country's Jesuits. Respect for popular culture is combined with commitment to promote and empower grass-roots initiatives. It is instructive to compare La Carucieña briefly with Barrio El Rodeo. As we have seen, pastoral agents and group members began Barrio El Rodeo with a similar commitment to building groups that did not have to be explicitly Christian. They concentrated instead on activism, praxis, and service to the barrio community. But whereas in La Carucieña the initial dispositions to action were steadily reinforced through a broad range of converging efforts (health committees, cooperatives, Bible study) in El Rodeo, as the left gained ground within the barrio, groups eventually divided along political lines, and the barrio's priests, who once were famous throughout Cali for their radical politics and uncompromising activism, delegitimized groups on the ground that they were no longer *sufficiently Christian*. Why?

Much of the explanation lies in how the evolving ideology of priests and pastoral agents cuts across the grain of group life. The Basque priests in Barrio El Rodeo were at once more rhetorically radical and more isolated from a support net than in Barquisimeto. They stressed immediate activism, not long-term organizational development. As a result, many initiatives were begun without ordinary residents being involved very much in getting things going or deciding on their proper direction. The result was a series of loose cannons, groups that lacked either the restraint imposed by top-down control (as in Facatativá) or the self-restraint that comes from a history of reflection and decision in common, as mediated through a series of links with other groups. When elements in Barrio El Rodeo, like groups elsewhere in popular sections of Cali, began to get deeply involved with insurrectionary groups, the priests became afraid and pulled back sharply.

Their change of heart does not seem to have come in response to outside pressure (e.g., from officials of the archdiocese) but rather from a kind of burnout. Isolated and facing a kind of organized clientele they had never imagined, these men in effect retreated to the traditions in which they had been raised, where groups are "Christian" by virtue of tight and explicit bonds with the church—groups may be smaller if necessary, but they are more secure. They made no effort to regain influence within existing groups, to struggle for example, to achieve a nonviolent but still radical position. Instead, groups and activists were cut loose, and the priests went back to basics, starting over on familiar and less perilous foundations.

Each of the organizational vehicles that became central in the cases examined in this and the preceding chapter carries with it a clear, if mostly unstated, set of messages about the character of the ideal member and the good citizen. In structural terms, the large, centrally coordinated, and hierarchically patterned organizations favored in the official Colombian view of things provide a subordinate and mostly passive role for ordinary people. Their identity is set by their links to these larger, hierarchical structures rather than by relations among themselves. The same holds true for groups that may be small in size but whose institutional connections are channeled and legitimated in this fashion. Members appear primarily as "the faithful," sheep in a flock led by their pastors, rather than as classes or communities. In such a scheme of things, the directive role of churches and pastoral agents is reinforced at every turn. As we have seen, the package is powerful and can be self-reinforcing. But if a few key elements are changed, it becomes possible to imagine alternatives, and to begin putting them into practice in the day-to-day routines of grassroots groups.

For change to take hold and endure, ordinary people must come to see themselves as individuals capable of change and of changing their community. Continuing religious linkages give the whole effort legitimacy; transforming the content and process of religious practice gives it a solid grounding in everyday routine; linking it firmly to expressed needs and evolving ideals makes it possible for abstract notions of equality, solidarity, and activism to take hold in the ordinary experiences of work, family, and community.

In his illuminating commentary on the life of Msgr. Oscar Romero of El Salvador, Jon Sobrino points out that for Romero, opting for the poor required much more than acting in their interests, serving as their voice, or doing things for them.[14] To be sure, under Msgr. Romero's leadership, the institutional church in fact did a great deal for popular groups in El Salvador, for example, in promoting cooperatives, providing legal aid, and defending human rights. But the fundamental thrust of Romero's option lay elsewhere. He believed that opting for the poor obligated the church to trust popular groups to act on their own, to empower them (with resources and a general grant of legitimacy), and

[14] Sobrino, "A Theologian's View."

to back them up when things got rough. Romero's wisdom and insight shines through the experiences reviewed in this book. If ordinary men and women are to think of themselves as the active, creative subjects they can be, they must be treated as adults in all walks of life. The experience can be difficult and frightening for those who already have power and status: prelates fear that church hierarchies will be undermined, political leaders worry about insurgencies or "excessive demand." But on the evidence of the Colombian and Venezuelan communities studied in these pages, such fears are exaggerated. Little rancor or class hatred is visible, and there is almost no challenge to the notion of authority itself. Group members want to be treated as equals, not to overturn society.

# SEVEN

## PRIESTS, SISTERS, AND PASTORAL AGENTS

I N PREVIOUS chapters, priests, sisters, and pastoral agents appear only in scattered snapshots: as categories in statistical tables ("resources" of the institutional church), givers of advice, shapers of agendas, and choosers of leaders. They have been depicted as occupants of defined roles who mediate the relations between institutions and popular groups, turn plans into action, and give general notions about "linkage" a firm grounding in everyday routine. Although these mediating roles are important, their impact cannot be satisfactorily understood in abstract terms. Because the ties that bind institutions and groups are also personal relations, it is important to take a close look at the men and women who fill the roles. Who are they? How and why did they come to this specific sort of commitment? What do they do every day, and what impact does their self-image and role definition have on the communities where they live and work?

Before we get to particulars, a few general comments on the relation among personal traits, beliefs and values, and role definitions are in order. Efforts to appreciate the depth and richness of personal experience and awareness should not obscure the fact that relations among them are not random but structured. They make sense in historical terms, and a close look reveals consistent differences of the now familiar kind between nations, genders, and specific organizational patterns.

To begin with, the general stress on a "preferential option for the poor" has spurred populist identification with the poor among clerical personnel all across the region. Since the late 1960s, this developing "option for the poor" has been associated with notable changes in residence, dress, language, and work habits that together have helped bridge long-standing social and cultural gaps between clerical personnel and popular groups. Although priests, sisters, and pastoral agents often consider such changes to be a sign of greater religious authenticity, and for this reason set out with great enthusiasm to rework their lives, the process can be wrenching and difficult for all concerned. This is especially so for nuns, whose previous education, training, and ordinary routines were generally undertaken within rigid, institutionally set boundaries. Exchanging habits for ordinary clothing, and leaving the sheltered settings and firm routines of schools or hospitals for the noisy, uncomfortable, and often chaotic ambience of popular barrios or hamlets, is understandably difficult and unsettling.

The change represented by decisions of this kind is not a one-shot affair; it does not happen overnight. Several mediations are required to get it started and give it a chance to last. There must be some kind of support system. Decisions to "opt for the poor" are rarely taken by priests or sisters in isolation. The more common response finds groups of men or women sharing the decision and working out the details of a new life together, step-by-step. Such personal networks are, of course, part of a general pattern of linkages to the institutional church, for example, through regular (and hopefully supportive) contact with each group's congregation.

The effort to legitimize new roles and routines has long-term consequences for church personnel, consequences that are only now starting to crystallize. More is at issue here than simply a reworking of the way church personnel reach out to popular groups. In conversation with priests, sisters, and pastoral agents, one often hears something like the following comment: "We came to teach and to give, but we are the ones who have learned and changed." This is an article of faith among many pastoral agents, and it bears a large measure of truth. Extended experience in these new settings can have an ongoing impact for those involved, reshaping their understanding of what religion is all about and what the proper tasks of "the church" (and of themselves as parts of that church) ought to be. Further, once these alternatives to conventional roles and activities are in place, they attract men and women who begin their careers seeking precisely the kind of experience that represented so major a change for their older colleagues. The result is a growing number of sisters and priests whose religious vocation is bound up, from the outset, with active commitment to the poor.

Changes of the kind just noted are not limited to those holding formal ecclesiastical roles. Over the last few decades, the Latin American churches have created many part- and full-time jobs, filled by laypersons, that are dedicated to managing the links between popular groups and the church. Examples include catechists, extension agents, cooperative specialists, and educators of all kinds who run occasional classes on topics ranging from literacy to sewing, accounting to history, health to theology. Such positions typically require little in the way of formal training or credentials. They are often filled by members of popular groups themselves. The whole process makes sense as part of the long-term impact churches can have in eliciting new kinds of leaders and leadership skills out of hitherto passive and silent groups.

The analysis undertaken here rests primarily on data from the programs, groups, and communities examined in the three preceding chapters. I begin with details on background, career, sources of involvement in popular work, perceived problems, and changing role definitions of priests, sisters, and pastoral agents. I then examine their positions on three issues that in combination make for coherent patterning of religious change, cultural transformation, and politics. I ask how they understand the *preferential option for the poor* and incorporate it (if at all) into their consciousness and daily routine. Who are the poor, and what exactly does it mean to *opt* for them? I then explore views on *popular religion*. Is popular religion simply a collection of inherited ignorance and superstition to be cleansed and purified? Or is it rather a valid expression of the life and culture of ordinary people, a source of valid lessons and values? Contrasts here undergird substantial variation in relations between pastoral agents and those they advise. Finally, I search for working definitions of *the ideal base community*. What does the ideal group or model member look like? How are they best linked to the institutional church? I close with life histories of two nuns that further illustrate alternative ways of opting for the poor, and suggest the broader implications of each path.

## Background and Personal History

A great many people are involved in work with popular groups. The overall numbers include high-ranking ecclesiastics (bishops, superiors of religious congregations, the vicar-general of Facatativá), staff of international or national organizations, full-time employees of dioceses or religious orders, and occasional collaborators or outside experts who may provide technical advice or material help of some kind. In principle, then, the option for the poor casts a very broad net, but for present purposes, attention is directed to a more restricted set. Although administration and office work are obviously important, those who carry out such tasks are peripheral to this analysis. Instead, I focus here on those with "hands-on experience": men and women who live in barrios and villages and work day-to-day establishing groups, identifying needs, and overcoming problems.

I interviewed and traveled with twenty-one individuals: nine priests, nine sisters, and three lay pastoral agents, all men. Country, gender, and institutional connection together set the initial tone and self-definition of the group: Venezuelans differ from Colombians, men from women, and those in religious congregations from clerics directly linked with dioceses. For purposes of exposition, I separate the discussion of priests and sisters from consideration of lay pastoral agents.

There was little variation in the ages of priests and sisters across the nations and communities (see table 7.1). At the time of my research, the whole group ranged in age from early thirties to early seventies. Women were substantially younger than men, with only two older outliers. These observations notwithstanding, differences in age do have an impact, but caution is required in drawing it out. The importance of age does not stem from the fact that younger people provide the sole (or even major) source of recruits for popular work. This is not the case. Rather, because the work is seen to be very exacting in physical and psychological terms, young people are deliberately chosen for such assignments. The fact that they are not so far along in career terms also makes involvement with popular groups less a wrenching change than an initial and enduring commitment.

The need for youth and physical stamina was repeatedly stressed to me. Especially for those working in rural areas, exhausting travel and difficult physical circumstances are common. Recall how Sister Sara's superiors justified her assignment by reference to her youth and presumed endurance. Her experience was widely echoed, for example, by this Venezuelan Jesuit, who stresses that anyone taking up this line of work must be both durable and adaptable. He loves his work: "I tell you, I am happy; without this work I would be a dead man." But he also points out that

> this is tough work, you know? The work itself is difficult and demanding, and thank God, God has given good health to all of us who work here. Sleeping every night in a different house, never knowing what you are going to eat, and not eating very well at that. Beans day after day, just beans and *arepas* [a fried cornbread universal in Venezuela]. Beans, *arepas*, and rice; beans, *arepas*, and rice. (V 222)

Physical strain makes those involved long for greater opportunities for rest, study, and reflection.[1] The problem is most acute in the cities, where priests and especially sisters are "on call" to barrio residents twenty-four hours a day. It is difficult to find time to get things done, harder still to manage regular periods of rest, prayer, or reflection. "What do you think you need most in your day-to-day activities?" got this response from two nuns in La Carucieña:

> For working here in the barrio? [*Yes*] Lots of things. I feel that I don't really understand the environment. I feel a great desire to be able to dedicate some time every day to reading and to study. You can learn a lot that way. (B 146)

> The very contact with the people that is part of our ordinary routine creates its own pressures and necessities. Knowing how to organize one's life so that rest is also possible. That's very hard. Here we struggle constantly to organize things, to create some kind of balance among tasks. So that there can be some rest, some kind of discipline, planning. Otherwise, each of us just goes off doing her own thing. And then there is no life in common, no community, no sense of closeness among us, even just taking a walk together. That's very important. (B 171)

Explicit provision for collective life helps ensure a measure of rest and psychological support. Small groups of men or women may share a house or apartment. There are also coordinated efforts among various groups to work together in a given barrio or rural area. Concrete examples in Venezuela include the Medical Mission Sisters and the nuns of La Carucieña, who live and work in groups of three or four and regularly have groups of novices (from their respective congregations) with them. The Jesuits also occupy a com-

---

[1] Cf. Katherine Gilfeather, "Women, the Poor, and the Institutional Church in Chile," and "Coming of Age."

pound (the Centro Gumilla) from which they fan out to urban and rural activities. A committee meets regularly to coordinate all these efforts. In Colombia, four Javierian sisters share a house in Meléndez; three priests jointly occupy a house in El Rodeo; four young priests work together out of the parish house in Caparrapí, and so on. In all these instances, the impact of common residence is reinforced by efforts to create a small, mutually supportive group: a focus for shared activities and a source of refreshment and encouragement. Of course, to some extent this stress on collective life is a continuation of long-standing traditions in the religious congregations themselves. But it is also a conscious response to felt needs and to the perceived danger of isolation and burnout.

National differences appear with respect to institutional affiliation, education, and place of birth. Among priests, those I encountered in grass-roots work in Venezuela were all members of religious congregations, were predominantly foreign-born, and, on the whole, had more education than did their Colombian counterparts. Colombian clerics in my fieldwork areas were all native-born, had little schooling beyond the seminary, and were predominantly diocesan priests.

The contrast between mainline ecclesiastical structures (dioceses/bishops/parishes/priests) and religious congregations is well known and much commented upon in Latin America. On the national or diocesan level, initiatives sponsored by bishops and religious orders commonly work on parallel lines, cooperative but jealous of their independence. The experience of Facatativá, where great effort was made to ensure cooperation between congregations and

**TABLE 7.1**
Priests and Sisters, Selected Traits

|  | Priests | | Sisters | |
|---|---|---|---|---|
|  | Venezuela | Colombia | Venezuela | Colombia |
| Assigned to Parish | 2 of 5 | 2 of 3 | none | 1 of 5 |
| Native-Born | 1 of 5 | all | 3 of 4 | 3 of 5 |
| Religious Order | all | 1 of 3 | all | all |
| Seminary Education Only | 1 | all | 3 | 3 |
| Advanced Studies | 4 | none | 1 | 2 |
| Uses Distinctive Clerical Dress* | none | 2 of 3 | none | 3 of 5 |
| Median Age (years)† | 45.5 | 58.3 | 46.5 | 44.75 |

* For men, cassock or clerical collar; for women, habit or modified headdress.
† At time of research

diocesan structures and personnel, remains very much the exception. As we have seen, the respective regional associations have taken very different tacks over the past few decades. CELAM focused on unity, orthodoxy, control, and campaigns against liberation theology, while its counterpart for religious orders, CLAR, became a major regional voice in support of efforts by male and female religious orders to identify actively with the poor in life-style, dress, values, and sociopolitical solidarity.[2]

These regional patterns find echo in our two countries. The bishops' conferences in both Venezuela and Colombia generally work out of a much more cautious, orthodox, and hierarchically focused agenda than do their counterparts for the religious orders. A recent survey of members of religious orders in Venezuela (carried out by their national confederation) puts these differences in perspective.[3] Most respondents indicated that they had only scant contact with bishops (one third reported no work-related contact at all). A large majority saw bishops as inefficient, strongly tied to the rich and powerful, and mired in an ecclesiology and image of "the church" that was little open to change. The impact of such unfavorable views and limited contact is magnified in Barquisimeto and Villanueva by the prominent role of the Jesuits. Jesuits are not only the largest male congregation in Venezuela; since the late 1960s, they have also been continental as well as national leaders in work for and with the poor.[4] One young Jesuit set his personal commitment to work with the poor in the context of the order's general position.

> We believe that that's the way to go. Our specific option here echos the one formally assumed by the whole Company of Jesus in 1975, to work for the promotion of justice and faith. We have stated formally that a commitment to justice has to be part of all our efforts. So that's why we do what we do wherever we find ourselves, be it in the university, working with peasants, or whatever. Our option must always be sought through active promotion of justice. (B 209)

Things are different in Colombia, where most of the priests I encountered were diocesan clergy, directly subject to the authority of the bishop. This makes them more vulnerable to sanction, including reassignment and (for foreigners like the Spaniards in Barrio Meléndez) termination of contract and expulsion from the country. Moreover, one often finds that clergy involved with base communities are simply the same priests who have attended a given

---

[2] See for example, CLAR, *La vida religiosa en America Latina: Respuestas y compromisos*; or P. Carlos Palacios, *Vida religiosa inserta en los medios populares*. Two recent studies focused on Venezuela are Mikel Viana, "¿Para que acontezca la vida religiosa?"; and Matilde Parra and Maria Gabriela Ponce, *Renovación y opción en la vida religiosa*.

[3] Conver-Ferve, *Los religiosos en Venezuela: Informe descriptivo de respuestas a la encuesta a los religiosos y religiosas de Venezuela*.

[4] Their activity spans many fields, including research and publication, along with organizational efforts like those reviewed earlier in these pages.

parish for years. A good example is Tabio, where the parish priest had already logged more than twenty years in the town when I met and interviewed him. Men like this take whatever programs or guidelines come down from the diocese as part of their overall responsibilities. Current stress on "the people," on participation, and on popular work in general must seem like just another turn of the wheel at times. Implementation is tempered by older habits and styles of direction and control. This is more than a question of age. Paternalistic orientations can also be found in younger priests, whose seminary education and training have led them to rarely question the notion that clergy should have a directive and monitoring role. Efforts by the four young priests in Caparrapí to subordinate all efforts to parish control are a case in point.

Ongoing links with religious congregations bring access to material and especially financial resources that otherwise would be unavailable in most communities. In Barrio El Rodeo, for example, where one resident told me that parish collections wouldn't keep a chicken alive, the Basque priests get regular contributions from their order at home. These provide for ordinary maintenance and also help get special projects going. All the clergy working in the Venezuelan communities I studied also receive extensive support, from their orders, from their home country, or both. The Jesuits combine jobs in teaching and publishing with money from the congregation to cover basic living and travel expenses, including the purchase and repair of vehicles and other equipment. Padre Vicente pointed to help from Melbourne: "They send me expenses every quarter. If there is any capital expense, they're always happy to supply it. Jeeps and things like that" (V 170). This pattern also applies to nuns. In the cities, they typically hold various jobs, most often in teaching, and pool salaries to support the household. In the countryside, it is harder for them to find regular work, but even here, teaching jobs are possible. Congregations chip in with funds to cover travel, equipment, rent, and to defray the expense of housing the novices who spend time with established groups of sisters as part of their training.

As noted, Venezuelan priests are better schooled and more likely to be foreign-born than are Colombians. Although the numbers involved here are small, the pattern is consistent with other data on the two nations and on Latin America as a whole.[5] Venezuela's clergy has long been predominantly (over three quarters) of foreign origin; these proportions have traditionally been reversed in Colombia. Moreover, until the mid-1970s, all the Jesuits in Venezuela were recruited from the Basque provinces in Spain. Since then, local talent has been pursued exclusively. One early result is that the only native son I encountered among Venezuelan priests was the youngest Jesuit. Venezuelan priests appear (in table 7.1) to be more educated than Colombians, but

[5] See, for example, the data in the *Statistical Yearbook of the Church* (1981).

this is more a by-product of the local predominance of Jesuits (who stress advanced studies) than of enduring national patterns.

As in Latin America generally, sisters outnumber priests, are more likely to be native-born, and have less formal education. The general rule with aspiring nuns seems to be to give them the basics, emphasize community life and its disciplines, and then set them off to work. With rare exceptions, ecclesiastical authorities have resisted pressure for more education for women, not to mention for access to the sort of advanced study in theology, philosophy, or law that makes for status in the church. The only cases of "more than basic" schooling for sisters that I encountered involved the Medical Mission Sisters (trained in nursing and medicine) and two Colombians who had gone to university before joining their respective congregations. Restricted educational opportunity is a source of considerable frustration for religious women. Indeed, the former nun I met in Barrio El Rodeo left her congregation precisely because of the official denial of her request to be allowed to pursue higher studies. Her perspectives on religious life had already begun to change, partly as a result of courses with progressive priests.

> I asked myself, what am I doing here? I can leave, get a job, help out my family, who at that time were really in need. I can study and get ahead. Another factor was that I had asked leave to enter university . . . but the mother superior said no, that the community had already given me a lot and that she didn't want me to study anymore. That hurt me a lot, because I think that when an individual betters herself, this helps the whole community, it helps everyone around her. . . . When I finally left, the superior herself cried, and they all begged me not to go. But I had made my decision, and so I came here looking for work. I spent a year without a steady job, but all the same I started at the university, without even a pencil to my name. (CR 285)

Resistance to higher education for women is illustrated by the case of ITER (Instituto de Teología para Religiosos). ITER was created by the joint confederation of male and female religious orders in Venezuela. By pooling resources, they hoped to make it possible for their constituent groups to educate new generations at home, rather than sending them to Europe, as had hitherto been the norm. Despite its sponsorship by both men and women, the nation's bishops have steadily refused to allow ITER to admit sisters as students on a equal basis. The sisters were thus compelled to establish a separate (separate but equal?) structure of courses. They were also prohibited from venturing into advanced theological areas that the bishops regard as irrelevant or unnecessary for women. Despite these restrictions, advanced education remains an important goal for many sisters, and organizations like ITER have had an impact, at the very least by diffusing innovative church documents and theological stances into the female congregations.

As women in a male-dominated institution, sisters confront a situation specific to themselves. This gives their personal histories and styles of action quite a different tone from that commonly encountered among men. Careers are typically played out within institutional confines; the range of choice is narrow. Education or health-care careers are common, for example, as teachers in schools for girls run by the congregation or as nurses in church-affiliated hospitals. As we shall see, this bounded and controlled experience means that for older sisters, making an option for the poor involves a wrenching midcareer change. This is commonly the case, for among those I interviewed, initial experience with popular work came on average about nine years after final vows, and followed a lengthy period of thinking and worrying about the need for a change. If we exclude the two youngest women (one in each country) who joined their orders precisely in order to do such work, then we find that the median experience the sisters have prior to opting for the poor rises to almost twelve years.

Those women who have made the change cite the opportunity for regular contact with ordinary people as one of the main attractions and most important benefits their new work has to offer. They experience such contact as liberating and enriching, and state that as a result, their religious faith is now more firmly grounded in real life. They believe themselves to be much less given to authoritarian ways than in the past. This elderly nun put it well:

> Before, when I started working, there was only nursing and religious education. But now our work is much more incarnated, more immersed in reality. In the past we always took as a starting point what we thought we had to offer. Now it is completely different. We try to take off from the people themselves, what they think. Why just insist on what I think? The important thing is what people think, it's sharing with them. (R 121)

The value of sharing in the richness and variety of everyday experience is contrasted favorably with the constricted life available in convents and schools. One of the sisters in La Carucieña told me that as a result of her change in work and in location, she had been transformed as a person. She now thinks in a completely different way. As for reasons, she states that

> well, it's *getting out*, just leaving the school. There, in the school, all your time is spent organizing the work with the girls. In that little world, you never know what's going on around you. I think I have really changed in that sense. The girls used to be everything for me. And now that I've opened my eyes, I can see another world, completely different: the needs of the people, the people themselves. And a person discovers lots of things that until then were invisible. You know, even now when I go back to our schools, I can see that nothing has changed there, they can't see beyond the walls. They still complain that there is so much to correct, so much work. They tell you that they have a hundred papers to mark, and that

Sundays it is nothing but grading and preparing for class. But there is nothing else, nothing beyond that. (B 172)

Other changes accompany the move to greater involvement with popular groups. Among these, the shift to ordinary clothing and the abandonment of exaggeratedly respectful forms of speech and terms of address deserve particular attention. Some changes are as simple as the use of ordinary names by sisters, who were often given a saint's name on entering their order. One of the nuns in La Carucieña began our interview by telling me that although she went by the name of Fatima, her real name was Maria del Socorro Alvarado. When she entered her order twenty-six years ago, "they named us after saints: Sister Luke, Sister Louis, and I don't know what" (B 158).

The general matter of titles and relaxation in social intercourse was discussed earlier. Here I wish to comment briefly on the significance of clothing. Until recently, it was common for nuns and priests to be marked off from the general population by details of dress and life-style. Priests were expected to wear cassocks or, at the very least, a black (occasionally gray) shirt with a clerical collar (known in Spanish as *un clergyman*). The norm for sisters was either a flowing habit or some variant involving a simple dress or, at minimum, some distinctive headdress and a skirt. Both sexes wore a visible cross, either as a pin or on a chain. These conventional indicators of clerical status are not very noticeable any more. Priests and sisters now regularly appear in the clothing common to ordinary men and women in the communities where they live. One hardly ever runs across a priest in a cassock anymore, the only exceptions being older men or students in traditional seminaries. Crosses are still worn, but they are now smaller and much less conspicuous, something on the order of a lapel pin.

Differences in external markers like clothing have long played a key part in undergirding social and cultural differences between clerics and ordinary believers. The issue has been particularly controversial for women, since, for many, use of the habit has been identified with being a nun. By the same token, abandoning the habit has often been taken as part of a general opening to society and a move to fuller and more equal participation by these women in all aspects of religious and social life. Habits neutralize women religious, hiding the body and thus desexualizing them in a way that makes them non-threatening. It also makes them look so different as to be anomalous, fitting into no ordinary category. One sister told me, amid great laughter, of a meeting she attended where signs were posted indicating that women should gather in one room, nuns in another. In her words, "I asked where I should go" (C 12).

Some of the women view the whole matter as simply a matter of convenience. They feel free to wear habits where local people expect it and ordinary dress elsewhere. Distinctive clothing, like habits (or clerical collars for men), is also believed to facilitate initial contacts by establishing that the person is of the church and (therefore) trustworthy. Once confidence is established, such external signs are no longer required and are set aside. This was the experience of Padre Vicente.

There are strong national differences on this score. None of the Venezuelans I encountered used any external marker of their status—no habit, no special headgear, no visible cross, no uniformlike clothing of any sort. In contrast, three of the five women active in Colombia used modified habits of some kind, although none wore the traditional flowing gown and headdress long identified as nun's clothing. A few sisters reported that when they moved to identify and live with the poor, they had violently (and sometimes bitterly) rejected the wearing of habits. But by now the controversy seemed remote, although efforts to reimpose habits and the like would certainly meet with considerable resistance. One of the more radical and intellectual sisters active in Meléndez rejected the easygoing stance just outlined and pointed out that habits were nothing more than the common clothing of late medieval women, frozen as a clerical standard some time in the Counter-Reformation. Her congregation has never used habits,

> but here in Colombia the majority of sisters still wear them. To my mind, habits are one of those things that show how much the church is out of phase with the times. Habits are nothing more than, well, you know, anyone who wears one is a little out of fashion. (CA 88)

In both countries, those who had deliberately abandoned clerical clothing, or who, like two younger sisters, had never used it at all, argued that habits placed unnecessary barriers between themselves and average people. By setting people off from one another, such distinctions made contact stilted and artificial. One older sister who abandoned the habit after many years explains why:

> I think it's better for the work that we do. Habits set up barriers between people. I first came to Tabio wearing a habit, and I can tell you that when people saw me dressed like that, they would give me fictitious answers, something to "please the sister." Now that I don't wear habits, they feel freer to tell me the truth. . . . You know, for us, not wearing the habit means that we demand more of ourselves. Because we have to demonstrate that with our own attitudes and actions that we really are consecrated. In contrast, with the habit, everyone could just assume it. (R 118)

Two Venezuelans put the matter in similar terms. The first is an older nun now deeply involved in cooperatives and local action committees throughout the city of Barquisimeto. In her view, dressing in ordinary clothing was simply better because it helps people get close to one another. With habits, or even with any kind of special religious clothing like what we had until recently, people are set apart. The "little sister" over there, and they point you out just like that! But now, dressed like this, normally, you've got more of a chance to approach people. (B 166)

Her colleague, a young member of the same congregation, said that the whole matter needed to be put into context. There was too much attention to clothing when the basic issue was not clothing but rather a general requirement that authentic faith be lived in the world, alongside ordinary people. Her comments are worth citing at some length.

Are you asking why it's better to live among ordinary people? Or are you just referring to clothing? [*That too.*] As for me, I think that it's because God called us to evangelize the world, and you can't do that shut up in a glass house. Of course, we need to make some special provision for those with a contemplative vocation, but apart from them, it's making yourself part of the mass, understanding and loving them just as he taught us to do. The Lord didn't isolate himself, the Lord went out among the people. He loved them, lived with them, and shared their experiences and their feelings. And that is what we religious are called to, to live with the people. And so I think that the only external sign we need to show is our love, right? A solid faith, and above all love—those are the only signs God has given us to be known by. And we need nothing else to distinguish us from others. To me, the real meaning of being a nun isn't somehow being more than others, but rather being in service to others. (B 139)

Most of the priests I met rejected distinctive clothing or other highly visible markers of clerical status on the same grounds: just more needless barriers between themselves and ordinary people. Indeed, when I asked one Colombian priest if all this did not in some way make for divisions (*muchas vallas*), he replied that yes, there was indeed a lot of nonsense (*muchas vainas*) about it all. The overall consensus among men and women was that the only meaningful and worthwhile markers of a consecrated life lay in visible signs of love and commitment.

An exception came in the conservative town of Tabio, where, as we have seen, the parish priest is very much cut to the old model. He has been in the town for decades, is on relatively easy terms with most groups, and can often be seen strolling around the town in his cassock. His view of the matter is revealing, for he suggests that external signs are an important part of the priest's general position and status as a role model.

I think we have to live in this world, and some external signs help us with this world. A priest won't go into a café wearing a cassock, but he will if he is in blue jeans. It isn't that he's doing something wrong. It's more a kind of control we exercise over ourselves. Now, with specific reference to the people, you've got to take their expectations into account. Around here I always wear a cassock, and if tomorrow I go into Bogotá dressed like that, no one says a word. Everyone sees me in a cassock and I feel comfortable that way. For me it's a habit; I've worn cassocks ever since I entered the seminary as a boy. But of course, how can they force today's young priests to wear them?

Now, with respect to being like others, you know that that's a double-edged sword. Of course we're like others; priests are human beings the same as everyone else. But set apart as the Holy Father has stated. Priests *should* be different; this business of being like others isn't good for priests anyway. Lots of people want priests to be different. They accept you as a priest, and they're only too happy to find things they can criticize, above all anything related to sex. And once they find something like that to criticize—and these are not bad people—from that point on they say, well, you have nothing to say to me. And that is the end of lots of sacraments, like confession. (R 54)

Clothing is not the only thing that sets clerics off from average men and women. Language also gets in the way. Clerical education is typically abstract, centered on philosophical and theological concepts. This means that many priests come out of the seminaries using words, forms of speech, and syntax that are so complex as to be practically unintelligible to ordinary people. Making a commitment to live and work with the poor is thus likely to require a deliberate effort to adapt to popular language and forms of speech. Biblical stories and examples are especially effective in this regard, and are widely used. I also found considerable recourse (especially in rural areas) to metaphors involving transport or energy. Reference is made, for example, to the need for tightening screws or checking tires if the car (the community) is to move ahead. Lanterns and flashlights also provide occasion for comment, as members are regularly urged to "charge your batteries" as a prerequisite to some sustained common effort.

Priests and sisters alike look back on their own education and training with critical eyes. Many point to excessive concern (in seminaries and convents) with discipline and organization. As one of the nuns in La Carucieña put it, "Of course, I'm not criticizing the formation I got as a novice. At least it gives you a foundation, right? But you know, it was so divorced from reality, it was a formation obsessed with schedules, with a bell for every little thing, and a concern with discipline that now we can see doesn't really matter at all" (B 171). There is general agreement that whatever value the moral virtues and theological principles provided in years of schooling may have had, there was too much stress on such issues, not enough on practical matters. A mild version of this point of view asserts simply that

from inside the seminary, you had a somewhat utopian view of the world. You went out thinking that it was just a matter of preaching, but you came up against all kinds of difficulties. . . . Yes, our formation was a little too theoretical and lacked a practical side, especially concerning details, for example, of how to run a parish office. You got the legal principles, but nothing about practical management. Of course, those are not what really matters. They did give you the fundamental orientations and values; as for the rest, it was catch-as-catch-can. That's all right. You wouldn't want lots of practical skills and no basic values. (R 55, 56)

Going further, one of the Venezuelan Jesuits insisted that his formal education had been useless and even harmful. The philosophy he learned was abstract and sterile, and new schools of thought like liberation theology were mentioned only to condemn them (B 63). He felt that more had been gained from direct insertion into popular milieus. As we have seen, this has since become a regular part of the preparation of all young Jesuits in the country. A younger Jesuit told me that the time he spent in popular work (in La Vega, an outlying barrio of the capital city, Caracas) had been the only valuable element in his own education. Formal studies were mostly a waste of time.

> Thank God they don't have that kind of novitiate any more. I would be the first to reject repeating all that, because it's useless, I tell you it is no good at all. . . . [In contrast,] my experience in La Vega was very positive both in practical terms and on a theoretical level. You know, even though many will deny this, it is still true that that kind of work requires theoretical reflection. The work itself draws you into it. . . . Yes, my education and training had lots of bad and lots of good elements, but for me that experience was absolutely fundamental. That, and the fact that I was lucky enough to wake up in time. (B 212, 213)

Priests and sisters are not the only agents the church sends to work "with the people." Many laymen and -women share the effort, and there is evidence that the role of these laypersons has expanded and gained importance in recent years. Madeleine Adriance argues that the convergence of political repression with moves by the Brazilian Catholic church to take up a strong and visible option for the poor helped bring many potential activists into full-time work with the churches. Her observations echo Albert Hirschman's recent discussion of grass-roots projects sponsored throughout Latin America by the Inter-American Foundation. Both authors point to the growing visibility and impact of groups and individuals who mediate between big structures (like governments or churches) and popular classes. They stress the critical role assumed by a new cadre of (mostly middle-class) men and women in getting such groups going and sustaining them with technical advice, political alliance, access to resources, and moral support.[6]

My experience in poor communities in Venezuela and Colombia differs in several noteworthy respects. I found hardly any such middle-class individuals (apart from priests and sisters). In part, this stems from the generally lower

[6] Adriance, *Opting for the Poor*; Hirschman, *Getting Ahead Collectively*.

levels of repression in our two countries: few activists are driven into the churches here. Further, all the programs studied here operate on a shoestring; at best, only modest resources are available. Even the limited staffing provided for in the CRS-Facatativá project is a rare exception. This means that fewer formal roles are available in the first place. The reduced scale of lay involvement is also related to the lower profile popular work has in the plans of each nation's central ecclesiastical structures. A specific commitment to the "option for the poor," backed up by concrete resources, remains the exception, not the rule, for the hierarchies of both countries.[7]

Whatever the reason, in my fieldwork I encountered only five full-time lay pastoral agents: four Colombians, one Venezuelan, and only one woman.[8] All the pastoral agents I encountered had lower-class backgrounds and little or no formal schooling. This suggests that the notion of "opting for the poor" does not capture their experience very well. These individuals have been poor all their lives. Their current positions are clearly a step up; they see these jobs as a chance to serve others like themselves. After conducting an initial round of interviews at the level of diocese, project, and communities, I returned for more detailed conversation with three young men (average age at time of research was thirty-three) who at that time held important positions in their respective areas. Two were Colombians linked to the CRS-Facatativá project: the diocese's main extension agent and cooperative specialist (Huberto Vanegas); and a catechist and organizer of lay training programs (Fernando Jiménez). Neither man has much formal education (five years of primary school for Fernando, none for Huberto). Each reports a history of great personal distress, including broken homes, illness, and unemployment, before he found this work. Each man describes the moment when he first realized that *he* could do this sort of work in terms that recall accounts of religious conversion. Eyes were opened and new possibilities appeared before them. The life and times of Huberto Vanegas are explored in detail in the next chapter. His colleague will occupy us here.

Fernando Jiménez was one of the first collaborators recruited by Román Cortés. Fernando recounts the origins of his involvement with Román as follows: He had been going through hard times. Economic difficulties (no skills, irregular work) were aggravated by illness and by the death of his parents, which had left him responsible for five younger siblings. He was depressed and aimless when he was invited to attend one of the first *cursillos* held in the diocese. He accepted, and

[7] Unlike Brazil, where Mainwaring (*The Catholic Church*) shows how such commitment developed through the 1970s and 1980s.

[8] I found no officially designated pastoral agents in rural Venezuela, where group members take responsibility for all tasks, and none in urban Colombia, where there is no money with which to pay anyone.

in that *cursillo* I met Father Román Cortés. That was more or less in 1970, around
the end of 1970, something like that. The *cursillo* led to big changes, changes in
my life that opened all kinds of new horizons. Perhaps my personality had just
been repressed because of all the hard times I was having. In any case, I was
liberated. I realized that despite everything, I could make it, that I wasn't alone.
I found friends, I found the support of Father Román, and you know, from then
on he was like a father, a real father to us. That was also the period of Msgr.
Zambrano Camader. With Father Román, he was just beginning the program for
training peasant leaders. Parish leadership schools were being founded, and promoters were needed to set them up in the parishes. For sure, I was interested, and
the bishop supported me, made me feel welcome, and encouraged me a lot. So
that's when I started working for the diocese, until I moved over to work full-time
alongside Román. (F 115)

Fernando and Huberto came to their current work through something like
the funnel effect I outlined earlier, whereby activities and commitments are
channeled to the church almost by default, given the scarcity of alternatives.
Their Venezuelan counterpart has had a very different experience. In the Centro Gumilla of Barquisimeto, I met and interviewed Humberto Pineda, a
young man from Barrio La Carucieña. One of the barrio's original invaders,
Humberto came from a fatherless family and had limited formal education
(two years of secondary school). From an early age, Humberto worked
(mostly at odd, unskilled labor) to support himself and his mother. While still
in his early teens, Humberto got deeply involved with leftist politics at the
barrio and citywide level. He had no contact whatsoever with religion or with
the Catholic church in particular. Around that time, the nuns in La Carucieña
had been spreading the idea of forming a cooperative. Humberto heard about
it through the neighborhood grapevine and was interested in the possibilities.

> That's why it was, it was because of that concern. When I got involved, I don't
> know why I first did it. More than anything else it was because I was looking for
> that kind of thing, because I wanted to see if what those people were talking about
> was any good. (B 36)

I asked if any of this had come as a result of contact with church-related
groups, as is sometimes the case. Humberto praised the sisters lavishly, but
noted that

> I didn't have much to do with Christian groups. I knew about them, but there was
> no real contact. Like I told you, I preferred working with political parties. But
> they [the nuns] were the ones who brought the idea. You know, here in the com-
> munity we're now used to the idea of having lots of groups. But really that's
> because of the work those nuns have done. They really put the Bible into practice,
> they say, let's carry it out. They have also helped interpret and explained it a lot.

For all those reasons, most of the groups there are the ones they have organized. (B 38, 39)

Humberto's experience is thus more radical and politicized and much less explicitly tied to the church than is common in Facatativá. Fernando is very wary of political entanglements and commitments, arguing that this leads to needless resentment and conflict. To Fernando, activist base communities in Nicaragua or El Salvador have been victims of political manipulation. "That's not the way to go," he told me, "but for sure something has to be done" (F 127). In contrast, Humberto Pineda believes that the critical point is to work on urgent problems, not to worry that groups may be too politicized or not Christian enough.

Humberto's position reflects the greater openness of city life, and the broader range of alternatives available there. It also makes sense in terms of the different norms that inform church programs in each of these settings. In contrast to Facatativá's pervasive concern with hierarchy and clerical control, in urban Barquisimeto little interest is expressed in keeping groups specifically and explicitly Christian. One of the Medical Mission Sisters put the matter in more general terms.

> Yes, participation has increased around here, but it's not really because of the people. Rather, the church began looking at it differently. Before, we only worked with religious organizations. If there was no religious motivation in a group, we didn't work with them. But now we don't care if people have a religious motivation or not. We didn't used to do this, but we learned the hard way. None of us had any preparation for working in barrios. Our preparation was in health. [Now] the church is willing to get into human problems, and this is a change. In parishes like this, we know which side we are on and they know too. As a result, we have lost some parishioners, mostly rich ones, who say we're preaching politics, not the Gospel. (B 190)

The choices and perspectives outlined thus far also make sense in terms of the general evolution of Latin American Catholicism. The changing concerns of clergy and sisters, the development of new roles for women, and, in general, the growing appeal of work "with the people" all resonate strongly with regional trends. These orientations and experiences also fit well within the national and structural contexts provided for popular action. Cutting across all these dimensions of variation, the intense experience of the changes experienced by religious women stands out sharply. Women's characteristic commitment to popular work and their predominant style of action also differ from men's. They are more likely to be found actually living with (and like) ordinary people in rented houses or apartments. They are also much less bound by training and tradition to the directive roles priests have long been expected to assume. Once out of the confines of convent or school, sisters may be therefore be considerably freer to act than are their male colleagues. Now that we know what sort of people they are, we can take a closer look at how their "option for the poor" is translated into the everyday routine of work.

## Working

The way pastoral agents go about the business of starting and nurturing groups depends greatly on their own self-image and sense of mission and on how they understand the core problems each community faces. Despite otherwise striking differences among themselves, most of the priests and sisters I interviewed agreed on two related points. First, they believe that "insertion" into popular life is a necessary prerequisite for effective group formation. In this view, popular groups will never endure unless someone is there to encourage and monitor them on a regular basis. Second, they believe that low levels of self-confidence and mutual trust, rather than, for example, isolation or poverty, are the most important obstacles to individual and collective progress that popular sectors face.

Putting these ideas into practice requires considerable physical mobility and an open attitude. Pastoral agents see themselves "going to the people" and calling them together to discuss their common experiences and needs. Thus, sisters in both Meléndez and La Carucieña rented houses in the barrio and spent lots of time just getting to know the terrain and the neighbors before attempting structured activity of any kind. They saw this as the only sure way to proceed, not only for themselves but also for the church as a whole. No longer can groups be created by fiat or be expected to revolve in automatic and unquestioned ways around the parish. They must arise out of the people's own needs and interests. One sister in La Carucieña states that the proper role for the church is to

> draw closer to the people, get closer to them and find ways to help them out. I don't know, the church seems to be a little removed from things. Even us, we are also a little bit apart from everything, we only get involved once in a while. You've got to really be with the people, live here, live alongside the people. Not just coming for a while, spending an hour with someone—but really being here. (B 160)

The youngest woman in this group came to La Carucieña on a temporary assignment but now finds the prospect of a return to teaching unthinkable. Her proper place is in the barrio, and her proper role is

> to listen to the people, to live with them, and by reading the word of God and reflecting together on it, to orient them so that they become aware of their rights,

their rights as persons, [and] to organize them so that they can move ahead, build community, and create a sense of fraternity among themselves. (B 138)

In the countryside, efforts at insertion in popular milieus are complicated by distance, rough topography, and difficulties of transportation. One solution is the circuit-riding strategy used so effectively by Padre Vicente around Villanueva. Recall that Vicente also spent years establishing bonds of trust in peasant communities. His efforts legitimated the idea of organization, made others welcome in the area, and created habits and dispositions of action that underwrote the later surge in organizational growth of all kinds. Obstacles to meeting with popular groups and getting to know them are even greater in Facatativá, where poverty and distance are overlaid with cultural isolation and suspicion and fueled by long-standing violence. As we have seen, one attempt at complete insertion ended with the expulsion of the priest in question from San Pedro.

This man distinguished his efforts sharply from the strategy used by Román Cortés. Román saw *cursillos* as the hook on which to organize base communities, using the same general plan throughout the diocese. He thus sacrificed depth for breadth, founding as many groups as possible without going very deeply into the character of any particular area. The resulting groups often had shallow roots and were overly dependent on the parish.

> I even proposed rethinking the communities. And he [Román] told me that since they were peasants, it wasn't necessary to get into much depth with them. I then asked him if that was because they were peasants, or rather because no effort was made to get to know their values. For example, given that the military had such a powerful impact, why not discuss that a little, why not explore the reasons for all that show of force? But he rejected that. Maybe it was because of his own spirit, the very zeal that made him the man he was, maybe that's why his ideas got blown out of proportion. He wanted to have so many communities and to show that it was possible, that all sense of balance was lost. We even once proposed to him that *cursillos* be suspended, and all our energies be put into rejuvenating the communities, deepening that experience and working closely with them. But he rejected that. (C 41a)

Those who worked closely with Román Cortés stress how hard it was to get groups started in this remote and troubled region. One of their main obstacles was a pervasive suspicion of outsiders, matched and reinforced by a distrust within the communities that kept people from working together. One of the sisters who was present at the creation of Román Cortés's program in Caparrapí told me how she and others coped.

> My area of responsibility was La Azauncha, and when I first got there in 1978, the guerrillas were coming into the zone, attacking in strength. That whole area was already flagged [by the authorities] as an antigovernment zone, a red zone.

So we were the first to arrive there, we missionaries. And I believe that our entry into the region helped reduce somewhat the distrust that was so common there. People in the same hamlet wouldn't even talk to one another, because they couldn't be sure who was a guerrilla and who was not. What's more, in the town when you mentioned La Azauncha, people would tell you that over there the people are bad, that they're *guerrilleros*, and all that. But we would say that no, they're fine people.

So I believe that our coming to the area helped mute the violence. People used to ask me, "Sister, how can you deal with those violent people?" But to me, no, they were wonderful people. So in this way we tried to start changing this image of violence. You know, when we first came there, people would run off the roads and hide from us. (C 85, 86).

Priests, sisters, and pastoral agents with extensive rural experience all cite inhibitions about self-expression as the principal obstacle to group formation. One sister with long experience in Río Frío told me that "it isn't so much that they had reservations, but rather that they didn't know how to express themselves. Ask them a question and they would hide under their *ruanas* [blanket-like wool capes]; nothing could make them come out. But if you ask now, they tell you that they've learned how to think and how to reflect on things" (R 115).

Getting started is particularly difficult where violence is endemic. The sister who had worked establishing groups in La Azauncha now points to major changes in self-confidence, sociability, and trust. Getting to that point was hard.

People there didn't talk to one another, no one said hello, there was no self-expression at all. I think that our arrival in the area helped a lot, especially in achieving greater sociability. They even tell you, for example, that before, we were embarrassed to say hello. We were embarrassed because we were only peasants, we had nothing to say. . . . But now they've learned to value themselves as persons. Before they had no awareness of their dignity as human beings, they thought they were like animals that neither needed nor merited anything. This was especially so in that part of La Azauncha where people are the most backward. (C 87, 88)

Her account is echoed by Huberto Vanegas, the lay pastoral agent charged by the diocese of Facatativá with starting up cooperatives throughout the hinterland of the parish of Caparrapí. He devoted over a year to preliminary work, trekking out to isolated *veredas* like La Azauncha, San Pedro, or Barro Blanco to discuss needs and involve local residents in planning the cooperative or related projects like water lines or bridges. His work began in 1980, and he relied heavily on the contacts this sister and her team had already established.

Well, we went in accompanied by a nun I met there and together we did the job. She already knew the people there, and they knew her—this nun was really committed to the rural people. Our procedure was to start with home visits, getting to know the families, to know their houses, and to understand the state of well-being here—really it is a state of ill-being. We tried to visit lots of families, dialogue with them, and then take the opportunity to invite them all to a meeting in the center—the center was the school—a meeting once every week or two where we would try to interchange ideas and concerns.

So we invited them to what was the first community meeting, attended by about thirty families. We described our two specific goals, which were first, organizing a cooperative, second, organizing a few socioeconomic projects, profit-making projects that would help them get some assets together, assets that they could use to solve the problems they faced. [We told them] that after all, the only way to resolve problems is through cooperation. (F 172)

These initial contacts were followed up by meetings in which the community got down to specifics and started to learn about cooperatives.

After a motivation [session] like that, we would plan a second visit, to exchange ideas in more detail. Then we would come back for a second visit, and learn more about their needs and concerns. At this time, they would give us details about their economic, political, and ideological situation. And also something about the state of local services. Then we would present to them the possibility of a short course on cooperatives, a course to be held there in the hamlet. This was done and about fifty-six people attended. I am talking now about Barro Blanco. People liked the course a lot. It was a very dynamic course, that is, it tried to sensitize people as much as possible so that they would start gaining awareness of the need to unify and to organize themselves to demand their rights.

The whole course lasted three days, and everyone attended. No one was missing for three entire days, and the course finished with a naming of a local committee, a committee of Cupocrédito. (F 173)

I witnessed a similar effort get underway a few years later in a gathering at La Magdalena, where the example of places like Barro Blanco was much discussed. Participants in this meeting of the area's leadership school (held on October 31, 1982) wanted help setting up a central marketing cooperative to service many of the *veredas* in the area. They knew about the earlier failures in Caparrapí, where private organizers got peasants to put up the initial capital for a cooperative and then ran off with the funds. The diocese's promoter used this disaster to underscore the difference that working with the church entailed. Those men were capitalists: they talked *only* about money; money was their sole concern, and so they left peasants holding the bag. He described his own efforts in these cases to this new audience, telling them that sure, when we began talking about cooperatives, they almost hit us, they almost stoned us. But we told them, no, we work with Father Román, and you know that Father Román would never hurt you. And we work with the church. And would you like to come to a meeting tonight? So they came, even the most suspicious, many of whom are now members and now defend the cooperative. Why?

They came because we did what those other gentlemen never did. They talked about nothing but money: what if we cut out the middleman, we could make more money, you would all have lots of money, that sort of demagoguery. And look how they left you in the lurch. But in contrast, we tell you about how organizing is the only way to save yourselves. Because the rich are organized, they have organizations, they're unified, and if the poor all go off each on his own, nothing can be done.

We asked them there, did those gentlemen ever provide any course about co-operatives? Show us the diploma. The answer was no, it was just a matter of putting in money, nothing more. But we are working with the church. Look how we talk about cooperatives in all our meetings. We do it all in the spirit of the church, with a real Christian spirit. (Q 17, 18)

All this went down very well with the audience. Plans were made for future visits to the *veredas*, and a series of courses about cooperatives was put on the drawing board. After the meeting, participants went home to spread the word among friends and neighbors. This may not be a very fast way to proceed, but as a practical matter, the very slowness and step-by-step character of growing popular involvement is vital to the construction of solidarity and mutual trust, and thus to success.

The failure of Río Frío's community business, EMCO, is now attributed by sisters and pastoral agents to the group's imposition from the outside (chap. 4, above). Because they did not live in the community (they visited from nearby Tabio), the sisters believe that they missed valuable chances to partic-ipate in local life and, thus, to understand community problems and perspec-tives more completely. As I suggested earlier, this may be overly optimistic. Río Frío also has a long history (that residents offer up with a combination of glee and bitterness) of gossip and factionalism. Still, in retrospect, dropping a fully formed package into an uninvolved community was bound to fail. With-out some prior foundation of trust and solidarity, the *vereda*'s pervasive gossip and envy worked unchecked to undermine the project. Sister Carmen com-ments:

Nothing could be done, things were undermined from the start by something I just don't understand. It destroyed all our work, and we never knew why it arose or exactly where it came from. Because, you see, it simply isn't possible that when twenty people meet regularly for over four years that they should all have run away. (R 113)

Román's death played a big part. After he died, there was sort of a general weariness, a conviction that nothing could be done. Given our experience in Río Frío, and what we know about how long it takes peasants to learn anything, it's now clear to me that twenty years were needed there for something lasting to be achieved. It's really our own fault, for not having had the patience to stay on. (R 122)

If isolation, low self-confidence, and lack of solidarity with others truly are characteristic of popular groups, then it is all the more imperative that priests and sisters identify fully with them as a prerequisite to getting change started. The presence of these men and women on a day-to-day basis helps break the prevailing isolation and legitimizes the notion of doing things in a new way. In the words of one sister in Barquisimeto, being on the scene "give[s] ordinary people a little more credibility." She regards such a presence as long overdue. By standing with the people, not with the rich and powerful, the church now has a chance to correct earlier mistakes. In the past, "we expected people to come to us, and kept ourselves apart. We didn't realize they are the majority, and that it's us who abandoned them" (B 138).

To those who opt for the poor in this way, being (or, rather, becoming) poor is more than a gesture of solidarity. It is also an indispensable part of their sense of self and of mission. Traditional religion no longer satisfies. Delivering moral guidelines, encouraging prayer, or sponsoring participation in religious sacraments or rituals no longer seem like enough. Such activities must now come wrapped within a broad reorientation of the institution and its commitment to and with the poor. What *must* they do? Here are two responses, first from a priest working alongside Padre Vicente, then from one of the nuns in La Carucieña.

The church has to give not only a moral judgment, but also a real witness through its institutions. A witness of closeness, of fidelity, right? And sometimes it also has to be the herald of new experiences, don't you think? (V 138)

What is the right stance for us to take in the face of social problems? I believe it is to throw yourself in, to help people to a truly integral promotion. I think that if we have a foundation like that, *then* we can move on to catechism, but the human base comes first. You can't just go to someone's house and say, "Well, how're you doing, now let's read the Bible, everyone has to be saved." Start off that way, and no one will understand a thing. You've got to begin differently, in a more humane way. Then, once the group has an idea of how things really are, then you can begin looking for ways to improve the situation. That's when you can say, "Look, on Sundays mass is said at such and such an hour." But this comes only after a whole process, right? (B 165)

Although isolation, mistrust, and suspicion are generally viewed as major problems, priests and sisters vary widely in how they explain these crippling conditions. Opinions vary, much as they do when the reasons for poverty are discussed. If being poor is seen to result primarily from individual failings, charity or perhaps education can help. But if poverty has structural sources, then activism, organization, and mobilization are possible and perhaps required. In the same way, if distrust stems above all from moral decay, then spreading the word of God appears both necessary and sufficient. But if the suspicion that runs through many communities is undergirded by structural conditions that weaken and divide the population, the solution lies elsewhere. Collective as well as individual change is needed.

Colombians and Venezuelans take very different positions on this issue. In Quebradanegra, where groups are highly devotional and limited in social or cultural spillover, the parish priest drew a simple and clear-cut analysis:

> The way I understand things, the principal problem is that we have shut our ears to the message Jesus Christ has for us. The message of the Gospels, the message that brings a profound change in our attitudes, in our relations with God and with our neighbors. The fullness of that message comes only through the church: through its hierarchy, its saints and scholars, its theologians, philosophers, and scripturalists. To me, that's the principal problem. (Q 60)

This man went on to highlight a series of positive changes in local life, especially the decline in drunkenness, fighting, and bad language (Q 64). His views were echoed in Tabio and Río Frío, where the priest attributes the collapse of base communities and of the community store to insufficient attention from the diocese and to an overwhelming dependence on clergy (i.e., on himself) that left groups unable to survive on their own. His position is curiously contradictory and reflects the ambiguities of the official Colombian stance concerning base groups. At one and the same time, he complains that groups are unable to survive on their own and notes their unwillingness to manage without clerical assistance. But why expect them to do anything else, if their formation has encouraged dependency from the very beginning?

Isolation and distrust appear in a different light when considered from the vantage point of those working in the barrios of Cali or Barquisimeto. Residents here are also poor, and despite the physical proximity barrio life imposes on them, contrasts in background, work conditions, and experiences often combine to make sociability difficult. But the sisters active here see the problem in structural, not individual, terms. A structural analysis of poverty is the basic component of this view. Barrio dwellers are conceived of above all as poor people, stuck at the short end of concentrations of economic power. From this vantage point, marginality and disorganization stem from weakness and poverty, not the reverse.[9] Even where special attention goes to the need for

[9] See Perlman, *The Myth of Marginality*; Archdiocese of São Paulo, Commission of Justice and Peace, *São Paulo: Growth and Poverty*; Eckstein, *The Poverty of Revolution*; and Wayne Corne-

cultural change, as in Barrio Meléndez, issues are framed in a way that underscores how inequalities of wealth and power make for cultural distortions, not how lack of education or initiative mire ordinary people in poverty. In this light, unmasking cultural manipulations appears as one step on the road to general activism. As one sister told me, barrio residents may think of themselves as "orphaned" (CA 76), but closer inspection shows that they really are *alienated*, in all the senses of the term.

> Resources are scarce, and this means that people can't dedicate themselves to this work; people have to eat, and so they don't have much spare time. That's one thing. [But] maybe the biggest problem of all, the biggest problem I face right now when I try to make people conscious of the reality around them, and of a program for changing it, [is that] most people are very alienated. They don't care about politics, and they don't care about their neighbors, and they don't care about anything. That makes it hard, that's a real obstacle. (CA 97)

Pervasive economic and political inequalities make for a general state of social and psychological oppression that is difficult to break. This often leads poor people to mask inner rage and humiliation with public silence, to keep "hidden transcripts"[10] along with the words and expressions they show to the world at large. The effort to break through these defensive facades begins with discovery of a common identity and with moves by the poor and powerless to work together, no matter how small the issue or proximate the goal. Ordinary people also need some kind of structural shield, some relation to larger institutions that gives a sense of protection and legitimacy to their efforts.[11] One Venezuelan sister articulated the point in these words:

> The people suffer from an oppression that comes from way back. It is moral, economic, psychological—everything that keeps them from becoming independent, from taking initiatives. Take for example the problem of the family, with the tremendous machismo we have here, all the families with no father at home. Things like that, I think that really they don't deserve all the blame; these things come as a result of that same overall oppression. They suffered from the same thing when they were growing up, that's what they saw every day.
>
> I believe that what we can contribute above all is understanding, love, being there for them. Because you see, they have been so completely abandoned in every respect—religion, sanitation, everything. I think it is a slow process, but the fact that they feel themselves to be accompanied, that someone is there to

---

lius, *Politics and the Migrant Poor in Mexico City*. See my "Urbanization in Latin America: Changing Perspectives" for comments on theory and method.

[10] The term is from James Scott. See his *Domination and the Arts of Resistance* for a full discussion.

[11] See Archdiocese of São Paulo, *São Paulo*, chaps. 5 and 6.

encourage them, to help them join together to become aware of their own problems—to me that is fundamental. (B 131)

The opportunity to work with others gives residents a sense that "they also have something to contribute to others, that they are really someone with abilities, that they can improve themselves. I've seen it happen, for example with our catechists. Even the way they look and hold themselves is different. I've been struck by the change" (B 135). Among those that do get involved in this way, spouses now treat each other with more respect, child abuse has declined, men and women dress better and look happier. Changes like these are the stuff of common conversation in the barrios.

An interesting and (for me) unexpected facet of the stress on building self-confidence appears in the development of health committees and in moves for dietary reform and natural medicine among the Venezuelan groups, both rural and urban.[12] Awareness of modern medicine is universal: like the well-to-do, poor people opt for doctors and for specific drug treatments if at all possible. But as a practical matter, medical help is costly and hard to get. For peasants, a long and difficult trip is usually required. For barrio dwellers, public facilities like social security clinics may be close at hand, but they are notorious in both countries for delays, poor service, and for the petty humiliations clients are forced to undergo. These prevailing conditions suggest that for many poor people, turning to doctors and pharmacists simply transfers personal dependence from saints and shrines to equally distant and powerful figures in clinics and hospitals.

When Father Manolo Moreno and the Medical Mission Sisters began to form health committees (around Villanueva and in the Barquisimeto barrios, respectively), they hoped to combine access to preventive care with dietary reform and holistic medicine. Central to the whole effort was a desire to empower people by giving them a kind of information about health that would let them take control of their own situation. Good health was presented as integral to God's plan. Local residents were urged to take responsibility and to believe that their own products (e.g., the fruits or vegetables they could grow) were as valuable (if not more so) than the prepackaged goods available in the marketplace. Father Moreno described his work as follows:

> Most of the time goes to educating people about health and nourishment, and trying to ensure that all these efforts (like growing vegetables) appear in the light of God's word. Making them see that God gave nature freely to us, and in this way removing the veil that covers their eyes and makes them think that processed goods are better than natural ones. . . . Above all, people here need to have greater faith in themselves, to value what they themselves produce. And this is

[12] Scott Mainwaring shows the importance of health committees in "Brazil: The Catholic Church and the Popular Movement in Nova Iguaçu, 1974–1985."

specifically relevant to health. I calculate the malnutrition [rate] here to be more than 80 percent. (V 131, 132)

Moreno's efforts at dietary reform included promoting family gardens alongside cash crops like coffee and encouraging consumption of fruits, vegetables, and dairy products that had long been ignored in favor of coffee and canned goods. Natural medicine centered on the use of herbal compounds and specific "healing earths" applied, for example, as mud packs to deal with knife wounds, stings, or snake bites. These are so cheap and effective that their use spread rapidly throughout the area, inspiring a number of popular folk songs that record and celebrate particular cures.

The mobile clinic established by the Medical Mission Sisters proved equally popular. The sisters agree with Moreno that health is inseparable from religious faith. As one told me,

Our work is related to salvation. Healing is an experience of salvation, and at a particular time in life can open people to something greater, to a religious giving of themselves. It is not just a hook [to attract residents]; it's valuable in itself, and it doesn't matter whether or not religion follows. (B 193)

These health-care efforts upset long-standing relations with doctors, pharmacists, and local bureaucracies. For example, as a result of their work with the clinic, the sisters have linked up with city- and state-wide movements of physicians seeking general improvements in health-care delivery. In Villanueva, local merchants complained bitterly to the state governor and to the archbishop that Moreno's efforts were ruining their business. He and the Jesuits were accused of maintaining links with guerrilla groups and of systematic antigovernment propaganda and subversion. As a result, Moreno himself was temporarily suspended as a priest, but the suspension was lifted after a large delegation of peasants (backed by clergy and sisters) came to Barquisimeto's episcopal residence in protest. Not long after this incident, Moreno was officially installed as curate and official successor to Padre Vicente, thus ensuring some continuity for the orientations that had been established in the area.

Priests and sisters who have made a commitment to the poor often share the popular view noted earlier that the institutional church has changed relatively little. Apart from making reference to scattered programs, no one in the group, even the most conservative among them, felt that the church had undergone any substantial transformation. Although most pointed to greater opportunities for lay participation, they saw such changes as too limited and without backing or reverberation in the institution as a whole. They also believe that their work remains for the most part isolated from and marginal to the institutional church.

Facatativá would seem to provide an exception to these comments, but it may be the exception that proves the rule. Reflection on the Facatativá experience suggests that close diocesan contact and supervision actually undermines the central goals of popular work that the diocese claims to preserve. The closer the contacts, the less able groups are to survive (at any stage) without them. A vicious circle is established in which chances for autonomy and independent growth are systematically cut off or, worse, never get a chance to emerge. The absence of such autonomy and independence is then lamented and taken as a pretext for continued close supervision.

As a practical matter, many of the clergy and sisters working at the grassroots level have only sporadic contact with the diocese, much less with the national church, for example, concerning documents or programs. Tabio's priest remarked that many of the diocese's efforts were more like campaigns than sustained programs: too much was attempted, too little accomplished.

> What we have are really campaigns. When these are national, we accept and try to implement them. As for specific programs, there are no properly national programs, just programs that come from the diocese. It's this way. The diocese writes a plan, and its own evaluations show that the plan is working. But the problem is that sometimes they try to do too much. They indicate a whole series of things that can't be done in the space of just one year. But then in the next year, they assume that all that has been done, and thus go on to set new goals. In human terms, it just hasn't been possible. (R 43, 44)

Later in this same interview, he went out of his way to note the enormous value of a recent document from the National Conference of Bishops. "I have not read it yet," he told me, "but I imagine it is very important, very profound" (R 52). At the very least, this offhand comment suggests a good deal of distance. Matters are worse in Cali and throughout Venezuela, where for all practical purposes those working at the grass roots have no contact whatsoever with the institutional church of bishops and dioceses. Only at moments of crisis, or perhaps at some once-a-year ceremony (a saint's day, confirmations), do the two levels meet.[13]

Of course, viewed from the base, lack of contact may not be all bad. It makes for considerable freedom of maneuver, and lets those seeking a space for popular work exploit contacts and networks of information or resources apart from those officially sanctioned by the church. In this kind of situation, groups can build more easily on one another. Thus the Javierian sisters already knew about the Spanish priests in Barrio Meléndez and wanted to work along-

---

[13] Talking with priests and sisters in these communities reminded me of an interview I carried out for an earlier study. In mid-1971, I interviewed the parish priest in La Raya, an invasion barrio in Valencia, one of Venezuela's fast-growing industrial cities. We were seated in the shade, outside his tiny house next to the church. He wore a cassock that was dirty and torn, and he needed a shave. His comment underscored the isolation he felt. Things are difficult in La Raya, he remarked, because "here we are marginal with the marginals, and our petitions don't get attention at higher levels" (*Religion and Politics in Latin America*, p. 271).

side them. The sisters in Barquisimeto were attracted to their specific barrio in part by the reputation local Jesuits had already established. The Jesuits themselves built on the base provided by Vicente. Recall the evocative metaphor they use: Vicente made the plate (Legion of Mary), we baked the cake (cooperatives), Manolo provided the icing and decorations (dietary reform, natural medicine). Apart from contacts of this kind, in each case local organizers drew support from alternative national networks for support: the Jesuits and CESAP in Venezuela; CINEP and *Solidaridad* in Colombia.

The men and women we are listening to in this chapter know very well that their work is only one of many possible alternatives in the church. They also know that the goals and styles of action embodied in the option for the poor now visible in Cali, Barquisimeto, Villanueva, or even in parts of Facatativá are often not well received in the church as whole. Commitment to the poor involves them in a difficult struggle, and as this penetrating comment from one of the sisters in Meléndez recognizes, the tide is not running in their favor.

It's not just that the church is conservative, and that's that. It is also that López Trujillo is very intelligent and able, and makes his presence felt across the board. He blocks change, and also keeps other bishops from exploring the possibilities of an opening, but he doesn't do it only through the exercise of authority. He has intellectual and ideological influence as well.

Another important factor, especially in the last year or year and a half, has been the conservative turn, the move to the right, in a number of religious orders, especially women. In 1978, 1979, and 1980, the years just before and after Puebla, we saw a real opening in the religious orders. Their own leadership allowed new experiences to go forward, provided freedom to go to the barrios, to the towns and villages. That's how lots of base-level sisters became committed to the poor in a serious way, as they began to discover a new world. But all that has changed in the last few years. And you can see that pressure and frictions start not in the base, but rather in the administration of the congregations. People at the base are left with no room for maneuver, and this leads to a situation where lots of sisters either leave their orders or remain, but with little they can do. So all those hopes and possibilities, they all go under. (CA 80, 81)

At this point, it may be useful to reflect for a moment on the exceptionally wide range of activities in which priests and sisters are involved. At a minimum, the list includes the following: catechism and Bible study; education (for adults and children); management of apostolic groups like *cursillos* or the Legion of Mary, community stores and cooperatives (local and regional); construction projects, including school buildings and water lines; dietary reform and farm gardens; preventive health care and natural medicine; accounting and leadership training. The list could easily be extended, but it is more important to identify the patterns through which these separate activities fit into a coherent vision of the proper role of the church and of its pastoral agents.

A critical element underlying the patterns that have emerged thus far is whether or not pastoral agents tie their efforts to goals of *re-Christianization*. Taking re-Christianization as a core objective presumes subordination of personal and group efforts to the greater interests of the institution, and to the directive role of its official leaders, clergy and bishops. When re-Christianization is a central goal, prevailing images of the church draw strength from notions of Christendom, according to which religious institutions are the proper source of binding norms for all areas of human life.

Re-Christianization also has clear implications for the nature and potential impact of group life. Organizations formed with this justification are not necessarily "more Christian" or "more religious" than others. All the groups studied here are linked in some way to the Catholic church. All hold to a common core of basic beliefs. At issue is more control and authority than religious authenticity. Where goals of re-Christianization predominate, it is difficult if not impossible for church people to break traditions of doing things to and for the poor. Because enlightenment and authority are presumed to flow only from the top down, ordinary people are never trusted to speak and act for themselves. Abandoning goals of re-Christianization commits priests and sisters to do more listening than talking, more sharing than handing out, and to focus on enabling and empowering others, not doing things for them. The effort is not an easy one, especially for priests raised in a system geared to domination by male clerics. But although difficult, it is not impossible, and on the evidence presented here, success is most likely to begin with the kind of multifaceted option for the poor visible in Cali and in the hamlets and barrios of Venezuela.

## Opting for the Poor, Popular Religion, and the Nature of Groups

Thinking about the poor raises a host of thorny questions. Are poor people best seen as passive objects, in the grip of larger, only dimly understood forces, or as active subjects in control of what they think and do? Should they be viewed as eternal victims (the poor who are "always with us"), as a social class, or rather as one element among many in the broad net the church casts? Are their beliefs no more than a hodgepodge of ignorance and superstition to be purified, or do these beliefs instead constitute a valid and authentic expression of faith mediated by experience? Are base communities and similar groups properly spiritual, social, or is some mix of the two appropriate? Finding answers to questions like these begins with the attempt to understand who the poor are in the first place.

*Opting for the Poor.* It is hard to find anyone in the church who is willing to reject the concept of opting for the poor in any explicit way. The poor have a special place in Christian imagery, and the general notion of a "preferential" option for them has become so deeply embedded in the ordinary discourse of Latin American Catholicism that it is unlikely to be dislodged by a frontal assault. The battle is fought on other terrain.

Discussions commonly take off from a distinction between the material poor and the spiritual poor. Those who accept this dual definition resist options for the poor that are made in "narrow" economic terms. From this vantage point, the materially rich can be spiritually poor, and the church is obliged to serve all without prejudice or exclusions. Such views are common in Facatativá, and move all involved to caution, especially in the tone and content of messages. Quebradanegra's parish priest spoke for many as he defined his version of the preferential option for the poor as a mixture of traditional spiritual care and charity. To be sure, opting for the poor means helping those in need. Further,

> On the positive side of the ledger, I see a considerable advance in the fact that so many of our small hamlets have gotten organized through the efforts of the base community promoters. This has led to many fine acts of charity and justice. Here in the parish center [the town itself] we have also witnessed extraordinary manifestations of this fraternal charity, directed at the poor and needy. (Q 60)

> Here in the parish, I have been intensely concerned with this option for the poor. And I want to tell you, humbly and without boasting of any kind, that I personally am providing almost the entire support for ten poor people. I support them with my alms, I look after them continuously, and I have taught those who work with me to treat the poor well, and to help them, so that here in the town, this kind of assistance for the poor should not falter. (Q 68)

A slightly more activist and less charity-focused version of this basic perspective comes from one of the sisters who worked with Román Cortes throughout the hinterland of Caparrapí. We have already heard her description of the distrust and violence endemic to this area. The following account of the meaning of opting for the poor suggests some of the contradictions that run through the whole effort. Service to all is enjoined but, at the same time, stress is placed on living with the poor (the materially poor) on a day-to-day basis. Thus:

> I think that the preferential option for the poor is important. Of course, we've got to get away from terms like "poor," because poor means someone who lacks everything. [But] the rich can be poor, with material and spiritual needs. I also think that our insertion with the poor gets us closer to them on a one-to-one [tu a tu] basis, and helps us understand their problems better. Directly from them, not from books. Living with them is different from learning about it only in theory. (C 89)

A far different view of the matter prevails among the Jesuits of Venezuela. The Centro Gumilla pitches its efforts (from publication to teaching and organizing) in support of popular groups, which are defined (as at Puebla) in highly specific social terms: peasants, slum dwellers, marginal classes, proletarians, and the like. Although he explicitly resists romanticizing the poor, this Jesuit argues strongly that

> it's not a question of *opting*, but rather, like Jesus, of betting that salvation, and the integral human liberation that we're fighting for, that all these come from the poor, from those who appear in Jesus' message as the privileged of God—the poor themselves. And it's them precisely because they are the ones who suffer all the consequences of this society, they are the ones who live all its ambiguities and feel all its deficiencies in themselves. I don't for a moment believe in the notion of the poor in spirit, who have not lived and felt poverty, and who are not also materially poor. (B 209)

The sisters in La Carucieña echo this activist position but add that although the preferential option for the poor is a great step forward for the church, it remains unfulfilled in practice (B 139). These women dismiss warnings about the perils of using a language of class to define church positions or about the dangers of any "exclusive" option (that is, one that focused more on one class than on another). They argue that as a practical matter, the church has long favored the rich. Thus the issue is changing the focus of activities, not creating one in place of a previous neutrality. One sister put it simply and well:

> It's something like finally realizing the need to attend to the people in specific terms, to the people around us. Until a few years ago, the church devoted herself solely to the middle and upper classes. And ordinary people, well, they had the attention of parish priests in the small towns, but the whole effort was minimal, and directed above all to the sacraments. Now there is a different understanding. (B 137)

The polar alternatives are clear. The poor can be the objects of the church's charity or spiritual guidance, or they can be seen as a social class with its own characteristic needs and perspectives. In the first case, the poor are defined primarily by their ties to the institution. They therefore appear as occupants of subordinate units within a hierarchical structure. That is what base means in this point of view. In the second case, they are approached as a group with an independent identity and autonomous values to offer. The term "base" has a more clearly social meaning here. Those "at the base" are the poor in concrete terms, and opting for them requires much more than choosing new programs, texts, clothes, or housing. It also requires actively siding with a social class, and joining its struggle to change the very conditions of its creation.[14]

---

[14] In chapter 2, above, I noted liberation theology's extensive borrowing from Marxism. The

So far in this section, I have focused on the extremes of the spectrum, but, as with much human experience, when it comes to figuring out precisely what opting for the poor means, most of the choices and decisions fall somewhere in between. Few people limit themselves to giving alms or blessings; fewer still move to revolutionary action. The matter is commonly seen in practical terms that underscore the need to choose but sidestep the kinds of conflict-ridden commitments or alliances the radical position often assumes. For this sister in Tabio, at issue is simply choosing to work with those in need.

> Well, yes, for example, in my work if I can choose between a well-paid job in a comfortable area and another that is not well paid but nonetheless works with the poor, then I have to prefer the poor. I don't deny that the rich have needs too, but I prefer to work with the poor.
>
> Also for example, in cases of conflict to side with the poor, as long as this doesn't create its own injustices. We don't want to canonize the poor either. (R 117)

This sort of middle-of-the-road position makes opting for the poor a matter of helping, backing, and standing up for poor people more than empowering them to do these things on their own. A broader commitment was justified by one of the priests working in rural Venezuela in terms that underscored the notion of choosing sides while still attempting to retain some sense of overall unity among all people. Metaphors of family serve this complex goal well.

> Well, you see with the church it's like with a family. If one of the children is sick, the parents have to give him preferential attention. And all the other children have to make a special effort to treat the sick one like a brother. It's the same thing here. In a society where the majority is malnourished and lacks education, giving preference means that we need to turn our attention to the neediest, so that we all come to treat them like brothers. (V 139)

For those who take a more radical stance, these views represent backsliding from the commitments made at Puebla and especially at Medellín.[15] In their eyes, things have been going downhill for years: Medellín's strong denunciations of injustice and institutionalized violence have been diluted, and its call for action shunted aside. Those who stick faithfully to the ideas of Medellín feel on the defensive. Still, work goes on, and the following comment from a sister in Barrio Meléndez indicates that some groups have continued backing, if not from the church as a whole, then at least from their own congregations. At issue is more than just helping existing movements or facilitating choice

---

broad commitment to the poor visible here recalls Marx's argument that freeing the proletariat was critical to human liberation because the condition of the proletariat summed up all exploitation. Their struggle will presumably be definitive.

[15] See my "Impact and Lasting Significance of Medellín and Puebla."

among the alternatives already in place. The task at hand is to create new
possibilities.

> The fundamental interest of my community lies in its clear option for the poor,
> the oppressed, the working class. Our commitment is to open new paths, to serve
> as something of a vanguard, with a real vanguard spirit. Because this is our gen-
> eral policy, each local group has lots of freedom to choose the sort of work it
> wants to pursue. Here in Colombia, we have three different groups. Two of them
> are involved in this kind of cultural work [and] we want to continue in this field
> because we see our particular contribution to the process of liberation as coming
> in ideological terms. That still leaves us free to get into many different areas and
> to start new kinds of projects. (CA 59, 60)

Debates about the meaning of opting for the poor are influenced strongly by
attitudes to popular religion. I asked priests and sisters to talk about what
"popular religiosity" meant to them, and to indicate how they dealt with it
(however defined) in their day-to-day work. The distinctions drawn concerning a "preferential option" color this topic as well, with noteworthy differences between the two countries and, especially, between priests and sisters.

*Popular Religion.*   The most common response to my question about the
meaning of popular religiosity was to highlight specific beliefs and practices.[16]
Respondents pointed, for example, to the strong cult for the dead, manifest in
repeated prayers to the dead, in special veneration for their spirits, and in
occasional efforts to mollify them or appeal to them for help. The pervasive
use of holy water as a charm or medicinal cure-all was also much mentioned.
Each region also has some custom or practice identified as its own: devotions
to a particular image or saint (e.g., Barquisimeto's Divina Pastora or Quebradanegra's San Roque); ribbons (color coded by sex) tied to the ankles or wrists
of newborns to ward off the evil eye; or recourse to amulets of one kind or
another to guard against the (literally) chilling effects of a recent death. Exaggerated devotionalism is placed in this category of what are frankly seen as
"curious" practices. Holy Week is a common focus of such intense devotions.
One sister told me that when she first arrived in the isolated hamlets around
Caparrapí, she found that residents were unwilling to do *anything* in those
days:

> Everyone stops work, especially on Good Friday. They are particularly devoted
> to Good Friday. Even though we have managed, with the catechism, to show the
> greater importance of Easter Sunday [and the Resurrection], Friday is still the key
> day for them. We became aware of this through surveys we carried out. On that
> day no one bathed, they wouldn't strike their animals, and no one worked. No
> one did any cooking either—they left everything prepared ahead of time.

[16] Kselman ("Ambivalence") states that this is a common view of the matter.

[*Why no bathing?*] Because they thought it was a sin, they believed they would be changed into water spirits [she laughs]. They also still believe in the souls in purgatory, and in the dead, they have a special veneration for the dead. For them, the dead have a sacred, almost mythical quality.

They see everything about Good Friday in terms of death, and I suppose they have good reason. They have suffered so much, they've been so martyred, that I suppose it's logical that death draws them so powerfully. It is such a strong part of their culture. (C 89)

When opinions differ about popular religiosity, variation is less a matter of the beliefs and practices reported than of the explanation offered for their origins and meaning. Those working in rural Colombia commonly present "popular religion" as a loose collection of items that have been passed down informally through the generations and carried forward with little conscious thought. As one sister put it, "These people are extremely religious as a matter of tradition, but they can't explain why. They hold to lots of religious customs and practices, without a clue as to what they mean" (R 119). By focusing on a set of heterodox and often decidedly "odd" or "quaint" practices, this view underscores the authority of clergy and sisters without questioning the faith of ordinary people. Some clearly feel comfortable with this situation because of the way traditional popular religiosity enhances their overall prestige and authority. They praise the deep and abiding quality of popular faith but stress the need for guidance to keep it on the right path. Quebradanegra's priest uses an organic analogy:

To me, popular religiosity is the humus of genuine holiness. Humus, you know, is a layer of soil that keeps things moist and lets seeds and plants germinate. It's the humus of a holy life, of the church, I'm sure of it. . . . Of course, there still are traces of superstition like amulets or good-luck charms—all those more-or-less superstitious objects. There's still quite a lot of that, and I have tried to control it as much as possible. Not in a moralizing way, but rather through theological instruction. (Q 71, 73)

The perspective just outlined takes popular religion as *something to be changed*, and therefore devotes little effort to understanding what it may signify to those involved, and why. But there is another position. When opting for the poor is taken to require "insertion" into popular milieus, accompanying rather than leading groups of poor people, pastoral agents are called upon to make a sustained effort to see the world through popular eyes, and to give special value to these new insights. Assuming a popular point of view requires more than a new sociology or a different vocabulary. Although it is clearly vital to acknowledge the poor as a group with independently valid experience, the idea must have religious significance if it is to carry much weight. The effort is never easy, but a first step to new understandings of popular religion is clearly to shed the baggage of authority—to remain, listen, and value what comes.

The nuns working in Barquisimeto's barrios show how this can be done. To them, popular religion is more than just a set of beliefs or practices and more than an expression of profound, if unlettered, faith. Although they acknowledge all this, they also stress that popular religion constitutes a source of wisdom and provides ordinary people with a way to live out their faith by drawing on the lessons of experience. Thinking about the matter in this way, the sisters do not so much go to the poor as engage in a real dialogue, learning and changing themselves in the process. Thus,

> it's part of my life, something I've gained as a result of living with these people. Because you see, in the education we received, all that was ignored and unknown, sometimes even criticized and looked down on. But you come to realize that these things are deeply rooted in people's experiences and that sometimes they have a lot to teach us: how to relate to one another; how to pray; how to have the kind of really festive celebration we had yesterday; the cult of the dead. For me it's been a whole education, a new life experience—an ambiguous one to be sure, but when you get down to it, a deeply valuable religious experience. (B 120)

Pretensions to an authoritative guiding role are abandoned here. The proper stance toward popular religion is thus not purification (in either conservative or radical directions) but rather approaching closer to share, learn, and understand.

> We've discussed this question a lot: how best to immerse ourselves in order to understand better, because you know, one tends to overlook things. A person comes in with her own preset ideas and plans and just proceeds without taking account of anything else. But really it's all a process, and the way you go about it is critical for all the work itself. It's vital to give full weight to what people themselves believe is important. Like in the case of holy water that we were talking about earlier. (B 123)

This position differs in subtle but important ways from the one that appears to guide activities in Cali's Barrio Meléndez. Remember that cultural reformulation is a central goal for the Javierian sisters there. They see popular religion as another of the distortions produced by alienating culture, warped and manipulated by the institutions which shape politics and culture generally. Working with these assumptions, the four Javierian sisters pitched all their efforts (in courses, libraries, celebrations, and daily discussions) toward *unmasking* alienating practices and thereby opening the community to alternative views of themselves and of the world. The problem is that such an orientation all too easily strips popular practices or devotions of the language and aesthetic values that make them meaningful to most people. Evangelization is reduced to social commitments; preaching and persuading nudge prayer aside; and in processions, placards and banners may come to replace costumes, music, or dancing.[17] The whole phenomenon is common in radical Catholic circles in Latin America lately, and the following description of how popular education is oriented in Barrio Meléndez makes the point well.

> We make an effort to provide ideas not only through exposure to reading the Bible and to some approximation to theology, but also to aspects of the social sciences. Along with this, we make a series of presentations that lay out an alternative vision of life. In that way, we try to create the seeds of a new man in the young adults with whom we work, the new man as defined by Che Guevara, by Saint Paul. That's more or less what we try to do. (CA 56)

It is instructive to set the alternative positions outlined here against the variations in popular belief and practices described in chapter 5, above. The exercise reveals a close association between the practices reported for and the views of pastoral agents active in each particular area. Traditional modalities predominate in San Isidro, Quebradanegra, Caparrapí, or Río Frío, where clergy have a notably more authoritarian and controlling bent. In contrast, experience in Agua Fría and in the communities scattered around Villanueva reveals new attitudes to the saints and shifting patterns of prayer, along with a belief that group solidarity can be a legitimate and even necessary expression of faith. Turning to the cities, we find that although there are close parallels between city and country people in Venezuela, this is not the case in Colombia. In both Barrio Meléndez and Barrio El Rodeo, residents have moved to a radical pattern of action and (especially of) discourse that stresses political solidarity with others and stretches common notions of church, sanctity, and sainthood well beyond conventional definitions.

If we adapt the typology of base communities laid out in chapter 2 and further specified for these communities in chapter 5 to the issues of the preferential option for the poor and popular religiosity (as discussed by priests and sisters), a rough correspondence emerges (see table 7.2). To radicals, popular religion requires purification to shed its alienating character. Such purification is best achieved through education, mobilization, and a diffuse activism that links local groups to a broad struggle over issues of class and power. CINEP has a separate department of "popular religiosity," which as a practical matter devotes its energies primarily to coordinating a scattered network of radicalized groups across the country. Conservatives also want to change popular religion, which they regard not as alienated but as insufficiently instructed. They praise popular religiosity as a sign of the people's "deep faith" but insist that any expressions of this faith be confined to moments and vehicles under ecclesiastical control. Clerics are portrayed as the sole legitimate judges of authenticity. The middle position is held down by those who strive to work

---

[17] Cf. Susan Rosales Nelson, "Bolivia: Continuity and Conflict in Religious Discourse."

within existing forms of popular culture and to use these as a means of energizing groups without gutting their characteristic language or aesthetic values, or reducing them to folkloric status: cultural remnants to be admired but never used. None of the three stances is simply a reaction to the other, nor is the middle to be understood as a residual category. To the contrary, as we have seen, each position has independent roots in the sociology and ecclesiology that inspire its adherents.

The preceding observations suggest an obvious question: If the correspondence is so close, is it not possible that popular groups do little more than parrot what they hear from trusted priests and sisters? Are the changes discussed in earlier chapters simply an echo effect, the old clericalism put to new ends? I do not think so, and at this point it is appropriate to advance a few reasons. To be sure, pastoral agents have considerable impact on popular ideas and practices, particularly at the outset of a process of change. At a minimum

**TABLE 7.2**

Priests and Sisters, A Typology of Positions on Key Issues

|  | Conservative | Sociocultural Transformation | Radical |
|---|---|---|---|
| **Preferential Option** |  |  |  |
| Cause of poverty | Individual Failings | Structural Sources | Structural Sources/ Oppression |
| Who are the poor? | All in need, spiritual and material | Material poor as a class | Material poor as a class |
| What should priests and sisters do? | Charity, self-help, avoidance | "Insertion," accompany | "Insertion," accompany, direct to change |
| **Popular Religiosity** |  |  |  |
| Definition | Heterodox practices | Valid expression of popular culture | Expression of alienated culture |
| Examples cited | Processions, holy water, cult of the dead, etc. | Processions, holy water, cult of the dead, etc. | Processions, holy water, cult of the dead, etc. |
| What should priests or sisters do? | Instruct, purify | Learn, adapt | Unmask, purify |
| Examples | Quebradanegra San Isidro Caparrapí | Villanueva Barquisimeto | Meléndez |

they may embarrass ordinary people and shame them into changing by insisting that much of what they were taught as children is foolish, mistaken, or unnecessary. But lecturing is unlikely to get the job done all by itself. Unless some change gets going within the group itself, instruction (however packaged) will probably do little more than drive older conventions underground. Recall that although few would admit to belief in ghosts, spirits, or apparitions, almost everyone knew someone else who did. As the old saying goes, "I don't believe in witches, but if they fly, they fly" ("No creo en brujas, pero que vuelan, vuelan").

*The Nature of Groups.*   The expected and hoped for character of base communities and related groups follows easily from what we have just seen. A critical element here is whether or not groups are required to be specifically Christian. The distinction surfaces most notably in disputes over the primacy of a spiritual or a social orientation for the group. Should they be devoted above all to Bible study, religious practice, and the perfection of personal spirituality, or is a broader range of concerns also appropriate? For most of the priests and sisters I interviewed, this is a distinction without a difference. One sister from Caparrapí put it this way:

> We always try to integrate the two, to join spirituality with human promotion. Because if you focus only on the spiritual, you're not being honest with people, telling them just to be calm and to have faith. No! I think that the diocese's whole effort provides important elements here. It is very much within the church, closely tied to the parish. We've always made a point of this, that groups not go off on their own, like loose cannons, but remain instead within the organizational structures of the parish. (C 87)

These views reflect the emphasis characteristic in Facatativá on authoritatively structured integration. From this vantage point, if base communities are to achieve a proper mix among faith, spirituality, and social issues, continuous links with the parish and with larger church structures are required. The experience of the Legion of Mary as founded around Villanueva by Padre Vicente provides a clear alternative. The groups he established started off from a base that was highly devotional and very concerned with the development of personal and group spirituality. But as Vicente saw matters, the best way to ensure religious legitimacy was to train, empower, and trust a cadre of local leaders to run things in his absence. Despite his concern for vertical as opposed to purely horizontal ties (God comes first, then the community), and his fear that the cooperative's rapid growth might obscure its religious dimension ("lots of coffee, little faith" ["mucho café, poca fé"], he is reported to have said), it was Vicente who set the whole process of change in motion and continues to praise it. The entire thrust of the cooperative's structure and ordinary routine has been to encourage a steady mix of faith with action. Solidary credit is justified in terms of the church as community, meetings begin with Bible study and end with a mass, and so forth. Further, in Villanueva as in cases like Agua Fría, the same people typically lead both religious and social/political groups. This effective fusion of the two dimensions belies efforts to impose a strict separation as the norm.

Let us be clear. The kind of groups just described are not less connected to the church than those in Facatativá. All the groups in question take off from links to the church, all prize the connection greatly, and, as we have seen, across the board, members regard themselves as Catholics in good standing. But the way these links and identities are understood and managed makes for noteworthy differences in resulting patterns of authority, commitment, culture, and action.

Self-managed transformations in group practice give new religious ideas an immediacy and conviction that instruction or preaching cannot achieve by themselves. They do so, for example, in Meléndez, Agua Fría or Villanueva, by involving members in the effort and, in this way, opening them to new sources of knowledge while instilling in them a broad-ranging self-confidence. Of course, such a process works to greatest effect when it is matched up with views among pastoral agents that respect and empower popular groups. They go together from the outset. Such a combination means that priests and sisters take off from a stance dedicated to listening and learning. After a while, the changes they help spark mean that there is something new to hear. Who provides the echo then? The point is not to decide which comes first but rather to locate patterns of synthesis, and explore the conditions that make them arise and either flourish or fail. The heart of the matter lies not in a dichotomy between spiritual and social orientations but rather in the way any orientation is put to work in ordinary practice. Even the most narrow and traditional beginnings can expand into other fields, given half a chance.

The next section profiles two sisters whose lives and careers illustrate some of the major possibilities of personal and religious change discussed in this chapter. These women differ on a number of dimensions, including age, education, and career pattern. Each is deeply committed to work with the popular groups, but, as we shall see, particularities of ideology and personal style make the undertaking very different in the two cases. Close inspection of these contrasting ways of working out a common commitment yields a richer understanding of what it means to be a nun in Latin America today.

## Two Matched Profiles

Gladys Bernal is one of three sisters from the Congregation of San José de Tarbes living and working in Barrio La Carucieña in Barquisimeto. Sister Gladys is a large, pleasant, and articulate woman who has been resident in La

Carucieña since early 1978. I first met her at the Jesuit residence in nearby Brisas del Aeropuerto, where she was conducting a series of meetings and classes (jointly with Jesuit priests) for barrio residents, for the novices of her order, and for young Jesuit students. Gladys is a well-known figure in La Carucieña, and her VW beetle is immediately recognized throughout the barrio. Indeed, Gladys spends a good part of every week in her car, visiting families and neighborhoods scattered throughout the barrio's extensive terrain. Her apparent omnipresence reflects her own boundless energy, and also reveals the extent to which residents feel free to call on Gladys and her housemates for advice or help at any time. If a family member is in trouble or help is needed confronting the bureaucracy (e.g., for access to hospitals, schools, or social agencies), Gladys or one of the other sisters is frequently enlisted for moral and material support. Services involving transport (the VW) are particularly welcome in a barrio where buses are scarce and taxis often refuse to go.[18]

When Sister Gladys chose to work with popular groups, she broke what until then had been a most conventional pattern of personal history and religious career. Gladys Bernal was born to middle-class parents in the city of Barquisimeto itself in early February 1934. Her primary and secondary education was all carried out in girls' schools run by nuns, and it was during her secondary school years that Gladys first felt a personal vocation to become a nun herself. An aunt was a sister of the same congregation that Gladys eventually joined, and this influence, added to the model provided by the sisters she encountered in school, helped to focus her decision. Gladys entered the order in 1959, and took final and definitive vows nine years later.

The conventional quality of this pattern was modified in small but significant fashion by the way she experienced military rule as a young girl. During the decade of dictatorship (1948–58), church schools and students were regularly mobilized to celebrate public holidays.[19] Gladys describes it this way:

I have had special concern for social issues ever since I was a young girl. In school I was involved with lots of organizations, including youth groups and catechism work. The dictatorship of Pérez Jiménez had a great effect on me. I was in *liceo* [high school], and I remember one occasion when friends of mine were beaten up and arrested; that had a big impact on me. I entered the novitiate during the dictatorship, and when the dictator fell, I was still a novice. Even so, all of us kept in touch with what was happening in the country; Pérez Jiménez himself once paid a visit to our town. As I said, I've always had strong social interests, and speaking as a Christian who shares in the search to change our own society, I can tell you that social issues have always been a focal point of my life. (B 124)

[18] For a similar (though more radical) case of omnipresence, see Jane Kramer, "Letter from the Elysian Fields," which describes the routine of a young priest in urban Brazil.
[19] See Luis Colmenares Díaz, *La espada y el incensario: La iglesia bajo Pérez Jiménez*, for details on these and similar public ceremonies.

The conventional pattern for aspiring nuns of the period was further modified in this case by two simultaneous events. The first was Gladys's participation (now as an advanced student) in a strike by students and faculty at the Institute of Theology of the Catholic University. Joining in a challenge to constituted church authorities was a wholly new experience for someone like Gladys. The strike brought out ideas about the legitimacy of siding with others against authority and of seeking alternative pathways for religiously valid work. These ideas were reinforced by the example of the 1968 Medellín conference, which Gladys and her colleagues followed closely. As things turned out, these conjunctures led Gladys to participate in some of the first public confrontations within the Venezuelan church during the late 1960s and early 1970s. As a nun, she was still relegated to the sidelines, but she felt present and involved all the same.

> The Institute of Theology really helped me a lot. At that time, there was a particular group of progressive professors there who were the focus of a lot of controversy. We sisters joined in the very first strike at the university [in their support] . . . so you could say that we lived through all of that. We felt the whole history of the Latin American church in our own lives.
>
> When I was working in our school in La Florida [an area of Caracas], I had a small group of boys and girls that was very involved with the life of the church, very aware. At the time of Medellín, we went to Bogotá. We were there, and we held meetings to discuss what we had seen. As a result, this group later joined with others in Caracas in occupying the Basilica of San Francisco [1969] as a symbolic gesture by young laypersons who wanted more openness and participation in the church. They were beaten and jailed. Of course, in those years we nuns weren't visible. The lay people were out in front, and we stayed on the sidelines. They wouldn't even let us visit them in jail. You know, these are the kind of things that leave a mark, they help you in your search. (B 124)

Despite these tentative forays into activism, on completing her studies and taking final vows, Gladys assumed the normal life of a full-fledged member of her congregation. She continued teaching in one of the order's elite girls' schools, logging a total of twelve years in this work. The initial break with convention came in 1975, when, along with a handful of companions, Gladys left the school and moved to a country town. Here she supported herself by teaching, first in a secretarial academy and then, after two years, in the local public high school. At the same time, she began experimenting with new kinds of work, especially in adult literacy courses, innovative catechisms, and a range of classes involving young people. In the early years, the sisters retained close ties with the local parish, although they attempted to share much of the ordinary life of the town, for example, in housing (renting a house by themselves), dress (abandoning the habit), and work routines.

Links with the parish affirm a valued sense of contact with the institutional church. But they can also make for constraint and conflict, particularly as the women involved gain confidence and move more forcefully to independent definitions of what they ought to be doing, how and where. In this instance, after a few years, escalating tensions with the local priest led the sisters, Gladys among them, to start looking for another place to live and work; a further round of experimentation began.

> We had problems with the parish priest, especially about how we were doing our work. Our pastoral style was very different from his, and we felt obliged to move. So first I came to Santa Isabel, a barrio here in Barquisimeto where our order has a residence. For the next three years I lived in Santa Isabel, gave classes in the Jesuit high school, and did a lot of work with youth groups in the barrio.
>
> During my final year in Santa Isabel, I got involved with a group of women making sweets [*dulces criollos*] for sale. We set up a small cooperative and had a stall in the Mercado San Juan. This began as something for the weekends, and lasted about a year and a half in all.
>
> As things turned out, the group was not economically viable. The women needed to earn more money, and in any case they lacked time for this, because most of them had to be both mother and father to their families. Nonetheless, their experience working as a group was valuable. It helped me explore new ways of working with groups, and they also learned a few critical lessons about how to press claims for help, how to work together, and how to build a sense of community.
>
> Then, in July 1978, two of the sisters living here left, one to become our provincial and the other to work with her as an assistant. That's when I came to join this community, to reinforce it, and I have been here ever since. (B 106–7)

This brief history raises a few points worth noting about Sister Gladys's early career and developing outlook. To begin with, over the years Gladys has drastically deinstitutionalized her life and work. She was raised in Catholic schools and, in a sense, never left them until the 1975 move to a country town. This was Gladys's first experience of living in an ordinary way with ordinary people since leaving her family home as a teenager to enter the convent. Further, the orientation Gladys brings to her work is intensely practical and localized. Wherever she is, Gladys and her companions work hard to meet and know the community and try to identify with it on issues that arise. In practical terms, this kind of orientation is highly activist and leads to commitments to projects ranging from cooperatives, health committees, or interbarrio housing efforts to participation in a range of confrontations with public authorities.

Gladys is a thoughtful person and sees the activist side of her work with the poor as the necessary result of long and careful reflection on the meaning of her commitment as a nun. Her comments on the preferential option for the poor illustrate the matter well.

I can tell you about my own experience. For me, it has meant a renovation of my whole commitment, my commitment as a Christian and as a nun. I think I had been searching for a long while, and by the time of Vatican II, I was already aware that things couldn't just continue in the same old way. Reading *Gaudium et Spes* opened new horizons for me, and I was very excited by what was going on in other countries. I read everything that came from CLAR, along with magazines from places like Brazil.

All that has been sort of like giving me guidelines, showing me ways to do things I already knew had to be done. So of course, for me the experience of meeting people and coming into contact with like-minded groups—groups that are getting strong now—this gives me lots of hope. (B 119)

For Gladys, opting for the poor means much more than simply coming *to* the poor from the outside. Her general perspective underscores the dialectical quality of the encounter: the impact is mutual. She and her sisters bring something to the communities and do so in a much less directive fashion than in the past. At the same time, immersion in the community is a learning experience for them. They offer windows for change, and are changed themselves.

In the early years of her commitment to popular work, Gladys was something of a radical. For example, she says that she rejected wearing the habit in a very strong way. In the same vein, her first encounters with popular religiosity (uses of holy water, particular devotions, local traditions or charms) spurred efforts to turn it immediately to more social and communitarian directions. Although Gladys and her companions remain committed to such efforts, they no longer see popular religiosity as just a collection of obstacles on the path to activism that must be swept away before "real work" can get underway. To the contrary, they now argue that if a satisfying and meaningful community life is to be established, such religious and cultural expressions must be engaged in a respectful and nonauthoritarian manner.

Gladys and the sisters who work with her see the new life they have undertaken as an active expression of what the church as a whole ought to be reaching for. Traditional concerns for the administration of sacraments are no longer sufficient to fill out an authentic religious mission. Salvation as traditionally defined also appears overly narrow, too focused on the individual to the detriment of community life. For Gladys, these basic elements of religious experience must be reunderstood and set in a more general context of human liberation. Just as body and soul cannot be separated, spiritual and material progress necessarily go together.

I believe that salvation, what today we call liberation, has to be an integral process. This means that the church must take open and decisive positions in support of human promotion and liberation. So that when we talk about saving people, we are also taking about freeing them. I believe that our commitment as a church has to be wide-ranging, and also very specific, very clear on the issues. We've got to be clear ourselves about the need—*for us!*—to make a deeper commitment, to work with others to make sure that our personal commitments contribute to a real process of liberation. (B 118)

As we have seen, this general stance meshes nicely with the theory and practice of the Jesuits of Centro Gumilla, who have acted as something of a magnet, drawing like-minded groups to the barrios of Barquisimeto, where each sets to work in its own characteristic style. The fact that so many different groups take the same path makes Gladys hopeful about the future.

One important change has been the growing awareness of the church that is being born in the people. In my own personal experience, I have seen how groups can grow and mature, take decisions and stick to them, gaining strength as they go. Mutual support is very important; what happened with Father Manolo [Moreno] is a sign of this. A big group of us backed him strongly, and so he felt supported, not isolated. I do believe that at the local and national levels, many groups are now becoming conscious of their role. They are learning that today the church has got to go to the people. (B 118)

A brief glance at Gladys's day-to-day routine may help put these broad commitments into more practical, down-to-earth terms. Basic expenses for rent, utilities, food, clothing, books, and materials must be met. The congregation helps out with a small subsidy, but all the sisters hold down regular jobs as well. Gladys teaches part-time (twelve hours weekly) at the local technical school. The rest of her week is devoted to religious education and to a diffuse presence in the barrio that boils down to providing services (as noted) and helping neighbors define and solve personal and community problems. Her days run more or less as follows: Mondays are kept free, and each of the women does what she wishes. Tuesdays and half of Wednesdays are dedicated to formal classes for novices (their own and also the young Jesuits). Gladys works part of each Wednesday and all day Thursday at the technical school. The other sisters use this time for their respective jobs as teachers, secretaries, and administrators. Fridays are devoted to general barrio issues, and Saturdays are reserved for household chores like laundry. Sundays are filled with church services and community meetings. Each evening is fully scheduled with a range of events including cooperative meetings, regular sessions of barrio education or health committees, study groups, gatherings of mothers' groups and catechists, and a regular weekly meeting of the barrio pastoral team composed of themselves, the Jesuits, the Medical Mission Sisters, Maryknoll workers, and elected lay leaders. As noted earlier, barrio residents feel free to knock on the sisters' door at any hour in case of emergency. They do so often. One month out of every year is reserved for a retreat or, at the very least, some joint trip away from the barrio.

Most of Gladys's explicitly pastoral efforts in the barrio are devoted to work with groups of mothers. Her long-range goal is to devolve religious education onto neighborhoods and families by recruiting a cadre of women who will be trained and motivated to carry on the work while stimulating and training others as well. After meeting with Gladys, these women also get together regularly on their own to plan out catechism and religious training. Many of the same women are also active in barrio cooperatives and health committees. Because the sisters know that their characteristic style of action may distress the hierarchy, they prefer to avoid public notice. According to Gladys, laypersons do most of the work themselves:

> For all practical purposes, nothing is done without them. All the leaders, especially the catechists and some *cursillo* members, are very aware of the importance of their role. Sundays are given over to organizational work, and when we are out of the city, they meet on their own in one another's houses. We leave them some mimeos, and they then organize the celebrations of the word. We even leave the sacraments with them, and they distribute communion. You know, sometimes you've got to keep these things a little hidden, because those in charge aren't likely to permit that kind of work. (B 114)

Explicitly social and political activities range from tree plantings and neighborhood clean-up efforts to participation in such popular protests as a demand for a local police station, better bus service, or covering nearby open sewage troughs. The protest described earlier that involved "taking" a highway around the barrio to protest faulty water service is repeatedly cited as a model of what popular involvement should be like. Whatever the specifics of the issue, the working ideal is for grass-roots groups to be simultaneously spiritual and social. Gladys puts it this way:

> I personally believe that you've got to join the two. Christians ought to have their feet on the ground, and carry out their commitment as Christians in all aspects of life. So, for example, when we meet with charismatic groups that concentrate on personal spirituality, we try to make them understand the need for social commitment as well. Sunday mass also gives a lot of weight to what real Christian commitment entails. There is always mention of community needs; that way, everyone can know about them, and a desire for commitment with the community can get going. Even though each group here has its own specific focus and identity, they all share a strong commitment to the community. (B 115)

The key to understanding how Gladys and her companions work in La Carucieña lies in grasping the way their visions of themselves, of the church, and of the community converge to make active involvement a fulfilling necessity. They see themselves as four independent women operating within a structure and set of normative guidelines provided by the institutional church that impel them to close identification with the community. Their perception of the community itself (La Carucieña and similar barrios) stresses how much its formation, history, and common culture are marked by structural inequalities of wealth and power. As the sisters see things, these elements have combined to isolate barrio residents from one another and, thus, blind them to shared needs and interests. For Gladys, this situation makes her own option all the more explicit and urgent:

> The first and most basic thing is to get for us to get close to the people. You know, we are so accustomed—I experienced this when I lived in our schools—to living behind walls. There in the school, it was impossible for me to feel the needs most people have, the needs of the majority. But the church has got to be where the majority is, that majority which is less able and less equipped to solve its problems.
>
> As I told you, to put it in personal terms, once I left those walls behind, I started to resonate with all sorts of things that had remained latent until then. They had never been expressed openly because there was no opportunity. But here in the barrio, you live so closely packed in, that if you're over here, they can hear you next door. So you're soaked in the community's life and in its problems. And this helps give us church people pointers about where the church's efforts have got to be directed.
>
> To me, Puebla's recommendation that we form communities is absolutely fundamental. Here in Venezuela we still don't have what you could call real communities, just groups. We need to multiply these groups and make people see the need to join together, express themselves, and support one another. For me, this comes first. Later you can tell people about sacraments and help them really experience the liturgy, but that comes only after they have really lived this new sense of fraternity. Around here, for example, we spent two years—no, more, two and a half—before we gave any thought to mass or any of that. "Sister [they would ask], and when is mass?" Well, let's see, and do you know your neighbor? Do you know what problems they have over there? (B 110–11)

Looking over the whole of Sister Gladys's life and career, one is struck by how much she has changed and how far she has moved from conventional starting points in family, upbringing, education, and vocational stirrings. Gladys Bernal's self-image is now framed by a tough-minded independence, and her ordinary work routine is clearly deinstitutionalized and open-ended. It is not that Gladys rejects the institutional church. Quite the contrary! Her ties to the church, her veneration for its traditions and leaders, and her sense of religious vocation are stronger than ever, but they find expression now in a very different range of options from those that occupied her in previous years.

Gladys actively pursues edification through any means available: courses, specialized seminars, journals, and the like. Reflecting on her own education and training, she sees the gaps but has a clear sense of what is required to fill them and where to go in the future.

All of us realize that the formation we got was not well suited to this kind of work, but we also know that in those years there was nothing else. In contrast, today special attention is paid each girl's particular vocation, so that the formation and training she gets are tailored to support it.

Societies change constantly, and so I believe that a person also needs to keep changing, so that she can be ready at any time. (B 125, 126)

It is instructive to compare Gladys Bernal with Carminia Navia Velasco, one of the Javierian sisters in Cali's Barrio Meléndez. Carminia is younger, better educated, and much more involved in regional and national networks of "progressive" clergy. Each woman clearly feels "part of the church," although the environment of the Colombian church makes Carminia quite accurately perceive herself to be much more subject to direct attack than does her Venezuelan sister.

Carminia Navia is a relatively short and heavy-set young woman who is exceptionally vigorous, intelligent, and erudite. I was given her name by contacts in Bogotá associated with the journal *Solidaridad*, who described Carminia as a key figure in a network of popular groups reaching across the barrios of Cali and out into surrounding areas. Because Carminia's work keeps her on the move throughout the western part of Colombia (giving talks, organizing meetings and courses), she is often hard to find. There is no telephone in her house, so I was fortunate to make contact on my first visit to Meléndez.

Carminia Navia is a daughter of Colombia's social and political elite. She was born in mid-1948 to one of Cali's most prominent families, and her immediate relatives have long been active in regional and national affairs. From the outset, this young woman had all the perquisites an upper-class background can bring in Colombia. She was educated at elite Catholic girls' schools in Cali, graduated in letters from the Universidad del Valle, and then spent a year traveling and studying in the United States. She also traveled widely in Latin America and, at one point, spent an entire year in Brazil. Her studies and travel put Carminia in contact with a range of experiences and change-oriented figures and thus helped her to crystallize long-standing concerns about faith, social justice, and the need for action.

As a girl, Carminia was not especially devout, not even very observant in conventional religious terms. When I asked if she could remember how she had first become aware of having a religious vocation, she responded,

Yes, of course I remember. But I don't know, it takes a while to tell, it's complicated. When I was a kid, I went to Catholic girls' schools here in Cali, schools run by nuns. At university I studied philosophy and letters, and I went through a period of skepticism, atheism, and all that—Marxism and the whole social question. I've always been drawn to social issues. My family has never experienced them directly, but the people, yes. When I went to the United States [1971] I was exposed to the Chicano movement, to Joan Baez and Bob Dylan, the anti-Vietnam protests, all of that. It was powerful stuff, and it influenced me a lot. I also met Ernesto Cardenal, who told me about his experiences in Gethsemane. Well, all these things. Later, after being in the U.S., I had a stronger sense of myself as a Latin American, a sense of a continent exploited by others. That also had an impact. (CA 94, 95)

All this restless searching was ultimately pushed in a religious direction by the example of Ernesto Cardenal,[20] by the people she met in Brazil, and by extensive readings in the then-emerging theology of liberation. Carminia returned to Colombia anxious to work with popular groups and ready to try out a commitment to and with the church.

Yes, and with a lot of resistance on my own part, because you know I have always been resistant to structures, and as a result, to lots of things that are common practice in the church. Then, the possibility arose of going to live in a popular barrio, forming part of its experiences. So, searching a little for how best to fit myself in, I joined up with a group of Javierians who were living in Barrio Belisario Caicedo, here in Cali.

I went there without a clear sense of what I was committing myself to. It was more like starting something. At that time, I was given to literature, I wrote poetry, so more than anything else it was part of a process of searching. But then I discovered that in fact I had something to contribute to the people, and that—and this is the basic point—that the church's project was the most complete and meaningful of all. (CA 96)

The decision to join a religious congregation grew out of these slowly crystallizing ideas. Carminia Navia is a young woman who chose to join a relatively youthful congregation. The Javierian Institute was founded in Spain in 1941 with an explicit commitment to "insertion in the world of work." From the outset, the Institute has pursued a style of education and training and has followed a model of work much at variance with conventional Catholic expectations for women's religious orders. Midcareer change was therefore not an issue for Carminia.

No, with us you know what you're getting into when you join. The Javierian Institute attracted me from the beginning because of its commitment to the poor, and what we might call its modern spirit. I think that lots of communities, in fact the vast majority of religious orders in the church, are out of sync with the times. They live in another age. Being in tune with the world is important to me. (CA 67)

---

[20] Ernesto Cardenal, the Nicaraguan poet and revolutionary, is a Trappist monk, long-time Sandinista militant, and served as minister of culture for the FSLN government. His poetry includes well-known modern (and very political) versions of the psalms, translated into English in Cardenal, *Psalms*.

I asked Carminia where she had pursued her studies with the Institute and what precisely was involved in becoming a member. She replied that the whole notion of separate and cloistered studies did not apply:

> Oh no, we have a different system. You affiliate with a group, like I did in Cali. First, there is what we could call a getting acquainted period, during which there are no commitments. You just participate, and take part in what is going on. Later, you work with all the Javierian communities in the area to draw up an individual plan of study and formation that is guided and directed by your fellow sisters. There is a kind of overall plan, which is revised continuously, but in any event each person carries out her own training in the same place where she lives and works, through a combination of reading, study, reflection, and daily activities. Small groups are formed, groups of two or three people, and each person can find a group that is suited to her own specific needs and circumstances. Through all this there is a basic common concern to deepen the meaning of religious experience while at the same time striving for a more complete knowledge of reality. That's very important to us: to know about the country we live in and to understand what has made us the way we are. Later, every five years or so, there are regular occasions of shared reflection with sisters of your own generation. And that is more or less how we do things. (CA 66, 67)

Carminia shares a rented house in the barrio with other women from her congregation. Like their Venezuelan counterparts, the four who live together in Barrio Meléndez combine individual study and work with pastoral efforts in the community, dedicating time, for example, to cultural centers, to the library, or to Bible study groups and the promotion of base communities. All residents of the house hold jobs outside the barrio (as teacher, secretary, and accountant), and they share in covering ordinary household expenses. As in La Carucieña, these contributions are supplemented by a regular grant from the congregation that covers additional costs for travel, library books, audiovisual gear, copying services, and the like.

Despite these similarities, Carminia's day-to-day routine varies notably from the one Gladys follows in La Carucieña. The core of the difference lies in Carminia's deep involvement with the national networks loosely collected around CINEP and *Solidaridad*. She travels widely outside Cali and is a frequent contributor to radical journals, including *Solidaridad*. All this makes Carminia's involvement in the everyday life of Meléndez less salient than is the case for Gladys in La Carucieña. Carminia's primary focus is elsewhere. Although she lives in the barrio, it serves her more as a point of departure than as a location for immersion into popular culture. For Carminia personally,

> My involvement in the barrio is not direct, but rather for the most part conjunctural. In fact, my work is a little hard to describe. I try to coordinate and stimulate groups that are doing work like the ones you can see here in the barrio. I work

both inside and outside the city, but above all here in Cali. We do this work in three barrios in Cali: in Villalaguna, in San Marino, and here in Meléndez. So we have our specific programs in those three, and we also work with youth and other groups on a citywide level. Most of my work involves coordination of all these efforts—planning, review, and also giving lots of courses. I do courses for leaders, for young people, for base groups (somewhat less), and also courses in theology and Bible. I suppose my role is really to provide feedback for all these base-level groups. I also work with a few other cities in the department. (CA 68)

Carminia's evident intellectual strength and erudition give a curiously detached flavor to her responses on questions about the preferential option for the poor, change in the church, or the proper nature of grass-roots groups. Commentary is typically elaborate, carefully crafted and nuanced; issues are framed in analytical and tactical terms. The following extended discussion of the preferential option for the poor is a case in point. Carminia begins by arguing that taking an option for the poor necessarily entails choosing sides in a class struggle, with all the dangers this can bring.

People talk about the preferential option for the poor, but what does this really mean? It must mean that you've got to choose, that in our work we must make a preferential choice, not exclusive but rather preferential, in favor of the poorest in society. We understand this in class terms, within the frame of reference Marxism defines for us. We live in a society divided in classes, and there is a class struggle. So we have to choose, to take on the interests of one of these classes, and that of course leads to confrontations with the interests of the other class. This means that Puebla's preferential option for the poor, or the Gospel's option for the oppressed, becomes part of the whole sociological process [of conflict] that Latin America is living through now. (CA 84, 85)

She notes that many in the church stop short of this logical conclusion. In her view, for most priests and sisters who work with popular groups, making a "preferential option" is something of a romantic act, an unfocused identification with the poor.

It's getting close to the poor, seeing how they live, sharing their lives a little, and accompanying them, not in a paternalistic way but really in what amounts to an idealistic kind of identification. . . . There is also the case of lots of Christians who are poor, above all Christians in the communities who are just poor. What preferential option can they make? It's them, they are the poor. They just live their lives and don't really know much about how the church is somehow "for them." (C 85, 86)

Carminia's discussion of this issue is flavored by a keen sense of the hostility she and her companions face from Colombia's church hierarchy. As we have seen, their work in Meléndez is independent of the archdiocese. They build their own buildings and rent others, finance their own programs and run them with complete autonomy, neither asking for nor receiving ecclesiastical approval (CA 92). Such independence is a necessary fact of life, because while in other countries the church may back popular groups, according to Carminia,

> To me it seems that the structures of the institutional church in Colombia haven't made any commitment whatsoever to the poor, not even a romantic one. Neither in the speeches nor in the writings of the hierarchy do the poor appear as preferred in any way. They appear because after all they have to appear; they've got to be mentioned in some way. They can't just be ignored. But it's almost always in abstract terms, from a distance, and wherever possible, they avoid the problem entirely. (CA 87)

What is remarkable about these responses is the high proportion of analytical and tactical to experiential elements. One might say (being unkind) that there is more commitment here to "the people" than to anybody in particular. When Carminia Navia sets out to reflect on the preferential option for the poor, her analysis is clear and penetrating but there is little personal identification. Part of this stems from the fact that Carminia's work frequently takes her out of the barrio. But this kind of work was deliberately chosen, and the orientation marks Carminia's approach as a whole, which combines sympathy with and a longing for identification with the poor (as in her poems, quoted below) with a heavy stress on instruction and tactics. The barrio appears to be less a community of belonging than a laboratory or case study in the dynamics of change. One searches in vain for the sort of deep and routine identification with the community that comes across Gladys Bernal's words about her work in La Carucieña.

Differences between the two perspectives become even sharper if we consider Carminia's vision of base communities. Like most of those who make a conscious and explicit "option for the poor," Carminia believes that groups like base communities need to have a strong social dimension. Social and political issues must be placed at the center of attention, infused with religious sensibility, and pointed toward greater participation and involvement at every stage of the game. Close inspection reveals that Carminia's view of the groups actually operating in the barrio is not very favorable. One hears a certain impatience, a desire to get on with the business of social and political transformation. The following commentary is a case in point. After telling me that, in effect, "participation here is really minimal, despite all the noise people make about it" (CA 70), she went on to note that participation remains limited because the move to social and political issues is held back by remnants of traditional religiosity.

> Concretely, our communities are communities whose fundamental motivation is faith. Their basic discourse centers on the Gospels, the Bible. But they are also

communities where social issues are strongly felt. On another level, and more stemming from the efforts of outsiders than of members themselves, there is politics too. But in any case, all this concern for social issues, this discovery of the need for commitment to change society, all of that is shot through with a very traditional spirituality, a very traditional kind of religiosity that sets limits to social action. (CA 72)

The most urgent needs Carminia experiences on a day-to-day basis are lack of money and time. Money is always in short supply. It is one of the ironies of work with popular sectors that those who do it are obliged to beg from the rich in order to be able to live with the poor. Few live as simple and undemanding a life-style as Padre Vicente, and even he fills basic needs like housing or a jeep from outside funds (from Australia). The more common situation is like Carminia's.

> Money is the basic problem in work like this, because when you try to do a kind of popular work that is neither paternalistic nor controlling, that's exactly the kind of work no one wants to support. Once in a while you may encounter European friends who are willing to help with no strings attached, and then you can accept. So economic questions influence us because we have no resources, because resources are very precarious, and because it means that people can't give themselves full time to the effort. They've got to eat, so they haven't got much spare time. That's the first thing. Another point, and probably the biggest difficulty I face as I try to make people aware of their reality and get them committed to a program of social change, is the power of the media. Most people are totally alienated: they don't care about politics; they don't care about their neighbors; they don't care about anything. I've also had to make extra time to study and write, but you know, once you get into this kind of work you realize that all that will be very difficult to manage. Maybe after a while, I might be able to take a year or two off, devote myself to study again, but here in the parish it's very hard. (CA 96, 97)

Pursuing a popular option in the barrios of Cali can be difficult and frustrating. Carminia's perception of the inconstancy of popular participation is all too accurate. As is the case with invasion barrios generally, participation in newer areas of Cali is extremely volatile. As we have seen, the norm is apathy punctuated by sporadic bursts of anger and energy that rarely consolidate into lasting movements. Nonetheless, in terms of the growth of a new kind of religious presence, Carminia and her sisters see the beginning edge of change, still fragile and limited to be sure, but present nonetheless. This is especially so

> if you take the life of the church in broader terms, and reach beyond all those formal barriers [of diocese or parish] and consider the dynamics of all the groups and communities being formed. These ecclesial groups are being established not at the margins of the church, not outside the church, but still with a certain mea-

sure of autonomy. . . . But even where sisters or clergy stand by the groups, and even in cases where their priests let them go forward on their own, even in these cases, groups commonly end up very dependent on the impulse they get from clergy. So it's critical that the role of priests and sisters be steadily reduced, so that they don't end up always in an orienting role, but rather that groups define their path for themselves. (CA 70–71)

Despite these beginnings, Carminia finds the raw material resistant to change. Expectations of deference and obedience are so deeply ingrained in the culture and consciousness of ordinary people that progress (e.g., in promoting critical awareness or fuller participation) is more a matter of defending inches gained than of consolidating new territories. Life is hard for most Meléndez residents, and as we have seen, they face the prospect of being forced out by developments intended to serve the middle class.

> But even so, there are no signs of fight in the people. Once in a while, yes, there's a march or a protest, but never an organized process. I think people are affected by the general apathy of national politics. In ecclesial terms, people are swamped with options, but at the level of the official church, most just go on obeying as before, obeying the orders of the bishop or the hierarchy. There is also a national campaign to discredit popular work and autonomous groups, and as a result, all these efforts are damaged. (CA 77)

Although most of her activities are focused outside the barrio, Carminia Navia's powerful intellect, manifest in forceful and often eloquent writings, has clearly done much to shape the thrust and impact of local efforts. Her ideas take form in the struggle to set and coordinate popular agendas throughout the region and are further sharpened in the many courses she gives, either alone or in collaboration with other activists and intellectuals she gets to participate. The character and tone of these efforts is familiar by now. As we have seen, for Carminia, urban barrios constitute a central locus of contradiction and change in contemporary popular culture, a culture that her work is dedicated to changing.

Some of Carminia's influence will also appear in one of the life histories (of a woman from Cali) presented in the next chapter. Rather than prefigure that discussion, I prefer to close this portrait of Carminia Navia by taking a different angle of view. Following are excerpts from several of her poems. These circulate widely in Cali and also through the networks mentioned above. Like all her writing, the poems that follow reveal a common concern with sharing, with social context and a strong social message, and with a self-conscious pursuit of ordinary experience.[21]

[21] All the poems presented here are drawn from a collection entitled *Caminando* (Walking).

### He Taught Like Someone with Authority

He sat them down at his table,
And sharing bread, shelter, and a glance
He gave them his word
>It is the word of a man on the path
>of a life of service

It is the word struggle
It is the word love
It is the outstretched hand
It is the answer to questions
His word became flesh in the poor, the dispossessed
his word was light
>it was part of our history.

### [Enseñaba Como Quien Tenía Autoridad]

[Los sentaba en su mesa
Y compartiendo pan, techo, y mirares,
les daba su palabra
>Es el hablar de un hombre del camino
>de una vida al servicio

Es la palabra brega
es la palabra amor
Es la mano tendida
es la respuesta para las preguntas
su verbo se hizo carne entre los débiles, en los desposeídos
su palabra fue luz
>fue gesto en nuestra historia]

### Prayer in the Nighttime Hours

Lord,
I've got to gather in myself
the prayers of many along the way
and I don't manage to do my own
Lord,
forgive me
for listening to an electronic verison of Ravel's *Bolero*
when my neighbor can't hear or make sense of it
personally . . .
I've got to gather
the smile from the tired lips of my brothers
and carry it to the world of rest and illusion
And I don't manage to rest from my own weariness

Lord
forgive me,
because I want to listen to tangos
while
one table . . . two . . . tables . . . many tables
are still empty
forgive me,
because I see them getting screwed over
and I don't know how to unscrew things
forgive me
my silence
my fear
the hours I pass without challenging those who embitter the lives of my friends.

### [Oración en Horas de la Noche]

[Señor
yo tendré que recoger en mí
la oración de muchos del camino
y no logro hacerla mía
Señor,
perdóname
por oír el bolero de Ravel en versión electrónica
cuando mi vecino
no puede oírlo ni lo sabe
personalmente . . .
Tendría que recoger
la sonrisa de los labios cansados de mi hermano
y llevarla hasta el mundo de la ilusión y del descanso
y no logro siquiera descansar mi cansancio
Señor,
perdóname
porque quiero oír tangos
mientras
una mesa . . . dos mesas . . . muchas mesas
permanecen vacías
perdóname,
porque los veo jodidos
y no sé desjoderlos
perdóname
el silencio
el miedo
las horas vividas sin reto a los que amargan a mi amigo.]

### In the Barrio Meeting

In the barrio meeting
the child is playing
And talk is slow and relaxed
nothing has the odor of a sermon
In the barrio meeting,
the grandmother smiles
the worker looks at his greasy hands
the boy smokes his cigarette
and we all talk while as a tremor runs through our bodies
Nobody has the floor.
In the barrio meeting the child is playing.
What will Christ tell us today about how to live?
Who will do it this morning?
In the barrio meeting
we are all searching for the cool move
              the liberating bread
              work that can build a city without walls
In the barrio meeting
the child is playing

### [En la Asamblea del Barrio]

[En la asamblea del barrio
el niño juega
Y la palabra es lenta y reposada
nada huele a sermón
En la asamblea del barrio,
la abuela se sonríe
el obrero se mira las grasas de sus manos
el muchacho se fuma un cigarillo
y todos conversamos mientras un currulao atraviesa los cuerpos
nadie posée la palabra.
En la asamblea del barrio el niño juega.
¿Que nos diremos hoy para vivir a Cristo?
¿Quien lo hará esta mañana?
En la asamblea del barrio
buscamos todos juntos la onda chévere
              el pan liberador
              el trabajo que construya la ciudad sin barreras.
En la asamblea del barrio
el niño juega]

Although I have stressed the contrasts in background, education, career, and outlook that set these two women on different pathways in their "option for the poor," it would be misleading to leave explanation at the level of individual characteristics. Structural and contextual variations also play a critical role. The structural isolation of radical experience in Colombia and the unremitting hostility that people like Carminia run up against on a regular basis clearly reinforce the mix of radical rhetoric with organizational fragility noted earlier in these pages. Pastoral agents and ordinary people alike are exposed to reprisals from civil and ecclesiastical authorities and, in certain cases, to police or military action as well. A vicious circle thus emerges, as all this vulnerability and danger combine to cut the ground from under efforts at long-term cultural change that are, after all, the Javierian sisters' stated priority.

In contrast, for the sisters in La Carucieña, the Jesuit connection combined with a much less threatening national and institutional setting makes a less directly politicized discourse and form of action both sensible and feasible. Their commitment to live and work with the people is phrased in simpler and more straightforward terms, without the theoretical apparatus one encounters in Barrio Meléndez. Nonetheless, the support provided by a powerful and close-knit infrastructure (all the groups concentrated in the area) makes it possible for these women to begin building more secure foundations for a kind of cultural change that can last.

## Conclusion

The patterns of social origin, education, religious experience, and general orientations that prevail among the priests, sisters, and pastoral agents we have encountered working with popular groups provide us with important grounds for reflection. First, these men and women undertake an exceptionally broad range of tasks and roles. Over a career, individuals work in many different areas; looking across the whole group, one finds occupations ranging from catechist to accountant, teacher to group organizer, nurse to agronomist, spokesperson and link to outside resources to all-purpose ear for listening to problems and shoulder to lean on whenever needed. This varied set points up the demanding quality of the work and explains some of the stress on physical stamina and the dangers of burnout that we have encountered. The trend to teamwork noted earlier is clearly an attempt to respond to these new role definitions.

A second general point concerns the mediating role priests, sisters, and pastoral agents play. By definition, they are part of the institutional church while also operating between it and popular groups. Legitimacy, resources, and moral strength are drawn from their connections to each. The way this in-between condition works out in much recent experience suggests how misleading it is to see these men and women as mere transmission belts in the machinery of the institutional church: delivering orders from above and monitoring compliance on the ground. Although some cases approximate that model, as we have seen, they do so at the cost of heightened frustration for the pastoral agents themselves. Smothering supervision and control keep "their groups" from getting off the ground in an enduring and independent way, leaving these pastoral agents trapped in an endless cycle of reinforcement.

In general, the experience of popular work clearly has important consequences for the way pastoral agents see themselves, their work, the church itself, and the popular groups they serve. Such work, and the broad effort to identify with the popular classes in which it is commonly embedded, requires commitment beyond a standard nine-to-five routine. Transformations in speech and forms of address, in clothing, diet, residence, and work routines are also common. These undercut traditional social and cultural distances dividing the church's agents from the mass of ordinary believers while at the same time opening the habits and consciousness of these agents to hitherto unknown perspectives on the world.

A third and final point is simultaneously theoretical and methodological. The centrality and dynamic character of linkages in the experiences sketched out here underscore the need for analysis to keep these linkages at the center of attention. In methodological terms, this requires us to "work the structures": tracing the way agendas are made, following the trajectory of ideas and programs, and, in this way, tracking sources and pathways of change in religion, culture, and organizational life. If analysis is to "work the structures" in the way I have suggested here, structures themselves need to be reunderstood in dynamic and behavioral terms. The structures in question are not mere collections of laws and regulations dedicated to grinding out documents and adjusting statuses. They are living, changing organizations that generate both power and meaning, projecting values and identities that bind members and leaders together over the long haul. These in turn lay a foundation for values of legitimacy, fellowship, loyalty, and support that may not be available elsewhere in the culture.

The next chapter extends the effort at life histories begun here with Gladys Bernal and Carminia Navia beyond the holders of formal ecclesiastical roles to include activists and group members generally. How are the changes witnessed thus far borne out in the personal experience of ordinary people? Let us listen one last time to the women and men of these comunities as they talk about their lives, their groups, their country, their faith, and their church.

# EIGHT

## SELECTED LIFE HISTORIES

THIS CHAPTER presents five ordinary lives, told insofar as possible in the voices of the men and women who have lived them. They discuss their youth and upbringing, describe education, work, and family, and speak at length about what faith, church, and community have meant to them, and how these have changed in the course of their lives. The life histories in this chapter are best understood as both individual and social documents. They represent the efforts of thoughtful men and women to make sense of their own experiences, and to give them meaning in a larger social and philosophical context in which their lives are played out. The accounts we are about to hear are not spontaneous. They are the product of formal and informal interviews, reinforced by visits to home and community that provided a chance to observe these individuals in a social setting that was meaningful to them. Throughout, I have tried to be faithful to the language, priorities, weighting, and sequencing of each person's self-description while retaining sufficient editorial judgment to allow for an organized presentation that can highlight parallels and differences as it sets each life firmly in context.

This is structured, not raw, transcript, and in selecting and organizing cases and materials, I have been guided by two basic methodological precepts. The first draws on C. Wright Mills's stress on the intersection of biography, history, and social structure, and leads me to highlight common problems and set each life in the context provided by time, place, gender, and class.[1] The second draws on Clifford Geertz's injunction to avoid turning individuals into matchstick figures that caricature social categories. As he points out, "To be human here is thus not to be Everyman; it is to be a particular kind of man, and of course men differ: 'Other fields,' the Javanese say, 'other grasshoppers.' "[2]

Each of the men and women reviewed in this chapter has a characteristic individual tone and style that deserves special attention. But this does not make our subjects totally unique, nor does it mean that they could be drawn at random from any population. Each is broadly representative of her or his time and place: the specific years, nations, and communities that frame these lives give every individual a full set of the particularities that make for a complete and meaningful human life. When viewed against the data provided in earlier

[1] *The Sociological Imagination.*
[2] "The Impact of the Concept of Culture on the Concept of Man."

chapters on the origins and dynamics of change in religion, culture, organization, and social life generally, these autobiographical reflections yield a richer and more complete portrait of the process than any single perspective can offer.

The five histories that follow offer a rough balance among the major categories of place and person presented in these pages. We shall listen to three men and two women, one barrio dweller and four peasants, two Venezuelans and three Colombians. I begin with the life of Huberto Vanegas, who came to work for the diocese of Facatativá after an extraordinary youth of wandering and deprivation. This account is followed by a look at two Colombian women: Olga Ceballos and Susanna Madrid, respectively from Cali's Barrio El Rodeo and the *vereda* of Barro Blanco, outside Caparrapí. Two peasant men follow: Patricio Alvarez from Agua Fría and Fortunato Duque from the Villanueva area. I close the chapter with a brief comparative discussion.

## Huberto Vanegas: A Lay Pastoral Agent

Huberto Vanegas works for the diocese of Facatativá. He is a full-time member of the Mobile Team set up to run the CRS-funded Procampesinos project. His specific work is to promote and supervise cooperatives, community stores, and individual projects of various kinds. A sample of his efforts would have to include the following: cooperatives near Caparrapí; community stores in Agua Fría, Río Frío, and other sites; and a series of small projects ranging from building bridges and installing wells and water lines to start-up and initial supervision of local profit-making ventures like apiaries, chicken farms, or raising rabbits for sale in regional markets. When I first met Huberto, he had just concluded a long and difficult effort to get the cooperative in Caparrapí established and operating. He was then on the verge of turning his attention and energies to some of the other endeavors just mentioned.

Huberto is a short, slight, and intense man, usually dressed in jeans, boots, a workshirt, and jacket. He speaks in very colloquial language with a pronounced regional accent and walks with a noticeable limp, the product of a congenital defect that left one leg shorter than the other. Huberto's life and times prior to his arrival in Facatativá constitute a personal odyssey that presents, often in exaggerated form, much of what has happened in Colombia since the late 1940s. His life is significant and deserves special attention not because it is typical but rather precisely because its endless searching and wild gyrations crystallize experiences that have touched the lives of many Colombians. That Huberto should have ended up working for the church, and the specific way he came to this work, also sheds helpful light on the church's appeal, and on the impacts it can have on ordinary lives.

Huberto Vanegas was born on April 9, 1952, in Santuario, a small town in the department of Risaralda, in the heart of Colombia's central coffee-growing region. In many respects, he is a product of The Violence, which was especially savage in this part of the country. Even his date of birth has connotations of violence in Colombia, for it was on April 9, 1948, that the assassination of a major political figure, Jorge Eliécer Gaitán, sparked rioting, protests, and extensive violence that began ten years of civil war. Indeed, mention of the "ninth of April" in conversations among Colombians still touches off discussions of violence. Huberto never knew his father, and even though he was born in a town, at an early age he moved with his mother to the countryside, where she found work as a day laborer. Huberto began to work as soon as he was physically able.

> There we worked the land: coffee, bananas, yucca. [*What kind of work was it?*]
> Well, we were day laborers, we had no land of our own. My mother had a small inheritance, but one of the sharp-eyed thieves of The Violence stole it from her. So we had to work as day laborers. I did this until I was fourteen years old. (F 8)

When Huberto was about fourteen, they moved from this mountain region to the hot climate of the Cauca Valley, where work was found on a large sugar estate (Ingenio Río Paila), once again as day laborers. After two years they moved again, to similar work, but now on coffee farms farther up the valley, in the area around the city of Trujillo. Around the time of Huberto's eighteenth birthday, the two moved on to the small nearby town of Apia. In Apia, Huberto's work changed, and he gradually became more independent.

> Later we went to a town called Apia, a really nice town. I've thought a lot about the path I have had to follow in, and I especially remember the time I spent in Apia. Now comes an interesting part. In Apia I worked in a whorehouse [*una zona de tolerancia*] selling beer. Yeah, in one of those places, selling beer, because I didn't know how to do anything else. I worked there selling beer, taking care of the drunks, taking care of the prostitutes—all in all, running one of those houses. I was in charge of one of those houses. (F 8)

His mother soon left Apia to seek work in the banana zone near Urabá, along the country's distant north (Caribbean) coast. After a while, Huberto joined her there and found work, successively, as cowboy, baker, and street vendor. He lasted only a few months in Urabá, returning first to Apia and then quickly hitting the road again. This time he landed in the Pacific port of Buenaventura, where he found work tending bar, once again in a local whorehouse. After a stint at day labor in construction, he used his earnings to buy a kit and set himself up full-time shining shoes in the street. A combination of difficulties, including personal entanglements with several local women, soon made him leave the coast for good.

I went to Trujillo again, to work in coffee. I did that for a year, and that is where the interesting story begins. I had never studied, I had no formal schooling at all. From night classes I knew enough to read and write, just barely, but nothing else. I was living in a *vereda* called Los Cristales, I had been living there about a year when a group of priests, Redemptorist Fathers, came in a mission to the area. I had already lived in Los Cristales for about a year, and had just moved to another *vereda*. But I came back to Los Cristales to visit, and heard that the fathers were there. Among other things, they organized youth groups, groups that had picked leaders and started work on lots of things, with concrete programs and goals. (F 9)

Although Huberto's contact with the mission was accidental, it has an air of destiny about it. Through the efforts of the mission, he learned to read and write well and joined a church-sponsored group in a series of local promotional activities. The ensuing involvement changed his life completely, opening doors to new and hitherto unimagined possibilities.

After a while they asked me, "Why don't you become a member of the group? why don't you come to the meetings?" So I did, for about a year. At that time, I was very timid, very withdrawn, traumatized; I never said anything. I went to the meetings, but I never said a word. And the group really did a lot; it was engaged in many community activities, Acción Comunal, adult education, things like that.

So I joined in all that and *boom*, my eyes were opened. I took a course on leadership training with Father Célico Caiccdo, and later another course on human relations with the Bishop of Buga, Msgr. Julián Mendoza, and I began to get more active. At that time Gilberto, the coordinator of the group, had to go to Medellín to continue his studies in the seminary, and the question arose of who would be the group's coordinator from then on. There was a secret vote, and I was elected. Me, Huberto, withdrawn and timid and all that. I told them it was impossible, that it could not be, but yes, they said, you're the one with all the necessary qualifications. That's how I became a group leader. (F 10)

The particular group Huberto had joined was part of a broad outreach program organized by the Instituto Mayor Campesino, a Jesuit foundation located in Buga. About six months after Huberto's election as a local leader, promoters from the Institute came through Los Cristales, seeking candidates for a five-year course on cooperatives and community organization. Huberto wanted desperately to attend, but was not among those selected. "The priest told me that now was not the time, that I should stay in the *vereda*; we are holding you for later, keep working in the *vereda*" (F 10). But for personal and family reasons, none of those originally chosen could commit themselves to go to the Institute's five-year program. Huberto was ready, packed his few things, and left immediately for Buga. He was then twenty-five years old. Of the sixty-eight people selected for the course, thirty turned up to begin studies. Of these, only five graduated, Huberto among them. After completing the training program, he spent thirteen months with the Institute itself as a rural promoter, working with neighborhood stores and small cooperatives, until accumulating tensions with the Institute staff led him to move on.

The Huberto Vanegas who hit the road now was very different from the wanderer of earlier years. He now had self-confidence, a set of skills, and a purpose. He also had contacts into the net of individuals working in development organizations and, in short order, found work with the diocese of Facatativá.

> As a result of some problems, including failure to attend a few meetings, Father Martínez suggested to me that it would be better if I resigned. And I did so completely without anger, with a formal letter—no resentment. I think that he was also concerned about my ideological formation, because around that time I began to think a lot about politics, about social and political questions at an ideological level. Why form local stores or cooperatives? Does that solve anything? Isn't it just aspirin? I talked that way with the people, and so I think it was not so much because I missed meetings as really for ideological reasons. . . . So I left and spent three months without a job. At first I wanted a job with ANUC [Asociación Nacional de Usuarios Campesinos, a peasant group], but that didn't work out. Then I got a telegram from a friend who was working with Peace on Earth around Sasaima, who told me to come because in Faca they were looking for a cooperative promotor, and so I arrived in Facatativá. (F 11)

Reflect for a moment on the incidents and accidents of this life. Huberto was born in the depths of The Violence and grew up in extreme poverty and hardship. He had no formal education and little likelihood of improving his lot. By all ordinary criteria, this man was doomed to a short and mostly unsatisfying life. In this light, Huberto's contact with the missionaries and his later hookup with the Institute at Buga may seem like just two more chance occurrences among many. To be sure, the fact that Huberto crossed paths with these organizations is of course something of an accident, but it is important to place these individual events in context.

For many years, the Colombian church has run missions, outreach programs, and a series of efforts aimed at finding and forming "leaders." Many of these initiatives have been focused on the part of the country where Huberto grew up. The towns and villages in this region are not only the agricultural heartland of Colombia; they also constitute its firmest core Catholic area. This suggests that Huberto's "chance encounters" are less surprising in themselves than in the fact that they did not happen earlier. In all likelihood, it was only his restless movement from place to place and job to job that delayed the encounter, and thus put off the moment Huberto's natural talents were uncovered until well into young adulthood.

The five years Huberto spent at Buga were decisive. After a rootless adolescence devoted to selling beer, punching cows, working in a bakery, shining shoes, and the like, the opportunity to remain in one place with secure and stable conditions of food, shelter, and human ties must have seemed like heaven. The content of the course was also critical, for it concentrated Huberto's energies on productive and satisfying work and shaped his clear inclination to service to others. Huberto describes the years at Buga with the term "detoxification," by which he means a gradual unlearning of old images and expectations. He views such detoxification as a necessary prerequisite to the ability to make a new life.

> Look. Before, what happened to me is what happens to lots of people, I don't know, to millions in Colombia and in the whole world. We have never gotten a real evangelization, and so we see religion as something secondary, without much importance. That is to say, we give a certain reverence to religion, to God, to the priests and bishops. We respect religious celebrations, we pay attention to them, but we don't understand them. That's how it was with me. Some fears, lots of anxiety, and religion over there, hidden, no? Mysterious. I saw things that way, with great respect for it all—priests, mass, sisters, and all that. To me, it was all superior, all above me.
>
> But when I entered the Instituto Mayor Campesino in Buga, we got a process of evangelization called "detoxification of concepts" over a two-year period. Two years. During those two years, I acquired a deeper spiritual formation, a truer one. And that made it possible for me to draw closer to the church as a layperson. At one point I explored entering the seminary, but then I realized that this was not for me. That I could do something, that I could serve church, nation, and society through marriage, through my own family, and that really you can serve from any place where you are actively working. (F 186, 187)

As an employee of the diocese of Facatativá, Huberto is a full-time pastoral agent. But his life experience and understandings differ sharply from those of pastoral agents in clerical roles—priests and sisters. They want to identify with the poor; he has always been poor. For them, "insertion" in the world of the poor is an act of liberation; for Huberto, liberation came from escape. I do not mean to suggest that Huberto seeks upward mobility above all. He loves his work and is content with the modest economic rewards it brings. But his own life history leaves Huberto with few illusions about the satisfactions of being poor. Romantic images of "the people" have little place in his view of the world: he knows very well how to distinguish the virtues of a simple life from the miseries most people endure most of the time. For example, Huberto has a tough and realistic understanding of what shapes peasant life in areas like Caparrapí. As he sees it, peasant communities have urgent and highly concrete economic needs. Such needs take on a sharp and often bitter edge when they are experienced in contexts of pervasive physical and psychological insecurity.

> The most serious problem, with the greatest social and psychological effect, has been ideological. Guerrilla groups, especially the FARC [Fuerzas Armadas Revolucionarias de Colombia, the oldest and largest of Colombia's guerrilla organizations] in this area, have been active for a long time, struggling to attract people to their ranks through campaigns and motivations that set people against the state, make the state fall into disfavor. This has made effective work of any kind difficult, because it leaves people full of resentment, angry and fearful. Although for the most part they are illiterates and have little knowledge of things, these people have grasped the message of all these guerrilla campaigns very well. And this has made things difficult.
>
> On the other hand, the military is also very drastic. They believe that the peasants of certain of these zones—for example La Azauncha, La Loma de Aldana, La María, Barro Blanco, and La Fría—that these people are tied in some way to the guerrillas. And so they try to force them to tell what they know. There are abuses, demands to come to the barracks for interrogation, intimidation, torture. That's how it is. People are caught, afraid of the Left on one side and the military on the other. And so nothing can be accomplished. In those areas, people don't even want to work. Lands are neglected, there is no technical advancement and no services, because people want nothing to do with anything. (F 170, 171)

Huberto values the supportive character of the diocese's Mobile Team and likes the chance for service to others this kind of work provides. He reads and studies on his own, using pamphlets and taking correspondence courses available through the diocese or provided by national organizations. Thus,

> I understand a few general points, for example, that about the need for a truly integral promotion. That people require not just economic, political, religious, cultural, or technical promotion, but rather that they need to have all these together in a package in order to make a fuller and more truly human life for themselves. That's how I see things, and so I try to learn something about all these areas, so that I can then bring it to them. (F 181, 182)

Overall satisfaction in work is tempered by two major difficulties that Huberto believes conspire to undermine his best efforts. The first is scarce resources. "What I dislike the most", he remarked to me, "is that you've got to work with your fingernails" (F 182). There is simply not enough to go around, and this makes for insufficient training as well as for difficult working conditions: long bus rides, poor food, no tape recorder, no books, limited clerical supplies, and infrequent rest or recreation in what are difficult and physically taxing endeavors. Of course, such complaints are common in popular work. But in this case they are reinforced by a second difficulty, which

Huberto describes as a permanent tension between promoters like himself and the parish priests bent on maintaining traditional patterns of clerical control.

For Huberto, this raises real dilemmas, not only for his work but also for his self-image as a person. Huberto owes a lot to the church and prizes the religious connection very greatly. But the thrust of his education, training, study, and work has moved him away from automatic acceptance of clerical authority. Huberto's "detoxification" at Buga led him to a demystified and much less fearful understanding of the church. Once he saw clergy and bishops as remote and powerful figures, but

> right now I see things differently. I see the church differently, I see the priests differently. Just as I make demands on myself in order to serve others, in the same way I look at the actions of bishops, priests, and sisters with demanding eyes. Because the Gospels are not just a matter of theory, are they? No. They require a deep commitment in practice. Being Christian is, it's like a whole life, a life of service. (F 187)

Huberto Vanegas is a man who discovered the liberating idea of himself as an active, creative subject at twenty years of age. After a youth spent wandering from place to place, buffeted by forces beyond his understanding and control, a chance encounter opened the doors to knowledge, self-knowledge, and action. Recall the way he put it: "Boom, I opened my eyes." Huberto's eye-opening experience is like a reverse image of the midcareer change many nuns report on breaching institutional boundaries and identifying fully with the poor. In both instances, the experience is profoundly liberating and releases creative energies that can then be put to all kinds of uses. In Huberto's case, the church provided a critical mediation for his own efforts to change his life. Through the church, he found instruction, direction, legitimation, and even a place to work.

Of course the underlying issue is not the church per se but rather the way personal and community transformations can draw strength from these ties. Once illiterate, untrained, shy, and silent, Huberto has become a confident, capable, and articulate man. He speaks easily before large groups, plays and composes music, and, when I last spoke with him, had just gotten married and was starting to write a book. His own life makes him sure that change is possible—not easy, but possible nonetheless.

> I believe that when I try to be a good community promoter, this means attempting to have a deep influence in the community by promoting, moving people to changes that come from within themselves, changes that are at first personal, family centered, communitarian. What I mean is, you see, just as I have changed, others have changed too, and many more can change if they can just manage to change, even a little bit, the distorted consciousness hard lives have given them.

We Colombians can serve for something good, we can try to bring our best to the life of the nation. (F 190)

## Two Colombian Women: Olga Ceballos and Susanna Madrid

Olga Ceballos Rendón has lived in Barrio El Rodeo since 1966, has raised a family there (twelve children surviving infancy, fifteen grandchildren by 1983), and has been active in barrio affairs from the outset. Olga is an energetic and determined woman, with brilliant black eyes and black hair pulled back in a ponytail. She tolerates neither fools nor falsehoods, punctuates her conversation with energetic and forceful gestures, and, as we shall see, prefers plain talk and earthy metaphors to the polite fictions of ordinary conversation.

Olga's involvement with the church grew out of a broader activism whose roots are found in neighborhood and especially political concerns more than in conventional religiosity. She returned to the church and to religion because of the commitment to justice it seemed to embody, not as a simple continuation of the devotion she knew as a child. As was the case with Huberto Vanegas, the life and times of Olga Ceballos epitomize much of the experience poor people have had in this part of Colombia. Olga is a true daughter of The Violence, and has known all the dangers and uprootings and has felt in full measure the insecurities and fears that experience left in survivors.

Olga Ceballos was born in mid-1940 to a peasant family in Giricarcia, a small village not far from the city of Armenia, in the department of Quindío. She was one of five children of a peasant family that was forced to move as a result of political and economic pressures associated with The Violence, which was severe in this region. When Olga was twelve, her parents fled to open lands in the eastern *llanos*, or "plains." Around this time, many rural families were on the move, trying to escape The Violence by migrating either to the cities or to remote rural areas that looked like safe havens. For a while, the *llanos* offered this kind of refuge, and Olga's family was able to establish a good farm on unclaimed and unused lands. There they lived in relative security for about two years until it became necessary to abandon the farm and flee again. The year was 1954, and there had already been signs of danger, including a recent raid and search of the house by armed men.

> People were still finding bodies all around the area, skeletons and all that. Well, time came for the fiesta of San Pedro—in those parts, people really go all out in celebrating that day. We were invited to a beautiful peasant fiesta, very beautiful. People were playing guitars, there was dancing, and tons of food. When we got there, a man came up—he was one of the group that had come to our house. He called my father over and told him, "Listen, I am going to tell you something, but I want you to keep it a secret. Don't tell anyone, because if it leaks out they

will get me. Because you are a good Liberal, nothing happened to you, but there are some who want to go back to get your daughter.'' Well, my father turned the color of ashes, and right there told my mother. They told me all this much later. He warned her not to tell anyone, but that it would be best to leave. It might have been a ruse to get him to abandon the farm, because it was a very good farm, and at that time the violence was all between red and blue [Liberals and Conservatives]. So my father started making arrangements, and my mother and I slipped away while he managed to save the crops that were ready. We wandered around totally lost in the countryside, and it was horribly scary until he got things arranged and brought us to the town. (CR 158, 159)

The family then began a five-year period characterized by hardship, short-term jobs, and frequent moves from one town to another. In 1959 they arrived in Tuluá, a major commercial center not far north of Cali, in the Cauca Valley. In that same year, Olga married and came with her husband to Cali. With all this movement, it is not surprising that Olga has had little in the way of formal education: two years of primary school in Giricarcia is all she could manage.

When we got to Barrio El Rodeo, we began to see other things. We had lived a life of—no, no! We didn't think about anything, we didn't know anything. I for one had never studied at all, and the only thing I read, and I did like to read, was *Selecciones* [the Spanish version of *Reader's Digest*]. That I liked a lot, and I also liked reading about the Second World War, but at that time I didn't know what a war was. I thought these were things people invented, like stories, I had no idea what a war was. (CR 160)

As these comments suggest, Olga is almost entirely self-taught, and for a girl from the country, there was a lot to learn. She saw her first movie at the age of seventeen, and was left for days in a cloud of images and illusions. Her country upbringing was ''so repressed'' that

when I got married, I knew nothing about babies. I knew nothing about sexuality, I knew nothing at all. I had a vague idea about those things of marriage, that what this and that were, what was feminine, but as for myself, nothing. Sometimes I sit down to think about it now and it makes me sad to see how I was. I remember that I got married and became pregnant, and when I started having pains they took me to the hospital. The doctor tried to calm me down, because I was in pain, and I was very worried. He said, ''Be calm, it's all right, you are going to have a baby.'' I told him, ''No doctor, I am calm and all that, but just give me something for this pain.'' You see I didn't know there were pains [in childbirth]; I never heard about that. When I got married, I don't know if it was that the people around me thought I was too dumb, or that they just never got around to telling me that when you're pregnant and it is time, that there are pains and all that. For me it was totally unexpected. (CR 187, 188)

Like other Colombian women whose voices we heard in earlier chapters, Olga married young (at age nineteen), mostly to escape the heavy hand of her parents. Because her parents opposed the match, she was forced to elope, but soon discovered that marriage was no solution. As Olga puts it, her parents "knew what was waiting for me. They knew the kind of waters I was getting into. Since they had raised me in such a repressed way, I was convinced that in marrying I would free myself, be a different person, that marrying would be a solution. That having been so repressed as a girl, that this would be an escape. But things went bad for me, bad, bad, like for dogs at mass. I left that man long ago" (CR 186). Olga had two children with her husband, and since the separation has made a life in free union with a companion who is the father of her other children.

Olga's first steps in community activism came not through the church but rather in the political campaigns of 1970. Along with many other poor Colombians (especially in the cities), she and her companion were swept up in that year in the enthusiasm surrounding General Rojas Pinilla's populist bid for the presidency. At the time, the couple knew little about politics and made minimal effort to find out. Politics came to them.

> So one night we went to bed very late, that was our usual custom. We had been sitting up in the night talking, the children were very small. My companion and I were talking about this and that when we saw a whole crowd of people passing by in the street. It was about 11 P.M., and I said to him, let's see what is going on. So we went out, and this was the time of Rojas Pinilla's campaign. And everybody was talking about *mi general*: *mi general* this and *mi general* that. One lady told us the whole story about how he was against poverty, told us all that he had done. I knew nothing about politics; when you're raised like I was, you don't know anything. But anyway we said fine, and they invited us to a headquarters, to a meeting. We went, and there too all they talked about was *mi general*. Well, we sort of liked the whole thing, and since we had no special political color [party identification], we got involved. (CR 160, 161)

Following her initial contact with ANAPO (Alianza Nacional Popular), Olga identified for a while with the Communist party, which, like many groups on the left, had looked to the Rojas Pinilla candidacy as a way of breaking the traditional two-party [Liberal-Conservative] monopoly of Colombian politics. But she and her companion soon got disillusioned with the Communists. At the same time, ANAPO's rapid decay led Olga to refocus her energies away from national issues or organizations and toward the barrio. Involvement with the church came later. At first, "we began working with the community board, with local groups, and things like that. At that time, I probably called myself a Christian, but I had not identified myself as a Christian, not like in the work we are doing now" (CR 163).

As a young girl, Olga had disliked going to church so intensely that when her parents forced her to attend mass, she always fainted. "After I got married, I never went back to church. To me it seemed so absurd to go there, things you couldn't understand, things you couldn't see. To me it had no meaning" (CR 163). Despite this general alienation from the church, Olga notes that her life has taken lots of curious turns ("la vida mía ha sido de curiosidades" [CR 163]). One of these turns was the accidental set of circumstances that led to her first contacts with the priests in El Rodeo.

One Easter, a Holy Week procession passed by her house, and when she and her companion emerged to watch and listen, they heard one of the priests vigorously denouncing injustice. She remembers him arguing that true Christian commitment meant much more than prayer; action was required to fight for justice and equality. Olga was favorably impressed, but since she never went to church, nothing happened for a while. Not long after, when she attended a neighbor's funeral, once again Olga heard the priest attack injustice, and talk about why things were the way they were. She decided to make an approach.

> So one day I went there, and since I had heard that they had groups in the parish, I showed up when they were in the middle of a meeting of the social action group. Since, like I told you, I had not been able to work with the local barrio board, I thought I would see if working with these people would be any different. So I told the priest, "Padre, I want to work here, I want to join your social action group, but the problem is that I am not a Christian. I am not into any of that stuff." Then he told me, "Yes, yes, I accept you."

At first some members had reservations, given Olga's well-known local career as a left-wing political activist. But she was soon accepted in the group, and

> later the padre told me, "How can you say you are not a Christian? You are one of the most Christian people I have, because, you see, look at that flock of sheep that comes every day to mass. They aren't Christians, they're just sheep who come here every day without knowing why. I am here saying mass and they don't have the slightest idea of what I am talking about." That's when we became good friends, and I gave lots of time working for the parish. (CR 165)

Olga began her activities by visiting some of the parish's poorest families and helping to distribute surplus food products acquired through Caritas and Catholic Relief Services of the United States. Despite being poor herself, this contact with poverty's extremes shocked Olga deeply and spurred her to search for better, more enduring solutions. Around this time, she also participated in her first Bible study class, organized in El Rodeo by Sister Carminia Navia of Barrio Meléndez, whom we have already met. Olga remembers this meeting with Carminia very clearly. All her frustrations with the church and with the general situation burst out:

> Well, I let slip a lot of things, a lot of anger. When I asked her about the church, about her commitment with the church—at that time I made no distinction between church, Christians, Catholics, and all that. Why didn't the church show that it was with the poor, and why were priests and sisters so remote and inaccessible? And what about the religious orders who talked and talked about equality but still kept separate dining rooms for the children who could afford it, and for the sisters too? (CR 167)

Although at first she was put off by Carminia's direct and abrasive manner, Olga soon realized that she had met a person who could be trusted. Her comments recall the way people in rural Facatativá describe their first encounter with Román Cortes, or how peasants from Villanueva talk about Padre Vicente. Fear is soon followed by conversion, then by trust and friendship.

> Then she began to answer me, seriously and with specifics. She didn't try to fool me, but rather said that acting in those ways was not being Christian. Being Christian involved more than saying so, just saying "I am Christian," but rather of showing it in actions. And that they were failing that test, and missing that truth because at those moments they were lying. So she gave me a lot of serious answers, and I loved her dearly, although I was terribly afraid of her.

*Why were you afraid?*

> Because of how she talks, the way she is. You've seen how sharp and brusque she can be, and so I was afraid. . . . But little by little I got to know her, and we spoke more directly. And looking in her eyes one sees who she really is, because she looks at you with total honesty and openness. That's how she is: frank and forthright. And so we got to know each other, and now I love her very much. (CR 167)

These fearful encounters were the beginning of a long and fruitful association between the two women. Through Carminia, Olga became aware of the ideas and organizations collected around *Solidaridad*, and subsequently attended numerous courses on theology and church, unions, history, and international issues. Her involvement with the parish also grew as the Basque priests drew her into their efforts at promoting housing and city services, and defending the weak and helpless. The priest was tireless, always there when needed:

> Sometimes he got involved in tremendous polemics in the barrio, where people had to pull him out. For example, once the police came to evict a woman from over there [points down a street]. So he called the people together, not in a conspiracy of any kind, but rather to ask them, what do you think about all this? And the whole barrio went down there, and so the police weren't able to carry out their

dirty work. We spent the whole night watching, it was a tremendous fighting spirit. That's what a priest should do, face up to painful and difficult things. We aren't here just to watch and do nothing, to look to others to give us alms and support us. No. Reality is different, there is a commitment. (CR 169)

The departure of Rodeo's founding priest and the subsequent shift to a more cautious and less activist stance by those who remain left Olga depressed and worried about the future. She hopes against hope that a new influx of sisters from Carminia's order will spur the clergy to renewed commitment and get things moving in the right direction again. This is essential, for without active help from the priests, it is hard to convince most people.

> They say that no one is a prophet in his own land, but this isn't so for the priests. Whatever they say is good and is accepted. They can get projects started and do things that you and I cannot do, because we are not clergy. It even gets to the point that if you go and talk about the Gospel and say that the Gospel says this or that, someone will tell you no, because it's you who says it, not a priest.

*And the sisters?*

> They are more involved with people, making friends and trying. . . . I think it is just one of those things, they can't come and try to organize groups and create communities without having a good friendship with the people, I think they are starting from there, with good relationships. I can see that they like people very much, and that they are hardworking. (CR 178, 179)

Olga's growing identification as activist Christian and her sustained involvement in popular organizations of religious inspiration have nurtured a sophisticated critique of the institutional church. Her views on the preferential option for the poor illustrate the point well. Forceful and often eloquent documents were written at Medellín and Puebla, but that was then, this is now. To Olga, the church's preferential option for the poor exists mostly on paper, and only weakly at that. It is a long and difficult step from documents to action, a step that bishops (especially Colombian bishops) are unlikely to take.

> To my mind, whatever happened at Medellín and Puebla stayed right there, at Medellín and Puebla. You know, at Medellín lots of things were said, and later people claimed that things were signed because they [the bishops] had been tired, were sleepy, and didn't realize what they were signing. What documents say is one thing, but with the kind of bishops we have . . . if we only could have some bishops who would pay attention to it, with even a little consciousness, who would issue a call to read the texts, to value what is written there, and not just invent things, like talking about communism. Instead of all that, they should simply *be true* to what is said there. I believe that the church is very great, and needs really to fulfill the Gospel message. But we don't even get that, they aren't even true to the Gospel. Instead, they take it and adapt it to whatever they want. So, to

me, in my view Puebla is something like this, something way above the clouds, like the God they taught us about in school. (CR 180)

As she looks outward from the parish to appraise the ecclesiastical institution as a whole, Olga is thus well aware of the ties that bind, and the way they operate to constrain and confine popular action. Her response to a question about possibilities for lay participation in the church is worth quoting at length. She pushes the issue firmly to the matter of what participation is supposed to be about in the first place.

But which church? Because look, what I see is that there are parts of the church that do this, because according to the hierarchy—no, no, no—the hierarchical church will never let priests get involved in these things. We see that they issue statements about not getting involved in politics, but politics means talking about hunger, and letting the people speak about injustice, poverty, and all that. They say we shouldn't slide over into other areas, but what are they really doing? What they are doing is denying the Gospel. Because if you read the Gospel—I tell you I am a Christian and I have a Bible. But I hardly know any of these biblical citations. I only know one, which is Isaiah 58, which talks about the offerings he wants, and it is to loosen the chains and break the yoke. They will tell you that yes, they accept that, but only in a nice way, through lots of praying [literally, "a punta de padrenuestros"] to who knows what kind of solutions. But in any case, there are parts of the church where people have become more aware, and we don't care that much about church hierarchies. What we see is that commitment with the people is more important than being more or less okay with them. So we go on, continuing with the real Christian commitment we have. (CR 173–74)

The kind of commitment Olga Ceballos wants from the church is especially important to communities like Barrio El Rodeo, where residents need all the allies they can muster. These are poor people who work hard at unsteady and insecure jobs. Constant political division and factional infighting make it all the more difficult to get much accomplished. From Olga's vantage point, the church ought to help the poor because that is the right thing to do. Poor people need help the most. Standing with the poor is also in the church's institutional self-interest. As Olga sees things, if the church is not committed to the people, it is doomed to disappear.

And it should disappear, because what good is that kind of church, what use is it for the poor? Just to tell us that we are going to hell? We live through hell every day we face floods, scarcities, and all those needs. What more hell is there than that? So why should anyone care if all they do is keep hammering away at the same old thing? (CR 182)

The stress on social and political activism that we hear in ordinary conversation with Olga should not obscure more conventional aspects of her spirituality or her religious belief and practice. Olga is deeply involved in religious education and works closely with parents and children in the barrio to give a new tone to traditional catechism. She attends mass at least once a week and prays regularly. When asked to whom she prays and for what, Olga replied in these terms:

> Many people think that praying is sitting by yourself with a rosary. [But] I think a lot about commitment, and I ask for strength, because I know that all the troubles and tangles we go through are going to bring lots of headaches. I believe there is a God, a force that lives inside each of us, and I pray to that force, to that light. (CR 189)

From Olga's vantage point, Jesus, Mary, and the saints are important role models but should always be seen as real people, warts and all. The saints "were people who gave themselves fully, who fought and gave their lives for others. Not the figures we see in images, those inventions." In her eyes, the Virgin Mary is above all "a suffering and sacrificing mother," and as for Jesus: "In Jesus I see a model of life. I see him and I accept him as just a man, a man who had women, who got drunk. But he came to fulfill God's plan, he denounced injustices and announced a better life." In her view, a good life must be made here and now, because after death Olga expects, frankly, "nothing" (CR 190).

Looking back on her upbringing and on her life as a whole, Olga is struck by how far she has traveled, how much she has changed. She sees herself now as being authentically religious, having fought her way through experience to a more meaningful understanding of what faith entails and requires. Thus,

> I tell you that I am a Christian. I have my own views, I have made my choice, and I am resolved. And I ask my God to give me lots of strength so that I can be part of what has to come, but that it be with the people. If people are convinced, and if you can show them a God who is really present, part of their lives, then they will accept that God. Right?
>
> Me, for example, I was raised with the idea of a God way above the rooftops, that you couldn't see. But tell someone they serve God in a person, because God is there; that you are church because the church is there, not in that pile of cement. Things change, we learn, and people need to see this. (CR 183)

Recall Olga's comment that her life had been full of curiosities. In her view, the most curious of all the twists and turns life has taken was her return to the religion she had rejected so strongly as a girl. Activism and a commitment to struggle against injustice were the bridge that brought her back to the church, no longer as a naive and, in her words, "repressed" young woman but now as an independent, responsible, and often highly critical believer. It is worth comparing this trajectory to that of another daughter of The Violence, Susanna

Madrid. The comparison takes us away from the streets and slums of Cali to Barro Blanco, one of the most isolated *veredas* in the parish of Caparrapí.

Susanna Madrid is a pleasant, slight, and gray-haired woman. She is a single parent and lives on a small farm in Barro Blanco with her own parents and her children. She has been deeply involved with the local church since arriving in the area in 1975. Susanna is also a strong and independent woman, but in sharp contrast to Olga Ceballos, Susanna sees her links to the church as original and primary: religion undergirds political activism, not the reverse.

Susanna Madrid was born to a much-traveled peasant family on January 21, 1940, in San Cayetano, a village in the rural part of the department of Cundinamarca, part of the general hinterland of the capital city of Bogotá. Her mother was raised in Cundinamarca, but her father grew up El Líbano (department of Tolima), a town that later became famous as one of the very worst centers of The Violence.[3] The Violence struck rural Cundinamarca hard, forcing Susanna and her parents to abandon their farm and flee to the capital city. In Bogotá, she finished primary school and then married while still relatively young. Like Olga Ceballos, Susanna had problems with her husband, and the two eventually separated.

> In Bogotá I got married and we had a small place. But my husband soon started making trouble, about why wouldn't I work and all that, and I got sick of it. So we sold the place and he stayed in Bogotá while I moved to Caldas, to a farm some friends sold to us. Friends! So-called friends they were, because that land was really poor, and full of mosquitos. You went around swollen all the time. I lasted six years in Caldas, but then I couldn't take it anymore, and I sold that spread. So then I came here, because through some friends of my father I petitioned INCORA [Instituto Colombiano de Reforma Agraria, the national land reform agency] to grant us title to this farm. But it's been hard here, with all the trouble the army gives us, they won't leave a body alone. (C 84)

Susanna was brought up in the conventional religiosity common to much of rural Colombia in the 1940s. Her parents attended mass whenever possible (given the constraints of work and transport) until her father broke with the church in reaction to its partisan entanglements in The Violence. Susanna took First Communion as a young girl and, generally speaking, led an ordinary religious life until the combination of periodic moves and the trauma of marital separation made her shy away from active participation, if not from belief.

All this changed soon after her arrival in Barro Blanco when Susanna encountered Román Cortes, who was then just beginning to promote *cursillos* and groups in the area. Her experience with Román and his team followed a

---

[3] See James Henderson, *When Colombia Bled: A History of the Violencia in Tolima*; Oquist, *Violence*; and for a perspective on nineteenth-century origins, Helen Delpar, *Red against Blue: The Liberal Party in Colombian Politics, 1863–1899*.

now-familiar pattern of growing involvement: initial contact and participation in a *cursillo* followed by group formation and selection for a leadership role, as a local *animadora*.

> When we first got here, all this was very remote, and not just because of the roads. It had also been neglected and abandoned. Then Román came to say mass and form the community. He came along with Celmirita [Sister Celmira Duque]. Me, I owe everything to the sister, to Celmirita. I really owe her everything, because you know how it is, you don't really get to talk much with priests. So it was by talking with her. Actually she arrived a little later, when was it? It hadn't been planned, but I have it all written down in my little notebook. Yes, yes, the first meeting of local leaders that I attended was on March 26, 1980. Look how worn my old notebook is! (C 74, 75)

Being a single parent separated from her husband is a difficult position for a woman to sustain amid the conventional morality of the Colombian countryside, but Susanna has stuck to her guns. Although Román and his aides repeatedly begged her to try for reconciliation, she has insisted that it was impossible to patch things up. Notwithstanding the anomaly her status posed in rural society, Susanna has had sufficient force of character not only to persevere but also to participate actively in a broad range of church-related efforts. As an activist and later as an officially designated *animadora*, Susanna's responsibilities have ranged from running catechism classes and study circles to promoting family gardens, cooperatives, and local water projects. Whatever the specific focus, every activity has been conducted in close concert with the parish, as it is represented by one or another of the priests or the sisters working there.

Susanna sees involvement with the church as both necessary and desirable. It is necessary because working with the church is a way of affirming the religious experience and sense of identity as a believer that she prizes so highly. It is also desirable because, as we have seen, in areas like the zone around Caparrapí, the church provides ordinary people with help that no other institution is willing or able to give. Moreover, as far as Susanna is concerned, unlike the army, the official school system, or powerful rural groups like the Federation of Coffee Growers, the church can be relied upon to have responsible, accountable, and morally upright individuals acting in its name.

> Anyone can see that the formation of church people is different. We were talking about that just a little while ago with the kids, about what a big difference there was between Huberto [Vanegas] who is the diocese's social promoter and the promoter who works for the Coffee Growers. You never hear Huberto utter a dirty word or speak ill of anyone. What a contrast with that one from the Federation! I would follow Huberto anywhere, even to Patagonia; I know he is incorruptible.

But I wouldn't even let my daughter take a walk with the man from the Federation.
(C 79)

The church is more than simply trustworthy in itself. Its programs and activities also help generate trust in others. They bring together individuals who would otherwise never see one another, let alone speak or work in cooperation. This is particularly important given the ever-present threat of violence, which makes people hang back from contact, suspicious of any outsiders. To Susanna, greater sociability is one of the most valuable benefits the church has brought to the area.

> Yes, yes, there have been changes. Earlier, people were like I told you when we started talking. They were the same at home as when they came to town—dirty, never neat or well-dressed, nothing. But now when a meeting is called, people try to look their best. It's a change. Another thing. People here lived in fear. Fear of the army, of the guerrillas. This hasn't gone away, but it is better now. Now people talk among themselves with more confidence.

> *Why?*

> It must be the meetings. Because as for the rest, what is there, what is there? We don't even have a schoolteacher. The only thing that functions is this. This is the only way people can meet others apart from those in their own hamlet. Before, there was a lot more distrust. Some remains, and that's why people don't accept the programs. But you know, if people are suspicious, it's because they have been tricked so often, so many things have been done to them. You can't blame them. But look at places where that distrust is gone, and you'll see that people can get moving, they really can. (C 76a)

The region around Caparrapí has an air of blocked opportunity about it. Despite good soil, a favorable climate, and decent farming conditions (which attracted Susanna's family to the area in the first place), isolation and poor transport make it hard to get crops out. Even with good harvests and stable weather and road conditions, peasants never know when they may be accosted by guerrillas, the army, or both. Like the peasants of San Pedro to whom we listened earlier, Susanna feels trapped between two equally abusive armed groups: the official military and the guerrilla forces. Each accuses peasants of aiding the other, and each is abusive, but Susanna reserves particular bitterness for the army.

> For me the toughest problem is the way the army treats people. The government never gets tired of talking about peace, peace, and people easily throw all the blame on the guerrillas. Now believe me, I have nothing good to say about the guerrillas, but if the army would just treat people decently, like human beings, they would get more cooperation. But people are afraid of the army, and what's

more *they make you afraid*. I know if someone confronts me that way, with those looks, I sure take a step back. But the army is like that. I think the army deserves most of the blame for the violence, because of how they treat people. Sure, the government says this is all lies, but no, that's the way it really is. The army is all screwed up. I wish our army were different. (C 76, 77)

The army's constant interference with travel in and out of the area makes it hard for peasants to earn a living. It also effectively shuts out those who want to help communities improve themselves. Teachers are intimidated, church workers threatened, agricultural technicians turned away. I told Susanna that I had been advised not to travel to one part of the parish, and she commented:

Yes, that's the way they are. They won't let people work, they won't let us progress. And if people want to come and help us get out from under, they won't allow it. To my mind, the army is responsible for everything bad around here. People won't help them, the government says that people won't cooperate with the army. But how can you work with them when they look at you that way, when they are so bad? People around here live with constant fear, they live in permanent anxiety. (C 84)

Susanna believes that the region's most critical needs are less credit, transport, or technical help than greater culture, and easier access to its tools, particularly schools and teachers. Barro Blanco has never been able to hold a teacher for long. They are appointed, stay for a while, and then leave.

It has been no use pleading. All our asking and still they ignore us, they trick us. They promise to come and enroll the children next week, or maybe in two weeks' time, but no one ever comes. Now they are talking about coming after Easter. The truth is that we are lost and forgotten. (C 73)

The lack of basic services in the *vereda* undermines the possibilities for cultural advancement. Recall how hard it was for people in San Isidro to gather much enthusiasm for books after a long day of hard physical labor. Susanna believes that much of the problem arises from poor living conditions.

Light is another problem. If we only had lights in the house, we could read, study. We like to study, but without lights, it is difficult. You get home all tired out, and it is hard. If there were lights, people could study more and acquire more skills. I have mentioned to people that if we had lights we could show a film, that would be even better. I know that I'm content with words, but a film lets you learn a lot, really a lot. We could really attract people with something like a film. Once in Bogotá I saw a film, it was a Russian film about growing wheat. Now, that isn't really very interesting, I don't care about agriculture over there. But if you had something for the people here, it would be interesting, we could really learn a lot. (C 74)

Susanna Madrid's understanding of the relation between church, society, and ordinary people like herself is complex and occasionally contradictory. Dependence and independence coexist in her view of things. To begin with, she recognizes the power of the institutional church and looks to it for help and guidance. "For me, the church is more powerful than any government or any army. Wherever the church is active trying to resolve problems, there you can see real progress" (C 78). But this visible power can also have negative consequences. People depend too much on the church, and are often reluctant to get involved unless there is an active and direct institutional presence. Thus Susanna notes, for example, that without a priest or sister in attendance, few are likely to show up for meetings, and fewer still remain to the end. Still, she values the chances for participation the church now provides, and sees this participation as part of a broad process of personal and collective change. In her view, over the long haul people must learn to help themselves; the best medium for accomplishing this end is study and hard work, not sterile confrontation or empty talk. In this regard, the church offers not only material help but also the moral support required to see the process through.

This ambiguous mix of self-esteem and dependence extends to other areas of life. Susanna's understanding of poverty and of the preferential option for the poor illustrates the contours of her position very well. Like most of her neighbors, Susanna is a hardworking person, blocked from advancement by forces beyond her control. Although she recognizes that poverty like hers has structural sources, Susanna's view of class relations retains powerful components of hierarchy. She aspires less to change the system than to effect reconciliation.[4] Rich and poor must come together, and the church is the logical intermediary.

> I often think that we poor people have reservations about the rich, and the rich have reservations about the poor. Maybe what has been missing is communication between one and the other. The church could be that communication. We said just that in our parish evaluation, that the parish team was dedicated to that goal, and that it was not necessary to try to do everything. Because how can we think that the rich are better than us, and still fear them, and then they are also afraid of the poor? How can such a thing be? (C 79, 80)

Susanna is very devout: she prays regularly and attends mass whenever possible. Her spirituality is relatively conventional, and after death she hopes for union with God, a kind of ecstatic fusion into one divine essence. "When I think about eternity, I don't imagine God there and me here, apart. Not apart, but rather him in me and me in him. If he were separate and I was separate, there would be just the same danger [as now]. To me, eternal salvation is

---

[4] Drogus ("Reconstructing the Feminine") states that this is a common response among women, who often filter out messages of conflict and opposition.

having God within my own being, that's what it is'' (C 83–84). Susanna simply cannot fathom a life without faith.

> For example, sometimes I try to imagine lots of things, piles of money, for example, but I get bored right away. I think about many things, like having the house I always dreamed of, but without God what would we do? There would be no reason for anything. I look at people who say they don't believe in God, and I wonder, what can they be like? (C 83)

Susanna is not only devout but also (unlike Olga Ceballos) highly devoted to the institutional church. One of her happiest moments came when her father was reconciled with the church. Like many victims of The Violence, he harbored deep anger and distrust of church and clergy. In his view, they had caused terrible harm by inciting, promoting, and legitimizing violence under the guise of defending ''religion'' from atheistic attacks.

> That brings me back to the point that when people are suspicious, they have reasons. With him it was The Violence. Ever since the time of The Violence in San Cayetano, he drew back and always said that you had to be very cautious dealing with priests and sisters. But now he has come back, and I am really happy. Now when he comes to town, he goes to mass. And he understands that today's clergy are not responsible for what others did. What blame do they have? I was sure my father would die far from our Lord, but now he sees that priests are our friends again, that the priest can be with rich and poor. How much better off we are with a good priest! Sure, they can also be failures, but how much we can benefit! (C 81)

Looking at the life stories of Olga Ceballos and Susanna Madrid together points up a number of striking parallels and differences. Both women are daughters of The Violence and were raised in the countryside amid fighting, danger, and family traumas. Both were unhappy in their marriages and sufficiently strong-minded to strike out on their own. They were not abandoned but decided to make independent lives. This is no mean feat, given the prevailing culture of Colombian domestic life. Each believes in God, and the two share a common commitment to work in and for the community through the church.

Now differences begin. The clearest variation arises in the path each woman took to involvement with the church. For Olga, the church represented another step on a path to fuller and more meaningful activism. As a teenager, Olga rejected religion and the church, and then drifted until being drawn into the radical urban politics of the early 1970s. But politics soon left her disillusioned. She wanted a message with more depth and authenticity, and hoped to find collaborators less focused on personal or factional gain and more devoted to serving others. Because she lived in the city, Olga was able to shop around until she finally found something suited to her needs and inclinations. In contrast, for Susanna Madrid, the church has been the only conceivable vehicle for action. As a young adult, she retained the faith of her childhood, but felt set apart from the church as a result of her marital problems. Renewed by contact with Román Cortes, her commitment soon blossomed into activism. Shopping around is not an option in a place like Barro Blanco. A few alternatives do exist, but these are so discredited that as a practical matter the church stands alone for people like Susanna. No other institution can be trusted.

The difference in starting points suggests possible variations in the focus and durability of the two women's commitments. Each is clearly a dedicated person, but for someone like Olga Ceballos, a shift in the medium chosen for her considerable energies—say, to a Protestant church, a trade union, or to some other political party—is certainly conceivable. Such a choice is unthinkable for Susanna, whose connection to the institutional church is clearly a personal and moral lifeline. The experiences of these two women offer elements for reflection that should be borne in mind as we turn to consider the lives of two peasant men: Fortunato Duque, a very poor Venezuelan coffee grower, and Agua Fría's Patricio Alvarez.

## Two Peasant Men: Fortunato Duque and Patricio Alvarez

Fortunato Duque and Patricio Alvarez have much in common. Each is a very poor peasant born to a poor peasant family well over half a century ago. Each is a firm believer who throughout his life has maintained deep faith in God, devotion to the church, and a religious practice as regular as could be managed under the circumstances. Each man also has a thoughtful and well-developed spirituality. Each life took a decisive turn as a result of encounters with extraordinary priests who brought religious reforms and socioeconomic organizations to their areas. For Fortunato Duque, contact with Padre Vicente sparked a new sense of church and community and of himself as an independent and responsible individual. For Patricio Alvarez, Román Cortes triggered an experience of personal conversion that set him on a path of learning and service to others.

Fortunato Duque was born on June 11, 1931, in Las Quebraditas, a very remote village in the western mountains of Venezuela, in the state of Lara. His father and mother were peasant farmers from villages in the same general area. He is a short, slight man who is rarely seen without a large hat and a welcoming expression. He is extremely poor, and over the years has worked in towns and villages all across the region, mostly as a day laborer with occasional access to rented land. When I met him, Fortunato had recently moved to Villanueva in search of work. Until then, he had been living for many years in El Silencio, a tiny *caserío* located nine hours by foot from Villanueva itself. Fortunato describes El Silencio in these terms:

> That community is very far away, extremely remote and forgotten. Forgotten by everyone, above all by the government. The government remembers about it only in moments like these, in election years. Then they come to the town with loudspeakers, making all sorts of promises. But nothing ever happens. The houses there are really poor. (V 110)

Fortunato has no formal education at all; there were no schools in the countryside when he was a boy. Even if there had been schools available, his family could not have afforded to send him. As long as he can remember, Fortunato has worked in agriculture, first to fill out his parent's household income, later to support his own family. He was able to learn a few basics (ABCs and some counting) at home and, as an adult, has attended various courses offered through the churches. These courses, reinforced by his experience in the Legion of Mary, provided a chance to master reading and writing.

> My mother taught me, and I learned a few things from others in the street. Also a course on adult catechism in El Hatillo. A schoolteacher from near home was in that course too, and he taught catechism and gave classes. So I joined up with him to form a local group, an adult education group. That was the theme, and in that way I also managed to grab a little education for myself. (V 109)

Major changes came to Fortunato Duque's life with the arrival of Padre Vicente. He recalls their first encounter:

> Padre Vicente arrived by himself, alone with Miguel Malgacía's family, from La Barranca. Over there they thought he was a *guerrillero*. There had been guerrillas around the area, and so they were sure he was one. After all, they had never seen him before; they didn't know him. You see, when an unknown person arrives, that draws a lot of attention. I could tell right away that he was no *guerrillero*; I looked at his face and saw that he was no *guerrillero*.

> *Just by looking at his face? He didn't have the face of a* guerrillero?

> No, he had the face of a saint. And that is the man who has prevailed in lots of towns, not only in El Silencio, but everywhere around here. (V 110)

Fortunato was an early recruit to the Legion of Mary. The Legion brought him a number of valuable new experiences, among them the chance to get together on a regular basis with others in his village and throughout the region. From the outset, each local or village unit of the Legion has held weekly meetings and has also sent elected representatives to monthly gatherings held in Villanueva. I asked Fortunato to describe a typical meeting in El Silencio. His account points up the importance of cooperative work and organizational responsibility.

In El Silencio? Over there we organize meetings to deal with catechism for children. Then there are Bible study meetings, sort of for the people to dialogue and teach one another about what God's word is, and then to talk it over. Also to provide guidance, because many of us are baptized but don't know anything about it. You know what I mean? So that is the goal of the Legion of Mary, and those are the teachings of the Legion of Mary. Each presidium has its weekly meeting, every week. They hold the meeting, and the meeting is for members to get together and talk over their problems. Then work is assigned to each member in pairs, two by two. They go to do such-and-such a thing here or there. And that is the week's work. (V 112)

The work assigned in these meetings ranges from teaching to visiting the sick, charity to some cooperative local effort. Over the years, different tasks have been taken up, but whatever the particulars of the issue at hand, each matter gets a full discussion in group meetings, with a complete report (in writing) to members. The report is entered in the records. At the time of my fieldwork, the groups were actively spreading the word about dietary reform and farm gardens as had been urged by Manolo Moreno, and members were especially active in attempts to get gardens started in a number of communities.

In Fortunato's eyes, no valid distinction can be drawn between the religious concerns of the Legion and the socioeconomic activities of the cooperative. Each reinforces the other, each commitment makes sense in light of what the other requires of members. Like others in Villanueva, Fortunato argues that experience in the Legion and ties to the church help guarantee that cooperative members are honest and trustworthy people. Religious affiliation may not be a formal test for cooperative membership, but belief and faith are essential to success. If members seek only personal gain, they undermine the group. But if they come in search of God, then they are likely to serve all. Belief in God is an essential basis for trust among human beings, a prior foundation for attempts at organization and cooperative effort. Without such belief, people are easily discouraged.

I don't know, they get discouraged easily. Let me tell you something. When we get together in a group meeting or in a religious event, really, what we are really seeking is God. When we aren't looking for God, then the search is for people, and they come to me. And I tell them that what you have got to do is seek God out. Because God is everywhere. The same God is here when I talk with you, when we speak here, he is also there in the meeting. So I think that with these people who get discouraged, who can't be interested in coming to the meetings, I think that the real reason they don't come is that they are looking for me, not for God. . . . We've got to keep pushing forward, but those people are likely to fade out. They are not constant. (V 117, 118)

Fortunato has a compelling vision of the church. He grasps its institutional quality clearly, and sees it realistically as a powerful and far-reaching set of structures. But at the same time, he argues eloquently that "we are all church." In his view, "being church" requires participation in formal religion (in mass, taking Communion, joining in religious festivals, participating in groups like the Legion of Mary) along with active involvement in community efforts, working alongside one's brothers and sisters for the good of all. The key word is *active*.

> You've got to participate in the mass. Sure, at mass they say what you do is hear mass, but there is more, you have to join in. If you don't participate, then really the priest is doing mass alone, just by himself and not shared with everyone. So we participate, that is our duty, to participate and not only in mass, but in lots of other things too. Let's just say that as Christians we are all church. . . . The Legion helps a lot. Now many people are aware, many have come to realize that we are all church. That everyone is church, a block of the church. That means that we have got to ratify what the priests do, and ratify the movements we find ourselves in. If we come to your country, then we must look for the groups you have there, we've got to seek them out. If we don't try to find them, then we are not being church. Wherever we are, we need to participate actively in the church, because the church is the same everywhere. (V 115, 116)

Fortunato's position combines a strong sense of personal and collective autonomy with great reverence for church and clergy. He is exceptionally devoted to Padre Vicente. We have already heard him describe Vicente's saintly face. On reflection, it is clear to Fortunato that Vicente's saintliness is more than a matter of looks. The key point is Vicente's complete dedication to others.

> He is a marvelous padre in those things. I think we have never seen a padre in those parts who is so totally selfless, who suffers hunger, suffering, yes, because he really does suffer. You never worry about him, there is no need to worry, because he has enough, at least people give him food to eat. But if you have no meal, he won't eat his. He worries because you are hungry. He sees you sitting there and starts asking, "Where will this one eat?" Everyone is looking at him, and meanwhile he is asking that poor unfortunate, "Where are you from, do you have a place to sleep, have you eaten?" He sees you over there, an unknown, and wants to know where you came from, what you are doing, where you are going. Meanwhile he just pushes on, and as to where *he* [Vicente] will eat or sleep, it's just "I will sleep somewhere out there, don't worry." (V 114)

Fortunato also has praise for Alberto Dorremochea (Padre Dorre), one of the main Jesuit organizers working in the region. Dorre is also seen as hardworking and self-sacrificing, but his blunt and forthright manner made many uncomfortable at first. They were used to a different style and manner in their clergy; it took a while to convince people that he was a priest.

> The priest from the cooperative, Padre Dorre, lots of people told me that they couldn't believe that that padre really was a padre. Because he talks so simply and bluntly in the cooperative meetings. Others thought he couldn't be a padre because of the way he went around in jeans in a Toyota, and above all because of the way he acted with people [this refers to joking and arguing]. But that's how they all are, especially Padre [Manolo] Moreno. (V 122)

The trust Fortunato and his companions had for Vicente and through him, for the other priests, helped smooth the transition from Legion to cooperative. The new cooperative structures were legitimized by the presence of Jesuit advisers and also by the contrast between the visible honesty and open style of operation of the Jesuits and the aloofness and corruption of established credit and marketing agencies like the PACCA (Productores Asociados de Café, a semiofficial agency established in 1968). PACCA is viewed as just another arm of the state, financed by peasant fees but remote and not accountable to peasants themselves. The cooperative is different.

> Around here for years we've had a group called PACCA, which belongs to the coffee growers. But those who joined still have no idea of what the group does, of what goes on there, because they've never gotten a report about anything. But with us, every two months we know all about the cooperative. We read a report the cooperative gives us, a complete account that tells us what resources we have. We know what our capital is, where it is going, what it is invested in, what we are contributing ourselves. And this makes us happy to contribute. We know that our group is clean, well run. The cooperatives are a very clean and healthy movement, and that is very good. (V 121)

Fortunato Duque has a clear and straightforward view of local and national problems. He knows that peasants are weak and poor, and recognizes their dependence on pricing and marketing decisions (e.g., for coffee) taken far away. Considerations like these make him stress the need for organization and collective action. He is particularly concerned with education, and hopes that coming generations can enjoy greater access to schools and schooling than was available to him. Facing a range of problems, Fortunato looks for a kind of help that will let peasants progress to a point where they can help themselves. Whatever the issue, the critical point is to work together. When I asked who should solve these problems, the answer was first general, then specific.

> Well, first of all God, and after God the community. The people of each *caserío* have got to get together, to get moving to press the government for help. They need to get together, have meetings, make representations, and see what can be done. (V 118–19)

At our level, for peasants like us what would be useful to those of us who work the land would be long-term credit, credits for improvements. We could use those credits to upgrade our holdings. At least with long-term credit you've got a chance to work better. We would improve what we have and that way at least something would get accomplished. But as for ordinary credits, like credits for supplies, they are not much real help, because they make you satisfied with things as they are. What they amount to is just more debt, nothing else. (V 120)

Participation in the Legion of Mary and later in the cooperative has brought much of great value to Fortunato's life. Although his personal economic situation is still not very good, Fortunato believes that he benefits from the overall improvement that the cooperative has helped bring to the region. Wages are higher, access to credit is easier, and, as we have seen, reforms in diet and medical care have cut household costs while improving the quality of life. Many of the changes Fortunato prizes most are noneconomic in character. He has been able to travel and to improve himself culturally through exposure to a wide range of courses. He has become a respected community leader, not only through the Legion and the cooperative, but also in the national Peasant Federation. In all these ways, Fortunato Duque has become an active subject. He is aware of the possibilities of change, and conscious of himself as a person able to change and to change others. Although he remains a polite, even courtly, individual, this man has decisively shed the shyness and self-imposed reserve of traditional peasant culture. He is ready to speak and act plainly, and knows that others look to him.

Oh, there's nobody like me when it comes to working. When I go to an agrarian reform settlement, I always go to the delegation offices, to talk with the Peasant Federation. That's how I manage to help people get things. There's always something, some kind of official help and they tell me no, since the last time you went there, they don't come around anymore. They always tell me, when we need to make up a delegation, we'll go if you will come with us. So I go along. But they need to go on their own too. They've got to get used to that, because someday I will die. [*They need to learn.*] Sure, they've got to learn to do things on their own. (V 119)

It is hard to disentangle religious from social motives and forms of action in Fortunato's view of the world. He recognizes that they fall in distinct areas but believes that at bottom they are properly seen together. If everyone is church and if being church requires sharing and mutual support, then exclusive stress on any single dimension—spiritual, social, or economic—is misplaced. According to Fortunato, an integral approach is needed. This is what he learned from Padre Vicente, this is how he tries to act, and, in his view, this is the surest way to progress.

You've always got to be teaching, that's how you can really get involved with people. They can be very proud, humble, or whatever, but all the same, you've got to work with them: teaching, educating, and talking about the community. That's how a person gets to be really someone, helping promote change and helping the community. But if you go too fast or jump in too abruptly, nothing takes hold. The church can help, but it's best the way I said, at least that is how the priests we have now have taught us. That, for example, we have a meeting in someone's house and the first thing Padre Vicente tells us is not to show up just talking about the Bible. That's not the way. Instead, we talk about the difficulties they face, about their problems, about all those things. Nowadays we know about motivation, that when people are motivated, a lot more can be accomplished. And that is the way the church can cooperate in the community. (V 122, 123)

Fortunato's understanding of the "preferential option for the poor" builds on his sense of himself as part of a community. His perspective echoes other voices we have heard in these pages. Equality is assumed and taken as a foundation for everything else; sharing and community are stressed over division, conflict, or bitterness. As far as this man is concerned, all are equal before God, all share in God's grace, and all are equally obliged to help one another if they consider themselves to be Christians. In Fortunato's view of the world, opting for the poor is therefore an integral part of loving one's neighbor and thus "being church."

The preference for the poor? Let's put it this way: What do we have to do in order to say that we are church? Suppose, at the very least, that we see a person who is in bad shape, without clothes and without food, and we think we're very Catholic but we never stop to think about him. I believe that then we are nothing, not church, not anything because we have no feeling for others. (V 123)

In addition to his strong focus on community, Fortunato is very devout in conventional terms. He prays regularly and holds to a number of traditional devotions. Fortunato was raised in a religious family and has been devoted to the church all his life.

I remember that I made my First Communion when I was seven years old. My mother taught me how, and she told me what it was, what I was going to receive. I still remember, it's like I can still hear her talking to me. Since then I have continued. Whenever there was a festival, even though we lived in the country, they would bring me to the town. That's where you could take Communion, in the church. (V 124)

Fortunato regards easier and more frequent access to church services as a major benefit of living in the town of Villanueva. He attends mass at least once a week and prays often, mixing traditional devotions like the rosary with prayers for family members, church, community, peace, and the like. He also reads the Bible frequently, alone or with his family, and also in Legion meetings. Fortunato no longer uses holy water in the old ways and is clear on the fact that religious pictures are pictures, nothing more.

> Yes, the images that we buy, well they are just pictures after all. We have the custom of lighting candles before them, but it's just a tradition, nothing more. (V 125)

In contrast to many group members we have heard, he still makes promises and is careful to carry them out. One promise made for the health of his mother is a vivid example. Fortunato prayed to Saint Anthony, pledging to dance before the Lord if she recovered.

> I remember once my mother was sick and so we got her out to the hospital. At first I carried her myself, in a hammock; it was a difficult path. Then we came to a river and I said good-bye and remained there alone. I got down on my knees and asked blessed Saint Anthony to help my mother and I promised that in fifteen days I would pay him with a *gaita*. You know what a *gaita* is? It's a dance. So, fifteen days later my father came and told me, "Son, your mother is walking." And when I went to see her, she looked fat and beautiful. I went and saw her in the hospital at El Tocuyo and at first even I did not recognize her.
>
> I was so happy to see her recovered, and I told her, "Mama," (you know you always think about your mother) I told her, "Mama, now that you are better I want you to know that I made a promise for you. Let me die if I don't carry it out." What was it? I told her, "a *gaita* for Saint Anthony." So when they released her from the hospital, I went down there and brought her home. And seven days later she heard the drums at the door of her room, drumming for Saint Anthony. That's why I have such affection for Saint Anthony, because he interceded before God. (V 128, 129)

Fortunato's personal spirituality is highly focused on Jesus, who is seen for the most part in conventional terms, with emphasis on how Christ sacrificed his life to free human beings from sin. He venerates the Virgin Mary because her acceptance of God's gift made Jesus' birth possible. He also sees Mary as something of an intermediary. The saints are a different matter. As we have seen, on occasion Fortunato prays to the saints, but on the whole he sees them less as figures of power than as role models.

> So there are saints, saints who were converted through their good works. And that is our goal, every person has a goal, and I tell you again, you come for your work to our communities, to our brothers. . . . You work according to your own image, from your community. You are sure that you are following a goal, searching for God. You go with God always, that is how life is, and so God is with you, and that is what the saints were doing too. Many people have become saints because of their good works, many have been converted. (V 129)

That Fortunato Duque has not abandoned traditional practices for the exclusive stress on preaching and Bible study found in many base communities and similar groups warrants separate comment. His ability to combine conventional spirituality with personal independence and community activism suggests that although changes in religious practice are a common part of group development, they are neither necessary nor sufficient. Indeed, excessive stress (for example, by pastoral agents) on the reform of religious practice may be counterproductive, turning people off by gutting their religious life of much of its color and vitality. Real democratization is more fundamental. It gives men and women a chance to invest even the most ordinary acts with new meaning, because they themselves have become new people.

Patricio Alvarez was born on March 17, 1930, in Agua Fría, which was also home to his parents and grandparents. Patricio is a short, thin, and somewhat stooped man, with a weather-beaten and grizzled face. Like most of his neighbors, Patricio has lived all his life in Agua Fría, eking out a difficult and precarious livelihood from several small plots of land on which he raises the typical local mix of coffee, sugar (for *panela*, a crude brown sugar made locally), and some subsistence crops. He suffers greatly from arthritis, which makes the day-to-day routine of agricultural work painful and even more laborious than usual. Although Patricio Alvarez resembles his friends and neighbors in many ways, he differs in the depth and intensity of his involvement with the church.

I first encountered Patricio at the monthly school for *animadores* in La Magdalena. There he was a soft-spoken but articulate and forceful participant whose views clearly commanded respect. I soon discovered that this was no accident. Patricio was one of the first to participate in the *cursillos* organized by Román Cortes. Since that initial contact, in 1970, Patricio Alvarez has attended a series of church-sponsored courses that eventually prepared him to take on a formal position as lay minister, one of only a handful in the entire diocese of Facatativá. He was a founder of the base community and the community store in Agua Fría, and works hard to spread the Gospel and promote community welfare in the surrounding towns.

> My real work has always been in agriculture. That's what I do. When I was a young man I tried carpentry and other things, but I got bored. I even tried building houses—I built this one [where we are sitting]. All work is hard, but the hardest of all is work with the base community. That is hard because you've got to know how to reach people. I always try, for example, to convince people to love work and hate drunkenness, but they pay no attention. (A 11)

Like most Colombian peasants of his generation, Patricio had only very limited access to formal schooling. There were few schools or places available for young peasant men, and in any event, families preferred to keep their sons and daughters at home.

Unfortunately, my time for school came when it was still not required to know how to read or write, that was just for a select few, space was limited. People would say, "No, my child is a boy, and since I am a peasant, he will follow the same path. You don't need letters or mathematics, none of that, for agriculture." That's what people thought at that time, and so they didn't worry about school for their children. (A 1)

As a result of a government campaign to enroll students, at the age of ten, Patricio got to spend a little time (less than a year) in primary school. Here he learned to recognize letters, got a start on reading, and picked up some rudimentary arithmetic. After leaving school, he tried to continue learning on his own. He was particularly anxious to read well: "My spelling is still not well developed, but I love to read, and I love to write, especially to read. Reading is a great thing!" (A 2). Patricio never got the chance to return to school after that year but has continued to study, above all through *cursillos* and church-related courses. As he put it,

It's a miracle that I managed to study at all; I only spent five months in a school. I give thanks to my parents, because when I had to leave after only five months, they were careful to ask me what I knew, and to practice the ABCs with me. That's how I learned to read and write, even though my spelling and punctuation are very bad. All the courses I have done have been Christian ones, like the course on Christian fundamentals in 1970 [with Román Cortés] or six advanced courses for *animadores*. . . . My formation for entering society is owed entirely to the meetings in our hamlet, and to conversations with my family. (A 11)

When Patricio talks about the *cursillos*, images of basic transformation turn up repeatedly: we were bad, we became good; once full of vices, we now lead a moral life; we moved from darkness to light; we were converted, and now we know what it really means to be a good Christian. After the initial flush of enthusiasm left by the first *cursillo*, Patricio and his companions faced the challenge of getting a base community set up and running. At first it was hard: people were accustomed to operating as separate individuals or, at best, within a limited family circle. To Patricio, many remain "lost in their own individualism. They care only about what touches them, but as for others, nothing" (A 4). They could not get used to the idea of acting as a group without outside help, and wondered,

How can we get started? Who will move us for these meetings? Who will read and what? We also faced the problem that those who had not gone to the *cursillo* were jealous and suspicious. They even thought we were not Catholics any more, but had joined some [Protestant] sect. (A 14)

Despite these misgivings, the group persevered, as we have seen, inspired by Román Cortés's insistence that organizing groups would lead to better lives as individuals and as a community. As the group evolved, the normal round of discussion and participation uncovered shared problems and spurred autonomous initiatives of mutual aid and self-help. Apart from the community store, discussed earlier, there is also a regular system of rotating voluntary labor, whereby members help one another with specific tasks like harvesting crops or building houses. The decision to focus on any particular issue or concern is determined mostly by reading diocesan programs, as interpreted by Sister Sara. Patricio explains: "The diocese's plans often don't arrive, and if they are very difficult, then Sister Sara is in charge of telling us how to carry them out" (A 15). As we have seen, official church guidelines are also modified in Agua Fría by reflection on local experiences, as the group strikes out on its own.

Patricio's role as lay minister is central to the way he assesses the meaning and worth of his own experience and the proper orientation of group life as a whole. He takes his role very seriously. "To me, this is a work of great responsibility; I have to be careful to call people. I try to know what is happening to them, and I suffer to draw out the truth with them" (A 15). Becoming a lay minister was the capstone of a long process of growing confidence and self-affirmation. Patricio still remembers being amazed when Román Cortés suggested to him that ordinary people could become ministers of the church.

> It sounded awfully strange, we couldn't make sense of it. To become a priest, a religious? Maybe at most a nun, but what could an ordinary peasant do, a person who is married is to have a ministry in the church? No, no, no. (A 23)

The centrality of lay ministry suggests that for Patricio Alvarez, religious belief and responsibility, organized and mediated by the church, undergird everything else. Although he has become an articulate and self-confident man, Patricio takes an exceedingly humble view of his ministry. He locates it at the bottom level of a hierarchical, trickle-down vision of religious life. He knows that lay ministries were central to primitive Christianity but then disappeared. His explanation is that the priests were careless and let such ministries slip into disuse.

> Later during the pontificate of John XXIII, he convoked the Second Vatican Council, and in this council they discovered that there had to be lay participation in the things of religion, that they [laity] could help in their own religious education, in so many aspects of the family, evangelizing in their own family. This is what we are called to. Later these documents began to come out, and the bishops distributed the documents to the parish priests, the priests started distributing them to us, we began interpreting them, and in this way I started to become aware and I committed myself. (A 8)

One becomes a lay minister only after extensive study of church documents along with practical training in church programs. Serving as a lay minister integrates Patricio's activities and general presence into the overall thrust of church programs in several ways. As noted earlier, the idea is to have the individual remain in family and community, serving both as teacher and model. In Patricio's words, "to serve in a loving way, first in the family and then with all our neighbors. To give witness to the life of Jesus to every one around us, to collaborate in all group meetings in the hamlet, to cooperate with the parish when necessary, and in other areas too, just as much as you can" (A 8–9). This kind of involvement reinforces the "funnel effect" noted earlier for Facatativá, whereby local initiatives are channeled into and through the churches. It also tempers Patricio's assessment of any group meetings or community efforts by making spiritual and moral regeneration primary bases for a better life in Agua Fría and in the nation as a whole.

In Patricio's eyes, self-control and self-mastery are central to the whole process. Being a good person requires taking active control of one's life. He once told me that people like to claim that *they* do not sin, because (they say), if God put temptation before us, how can the acts be sinful? Patricio dismisses this view with some impatience: "No sir, it's not that way at all. No. He gave temptations to us as a kind of test, to see if we are capable of self-control, if we can live our lives with a little order and self-control. If you think about it, that's really the way to live well" (A 25). As Patricio sees matters, the ideal base community is the one that follows through:

> I believe that the perfect base community is the one that moves from prayer to action. (A 16)

Patricio's understanding of local and national problems flows directly from his root religious beliefs and commitments. He sees steady progress in Agua Fría, and believes that if his children and grandchildren stay on the right path, their lives will continue to improve in every way. The basic change is moral.

> In moral terms, the changes I see leave me really satisfied. Before we had the base community, there was lots of disorder, lots of marital problems. The couple that did not fight was a real rarity. But ever since we began participating in the world of God, morals have improved a lot. (A 16)

When I asked about specific local problems, Patricio concentrated on the lack of wholesome recreational facilities for youth. These left them open to the temptations of *tejo* (a gambling game ubiquitous in rural Colombia), and to the drunkenness associated with it. Inadequate schooling also hurts the community, and after some reflection, Patricio added that "there is no work here. That's why people leave to take jobs as policemen, or join the army. Women turn to prostitution in the cities or find jobs as maids. Solving problems like these is the job of Communal Action, but here, at least, that doesn't work. It used to exist, but the whole thing fell apart. There were organizational problems" (A 14). When he turns his attention to the national level, Patricio also puts moral issues first, noting that the insecurity and violence so visible in Colombian life "are all caused by libertine attitudes" ("se deben al mucho libertinaje") (A 16).

Patricio's vision of politics is complex. He listens to the radio often, is aware of national and international events, and mentions them regularly in conversation. He draws many of his ideas about the good society and the possibilities of self-moved change from the example of Israel, whose experience of cooperatives fills him with admiration. But the same trickle-down notions that undergird his concept of lay ministry also appear when he looks to the political world. Despite scant faith in politicians or their promises, Patricio does not look to other kinds of collective action or to alternative links to power that might change the political landscape in some basic way. Leaders seem like facts of nature. For example, although Patricio knows that many in Colombia see elections as irrelevant and abstain from voting, he nonetheless votes in good faith. "When there are elections, I always vote for the one I like the best, the one I prefer, who seems most committed, in spite of the fact that they have fooled us so often, that we have always been victims of trickery" (A 7). In his view of the world, people have a moral obligation to help each other struggle against exploitation. As a practical matter, this stance makes for support of self-help programs and community organization while it excludes violence of any kind. Thus,

> for ten or eleven years now, I have dedicated myself to studying the situation. This has led me to rebellion, but to a Christian rebellion, a peaceful rebellion, not rebellion like those groups who say, No, I will not go along with the government anymore, I will not go along with this group or with the other. I'll get a rifle or a revolver or even just a machete and go out to kill. No, no, this is not what we are called to. (A 2)

Patricio has a clear vision of his own poverty and understands the limited possibilities for action that his personal and community situation present. He sees the preferential option for the poor as fundamental but obviously unfulfilled. He defines this option in the following terms: "It refers to Jesus' mandate, to the only real reason that he came into the world, which was to give some help to the poor. So far, it looks like a failure, because there is still injustice" (A 16). Despite this statement, as a rule when Patricio talks about being poor, one hears little resentment or bitterness. Hope is the dominant note.

> So you see, even in the midst of the economic miseries I live in, I have found good things. I am poor, but I don't make a big deal about it. I don't get all excited because I am poor, because I don't have a farm, or money to spend. If I did, I would probably be just another jerk, wasting my life, like the others, with alcohol or maybe marijuana. But since I don't have anything, I'm free of all that filth.

Instead, I stop and reflect and look around at the reality we human beings live in. And I see that it's not really a question that people have no resources to support themselves with. There are plenty of resources, but either they are not found, or when they are found, people don't know how to use them. There is nothing in God's creation that isn't useful to man. (A 24)

This general view of the world is reinforced by a growing sense of personal capacity that makes Patricio ready and willing to work in any nonviolent way to help the community. Thus, in one conversation he told me that he was trying to get money together to join a small local cooperative organized by the Coffee Grower's Federation. Once he was a member, he planned to take the first opportunity to protest the unfair practices of the Federation's local affiliated stores, and to seek some redress.

So I have been struggling now for a while to get together 1,200 pesos [then about 6 United States dollars] to become a member of that cooperative, so that I can have a voice, to go there and talk about these things. Because, after all, if we know about things that are unjust, then it's our duty to tell everyone about them, once and for all. You know, there are people who join a group that claims to be in favor of everyone but who still keep quiet when they see injustices happening. They tell us to have patience, to bow our heads and cover our ears. Better not to join at all, if you're not going to do anything about it! (A 30)

There is little evidence here of the traditional mask of personal passivity and public submission that covers inner rage with outward deference. Patricio Alvarez has no awe of the wealthy and powerful. Witness this account of the difficulties of sharing experiences with people from the larger towns. It is hard, he points out,

because in Villeta they are businessmen, people with money. It is very difficult to share with a group from Quebradanegra, because we are peasants, with no more than a few months of primary school, and over there are very well-prepared people, university graduates, doctors, and all that. But no matter, this year we had a one day get-together with them, and they had to hang their heads before us. We bested them, we surpassed their level, and they were convinced. Economic resources don't matter at all. They have no effect on anything. Money is money, morals are morals. (A 10)

Patricio has a very high regard for clergy and sisters, particularly those now active in his area. "They have been magnificent; the more we work, the more they help us" (A 15). He thinks that the church has come far since his youth, and he especially prizes the opportunity it provides for greater lay involvement. Nonetheless, Patricio's enthusiasm for this participatory image of the church is tempered by a clear-eyed sense of the power of the institution. People still need the money and resources the church has to offer. Patricio's comments on the church's proper social role are exceedingly concrete:

> The church's contribution might be, for example, to do what the diocese of Facatativá is doing, which is to lend money to the poor peasants, to promote small businesses like raising pigs, chickens, or rabbits, or small sewing shops. Things like that. They are putting money there that used to be used for building fancy schools. (A 16)

Patricio Alvarez is a very devout man. His spirituality and ordinary religious practice combine elements of traditional religiosity like promises and pilgrimages with more recent innovations. Reflecting on his own First Communion, Patricio points to the changes he sees:

> Yes, my mother got me ready. At that time we had no catechists. You had to record questions and answers in your memory [literally, "tape them"]. But later I came to realize that Catholicism isn't learning prayers by rote, but rather that we have to incarnate them in ourselves, and live them in our actions. (A 12)

Patricio attends mass every Sunday, taking the long walk from Agua Fría to La Magdalena. If he is traveling away from home, he makes every effort to find a church. He reads the Bible regularly: alone, with his family, and in group meetings. He also keeps a number of religious objects in his house, including pictures of the Sacred Heart and of the Virgin Mary, several homemade crosses, and a rosary. Patricio prays on arising and on going to bed, and also says the rosary regularly with his family. His prayers are directed above all to God and to the Virgin Mary, who, as he puts it, "is just one, but who has appeared in different places. That's why we give her names like the Virgin of Bojacá or the Virgin of Chiquinquirá" (A 13). He sees the saints in mostly traditional terms, as workers for Jesus, and regularly makes promises to locally favored saints, above all for health. After describing prayer to me in this way, he commented that lately praying had begun to appear in a different light.

> Yes, I pray continuously to find myself with the Lord when I get up, when I go to bed, and lately, for a year or so now, I have become aware that when I am with other people, at work, playing, resting, I am praying then too, because I am communicating with my brothers. (A 13)

In what remains to him of this hard life, Patricio wants little. His personal goals center on the church's specifically religious work. He wants to do more:

> The apostolate, concretely this year. To make myself useful to the church, to be able to leave this hamlet for others, and promote the Christian movement. Thanks to this, the church noticed me and gave me the ministry.

*And for the future?*

To prepare myself better for the apostolate. I want nothing else. I don't care about the cooperatives, Acción Comunal, or any of that. They are not important. I am going to dedicate myself only to the apostolate. One of the conditions of my ministry is not to sell my land, in case the hamlet fails to support me. But this worries me because I would not leave the apostolate. If the people here don't support me, I would go elsewhere to continue. (A 12)

All in all, Patricio feels fulfilled. Despite great poverty, he has little sense of material deprivation. His world has opened up immeasurably and changed in ways he finds pleasing and satisfying. He has a clear sense of himself as a person of dignity and realized potential, doing his duty and serving God, church, family, and community. In the years to come, he hopes to continue serving, and perhaps to write a book.

I might have had the material for a book if I had just been a little more orderly, made notes and kept them. You know, they say that everyone has three goals in life: to plant a tree, to raise a child, and to write a book. I haven't done the book. It's the hardest of all, I guess it takes many years. On the other hand, with a tree, if you plant it in a good place and give it some care, in four or five years, there it is. To give you a concrete example, and here I'm speaking very sincerely, over there you can see a tree—around here we call it a *cachipay*. Years ago I got the idea of bringing some seeds here and planting them. One of my friends told me, "No, no Patricio. What are you thinking about? Do you expect to get *cachipays* from those little saplings you're tending there?" Well yes, of course. You know even if I can't eat their fruit, my children will. Don't you see? I have eaten lots of fruit from trees I didn't plant myself, that were planted by my father or by my grandfather. So, I have to do the same, I have to plant trees so that tomorrow my children and my grandchildren can eat their fruit and lie in the shade they give. I've eaten a lot of *cachipay*.

That little palm tree over there, I planted it three days after getting back my very first *cursillo de cristiandad*, about eleven years ago. I brought the seeds back from trees in the square at El Ocaso. When my boy Ambrosio took my bag, he said, "Let's see what Papa is bringing from there." It was the seed. "And what's this?" A palm. "Well, let's plant it." And that's the one. (A 30, 31)

Fortunato Duque and Patricio Alvarez have much in common. Children of the same generation, each is poor, devout, and became literate only as an adult. Both lives have been transformed as a result of involvement in and through the church. Despite these parallels, the two men differ notably in outlook and in the sense they give to experience. Fortunato is more open to extensive social and economic involvement and much more egalitarian in his basic presuppositions. Although Patricio feels no particular awe of the rich and powerful, at the same time he sees himself as a subordinate player in a hierarchically ordered world. In part, these contrasts arise from variations in the orientation of the pastoral agents who recruited and influenced them: Padre Vicente and the Centro Gumilla Jesuits or Román Cortes and the diocese of Facatativá. The ideology and organizational culture that prevail in each region and nation also play a part in setting key dimensions of openness and breadth of vision that characterize each of these men.

The initial stimulus for change in both lives came from religion, but in Facatativá, change is undertaken in close connection with the institutional church and remains focused for the most part on small-scale community projects. Fortunato Duque's experience differs sharply. Here, small groups have been a beginning, not an end point, for change. Larger structures with a social and economic mandate have built on the religious base. Of course, as we have seen, these differences in scale and purpose are reinforced by the greater autonomy peasant leaders enjoy in the Venezuelan case. Each man is something of a model citizen, in the terms that prevail in his environment. Patricio reflects in full measure the hierarchical expectations that permeate Colombian organizational life; Fortunato works with assumptions of democracy and egalitarian relations that make sense in Venezuela.

## Conclusion

In this chapter, we have listened to very distinct individuals with strong personalities and a well-defined sense of themselves as men and women actively changing their own lives. Their biographies resist fusion into a composite image: too much detail is lost to make the results satisfactory. Yet these experiences are not unique. Each makes sense in the context of the broad patterns of culture and ideology, leadership and institutional arrangements, linkage patterns, and local or national constraints and opportunities laid out in these pages. Consideration of these five life histories thus offers a window on broader processes of change and accomodation that shape the emergence of new cultural formations. As George Eliot wrote,

> We should not shrink from this comparison of small things with great, for does not science tell us that its highest striving is after a unity which shall bind the smallest things with the greatest? In natural science, I have understood, there is nothing petty to the mind that has a large vision of relations, and to which every single object suggests a vast sum of conditions. It is surely the same with the observation of human life.[5]

To draw this chapter to a close, I prefer not to summarize or repeat the arguments presented thus far but to draw comparisons by examining briefly

[5] *The Mill on the Floss*, p. 287.

the pattern of response to seven statements.[6] The text of each statement is given in table 8.1. Taken together, the reactions collected in table 8.1 reveal a group whose deep involvement with the church is marked by a growing sense of independence from its direction. They remain persons committed to the church but who no longer see themselves as lesser or subordinate individuals. They regard priests and sisters as people like themselves, and, with the exception of Susanna Madrid, welcome the move to ordinary clothing and lifestyles by the church's representatives. Only Patricio agrees with the traditional practice of charging money for mass. He sees this as fair pay for services rendered. Others reject fees, although they agree that if "we are all church," then all must pitch in to support clergy and sisters.

The practical ecclesiology that guides these individuals in everyday life also comes through in their responses to the first and second statements. With the continued exception of Susanna Madrid, they agree that the church is not the proper place to solve one's problems. People must learn to act on their own, alone and, above all, as communities. In this regard, even if the church is not the place to solve problems, it can be a means for acquiring the resources and tools needed to move ahead. Although everyone is respectful of the church, no one agrees with a statement requiring total obedience. At best, obedience depends on the issues: on matters of faith or morals, "of course" one needs to obey; on other matters, perhaps.

The strongest common vision that emerges from these responses concerns the need to work together. The stress we have already seen on self-help is powerfully undergirded by a sharp rejection of passivity in the face of injustice and by a commitment to mutual help and common work as moral obligations for Catholics. All make common effort a critical value, but are careful to downplay the disciplinary sense of "obligation." This is a free choice. Patricio's rejection of passive resignation is thoughtful:

> Yes, life brings injustices one after another. Some people put it all in God's hands, even though we have in our own hands the power to change things. It's better to fight, to struggle. When you see that nothing can be done, then there is no alternative but to resign yourself. But a person should always look for solutions. (A 17)

The similarity of Olga, Susanna, Fortunato, and Patricio on these points suggests that a common process may be at work, pushing consciousness and action to shared positions, even in the very different circumstances in which these four lives are played out. The main elements of this shared position include giving very high value to participation, along with individual and community responsibility. Personal independence is also prized and is best ex-

[6] Responses from Huberto Vanegas are not included here, as he was given a different questionnaire, intended specifically for pastoral agents.

**TABLE 8.1**
Responses to Statements of Opinion

| | Olga Ceballos | Susanna Madrid | Fortunato Duque | Patricio Alvarez |
|---|---|---|---|---|
| The church is not the place to solve one's problems. | One needs to resolve problems in common. | It is not the place—it is the medium. | Praying without acting means we die of hunger. We are the church. | You have to help yourself. |
| Even if one does not agree with the Church, Catholics are obliged to obey. | No | No. If you agree, then yes; otherwise no. | Of course | Depends on the issue. |
| Priests and sisters are Catholics like all the rest, with the difference that they have chosen a consecrated life. | We need to see what they really devote themselves to. | Yes | Yes | Yes |
| It is better to accept what life brings rather than to constantly fight to change things. | No | No | We have to fight. | No, it is better to struggle. |
| Mutual help and working together are a moral obligation for Catholics. | Yes, and for non-Catholics, too. | Yes, that is obvious. | Yes | It is not an obligation, but rather a free choice. |
| There should be no charges for mass. | Yes | We ought to collaborate voluntarily. No changes. | Yes, we take a collection. | No. There should be a charge, to support the clergy. That's their work, their job. |
| It is better that priests and sisters dress and live a different life-style than others. | No | Yes, but the key is good behavior, to avoid immorality. | No, they are different anyway when they celebrate mass. | When there is no distinction in clothes or life-style, then we have a real test. They are obliged to avoid vulgar acts and words. Sometimes distinctions are good; other times, it does not matter. |

pressed in the ethic of rough egalitarianism that emerges in attitudes toward priests and sisters and to the general question of obedience.

To be sure, no collection of individual lives can provide enough evidence to establish or prove a trend or reality. But that is not my intention. I present these experiences in order to illustrate as fully as possible what change can mean to individuals and communities. Lives are never lived in the abstract. To make sense of the experience and developing outlook of men and women like these, their biographies must be situated in the relevant social, cultural, and institutional contexts of youth and adulthood. When this is done, the outlines of a possible long-term shift in popular culture begin to appear.

What might this popular culture look like in the end? Whatever other characteristics it may present, the popular culture being nurtured in the base communities and related groups reviewed in these pages will be more capable of sustained cooperative action and much less riven by distrust or by the family or kin-based divisions that characterized earlier experiences. Through self-education and growing participation, individuals and groups have groped their way to a clearer understanding of the economic and social bases of their own situation. Grounding themselves in an active reading of the Bible, they have begun to craft an independent perspective on these situations.

The whole process bears superficial resemblances to the "ideological unmasking" of which Marxist terminology speaks. But there is little resentment here, and less open conflict, and a term like "unmasking" seems overly harsh and unyielding. At issue in cases like these is something more on the lines of James Scott's notion of "ideological work."[7] Scott insists that it is misleading to search for explicitly structural discourse, and finding none, to conclude that there is false consciousness or, worse, no consciousness at all. What is happening is not lack of awareness but rather a process in which ordinary speech and daily experience provide arenas for making sense of events and responding to them. Working through and chewing over their own experiences, these ordinary men and women make sense of big issues by placing them in small and familiar contexts. Church-supported values of reconciliation and fraternity clearly help to blunt the edge of confrontation, as do the links these values promote to other levels.

Throughout Part II, I have intentionally stayed "close to the data," letting popular voices speak with minimal interference. I have suggested lines of comparison and pointed to possible explanations but, thus far, have deliberately refrained from putting together a comprehensive explanation. The next two chapters address this task with particular attention to issues of linkage and the relation between popular culture and institutions.

[7] *Weapons*, pp. 184–240.

# PART III

## THEORETICAL AND COMPARATIVE

## REFLECTIONS

Eighteenth-century philosophers had a very simple explanation for the general weakening of beliefs. Religious zeal, they said, was bound to die down as enlightenment and freedom spread. It is tiresome that the facts do not fit this theory at all.

—Alexis de Tocqueville

# NINE

## LINKING EVERYDAY LIFE WITH BIG STRUCTURES

IN THIS CHAPTER, I will draw the threads of evidence and argument together around themes of linkage. As we reflect on the emergence of popular voices in Latin American Catholicism, and on the possibilities they hold for cultural and political transformation on a large scale, continuing links between popular groups and big structures assume particular importance. Popular culture grows not in isolation but linked to the explicit programs and messages of institutions, and also to the tacit models they leave embedded in social relations and public images of power and authority. The very notion of "popular" rests on relations between the everyday lives of poor people and the big structures of power and meaning that set parameters of change for the society as a whole. Acknowledging the importance of these continuities and connections suggests that the proper task for analysis is not to discover whether linkages exist or to measure their strength. Our task instead is to elucidate how such ties are organized, legitimated, and put into practice, and then to figure out what difference this makes to the character of popular voices, to their viability, and to their impact.

Earlier I pointed to links between institutional and popular aspects of religion, culture, and social and political life. Here I extend the analysis to include a broad range of links between everyday life and big structures. As used here, *everyday life* refers to the structured patterns of action, discourse, norms, and established social roles that appear when religious and cultural change is considered "from below." A partial list includes particular forms of speech, the experience of class and gender distinctions, the impact of work and poverty on routines and expectations, relations within families and among friends and neighbors in a community, the experience of authority, and central expressions of faith such as prayer, religious celebrations, and conceptions of key religious figures like the saints, or Jesus and Mary.[1] The term *big structures* refers to institutional formations like church, state, or major economic groups. These control real resources, both symbolic and material, which they use to project messages and power over time, space, and social boundaries. Big

---

[1] My usage is close to de Tocqueville's concern with "mores," which he used to include manners and styles of social interaction, patterns of family life, prevailing norms about hierarchy, equality, and authority, and the mutually reinforcing links between civil and political associations. The title he gave to chapter 9 of the first volume of *Democracy in America* is suggestive: "The Laws Contribute More to the Maintenance of the Democratic Republic in the United States than Do the Physical Circumstances of the Country, and Mores Do More than Laws."

structures find expression in everyday life as they shape the general contours of opportunity. They are also manifest in the efforts of mediating agents like communications or transportation services, cooperative extension agents, teachers, soldiers, and local government officials, and, of course, the priests, sisters, and pastoral agents we have met and listened to in these pages.

Everyday life and big structures evolve and change in close concert, bound together by linkages of identity, affect, shared belief, habit, and interest. Linking the two entails searching for mutual influences and points of contact and potential conflict. These are dialectical relations that generate long-term cultural and social transformations through the exchange (often tacit, unacknowledged, and unequal) of guiding values and ideas. As we have seen, popular groups and institutions both spend a lot of time discussing understandings and explanations, striving for a sense of legitimate roles and proper behavior, and reworking the nature of experience in the "in-between spaces" created by organizational and ideological innovation. My earlier discussions about the emergence and diffusion of norms of hierarchy or equality, of concerns about authenticity or commitment, of the perceived legitimacy of politics, and of models of election or accountability, and about the spread of concepts of class and conflict are all cases in point.

The relationships at issue are complementary and overlapping. One that has occupied us here concerns the social construction of ideas. Ideas gain social force through a process that extends individual attitudes and values into collective forms. In part, this is a matter of language, which of course is necessarily both individual and social. But the social force of ideas also reflects and draws strength from the way collective organization appears in individual consciousness: as ideologies (plans and action programs tied to specific groups) and as broad cultural norms (the stuff of common sense, basic notions of right and wrong, of proper and possible). A second kind of linkage is concrete and material: actual structures (buildings), organizational routines, texts or publications. Tangible resources like these turn the relation among levels of action and scattered experiences into matters of routine. With a place to meet and a model agenda to follow, meeting can become a standard operating procedure. Linkage is also a matter of human agency, carried in the actions of individual men and women who commit themselves to bringing big structures to the lives and values of ordinary people, and vice versa. Together, these aspects of the role of linkage—as a latticework binding personal and collective understandings to one another, as material infrastructure, and as human agency—provide fruitful ground for reflection on the broader significance of popular voices in Latin American Catholicism.

A sustained focus on linkages solidifies and enriches phenomenological analysis of the kind undertaken in this book by placing discussions of values and perspectives in meaningful and realistic social contexts. This is important because human agents do not operate in a void. They move from day to day through thickets of particulars to make sense of themselves and their situations and to create acceptable and possible forms of action. Concern with linkages is particularly useful for comparative analysis of the kind undertaken in this chapter, which ranges widely across cultures and traditions in search of parallels to Latin American experience. By pointing to sources of variation that arise in comparable processes and settings, attention to linkage enhances the richness and specificity of the discussion. Charles Tilly states,

> In tracing the encounter of individuals and groups with the big structures and large processes, we make the necessary link between personal experience and the flow of history. The structures at issue are now relationships among persons and groups, the processes are transformations of the human interactions constituting these relationships. . . . The necessary comparisons among relationships and their transformations are no longer huge, but they gain coherence with attachment to relatively big structures and large processes.[2]

Religion is an apt medium for studying the creation, maintenance, and impact of linkages. The symbols and central norms advanced by organized religions of all kinds acquire social presence through forms of repeated practice (prayer, processions, passion plays, base community meetings, and so forth) that are at once individual and collective. Religions thus bridge levels of analysis and experience with great power, setting proximate acts in ultimate contexts and changing the lens through which events and experience are understood. Linkages are especially important for Catholicism, whose dense and overlapping structural networks facilitate continued relations among levels.

Many of these ties still take shape within conventional trickle-down models, in which authority, legitimacy, and knowledge descend vertically (it is assumed) from pope to bishop, bishop to priest, priest to sister, and then on to lay ministers (if any) and ordinary believers. But even when the tables are turned in ways that enhance the validity and autonomy of popular insight, linkage itself is not rejected. Like their conservative counterparts, radical groups or those focused on sociocultural transformations prize membership in the church, and look for validation of their ideas and actions to its central norms and structures.

A common view of linkages emphasizes the inequalities of power that run through these relationships. It is true that big structures like the institutions of state or church represent concentrations of material and cultural power. They use this power to project repertoires of terms, symbols, norms, and models of the good life to their members, along with culturally sanctioned ways of earning a living, raising a family, and making contact with others. The men and women of popular groups are well aware of the gap that separates their world from that of the powerful. They see and understand how cultural, economic,

---

[2] *Big Structures, Large Processes, Huge Transformations*, p. 64.

and political differences combine to solidify and strengthen that gap. But although power is important, by itself, attention to power fails to satisfy.

Differences in raw power have no predetermined outcome for the poor. They cannot be assumed to lead inevitably to either fatalistic resignation, passive acceptance, exit, or revolt. Along with differences in power and in the way it is created and used, issues of meaning must also be addressed. Even where enduring collective action never develops, a search for meaning and control goes on in the spaces of everyday life. The powerless work with the tools at their command, recombining and reinterpreting ideological and material elements to make an edge, however small, of difference in their situation. This means that new beliefs may be nurtured and predispositions to action created in ways that remain hidden if analysis focuses exclusively on power or on the short-term outcome of particular conflicts.

Throughout this book, I have insisted on the need to "work the linkages" between everyday life and big structures. Working the linkages is a matter of experience, something that popular groups and elites do all the time as programs are founded, groups established, members recruited, and efforts made to satisfy individual and community needs. Working the linkages is also a strategy for research, a methodological injunction to pay close attention to mediations, connections, and to the general process through which different levels of organization and action are bound together over time and space. This overall position, and the focus on small and intermediate settings for analysis reflected in the core data for this book, rests on several related assumptions.

In this book, I have proceeded from the assumption that participation at different levels and in different spheres reflects and reinforces a common social process. More is involved here than simple parallelism in participation, as if voting in elections (for example) were part of the same general disposition to participate that is visible in family decisions or activism in neighborhood assemblies.[3] The issue is less participation per se than the development of new personal and group self-images and their crystallization in enduring forms of associational life. Participation is too gross a concept, for, as we have seen, the act of participating can be an exercise in dependence and subordination or a liberating affirmation of reason and capability.

The next two assumptions underscore the role of agents and mediators and the need to reach beyond everyday life (just as ordinary people do) to grasp the likely direction and viability of changes undertaken at that level. Attention to ideas and to norms and values is necessary but not sufficient. To be sure, ideas are important. They can legitimize the very notion of change or inhibit it, help institutions disengage from traditional alliances or reinforce them. But ideas die on the vine without agents to carry them and clients whose needs and

---

[3] For example, Harry Eckstein, *A Theory of Stable Democracy*; or Carole Pateman, *Participation and Democratic Theory*.

situations make the ideas resonate and give them a chance to work. For changes in popular culture to have enduring impact on a larger stage, allies and connections are indispensable. They provide moral and material support that make it possible for ordinary people to expand their horizons and, after a while, to imagine and to make new connections of their own.

Cultural analysis often has the defect of restricting attention to values and meaning alone. But this will not do, for it leaves both meaning and material structures reified and separate, and cannot explain why they combine in regular and predictable ways. Culture as norms and symbols must be set against the material structures that make it possible for ideas to diffuse over time and space. We must therefore pay systematic attention to such issues as the printing and distribution of pamphlets, the organization and scheduling of trips and meetings, the search for resources for celebrations or festivals, and so forth. Questions like these are as much a part of cultural analysis as are ideas themselves.[4]

Combining symbolic and normative with organizational and material aspects of culture underscores the potential for conflict and struggle at all points. The assertion by subordinate groups of a right to sacred power and a capacity for autonomous interpretation and action is a conflict-charged and, in this sense, necessarily political act. Explicitly political motives need not be primary for this to be true. Indeed, the evidence from Latin America and elsewhere suggests that religious values are often primary.[5] Groups and individuals take off from a desire (often experienced as an urgent requirement) to do good, to be authentically faithful to divine will, and so forth. But no matter, for such initiatives are viewed as political by the powers that be, who correctly understand the assertions of sacred power to be just a short and easy step away from efforts to acquire material power and to challenge authority in general. Karen Fields shows that colonial administrators in Central Africa viewed independent religious movements as "ecclesiastical bolshevism."[6] Similar terms are rarely far from the lips of conservative prelates and politicians in Latin America today.

[4] On these points, see Clifford Geertz's classic essays "The Impact of the Concept of Culture," and "Thick Description," and also *Negara*. Fischer (*From Religious Dispute*); Arjomand (*The Shadow of God and the Hidden Imam* and *The Turban*); and Ileto (*Pasyón*) provide illuminating discussions of the social bases and political impact of passion plays. Much recent neo-Marxist research unfortunately centers attention on intensive symbolic analysis with only a general and abstract study of the relation of symbols to contexts and power. Roger Lancaster's *Thanks to God and the Revolution*, discussed in detail below, is a case in point.

[5] See, among others: James Davison Hunter, *American Evangelicalism*; Fields, *Revival and Rebellion*; Ranger, "Religious Movements and Politics"; and Levine, "Religion and Politics in Comparative and Historical Perspective."

[6] *Revival*, p. 238. Both MacGaffey (*Modern Kongo Prophets*) and Asch (*L'Eglise*) report similar attitudes by Belgian colonial authorities toward the efforts of Simon Kimbangu.

## Consciousness, Ideology, and Culture

Scholarship and public commentary refer often to the *ideologization* of religion and religious discourse. The notion has much in common with concerns about religion's supposed *politicization*, including a sense of threat and a suggestion that the indicated phenomenon (*ideologization* or *politicization*) is an aberration: a (hopefully temporary) detour on the road to secularization. I have already discussed the concept of politicization at some length in earlier chapters. At this point, I want to consider possible meanings of *ideologization* and to weigh its relevance for this analysis.

The term itself ("ideologization of religion") implies a conversion of discourse that is proper to individual spirituality (and hence, for the most part, private and limited) into programs of action for organized collective groups. Active involvement with power and conflict is implied. Ideologization thus appears as a middle step in a chain that ties personal values to broad cultural norms. Serif Mardin comments that cultures provide ordinary people with working maps that offer both personal guidance and portraits of the ideal society. They also provide "items in a cultural knapsack" that integrate "the individual's perceptions of social rules and positions with signifiers for images, sounds, and colors."[7] In these terms, a concept like ideologization points to the complex infrastructures dedicated to producing and distributing maps and signposts and to finding and holding users.

The difficulty with notions of ideologization lies not in the idea itself but rather in the suggestion that such uses of religious discourse, belief, and structures are somehow improper or aberrant. Geertz's influential formulation, for example, holds that the declining coherence of a religious worldview leads to ideologization of religion.[8] But the record in Latin America and elsewhere reveals not declining coherence but rather a search for new coherence driven by men and women making themselves into different individuals and communities. The stances they now take are neither more nor less "ideological" than what went before. What has changed is their own sense of self and their capacity to act and to judge. The matter is also not well addressed by simple contrasts of popular to elite outlooks that attribute the gap to divergent class interests. There are class differences, of course, but in all cases, the influence of class is mediated by connections of ideology and institutional affiliation that underscore continued ties and repeated efforts at synthesis, not simple demarcation.

How we think about things organizes the way we see and interpret reality, what we value and seek, and how we act. A peculiar value of studying religion is how strongly it reinforces our sense of the creative power of ideas, and of

---

[7] *Religion and Social Change in Modern Turkey*, p. 7.

[8] Clifford Geertz, *Islam Observed: Religious Development in Morocco and Indonesia*.

their ability to move individuals, groups, and collectivities in new and unexpected ways. For believers, religion is an active force at all stages of the process: not a mere reflection of reality, but a template for it; a paradigm, not a mirror. Religious ideas provide the underpinnings for a series of elective affinities between individual consciousness and values, group ideologies, and broad cultural norms. The resulting correspondences are visible not only in religion as conventionally defined but also in relations between religious ideas and basic categories of social, economic, and political understanding.

In his comparative and historical studies, especially those concerned with religion, Weber emphasized the need to keep ideas, institutions, carriers, and clients in dynamic balance. He gave special stress to elective affinities, in a consistent effort to explain why certain ideas make sense to particular groups at specific moments, or why a given pattern of organizational growth or leadership style finds audiences and has an impact in one situation and not another. Elective affinity meant more to Weber than passive conjunction, simple correlation, or attempts at mutual influence. He used the concept to point to similarities in the inner structure of discourse and meaning visible in otherwise disparate entities: religious doctrine and economic ethos, group structure and worldviews, class interests and cultural orientations. By putting matters in this way, Weber could take account of correspondences in the inner structure of ideas and in their converging social appeals without falling into determinisms. Choice and human agency remained important at all levels.[9]

According to Weber, groups seek and accept religious ideas according to their place in the social order. He argued, for example, that artisans and the petty bourgeoisie were disposed to accept rational ethics and congregational forms of organization because such ideas and practices fit their situation well, giving religious meaning and sanction to the kind of social order they were already striving to create. A rational world with an ethic of compensation where "honesty is the best policy" made sense to groups like these.[10] Their work and home life already exemplified the rational organization, totalizing orientation, and stress on independent self-management that such religions

---

[9] To Weber, the social and cultural impact of any religion rested on the practical ethic embodied and advanced in everyday life. His well-known work on Protestantism and the spirit of capitalism, for example, argues that the Calvinist ethical codes were reinforced by the congregational structure of the churches in ways that enjoined average people to fuse religion with daily life in a never-ending process of conversion and religious control. Although he insisted that the life conditions of artisans and the bourgeoisie made them find rational ethical religions sensible and attractive, as a general matter, he held that "there is certainly no uniform determination of religion by these general conditions in the life of artisans and petty bourgeois groups. . . . The mere existence of artisans and petty bourgeois groups has never sufficed to generate an ethical religiosity" (*Economy and Society* 1:482). Michael Lowy provides an insightful discussion of the concept of elective affinity in *Rédemption et utopie*, chap. 1.

[10] *Economy and Society* 1:481–84.

(like the Puritan sects that occupied Weber's attention) articulated as doctrine.[11]

Weber thought religious and cultural change unlikely to come from peasants or the urban poor, or from Catholicism in general. The stifling effect of hierarchy and structure in the Catholic church made innovation difficult, and Weber believed peasants to be generally unsuited to the demands of ethical religion. The rhythms of their life and work—which were at the mercy of the elements—predisposed them to rely on magical explanations and powerful intermediaries. At the same time, economic weakness, physical isolation, and overall social subordination made peasants especially prone to domination by a stratum of religious officials. As to the urban poor, although it was apparent that they were estranged from the churches of his day, Weber argued that their expressive needs were simply transferred to new vehicles, especially to the proletarian political parties, whose "soteriological orgies" he viewed with evident distaste.[12]

To assess the relevance of these ideas for popular Catholicism in Latin America, two questions must be posed. First, what has changed among rural and urban popular sectors that can explain why they should now appear on the public stage as leading carriers of religious innovation? Second, do these changes make sense of the particular kind of innovation we have observed? Weber offers a few hints. He remarks, for example, that "the peasantry will become a carrier of religion only when it is threatened by enslavement or proletarianization, either by dominant forces (financial or seignieurial) or by some external political power."[13] He also stresses how crisis turns popular attention to religion as a source of cultural innovation.

The economic, social, and political changes of recent decades have opened popular groups in Latin America to innovations of all kinds, religious among them. In the countryside and in spreading urban barrios, poor men and women have become not only more available but also distinctly more responsive to new possibilities. In part, this reflects the decay of traditional legitimations and the discrediting of long-standing paternalistic ties (with landlords, employers, or political entrepreneurs) that could once be relied upon to ensure

---

[11] It is a classic Weberian point that the privileged seek legitimation of their position and acknowledgment of their role in divinely established arrangements. Strivers seek confirmation of God's favor in their own social climbing. As for the underprivileged, "they make up for their lack of any claim to be anything *either* by insisting on the worth of what they will one day be, of what they are called to be in future life either in this world or the next, *or* (and usually at the same time) by insisting on their 'significance' and their 'achievements' in the eyes of Providence. Their hunger for a dignity that has not come to them, they and the world being what they are, leads them to form this conception, from which arises the rationalistic idea of a 'Providence' and the importance which they have before a divine court with quite different standards of human worth." ("The Soteriology of the Underprivileged," pp. 182–83.)

[12] Ibid., p. 178.

[13] *Economy and Society* 1:468.

conformity. The old order's decay has also meant greater access by challengers, weakened control, and a decided drop in the power of older symbols of authority and leadership to compel obedience. Changes of this kind have been magnified and accelerated by the new religious messages and metaphors (equality, justice, Exodus, the Prophets) that appeal to groups on the move and that open religion itself to change—not least as a result of drawing in this new and newly active clientele.[14]

In sum, new circumstances and changing ideas combined to shift the center of gravity of religious experience and to change the character of its organized social and political impact. Change is constant in both the content and the form of expression. The centrality and regularity of change may seem obvious, but the point must be made directly here. Stress on the fact of change in cultural norms is particularly important in the case of Latin America. There is a widely held theory according to which the character of social relations and politics in the region can be derived from Iberian cultural patterns laid down centuries ago. In this view, the contemporary Latin American ethos is defined by norms of inequality and deference to hierarchy, by paternalistic expectations, and by a model of organization and of the good citizen that encourages and rewards submission. Associational life is sponsored and manipulated from above by state and other elites. Class-based collective action is inhibited, and corporatist patterns predominate.[15]

This argument is deeply flawed. Exclusive stress on the continuities of some presumed Iberian cultural ethos washes out critical dimensions of conflict and power, ignores variation, and obscures sources of change. In these ways, static views of culture beg the question of why particular configurations are advanced and accepted in the first place. As Barrington Moore suggests, the very notion that cultural persistence is normal assumes what must be explained.

> The assumption of inertia, that cultural and social continuity do not require explanation, obliterates the fact that both have to be re-created anew in each generation, often with great pain and suffering. To maintain and transmit a value system, human beings are punched, bullied, sent to jail, thrown into concentration camps, cajoled, bribed, made into heroes, encouraged to read newspapers, stood up against a wall and shot, and sometimes even taught sociology. To speak of cultural

---

[14] Cf. Richard N. Adams, *The Second Sowing: Power and Secondary Development in Latin America*; or Susan Eckstein, "Power and Popular Protest." Only lately is the salience of religion being recognized. Janice Perlman's otherwise excellent *Myth of Marginality*, for example, excludes religious groups a priori, a curious and short-sighted decision.

[15] The following are representative of this school: Howard Wiarda, "Toward a Framework for the Study of the Ibero-Latin Tradition: The Corporative Model"; Glen Dealy, "Prologomena on the Spanish American Political Tradition"; Richard Morse, "The Heritage of Latin America"; Claudio Veliz, *The Centralist Tradition of Latin America*; and most recently, Lawrence Harrison, *Underdevelopment is a State of Mind*.

inertia is to overlook the concrete interests and privileges that are served by in-doctrination, education, and the entire complicated process of transmitting culture from one generation to the next.[16]

Struggles over cultural persistence and change are shot through with power and punctuated by conflicts about what makes authority legitimate. That is why disputes over "the popular" are so acute. At stake is not just acceptance of some abstract propositions but rather control over access to knowledge, power, and legitimacy, both sacred and profane. Dimensions of power and conflict appear immediately if we ask how abstract religious concepts arrive to groups and communities. Struggle and change are visible not only in dis-putes among theologians who (like Leonardo Boff, Hans Kung, or Charles Curran) may be called to account by church authorities; they are also manifest in the competition between different organizing principles applied to individ-ual and community life. Ideas gain social impact not only through explicit preaching and instruction but also (and more importantly) by virtue of the way they are embedded in the structure of groups, in repeated practices and oppor-tunities for socializing, and in common understandings of right and wrong.[17]

Ideas find social effect, linking consciousness to ideology and culture, through regular actions they sponsor or through which they find regular ex-pression. Examples that we have considered include arrangements for Bible study and community organization and also periodic celebrations like bap-tisms and funerals, vigils and processions, dances, and prayer. Simple matters like helping others in need also bring individuals together on a regular basis. The repetitive quality of action given by religious routine has important con-sequences for the ability of popular groups to take up and change the ideas that come to them. The whole effort may be reinforced by other structural changes, as a Weberian perspective would insist. But structural considerations are not enough. We must also address the force of the ideas themselves. Albert Raboteau's work on the religion of American slaves is a case in point.[18]

Raboteau shows how the slaves transformed a religion of conquest and domination into a justification for resistance and, ultimately, a charter for lib-

---

[16] *Social Origins of Dictatorship and Democracy*, p. 486.

[17] Consider, in this light, the "see-judge-act" methodology that is often cited as central to contemporary Latin American Catholic discourse and action. According to this approach, reli-giously legitimate action comes not through deduction from doctrinal principles but rather from reflection on the meaning of active involvement in the world. But if believers are truly to see, judge, and act, much depends on what they look for and on the interpretation given to that "see-ing." By promoting and diffusing new expectations and visions of church, society, and politics, events like Medellín and Puebla helped change many of the assumptions on which this seeing was founded. The impact of new definitions of poverty on institutions, understandings, and actions is an obvious case in point. On the "see-judge-act" methodology, see, for example, Edward Cleary, *Crisis and Change: The Church in Latin America Today*.

[18] *Slave Religion*.

eration. Some traditional elements (like the salient role of dance, or the "shout") were carried over from African experience, and helped affirm identity and solidarity even in the conditions of helplessness and atomization the slaves faced. Central ideas were also appropriated from the dominant religious tradition, and then used to counter abuse and to create obverse images that justified liberation over servitude. Like the Latin Americans we have listened to, slave voices were particularly attracted to the Exodus story, which made obvious sense to people who themselves were captives far from home. An infrastructure of capable leaders and independent churches gradually developed, often with the help of strategic white allies.

These ideas and institutions later played a central role in the emergence and consolidation of the civil rights movement in the 1950s and 1960s. The churches helped legitimize resistance to segregation while also providing members and the black community at large with infrastructures of solidarity, contacts, and organizational resources that made resistance viable. Effective leaders drawn from a new generation of ministers and student activists were then able to turn discontent into sustained collective action. Scholars of social movements who work with theories of resource mobilization have stressed this point, but their emphasis on movement entrepreneurs runs the risk of missing the way that broader elements of cultural and social change condition perception and action.[19]

The culture and rhetoric of the civil rights movement was thoroughly steeped in religious imagery, for example, in the speeches of the Reverend Martin Luther King, Jr. Looking back, Raboteau argues that the apparently unworldly ideas of black religion had considerable power to change perspectives and actions in this world.

It does not always follow that belief in a future state of happiness leads to acceptance of suffering in this world. It does not follow necessarily that a hope in a future when all wrongs will be righted leads to acquiescence to injustice in the present. . . . The slaves believed that God had acted, was acting, and would continue to act within human history and within their own particular history as a peculiar people just as long ago he had acted on behalf of another chosen people, biblical Israel. Moreover, slave religion had a this-worldly impact, not only in leading some slaves to acts of external rebellion, but also in helping slaves to assert and maintain a sense of personal value—even of ultimate worth. . . . By obeying the commands of God even when they contradicted the commands of

[19] On these aspects of the civil rights movement, see Morris, *Origins*, and Branch, *Parting*. Morris does a particularly good job of showing how changes in the content and context of Southern black churches together made the civil rights movement possible, likely, and viable. See *Origins*, especially chapters 1 through 4. Susan Eckstein's comments on resource mobilization theory in "Power and Popular Protest" are instructive.

men, slaves developed and treasured a sense of moral superiority and actual moral authority over their masters.[20]

Religious traditions in the black community thus provided both a moral vocabulary and a context that could be turned to new uses. Like the English Puritans, they could ask "if all men were equal before Christ, should they not also be equal before the law?"[21] Although there is nothing necessary or automatic about this kind of shift from passivity to activism, once underway, it has self-sustaining capacities that allow new leaders to emerge and new paths to be taken. In cases like these, religious ideas need not serve as a direct charter for action. It suffices that they provide what June Nash calls a "generative base" for group identities and commitments.[22] Michael Walzer comments on the power of the Exodus story:

> The Exodus, or the later reading of the Exodus, fixes the pattern. And because of the centrality of the Bible in Western thought and the endless repetition of the story, the pattern has been etched deeply into our political culture. It isn't only the case that events fall, almost naturally, into an Exodus shape; we work actively to give them that shape. We complain about oppression, we hope (against all the odds of human history) for deliverance; we join in covenants and constitutions; we aim at a new and better social order.[23]

Religious ideas provide enduring linkages between different levels and areas of life in several ways. The weak may be attracted by and may appeal to the central legitimating ideas and images of a religious tradition. This is the case of American black history, and of many of the experiences studied in this book, where dominated groups use religious sanction as a ground for expanding their sphere of autonomous action. But popular groups do more than latch on to one idea or another. They also put religious norms and practices together in new ways. This makes it possible to hold on to the power, for example, of belief in prayer and salvation while refocusing these sources of strength in a

[20] Raboteau, *Slave Religion,* pp. 317–18. See also Fields, *Revival*; Asch, *L'Eglise*; Comaroff, *Body of Power*; MacGaffey, *Modern Kongo Prophets*; and Bengt G. M. Sundkler, *Bantu Prophets in South Africa.*

[21] Hill, *Century of Revolution*, p. 147.

[22] "Cultural Resistance and Class Consciousness in Bolivian Tin-Mining Communities," p. 197. To be sure, influence is not unidirectional, and categories like "religion" and "politics" are not mutually exclusive: there is continuous borrowing and adaptation. Suzanne Desan shows, for example, how rural French Catholics appropriated the language of liberty intended by the Jacobins to carry anticlerical messages and adapted it to defend their religious rights against revolutionary power. See her "Redefining Revolutionary Liberty: The Rhetoric of Religious Revival during the French Revolution." That experience finds many echoes, for example in the modern Philippines (Ileto, *Pasyón*), in Africa (Ranger, "Religious Movements and Politics") or, from a different perspective, T. Dunbar Moodie, *The Rise of Afrikanerdom* and in the Islamic world (Gilsenan, *Recognizing Islam*).

[23] *Exodus and Revolution*, p. 134.

community context. There is continuity in change here, and continuity has its uses, among them allowing religious transformation to emerge as a cumulative process. This enhances the ability of popular groups to build, or, more precisely, to reassemble, a compelling vocabulary of moral choice and concern.

Some concepts and experiences are more effective at working the linkages than others, and thus may be likely to occupy the attention of emerging popular groups. Understanding what makes for success in turning popular religious culture from a warrant for submission to a charter for resistance and liberation may therefore be furthered by a close look at several ideas in particular. I have already suggested how new ecclesiologies enhance the status of ordinary people and justify new roles for them. References to Exodus, to practical love, and to prophetic stress on justice and action in human history have also popped up repeatedly. Any account of central religious concepts must also include the following: holiness and faith, death and salvation, authenticity and solidarity.

The relation of holiness and faith to organization, politics, and power is complex and often confusing. Ordinary speech assigns holiness and faith to religion, evoking images of sanctity, grace, devotion, and their institutionalization in churches or similar structures. Power and politics have a different aura, and commonly call up images of coercion, conflict, and violence. Different claims to leadership are advanced and varied styles of action promoted in each case.[24] Everyday usage recognizes ambiguities and overlaps as it speaks, for example, of the power of holy men or notes that politics involves both partisan or state-focused actions as well as more general relations of power and authority in all spheres, religion among them. Still, for practical purposes, the distinction is meaningful, and clear enough to serve as a rough guide in daily life.

In political terms, holiness and faith are empty vessels. Churches and holy men have supported everything from revolution to reaction (and reactionary revolution as well, as the recent experience of Iran demonstrates), equality to hierarchy, activism to personal withdrawal. But in the modern age, the direction of change for both has been consistent: away from quietism and passive resignation and toward a vision of self-mastery and action in the promotion of justice as the most faithful expression of God's will. What makes holiness quietist or activist and turns holy women or men into reliable friends of power or its militant opponents rests in the last analysis on what sorts of people recognize the claim and what such recognition entails.

Instructive examples of the impact of changing definitions of holiness come from recent Islamic and African experience. Fouad Ajami's biography of Leb-

---

[24] This is surely what prompted Weber to warn that "the man who is concerned for the salvation of his soul and the salvation of the souls of others does not seek these aims along the path of politics. Politics has quite different goals, which can only be achieved by force" ("Politics as a Vocation," p. 223).

anon's Imam Musa Al Sadr explores the connections between this man's claim to religious legitimacy and holiness and the origins of Shi'ite activism in Lebanon.[25] Musa Al Sadr stretched the definition of clerical leadership far beyond conventional bases of lineage and tradition. He created new institutions, reshaped religion's political meaning for the Shi'ite masses, and set a new course for them in society and politics. The whole effort gained strength from urgent, changing popular needs that led the faithful to recognize this man as holy (with the highly charged title of Imam)[26] while they readily moved down the new paths he charted. In a similar way, Roy Mottahaddeh's study of the education and changing role of clerics in Iran underscores the malleability of official and popular views of holiness, and the many and changing relations to power to which these views can be put.[27]

Terence Ranger and David Lan underscore the key role played by holy men (Christian leaders and spirit mediums) in Zimbabwe's struggle for independence. Ranger comments that "Christian holy men played the essential role of mediator between guerrillas and peasants, . . . lent their sacred authority to the guerrillas' cause, and imposed the bye-laws and ground rules for guerrilla interaction with a Christian peasantry."[28] They assumed this role not only in response to demands from below but also as a result of inner conviction about the rightness of the revolutionary cause. Lan's account of the apparently incongruous alliance between spirit mediums and theoretically rationalist Marxist guerrillas points to converging ideas and interests that went far beyond tactical considerations. Acceptance by the mediums helped make guerrillas "at home" in lands that were not their own. Mediums gave young guerrilla fighters moral and material guides to the territory, joining their struggle for independence to established traditions that made current generations stewards of the land, holding it in trust for ancestors who made themselves manifest through the mediums. Lan states that

> it is the unique quality of the Shona spirit mediums that they are able to present a complex "performance" of the past combined with a vision of the future in a way that enhances the peoples' belief in the value of their much maligned history and thereby strengthens their belief in their ability to create a better future. Among the particular skills of the mediums that were called upon during the war was their ability to accumulate followings that crossed chiefly boundaries. These they put at the disposal of the nationalist leaders.[29]

[25] *The Vanished Imam.*

[26] For Shi'ites, the title calls up millennial images of religious leaders (Imams) whose appearance will usher in a new age of justice.

[27] *The Mantle of the Prophet.*

[28] Ranger, *Peasant Consciousness and Guerrilla War in Zimbabwe*, p. 215.

[29] *Guns and Rain*, p. 222.

Redefinitions of holiness and faith in Latin American Catholicism have centered less on the aura of particular men or women than on broad institutional and ideological changes that locate the church's sense of self and mission within popular groups. The general stress on going to and opting for the people, and related efforts to root authority more in witness and shared experience than in formal roles and statuses, is relevant here. The moral authority of venerated figures like Archbishop Oscar Romero, for example, rested on his institutional role as archbishop of San Salvador, not on his personal charisma. Moving the center of gravity of religious ideas away from the individual and toward the community undergirds commitments to collective action and makes them a logical outgrowth of being "truly" religious. The transformations of prayer and of concepts of sainthood outlined in previous chapters are further cases in point, as is the general shift of markers of holiness and faith away from personal piety to expressions of communal solidarity.

Evolving views of death and salvation warrant separate attention. Although grappling with the meaning of death is important to all religions, it is especially so for those like Christianity, in which the promise of salvation plays a central role. As we have seen, death and the cult of the dead are central to the working catalog of "popular religion" that most pastoral agents carry about with them. How does a changing concern with death affect the social and cultural impact of religion? The matter has obvious historical and comparative referents. Thomas suggests, for example, that as magic declined in early modern England, the dead gradually faded as a presence in everyday life. This freed the living to attend to community and society in creative ways; they were no longer constrained by the need to placate the dead.[30] But this may be an overly simplistic view that fails to take account of other continuing links between the living and the dead. Lan comments that peasants in Zimbabwe combine Christian and ancestral rituals and understandings of death with an ease that puzzles outsiders.

> For some people, the existence of alternative belief systems is problematic and occupies a great deal of intellectual energy, not so much in an attempt to reconcile the two as to decide which is appropriate in which circumstances. For others the two systems are easily reconciled. After all, Jesus died and rose again after three days. The only difference this illustrates between Jesus and the Shona ancestors is that the ancestors wait a year after their deaths before they rise up and become active again. Furthermore, it is argued, the Bible instructs us to love, honour and obey our parents. It does not say that we have to stop this after they are dead.[31]

Indeed, the dead are not forgotten. They continue to be remembered and are venerated, but in new ways. In the midst of Central America's conflict and

[30] *Religion and the Decline of Magic*, pp. 602, 606.
[31] *Guns and Rain*, p. 41.

civil wars, for example, funerals and funeral processions assumed new and even greater roles in popular religious culture.[32] The prevailing understanding of death and the kind of religious expression favored to deal with it changed in ways that promoted belief and mutual solidarity in the face of continued violence and personal tragedy. Berryman comments:

> Many Christians were being killed, and their death was widely regarded as martyrdom—following the death of Jesus the Great Witness (Martyr) and this closeness to martyrdom tended to give a sense of ultimacy to people's actions and options. . . . One revealing indicator is that the main liturgical celebrations have often been funerals for those who have "fallen" (usually not in armed combat). On these occasions, there is a sense of shared community, commitment, risk, and joy, and a certitude that this death is not in vain.[33]

Berryman goes on to argue that a new sense of life is what ties religious change in Central America into a coherent body of theory and practice. This sense of life is rooted in basic Christian beliefs about resurrection, which provide the strength and conviction required to change both personal and communal dimensions of action. "It seems to me," he writes, that

> perhaps the most powerful element in the motivation of Christians in their struggle in Central America is a paschal sense of life: what Archbishop Romero meant when he said, "if they kill me I will rise in the Salvadoran people." This statement was not a secularized or a purely horizontal view of the resurrection. On the contrary it came from one whose belief in final resurrection was utterly orthodox. But it expressed his view that the ultimate meaning of present struggle is revealed in the death/resurrection of Jesus. Romero was able to combine the most traditional view of "offering up" sacrifice with that of struggle.[34]

This stress on resurrection over death, and related efforts to link both life and death to the quality of community, give a new social edge to ideas about salvation. Salvation does not begin after death but in life, here and now. It is not a matter for disembodied spirits alone, but for spirits incarnated in living men and women: not salvation but, as Gladys Bernal put it, "what today we call liberation." The vigorous rejection of the idea of hell that we heard in the barrios of Cali has much in common with more elaborate theological changes that insist on fusing human with salvation history.[35]

[32] This is, of course, not an isolated instance. The importance of funerals as cultural and political statements stretches back to Pericles' famous oration and beyond. Contemporary instances abound, and two may be noted here: the salience of passion plays and images of martyrdom in Iran, and the use of passion plays in popular movements in the Philippines. On Iran, see Michael M. J. Fischer, *Iran: From Religious Dispute to Revolution*, or Arjomand, *The Turban for the Crown*. On the Philippines, see Ileto, *Pasyón*.

[33] *Religious Roots*, p. 392.

[34] Ibid., p. 391.

[35] Gustavo Gutiérrez, *The Power of the Poor*.

Religious ideas that serve as markers of solidarity and authenticity are particularly important for linkage. Solidarity itself is a logical core value in congregational religions. There is bound to be considerable peer pressure in such intense settings where face-to-face contact is the rule. The transition from individual to community-focused criteria is further reinforced by the conviction that authenticity stems from witness, especially the witness that comes from "accompanying" the poor. To witness is to share experience, to express solidarity through that sharing, and perhaps to be changed in the process. One witnesses to the worth and truth of values by living them. Grounding religious authenticity in witness of this kind changes the basis for authority and for its claims in far-reaching ways. Ordinary experience becomes a source of religiously valid values, and leadership is made accountable to norms of solidarity. Trickle-down models are gradually displaced by the acknowledgment that authority can have a number of legitimate sources and voices. Words like *accompany* begin to define what makes leadership legitimate.

The critical role played by Bible study and biblical images in our cases suggests the utility of a fresh look at precisely how use of the Bible can shape linkages. The content and effect of biblical images and metaphors is clearly mediated by social context and by the specifics of experience. As E. P. Thompson remarks in another context, cultural formations are "a profoundly important component not only of ideology, but [also] of the actual institutional mediation of social relations."[36] When social relations are particularized by physical isolation, organizational weakness, or deliberate and successful elite attacks on autonomous group structures, it is not surprising to find a stress on reconciliation over conflict, on individual ties and improved communication between the classes over joint revindicative action. In each case, the former is less risky and does not expose ordinary people to the uncertainties of politics and the hazards of scarcity. In this vein, Portes comments that the economic ethos of peripheral groups entails no sense of entitlement to anything and rejects activism as illegitimate and risky. This accounts for the absence of structural blame in popular discourse and for the pervasive reliance on individually constructed networks.[37] Class discourse is often converted to personal terms and action appears fated to ambiguity, as hope and expectation are constrained by a self-image of weakness and a realistic sense of the possible. Peasants in Caparrapí thus point easily to economic injustice or army abuses while they continue to articulate values of reconciliation.

Jennifer Hochschild found a similar pattern in her work on American con-

[36] "Eighteenth-Century English Society: Class Struggle without Class?" p. 137. See also Scott, *Weapons*, p. 44.

[37] Alejandro Portes, "Rationality in the Slums." See also Susan Eckstein, *The Poverty of Revolution*; Perlman, *The Myth of Marginality*; and Carlos Vélez-Ibanez, *Rituals of Marginality: Politics, Poverty, and Cultural Change in Central Urban Mexico, 1969–1974*.

cepts of distributive justice.[38] She points to a notable gap between norms of equal treatment that respondents absorb from the larger culture and differentiating principles they learn from experience. The resulting ambivalence feeds diffuse anger and frustration, confusion, inconsistency, nerves and personal stress, and a general feeling of helplessness. Ambivalence is fueled by habit and inertia, by the tendency of the poor to make social relations into natural (and hence inevitable) phenomena, and by the role of institutionalized power in promoting acquiescence. Cultural change is a risky and uncertain enterprise for the poor,

> exposing an unaware, even if ambivalent population to a new set of ideas—that is, simply throwing out an analysis, no matter how correct, will have little effect. Rather, there must be class-wide rethinking, conducted not in the abstract but firmly in the context of everyday life. This requires not only leaders but also a larger social stratum within the class which can facilitate the growth of consciousness, practically and intellectually.[39]

Hochschild correctly underscores the need for change to be rooted in points of convergence between everyday life and big structures. But her insistence on "class-wide change" is too stringent. The essential point is not to rework the consciousness of an entire social class. This is probably illusory in any case. Homogeneity of consciousness cannot be assumed but must, rather, be created. This requires deliberate efforts to create solidarities that can bridge the gap between personal and collective life in meaningful, satisfying, and enduring ways.

If ideas are to change behavior over the long term, they must be built into the routine expectations and operating procedures of groups and institutions. This involves both change and continuity, risky innovation and networks of legitimate structures, words, symbols, and ideas.[40] Religion can be central to this process, not only for the popular voices of today's Latin American Catholicism but also, as I have indicated in this chapter, for a broad range of cultures, traditions, and historical periods. Religions make for linkage by placing proximate acts in ultimate contexts as a matter of routine, giving public social meaning to personal acts like prayer, gathering believers together repeatedly, and binding very different kinds of people in shared identities, however minimal. Connections like these are crystallized in complex (sometimes elaborate and beautiful) structures of doctrine, law, wood, concrete, steel, and stone. To be sure, although linkage is a constant, its direction and

---

[38] *What's Fair?*

[39] Ibid., pp. 273–74.

[40] Change is rarely inscribed on a blank slate but rather uses and reworks materials already present—ideas, symbols and metaphor, and forms of experience. Liberation theology, for example, works with basic Christian categories of sin, grace, and salvation. It could scarcely do otherwise. But that does not take away from its fundamentally innovative character.

impact are variables. The next section examines the mediations and specific human mediators that constitute these linkages, day to day, and considers the impact of different kinds of mediation for democracy.

## Mediators, Mediations, and the Question of Democracy

Throughout this book, I have stressed the critical role of mediators and mediations. Mediators provide structured access to resources, valued alliances, and a sense of legitimacy. They help constitute spaces (often literally, as in buildings or arrangements for meeting) where innovations can be tried out. As they work the linkages between everyday life and big structures, mediators *become*, for all practical purposes, the institution in whose name they act. They are certainly seen that way by popular groups, who draw guidelines for action and evaluation not only from the explicit messages they hear but also from the models of authority, leadership, and accountability set before them by the behavior mediators display.

Those who undertake to make mediations work are more than transmission belts. Like the institutions they serve and the people they live among, mediators are themselves subject to change. This means that neither mediators nor mediations can be understood in static terms, as if arrangements could just be put in place and then relied upon to operate as intended. The whole matter is shot through with change, and debate over these changes has had a prominent place in the discourse and practice of liberation theology, of base communities, and of popular voices generally. In recent years, statements by liberation theologians and activist Catholics have fallen into a common pattern. Along with formal expressions of theology and enunciation of programs, one commonly encounters stress on experience and praxis. The systematic reader is likely to encounter many versions of "we went to teach and ended up learning," "we went to change others and returned changed ourselves," and so forth.

On beginning this study, I was skeptical of statements of this kind. They seemed more programmatic than experiential, more a post hoc justification for siding with "the people" than a genuine outgrowth of work with anybody in particular. Living among the people will not guarantee change. Priests, sisters, and pastoral agents have to make conscious decisions to identify as far as possible with popular groups, sharing not only their day-to-day routine, but also the possibilities and dangers they face, the hopes and fears they experience.[41] As we have seen, the evidence is ambiguous, and the record shows considerable variation resulting from differences in ideology, personal style,

---

[41] See Noone, *The Same Fate*; Carrigan, *Salvador Witness*; and Brett and Brett, *Murdered in Central America*, for case histories.

career pattern, and institutional connections. But if we search for elements likely to predispose mediators to change in ways that lead them to open and empower popular groups rather than to close and restrict them, a few points emerge.

Gender is a primary consideration in the day-to-day experience of mediation in the Latin American churches. For several reasons, women are better situated to take up roles of this kind. They are more numerous than men, not only in group membership but also among pastoral agents. Interactions are therefore more likely to be among women than between the sexes. Even if numbers were equal, traditional divisions between the sexes would probably predispose women to interact more with other women. Religious sisters and women in the communities are also similarly marginalized in cultural and power terms. This leaves sisters freer to innovate than priests, who remain subject to tighter hierarchical supervision and control. It also drives ordinary women to join groups at a higher rate than men. This has little to do with the supposedly greater spirituality or piety of women, an explanation popular among church officials. It has a great deal to do with the fact that groups satisfy needs addressed nowhere else in the social order: education, companionship outside the home, and so forth. Over time, experience in the groups can undergird changes not only in family and community but also in women's self-image.[42]

If mediators are to contribute to openness rather than closure, conscious efforts are required to cut the social and cultural gap dividing them from ordinary people. Demystifying the power and the person of mediators helps demystify authority in general. Commonalities in language, dress, work, and residence clearly do this, leaving ordinary people freer to express ideas and to act. When Patricio Alvarez of Agua Fría (certainly no radical) comments that he and his companions outshone Villeta's middle classes, he underscores the dying validity of the idea that only the educated can be truly orthodox. Recall his words: "It doesn't matter at all. Money is money, morals are morals." It also makes a difference how and why mediators come to work with the people in the first place. Those who take up this work as an assignment (like Sister Sara) or who have been among the poor all along and now find themselves subject to new expectations (like the parish priests of Tabio or Quebradanegra) are less likely to change than are individuals whose commitment to popular groups is a conscious and freely taken choice.

---

[42] Because relatively few adult women have full-time jobs outside the home, they are more able (at least in principle) to get together. Katherine Gilfeather refers to the whole process as a "coming of age" and provides evidence of substantial change in women's self-image and in their religious as well as sociopolitical orientations over a twenty-year period in Chile. See her "Coming of Age in a Latin Church." For a discussion of the differential recruitment of urban Brazilian women to Catholic base communities, pentecostal churches, and umbanda temples, see John Burdick, "Gossip and Secrecy: Women's Articulation of Domestic Conflict in Three Religions of Urban Brazil."

The implications of these career differences reach beyond personal taste or commitment. Choices by individuals also reflect and reinforce larger decisions about how religious influence is to be exercised. Take the matter of preaching, pastoral care, and prophetic roles. Weber argued that preaching and pastoral care were likely to be the norm for stable groups attending to settled populations.[43] In contrast, prophets stand apart from established structures. They act and speak in ways that cut across established expectations and lines of authority, shaking them up when not ignoring or undermining them completely. Most of what we find in contemporary Latin American Catholicism fits under the rubric of preaching and pastoral care. Truly prophetic roles are rare. Even the most innovative and critical voices are raised within ecclesiastical structures, and point to their renovation, not their substitution for other structures. The common pattern is less that of a Camilo Torres, or even of an Archbishop Romero, but rather of someone like Román Cortés, who labored to develop pastoral strategies on the ground that change was essential if continuity were to be ensured.

Why are prophetic roles scarce in Latin America today? With rare exceptions, grass-roots activists, members of religious congregations, and middle-level religious officials (all on "the firing line" and hence at least potential candidates for prophetic action) cannot count on support and protection from their superiors. Traditional concerns with hierarchy and top-down control make innovation suspect from the start. Long-standing bonds of interest and circumstance binding religious with other elites also mean that opportunities to innovate are constricted from the outset and are very likely to encounter stiff opposition.

The institution as a whole is less likely to assume prophetic stances (even in the loose sense of the term, where "prophetic" means critical) because traditions of separate identity and potential opposition to the state are weak. Latin America contrasts sharply to a case like Iran, where Arjomand documents the extraordinary ability of the Iranian hierocracy to concentrate opposition while advancing a coherent set of religious and legal claims to alternative authority.[44] A better parallel to Latin America comes from the European Middle Ages, where before the Reformation, religious orders (like the Franciscans) often raised banners of reform and authenticity against the excesses of religiopolitical alliances.

The evidence from Latin America suggests that innovation is more likely to succeed when its sources are marginal to (but not isolated from) central lines of authority in the institution itself. Religious congregations of men and particularly of women have played a key role by virtue of their ability to bring

---

[43] For example, in *Economy and Society* 1:464–65.

[44] "Iran's Islamic Revolution"; "Religion, Political Order, and Societal Change"; and *The Turban for the Crown*.

independent traditions, resources, and connections to the tasks at hand. This frees them (at least in principle) from the subjection to alliances and connections visible in mainline church structures. To be sure, they face their own constraints and operate under disciplines specific to each congregation, but it is still fair to say that in the ordinary course of events, they are relatively shielded from external pressure.

Understanding the nature and long-term impact of mediations is important to grasping the relation between religious change and the theory and practice of democracy. The relation is a dialectical one. Democracy can promote religious change not only by projecting new standards for defining the good citizen and the good leader but also by spreading the idea that agendas can bubble up from below just as legitimately as they can trickle down from above. I asked in chapter 3 if democracy as it exists in Venezuela and Colombia has made a difference to churches and popular groups. Throughout this book I have made internal democratization a centerpiece of change within the groups themselves. Now it is time to turn the question around and ask how much and in what ways religious change can contribute to political democracy and to the further democratization of culture and social relations.

The significance of the issue has been magnified by the wave of transitions to civilian rule and political democracy that spread throughout the region in the 1980s. These restorations of democratic political arrangements have aroused considerable scholarly interest, and have spurred much rethinking of the bases of regime change and political transformation. Many observers have pointed to the importance of civil society in the process, visible, for example, in the creation of "new" social movements distinct from and opposed to the state, base communities among them. These movements constitute "popular spaces" where resistance to official control can evolve and issues can be advanced that find no place in the official scheme of things. Their prominence reflects the decay of alliances that once bound institutions like churches, corporations, or professional societies to the elites and interests of the state. They further contribute to the erosion of authoritarian norms through their effect in spreading less elitist and more participatory understandings of authority and social relations.[45]

Elsewhere I have criticized this literature for focusing too much on groups

---

[45] Susan Eckstein, *Power and Popular Protest*; Scott Mainwaring and Eduardo Viola, "New Social Movements, Political Culture, and Democracy: Brazil and Argentina in the 1980s"; Alfred Stepan, "State Power and the Strength of Civil Society in the Southern Cone of Latin America"; Manuel Antonio Garretón, "Popular Mobilization and the Military Regime in Chile: Complexities of the Invisible Transition"; Guillermo O'Donnell, "Tensions in the Bureaucratic Authoritarian State and the Question of Democracy"; Guillermo O'Donnell, Phillippe Schmitter, and Laurence Whitehead, eds., *Transitions from Authoritarian Rule: Prospects for Democracy*, *passim*, but especially vol. 4.

alone while showing insufficient concern for analysis of linkages.[46] The resurrection of civil society and the creation of popular spaces cannot be understood as if popular groups existed wholly apart from structures and elites.
Popular groups do not spring unbidden and unaided from the needs and concerns of the poor. Understanding the origins and character of groups requires
analysis of how social and political linkages are put together in structured
ways. The ties that bind leaders and followers are constructed through day-to-
day struggles in which issues are formed and legitimating arguments advanced, then accepted or rejected. Without paying attention to all these issues,
we can gain little insight into how democratic life can be built in open systems,
why it is valued by elites and average citizens, or what the specific ways are
in which democracy can be reinforced or undermined in ordinary practice.

The theory and practice of popular religious groups illustrates the point
well. The Radical Ideal, for example, is founded on the belief that base communities constitute the seedbed of a thoroughly democratizing renovation of
culture, social life, and politics. But after the first flush of enthusiasm, scholars have grown wary of these exaggerated expectations. They were the product
of writing that often confused hopes with realities, theological reflection with
empirical research. Brazil is an instructive case in this regard, and provides
the clearest instance in all Latin America of strong hierarchical backing for the
popular church. Over the last twenty-five years, church leaders actively staked
out a position that opposed the state in the name of popular classes. They
created new structures and devoted considerable resources and energies to empowering popular groups. Radical church intellectuals were prominent, base
communities were founded in large numbers, and significant social movements were created.[47] With all this in mind, Della Cava attributes a "new
hegemony" to what he calls "the People's Church" during the 1970s.[48] I shall
have more to say about the notion of hegemony below. For the moment, a
common-sense definition suffices, in which "hegemony" refers to overwhelming acceptance of a single pattern of discourse, explanation, and action.

Even in these limited terms, the evidence for hegemony by the People's
Church (in our terms, the Radical Ideal) is very weak. The movements (leaders, activists, and organizations) never accounted for more than a small proportion of church members in Brazil. They have steadily lost ground over the
few decades to religious alternatives like Umbanda and, especially, evangelical Protestantism. Even when pursued vigorously by the Catholic church,
commitments to popular organization have had little discernable impact on

[46] "Paradigm Lost: Dependence to Democracy."

[47] See Mainwaring, *The Catholic Church*; Bruneau, *The Church in Brazil* and "Church and
Politics in Brazil."

[48] Della Cava, "The 'People's Church,' The Vatican, and *Abertura*."

everyday consciousness and action.[49] Doimo's rich account of grass-roots movements in one Brazilian city points to ambiguities in the groups' relations with the church and notes the pervasive weakness of groups and the difficulty they encounter in changing local priorities.[50] Della Cava's own discussion suggests that the experience of the People's Church in Brazil is best understood as an attempt (short-lived at that) to establish a new hegemony. He thus points to the ongoing scarcity of grass-roots leaders, the continued ability of conservatives to appropriate popular religiosity to their ends, and the increasing power of a "conservative restoration."[51] If the evidence is this weak for Brazil, where commitment, expectation, and rhetoric have been so powerful, what can we say about the contribution of religious change (especially in popular settings) to the theory and practice of democracy?

Three issues are critical. The first points to the role religious change can play in breaking the culture of silence in which the powerless find themselves. The second underscores the emergence of new leadership strata, and of an image of leadership that advances hitherto unknown norms of accountability. The third addresses the general impact associational life can have for the powerless by providing practical experience in democracy along with a shield, however minimal at first, behind which individuals and groups can begin to change. In combination, these elements undergird the extension of democracy to marginal groups and the creation of a place for them as active and responsible citizens.[52]

To be powerless is to be locked in a culture of marginality and silence. Being without voice makes the powerless nonparticipant: for all practical purposes invisible when decisions are taken that affect their lives, livelihoods, and self-image. When powerlessness and silence are considered from below, it becomes clear that more is at issue than being on the losing side of issues that come up for resolution on the public agenda. Power is expressed not only in explicit decisions and outcomes. It also works through arrangements that keep issues from reaching the public eye in the first place. The silence that cloaks the powerless reflects internalization of those arrangements in ways that make ordinary people assume that nothing can be done. Silence thus contributes to the naturalization of poverty by converting social arrangements into

---

[49] On religious competition, see John Burdick, "Looking for God in Brazil: The Progressive Catholic Church in Urban Brazil's Religious Arena." For a discussion of Catholic influence on political change, see Thomas Bruneau and William E. Hewitt, "Patterns of Church Influence in Brazil's Political Transition."

[50] Ana Maria Doimo, "Social Movements and the Catholic Church in Vitória, Brazil." See also Teresa Caldeira, "Electoral Struggles in a Neighborhood on the Periphery of São Paulo" and *A política dos outros*.

[51] Doimo, "Social Movements," pp. 155–60.

[52] Cf. Archdiocese of São Paulo, *São Paulo*, chap. 6.

facts of life. Gaventa's work on power and consciousness among Appalachian miners argues, for example, that

> the quietness of this segment of America's lower and working class perceived at a distance cannot be taken to reflect consensus to their condition or seen to be innate within their socio-economic or cultural circumstances. As one draws closer, in fact, the silence is not as pervasive as it appears from other studies, or even from initial inquiry among them. Generalized discontent is present, but lies hidden and controlled.[53]

The point holds for popular communities in general, and base communities can help to break this culture of silence under several conditions. Democratic internal arrangements are necessary but not sufficient. They are a necessary step in converting group process from an exercise in subordination or, at best, a game of charades (as in Caparrapí) into a medium that encourages ordinary people to bring grievances and needs to the surface, and helps them to do so. As we have seen, egalitarian norms and democratic arrangements reinforce trust and solidarity, particularly in small settings where the intensity of personal interaction helps elicit discussion and makes persuasive argument more effective. New members are thus socialized by older ones, and experience has a chance to accumulate. In these ways, democratization helps bring what Scott calls the "hidden transcripts" of the powerless to light. But by itself, democratization is insufficient because group survival is not determined only (or even primarily) by what happens within groups themselves. The continued presence of larger forces means that groups need alliances and connections. These provide a floor of security, whose importance is most apparent when groups make their first tentative efforts at activism beyond the scope of religious concerns or very localized issues. The transition from satisfying particular needs for housing or schools to affirming a general disposition to activism is difficult in any case. It is harder still for the poor and weak, who often personalize social relations and who lack the information required to reach beyond local levels effectively.[54]

For linkages and alliances to have a chance of breaking the culture of silence, paternalism must be discarded. This is hard for clerics and not much easier for their clientele. Clerics are socialized into traditions that reinforce expectations of control in roles that are caring but clearly dominant. At the

---

[53] *Power and Powerlessness*, p. 252. Gaventa provides an exhaustive review of theoretical and methodological debates surrounding the study of power.

[54] Goldrich's early studies on barrio dwellers in Chile ("Political Organization") affirm the critical role organizers (in that case, from the political parties) played in getting groups started and keeping them going. Only when these organizers advanced the notion of activism as normal, desirable, and legitimate were groups likely to remain in the struggle after the short-term needs of members were met. On these points, see also Susan Eckstein's "Power and Popular Protest" and the extensive bibliography she cites.

same time, long experience has accustomed popular groups to seek favors by cultivating dependent relations with the powerful or their agents. Seeking favors implies going hat in hand to the offices of politicians for a job or a reference, to middlemen or money lenders for an advance, and to clergy for help in managing the system. Eckstein calls this "structurally induced personalism," and argues that it cannot be understood with a focus on individual or group traits. Attention must be directed instead to structural and organizational patterns that make such dependence seem an inevitable and necessary choice to those on the bottom.[55] To be sure, assistance of this kind is helpful and sometimes indispensable, but whatever the immediate outcome, it clearly reinforces both the ideology and the practice of dependence. Only when institutions (or elements within them) make empowerment a central goal do popular groups get a chance to turn such ties from warrants for silence to opportunities for speech.

Cultural and organizational changes of the kind outlined in these pages do not necessarily translate into greater power, resources, or comfort for the poor. They will not eliminate differences of wealth, power, and knowledge. If implemented, they cannot guarantee greater equity, justice, or liberty in the larger society. In short, the world is unlikely to be "turned upside down" here, as it seemed to be at the height of the English revolution.[56] Were all utopian dreams to be realized, there could in any case be no assurance of egalitarianism or democracy over the long haul. As Weber reminds us, the more common case is that "emotional revolution is followed by traditionalist routine."[57] Reconceiving authority and empowering resistance depends less on the construction of utopias than on the ability of ordinary people and middle-level actors to craft new organizations and routines of action. This is the best way to establish the legitimacy and viability of associational life, and to change the assumptions about ordinary people that are built into political arrangements.

The kind of social and political order at issue in such changes is brought into focus by C. B. McPherson, who distinguishes models of liberal democracy with respect to their assumptions "about the whole society in which the democratic political system is to operate and their assumptions about the essential nature of the people who are to make the system work (which of course, for a democratic system, means the people in general, not just a ruling or leading class)."[58] According to McPherson, early liberal views (utilitarian theory, for example) stressed the need to defend property and class power

[55] *The Poverty of Revolution*, p. 93, and *passim*.

[56] Even in that memorable case, such inversions were short-lived, although they left a recognizable basis for eventual claims of independence from the state. See the essays in J. F. McGregor and B. Reay, eds., *Radical Religion in the English Revolution*.

[57] "Politics as a Vocation," p. 222.

[58] Ibid., p. 5.

against threats posed by pressures for equality. Mill and de Tocqueville later modified this position by arguing that

> compared with any oligarchic system, however benevolent, democracy drew the people into the operations of government by giving them all a practical interest, an interest which could be effective because their votes could bring down a government. Democracy would thus make the people more active, more energetic; it would advance them "in intellect, in virtue, and in practical activity and efficiency."[59]

Faith in democracy's transformative powers (*developmental democracy*, in McPherson's terms) was gradually abandoned in political theory in favor of a model that defined democracy in terms of competition between elites who lead groups that need not be (and, in fact, most often are not) democratic within.[60] Emphasis was placed on the balance of forces and on a periodic exchange of leaders chosen by a clientele that was only occasionally active, and that was assumed in any event to lack interest in and information about politics. McPherson rejects such views in favor of *participatory democracy*, a model that in his definition combines elements from the developmental school (especially the notion that democracy makes for improvement) with a call to transform existing relations of class and power.

Sklar outlines a "political theory for development" in similar terms.[61] He states that prevailing understandings of democracy, and of the possibilities for building and sustaining it in the Third World, have been overly influenced by a view that takes democracies as fully formed products, and then proceeds to underscore the complexity and difficulty of success at getting them started and making them last.[62] Sklar points out that this position is unduly constrained by what already exists, and hence underrates the possibility of building democracy step-by-step. "Democracy," he writes, "comes to every country in fragments or parts; each fragment becomes an incentive for the addition of another."[63] Sklar emphasizes the creation of democratic norms and practices in organizational clusters at subnational and subinstitutional levels. Participation in these settings, with effective guarantees of protection, furthers norms of accountability that can then be put to work elsewhere, for example, in reshaping relations between these groups and others or in setting the character of emergent leadership. Echoing John Stuart Mill, he writes that

> in all societies, men and women in all walks of life are motivated by personal incentives and seek assurances of personal security for themselves, their families,

---

[59] Ibid., p. 51.
[60] As exemplified in Joseph Schumpeter, *Capitalism, Socialism, and Democracy*. For a sharp criticism, see Jack L. Walker, "A Critique of the Elitist Theory of Democracy."
[61] "Developmental Democracy."
[62] Ibid., pp. 690, 707.
[63] Ibid., p. 714.

and friends. From that standpoint, it is only logical to assume that increasing degrees of mass political participation will enhance constitutional liberty and foster the creation of political environments that, in turn, would be conducive to economic achievements by industrious persons, particularly entrepreneurs. A political theory for development, then, would elucidate complementary relationships among democratic participation, constitutional liberty, social pluralism, and economic efficiency.[64]

The theory and practice of popular voices as examined in this book draw freely on developmental and participatory models of democracy. From developmental democracy comes the conviction that participation can change consciousness and enhance both personal and collective capabilities. From the participatory tradition comes a faith in decentralization, reinforced by a conviction that popular insights and decisions are more authentic than those stemming from conventional representative arrangements.[65] By focusing attention on the need to break the culture of silence, democratic norms that incorporate popular groups into their legitimating structures can do much to replace expectations of quiescence with assumptions of interest and capacity. This makes it possible for group actions to become regular and routine, no longer confined to occasional outbursts like the taking of Fifth Street in Cali or to marginal expressions of dissent such as gossip, envy, or foot-dragging.[66] The operative norms built into mediating structures and the character and orientations of specific mediating agents are critical to possibilities for the affirmation of reason and responsibility and, hence, of sociability and associational life. Change goes forward in what I have termed "in-between" spaces, and conflict is therefore likely to remain centered on how these spaces are defined, organized, and given content and value. The next section sets these concerns against considerations of class. How do class formation and the inequalities reflected and reinforced by class shape the linkages we are exploring here?

## A Note on Class

Social class plays an important but not a determining role in the analysis of this book. This is as it should be. It is a sociological truism that objective class identity (based, for example, on income, ownership of the means of production, or employment) does not translate directly into subjective awareness of common circumstances, not to mention dispositions to collective action. We

---

[64] Ibid., p. 709.

[65] There are echoes here of the work of Paulo Freire (*Pedagogy of the Oppressed* or *Education for a Critical Consciousness*) and of the ideas in Paul Goodman's classic *Growing Up Absurd*.

[66] On repertoires of protest and on the conditions shaping their use, see Susan Eckstein, "Power and Popular Protest."

have seen that distinctions of class are present in popular discourse and in the guiding ideas that institutions and their agents work with every day. But in no case can patterns of consciousness, organization, or action be directly attributed to class. How can the impact of class and class differences on popular culture be assessed most fruitfully? How does class contribute to the re-creation and reinterpretation of linkages? I address the matter here through brief reflection on the relation of class (and of particular classes) to needs and perceptions; on the relation of class to community; and on the links between class and culture.

Social needs are not natural phenomena, once established and forever the same. They are historical creations and, as such, are subject to constant change. Each generation's efforts to satisfy these needs produces new problems and opportunities for its heirs. In a famous passage, Marx comments that "mankind therefore sets itself only such tasks as it can solve; since looking at the matter more closely, it will always be found that the task itself arises only when the material conditions for its solution already exist, or are at least in the process of formation."[67]

The needs and tasks that make sense to popular religious groups in Latin America, and that they acknowledge as authentically their own, carry seeds of change that are shaped by class in important but not exclusive ways. The instrumental needs, mediated social needs, and broad cultural needs detailed in chapter 6 are also shaped by gender, by ideology, and by ties to the outside. All this is unexceptionable. The matter becomes more complicated when we move from generalities of this kind to ask whether the class position of popular groups gives them any special capacity or disposition to challenge the social order and its ideological apparatus.

Recent research in São Paulo, Brazil (a major center for base commuities), shows "very little impact of class" on the orientation, priorities, or activities that base communities took as their own. Hewitt's exhaustive studies of the matter suggest that if we ask why ordinary people join groups and what determines thought and action once they get involved, class alone explains little. Instead, "what [base communities] do and how they are is influenced as much by church related variables as by their social class position."[68] Although it is clear that class establishes important commonalities in work, speech, residence, and the like, in all cases the impact of class is overshadowed by other factors, despite a powerful commitment by many pastoral agents to ideologies of class.

Conclusions of this kind are often countered by assertions that expressed attitudes and visible patterns of behavior (the kind of data on which Hewitt relies) fail to get at the deeper structure of meaning and commitment that gives

---

[67] In Tucker, *The Marx-Engels Reader*, p. 5.
[68] Hewitt, "The Influence," p. 141.

form and meaning to popular consciousness. Those advancing this view work with Gramscian concepts of hegemony, and make the indisputable point that domination is ensured not only or even primarily by coercion but also through effective control over the language, discourse, and consciousness of the dominated. Ruling ideas are projected by the powerful, carried by mediators (e.g., clerics, educators, and others labeled "organic intellectuals" by Gramsci), and internalized by the weak in ways that, in effect, turn the powerless into their own policemen.[69]

Otto Maduro has presented the most elaborate and general Gramscian account of religious change in Latin America. Maduro stresses the role priests can play as "organic intellectuals" for the subordinate classes. Priests fit this role, he states, when they are "gathering, systematizing, expressing and making a response to the aspirations and needs of the subordinate classes." They

> have been able to mold and mobilize vast middle and popular sectors with significant antihegemonic impact. . . . They have conveyed to the subordinate classes of the continent a series of innovations . . . favoring the development of a Catholic world view opposed to the relationships of dominance that prevail in Latin America but capable of preserving continuity with the religious traditions of Latin American popular classes. Hence these innovations could function as religious channels for alliances among the various social sectors oppressed by their dependence and by capitalist industrialization.[70]

Such a role is of course possible, but on the evidence, it is very unlikely. The more common pattern finds clerics and pastoral agents unable or unwilling to break through paternalistic expectations. Conservatives remain wedded to a vision of fathers and children, shepherds and flocks, with ordinary people waiting to be led to pasture. For their part, radicals benefit from clerical status to cut across the grain of popular culture and advance their own agenda, dismissing local traditions and clashing with local leaders. Nelson documented an all-too-frequent pattern in Bolivia, in which reformist clergy and sisters are committed to a purified version of religious practice that stresses preaching, edification, and social action so much as to gut local religious life of color, aesthetic values, and appeal.[71] The result is conflict. More recently, Azevedo

---

[69] The root source of this view is Marx, *The German Ideology*: "The ideas of the ruling class are in every epoch the ruling ideas. . . . The class which has the means of material production at its disposal has control at the same time over the means of mental production, so that thereby, generally speaking, the ideas of those who lack the means of mental production are subject to it" (Tucker, *The Marx-Engels Reader*, p. 172). Note also Marx's well-known comment that "it is not the consciousness of men that determines their being, but on the contrary, their social being that determines their consciousness" (ibid., p. 5). For Antonio Gramsci, see *The Modern Prince and Other Writings* and the *Prison Notebooks*. David Laitin tries to apply Gramscian constructs to the study of religion, culture, and politics in Nigeria in *Hegemony and Culture*.

[70] *Religion and Social Conflict*, p. 145.

[71] Cf. Susan Rosales Nelson, "Bolivia."

has underscored the vast social and cultural gap separating progressive pastoral agents from base community members in Brazil. Pastoral agents, he suggests, are thrilled by popular culture, and appropriate its expressions (e.g., metaphors, painting, woodwork) in ways intended to "make one's *immersion in the people* and one's *complete identification with them* appear authentic. But no account is taken of the hiatus underlying the process: the dissociation of the social and cultural realms that compromises the effort in the long run."[72]

The problem has important methodological dimensions. With rare exceptions,[73] studies that work with assumptions of hegemony rarely set symbolic analysis in a sufficiently dense context to allow us to judge their validity. There is not enough data on the material infrastructure of religious change, or on how power shapes ideological projects generally.[74] James Scott has argued that insistence on the normative incorporation of the powerless is flawed in several ways. It ignores what are often weak and ineffective ties, produced, for example, by the scarcity of schools or media connections in much of the third world. It also fails to account for what in Scott's view is a generalized latent predisposition to cultural inversion on the part of popular groups. He asserts that there is a "structural slippage" between great and little traditions (institutional and popular culture in our terms) manifest most notably in the rough egalitarianism of popular culture and in the persistence of utopian ideals of a world where the rich shall be brought down and the poor exalted.

> The imaginative capacity of subordinate groups to revise and/or negate dominant ideologies is so widespread—if not universal—that it might be considered part and parcel of their standard cultural and religious equipment. . . . [Indeed,] subordinate classes—especially the peasantry, are likely to be more radical at the level of ideology than at the level of behavior, where they are more effectively constrained by the exercise of power.[75]

Scott's work has been very influential in shaping strategies of analysis to uncover the "hidden transcripts" of subordinate groups by probing deeply into the structure and discourse of everyday life, including central religious celebrations, for indicators of resistance. But his insistence on the power of utopian predispositions and countercultural elements in popular consciousness may be misleading. The evidence from Latin America suggests that pursuit or

[72] *Basic Ecclesial Communities*, p. 95.

[73] Scott, *Weapons*; Gaventa, *Power and Powerlessness*; Shepard Forman, *The Brazilian Peasantry*; Nash, "Cultural Resistance."

[74] Much recent work on religion in the Nicaraguan Revolution falls into this trap, confusing unquestioned support for the revolution by some religious groups with the successful construction of a new and uniquely powerful hegemonic ideology and culture from the mix of Sandinista militancy, revolutionary mythology, and liberation theology. For a fuller discussion, see my "How Not to Understand Liberation Theology, Nicaragua, or Both."

[75] *Weapons*, p. 331. See also his influential two-part article, "Protest and Profanation: Agrarian Revolt and the Little Tradition."

construction of utopias is in fact much less salient in popular discourse than are more modest shifts in the social and cultural balance that over the long haul can lay a foundation for support of authority or resistance to its claims.[76]

The experience of El Salvador is relevant here. El Salvador provides the clearest and best-documented example in contemporary Latin America of close, long-term links between popular religious organization and peasant rebellion. Berryman has documented the tight association (in origins, membership, and regional distribution) between base communities, popular movements, and revolution.[77] Pearce's detailed account of life in rebel-held territory around Chalatenango points further to the role local church leaders and organizations have played in constituting new norms and patterns of social life.[78] Her study comes close to validating the concept of clergy as organic intellectuals in Maduro's terms. Pearce also does much to uncover the hidden transcripts to which Scott refers, and to make them central to understanding how and why rebellion prospers.

But a closer look at the evidence shows that class plays a less compelling role in El Salvador than do elements of culture, community, and politics. Kincaid's historical comparison of peasant rebellions found no clear correspondence of group development or political outlook with class.[79] Base communities and peasant movements arose not in areas of proletarianization (as much social theory would suggest) but rather in zones where retention of a minimal land base facilitated organization. As in Venezuela and Colombia, most group members were in the middle ranges of poverty, not at the bottom. Kincaid underscores the mediating role of community solidarity in energizing peasant mobilization and resistance. Such solidarity is not simply available as a permanent source of identity motivation waiting only to be tapped. Peasants in El Salvador drew neither on tradition nor on desires to reconstruct some lost utopia. Rather, community was created fresh in each generation.

> The contemporary strength of community solidarity was in a recreated form, the product of popular religious organizing efforts around residual community bonds. . . . These ties and externally promoted organizational forms appeared mutually indispensable elements in the formation of a contestatory peasant movement.[80]

Religion provided both motivation and constraint in this process. Religion, writes Kincaid, "seems to have played an important role only in the contemporary period. The creation of the base communities in the 1970s drew

---

[76] As I suggest in the next chapter, elites are often considerably more radical than those they claim to represent.

[77] *Religious Roots*.

[78] *The Promised Land*.

[79] Douglas Kincaid, "Peasants into Rebels: Community and Class in El Salvador."

[80] Ibid., p. 490.

strength from the traditional Catholic religiosity of Salvadoran peasants even as it sought to redefine that outlook in a more worldly and activist manner. But the fact that religious tradition also encompassed the Salvadoran ruling elite (whose interests the Church had once faithfully served) made it difficult for Church organization to be utilized directly as an instrument of intra-societal conflict. This helps to explain both the severity of contemporary doctrinal disputes in this church and the rapprochement of the Catholic Left movement with Marxist theories and organizations."[81]

The historical and comparative record shows that communal solidarities have undergirded many movements that challenge established power. They provide resources for mobilization and support networks that help sustain resistance over time, even in the face of intense repression and what seem like impossible odds.[82] Community solidarities (backed by ties with clerical institutions) played a key role in the making of the Iranian revolution.[83] They have also been central to the constitution of identity and the establishment of bases for resistance to colonial rule in modern Africa.[84] Recent Latin American experience of popular religious change affirms the importance of solidarities like these, while underscoring how much they are the result of specific, identifiable, creative efforts. Institutional interventions play a critical role here by shaping culture, and in this way giving concrete expression to class needs. They do so not only by advancing new ideas about justice, equity, and the like, but also—and this is the fundamental point—through the deliberate creation of community.[85]

To be sure, community cannot be made of whole cloth. The example of Río Frío suggests that some towns are so riven by distrust and envy that efforts to promote solidarity are fatally undermined. Still, I underscore the deliberate creation of community and sociability because it is clear that with rare exceptions such as in the ethnically and linguistically distinct Indian communities of Southern Mexico, Guatemala, or Bolivia, popular groups in Latin America today cannot rely on elements drawn from the preexisting social fabric.[86]

---

[81] Ibid., p. 492.

[82] A vast literature also exists that documents the enormous force such ties can generate. See, for example, Craig Calhoun, *The Question of Class Struggle: Social Foundations of Popular Radicalism during the Industrial Revolution*, and his "Radicalism of Tradition: Community Strength or Venerable Disguise and Borrowed Language."

[83] Arjomand, *The Turban for the Crown*. Arjomand provides grounds for assessing the more general significance of this and other aspects of the Iranian revolution in the last chapter of *The Turban for the Crown*.

[84] Ranger, "Religious Movements and Politics."

[85] This has implications for the theory of social movements, in particular by changing perspectives on the role of external political entrepreneurs, stressed, for example, in resource mobilization theory. See Susan Eckstein's review of the issues and relevant literature in "Power and Popular Protest."

[86] On Boliva, see Nash, "Cultural Resistance," and also her classic *We Eat the Mines and the*

There has been too much change; change of a kind that has fragmented and localized the process of class and cultural formation in ways that make tradition irretrievable, when it is not simply an illusion to begin with.

## Conclusion

I have argued in this chapter that a theoretical focus on linkages and mediations yields a rich and compelling portrait of how cultural change begins, why it takes specific form, and what makes it last. Approaching culture and culture change through analysis of linkages is theoretically and methodologically sound, and much more fruitful empirically than attempts to work up lists of "culture traits."[87] If we are to grasp transformations in popular religious culture as they appear and make sense to popular groups, both perceptions and available tools of action must be placed in a context of continuing ties between the everyday life of individuals and the big structures.

The matter has important implications for any effort at reconstructing experience and history "from below." Popular groups are not alone, nor are they isolated. There is much interchange and borrowing across social levels, even in situations marked by conquest or by sharp distinctions of ethnicity or language. This does not mean that popular groups accept everything that comes down the hierarchical ladder. They are not infinitely malleable, but rather take the images and messages of the dominant culture and work them into the particular context of their own time and place. The central question for theory and practice is to identify conditions under which mediations and linkages work not to affirm what already exists but to transform it.

What turns these multiple and overlapping ties from instruments of control into tools of empowerment? What makes it possible for the localized and mostly innocuous activities of groups like base communities to connect with and perhaps to influence larger processes of change? Change within institutions is a prerequisite. Institutions are more than just machines that allocate roles and statuses, that grind out a steady flow of rules, regulations, and edicts. They are also communities of identity and loyalty through which meaning and action are bound together over time, space, and social boundaries. If we take a dynamic, social view of institutions and institutional change, it becomes apparent that the required transformations in ideas and organizational forms

---

*Mines Eat Us*; on Southern Mexico, Victoria Bricker, *The Indian Christ, The Indian King*; Robert Wasserstrom, *Class and Society in Central Chiapas*; and for a sharply critical view, Judith Friedlander, *Being Indian in Hueyapán*.

[87] In "Thick Description," Clifford Geertz ridicules this tendency in anthropology, which has reappeared lately with some vigor in work on "political culture." For example, see Samuel H. Barnes, *Political Culture*, pp. 37–41; and for a general restatement by one of the major promoters of "political culture" studies, Gabriel Almond, "The Study of Political Culture."

come not only from change at the top but also from efforts by intermediate strata and ordinary people to understand what being religious requires in changing circumstances.

Acknowledging change is important, but it is not enough. We must also ask why some innovations take hold at specific times and places while others are ignored or rejected. Receptivity to religious innovation makes sense as part of broader social changes that undermine existing relationships and understandings, making clients available in new ways. Religious institutions and those who lead them must also disengage from alliances with other elites, especially in the state. Only then can religious legitimacy attach itself to criticism and resistance in ways that are meaningful and convincing to ordinary people. The poor are neither foolish nor foolhardy. They are willing to take risks, but only after due reflection and careful judgments about the authenticity and the power of those who claim to serve and help them.

Changes that promote participation and sociability in egalitarian terms are more effective in transforming linkages than those that simply advance a new message. This is so because of the self-affirming and self-sustaining character this kind of participation has. Vigorous associational life draws strength from the creation of the idea and the reality of an active, responsible citizenry. In this light, it is clear that one of liberation theology's most enduring contributions has been to demystify authority by giving the tools of association to everyone, and by making the effort legitimate in religious terms. The development of strong associational life provides underpinnings for a truly independent civil society. The resulting shift of popular culture from resignation, fatalism, and silent powerlessness to equality, activism, organization, and voice is a cultural and political change of major proportions.

It is too soon to be sure if all this will last. Although transformations within religion can energize and promote change with great power, they also suffer from a few built-in limitations. Religion's transformative powers stem above all from its ability to cloak any activity with symbolic significance in ways that mobilize individual and group resources. Limitations rest on the difficulty that clerically focused institutions have in shedding authoritarian and paternalistic habits. Religious elites will find it hard to escape a crippling fear of challenges to their authority as long as the concept and conduct of authority remains wedded to hierarchy and to conditions that separate them from the people they lead. Although this point is especially evident in Catholicism, parallels exist with any religion that accords special status and authority to an officially designated clerical stratum.

Religion's potential for energizing and driving change has much to do with a capacity for synthesis in both thought and action. Synthesis is not limited to ideas, audiences, and structures but also extends to the relations between religion and politics more generally conceived. Conventional models that point to religion's inevitable privatization and anticipate the secularization of culture and politics hold little promise for making sense of change. They are in the same position as the functionalist sociological models whose stress on harmony and cohesion utterly failed to anticipate or explain the rise of the civil rights movement in the United States in the 1950s, not to mention the protests and contestations of subsequent decades.

To reject these models does not require us to accept the notion, reviewed earlier in this chapter, that the poor have some latent disposition to cultural inversion. Reference to supposed utopian hopes of turning the world upside down is neither realistic nor necessary to explain and understand change. The popular voices raised in Latin America today have more modest goals and look to a surer foundation for the future.

They want more dignity, better jobs, decent houses, and fair futures for family and community. They seek these ends by working in the open spaces made available by change elsewhere in the system. Once active, they can and do expand these spaces, making themselves into new women and new men in the process. The linkages considered in this chapter are in some sense empty vessels, to be filled anew by every generation according to its lights and its circumstances. Over the years, this gives growing weight in theory and practice to popular understandings of what religion justifies and faith requires in the world that power and politics gives to average people, which, in meeting, they make anew.

# TEN

## THE FUTURE OF POPULAR VOICES

THIS BOOK has taken a close look, from several different angles of view, at how popular voices emerge and what they have to say. I have stressed how changes in popular culture emerge and are linked to associational life and to institutions. I have also considered the implications of all this for politics defined not only with respect to states and regimes, but also to politics as defined in terms of the dimensions of conflict, power, and authority that run through all spheres of life. Religion has been central to our story because in Latin America, as elsewhere in contemporary and historical experience, religion is critical to the legitimation and self-image of popular voices, as well as of their allies and opponents.

Although religion is not all there is to popular culture, religion does play a key role in the formation and diffusion of that culture. Religions of the most different kind do this by providing values, images, metaphors, and symbols that give particular meaning to ordinary speech; they also provide structures— regular and routine times and places where voices can be raised and heard. Seeing popular culture through the lens of religion helps us people the hitherto empty structures of politics and economy with recognizably human individuals: real people, not just "the people." Instead of seeing classes or groups who act and react in mechanical fashion, we face real men and women whose evolving day-to-day thoughts and concerns move them to act in and on the world—not only as isolated individuals, but also as citizens, groups, and communities.

Making religion central to the presentation of popular voices is also a way to redress the theoretical balance. The conventional wisdom of earlier generations of social scientists—who viewed religion for the most part as irrational, epiphenomenal, and doomed in the long run to decline and privatization—is pretty much exploded by now. At best, such expectations were misspecified, confusing the particulars of restructuring ties between religion, culture, and politics with general secularizing tendencies.[1] At worst, the neoevolutionary assumptions on which they rest simply perpetuate nineteenth-century prejudices. By depicting religion and religious institutions as necessarily static and doomed to decline in the face of modernization and the rationalization of cul-

---

[1] See Robert Wuthnow, "Understanding Religion and Politics"; N. J. Demerath, "Religious Capital and Capital Religions: Cross-Cultural and Non-Legal Factors in the Separation of Church and State"; and John Coleman, "The Situation for Modern Faith."

ture, they ignored dynamics of change within religion, and obscured religion's evident role in generating and empowering other transformations and movements. They also failed to grasp the power of claims to reason advanced within religion, and to understand their impact on culture and politics.

This concluding chapter offers an opportunity to confront the evidence with a few basic questions. After a brief review of the evidence and argument in the preceding chapters, I will explore parallels between Latin American experiences and moments of change in other times and places. I then ask if the men and women we call "popular" have something special to say. How can we best hear their words, understand their meanings, and grasp what, if anything, makes them unique? A further set of questions concerns the future of popular voices, and what they are likely to leave behind. I argue that the legacy of popular voices in Latin American Catholicism is best found in a revitalized religious and moral discourse, in the working out of new forms of sociability through groups and movements, in changed interinstitutional relations, and in efforts to redefine the meaning and presence of "religion" on the Latin American scene. I conclude with reflections on what we need to know about the future of popular voices, and why the effort is worthwhile.

## Reprise

The voices we have listened to and the groups we have observed in this book are broadly representative, without extremes either of conservatism or radical activism. These midrange results reflect the middling status that Venezuela and Colombia hold in the overall Latin American scheme of things. Despite the differences between them that have occupied us here, in neither case has change been driven by exceptional levels of economic crisis, war, or similar disasters. Religious transformations in the two cases also fall within the mainstream, and, as such, offer a plausible window on the likely future of change for the region as a whole. A composite portrait can be built from our cases with reference to the following points.

First, the history and structure of major institutions and of the relations between them creates very different environments for popular religious groups. Environments in Colombia are hostile even when encouragement is intended, while Venezuelan settings legitimize the very idea of popular groups and give change room to get off the ground.

Second, poverty shapes the needs that members bring to groups and, through them, to their encounter with big structures. This makes class important, but as we have seen, in all cases the impact of class differences is mediated by other factors, including most notably gender, urban or rural context, and institutional connections of identity, loyalty, and affiliation.

Third, prevailing images of the church and of what religion requires and promotes are critical to how popular groups see themselves, what they say and do, and how they organize. Stress on hierarchy and institutional control produces dependent groups that can neither generate nor sustain change. Provision for democracy and equal participation is a surer basis for lasting personal and collective action.

Fourth, by making the exercise of reason a path to valid religious truth, base communities' reliance on Bible study changes the character of legitimate religious knowledge in ways that reinforce confidence in one's own ability to reason, judge, and act independently. Authentic understanding and interpretation no longer appear reserved to officially sanctioned intellectuals, and communities generate intellectuals of their own who can provide family, friends, and community with interpretation and leadership.[2]

Fifth, the plans, programs, and overall culture of institutions find practical expression through mediating roles like those of priests, sisters, and pastoral agents. Sisters take especially prominent roles because their own self-image and role definition have changed in ways that enhance commitment and access to popular groups.

Sixth, innovation in the church is more likely to arise from sources that are marginal to, but not isolated from, the institution's central structures and lines of authority. Marginality frees potential innovators from tight hierarchical control, while isolation undercuts innovation by cutting groups off from resources, a sense of identity and legitimacy, and protection. Autonomy within a framework of stable linkages to big structures works best, not only for mediators like religious congregations or marginal sectors like women, but also for base communities in general.

Seventh, religion is clearly both a constant and a variable for popular groups. Important variations in religious sensibility are associated with differences in group structure, roles, and practice. Greater equality and reduced sociocultural differences between church and people are critical in this regard. It is also clear that religion cannot be addressed as no more than a source of energy for social and political struggle. Religion is valued for itself and provides underpinnings of trust and legitimacy that make it possible for groups to recruit members and operate.

Eighth, and most generally, nothing is preordained or fixed in values or culture. Throughout this book we have seen how experiences change beliefs, and how beliefs change behavior both at the individual and collective levels. Neither values nor culture are static, nor can they be dismissed as superstruc-

---

[2] Commenting on rural South Africa in the 1920s, William Beinart and Colin Bundy point out that "local struggles constantly threw up intellectuals, individuals capable of expressing the economic, social, and political interests of a social group. . . . Too much is sometimes made of the archaic or primitive elements in rural politics. . . . Such millennial and archaic features that were present were almost always linked with more instrumental thinking" (*Hidden Struggles in Rural South Africa*, pp. 27, 35–36).

ture, the epiphenomena of presumably more fundamental movements of economic or political forces and interests. The interests that individuals and groups pursue do not flow only from their from positions in the social structure. They are suffused with cultural significance and are value-laden from the outset, and are as much affected by the dynamics of cultural, as by economic or political, change.

The list could easily be extended, but the point is not to enumerate traits and defining characteristics but rather to explain how and why they fit together in real life. On the ground in communities throughout Latin America, one encounters not separate traits but packages of belief, practice, and structure that are either preformed or put together on the spot by popular groups and pastoral agents. How do the choices available in our communities fit broader Latin American patterns? Further reflection on the typology of base communities outlined in earlier chapters provides a few answers. In developing and naming that typology, I chose a language derived from politics (Conservative Ideal, Radical Ideal, and Sociocultural Transformation) because that is how the issue is posed in most contemporary Catholic discourse in the region. But labels like these should not obscure the determining role of religious and cultural elements, and their centrality in setting the form and content of linkages between base communities and politics. How do the types stand up?

The Conservative Ideal as exemplified in Facatativá is clearly a core option in Latin American Catholicism today. It provides for grass-roots organization and a creative reach into popular experience without sacrificing continuity or hierarchy. The *popular* is domesticated, its potential dangers declawed. It may be that the preponderance of hierarchy in the Colombian scheme of things makes popular groups likely to end up authoritarian in spirit, popular in name alone. Still, experiences like Agua Fría affirm that popular groups can break through even this confining straitjacket, given a little isolation and an opening for independent leadership. Bear in mind that this Colombian version of the Conservative Ideal is not the most conservative option available. In other cases, popular organization finds almost no legitimate room, the church remains confined to hierarchy, bound to close alliances with political (especially military) power, and wedded to a world where poverty remains a burden to be borne, more an affliction than a social condition.[3]

There is broad agreement that much of the initial stimulus to create base communities came as a reaction to the scarcity of clergy. Church leaders were searching for ways to organize and hold masses without the regular presence of clergy. This remains a powerful motive. But continued resistance by church elites to the incorporation of ordinary people, and especially of women (nuns and women in the communities), makes it hard to see how in the long run the Conservative Ideal can reach much beyond creating second-best alternatives,

---

[3] Argentina is perhaps the clearest case in point.

or short-lived transmission belts, for the ecclesiastical institution. In this light, the distinction between Radical and Sociocultural Ideals, assumes particular importance. Consider the Radical Ideal for a moment.

Despite their repeated claims to be nondirective and to constitute a "church born of the people," groups of this kind have important authoritarian tendencies of their own. Popular understandings are viewed as either dangerous and uncontrollable (for example, in Barrio El Rodeo), inchoate, or limited by what Lenin would have called a "trade union mentality." In a recent study of what he calls Peru's "leftist angels," Luis Pasara points to a radical Catholic style (found among many of the priests, sisters, and pastoral agents who "go to the people"). This style (compounded of utopianism, clericalism, elitism, intellectualism, and verticality) leads, in Pasara's view, to ideological rigidity and organizational inefficacy. The net result is to weaken popular movements while energizing and motivating right-wing opponents.[4]

The combination of exaggerated rhetoric with organizational weakness leaves ordinary people exposed to countermeasures and to fluctuations beyond their control. The reservations about links to other levels that are so visible in the barrios of Cali in effect make it harder for popular groups to legitimate contacts up and out of the base. These are commonly painted as sellouts. Even in cases most often cited as exemplars of the Radical Ideal, like El Salvador or Brazil, support for popular groups has been much more fragmented, short-lived, and conflict-ridden than conventional wisdom admits. Thus it was not the Salvadoran church "as a whole" but rather the archdiocese of San Salvador (led by Archbishop Romero) that supported and sustained this position, often in the teeth of bitter opposition from other prelates. After Romero's murder, church leaders backed off from prophetic criticism and sought accommodation and mediating roles instead. Grass-roots groups and pastoral agents were left stranded, confused, and exposed.[5] These considerations suggest skepticism and grounds for concern about the future if too much reliance is placed on the Radical Ideal.

Both conservatives and radicals praise the people lavishly. Conservatives like the parish priest of Quebradanegra laud what they suppose to be the inherent piety of popular groups. They welcome the dependence that leads to respect for and deference to clergy, viewing these as guarantees of orthodoxy and reliability. Unity in the church and around the church's official leaders is stressed; authority and obedience are seen as cardinal virtues. From this vantage point, they condemn radicals for not being authentically religious and for manipulating the poor in service to a Marxist political agenda. Radicals also praise the values of popular groups, but typically cast their comments in terms of class unity and solidarity. The matter is often put in utopian terms, as if

[4] "Peru: The Leftist Angels," pp. 291–301.
[5] Cáceres, "Political Radicalization."

authenticity were to be found only among the poor and hope for the future possible only with a complete change of social and political structures.[6] Their position recalls Marx's image of the proletariat as the group whose oppression was so extreme and concentrated that its negation through revolution would lead to complete change and the elimination of all repression.[7] The point here is that despite shared praise for the poor, neither conservatives nor radicals give much credit to popular groups themselves as independent sources of values, ideals, leadership, and sustained common action. The Sociocultural Ideal differs in noteworthy ways.

This position is not a residual category but an independent variant of the life and culture of popular religious groups. Given a chance to acquire experience, a corps of leaders, and some institutional identity without exclusive focus on social or political activism, groups survive better for several reasons. Early and potentially devastating conflict with the big structures of church and state is avoided. Making religious practice central in a context of democratic organizational traits gives the groups continuing appeal to members, for whom both religion and the experience of self-governance have independent value. It becomes possible to incorporate and draw strength from a broad range of religious beliefs and practices, and to put these to communitarian uses. Recall how in Villanueva, early decisions to give the groups a multiple character (simultaneously religious, social, and economic) made for more complex solidarities and greater resilience in the face of setbacks. In this particular case, survival was enhanced by rural location that, as a practical matter, undercut competition and the resulting drain on clientele.[8] Groups of this kind are not free of clerical intervention, nor do they wish to be. But the clerics here, Jesuits and independent figures like Padre Vicente, assumed a self-limiting role that enhanced groups' ability to survive on their own.

One way to grasp the validity of these models in theory and practice is to ask how the agenda each advances for religion fits with prevailing images of church and people. Conservatives emphasize individual spirituality and conventional moral concerns. Radicals make structural change and elaboration of collective identity and class consciousness central. Those following a Sociocultural Ideal mix changes in spirituality and religious practice with material improvement and community organization. If we set these alternatives against current Vatican policy, the long-term implications come clear.

A central aim of recent Vatican policy in Latin America has been to move the agenda of religious discourse and action away from egalitarian norms and

[6] Azevedo, *Basic Ecclesial Styles*, and Pasara "Peru: The Leftist Angels," emphasize this point very well.

[7] For example, in his *Contribution to the Critique of Hegel's Philosophy of Right*.

[8] For a comparison of urban and rural settings, see Levine and Mainwaring, "Religion and Popular Protest." See also Kincaid, "Peasants into Rebels"; Mainwaring, *The Catholic Church*; and Bruneau, *The Church in Brazil*.

religious categories like *structural sin* with their associated stress on activism and toward (or better, back to) more traditional concerns like personal and family morality, censorship, sexual mores, subsidies to education, and so forth. The predominance of such issues fits well with a conservative sociology that attributes visible social ills (including poverty and conflict) to the "strains of change" rather than to a structural opposition between powerful and powerless. It also enhances traditional lines of authority by reserving all power of interpretation and guidance once again to institutional elites.[9]

One way to look at these initiatives is to see them as a reaction to the threat of Protestantization in the region's Catholic churches and groups. There is something to this fear, for as we have seen, base communities often have decidedly Protestant-like qualities. They stress the Bible and the value of literacy, they make informed participation a marker of faith, and they look to personal responsibility within congregational structures. As was the case for the Puritans who occupied Weber's attention, the spirituality common to many base communities of the Radical or Sociocultural kind is decidedly *of this world*. Mastery of the environment is valued and comes hand in hand with assertions of personal worth and commitment to individual and community improvement. Religious expression is fused with an ever-expanding range of commitments in everyday life. Note that conversion experiences play a key role in each case. Conversion is a powerful, often shattering experience that opens men and women to new horizons and commitments. Cohen states that for the Puritans, "Grace imparted by the Spirit regenerates the convert and issues forth in a life of sanctified works. . . . Grace leads ultimately to heaven, but penultimately to a career of holy service suggested by the Moral Law. Turning does not inhere in a single event; it stretches out through a lifetime of faithful discipline."[10] Similar changes in family and community life are associated with conversion and group membership among base community members and their Protestant counterparts. Greater equality between the sexes is enjoined; self-control, self-discipline, and savings are promoted; and mutual aid is taken as an obligation.

How do popular Catholic voices fit with concurrent developments in the Protestant churches of Latin America? The translation of texts and liturgies into local languages and the stress given to Bible study and small group organization has moved these Catholics much closer to the pattern of Protestant experience. In terms of doctrine and ideology, progressive Latin American Catholics share with Protestants a commitment to seeing community life in linear, historical terms. Both groups therefore place considerable stress on change over time, with history seen as God's project for humanity. In this light, distinctions between salvation history and ordinary human events are

[9] Cf. Lowy, *Marxisme*; Lernoux, *People of God*.
[10] Charles Lloyd Cohen, *God's Caress: The Psychology of Puritan Religious Experience*, p. 6.

rejected as false. Instead of the secularization much social science theory expects to find, instances like these point to a notable sacralization of the ordinary world. The religious resurgence visible in Latin America's Catholic base communities and expanding Protestant churches underscores the continuing (indeed, the growing) power of religious motivation to reach out, infusing an ever-broadening range of events and experiences with sacred meaning.[11]

Protestant churches differ from Catholic groups in a number of important ways. In ideological terms, both reject poverty, but for different reasons and with contrasting implications. The Catholic discourse crystallized in liberation theology makes poverty hinge on structural exploitations and inequalities. Overcoming poverty is thus a matter of collective struggle, ultimately of power. But Protestant tradition attributes poverty ultimately to evil, and makes overcoming poverty contingent on conversion and self-mastery.[12] Related contrasts in political messages come from the way social conflict is understood and ordinary experience is accorded religious value. Wolterstorff argues that liberation theology shares with modern Protestant reformers (like nineteenth-century neo-Calvinists) a disposition to see conflict as the result of injustice. For liberation theology, conflict arises from the domination of some groups by others. Domination is explained in terms of class and class conflict and is given religious sense through the incorporation of these Marxist categories into expanded notions of sin. For neo-Calvinists, the root of the problem was idolatry, specifically an exaggerated faith in growth. The solution was personal conversion and reaffirmation of communitarian values.

The preceding contrasts are accentuated in Latin America by the fact that the fastest growing sector of the region's Protestantism has been its evangelical and fundamentalist churches. These draw heavily on a "prosperity theology," in which prosperity appears as a visible sign of grace; individual advancement is enjoined. All this is far from the common ideology of most base communities, which stress community and collective action. Institutional and especially international connections also move political orientations in different directions. Latin American evangelical churches commonly have close ties

---

[11] For comparative perspectives see my "Religion and Politics"; and also Arjomand, *The Turban for the Crown*; Lan, *Guns and Rain*; and Fields, *Revival and Rebellion*. Doimo ("Social Movements," pp. 217–18) stresses how changes in the Brazilian church "encouraged participation and organization as components of faith and the duty of Christians. When a housewife and mother of eight like Dona Maria Clara, who became a symbol of the Vila Velha CEBs through her active participation in social movements, gets up on a platform and speaks to a gathering of demonstrators of her daily suffering, denounces capitalist exploitation, and calls for the social justice and equity achieved through the participation and organization of the people; she speaks in the name of her faith. Her cry was for a better existence in the name of the struggle for liberation and in the name of Christ. . . . This points out a process of sacralization of the profane: politics. The practice of politics by the people will now enter a domain of faith. The need for a 'critical reflection on reality,' for participation and for organization is now an attribute of faith."

[12] Wolterstorff, *Until Justice*.

with North American groups. Once beyond the local level, they have tended to assume the political agenda of North American fundamentalism, above all its stress on anticommunism and on submission to constituted authority. Evangelicals have been active in support for military rule and right-wing parties.[13]

There are structural differences as well. Evangelicals find greater opportunities for mobility in and through their churches than do ordinary Catholics. It is easier, for example, to become a pastor in a Protestant congregation than to become a Catholic priest. Less time is involved, there is less isolation from the community, and barriers of social class, culture, and ethnicity are distinctly lower. On the whole, Catholic clergy remain significantly whiter and more middle class than the popular congregations they serve.

Do evangelical Protestants constitute an alternative to base communities and similar groups in Latin America today? If the drive for greater unity and the reaffirmation of hierarchy and control now underway in the Papacy of John Paul II continues to advance, may we anticipate a loss of members to the Protestant churches? There are compelling reasons to think so. Expansion among evangelical and fundamentalist churches has not only outstripped growth among other Protestants, but has also competed directly with the Catholic church, drawing members in large numbers from traditional groups and parishes and from base communities.

Group members prize the intensity, warmth, and egalitarian character of base communities. Because evangelical and fundamentalist churches are comparable in intensity of experience, personal warmth, and the equality of believers, the effort to domesticate base communities would therefore seem a likely spur to defection. Movement to evangelical churches may also be spurred by some traits of progressive base communities that members find onerous: the intense commitments of time and energy they demand or the stress on words and preaching over expressive behavior and aesthetic satisfaction.[14]

There are other alternatives than conversion. Quiescence would be easy, as it requires little more than slipping back into familiar routines. Some valued elements, like Bible study, would doubtless remain, but the surrounding infrastructure of a cooperative egalitarianism would go, taking with it much of

[13] Rose and Brouwer ("Guatemala's Upper Classes Join the Evangelicals") point out, for example, that during the short-lived but exceptionally violent presidency of Guatemala's General Rios Montt, who was an elder of one large evangelical church, his fellow church leaders were active in soliciting international support for military rule. Detailed research on growth and change in Latin American Protestants is just getting underway, but see especially Stoll, *Is Latin America Turning Protestant?* and Martin, *Tongues of Fire*.

[14] Burdick argues that the stress on collective solutions and political action that characterizes many progressive base communities in Brazil makes it hard for members to articulate and resolve critical problems of everyday life (such as domestic conflict, sexuality, or racism) within the group. This drives members to the evangelicals, which function effectively as cults of affliction. See "Gossip and Secrecy" or *Looking for God in Brazil*.

what helped turn personal experience to collective action. For those who remain committed to work within groups of religious inspiration in general or in circumstances where free organization remains difficult, a move to associations "of Christian inspiration" but independent of the institutional church seems most likely. The case of CESAP finds many echoes, for example, in Chile, where the hierarchy's withdrawal from activism and its efforts to reassert control have been answered by the construction of "popular Christian communities." With the help of sympathetic allies in the church (especially the religious congregations) and politics, these groups have asserted their autonomy and their ability to act independently in the future.

## Explaining Change

The preceding review raises an obvious question: Why Latin America? Why should Latin America have been the scene of such profound and for the most part unanticipated changes? One answer lies in the way crisis opened the door to religious innovation. Religion has been so closely intertwined for so long with the structure of domination in Latin America that crisis (in the Weberian sense of expanded trade, broadened scale of action, and emerging challenges to legitimacy) made religion a particularly likely focal point for change. Such transformations generate new roles for clergy and ordinary believers, spark different kinds of social formations, and lead to shifts in the moral and cultural discourse of elites and mass publics alike.

Acknowledging the salience of religion in moments of crisis and change is important but by itself tells us little about precisely which kinds of individuals and groups are likely to press for a new message and be open to hearing and acting on it. Drawing on the experience of the Puritan revolution, many observers have pointed to the rise of "masterless men," individuals free of old constraints but not yet bound to definitive new arrangements.[15] New urban migrants, displaced peasantries, and, despite the gender-specific formulation, women, are often cited as especially critical audiences for and carriers of change. The marginality in question is not just a matter of being on the "wrong side" of lines of class, wealth, ethnicity, or gender. Marginality also characterizes aspiring classes whose experience of movement leaves them bereft of footing either in the traditional order or in the new arrangements being put together. Such "masterless men" are a prime source of new leadership and an avid clientele for innovations in religious discourse that underscore equality, identity, and an independent capacity to reason, judge, and act.[16]

---

[15] Hill, *The World Turned Upside Down*; Michael Walzer, *Revolution of the Saints*; and for a recent statement, Don Herzog, *Happy Slaves: A Critique of Consent Theory*.

[16] Cf. Karen Fields (*Revival and Rebellion*, p. 22): "Sociologists of religion did not predict the political resurgence of 'old-time religion' here in America, this most secular of modern societies.

Singly and in combination, all these elements are apparent in Latin America. As in other great transformative moments of cultural and political history, contemporary Latin American experience has generated vast enthusiasms along with a sense of openness and unbounded movement. Institutions are shaken up, and individuals have the feeling, as one Venezuelan put it, that "I have had a historic life."[17] Habermas argues that in the modern age, traditional bases of community (what he terms "lifeworlds") are penetrated and colonized (by "systems") and undercut without satisfying and meaningful equivalents being provided. This makes free communication and undistorted reason more and more difficult. In his view, this process makes legitimacy conflicts prominent and sparks the creation of social movements likely to stress identity, community, and autonomous claims to reason.[18]

Conflicts over legitimacy come to center stage when the principles and justifications that institutions project no longer find significant response from, or correspondence in, ordinary life. In this vein, Habermas sees social movements as primarily defensive, dedicated to the reconstruction of coherence in daily life and to the defense of a particular kind of linkage or stitching between levels. They advance a "revaluation of the particular, the natural, the provincial, of social spaces that are small enough to be familiar, or decentralized forms of commerce and despecialized routines, of segmented pubs, simple interactions, and dedifferentiated public spheres—all this is meant to foster the revitalization of possibilities for expression and communication that have been buried alive."[19]

Much recent commentary has focused on the relation between religion and protest. The issue is important but the focus is too limited. It is important because it highlights the turn of religious motivation and legitimacy from submission to resistance, from apathy to activism. However, in common usage, words like *protest* slip all too easily into definitions that are limited to overt (and most often violent) actions. But as we have seen, overt or violent activism do not exhaust the possibilities of resistance. A more flexible and varied usage is indicated, at the very least to distinguish between forms of protest and resistance in everyday life and big structures, between the activism likely to emerge in different spheres and levels of action, and so forth. Indeed, exces-

---

And we did not foresee that religion would fire a potent revolutionary engine in Iran. Indeed, we have done no better than economists have in predicting major new developments of our times. I do not know what ails economics. But I have become convinced that the problem of rationality, as applied to churches militant, is little more than a translation into scholarly terms of the native folklore about religious belief that is current in secular societies."

[17] Cited in Peattie, *The View from the Barrio*, p. 21.

[18] For Habermas, see *The Theory of Communicative Action*, 2 vols.; Richard Bernstein, ed., *Habermas and Modernity*; and John B. Thomas and David Held, eds., *Habermas: Critical Debates*.

[19] *The Theory of Communicative Action* 2:395. See also Anthony Giddens, "Reason without Revolution? Habermas's *Theorie des kommunikativen handelns*," p. 110.

sive focus on protest as an outgrowth of religious ideas and structures probably tells us more about the prejudices of analysts than about the beliefs of ordinary people. The assumption that religion necessarily supports apathy and fatalism is not only historically false. It also confuses the externals of action, often sharply constrained by circumstance, with what these mean to ordinary people. To those involved, religious belief and action may further solidarity and mutual support despite remaining (for structural reasons) so fragmented that the result ends up looking like resignation. Facades of deference may be laboriously maintained to hide dangerous feelings of anger and humiliation. Getting behind the mask and breaking the silence is a question of power and opportunity, not of basic belief.

Although his ideas throw useful light on the character of the changes central to this book, Habermas exaggerates the closed and static quality of everyday existence—what he terms the "lifeworld." He fails to give adequate weight either to changes *within* the ambit of everyday life or to efforts by ordinary people and small-scale groups to manipulate and rework linkages in ways they see as likely to make for a better life.[20] But issues of this kind must be addressed if we are to understand how and in what sense popular voices are, indeed, unique.

I do not mean to suggest that the link of religion to social and cultural change, and to the creation of new self-images and structures with political impact, is limited to popular groups. The events of late 1989 in Eastern Europe demonstrate that changes of this sort find expression throughout the social order. The churches of Eastern Europe provided indispensable networks of solidarity, places to gather and organize, and a moral vocabulary that energized and empowered resistance. There are obvious echoes here of the churches' role in recent Latin American history, where authoritarian rule drove resistance into the churches and dramatically enhanced the visibility and appeal of religious messages about freedom and justice.[21] Still, the question of popular uniqueness must be addressed here, if only because of the enormous attention it has garnered in the recent discourse and action of Latin American Catholicism. The next section considers the matter from several points of view. Are popular voices unique for structural reasons, as a reading of Habermas would indicate? Are they particularly open to messages of simplicity, identity, and purity, as much liberation theology affirms? Or do structural changes and cultural transformations act on one another to create mo-

---

[20] As Giddens ("Reason without Revolution?") suggests, there is probably too much influence of Parsonian structural functionalism in Habermas for him to give due weight to change.

[21] See "Lutheran Church Gets a Bigger Role," *New York Times*, December 7, 1989. There were substantial differences in the role played by churches across Eastern Europe. In Poland, for example, the Catholic church exercised more centralized control early on. In East Germany, strong Lutheran traditions encouraged more diversity. See Greschat, "The Relationship of the Protestant Church to the Governments of the Two Germanys."

ments during which popular voices are at once targets of opportunity and active subjects pursuing their own transformation?

## Are Popular Voices Unique?

The best answer is no, or to be more precise, no with an explanation. Popular voices and the people who bear them are not unique. They embody no particular virtue, display no unusual piety, have no special insight to offer about the nature of social relations or politics. I have called them ordinary or average people throughout this book, and that is what they are: neither better nor worse than others, neither especially good nor especially capable as such. Although they are often depicted as unique, closer inspection shows that the portraits painted for us by outsiders (pastoral agents among them) rarely match up well with what observation reveals, much less with the self-images these men and women hold.

The evidence shows popular groups to be consistently less radical and much less prone to utopian expectations those who come to or write about them. There are also few grounds for assigning them a particular capacity to hear and accept messages of liberation. If we set aside purely theological or political argument, which endows the poor with this ability more or less by definition, only ambiguous and contradictory evidence remains.

A shift in perspective may help. If we rephrase the question about uniqueness to make it depend not on qualities inherent to popular voices, but rather on their place in a particular kind of culture and social order, a more complete understanding is possible. Because the life conditions and experiences of popular groups differ in systematic ways from those faced by members of upper and middle classes, their worldviews are built of other materials and rest on different foundations. Structural position and the pattern of social and cultural change makes popular groups both available for and particularly open to opportunities for the construction of reason, sociability, and community that are, at least for them, fundamentally new.

The growth of personal and collective claims to understand and act on the world in rational ways and to create and hold knowledge independent of authority run through the experiences reviewed in this book like an underground river. They may not always be explicit or visible, but their continued presence is nonetheless essential to fertility and growth. Once worked into everyday social practice, the claim to reason acquires "a stubbornly transcending power, because it is renewed with each act of unconstrained understanding, with each moment of living together in solidarity, of successful individuation, of saving emancipation."[22] Concern with reason and efforts to rationalize re-

---

[22] Bernstein, Introduction to *Habermas and Modernity*, p. 25. Concern with conflicts and trans-

ligion and social life are of course not unique to popular groups, but it is important to see how and why they take a place in their working agenda of daily life. What gives claims to reason a basis in hitherto disorganized and dispirited groups? How are such claims detached from the demands of specific problems, like organizing a cooperative or building a school, and diffused throughout the social order?

Reading and the independent access literacy provides to knowledge and power appear to be critical. The experiences of base community members, for whom reading opens doors to self-creation and self-assertion, have important historical antecedents. Zaret states that in the run-up to the Puritan revolution, a virtual "charisma of reason" became central to the life of dissenting churches. Armed with confidence in their own reason and in their interpretive ability, and further supported by networks of solidarity in church, commerce, and community, the Puritans advanced what Zaret calls a "democratization of criticism" in which literacy played a central role.[23]

> The importance of printing and literacy for popular dissent involved more than the mere dissemination of critical ideas. Equally important was their role in facilitating the high level of ideological competence that is inherent in popular dissent. Dissent depends on this competency. Dissent is heresy made legitimate in varying degrees by the recognition that it is normatively wrong or practically impossible to repress it. This is so because dissent and orthodoxy can refer to the same or similar abstract beliefs and values in order to justify their contrary tenets. . . . There is an important link between lay literacy and the kind of religious dissent in which rank and file dissenters are able to make convincing and critical normative judgments. Compared to oral instruction by priests, reading contains much greater potential for promoting assertive and independent styles of thought among laymen.[24]

It is important not to conflate rationalization and claims to reason with secularization. All that rationalization requires is order, explainable and predict-

---

formations of this kind are not just a matter of intellectual fancy or fashion. Everyday life opens itself to our inquiry and demands our attention precisely because crisis is undermining conventional ties and explanations. Ordinary men and women reach out from family and community to challenge and rework long-established arrangements. At the same time, institutions search for new legitimations and bases of action. Allies and mediators are about and support is possible.

Latin America is only one instance among many. The stress on undistorted communication and the social construction of reason visible in more democratizing base communities bears comparison not only with the oft-cited Puritans of sixteenth-century England, but also, for example, with modern Africa's conflicted encounter with Christianity and colonialism. Acknowledging the rationality of religious actors and the power of their claim to possess and use reason is central to grasping the link between religious change and political resistance. See, for example, Fields, *Revival and Rebellion*; or Ranger, "Religious Movements and Politics."

[23] *The Heavenly Contract*, pp. 20, 21.
[24] Ibid., p. 29.

able rules, and a sense of control. The advance of rationalization within religion, for example, may undermine belief in magical manipulation and undercut traditional bases of clerical authority. Many of the comments cited earlier that contrast the authenticity of faith expressed in action with the hypocrisy of reliance on ritual and external signs are remarkably evocative of the Protestant Reformation in general and of Puritans in particular. But in no way do claims to reason or the creation of a general capacity for independent judgment require abandoning religion as faith, practice, or membership.

Certain functions clearly move in and out of the orbit of explicitly religious judgment and ecclesiastical control. Health is a good example. With the growing availability of technical medicine, most people turn for help to clinics, hospitals, nurses, and doctors rather than to prayer and pilgrimage—at least as a first step. Roles such as the registry of births, deaths, or marriages or the management of education follow a similar pattern. All shift to some extent from religious to secular hands. But we cannot leap from this narrow ground to assert a generalized retreat of religious concerns and definitions in the face of others. That misspecifies the meaning of secularization and confuses rearrangement and restructuring with long-term trends.

In all likelihood, we remain overly committed to a false image of European history in which secular worldviews and state control grew along with one another. An alternative perspective would suggest that today, as in the past, transformations in religious consciousness and organization entail less the secularization of private life than the sacralization of the world. The most proximate events and actions are placed in a context of divine creation, left now to individuals and groups to follow on their own. The Protestant legacy emphasizing spiritual self-possession, self-control, and congregational independence had far-reaching consequences for culture, politics, and law. In Christopher Hill's words, "If there is a spark of the divine in all men, preaching should not be a clerical monopoly. No spoken or printed word should be suppressed, lest God's truth be lost. If all men were equal before Christ, should they not also be equal before the law?"[25]

The particular way in which reason, sociability, and community converge in recent Latin American experience suggests a sense in which the popular voices of Latin American Catholicism may indeed be unique. With growing confidence in personal and collective reason and a sense of structural support (from the institution), groups like base communities have crafted a solution to the problem of combining change with a sense of community and a connectedness to something beyond self and family. Here the pervasive sense of linkage is especially enriching. Bellah and his collaborators have pointed to the absence of ties like these in contemporary American society, where, in their view, therapeutic metaphors and a focus on the individual unconnected to

[25] *The Century of Revolution*, p. 147.

community reign supreme. The result is impoverishment of both private and public life.[26] There is little evidence of such a turn in the popular Catholic voices of Latin America. Instead, the powerful stress on community and solidarity actively furthers the legitimacy of transpersonal identities and concerns without smothering individual growth.

## Facing the Future

Understanding the future of popular voices requires answers to two kinds of questions. First come experiential questions that direct our attention to the likely fate of the individuals, groups, and perspectives that together constitute what Latin Americans know as *lo popular*. What legacy will these men and women leave to their children, their communities, their churches and nations? Are the changes we have studied here just a bubble, a blip on the historical screen? Or will they continue to evolve as popular understanding and empowerment grow? Reflection on these issues raises two further questions: What must we know to know about the future of popular voices? What is the impact of those voices on how we go about the process of research and reflection in the future?

To begin with experience, the first thing to say about the future of popular voices is that it is only partly in the hands of popular groups themselves. If the arguments and evidence of this book establish nothing else, they do make clear that change in popular culture cannot be understood in isolation from institutions and formal expressions of ideology or doctrine. They may and do overflow previously established boundaries, but only rarely do they reject the boundaries altogether. There has been no significant schism or open division in Latin American Catholicism, and only modest inroads by alternative religions. There is little yearning for a "world turned upside down."

That popular voices are neither alone nor isolated helps account for the richness and nuanced quality of their views. As Marjorie Becker has noted in a different context, popular views come in color, not black and white, and there-

---

[26] Bellah et al., *Habits of the Heart*. The authors state (pp. 47–48) that "Between them, the manager and the therapist largely define the outlines of twentieth century American culture. . . . [This] new culture is deeply ambiguous. It represents both the easing of constraints and dogmatic prejudices about what others should be and an idealization of the coolly manipulative style of management. In our society, with its sharply divided spheres, it provides a way for the beleaguered individual to develop techniques for coping with the often contradictory pressures of public and private life. Yet it does so by extending the calculating managerial style into intimacy, home, and community, areas of life formerly governed by the norms of a moral ecology." On therapeutic metaphors, see the penetrating comments of James Davison Hunter in *American Evangelicalism*. For general commentary on the issues raised by Bellah and his collaborators, see C. Reynolds and R. Norman, eds., *Community in America: The Challenge of "Habits of the Heart."*

fore resist all-or-nothing perspectives on the world.[27] Being so deeply and so consciously embedded in social relations and in a sense of community acts as a brake on the ability of all-out definitions of conflict (e.g., around class, gender, ethnicity, language, or even religion) to occupy the exclusive center of popular attention.

At the same time, the connection to larger structures makes popular voices and popular groups vulnerable to pressures and efforts at control. The centrality of linkages to the theory and practice of popular religious culture poses obvious limits for the future. Growing national and international pressures within the churches have begun to take a toll, cutting the ground from under the most activist groups. Leaders are transferred, resources withdrawn, and legitimate tasks and roles are redefined. As a result, popular groups find that the road gets harder and its direction more and more uncertain. Pressures of this kind have increased steadily throughout the papacy of John Paul II, whose vigorous affirmation of authority and unity in the church are manifest in a host of conservative ecclesiastical appointments, purges of seminaries, training programs, and publishing outlets, and a consistent effort to control autonomous groups. The net result has been to push religious discourse and action back to older definitions of critical issues and concerns.[28]

The impact of such pressures within the churches has been magnified by the notable economic and political decay that the 1980s brought to Latin America. Accelerated economic crisis in a context of weak and ineffective government reduces the survivability of social movements inspired by religion and cuts the ground from under their potential for sustaining and enriching democracy. This is so for several reasons. The political liberalization that came to much of Latin America with transitions to democracy has undermined the unity of popular groups. With the restoration of civil rights and political democracy, many who had joined religious groups because they were the only available options now moved on to other affiliations. In addition, the association of political democracy with economic disasters left over from now-defunct military regimes has reinforced disillusionment with democratic politics at both ends of the ideological spectrum. Conservatives in many churches never thought much of democracy to begin with: Argentina is perhaps the best-known example. The Argentine hierarchy actively supported the military's self-styled crusade against communism. Progressive Catholic initiatives were eliminated and their promoters often fingered for the police. Argentina's Catholic bishops voiced support for democracy only when it was already inevitable. The example suggests that as conditions worsen, conservative Catholics may look once again to alliances with the powerful. Radicals find their own

---

[27] "Black and White in Color: *Cardinismo* and the Search for a Peasant Ideology."
[28] Lernoux, *People of God*; Caldeira, *A política dos outros*.

suspicion of bourgeois politics all too readily confirmed when the give-and-take of liberal democratic arrangements produces only deepening despair.

Whatever the case, there is growing tension and ambiguity. It is rare to find an ecclesiastical hierarchy that is willing to empower ordinary people in politics and religion, and to stand with them. Such a position seems imprudent to church elites and runs counter to deeply held principles that make maintenance of the institutional church a primary and critical concern. As we enter the 1990s, it seems clear that the pendulum has swung against popular groups and their promoters. Social, economic, and political transformations have weakened and split their base, making it harder to recruit members to activist roles.

Still, it may be that a sufficient foundation has been laid to allow change to go forward, albeit in what are likely to be nonreligious channels. The long-term cultural and political impact of religious change will probably find effect less within explicitly religious structures than in the diffusion of new leaders and norms of accountability to other areas of social life. Putting the matter in this way does not mean that religion disappears from the equation, but rather that we need to see its place and presence in different terms.

Without losing sight of the continuities that religious structures and identities provide, we can see how the emergence of popular voices, no matter how vulnerable at first, shifts the focus away from religion as such (a bounded set of rules and structures) to the workings of faith and action in day-to-day life. Citing Bonhoeffer, Gustavo Gutiérrez has repeatedly stated that the true challenge facing Catholics in Latin America today is to mount a critique of organized religion in the name of faith.[29] In this light, liberation theologians argue consistently that seeing things from the vantage point of the poor is not just a matter of rereading history, but also a commitment to remaking it; not only an explanation of injustice, but also a conversion to struggle for something better. Base communities themselves are not the heart of the matter. The central issue is not one organizational form or another, but rather a transformation of culture that makes any organization likely to be taken up and sustained. The real challenge, as I noted at the very beginning of this book, lies not in opting for the poor or becoming a voice for the voiceless. It is, rather, to empower popular voices, to trust them, and to set them to work.

If the future of popular voices is uncertain when not just simply bleak, and the evidence is at best ambiguous, one might well ask why anyone should bother to study popular groups and listen to popular voices in the first place. The answer is complex and bears both on values and on a judgment about the kind of research that is most likely to yield reliable knowledge about cultural, social, and political change.

[29] *The Power of the Poor*, chaps. 7 and 8.

## Knowing about the Future

We do not study the poor because they are likely winners of short-term conflicts. On the whole they are not. But exclusive focus on such immediate outcomes yields an impoverished and misleading vision of change. By centering attention on struggles that are joined within existing parameters, this point of view makes it hard to see developing challenges to the entire system, or to grasp how individual changes and small-scale solidarities can gradually become charters for collective resistance to authority and to its claims. In Scott's words,

> Everyday resistance makes no headlines. Just as millions of anthozoan polyps create, willy-nilly, a coral reef, so do thousands upon thousands of individual acts of insubordination and evasion create a political or economic barrier reef of their own. There is rarely any dramatic confrontation, any moment that is particularly newsworthy. And whenever, to pursue the simile, the ship of state runs aground on such a reef, attention is typically directed to the shipwreck itself, and not to the vast aggregation of petty acts that made it possible.[30]

A desire to understand the cultural and social construction of bases for resistance does not exhaust the reasons for studying the poor. We study the poor and record their voices also to redress a balance. History, they say, is written by victors, and most people are not victors on a large scale. If we are to grasp how human beings grow and change, attention has to reach beyond the records of triumph and domination recorded by elites and preserved in institutions, to incorporate the ideas and experiences of most of the world. To cite Walt Whitman:

> Have you heard that it was good to gain the day?
> I also say it is good to fail, battles are lost in the same spirit in which they are
> won . . .
> Vivas to those who have fail'd!
> And to those whose war-vessels sank in the sea!
> And to those themselves who sank in the sea!
> And to all generals that lost engagements, and all overcome heroes!
> And the numberless unknown heroes equal to the greatest heroes known![31]

---

[30] *Weapons*, p. 36. Cf. the words of one Filipino peasant organizer quoted by Reynaldo Ileto; "No insurrection fails. Each one is a step in the right direction" (*Pasyón*, p. 7). The judgment cannot be lightly dismissed, nor should it be incorporated into a neo-Marxist framework of inevitable revolution. To say that no insurrection fails means that each act of resistance contributes to nurturing an independent popular consciousness, thus making continued effort possible.

[31] "Song of Myself," quoted in *Leaves of Grass*, p. 37.

A further reason to study popular groups and listen to popular voices comes from the force with which they remind us of the energizing and creative power that moral argument can have. The point is too often forgotten in the social sciences, whose characteristic understanding of the world remains steeped in liberal and Marxist assumptions that make values and belief subordinate to interest narrowly defined. But as we have seen, the drive to construct meaningful vocabularies of moral concern and to build them into community and social life has an autonomous logic. As Habermas puts it, "We must finally relearn what we forgot during the fascist period . . . that humanitarian and moral arguments are not merely deceitful ideology. Rather, they can and must become central social forces."[32]

What do we need to know in order to achieve reliable and enduring knowledge about popular voices? How can we best grasp the impact of evolving patterns of popular religious experience and understanding on cultural and political change on a large scale? What is the next step in research? Agendas for future work can be put together in several ways. The easiest is to compile lists of empirical questions. In all probability, we will never have complete coverage of contemporary, let alone historical, aspects of religion, culture, and politics: leaders, symbols ideologies, shrines, movements, parties, and the like.

This building-block approach is likely to disappoint. The problem is not simply to get "all the facts." We must first establish what the relevant facts are, and this task calls for theoretical clarification, not data collection. In the study of religion, culture, and politics, the very definition of the field, and hence of key questions for research, is very much up for grabs. Little is truly settled. Therefore, construction of an agenda for future work must start with reflection on the proper lines of research. What are the kinds of acts we need to study? Which questions can and should be asked? Reflection on the arguments and evidence of this book make a few points stand out.

Research must focus on the sources of transformation in religious ideas. This involves not only formal theological or doctrinal debates but also the kinds of religious innovation that occur as ideas are taken up and transformed on the peripheries of power. I have argued in this book for a methodological and theoretical approach to the study of religious change that combines attention to institutions and popular groups, ideas and structures, values and contexts. Much of the creative rethinking of the Christian faith now occurring in Latin America is happening not in seminaries and universities but among the poor and at the grass roots. We need to specify how new ideas fit the needs and practices of emergent or already existing social formations. What sorts of structural changes make some kinds of ideas more or less appealing, more or less meaningful? The spread of democratic forms in grass-roots Catholicism

[32] Habermas citing Marcuse in "Psychic Thermidor and the Rebirth of Rebellious Subjectivity," p. 76.

today, the meaningfulness of ideas about sacrifice and suffering, and the diffusion of new concepts of leadership and activism are all cases in point.

Competing attempts to shape religion must be specified and each associated with an identifiable power base and organizational net. It makes a substantial difference how groups are started, who defines their agenda, and what sort of structures mediate action. This point is all the more important given the fact that for most popular groups, the experience of change is not only one of movement on a continuum from one kind of action or group to another, but also of competition and choice between alternatives. Finally, attention to change must not obscure continuities. These rest in part on the staying power of institutions but, in a more basic sense, arise from the conjunction of everyday needs with the structure of opportunity.

Much of the task of understanding religion, culture, and politics is to identify the structural conditions that make religion salient as a vehicle for the pursuit or expression of meaning and interest. At a minimum, these include the decay of some older system, the delegitimation of its characteristic symbols and mediations (leaders, organizations, rituals), and a further process that changes the routines of ordinary people to bring them together in new ways, make them more available for organization, and enhance popular imagery and solidarity in the process.

The key point for analysis is to avoid reifying a particular unit or orientation, freezing it in time and treating it as once and forever the same. The orientation of a given class, group or institution—and even the definition of "religion"—cannot be assumed to hold now or in the future as in the past, here as there. Instead, research must address the formation of packages, of clusters of elements, and of legitimations. Future studies could then specify how such configurations are put together, by whom, and under what circumstances. How are packages related to one another in a given social order, what makes for success or failure, why the appeal to specific groups? The result of all this would be a comparative historical sociology concerned less with specific outcomes or even tendencies as with the clustering of ideas, leadership, followers, resources, and opportunities that makes any of these emerge and gives them enduring impact.

Normal times are not hospitable to dramatic innovation; movements of religious revitalization find a readier hearing in transformative moments, when crisis sharpens the edge of change and raises the stakes. As new visions emerge and established arrangements are challenged and undermined, the contours of change become clearer. But this sharper vision is not a product only of improved concepts or research tools. Awareness of change is also thrust upon us by those who are caught up in its midst and whose thoughts and actions, projected time after time on a larger scale, give it life and make it go. The men and women who constitute Latin America's popular sectors resist being confined to the status of objects available for others to study and evaluate. They are active, creative subjects, and it is through their efforts that the familiar is "brought to consciousness as something in need of being ascertained."[33] Listening to their voices and trying to make sense of the world as it appears to them gives us a clear view of how much the landscape of life has changed, where new horizons lie, and how things look to ordinary men and women as, with some hope and lots of faith, they make their way to an uncertain future.

## Envoi

In the prelude to *Middlemarch*, George Eliot reflects on the example of Teresa of Avila, and asks how many potential Saint Teresas lead ordinary and unnoticed lives. Lacking opportunity or an appropriate medium, their vision and energies find only halting expression in daily life. In the concluding paragraph of the book, Eliot returns to this theme and notes that although the heroine, Miss Brooke, left no great name or monument behind,

> the effect of her being on those around her was incalculably diffusive: for the growing good of the world is partly dependent on unhistoric acts; and that things are not so ill with you and me as they might have been, is half owing to the number who lived faithfully a hidden life, and rest in unvisited tombs.[34]

So it is with the people we have listened to in these pages. The world is indeed not so ill with us as it might have been in no small measure because these men and women have shown us how to challenge and change immemorial patterns of silence and subordination. Their voices affirm the power of human creativity and the continuing value of solidarity and common effort. Anyone can be a saint, or so they tell you now in the barrios and villages of Latin America. With a little empathy and some imagination, we can begin to see the potential and as yet unnoticed saints all around us.

[33] Habermas, *The Theory of Communicative Action* 2:400. Habermas goes on to comment that sometimes "it takes an earthquake to make us aware that we had regarded the ground on which we stand every day as unshakeable" (ibid.).

[34] *Middlemarch*, p. 896.

# BIBLIOGRAPHY

## DOCUMENTS

*Annuario Pontifico*. Vatican: Libería Editrice Vaticana, selected years.
*Catholic Almanac*. Huntington, Ind.: Our Sunday Visitor, selected years.
*Identidad cristiana en la acción por la justicia: Una version alternativa*. Bogotá: n.p., 1977.
*Liberation Theology and the Vatican Document*. Vol. 1, *The Vatican Document and Some Commentaries*. Quezon City: Claretian Publications, 1988.
*Liberation Theology and the Vatican Document*. Vol. 2, *A Philippine Perspective*. Quezon City: Claretian Publications, 1986.
"Presentación de la experiencia de las comunidades cristianas populares del Barrio Meléndez (Cali)." Mimeographed, n.d.
"Sacramental." *The Catholic Encyclopedia Dictionary*. New York: Gilmary Society, 1929.
*SAL Un compromiso sacerdotal en la lucha de clases, documentos, 1972–1978*. Bogotá: SAL, 1978.
*Statistical Abstract of Latin America*. Los Angeles: University of California, Latin American Center, selected years.
*Statistical Yearbook of the Church*. Vatican: Tipografria Poliglota Vaticano, 1981, 1983.

## BOOKS AND ARTICLES

Abel, Christopher. *Política, iglesia, y partidos en Colombia*. Bogotá: Universidad Nacional de Colombia, 1987.
Abouhammad, Jeannette. *Los hombres de Venezuela. Sus necesidades, sus aspiraciones*. Caracas: Universidad Central de Venezuela, 1970.
Adams, James. "CEBs as Groups: The Implications of Social Influence Theory." Seminar paper, Ann Arbor, Mich., 1989.
Adams, Richard N. *The Second Sowing: Power and Secondary Development in Latin America*. San Francisco: Chandler Publishing Co., 1967.
Adriance, Madeleine. *Opting for the Poor: The Brazilian Church in Transition*. New York: Sheed and Ward, 1986.
Agulhon, Maurice. *The Republic in the Village*. New York: Cambridge University Press, 1982.
Ajami, Fouad. *The Vanished Imam: Musa Al Sadr and the Shia of Lebanon*. Ithaca: Cornell University Press, 1986.
Alape, Arturo. *El bogatazo: Memorias del olvido*. Bogotá: Fundación Universidad Central, 1983.
———. *La paz, la violencia: Testigos de excepción. documentos*. Bogotá: Planeta Colombiana Editorial, S.A., 1985.
Almond, Gabriel. "The Study of Political Culture." In Gabriel Almond, *A Discipline*

*Divided: Schools and Sects in Political Science*, 138–56. Beverly Hills: SAGE Publications, 1989.

Americas Watch. *The Central Americanization of Colombia? Human Rights and the Peace Process*. New York: Americas Watch Committee, 1986.

Amnesty International. *Colombia Briefing*. New York: Amnesty International Publications, 1988.

Annis, Sheldon. *God and Production in a Guatemalan Town*. Austin: University of Texas Press, 1987.

Annis, Sheldon, and Peter Hakim, eds. *Direct to the Poor: Grass Roots Development in Latin America*. Boulder, Colo.: Lynne Rienner Publishers, 1987.

Antillo Armas, Sergio, Frank Bracho, and Sara Aniyar. *El venezolano ante la crisis*. Caracas: Ediciones Aman, 1988.

Antoncich, Ricardo. *Christians in the Face of Injustice: A Latin American Reading of Catholic Social Teaching*. Maryknoll, N.Y.: Orbis Books, 1987.

Arjomand, Said A. "Iran's Islamic Revolution in Comparative Perspective." *World Politics* 38, no. 3 (April 1986): 383–414.

———. "Religion, Political Order, and Societal Change: With Special Reference to Shi'ite Islam." *Current Perspectives in Social Theory* 6 (1985): 1–15.

———. *The Shadow of God and the Hidden Imam Religion, Political Order, and Societal Change in Shi'ite Iran from the Beginning to 1890*. Chicago: University of Chicago Press, 1984.

———. "Social Change and Movements of Revitalization in Contemporary Islam." In James Beckford, ed., *Rapid Social Change and New Religious Movements*, 88–127. Beverly Hills: SAGE Publications, 1986.

———. *The Turban for the Crown*. New York: Oxford University Press, 1988.

Asch, Susan. *L'Eglise du Prophète Kimbangu de ses origines a son role actuel au Zaire*. Paris: Karthala, 1983.

Assmann, Hugo. *Theology for a Nomad Church*. Maryknoll, N.Y.: Orbis Books, 1976.

Azevedo, Marcelo de. *Basic Ecclesial Communities in Brazil: The Challenge of a New Way of Being Church*. Washington, D.C.: Georgetown University Press, 1987.

Badone, Ellen, ed. *Religious Orthodoxy and Popular Faith in European Society*. Princeton: Princeton University Press, 1990.

Bagley, Bruce M. *The State and the Peasantry in Contemporary Colombia*. Latin American Issues no. 6. Meadville, Pa.: Allegheny College, 1989.

Bak, Janos M., and Gerhard Benecke, eds. *Religion and Rural Revolt*. Manchester: Manchester University Press, 1984.

Baloyra, Enrique. "Reactionary Despotism in Central America." *Journal of Latin American Studies* 15, no. 2 (November 1983): 295–319.

Barnes, Samuel H. *Politics and Culture*. Ann Arbor, Mich.: Center for Political Studies, Institute of Social Research, 1988.

Bastien, Jean Pierre. "Protestantismos latinoamericanos entre la resistencía y la sumisión, 1961–1983." *Cristianismo y sociedad* 12, no. 82 (1984): 49–68.

Becker, Marjorie. "Black and White in Color: *Cardinismo* and the Search for a Campesino Ideology." *Comparative Studies in Society and History* 29, no. 3 (July 1987): 453–65.

Beinart, William, and Colin Bundy. *Hidden Struggles in Rural South Africa: Politics and Popular Movements in the Transkei and Eastern Cape, 1890–1930*. Berkeley: University of California Press, 1987.

Bellah, Robert. *Beyond Belief: Essays on Religion in a Post-Traditional World*. New York: Harper and Row, 1970.

Bellah, Robert N., Richard Madsen, William Sullivan, Ann Swidler, and Steven M. Tipton. *Habits of the Heart: Individualism and Commitment in American Life*. Berkeley: University of California Press, 1985.

Berger, Peter L., and Thomas Luckmann. *The Social Construction of Reality*. Garden City, N.Y.: Anchor Books, 1967.

Bergquist, Charles. *Coffee and Conflict in Colombia, 1886–1910*. Durham, N.C.: Duke University Press, 1978.

———. *Labor in Latin America: Comparative Essays on Chile, Argentina, Venezuela, and Colombia*. Stanford, Calif.: Stanford University Press, 1986.

Bernstein, R., ed. *Habermas and Modernity*. Cambridge: MIT Press, 1985.

Berry, Albert. "Rural Poverty in Twentieth Century Colombia." *Journal of Latin American Studies and World Affairs* 20, no. 4 (November 1978): 355–76.

Berry, Albert, Ronald Hellman, and Mauricio Solaun, eds. *The Politics of Compromise: Coalition Government in Colombia*. New Brunswick, N.J.: Transaction Books, 1980.

Berryman, Phillip. *Liberation Theology*. New York: Pantheon, 1987.

———. *Our Unfinished Business*. New York: Pantheon, 1989.

———. *Religious Roots of Rebellion: Christians in the Central American Revolutions*. Maryknoll, N.Y.: Orbis Books, 1984.

———. "What Happened at Puebla." In Daniel H. Levine, ed., *Churches and Politics in Latin America*, 55–86. Beverly Hills: SAGE Publications, 1980.

Boff, Leonardo. *Church: Charism and Power. Liberation Theology and the Institutional Church*. Minneapolis, Minn.: Winston Press, 1986.

———. *Ecclesiogenesis*. Maryknoll, N.Y.: Orbis Books, 1986.

———. *Jesus Christ Liberator*. Maryknoll, N.Y.: Orbis Books, 1978.

———. *When Theology Listens to the Poor*. San Francisco: Harper and Row, 1984.

Boff, Leonardo, and Clodovis Boff. *Liberation Theology: From Confrontation to Dialogue*. Maryknoll, N.Y.: Orbis Books, 1985.

Bouvier, Virginia. *Alliance or Compliance: Implications of the Chilean Experience for the Catholic Church in Latin America*. Syracuse: Syracuse University, Maxwell School of Citizenship and Public Affairs, Foreign and Comparative Studies, 1983.

Branch, Taylor. *Parting the Waters: America in the King Years, 1954–1963*. New York: Simon and Schuster, 1989.

Braun, Herbert. *The Assassination of Gaitán: Public Life and Urban Violence in Colombia*. Madison: University of Wisconsin Press, 1985.

Brett, Donna Witson, and Edward T. Brett. *Murdered in Cental America: The Stories of Eleven U.S. Missionaries*. Maryknoll, N.Y.: Orbis Books, 1988.

Bricker, Victoria. *The Indian Christ, The Indian King*. Austin: University of Texas Press, 1986.

Brockman, James. *The Word Remains: A Life of Oscar Romero*. Maryknoll, N.Y.: Orbis Books, 1983.

Broderick, William J. *Camilo Torres*. Garden City, N.Y.: Doubleday, 1975.

Brown, Diana DeGroat. *Umbanda: Religion and Politics in Urban Brazil*. Ann Arbor, Mich.: UMI Research Press, 1986.

Bruneau, Thomas C. "Church and Politics in Brazil: The Genesis of Change." *Journal of Latin American Studies* 17, no. 2 (1985): 271–93.

———. *The Church in Brazil: The Politics of Religion*. Austin: University of Texas Press, 1982.

Bruneau, Thomas, and William E. Hewitt. "Patterns of Church Influence in Brazil's Political Transition." *Comparative Politics* 22, no. 1 (October 1989): 39–61.

Burdick, John. "Gossip and Secrecy: Women's Articulation of Domestic Conflict in Three Religions of Urban Brazil." *Sociological Analysis* 50, no. 2 (1990): 153–70.

———. *Looking For God in Brazil: The Progressive Catholic Church in Urban Brazil's Religious Arena*. Ph.D. diss., City University of New York, 1990.

Busquets, Carmen Elena. *La ruta de Don Miguel*. Caracas: Universidad Católica Andres Bello, 1988.

Bussmann, Claus. *Who Do You Say? Jesus Christ in Latin American Theology*. Maryknoll, N.Y.: Orbis Books, 1985.

Caballero Calderón, Eduardo. *El Cristo de espaldas*. Medellín: Editorial Bedout, n.d.

———. *Siervo sin tierra*. Medellín: Editorial Bedout, n.d.

Cáceres, Jorge. "Political Radicalization and Popular Pastoral Practice in El Salvador, 1969–1985." In Scott Mainwaring and Alexander Wilde, eds., *The Progressive Church in Latin America*, 103–8. Notre Dame, Ind.: University of Notre Dame Press, 1989.

Caicedo, Daniel. *Viento seco*. Bogotá: Fundación para la Investigación y la Cultura FICA, 1982.

Caldeira, Teresa. "Electoral Struggles in a Neighborhood on the Periphery of São Paulo." *Politics and Society* 15, no. 1 (1986–87): 43–66.

———. *A política dos outros: O cotidiano dos moradores de periferia e o que pensam do poder e dos poderosos*. São Paulo: Brasilense, 1984.

Calhoun, Craig. *The Question of Class Struggle: Social Foundations of Popular Radicalism during the Industrial Revolution*. Chicago: University of Chicago Press, 1982.

———. "The Radicalism of Tradition: Community Strength or Venerable Disguise and Borrowed Language." *American Journal of Sociology* 88, no. 5 (1983): 886–914.

Canak, William L., ed. *Lost Promises, Debt, Austerity, and Development in Latin America*. Boulder, Colo.: Westview Press, 1989.

Cardenal, Ernesto. *Antología*. San Jose, Costa Rica: Educa, 1975.

———. *Psalms*. New York: Crossroad Publishing, 1981.

Cardona, Ramón G. *Las migraciones internas*. Bogotá: ASCOFAME, 1972.

Carillo Bedoya, J. *Los paros cívicos en Colombia*. Bogotá: Editorial la Oveja Negra, 1981.

Carney, James G. *To Be a Christian Is to Be a Revolutionary*. San Francisco: Harper and Row, 1987.

Carrigan, Anna. *Salvador Witness: The Life and Calling of Jean Donovan*. New York: Ballantine Books, 1985.

Castells, Manuel. *The City and the Grassroots: A Cross-Cultural Theory of Urban Social Movements*. Berkeley: University of California Press, 1983.

CELAM. *Aportes de las conferencias episcopales: Libro auxiliar 3*. Bogotá: CELAM, 1978.

Centro Gumilla. "Proyecto campesino." Barquisimeto: Centro Gumilla, 1979.

———. "Rescatando campesinos caficultores." Barquisimeto: Centro Gumilla, 1980.

CESAP. *Formación y organización popular: Conceptos educativos y elementos metodológicos del trabajo de CESAP*. Caracas: CESAP, 1981.

———. *Un centro al servicio de la acción popular*. Caracas: CESAP, 1981.

———. *Nosotros y Puebla I: El designo de Dios en la realidad de America Latina*. Caracas: CESAP, 1980.

———. *Nosotros y Puebla II: Los obispos y la realidad*. Caracas: CESAP, 1981.

Childers, Vernon. *Human Resources Development: Venezuela*. Bloomington, Ind.: International Development Research Center, 1974.

Christian, William. *Local Religion in Sixteenth Century Spain*. Princeton: Princeton University Press, 1981.

Circulo de Análisis Social. "Análisis de coyuntura politica ecclesial." Santiago, Chile: May–June 1989, mimeographed.

———. *El episcopado chileno en crisis: Documentos y análisis*. Santiago, Chile: 1989, mimeographed.

CLAR. *La vida Religiosa en America Latina: Respuestas y compromisos*. Bogotá: CLAR, 1969.

Clawson, David L. "Religious Allegiance and Economic Development in Rural Latin America." *Journal of Inter-American Studies and World Affairs* 26, no. 4 (November 1984): 499–524.

Cleary, Edward. *Crisis and Change: The Church in Latin America Today*. Maryknoll, N.Y.: Orbis Books, 1985.

———, ed. *Born of the Poor: The Latin American Church since Medellín*. Notre Dame, Ind.: University of Notre Dame Press, 1990.

———, ed. *Paths from Puebla: Significant Documents of the Latin American Bishops Since 1979*. Washington, D.C.: United States Catholic Conference, 1988.

Cohen, Charles Lloyd. *God's Caress: The Psychology of Puritan Religious Experience*. New York: Oxford University Press, 1980.

Coleman, John. "The Situation for Modern Faith." *Theological Studies* 39, no. 4 (December 1978): 601–32.

Colemenares Díaz, Luis. *La espada y el incensario: La iglesia bajo Pérez Jiménez*. Caracas: 1961.

Collier, David, ed. *The New Authoritarianism in Latin America*. Princeton: Princeton University Press, 1979.

Comaroff, Jean. *Body of Power, Spirit of Resistance: The Culture and History of a South African People*. Chicago: University of Chicago Press, 1985.

Comaroff, Jean, and John Comaroff. "Christianity and Colonialism in South Africa." *American Ethnologist* 13, no. 1 (February 1986): 1–22.

Comblin, Joseph. *The Church and the National Security State*. Maryknoll, N.Y.: Orbis Books, 1979.

Conferencia Episcopal de Colombia. *Agentes de comunión y participación: Diáconos permanentes y ministros laicos.* Bogotá: SPEC, 1979.

———. "Aporte la conferencia episcopal de Colombia." In CELAM, *Aportes de las conferencias episcopales: libro Auxiliar 3.* Bogotá: CELAM, 1978.

———. *Aproximación a la realidad colombiana.* Bogotá: SPEC, 1981.

———. "Las comunidades eclesiales de base y la parroquia." In *Revista de misiones.* Bogotá: May-June 1981.

———. *Identidad cristiana en la acción por la justicia.* Bogotá: SPEC, 1976.

———. *La iglesia ante el cambio.* Bogotá: SPEC, 1969.

———. "Lección no. 9: La pastoral social en Colombia." Bogotá: SPEC, 1982.

———. "Lección no. 10: Compromiso político del cristiano." Bogotá: SPEC, 1982.

———. *Mensaje pastoral.* Bogotá: SPEC, 36 Asamblea Plenaria, 1981.

———. *Vivamos la iglesia comunidad eclesial.* Bogotá: SPEC, 1981.

Conferencia Episcopal Venezolana. *Cartas, instrucciones y mensajes, 1883–1977.* Vol. 1–A. Caracas: Universidad Católica "Andres Bello," Centro Venezolano de Historia Ecclesiástica, 1978.

———. "Declaración" (on thirty years of democracy). *SIC*, no. 502 (February 1988): 86–91.

Conver-Ferve. *Los religiosos en Venezuela: Informe descriptivo de respuestas a la encuesta a los religiosos y religiosas de Venezuela.* Caracas: Secretariado Conjunto de Religiosos y Religiosas de Venezuela, Conver-Ferve, 1975.

Cornelius, Wayne. *Politics and the Migrant Poor in Mexico City.* Stanford, Calif.: Stanford University Press, 1975.

Cortes Tossal, Román. "Testimonio y mensajes del P. Román Cortes Tossal." *Comunidad Diocesana* (Diocesis de Facatativá) 14, no. 15, 1982.

Davis, Natalie. "Some Tasks and Themes in the Study of Popular Religion." In Charles Trinkaus and Heiko Oberman, eds., *The Pursuit of Holiness in Late Medieval and Renaissance Religion*, 307–36. Leiden: E. J. Brill, 1974.

Dealy, Glen. "Prologomena on the Spanish American Political Tradition." *Hispanic American Historical Review* 48 (February 1968): 37–58.

De Armas, Frank, and Manuel Rodríguez Mena. *La crisis: Responsabilidades y salidas.* Caracas: Expediente Editorial, 1986.

Deas, Malcolm. "Colombia, Ecuador, and Venezuela, c. 1880–1930." In Leslie Bethell, ed., *The Cambridge History of Latin America*, Vol. 5, *c. 1870–1930*, 641–84. Cambridge: Cambridge University Press, 1980.

Della Cava, Ralph. "Brazilian Messianism and National Institutions: A Reappraisal of Canudos and Joaseiro." *Hispanic American Historical Review* 48 (1968): 402–30.

———. "Catholicism and Society in Twentieth Century Brazil." *Latin American Research Review* 11, no. 2 (1976): 7–50.

———. *Miracle at Joaseiro.* New York: Columbia University Press, 1970.

———. "The 'People's Church,' The Vatican, and *Abertura*." In Alfred Stepan, ed., *Democratizing Brazil*, 143–67. New York: Oxford University Press, 1989.

Delpar, Helen. *Red against Blue: The Liberal Party in Colombian Politics, 1863–1899.* University, Ala.: University of Alabama Press, 1981.

Demerath, N. J. "Religious Capital and Capital Religions: Cross-Cultural and Non-

Legal Factors in the Separation of Church and State." *Daedalus* 12, no. 3 (Summer 1991): 21–40.

Desan, Suzanne. "Redefining Revolutionary Liberty: The Rhetoric of Religious Revival during the French Revolution." *Journal of Modern History* 60 (1988): 1–27.

de Tocqueville, Alexis. *Democracy in America*. 2 vols. New York: Schocken Books, 1961.

Dix, Robert. *The Politics of Colombia*. New York: Praeger Publishers, 1987.

Dodson, Michael. "The Christian Left in Latin American Politics." In Daniel H. Levine, ed., *Churches and Politics in Latin America*, 111–34. Beverly Hills: SAGE Publications, 1980.

————. "Liberation Theology and Christian Radicalism in Contemporary Latin America." *Journal of Latin American Studies* 11, no. 1 (May 1979): 203–22.

Dodson, Michael, and Laura O'Shaughnessy. *Nicaragua's Other Revolution: Religious Faith and Political Struggle*. Chapel Hill: University of North Carolina Press, 1990.

Doimo, Ana Maria. "Social Movements and the Catholic Church in Vitória, Brazil." In Scott Mainwaring and Alexander Wilde, eds., *The Progressive Church in Latin America*, 193–233. Notre Dame, Ind.: University of Notre Dame Press.

Drogus, Carol. "Reconstructing the Feminine: Women in São Paulo's CEBs." *Archives de sciences sociales des religions* 71 (July–September 1990): 63–74.

Dulles, Avery. *Models of the Church*. New York: Doubleday, 1974.

Dunkerly, James. *Power in the Isthmus: A Political History of Modern Central America*. London: Verso, 1990.

Dussell, Enrique. *Ethics and Community*. Maryknoll, N.Y.: Orbis Books, 1988.

————. *Ethics and the Theology of Liberation*. Maryknoll, N.Y.: Orbis Books, 1978.

————. *History and Theology of Liberation: A Latin American Perspective*. Maryknoll, N.Y.: Orbis Books, 1971.

Eagleson, John, and Phillip Scharper, eds. *Puebla and Beyond*. Maryknoll, N.Y.: Orbis Books, 1979.

Eckstein, Harry. *A Theory of Stable Democracy*. Princeton: Center of International Studies, 1961.

Eckstein, Susan. *The Poverty of Revolution: The State and the Urban Poor in Mexico*. Princeton: Princeton University Press, 1978.

————. "Power and Popular Protest in Latin America." In Susan Eckstein, ed., *Power and Popular Protest: Latin American Social Movements*, 1–60. Berkeley: University of California Press, 1989.

————, ed. *Power and Popular Protest: Latin American Social Movements*. Berkeley: University of California Press, 1989.

Eliot, George. *Middlemarch: A Study of Provincial Life*. New York: Penguin, 1983.

————. *The Mill on the Floss*. New York: New American Library, 1981.

Ellner, Steve. *Generational Identification and Political Fragmentation in Venezuelan Politics in the Late 1960s*. Latin American Issues no. 7. Meadville, Pa.: Allegheny College, 1989.

Estrada, Nora. "Vivencias campesinas." *Revista javieriana* 451 (January–February 1979): 8–12.

Facatativá, Diocese of. "Aspectos de la realidad local y diocesana observados por los promotores y comunidades eclesiales de base para confrontar posteriormente con las realidades sentidas para las mismas comunidades." Facatativá, 1978.

―――. *Diócesis de Facatativá, 1962–1982: 20 años de lucha y esperanza*. Factativá, 1982.

―――. "Encuentro campesino." Special issue of *Comunidad diocesana* (Facatativá), no. 91 (September 1978).

―――. "Experiencia de comunidades eclesiales de base y ministerios laicales en la diócesis de Facatativá, Colombia." *Comunidad diocesana*, no. 91 (September 1978).

―――. *Premonografía*. Facatativá: 1982.

Faroohar, Manzar. *The Catholic Church and Social Change in Nicaragua*. Albany, N.Y.: SUNY Press, 1989.

Fields, Karen. *Revival and Rebellion in Colonial Central Africa*. Princeton: Princeton University Press, 1985.

Fischer, Michael M. J. *Iran: From Religious Dispute to Revolution*. Cambridge: Harvard University Press, 1980.

Forman, Shepard. *The Brazilian Peasantry*. New York: Columbia University Press, 1975.

Freire, Paulo. *Education for a Critical Consciousness*. New York: Seabury Press, 1974.

―――. *Pedagogy of the Oppressed*. New York: Seabury Press, 1968.

Friedlander, Judith. *Being Indian in Hueyapán: A Study of Forced Identity in Contemporary Mexico*. New York: St. Martin's Press, 1975.

Galilea, S. *The Way of Living Faith: A Spirituality of Liberation*. San Francisco: Harper and Row Publishers, 1988.

García Márquez, Gabriel. *La mala hora*. Buenos Aires: Editorial Sudamericana, 1969.

Garretón, Manuel Antonio. "Popular Mobilization and the Military Regime in Chile: Complexities of the Invisible Transition." In Susan Eckstein, ed., *Power and Popular Protest: Latin American Social Movements*, 259–77. Berkeley: University of California Press, 1989.

Gaventa, John. *Power and Powerlessness: Quiescence and Rebellion in an Appalachian Valley*. Urbana: University of Illinois Press, 1980.

Geertz, Clifford. "The Impact of the Concept of Culture on the Concept of Man." In Clifford Geertz, ed., *The Interpretation of Cultures*, 33–54. New York: Basic Books, 1973.

―――. *Islam Observed: Religious Development in Morocco and Indonesia*. Chicago: University of Chicago Press, 1968.

―――. *Negara: The Theatre State in Nineteenth Century Bali*. Princeton, N.J.: Princeton University Press, 1980.

―――. "Religion as a Cultural System." In M. Banton, ed., *Anthropological Approaches to the Study of Religion*, 1–46. London: Tavistock, 1968.

―――. "Thick Description: Toward an Interpretive Theory of Culture." In Clifford Geertz, *The Interpretation of Cultures*, 3–22. New York: Basic Books, 1973.

Gellner, E. *Muslim Society*. Cambridge: Cambridge University Press, 1981.

Gibellini, Rosino. *The Liberation Theology Debate*. Maryknoll, N.Y.: Orbis Books, 1988.

Giddens, Anthony. "Reason without Revolution? Habermas' *Theorie des kommuni-kativen handelns.*" In Richard Bernstein, ed., *Habermas and Modernity*, 95–121. Cambridge: MIT Press, 1985.

Gilbert, Alan, and Peter M. Ward. *Housing, the State, and the Poor: Policy and Practice in Three Latin American Cities.* New York: Cambridge University Press, 1985.

Gilfeather, Katherine. "Coming of Age in a Latin Church." In C. B. John and Ellen Loro Webster, eds., *The Church and Women in the Third World*, 58–73. Philadelphia: Webster Press, 1985,

————. "Women Religious, the Poor, and the Institutional Church in Chile." In Daniel H. Levine, ed., *Churches and Politics in Latin America*, 198–224. Beverly Hills: SAGE Publications, 1980.

Gilsenan, Michael. *Recognizing Islam: Religion and Society in the Modern Arab World.* New York: Pantheon, 1982.

Ginzburg, Carlo. *The Cheese and the Worms: The Cosmos of a Sixteenth Century Miller.* New York: Penguin, 1980.

Giraldo, Jaime. *Paros y movimientos cívicos en Colombia.* Controversia 128. Bogotá: CINEP, 1985.

Glock, Charles Y., and Philip E. Hammond, *Beyond the Classics: Essays in the Scientific Study of Religion.* New York: Harper and Row, 1973.

Goldrich, Daniel. "Political Organization and the Politicization of the Poblador." *Comparative Political Studies* 3, no. 2 (July 1970): 176–202.

Gómez Jiménez, Alcides, and Luz Marina Díaz Mesa. *La moderna esclavitud los indocumentados en Venezuela.* Bogotá: Editorial la Oveja Negra, 1983.

Goodman, Paul. *Growing Up Absurd.* New York: Random House, 1962.

Gott, Richard. *Guerrillas in Latin America.* Garden City, N.Y.: Doubleday and Co., Anchor Books, 1972.

Gramsci, Antonio. *The Modern Prince and Other Writings.* New York: International Publishers, 1957.

————. *Selections from the Prison Notebooks.* New York: International Publishers, 1971.

Greschat, Martin. "The Relationship of the Protestant Church to the Governments of the Two Germanies." MS., 1989.

Grindle, Merilee S. *State and Countryside: Development Policy and Agrarian Politics in Latin America.* Baltimore: Johns Hopkins University, 1986.

Gutiérrez, Gustavo. *The Power of the Poor in History.* Maryknoll, N.Y.: Orbis Books, 1983.

————. *Teología de la Liberación.* Lima: CEP, 1971.

————. *A Theology of Liberation.* Maryknoll, N.Y.: Orbis Books, 1973.

————. *We Drink from Our Own Wells.* Maryknoll, N.Y.: Orbis Books, 1985.

Habermas, Jurgen. "Psychic Thermidor and the Rebirth of Rebellious Subjectivity." In Richard Bernstein, ed., *Habermas and Modernity*, 67–77. Cambridge: MIT Press, 1985.

————. "A Reply to My Critics." In John B. Thomas and David Held, eds., *Habermas: Critical Debates*, 219–83. Cambridge: MIT Press, 1982.

————. *The Theory of Communicative Action.* Vol. 1, *Reason and the Rationalization of Society;* vol. 2, *Lifeworld and System: A Critique of Functionalist Reason.* Boston: Beacon Press, 1984, 1985.

Haight, Roger. *An Alternative Vision.* New York: Paulist Press, 1985.

Hansen, Eric. *The Catholic Church in World Politics.* Princeton: Princeton University Press, 1986.

Harding, Susan. "Convicted by the Holy Spirit." *American Ethnologist* 14, no. 1 (February 1987): 167–81.

Harrison, Lawrence. *Underdevelopment Is a State of Mind.* Lanham, Md.: University Press of America, 1985.

Hartlyn, Jonathan. *The Politics of Coalition Rule in Colombia.* Cambridge: Cambridge University Press, 1988.

Hatch, Nathan. *The Democratization of American Christianity.* New Haven: Yale University Press, 1989.

Hebblethwaite, Peter. *John XXIII: Pope of the Council.* London: Geoffrey Chapman, 1984.

———. *The Year of Three Popes.* New York: Collins, 1979.

Hellwig, Monika. "Good News to the Poor: Do They Understand It Better?" In James Hug, ed., *Tracing the Spirit: Communities, Social Action, and Theological Reflection,* 122–45. New York: Paulist Press, 1983.

Henderson, James D. *Conservative Thought in Twentieth Century Latin America: The Ideas of Laureano Gomez.* Ohio University Monographs in International Studies, Latin American Series, no. 13. Athens: 1988.

———. *When Colombia Bled: A History of the Violencia in Tolima.* University, Ala.: University of Alabama Press, 1985.

Herzog, Don. *Happy Slaves: A Critique of Consent Theory.* Chicago: University of Chicago Press, 1989.

Hewitt, W. E. *Base Christian Communities and Social Change in Brazil.* Lincoln: University of Nebraska Press, 1991.

———. "The Influence of Social Class on Activity Preferences of Comunidades Eclesiaes de Base (CEBs) in the Archdiocese of São Paulo." *Journal of Latin American Studies* 19, no. 1 (May 1987): 141–56.

———. "Strategies for Social Change Employed by Comunidades Eclesiaes de Base (CEBs) in the Archdiocese of São Paulo." *Journal for the Scientific Study of Religion* 25, no. 1 (March 1986): 16–30.

Hill, Christopher. *The Century of Revolution.* New York: W. W. Norton, 1982.

———. *God's Englishman: Oliver Cromwell and the English Revolution.* New York: Harper and Row, 1973.

———. *The World Turned Upside Down: Radical Ideas in the English Revolution.* New York: Penguin, 1982.

Hirschman, Albert. *Getting Ahead Collectively: Grassroots Experiences in Latin America.* New York: Pergamon Press, 1984.

Hochschild, Jennifer. *What's Fair? American Beliefs about Distributive Justice.* Cambridge: Harvard University Press, 1981.

Hogar-Escuela. *Hogar-Escuela.* Factativá: Mimeographed pamphlet, n.d.

Hunter, James Davison. *American Evangelicalism: Conservative Religion and the Quandary of Modernity.* New Brunswick, N.J.: Rutgers University Press, 1983.

Huntington, Deborah L. "The Salvation Brokers: Conservative Evangelicals in Central America." *NACLA Report on the Americas* 18, no. 1 (February 1984): 7–36.

Hvalkof, Soren, and Peter Aaby, eds. *Is God an American?: An Anthropological Perspective in the Missionary Work of the Summer Linguistics Institute.* Copenhagen: IGWIA, 1971.

Ileto, Reynaldo. *Pasyón and Revolution: Popular Movements in the Philippines, 1840–1910.* Manila: Anteneo de Manila Press, 1979.

Inglehart, Ronald. *Culture Shift in Advanced Industrial Society.* Princeton: Princeton University Press, 1989.

———. "The Renaissance of Political Culture." *American Political Science Review* 82, no. 4 (December 1988): 1203–30.

Inter-American Development Bank. *Economic and Social Progress in Latin America, 1987, Special Section: Labor Force in Employment.* Washington, D.C.: Inter-American Development Bank, 1987.

———. *Economic and Social Progress in Latin America, 1986, Special Section: Agricultural Development.* Washington, D.C.: Inter-American Development Bank, 1986.

Jacquette, Jane, ed. *The Women's Movement in Latin America.* London: Unwyn Hyman, 1989.

Kincaid, Douglas. "Peasants into Rebels: Community and Class in El Salvador." *Comparative Studies in Society and History* 29, no. 3 (July 1987): 466–94.

Kirk, John. *Between God and the Party: Religion in Revolutionary Cuba.* Tampa: University of South Florida Press, 1988.

Kornblith, Miriam. "Deuda y democracia en Venezuela: Los sucesos del 27 y 28 de febrero de 1989." *Revista del CENDES*, no. 10 (1989): 17–34.

Kramer, Jane. "Letter from the Elysian Fields." *New Yorker*, March 2, 1989, 40–75.

Kselman, Thomas. "Ambivalence and Assumption in the Study of Popular Religion." In Daniel H. Levine, ed., *Religion and Political Conflict in Latin America*, 27–41. Chapel Hill: University of North Carolina Press, 1986.

———. *Miracles and Prophecies in Nineteenth Century France.* New Brunswick, N.J.: Rutgers University Press, 1985.

———, ed. *Belief in History: Innovative Approaches to Religious History in Europe and North America.* Notre Dame, Ind.: University of Notre Dame Press, 1990.

Kuczinski, Pedro-Pablo. *Latin American Debt.* Baltimore: Johns Hopkins University Press, 1988.

La Feber, Walter. *Inevitable Revolutions.* New York: W. W. Norton, 1984.

Laitin, David. *Hegemony and Culture: Politics and Religious Change Among the Yoruba.* Chicago: University of Chicago Press, 1986.

———. "Religion, Political Culture, and the Weberian Tradition." *World Politics* 30, no. 4 (July 1978): 563–92.

Lan, David. *Guns and Rain: Guerrillas and Spirit Mediums in Zimbabwe.* Berkeley: University of California Press, 1985.

Lancaster, Roger. *Thanks to God and the Revolution: Popular Religion and Class Consciousness in the New Nicaragua.* Berkeley: University of California Press, 1989.

Lang, James. *Inside Development in Latin America.* Chapel Hill: University of North Carolina Press, 1988.

Leal Buitrago, Francisco. *Estado y Política en Colombia*. Bogotá: Siglo 21 de Colombia, 1984.

Lernoux, Penny. *Cry of the People*. New York: Penguin, 1982.

―――. "The Latin American Church." *Latin American Research Review* 15, no. 2 (1980): 201–11.

―――. *People of God: The Struggle for World Catholicism*. New York: Viking Press, 1989.

Levine, Daniel H. "Assessing the Impacts of Liberation Theology in Latin America." *Review of Politics* 50, no. 2 (Spring 1988): 241–63.

―――. "Authority in Church and Society: Latin American Models." *Comparative Studies in Society and History* 20 (October 1978): 517–44.

―――. "Colombia: The Institutional Church and the Popular." In Daniel H. Levine, ed., *Religion and Political Conflict in Latin America*, 187–217. Chapel Hill: University of North Carolina Press, 1986.

―――. *Conflict and Political Change in Venezuela*. Princeton: Princeton University Press, 1973.

―――. "Conflict and Renewal." In Daniel H. Levine, ed., *Religion and Political Conflict in Latin America*, 236–55. Chapel Hill: University of North Carolina Press, 1986.

―――. "Considering Liberation Theology as Utopia." *Review of Politics* 52, no. 4 (Fall 1990): 603–20.

―――. "Continuities in Colombia." *Journal of Latin American Studies* 17, no. 2 (November 1985): 295–317.

―――. "Democracy and the Church in Venezuela." *Journal of Inter-American Studies and World Affairs* 18, no. 1 (February 1976): 3–22.

―――. "Holiness, Faith, Power, Politics." *Journal for the Scientific Study of Religion* 26, no. 4 (December 1987): 551–61.

―――. "How Not to Understand Liberation Theology, Nicaragua, or Both." *Journal of Inter-American Studies and World Affairs* 32, no. 3 (Fall 1990): 229–46.

―――. "The Impact and Lasting Significance of Medellín and Puebla." In Edward Cleary, ed., *Born of the Poor: The Latin American Church since Medellín*, 64–74. Notre Dame, Ind.: University of Notre Dame Press, 1990.

―――. "Paradigm Lost: Dependence to Democracy." *World Politics* 40, no. 3 (April 1988): 377–94.

―――. "Popular Groups, Popular Culture, and Popular Religion." *Comparative Studies in Society and History* 32, no. 4 (October 1990): 718–64.

―――. "Religion." In Paula Covington, ed., *Latin American and Caribbean Studies: A Critical Guide to Research*. Westport, Conn.: Greenwood Press, 1991.

―――. "Religion and Politics: Drawing Lines, Understanding Change." *Latin American Research Review* 20, no. 1 (Winter 1985): 185–201.

―――. "Religion and Politics in Comparative and Historical Perspective." *Comparative Politics* 19, no. 1 (October 1986): 95–122.

―――. *Religion and Politics in Latin America: The Catholic Church in Venezuela and Colombia*. Princeton: Princeton University Press, 1981.

―――. "Religion, the Poor, and Politics in Latin America Today." In Daniel H.

Levine, ed., *Religion and Political Conflict in Latin America*, 3–23. Chapel Hill: University of North Carolina Press, 1986.

———. "Urbanization in Latin America: Changing Perspectives." *Latin American Research Review* 14, no. 1 (Spring 1979): 51–79.

———. "Urbanization, Migrants, and Politics in Venezuela." *Journal of Inter-American Studies and World Affairs* 17, no. 3 (August 1975): 358–72.

———. "Venezuela: The Sources, Nature, and Future Prospects of Democracy." In Seymour Lipset, Juan Linz, and Larry Diamond, eds., *Democracy in Developing Countries*, vol. 4, *Latin America*, 247–90. Boulder, Colo.: Lynne Rienner Publishers, 1989.

———. " 'Whose Heart Could Be So Staunch?' " *Christianity and Crisis* 22 (July 1985): 311–12.

———, ed. *Religion and Political Conflict in Latin America*. Chapel Hill: University of North Carolina Press, 1986.

Levine, Daniel H., and Scott Mainwaring. "Religion and Popular Protest: Contrasting Experiences." In Susan Eckstein, ed., *Power and Popular Protest: Latin American Social Movements*, 203–40. Berkeley: University of California Press, 1989.

Levine, Daniel H., and Alexander Wilde. "The Catholic Church, 'Politics,' and Violence: The Colombian Case." *Review of Politics* 39, no. 2 (1977): 220–49.

Lipton, Michael. *The Poor and the Poorest: Some Interim Findings*. Washington, D.C.: World Bank, 1988.

Lomnitz, Larissa A. *Networks and Marginality: Life in a Mexican Shantytown*. New York: Academic Press, 1977.

López Trujillo, Msgr. Alfonso. *De Medellín a Puebla*. Madrid: Biblioteca de Autores Cristianos, 1980.

———. *Opciones e interpretaciones a la luz de Puebla*. Bogotá: CELAM, n.d.

Lowy, Michael. *Marxisme et théologie de la libération*. Paris: Cahiers d'étude et de récherche, Institut International de Recherche et de Formation, 1989.

———. *Redemptión et utopie: Le Judaisme libertaire en Europe Centrale*. Paris: Presses Universitaires de France, 1988.

MacGaffey, Wyatt. *Modern Kongo Prophets: Religion in a Plural Society*. Bloomington: Indiana University Press, 1983.

———. *Religion and Society in Central Africa: The Bakongo of Lower Zaire*. Chicago: University of Chicago Press, 1986.

Mackay, John. *The Other Spanish Christ: A Study in the Spiritual History of Spain and South America*. London, 1932.

Maduro, Otto. *Religion and Social Conflict*. Maryknoll, N.Y.: Orbis Books, 1982.

Mainwaring, Scott. "Brazil: The Catholic Church and the Popular Movement in Nova Iguaçu, 1974–1985." In Daniel H. Levine, ed., *Religion and Political Conflict in Latin America*, 124–55. Chapel Hill: University of North Carolina Press, 1986.

———. *The Catholic Church and Politics in Brazil, 1916–1985*. Stanford, Calif.: Stanford University Press, 1986.

Mainwaring, Scott, and Eduardo Viola. "New Social Movements, Political Culture, and Democracy: Brazil and Argentina in the 1980s." *Telos*, no. 61 (1986): 17–52.

Mainwaring, Scott, and Alexander W. Wilde, eds. *The Progressive Church in Latin America*. Notre Dame, Ind.: University of Notre Dame Press, 1989.

Malavé Mata, H. *Los extravíos del poder euforia y crisis del populismo en Venezuela*. Caracas: Universidad Central de Venezuela, 1987.

Maldonado, Oscar, Guiteme Oliveri, and Germán Zabala. *Cristianismo y revolución*. Mexico City: Ediciones Era, 1970.

Mannheim, Karl. *Ideology and Utopia*. New York: Harcourt, Brace, and World, 1936.

Mardin, Serif. *Religion and Social Change in Modern Turkey: The Care of Bediuzzama Said Nursi*. Albany, N.Y.: SUNY Press, 1989.

Margolies, Lise, ed. *The Venezuelan Peasant in Country and City*. Caracas: EDIVA, 1979.

Marín, Ivan. "Experiencia de ministerios en Colombia." In Conferencia Episcopal de Colombia, *Renovación pastoral y nuevos ministerios*. Bogotá: SPEC, 1975.

Mariz, Cecilia L. "Popular Culture, Base Communities, and Pentecostal Churches in Brazil." Presented at the annual meeting of the Society for the Scientific Study of Religion, Chicago, November 1988.

Marsh, Robin Ruth. *Development Strategies in Rural Colombia: The Case of Caquetá*. Los Angeles: UCLA Latin American Center Publications, 1983.

Martin, David. *Tongues of Fire: The Explosion of Evangelical Protestantism in Latin America*. Oxford: Basil Blackwell, 1990.

Mauss, Marcel. "La oración." (1909) In M. Mauss, *Lo sagrado y lo profano obras 1*, 95–142. Barcelona: Barral Editores, 1970.

McGavick, James E. *Catholic Belief and Practice*. 3d ed. Baltimore: 1907.

McGovern, Arthur. *Liberation Theology and Its Critics*. Maryknoll, N.Y.: Orbis Books, 1989.

McGregor, J. F., and B. Reay, eds. *Radical Religion in the English Revolution*. New York: Oxford University Press, 1984.

McPherson, C. B. *The Life and Times of Liberal Democracy*. New York: Oxford University Press, 1977.

Mecham, J. Lloyd. *Church and State in Latin America*. Chapel Hill: University of North Carolina Press, 1934.

Medhurst, William. *The Church and Labour in Colombia*. Manchester: Manchester University Press, 1984.

Micheo, Alberto. "Una experiencia campesina." *SIC*, no. 431 (January 1988): 4–7.

———. "El hambre no tiene color." *SIC*, no. 493 (March 1987): 105–7.

———. "La política como opresión: el caso de los caficultores." *SIC*, no. 470 (December 1984): 440–42.

———. "La religión del pobre." *SIC*, no. 417 (November 1983): 417–19.

Mignone, Emilio. *Witness to the Truth*. Maryknoll, N.Y.: Orbis Books, 1988.

Mills, C. Wright. *The Sociological Imagination*. New York: Grove Press, 1961.

Moodie, T. Dunbar. *The Rise of Afrikanerdom: Power, Apartheid, and the Afrikaner Civil Religion*. Berkeley: University of California Press, 1975.

Moore, Barrington. *Social Origins of Dictatorship and Democracy*. Boston: Beacon Press, 1966.

Mora, Leonardo. "Café amargo." *SIC*, no. 446 (June 1982): 259–61.

Morris, Aldon. *The Origins of the Civil Rights Movement*. New York: Free Press, 1984.

Morse, Richard. "The Heritage of Latin America." In Louis Hartz, ed., *The Founding of New Societies*, 123–72. New York: Harcourt, Brace, and World, 1964.

Mottahaddeh, Roy. *The Mantle of the Prophet*. New York: Pantheon, 1985.

Nash, June. "Cultural Resistance and Class Consciousness in Bolivian Tin-Mining Communities." In Susan Eckstein, ed., *Power and Popular Protest: Latin American Social Movements*, 182–202. Berkeley: University of California Press, 1989.

———. *We Eat the Mines and the Mines Eat Us*. New York: Columbia University Press, 1979.

Navarro, Juan Carlos. *Contestación en la iglesia venezolana, 1966–1972*. Caracas: Mimeograph 1981.

Navia V., Carminia. *Caminando: Poemas*. Bogotá: Edición de la Corporación Para la Promoción Popular, 1981.

———. "Las semanas culturales y el problema de la organización popular." *Causa justa* (Bogotá), no. 2 (1980): 39–42.

Noll, Mark A. *Religion and American Politics from the Colonial Period to the 1980s*. New York: Oxford University Press, 1990.

Noone, Judith. *The Same Fate as the Poor*. Maryknoll, N.Y.: Maryknoll Sisters, 1984.

Novak, Michael. *Will It Liberate? Questions about Liberation Theology*. New York: Paulist Press, 1986.

Obelkevich, James, ed. *Religion and the People, 800–1700*. Chapel Hill: University of North Carolina Press, 1979.

O'Donnell, Guillermo. "Tensions in the Bureaucratic Authoritarian State and the Question of Democracy." In David Collier, ed., *The New Authoritarianism in Latin America*, 288–318. Princeton: Princeton University Press, 1979.

O'Donnell, Guillermo, Phillipe Schmitter, and Laurence Whitehead, eds., *Transitions from Authoritarian Rule: Prospects for Democracy*. 4 vols. Baltimore: Johns Hopkins University Press, 1986.

Opazo Bernales, Andrés. *Popular Religious Movements and Social Change in Central America*. Boulder, Colo.: Lynne Rienner Publishers, 1991.

Oquist, Paul. *Violence, Conflict, and Politics in Colombia*. New York: Academic Press, 1980.

Ortega, Juanita. "La salud es un derecho: Una experiencia popular." *SIC*, no. 440 (December 1981): 446–47.

Pagels, Elaine. *Adam, Eve, and the Serpent*. New York: Vintage Books, 1989.

Palacios, Marco. *Coffee in Colombia, 1850–1970: An Economic, Social, and Political History*. Cambridge: Cambridge University Press, 1980.

Palacios, P. Carlos. *Vida religiosa inserta en los medios populares*. Bogotá: CLAR, 1982.

Parra, Maltide, and Maria Gabriela Ponce. *Renovación y opción en la vida religiosa*. Caracas: UCAB, Facultad de Ciencias Economicas y Sociales, 1985.

Pasara, Luis. "Peru: The Leftist Angels." In Scott Mainwaring and Alexander Wilde, eds., *The Progressive Church in Latin America*, 276–327. Notre Dame, Ind.: University of Notre Dame Press, 1989.

———. *Radicalización y conflicto en la iglesia peruana*. Lima: Ediciones Virrey, 1986.

Pateman, Carole. *Participation and Democratic Theory*. Cambridge: Cambridge University Press, 1970.

Pearce, Jenny. *The Promised Land: Peasant Rebellion in Chalatenango, El Salvador*. London: Latin American Bureau, 1986.

Peattie, Lisa. *Planning: Ciudad Guayana Reconsidered*. Ann Arbor: University of Michigan Press, 1987.

———. *The View from the Barrio*. Ann Arbor: University of Michigan Press, 1968.

Peeler, John. *Latin American Democracies: Colombia, Costa Rica, and Venezuela*. Chapel Hill: University of North Carolina Press, 1985.

Pérez Esquivel, Adolfo. *Christ in a Poncho: Witnesses to the Nonviolent Struggles in Latin America*. Maryknoll, N.Y.: Orbis Books, 1985.

Perlman, Janice. *The Myth of Marginality: Poverty and Politics in Rio de Janeiro*. Berkeley: University of California Press, 1976.

Piven, Frances F., and Richard Cloward. *Poor People's Movements: Why They Succeed, How They Fail*. New York: Vintage Press, 1979.

Poggi, Gianfranco. *Catholic Action in Italy: The Sociology of a Sponsored Organization*. Stanford: Stanford University Press, 1967.

Pope, Liston. *Millhands and Preachers*. New Haven: Yale University Press, 1942.

Popkin, Samuel L. *The Rational Peasant: The Political Economy of Rural Society in Vietnam*. Berkeley: University of California Press, 1979.

Porras, Baltazar. *Los obispos y los problemas de Venezuela*. Caracas: Trípode, 1978.

Portes, Alejandro. "Latin American Class Structures: Their Composition and Change during the Last Decades." *Latin American Research Review* 20, no. 3 (1985): 7–40.

———. "Latin American Urbanization in the Years of the Crisis." *Latin American Research Review* 24, no. 3 (1989): 7–44.

———. "Rationality in the Slum: An Essay in Interpretive Sociology." *Comparative Studies in Society and History* 14, no. 3 (June 1972): 268–80.

Portes, Alejandro, and John Walton. *Urban Latin America: The Political Condition from Above and from Below*. Austin: University of Texas Press, 1976.

Putnam, Robert D. "Institutional Performance and Political Culture: Some Puzzles about the Power of the Past." Presented at the 1987 annual meeting of the American Political Science Association, Chicago, September 1987.

Raboteau, Albert J. *Slave Religion: The "Invisible Institution" in the Antebellum South*. New York: Oxford University Press, 1978.

Ranger, Terence O. *Peasant Consciousness and Guerrilla War in Zimbabwe: A Comparative Study*. Berkeley: University of California Press, 1985.

———. "Religious Movements and Politics in Sub-Saharan Africa." *African Studies Review* 29, no. 2 (June 1986): 1–69.

Ranger, Terence O., and Eric Hobsbawm, eds. *The Invention of Tradition*. Cambridge: Cambridge University Press, 1983.

Ratzinger, Joseph Cardinal. "Instruction on Certain Aspects of the 'Theology of Liberation.' " *Origins NC Documentary Service* 14, no. 13 (September 1984): 193–204.

———. "Instruction on Christian Freedom and Liberation." *Origins NC Documentary Service* 15, no. 44 (April 17, 1986): 714–28.

————. *The Ratzinger Report*. San Francisco: Ignatius Press, 1985.

Ray, Talton. *The Politics of the Barrios of Venezuela*. Berkeley: University of California Press, 1969.

Relensberg, Norbert S., Härmut Karner, and Volkmar Köhler. *Los pobres de Venezuela: Auto-organización de los pobladores. Un informe crítico*. Caracas: El Cid, 1978.

Reyes Oviedo, Nacho. "Los comités de salud." *SIC*, no. 488 (September–October 1986): 348–49.

Reynolds, C., and Ralph V. Norman, eds. *Community in America: The Challenge of "Habits of the Heart."* Berkeley: University of California Press, 1988.

Richard, Pablo. *Death of Christendoms, Birth of the Church*. Maryknoll, N.Y.: Orbis Books, 1987.

Roelefs, H. Mark. "Liberation Theology: The Recovery of Biblical Radicalism." *American Political Science Review* 82, no. 2 (June 1986): 549–66.

Romero, Catalina. "The Peruvian Church: Change and Continuity." In Scott Mainwaring and Alexander Wilde, eds., *The Progressive Church in Latin America*, 253–73. Notre Dame, Ind.: University of Notre Dame Press, 1989.

Romero, Oscar. *Voice of the Voiceless: The Four Pastoral Letters and Other Statements*. Maryknoll, N.Y.: Orbis Books, 1985.

Rosales Nelson, Susan. "Bolivia: Continuity and Conflict in Religious Discourse." In Daniel H. Levine, ed., *Religion and Political Conflict in Latin America*, 218–35. Chapel Hill: University of North Carolina Press, 1986.

Rose, Susan, and Steve Brouwer. "Guatemalan Upper Classes Join the Evangelicals." Presented at the joint session of the American Sociological Association and the Association for the Sociology of Religion meetings, Atlanta, August 1988.

Roseberry, William. *Coffee and Capitalism in the Venezuelan Andes*. Austin: University of Texas Press, 1983.

————. "Images of the Peasant in the Consciousness of the Venezuelan Proletariat." In Michael Hanagan and Charles Stephenson, eds., *Proletarians and Protest. The Roots of Class Formation in an Industrializing World*, 149–69. New York: Greenwood Press, 1986.

Ruiz Quijano, María Concepción. *Inserción de minoría activa*. Caracas: Universidad Católica Andres Bello, 1984.

Sánchez, Gonzalo. *Colombia: Violencia y democracia, informe presentado al ministerio de gobierno*. Bogotá: Universidad Nacional de Colombia Colciencias, 1988.

————. *Los Días de la revolución: Gaitanismo y el nueve de abril en provincia*. Bogotá: Centro Cultural Jorge Eliécer Gaitán, 1983.

Sánchez, Gonzalo, and Donny Meertens. *Bandoleros, Gamonales, y Campesinos: El Caso de la Violencia en Colombia*. Bogotá: El Ancora Editores, 1983.

Santamaría Salamanca, R., and G. Silva Luján. "Colombia in the 1980s: A Political Regime in Transition." *Caribbean Review* 14, no. 1 (1986): 12–15.

Santana, Pedro. *Desarrollo regional y paros cívicos en Colombia*. Controversia 107–8. Bogotá: CINEP, 1983.

São Paulo, Archdiocese of. *São Paulo: Growth and Poverty*. London: Bowerdean Press, 1978.

Schoultz, Lars. *National Security and United States Policy toward Latin America*. Princeton: Princeton University Press, 1987.

Schumpeter, Joseph. *Capitalism, Socialism, and Democracy*. London: George Allen and Unwin, 1961.

Scott, James. *Domination and the Arts of Resistance: Hidden Transcripts*. New Haven: Yale University Press, 1990.

———. *The Moral Economy of the Peasant*. New Haven: Yale University Press, 1976.

———. "Protest and Profanation: Agrarian Revolt and the Little Tradition." 2 parts. *Theory and Society* (1977): 1–38, 211–45.

———. *Weapons of the Weak: Everyday Forms of Peasant Resistance*. New Haven: Yale University Press, 1985.

Segundo, Juan Luis. *The Hidden Motives of Pastoral Actions: Latin American Reflections*. Maryknoll, N.Y.: Orbis Books, 1978.

———. *The Liberation of Theology*. Maryknoll, N.Y.: Orbis Books, 1976.

———. *Theology and the Church*. Minneapolis, Minn.: Winston-Seabury Press, 1985.

———. *Theology for Artisans of a New Humanity*. 5 vols. Maryknoll, N.Y.: Orbis Books, 1973–74.

Sheahan, John. *Patterns of Development in Latin America*. Princeton: Princeton University Press, 1987.

Sheehan, Thomas. *The First Coming: How the Kingdom of God Became Christianity*. New York: Vintage Books, 1986.

Sigmund, Paul. *Liberation Theology at the Crossroads: Democracy or Revolution?* New York: Oxford University Press, 1990.

Sklar, Richard L. "Developmental Democracy." *Comparative Study in Society and History* 29, no. 4 (October 1987): 686–714.

Slater, Candace. *Trail of Miracles*. Berkeley: University of California Press, 1985.

Sloan, John. "The Policy Capabilities of Democratic Regimes in Latin America." *Latin American Research Review* 24, no. 2 (1989): 113–126.

Smith, Brian H. *The Church and Politics in Chile: Challenges to Modern Catholicism*. Princeton: Princeton University Press, 1982.

———. "Churches and Human Rights: Recent Trends on the Subcontinent." In Daniel H. Levine, ed. *Churches and Politics in Latin America*, 155–93. Beverly Hills: SAGE Publications, 1980.

Sobrino, Jon. *Christology at the Crossroads*. Maryknoll, N.Y.: Orbis Books, 1978.

———. *Spirituality of Liberation: Toward Political Holiness*. Maryknoll, N.Y.: Orbis Books, 1988.

———. "A Theologian's View of Oscar Romero." In Oscar Romero, *Voice of the Voiceless: The Four Pastoral Letters and Other Statements*, 22–51. Maryknoll, N.Y.: Orbis Books, 1985.

*Solidaridad* 10, no. 100 (1988) (tenth anniversary edition).

———. "Desde la perspectiva de la iglesia de los pobres." *Solidaridad* 10, no. 100: 4–10.

Sosa, Arturo. "Iglesia y democracia y Venezuela." *SIC*, no. 501 (January 1988): 14–19.

Sosa, Arturo, and Eloi Lengrand. *Del garibaldismo estudiantil a la izquierda criolla, 1928–1935.* Caracas: Ediciones Centauro, 1981.

Stallings, Barbara, and Robert Kaufman, eds. *Debt and Democracy in Latin America.* Boulder, Colo.: Westview Press, 1989.

Stepan, Alfred. "State Power and the Strength of Civil Society in the Southern Cone of Latin America." In Peter B. Evans, Dietrich Rueschmeyer, and Theda Skocpol, eds., *Bringing the State Back In*, 317–43. New York: Cambridge University Press, 1985.

———, ed. *Democratizing Brazil.* New York: Oxford University Press, 1989.

Steward, J. H. *Theory of Culture Change.* Urbana: University of Illinois Press, 1955.

Stoll, David. *Is Latin America Turning Protestant?* Berkeley: University of California Press, 1990.

Sundkler, Bengt G. M. *Bantu Prophets in South Africa.* New York: Oxford University Press, 1961.

Támez, Elsa, ed. *Through Her Eyes: Women's Theology from Latin America.* Maryknoll, N.Y.: Orbis Books, 1989.

Thomas, Keith. *Religion and the Decline of Magic.* New York: Charles Scribner's Sons, 1971.

Thompson, E. P. "Eighteenth-Century English Society: Class Struggle without Class?" *Social History* 3, no. 2 (May 1978): 133–65.

Thompson, John B., and David Held, eds. *Habermas: Critical Debates.* Cambridge: MIT Press, 1982.

Tilly, Charles. *Big Structures, Large Processes, Huge Transformations.* New York: Russell Sage Foundation, 1984.

Torres, Sergio, and John Eagleson, eds. *Theology in the Americas.* Maryknoll, N.Y.: Orbis Books, 1976.

Trigo, Pedro. "La cultura en los barrios." *SIC*, no. 507 (July–August 1988): 292–96.

———. "Una utopía concreta para nuestra iglesia." *SIC*, no. 438 (September–October 1981): 340–42.

———. "Vida é historia en America Latina." *SIC*, no. 497 (July–August 1987): 314–19.

Tucker, Robert, ed. *The Marx-Engels Reader.* New York: W. W. Norton, 1972.

Turner, Victor. *Dramas, Fields, and Metaphors: Symbolic Action in Human Society.* Ithaca: Cornell University Press, 1974.

Turner, Victor, and Edith Turner. *Image and Pilgrimage in Western Culture.* New York: Columbia University Press, 1978.

Ugalde, Luis. "La nueva presencia de la iglesia en los procesos históricos de la sociedad." *SIC*, no. 491 (January 1987): 10–14.

———. "¿Tiene algo que aportar la doctrina social de la iglesia?" *SIC*, no. 497 (July–August 1987): 320–21.

———. "30 años de democracia y vida religiosa." *SIC*, no. 500 (December 1987): 560–63.

Urrutia, Miguel. *Winners and Losers in Colombia's Economic Growth of the 1970s.* New York: Oxford University Press, 1985.

Vallancourt, Jean-Guy. *Papal Power: A Study of Vatican Control over Lay Catholic Elites.* Berkeley: University of California Press, 1980.

Velásquez, Ramón J. *La caída del liberalismo amarillo*. Caracas: 1973.

Velásquez Lutero, Msgr. Hernando. "Alocución del Monseñor Hernando Velásquez Lutero en el encuentro campesino." *Comunidad Diocesana* 10, no. 91 (September 1978): 2–5.

Vélez-Ibanez, Carlos. *Bonds of Mutual Trust: The Cultural System of Rotating Credit Associations among Urban Mexicans and Chicanos*. New Brunswick, N.J.: Rutgers University Press, 1983.

———. *Rituals of Marginality: Politics, Process, and Culture Change in Central Urban Mexico, 1969–1974*. Berkeley: University of California Press, 1983.

Veliz, Claudio. *The Centralist Tradition of Latin America*. Princeton: Princeton University Press, 1980.

Viana, Mikel. "¿Para que acontezca la vida religiosa?" *SIC*, no. 438 (September–October 1981): 348–49.

Vidich, Arthur J., and Joseph Bensman. *Small Town in Mass Society*. Princeton: Princeton University Press, 1958.

Walker, Jack L. "A Critique of the Elitist Theory of Democracy." *American Political Science Review* 60 (1966): 285–95.

Walshe, Peter. *Church versus State in South Africa: The Case of the Christian Institute*. Maryknoll, N.Y.: Orbis Books, 1983.

Walton, John. *Elites and Economic Development: Comparative Studies in the Political Economy of Latin American Cities*. Austin: University of Texas Press, 1977.

Walzer, Michael. *Exodus and Revolution*. New York: Basic Books, 1985.

———. *Revolution of the Saints*. Cambridge: Harvard University Press, 1965.

Washington Office on Latin America. *Colombia Besieged: Political Violence and State Responsibility*. Washington, D.C.: Washington Office on Latin America, 1989.

Wasserstrom, Robert. *Class and Society in Central Chiapas*. Berkeley: University of California Press, 1983.

———. *Grass Roots Development in Latin America and the Caribbean: Oral Histories of Social Change*. New York: Praeger Publishers, 1985.

Weber, Max. "The Concept of Following a Rule." In W. G. Runciman, ed., *Max Weber: Selections in Translation*, 99–110. New York: Cambridge University Press, 1978.

———. *Economy and Society*. Edited by Guenther Roth and Claus Wittich. 2 vols. Berkeley: University of California Press, 1968.

———. "Politics as a Vocation." In W. G. Runciman, ed., *Max Weber: Selections in Translation*, 212–25. New York: Cambridge University Press, 1978.

———. "The Social Psychology of the World Religions." In H. H. Gerth and C. W. Mills, eds., *From Max Weber: Essays in Sociology*, 267–301. London: Routledge and Kegan Paul, 1948.

———. *The Sociology of Religion*. Boston: Beacon Press, 1963.

———. "The Soteriology of the Underprivileged." In W. G. Runciman, ed., *Max Weber: Selections in Translation*, 174–91. New York: Cambridge University Press, 1978.

Weisbrot, M. *Father Divine*. Boston: Beacon Press, 1983.

Whitman, Walt. *Leaves of Grass*. New York: Bantam, 1983.

Wiarda, Howard. "Toward a Framework for the Study of the Ibero-Latin Tradition: The Corporative Model." *World Politics* 25 (January 1973): 206–35.

Wickham-Crowley, Timothy. "Winners, Losers, and Also-Rans: Toward a Comparative Sociology of Latin American Guerrilla Movements." In Susan Eckstein, ed., *Power and Popular Protest: Latin American Social Movements*, 137–81. Berkeley: University of California Press, 1989.

Wilde, Alexander. "Creating Neo-Christendom in Colombia." Kellogg Institute Working Paper no. 92. Notre Dame, Ind.: University of Notre Dame, March 1987.

Williams, Peter. *Popular Religion in America*. Chicago: University of Illinois Press, 1989.

Williams, Phillip A. *The Catholic Church and Politics in Nicaragua and Costa Rica*. Pittsburgh: University of Pittsburgh Press, 1989.

Wilson, Bryan. "Secularization: The Inherited Model." In Phillip Hammond, ed., *The Sacred in a Secular Age*, 1–20. Berkeley: University of California Press, 1985.

Wolf, Eric R. "Kinship, Friendship, and Patron-Client Relations in Complex Societies." In M. Banton, ed., *The Social Anthropology of Complex Societies*, 1–22. London: Tavistock, 1966.

Wolterstorff, Nicholas. *Until Justice and Peace Embrace*. Grand Rapids, Mich.: William B. Eerdmans Publishing Co., 1983.

Worseley, Peter. *The Trumpet Shall Sound: A Study of Cargo Cults in Melonesia*. New York: Schocken, 1968.

Wuthnow, Robert W. "Quid Obscurum: The Changing Terrain of Church-State Relations." In Mark Noll, ed., *Religion and American Politics from the Colonial Period to the 1980s*, 337–54. New York: Oxford University Press, 1990.

———. *The Restructuring of American Religion*. Princeton: Princeton University Press, 1988.

———. "Understanding Religion and Politics." *Daedalus* 120, no. 3 (Summer 1991): 1–20.

Wyssenbach, Jean Pierre. "La biblia entre nosotros." *SIC*, no. 491 (January 1987): 8–9.

———. "Comunidad de barrio." *SIC*, no. 438 (September–October 1981): 343–44.

———. "La organización en los barrios marginales." *SIC* (January 1981): 11–14.

Zamosc, Leon. *The Agrarian Question and the Peasant Movement in Colombia*. Cambridge: Cambridge University Press, 1986.

Zaret, David. *The Heavenly Contract: Ideology and Organization in Pre-Revolutionary Puritanism*. Chicago: University of Chicago Press, 1985.

# INDEX

Acción Comunal, 98
ACPO (Acción Cultural Popular), 184n, 185
activism, 45, 51
Adrience, Madeleine, 226
agenda setting, 358–59; radicals and conservatives compared, 357
Agrarian Bank, 105
agricultural proletarianization, 37
agriculture: Colombia, 60; Venezuela, 59
Agua Fría, 106, 135, 151–53, 170, 173, 176, 191, 193
Agulhon, Maurice, 194
Ajami, Fouad, 15, 329
Allende, Salvador, 36
All Saints Day, 173
Alvarez, Patricio, 152, 302–9; base community, 303; birth and family, 302; class relations, 307; and Román Cortés, 303–5; education and *cursillos*, 303; lay ministry, 304; politics, 306; poverty, 306; preferential option for the poor, 306; spirituality, 308; views on clergy and role of church, 307–8; work, 302
Amos, 4
ANAPO (Alianza Nacional Popular), 282
ANUC (Asociación Nacional de Usuarios Campesinos), 276
Arjomand, Said, 15, 337
Ash Wednesday, 170
associations, 12, 340
authority, 8, 11
Azevedo, Marcelo, 346

Barquisimeto, 87, 107–16; agriculture, 107; urban organization, 114; violence, 107
Barrio El Rodeo. *See* El Rodeo, Barrio
barrio invasions, 185–86
Barrio Meléndez. *See* Meléndez, Barrio
Barrio Nuevo, 114
Barro Blanco, 105, 233, 288
base, 10, 44; in Colombia, 80–81; in Venezuela, 81–82
base communities: agendas, 50–51, 358–59; agenda setting, 358; cases compared, 148; common elements, 147–48; compared to Protestants, 339, 359–62; and culture

change, 13; definitions, 12, 45; and democracy, 164; egalitarian practices, 50; failures, 46; fear of reprisals, 270; ideal group in, 47; ideal leader in, 47; ideal member in, 47; images of Kingdom of God, 138, 139; issues of concern, 27; and liberation theology, 44–45, 51; occupations of members, 183, 187; origins, 46; religious values, 27; and scarcity of clergy, 356; spirituality, 351; typology, 45, 47–48, 164, 356–59; variation, 13, 45
Basilica of San Francisco, 87
Batatal, 111
Beinart, William, 355n
"being church," 146; popular images, 143
"being religious," 133
Bellah, Robert, 367
Bernal, Gladys, 252–69, 332; career, 254–55; and Centro Gumilla, 257; education, 253–54; local activities, 258; on popular religion, 256; vocation, 253
Berryman, Phillip, 15, 16n, 39, 49, 332, 348
Bible reading, 134, 136; preferred texts, 139; and self-confidence, 137
Bible study, 49; and liberation theology, 40; and linkages, 333
big structures, 317
Biscucuy, 111
Boff, Leonardo, 326
Bogotá, 94
Bonhoeffer, Dietrich, 370
Brazil, 31
Brisas del Aeropuerto, 114
Buga, 84n, 171, 275, 277
Bundy, Colin, 355n

Calderas, 111
Cali, 116–24, 179; agriculture, 116; taking of Fifth Street, 158, 344; urban geography, 117; violence, 129
Caparrapí, 97, 104–5, 144, 146, 148, 154, 156, 169, 193, 232; agriculture, 105; and the Conservative Ideal, 145; *cursillos*, 105; group meetings as charades, 144; holy water in, 175; Holy Week in, 246; Vicarías de Religiosas, 105

Cardenal, Ernesto, 261
Catholic Action, 6, 26, 78, 81
Catholic Relief Services, 103–4, 148, 277; and Caritas, 284; and Procampesinos, 105
Cauca Valley, 116, 274, 282
Ceballos, Olga, 280–87; activism, 282; attitude to church, 282–84, 286; and Bible study, 284–85; family history, 280; migration, 281; and Carminia Navia, 283–84; and Rojas Pinilla, 282; and *Solidaridad*, 284; spirituality, 287; views on Medellín and Puebla, 285
CELAM (Conferencia Episcopal Latinoamericana), 35–36, 71; Colombian role, 69
Central America, 14, 24, 36
Centro Gumilla, 87–88, 113, 115, 228, 257; origins and organization, 88; and popular religiosity, 88
CESAP (Centro al Servicio de la Acción Popular), 87–89, 113, 241, 362; origins, 89; pamphlets, 89
Chabasquén, 111
Chile, 31, 43
Chirinos, Pastora, 3
christendom, 70
Christian Democrats, 39; and popular religious movements, 39
christology, 140
church, 8–9; Colombia and Venezuela compared, 65–82; and democracy, 74, 77; as Institution, 9, 69; organizational strategies, 78–81; as Pilgrim People of God, 9; popular view, 195–96, 203; unity as value, 9; working definitions, 25
church-state conflict, 5
CINEP (Centro de Investigación y Educación Popular), 83–86, 123; Colombian bishops' attack on, 85–86; and *Solidaridad*, 241
civil rights movement, 327
civil society, 338
CLAR (Conferencia de Religiosos de America Latina), 35, 36; and Gladys Bernal, 256
class. *See* poverty
clerical populism, 50, 213
Cohen, Charles, 359
Colombian Bishops' Conference, 68; National Advisory Team on Base Communities and Lay Ministries, 97; National Coordination for Social Action, 78; organizational models, 199; organizational strategies, 78; and popular religion, 71–72; rural organization,

62; social analysis, 72–74; unity as value, 71; view on class division, 79
Comaroff, Jean, 15, 18
community, 3, 367; getting started, 232; meaning in Facatativá, 99; newness, 349
congregational religion, 178
Conservative Ideal, 47, 145, 356–57; hierarchy, 145. *See also* base communities
Conservative party (Colombia), 55
conversion, 134–45
COPEI (Comité de Organización Política Electoral Independiente), 81
Cortés, Román, 97, 98, 99, 104, 105, 108, 143, 144, 146, 151, 162–63, 175, 192, 227, 228, 337; organizational strategies, 97–98; use of *cursillos*, 231
cost of living, 191
CRAMCO (Centro Regional de Abastecimiento y Mercadeo Centro-Occidental), 111–13, 140–41; credit system, 112–13; roles, 113
crisis, 324, 362; and legitimations, 324
crisis-solace model, 22
Cristo Rey, parish of, 114, 175
cult of the dead, 321
culture: analysis of, 321; change, 325; of silence, 340
Cupocrédito, 104
Curran, Charles, 326
*cursillos*, 98–100, 105, 135, 151, 185, 210
*cursillos de cristiandad*, 98–99

Davis, Natalie, 15
deacons, 47, 81
Deas, Malcom, 57n
death and salvation, 331–33. *See also* popular religion
decay: political and economic, 369
Delegates of the Word, 101
Della Cava, Ralph, 331
democracy, 164, 338–39, 342–44; and religious change, 164, 338; Venezuela and Colombia compared, 91–92
Desan, Suzanne, 328n
De Tocqueville, Alexis, 11, 12, 147n, 148n, 343
Divina Pastora, La, 246
Dorremochea, Alberto, xx, 296
Duque, Fortunato, 294–302; on being church, 297; birth and family, 294; on clergy, 297; and the cooperative, 296; education, 295;

on Jesus, 301; Legion of Mary, 299; on PACCA and cooperative, 298; on Padre Vicente, 297; on Peasant Federation, 299; preferential option for the poor, 300; on religion and trust, 296; saints, 301; spirituality, 300–301

Eckstein, Susan, 28n, 151, 342
El Cauro, 141
elective affinities, 16, 323
El Hatillo, 185
Eliot, George, 310, 374
El Jordan, 120
El Líbano, 288
El Rodeo, Barrio, 118–20, 170, 172, 185, 188, 210, 281; Basque priests, 119; changes, 119; origins, 118; popular organization, 120; red reputation, 202
El Salvador, 31, 348
El Silencio, 295
EMCO (Empresa Comunitaria), 106; failure of, 234
Ephesians, Paul's epistle to, 144
ethical religion, 178
everyday life, 317
Exodus, 40, 139, 327, 329

Facatativá, diocese of, 94–107, 125, 144, 155, 164, 179, 183, 229, 232, 239–40, 276; agriculture, 94; compared to Barrio Melendez, 155; compared to Venezuela, 155; Conservative Ideal in, 356–57; experimentation in, 96; group agendas, 100; image of ideal group, 125; leadership schools, 100; Mobile Team, 103, 104, 273, 278; organizational style, 164; Vicarate of Pastoral Action, 102; Vicarías de Religiosas, 94, 105
FARC (Fuerzas Armadas Revolucionarias de Colombia), 278
Federation of Coffee Growers (Colombia), 105, 184, 188, 289, 307
Fields, Karen, 16n, 321
Franciscans, 337
Francis of Assisi, 172
Freire, Paulo, 344n
Fundación Carvajal, 116
funnel effect, 187

Gaitán, Jorge Eliécer, 56
García Márquez, Gabriel, 106

Gaudium et Spes, 256
Gaventa, John, 341
Geertz, Clifford, 272, 322, 350n
Gilfeather, Katherine, 336n
Gilsenan, Michael, 15
Golconda Group, 82, 83
Goldrich, Daniel, 341n
Goodman, Paul, 344n
Gramsci, Antonio, 346
grass roots groups, 5. See also base communities; individual organizations
Guárico, 111
Guevara, Che, 172
Gutiérrez, Gustavo, 41n, 43, 167, 370

Habermas, Jurgen, 363, 364, 372, 374n
health committees, 238
heaven, 177. See also popular religion
Hebblethwaite, Peter, 236n
Hebrew Prophets, 139
hegemony, 339–40, 346; and symbolic analysis, 347
hell, 177. See also popular religion
Hewitt, William E., 345
hidden transcripts, 237, 341, 347
Hirschman, Albert, 228
Hochschild, Jennifer, 333–34
Hogar-Escuela, 101–45
holiness. See popular religion
holy water, 173, 175, 246
Humanae Salutis, 35n
human rights, 5
hypocrisy, 170

Iberian cultural patterns, 325
ideologization of religion, 322–23. See also politicization of religion
ideology, 19
Iglesia ante el cambio, La, 70
Ileto, Reynaldo, 15, 371
innovation, 355
Instituto Mayor Campesino, 84n, 279
interviews, xxiii, 25
Iranian revolution, 3, 14, 329, 349
Isaiah, 40, 139, 140, 285
isolation, local, 240–41
ITER (Instituto de Teología para Religiosos), 220

Javierian Institute, 121–22, 261; views on popular culture, 122

Jeremiah, 40
Jesuits, 210; in rural Venezuela, 110, 125
Jesus, 140, 141; in liberation theology, 41
Jiménez, Fernando, 227
John XXIII (pope), 35n, 304
John Paul II (pope), xx, 361, 369
Jóvenes de Acción, 89

Kennedy, John, 172
Kincaid, Douglas, 348
King, Rev. Martin Luther, 327
Kingdom of God, 138–39
Kung, Hans, 326

La Azauncha, 231, 232, 278
La Carucieña, 114, 186, 210, 228, 230; invasion of, 186
laicism, 72
La Magdalena, 104, 233
Lan, David, 330
La Palma, 97
Latin American Catholicism: periods of, 33
La Vega, 87, 226
lay ministers, 47, 81
leadership, 19, 340
Legion of Mary, 108, 109, 112, 135, 138,
   161, 189; and cooperative, 109, 161; habits
   inculcated, 163; values, 109
legitimacy, 19, 363; grant to churches, 195;
   popular notions, 181; Weberian categories,
   19
Lenin, Vladimir, 357
Liberals (Colombia), 55
liberation theology, xx, 7, 8, 18, 24, 32, 37,
   38, 39–44, 50; attacks on, 37; audience for,
   37; and Bible study, 40; biblical sources,
   40; central ideas, 39; christology, 41; context of, 37; definition, 39; demystification
   of authority, 351; and history, 40; impacts
   of, 52; and Marxism, 40, 42; method, 42;
   and poverty, 39–41; sociology of, 44
linkage, xix, 19, 180, 270, 317, 350; and religion, 334; transforming, 350–51
literacy, 22, 37; and access to media, 22
liturgy, 49; translation to local languages, 35,
   49
Lopez Trujillo, Msgr. Alfonso, 36, 72, 79,
   241
Los Cristales, 275
love, 142, 329

McPherson, C. B., 342, 343
Madrid, Susanna, 288–93; as *animadora*,
   289–90; attitude to military, 290–91; and
   Román Cortés, 288–89; and education,
   291; family and migration, 288; sociability,
   290; spirituality, 292–93; views on class relations, 292
Maduro, Otto, 340, 348
Magdalena Valley, 94
Mainwaring, Scott, 15
Mannheim, Karl, 180
Mardin, Serif, 15, 322
marginality, 362; and innovation, 355
Marx, Karl, 43, 345
Marxism, 5, 35; and liberation theology, 40,
   42
marxist-christian alliances, 43
Mary Magdalene, 122
masterless men, 362–63
Mauss, Marcel, 168
Medellín, 33, 35, 36, 245, 326n; limited impact in Venezuela, 75
mediation, 320, 335; demystifying, 326; and
   gender, 336; reducing cultural differences,
   336; roles, 355
Medical Mission Sisters, 112, 114, 115, 163,
   229, 238–39
Meléndez, Barrio, 118–23, 135, 142, 155–
   58, 160, 171, 185, 187, 194, 230; Center
   for Popular Culture, 122; Javierian sisters
   in, 155; links with CINEP/*Solidaridad*,
   123, 157; organizational weakness, 160; origins, 118; radicalized discourse, 158; Social Action, 159; Spanish priests, 122,
   156–57; taking of Fifth Street, 158, 344
methodology, 23–29; contexts, 28; and decentralization, 26; and distance, 26; and language, 27; phenomenological, 28
migration, 21, 22, 62; intra-urban, 185–86
Mill, John Stuart, 343
Mills, C. Wright, 272
Mobile Team. *See* Facatativá
Moore, Barrington, 325
moral argument, 372
Moreno, Fr. Manuel (Padre Manolo), 112,
   238–39
Mottahadeh, Roy, 330
Movement of Third World Priests, 82n
Musa Al Sadr, Imam, 330

Nash, June, 328
National Front, 55, 55n, 56, 91
National Pastoral Institute, 81, 113
Navia Velsco, Carminia, 260–70; career, 261; and CINEP/*Solidaridad*, 262; education, 260–62; family, 260; option for the poor, 264–65; outside financing, 265; view of popular groups, 264–65; work, 263–64
Nazareth, 140
Nelso, Susan Rosales, 346
Nicaragua, 36

One Hundred Pastoral Agents, 80
ONIS (National Office of Social Information), 82n
option for the poor. *See* preferential option for the poor
organic intellectuals, 340
Osorio, Sister Sara, 148, 149, 150

PACCA (Productores Asociados de Café, C.A.), 162, 298
Padre Vicente, 108, 162, 163, 231, 239; use of Legion of Mary, 108–9
participation, 35, 50, 320
Pasara, Luis, 357
pastoral agents, 7, 50, 53; concentrations of, 120; social origins, 226–27; training in Colombia, 80
Pastoral Weeks, 33
paternalism, 52, 341
Pearce, Jenny, 38, 348
Peattie, Lisa, 59
Pharisees, 141
Pineda, Humberto, 228
Poland, 14
political parties in Venezuela and Colombia, 56, 57
politicization of religion, 7, 17, 322–23. *See also* ideologization of religion
politics, 7; Colombian bishops' view, 73–74, 79; and organization in Venezuela and Colombia
Polvorines, 120
poor: as focus, 7; in spirit, 8; viewed by radicals and conservatives, 357–58. *See also* poverty
popular, the, 6, 10, 317; in Venezuela and Colombia, 91

popular culture, xix; CINEP views, 85; claims to reason, 365–66; expectations, 126; future shape, 313; image in Venezuela and Colombia, 91; images of church and clergy, 199–200, 205, 311; responsibility in, 178, 311; rural self-images compared, 198–99; silence in, 237, 340; solidarity in, 31, 333, 348
popular groups, xix, 23; cases compared, 124–27; contexts for, 354; independence, 178; occupations of members, 183, 187; organizational models in Venezuela and Colombia, 199; and social class, 125
popular needs, 190, 191, 193, 345
popular religion, 6–7, 15, 16, 167–77, 203, 245, 247, 249; in Barquisimeto, 248; Centro Gumilla view, 88; CINEP view, 249; Colombian church view, 71–72, 247; cult of the dead, 173, 246; death in, 175–76; heaven, 177; hell, 177; holiness, 359; holy water, 173–75; in Meléndez, 248–49; prayer, 168–70; radicals and conservatives compared, 249; rationalization of ethics, 179; saints, 171–73; transformations, 167–77; view of church, 354–55; view of clergy and sisters, 195–96, 204, 215, 246–51; view of Venezuelan bishops, 76–77; Virgin Mary, 172
popular work: strategies in Venezuela and Colombia, 82–91
Portes, Alejandro, 3, 333
poverty, 5, 8, 181, 182; and class, 9, 354; and gender, 182–83, 199; in liberation theology, 39–41; and needs, 182; viewed as natural fact, 197
practical ethic, 323n
prayer, 49, 168–70
preaching, 337
preferential option for the poor, 36, 42, 213; clergy views, 214–15; popular views, 195–96, 201; Huberto Vanegas, 278–79; Venezuela and Colombia compared, 236
priests and sisters: activities, 241; age, 215; career patterns, 270; career shifts, 213, 221; clothing, 222–23, 225; collective life, 216–17; education, 220, 225; language, 225; mediating roles, 217; national differences, 217, 219, 220; opting for the poor, 213, 221, 242–46; physical stamina, 216; religious orders and church structures com-

priests and sisters (*cont.*)
    pared, 217–18, 219; self-image, 271; views
    of popular groups, 251–52; views of popu-
    lar religion, 246–51; views of poverty,
    243–51; youth, 216
Prieto, Msgr. Jaime, 102
Procampesinos, 102, 105, 273. *See also* Cath-
    olic Relief Services; Facatativá
prophetic roles, 38, 40, 139–40, 337; in liber-
    ation theology, 41
prophets, 140, 329, 337; compared to priests,
    337; Hebrew, 40
protest, 363
Puebla, 33, 35, 36, 42, 245, 326n; Colom-
    bian bishop's report, 71; popular view, 196;
    Venezuelan bishops' report, 75
Puritan revolution, 3, 40, 160, 324, 328, 362;
    role of Bible, 40

Quebradanegra, 104, 106, 148, 150, 151,
    169, 173, 193, 236, 307

Raboteau, Albert, 325, 326
Radical Ideal, 45, 101, 143, 339, 357. *See
    also* base communities
Ranger, Terence, 330
rationalization, 366–67
reason, 3, 355, 365–67
re-christianization, 207–9, 242
Reformation, 3. *See also* Puritan revolution
religion, 9, 14, 31, 372; and authenticity, 9,
    35; and authoritarianism, 21; and class,
    323, 324; and democracy, 21; populism,
    31; privatization, 351; and resistance, 31;
    and revolution, 219; theoretical changes,
    14. *See also* liberation theology; popular re-
    ligion
revitalization, 333
Río Bravo, 141
Río Frío, 106, 189, 232, 234, 236, 348
Rojas Pinilla, Gen. Gustavo, 282
Romero, Msgr. Oscar A., 10n, 176, 211,
    331, 332, 337, 357

saints, 170–72. *See also* popular religion
SAL (Sacerdotes para America Latina), 82,
    83
San Carlos, 105
San Isidro, 148, 166, 169, 176, 194; base
    community foundation, 149–50; lending li-
    brary, 191

San José de Tarbes: congregation of, 114,
    252, 253
San Luis, 141
San Pedro, 105, 173, 192–93, 231
San Roque, 246
Sao Paulo, 345
Scott, James, 28n, 313, 327n, 341, 347, 371
Second Vatican Council, 5, 33, 39, 305. *See
    also* Vatican II
secularization, 14–15, 351; and rationaliza-
    tion, 367. *See also* popular religion; reli-
    gion
"see-judge-act," 326n
SENA (Servicio Nacional de Aprendizaje),
    184
sexuality, 189
signs of the times, 35
sisters, 204, 213, 221, 355; clothing, 222–23,
    225; educational opportunities, 220; experi-
    ence of change, 229–30; as innovators,
    336; opting for the poor, 235. *See also*
    priests and sisters
Sklar, Richard, 343–44
Smith, Brian, 15
Sobrino, Jon, 211
sociability, 3, 179, 194, 367
social thought of the church, 10–11
Socio-cultural Transformation Ideal, 47, 164,
    358. *See also* base communities
*Solidaridad*, 83, 84, 85, 86, 123
solidarity. *See* popular culture
spirituality. *See* popular religion

Tabio, 106, 196, 236, 240
*tejo*, 305
*Theses on Feuerbach*, 43
Thomas, Keith, 331
Thompson, E. P., 333
Titicare, 114
Tocqueville, Alexis de, 11, 12, 147n, 148n,
    343
Torres, Camilo, 82, 83, 172, 337
Tulua, 281
two swords theory, 200

Umbanda, 339
Unicentro, 121
Universidad Campesina, 84n
Universidad del Valle, 121
Universidad Obrera, 84n
Uraba, 274

urbanization, 37; Venezuela and Colombia compared, 61, 63

Vanegas, Huberto, 3, 227, 232, 273–80; birth and family, 273–74; detoxification, 277, 279; education, 275–76; migration, 274–75; view on option for the poor, 277–78; and The Violence, 274–76; work, 274–75, 277–79
Vatican II, 40, 86, 256. *See also* Second Vatican Council
Venezuelan Bishops' Conference, 68–69, 74, 77; and democracy, 74–75; organizational strategies, 81–82; and popular religion, 76–77
Villanueva, 108–13, 138, 173, 307; debt, 110; dietary reform in, 238; group agendas, 141; group origins, 164. *See also* Barquisimeto; CRAMCO; Legion of Mary; Padre Vicente
Vincent Arthur. *See* Padre Vicente
Violence, The, 55, 55n, 56, 91, 184, 192; in San Pedro, 192–93

Virguez, Daniel, 3
voice for the voiceless, 5. *See also* preferential option for the poor

Walzer, Michael, 328
Weber, Eugen, 194
Weber, Max, 16, 28n, 140, 178, 323, 323n, 324, 337, 342, 360; on crisis, 324; on prophets, 337
Whitman, Walt, 371
Wilson, Bryan, 134
Wolterstorff, Nicholas, 360
Worsley, Peter, 17n
Wuthnow, Robert, 15
Wuytack, Francis, 87

Yacopí, 97, 104
Yumbo, 123

Zambrano Camader, Msgr. Raul, 228
Zaret, David, 366
Zimbabwe, 330, 331n